I0306486

John L Ransom

Andersonville Diary, Escape, and List of Dead

With Name, Company, Regiment, Date of Death and Number of Grave...

John L Ransom

Andersonville Diary, Escape, and List of Dead
With Name, Company, Regiment, Date of Death and Number of Grave...

ISBN/EAN: 9783337118914

Printed in Europe, USA, Canada, Australia, Japan

Cover: Foto ©ninafisch / pixelio.de

More available books at **www.hansebooks.com**

Andersonville Diary,

ESCAPE,

—AND—

LIST OF THE DEAD,

—WITH—

NAME, CO., REGIMENT, DATE OF DEATH

—AND—

No. of Grave in Cemetery.

JOHN L. RANSOM,

LATE FIRST SERGEANT NINTH MICH. CAV.,

AUTHOR AND PUBLISHER.

AUBURN, N. Y.
1881.

"Entered according to act of Congress, in the year 1881, by JOHN L. RANSOM, in the office of the Librarian of Congress, at Washington."

DEDICATION.

TO THE

MOTHERS, WIVES AND SISTERS

OF THOSE WHOSE NAMES

ARE HEREIN RECORDED AS HAVING DIED

—IN—

ANDERSONVILLE,

THIS BOOK IS RESPECTFULLY DEDICATED

BY THE AUTHOR.

John L. Ransom.

(From a photograph taken two months before capture.)

INTRODUCTION.

The book to which these lines form an introduction is a peculiar one in many respects. It is a story, but it is a true story, and written years ago with little idea that it would ever come into this form. The writer has been induced, only recently, by the advice of friends and by his own feeling that such a production would be appreciated, to present what, at the time it was being made up, was merely a means of occupying a mind which had to contemplate, besides, only the horrors of a situation from which death would have been, and was to thousands, a happy relief.

The original diary in which these writings were made from day to day was destroyed by fire some years after the war, but its contents had been printed in a series of letters to the Jackson, (Mich.) *Citizen*, and to the editor and publisher of that journal thanks are now extended for the privilege of using his files for the preparation of this work. There has been little change in the entries in the diary, before presenting them here. In such cases the words which suggest themselves at the time are best—they cannot be improved upon by substitution at a later day.

This book is essentially different from any other that has been published concerning the "late war" or any of its incidents. Those who have had any such experience as the author will see its truthfulness at once, and to all other readers it is commended as a statement of actual things by one who experienced them to the fullest.

The annexed list of the Andersonville dead is from the rebel official records, is authentic, and will be found valuable in many pension cases and otherwise.

THE CAPTURE.

A REBEL RUSE TO GOBBLE UP UNION TROOPS—A COMPLETE SURPRISE—CARELESS OFFICERS—HEROIC DEFENCE—BEGINNING OF A LONG IMPRISONMENT.

BELLE ISLAND, Richmond, Va., Nov. 22, 1863.—I was captured near Rogersville, East Tennessee, on the 6th of this month, while acting as Brigade Quarter-Master Sergt. The Brigade was divided, two regiments twenty miles away, while Brigade Head-Quarters with 7th Ohio and 1st Tennessee Mounted Infantry were at Rogersville. The brigade quarter-master had a large quantity of clothing on hand, which we were about to issue to the brigade as soon as possible. The rebel citizens got up a dance at one of the public houses in the village, and invited all the union officers. This was the evening of Nov. 5th. Nearly all the officers attended and were away from the command nearly all night and many were away all night. We were encamped in a bend of the Holston River. It was a dark rainy night and the river rose rapidly before morning. The dance was a ruse to get our officers away from their command. At break of day the pickets were drove in by rebel cavalry, and orders were immediately received from commanding officer to get wagon train out on the road in ten minutes. The quarter-master had been to the dance and had not returned, consequently it devolved upon me to see to wagon train, which I did, and in probably ten minutes the whole seventy six mule army wagons were in line out on the main road, while the companies were forming into line and getting ready for a fight. Rebels had us completely surrounded and soon began to fire volley after volley into our disorganized ranks. Not one officer in five was present; Gen. commanding and staff as soon as they realized our danger, started for the river, swam across and got away. We had a small company of artillery with us commanded by a lieutenant. The lieutenant in the absence of other officers, assumed command of the two regiments, and right gallantly did he do service. Kept forming his men for the better protection of his wagon train, while the rebels were shifting around from one point to another, and all the time sending volley after volley into our ranks. Our men did well, and had there been plenty of officers and ammunition, we might have gained the day. After ten hours fighting we were obliged to surrender after having lost in killed over a hundred, and three or four times that number in wounded. After surrendering we were drawn up into line, counted off and hurriedly marched away south. By eight o'clock at night had probably marched ten miles, and encamped until morning. We expected that our troops would intercept and release us, but they did not. An hour before daylight we were up and on the march toward Bristol, Va., that being the nearest railroad station. We were cavalrymen, and marching on foot made us very lame, and we could hardly hobble along. Were very well fed on corn bread and bacon. Reached Bristol, Va., Nov. 8th and were soon aboard of cattle cars en-route for the rebel capital. I must here tell how I came into possession of a very nice and large bed spread which is doing good service even now these cold nights. After we were captured everything was taken away from us, blankets, overcoats, and in many cases our boots and shoes. I had on a new pair of boots, which by muddying them over had escaped the rebel eyes thus far, as being a good pair. As our blankets had been taken away from us we suffered considerably from cold. I saw that if I was going to remain a prisoner of war it behooved me to get hold of a blanket. After a few hours march I became so lame walking with my new boots on that the rebels were compelled to put me on an old horse that was being lead along by one of the guard. This guard had the bed spread before spoken of. Told him I was going into prison at the beginning of a long winter, and should need a blanket, and could'nt he give me his. We had considerable talk, and were very good friends. Said he rather liked me but wouldn't part with his bed spread. Didn't love me that much, treated me however with apple jack out of his canteen. I kept getting my wits together to arrange some plan to get the article in question. Finally told him I had a large sum of money on my person which I expected would be taken away from me anyway, and as he was a good fellow would rather he would have it than any one else. He was delighted and all attention, wanted me to be careful and not let any of the other rebels see the transfer. I had a lot of Michigan broken down wild cat money, and pulled it out of an inside pocket and handed him the roll. It was green paper and of course he supposed it greenbacks. Was very glad of the gift and wanted to know what he could do for me. My first proposition to him was to let me escape, but he couldn't do that, then I told him to give me the bed spread, as it might save my life. After some further parley, he consented and handed over the spread. He was afraid to look at his money for fear some one would see him, and so did not discover that it was worthless until we had become separated. Guards were changed that night and never saw him any more.

The cars ran very slow, and being crowded for room the journey to Richmond was very tedious. Arrived on the morning of Nov. 13th, seven days after capture, at the south end of the "long bridge," ordered out of the cars and into line, counted off and started for Belle Isle. Said island is in the James River, probably covers ten or twelve acres, and is right across from Richmond. The river between Richmond and the island is probably a third or half a mile. The "long bridge" is near the lower part of the island. It is a cold, bleak piece of ground and the winter winds have free sweep from up the river. Before noon we were turned into the pen which is merely enclosed by a ditch and the dirt taken from the ditch thrown up on the outside, making a sort of breastwork. The ditch serves as a dead line, and no prisoners must go near the ditch. The prison is in command of a Lieut. Bossieux, a rather young and gallant looking sort of fellow. Is a born Southerner, talking so much like a negro that you would think he was one, if you could hear him talk and not see him. He has two rebel sergeants to act as his assistants, Sergt. Hight and Sergt. Marks. These two men are very cruel, as is also the Lieut. when angered. Outside the prison pen is a bake house, made of boards, the rebel tents for the accommodation of the officers and guard, and a hospital also of tent cloth. Running from the pen is a lane enclosed by high boards going to the water's edge. At night this is closed up by a gate at the pen, and thrown open in the morning. About half of the six thousand prisoners here have tents while the rest sleep and live out of doors. After I had been on this island two or three days, I was standing near the gate eating some rice soup out of an old broken bottle, thoroughly disgusted with the Southern

Confederacy, and this prison in particular. A young man came up to me whom I immediately recognized as George W. Hendryx, a member of my own company "A" 9th Mich. Cavalry, who had been captured some time before myself. Was feeling so blue, cross and cold that I didn't care whether it was him or not. He was on his way to the river to get some water. Found I wasn't going to notice him in any way, and so proceeded on his errand. When I say that George Hendryx was one of the most valued friends I had in the regiment, this action on my part will seem strange as indeed it is. Did not want to see him or any one else I had ever seen before. Well, George came back a few moments after, looked at me a short time and says: "I believe you are John L. Ransom, Q. M Sergt. of the same Co. with me, although you don't seem to recognize me." Told him "I was that same person, recognized him and there could be no mistake about it." Wanted to know why in the old harry I didn't speak to him then. After telling him just how it was, freezing to death, half starved and gray backs crawling all over me, &c., we sett'ed down into being glad to see one another.

Nov 23.—Having a few dollars of good yankee money which I have hoarded since my capture, have purchased a large blank book and intend as long as I am a prisoner of war in this confederacy, to note down from day to day as occasion may occur, events as they happen, treatment, ups and downs generally. It will serve to pass away the time and may be interesting at some future time to read over

Nov. 24.—Very cold weather. Four or five men chilled to death last night. A large portion of the prisoners who have been in confinement any length of time are reduced to almost skeletons from continued hunger, exposure and filth. Having some money just indulged in an extra ration of corn bread for which I paid twenty cents in yankee script, equal to two dollars confederate money, and should say by the crowd collected around that such a sight was an unusual occurrence, and put me in mind of gatherings I have seen at the north around some curiosity. We received for to day's food half a pint of rice soup and one-quarter of a pound loaf of corn bread. The bread is made from the very poorest meal, coarse, sour and musty; would make poor feed for swine at home. The rice is nothing more than boiled in river water with no seasoning whatever, not even salt, but for all that it tasted nice. The greatest difficulty is the small allowance given us. The prisoners

are blue, downcast and talk continually of home and something
good to eat. They nearly all think there will be an exchange of
prisoners before long and the trick of it is to live until the time
approaches. We are divided off into hundreds with a sergeant to
each squad who draws the food and divides it up among his men,
and woe unto him if a man is wronged out of his share—his life is
not worth the snap of the fin er if caught cheating. No wood to-
night and it is very cold. The nights are long and are made hideous by the moans of suffering wretches.

Nov 25.—Hendryx is in a very good tent with some nine or ten
others and is now trying to get me into the already crowded shelter. They say I can have the first vacancy and as it is impossible
for a dozen to remain together long without losing some by sickness, my chances will be good in a few days at fartherest. Food
again at four o'clock. In place of soup received about four ounces
of salt horse, as we call it.

Nov. 26.—Hendryx sacrificed his own comfort and lay out doors
with me last night and I got along much better than the night
before. Are getting food twice to day; old prisoners say it is fully
a third more than they have been getting. Hardly understand how
we could live on much less. A Michigan man (could not learn
his name) while at work a few moments ago on the outside with a
squad of detailed yankees repairing a part of the embankment
which recent rains had washed away, stepped upon the wall to give
orders to his men when one of the guards shot him through the
head, killing him instantly. Lieut. Bossieux, commander of the
prison, having heard the shot, came to learn the cause. He told
the guard he ought to be more careful and not shoot those who
were on parole and doing fatigue duty, and ordered the body carried to the dead house. Seems tough to me but others don't seem
to mind it much. I am mad.

Nov. 27.—Stormy and disagreeable weather. From fifteen to
twenty and twenty-five die every day and are buried just outside
the prison with no coffins—nothing but canvas wrapped around
them. Eight sticks of four foot wood given every squad of one
hundred men to-day, and when split up and divided it amounted to
nothing towards warming a person. Two or three can put their
wood together and boil a little coffee made from bread crusts. The
sick are taken out every morning and either sent over to the city or
kept in the hospital just outside the prison and on the island.
None admitted unless carried out in blankets and so far gone there

is not much chance of recovery. Medical attendance is scarce.

Nov 28.—Very cold and men suffer terribly with hardly any clothing on some of them. A man taken outside to-day, bucked and gagged for talking with a guard; a severe punishment this very cold weather.

Nov. 30.—Came across E. P. Sanders, from Lansing, Michigan, and a jolly old soul is he. Can't get discouraged where he is. Talk a great deal about making our escape but there is not much prospect. We are very strongly guarded with artillery bearing on every part of the prison. The long bridge I have heard so much about crosses the river just below the island. It is very long and has been condemned for years—trains move very slow across it. There was a big fire over in Richmond last night about 2 o'clock; could hear all the fire bells and see the house tops covered with people looking at it. Great excitement among the Johnny Rebs.

Dec. 1.—With no news concerning the great subject—exchange of prisoners Very hungry and am not having a good time of it. Take it all around I begin to wish I had stayed at home and was at the *Jackson Citizen* office pulling the old press. Dream continually nights about something good to eat; seems rather hard such plenty at the North and starving here. Have just seen a big fight among the prisoners; just like so many snarly dogs, cross and peevish. A great deal of fighting going on. Rebels collect around on the outside in crowds to see the Yankees bruise themselves and it is quite sport for them. Have succeeded in getting into the tent with Hendryx. One of the mess has been sent over to Richmond Hospital leaving a vacancy which I am to fill. There are nine others, myself making ten. The names are as follows: W. C. Robinson, orderly sergeant, 34th Illinois; W. H. Mustard, hospital steward 100th Pennsylvania; Joe Myers, 34th Illinois; H Freeman, hospital steward 30th Ohio; C G. Strong, 4th Ohio cavalry; Corporal John McCarten, 6th Kentucky; U. Kindred, 1st East Tennessee infantry; E. P. Sanders, 20th Michigan infantry; George Hendryx and myself of the 9th Michigan cavalry. A very good crowd of boys, and all try to make their places as pleasant as possible Gen. Neil Dow to-day came over from Libby Prison on parole of honor to help issue some clothing that has arrived for Belle Isle prisoners from the Sanitary Commission at the North Sergeant Robinson taken outside to help Gen. Dow in issuing clothing and thinks through his influence to get more out for the same purpose. A man froze to death last night where I slept. The body lay until nearly dark before it was removed. My blanket comes in good play, and it made the boys laugh when I told how I got it. We tell stories, dance around, keep as clean as we can without soap and make the best of a very bad situation.

Dec. 2 —Pleasant weather and favorable for prisoners. At about nine in the morning the work of hunting for vermin commences, and all over camp sit the poor starved wretches, nearly stripped, engaged in picking off and killing the big gray backs. The ground is fairly alive with them, and it requires continual labor to keep from being eaten up alive by them I just saw a man shot. He was called down to the bank by the guard, and as he leaned over to do some trading another guard close by shot him through the side and it is said mortally wounded him. It was made up between the guards to shoot the man, and when the lieutenant came round to make inquiries concerning the affair, one of them remarked that the ——————— passed a counterfeit bill on him the night before, and he thought he would put him where he could not do the like again. The wounded man was taken to the hospital and has since died. His name was Gilbert. He was from New Jersey Food twice to-day; buggy bean soup and a very small allowance of corn bread. Hungry all the time.

Dec. 3.— Rumors of exchange to be effected soon. Rebels say we will all be exchanged before many days. It cannot be possible our government will allow us to remain here all winter. Gen. Dow is still issuing clothing, but the rebels get more than our men do of it. Guards nearly all dressed in Yankee uniforms In our mess we have established regulations, and any one not conforming with the rules is to be turned out of the tent. Must take plenty of exercise, keep clean, free as circumstances will permit of vermin, drink no water until it has been boiled, which process purifies and makes it more healthy, are not to allow ourselves to get despondent, and must talk, laugh and make as light of our affairs as possible. Sure death for a person to give up and lose all ambition Received a spoonful of salt to-day for the first time since I came here.

Dec. 4.— Exchange news below par to-day. Rather colder than yesterday; a great many sick and dying off rapidly. Rebel guards are more strict than usual, and one risks his life by speaking to them at all. Wrote a letter home to-day, also one to a friend in Washington. Doubtful whether I ever hear from them. Robinson comes inside every night and always brings something good.

We look forward to the time of his coming with pleasure. Occasionally he brings a stick of wood which we split up fine and build a cheerful fire in our little sod fireplace, sit up close together and talk of home and friends so far away. We call our establishment the "Astor House of Belle Isle." There are so many worse off than we are that we are very well contented and enjoy ourselves after a fashion.

Dec 5.—Cold and raw weather with no wood. Men are too weak to walk nights to keep warm, sink down and chill to death. At least a dozen were carried out this morning feet foremost. Through Robinson's influence Hendryx and myself will go out to morrow to issue clothing, and will come in nights to sleep. We are to receive extra rations for our services. In good spirits tonight with a good fire and very comfortable for this place.

Dec. 6.—One month a prisoner to-day—longer than any year of my life before. Hope I am not to see another month in the Confederacy. A great deal of stealing going on among the men. There are organized bands of raiders who do pretty much as they please. A ration of bread is often of more consequence than a man's life. Have received food but once to-day; very cold; at least one hundred men limping around with frozen feet, and some of them crying like little children. Am at work on the outside to-day; go out at nine in the morning and return at four in the afternoon, and by right smart figuring carry in much extra food for tent mates, enough to give all hands a good square meal.

Dec. 7.—No news of importance. The rebels say a flag of truce boat has arrived at City Point and Commissioner Olds telegraphed for and undoubtedly will agree upon terms for an exchange of prisoners. Men receiving boxes from their friends at the north and am writing for one myself without much hope of ever getting it.

Dec. 8.—The men all turned out of the enclosure and are being squadded over. A very stormy and cold day; called out before breakfast and nearly dark before again sent inside Very muddy and the men have suffered terribly, stand up all day in the cold drizzling rain, with no chance for exercise and many barefooted. I counted nine or ten who went out in the morning not able to get back at night; three of the number being dead.

Dec 9.—Rumors that one thousand go off to-day to our lines and the same number every day until all are removed. It was not believed until a few moments ago the Lieutenant stepped upon the bank and said that in less than a week we would all be home again, and such a cheering among us; every man who could yell had his mouth stretched. Persons who fifteen minutes ago could not rise to their feet are jumping around in excitement, shaking hands with one another and crying, "A general exchange! a general exchange!" All in good spirits and we talk of the good dinners we will get on the road home. Food twice to-day and a little salt

Dec. 10.—Instead of prisoners going away five hundred more have come, which makes it very crowded. Some are still confident we will go away soon, but I place no reliance on rebel reports Rather warmer than usual, and the men busying themselves hunting vermin. A priest in the camp distributing tracts. Men told him to bring bread; they want no tracts. Exchange news has died away, and more despondent than ever. I to-day got hold of a Richmond *Enquirer* which spoke of bread riots in the city, women running around the streets and yelling, "Peace or bread!"

Dec. 11.—Was on guard last night over the clothing outside. Lieut. Bossieux asked Corp. McCarten and myself to eat supper with him last night, which we were very glad to do. Henry, the negro servant, said to the lieutenant after we had got through eating: "I golly, masser, don't nebber ask dem boys to eat with us again, dey eat us out clean gone;" and so we did eat everything on the table and looked for more.

Dec. 12.—At just daylight I got up and was walking around the prison to see if any Michigan men had died through the night, and was just in time to see a young fellow come out of his tent nearly naked and deliberately walk up the steps that lead over the bank. Just as he got on the top the guard fired; sending a ball through his brain, and the poor fellow fell dead in the ditch. I went and got permission to help pull him out. He had been sick for a number of days and was burning up with fever, and no doubt deranged at the time, else he would have known better than to have risked his life in such a manner. His name was Perry McMichael, and he was from Minnesota. Perhaps he is better off, and a much easier death than to die of disease as he undoubtedly would in a few days longer. The work of issuing clothing slowly goes on. In place of Gen. Dow, Col. Sanderson comes over on parole of honor; and is not liked at all. Is of New York and a perfect tyrant; treats us as bad or worse than the rebels themselves. Col. Boyd also comes occasionally and is a perfect gentleman. Talked to me to-day concerning Sanderson's movements, and said if he got through to our lines should complain of him to the authorities at Washington. He took down notes in his diary against him.

Dec. 13.—Nothing of any importance to note down. The officers come over from Richmond every day or two, and make a showing of issuing clothing The work goes on slowly, and it would seem that if clothing was ever needed and ought to be issued, it is now; yet the officers seem to want to nurse the job and make it last as long as possible. Many cruelties are practiced, principally by the rebel sergeants. The lieutenant does not countenance much cruelty, still he is very quick tempered, and when provoked is apt to do some very severe things. The Yankees are a hard crowd to manage; will steal anything, no matter what, regardless of consequences. Still I don't know as it is any wonder, cooped up as they are in such a place, and called upon to endure such privations. The death rate gradually increases from day to day. A little Cincinnati soldier died to-day. Was captured same time as myself, and we had messed together a number of times before I became identified with the "Astor House Mess." Was in very poor health when captured, but could never quite find out what ailed him. I have many talks with the rebels, and am quite a priveleged character. By so doing am able to do much for the boys inside, and there are good boys in there, whom I would do as much for as myself,

Dec. 17.—I have plenty to eat. Go outside every day whether clothing is issued or not. To explain the manner of issuing clothing: The men are called outside by squads, that is, one squad of a hundred men at a time; all stand in a row in front of the boxes of clothing. The officer in charge, Col. Sanderson, begins with the first at the head of the column, looks him over, and says to us paroled men: "Here, give this man a pair of pants," or coat, or such clothing as he may stand in need of. In this way he gets through with a hundred men in about half an hour. Us boys often manage to give three or four articles where only one has been ordered. There seems to be plenty of clothing here, and we can see no reason why it should not be given away. Have to be very careful, though, for if we are caught at these tricks are sent inside to stay. Officers stay on the island only two or three hours, and clothe four or five hundred men, when they could just as well do three or four times as much. It is comical the notes that come in some of the good warm woolen stockings. These have evidently been knit by the good mothers, wives and sisters at the North, and some of the romantic sort have written letters and placed inside, asking the receiver to let them know about himself, his name, etc., etc. Most of them come from the New England states, and they cheer the boys up a great deal.

Dec. 18.—To-day as a squad was drawn up in front of us, waiting for clothing, I saw an Irishman in the ranks who looked familiar. Looked at him for some time and finally thought I recognized in him an old neighbor of mine in Jackson, Michigan; one Jimmy Devers, a whole souled and comical genius as ever it was my fortune to meet. Went up to him and asked what regiment he belonged to; said he belonged to the 23d Indiana, at which I could not believe it was my old acquaintance. Went back to my work. Pretty soon he said to me: "Ain't you Johnny Ransom?" And then I knew I was right. He had lived in Jackson, but had enlisted in an Indiana regiment. Well, we were glad to see one another and you may just bet that Jimmy got as good a suit of clothes as ever he had in our own lines. Jimmy is a case; was captured on the 1st day of July at the Gettysburg battle, and is consequently an old prisoner. Is very tough and hardy. Says the Johnny Rebs have a big contract on their hands to kill him. But I tell him to take good care of himself anyway, as there is no knowing what he will be called upon to pass through yet.

Dec. 20.—James River frozen nearly over, and rebels say it has not been so cold for years as at the present time. There are hundreds with frozen feet, ears, hands &c., and laying all over the prison; and the suffering is terrible. Hendryx and myself are intent on some plan for escape. The lieutenant has spies who are on the watch. The authorities know all about any conspiracy almost as soon as it is known among ourselves. Last night just after dark two or three Yankees agreed to give the guard $10 if he would let them get over the bank, to which he promised; and as soon as they got nearly over fired and immediately gave the alarm. One of them received a shot in one of his legs and the others scrambled back over the bank; the three minus their $10 bill and a sound leg. They cannot be trusted at all and will promise anything for greenbacks. Sergt. Bullock of our regiment is here and very sick with fever; cannot possibly live many weeks in such a place as this. Col. Sanderson still issuing clothing, but very unfair, and the men who need it most get none at all. All the outsiders received a suit throughout to-day, myself among the rest. Got a letter from home, everybody is well. They say keep up good heart and we will be exchanged before many weeks.

Dec. 21.—Still cold. Have enough to eat myself, but am one of a thousand. The scurvy is appearing among some of the men, and is an awful disease—caused by want of vegetable diet, acids, &c. Two small pox cases taken to the hospital to-day A sutler has been established on the island and sells at the following rates: poor brown sugar, $8 per pound; butter, $11; cheese, $10; sour milk $3 per quart and the only article I buy; eggs, $10 per dozen; oysters, $6 per quart and the cheapest food in market.

Dec. 22.—A large mail came this morning, but nothing for me. A man who gets a letter is besieged with questions, and a crowd gathers around to learn the news, if any, regarding our future. Rations smaller than usual, and Lieut. Bossieux says that it is either exchange or starve with us prisoners sure, as they have not the food to give us. To-day saw a copy of the Richmond Enquirer in which was a long article treating on exchange of prisoners, saying our government would not exchange owing to an excess held by us, and unless their terms were agreed to, as they could not afford to keep us, the coming summer would reduce our ranks so that they would not have many to feed another winter. Rather poor prospects ahead for us poor imprisoned yanks. Lots of Sanitary stores sent on to the island for us, but as yet none have been issued, the rebels (officers in particular), getting fat on what rightfully belongs to us.

Dec. 23.—Almost Christmas and we are planning for a Christmas dinner. Very cold. The rebels are testing their big guns on the opposite shore of the river and fairly shake the ground we stand on. We can see the shells as they leave the guns until they explode, affording quite a pastime for us watching their war machines. Militia in sight drilling over in Richmond. A woman found among us—a prisoner of war. Some one who knew the secret informed Lieutenant Bossieux and he immediately had her taken outside, when she told him the whole story—how she had "followed her lovyer a soldiering" in disguise, and being of a romantic turn, enjoyed it hugely until the funny part was done away with and Madame Collier, from East Tennessee, found herself in durance vile; nothing to do but make the best of it and conceal her sex if possible, hoping for a release, which, however, did not come in the shape she wished. The lieutenant has sent her over to Richmond to be cared for and she is to be sent north by the first flag of truce boat. She tells of another female being among us, but as yet she has not been found out.

Dec. 24.—Must hang up my stocking to-night for habit's sake if nothing else. I am enjoying splendid health, and prison life agrees with me. Wrote home to-day

Dec. 25—and Christmas.—One year ago to-day first went into camp at Coldwater, little dreaming what changes a year would bring around, but there are exchange rumors afloat and hope to see white folks again before many months. All ordered out to be squadded over again, which was quite a disappointment to our mess as we were making preparations for a grand dinner, gotten up by outside hands, Mustard, Myers, Hendryx and myself. However, we had our good things for supper instead of dinner, and it was a big thing, consisting of corn bread and butter, oysters, coffee, beef, crackers, cheese &c.; all we could possibly eat or do away with, and costing the snug little sum of $200 Confederate money, or $20 in greenbacks. Lay awake long before daylight listening to the bells. As they rang out Christmas good morning I imagined they were in Jackson, Michigan, my old home, and from the spires of the old Presbyterian and Episcopal churches. Little do they think as they are saying their Merry Christmases and enjoying themselves so much, of the hunger and starving here. But there are better days coming.

Dec. 26 —News of exchange and no officers over from Libby to issue clothing. Extra quantity of wood. Rebels all drunk and very domineering. Punish for the smallest kind of excuse. Some men tunneled out of the pen but were retaken and were made to crawl back through the same hole they went out of and the lieutenant kept hitting them with a board as they went down and then ran back and forward from one hole to the other and as they stuck up their heads would hit them with a club, keeping them at it for nearly an hour. A large crowd of both rebels and Yankees collected around to see the fun.

Dec. 27.—Col. Sanderson and Col. Boyd came over this morning in a great hurry and began to issue clothing very fast saying an exchange had been agreed upon and they wanted to get rid of it before we all went away. Pretty soon the news got inside and the greatest cheering, yelling, shaking of hands and congratulating one another took place. Just before dinner five hundred were taken out, counted and sent away. Everybody anxious to go away first which of course they cannot do. Sergts. Hight and Marks stand at the gate with big clubs keeping order, letting them out two at a time, occasionally knocking a man down and it is seldom he gets up again very soon. Some of the outside went and the rest go to-morrow. It is a sure thing—a general exchange and all will be sent away immediately. Everybody in good spirits. Guess northern folks will be surprised to see such looking objects come among them. They are the worst looking crowd I ever saw. Extra ration of food and wood to-night and am anxiously waiting for the morrow.

Dec. 28.—For some reason or other no more being taken away and more despondent than ever. Very cold.

Dec. 29.—Nearly as cold weather as I ever saw at the North. All the supplies brought by hand over the long bridge, owing to the river being frozen over and not strong enough to hold up. Rebel officers all drunk during the holidays. Snow an inch deep.

Dec. 30.—No rations issued yesterday to any of the prisoners and a third of all here are on the very point of starvation. Lieut. Bossieux sympathizes with us in word but says it is impossible to help it as they have not the food for us. This is perhaps true as regards edibles but there is no excuse for our receiving such small supplies of wood. They could give us plenty of shelter, plenty of wood and conveniences we do not now get if they felt so disposed.

Dec 31.—Still very cold and no news encouraging. Rebels very strict. One prisoner found a brother among the guards who had been living in the south for a good many years and lately conscripted into the Confederate army. New Year's eve. Man wounded by the guard shooting, and ball broke his leg. Might better have shot him dead for he will surely die. Raw rice and corn bread issued to day in small quantities. Richmond *Enquirer* spoke of the five hundred who left here day before yesterday and they have reached Washington.

NEW YEAR'S DAY

AND THE PLACE IT FINDS US.—APPLES TO EAT AND AN OLD COMRADE JOINS US.—MATTERS GETTING WORSE WITH OCCASIONAL RUMORS OF EXCHANGE, ETC., ETC.

Jan. 1, 1864.—A great time this morning wishing one another a Happy New Year. Robinson bought on the outside a dozen apples and gave us all a treat. Nothing but corn bread to eat and very poor quality. Dr. F. L. Lewis, Vet. Surg. 9th Mich. cavalry, came in to day; was captured at Dandridge, East Tennessee, where our regiment had a severe engagement. Tells me all the news. Col. Acker wounded, etc., etc. Thinks it a queer New Year trip, but also thinks we will be exchanged before many weeks.

Jan. 2.—Rebel congress about to meet, and the people of Richmond demand through the papers that the prisoners confined here be removed immediately, as there is hardly enough for themselves to eat, aside from feeding us "Northern Hirelings." Hear of bread riots and lots of trouble across the river. A big fire last night in the vicinity of Libby Prison.

Jan. 3.—Received a letter from Michigan. Not quite so cold, but disagreeable weather. Nine men bucked and gagged at one time on the outside, two of them for stealing sour beans from a swill-barrel. They would get permission to pass through the gate to see the lieutenant, and instead, would walk around the cookhouse to some barrels containing swill, scoop up their hats full and then run inside; but they were caught, and are suffering a hard punishment for it.

Jan. 4.—Some ladies visited the island to see us blue coats, and laughed very much at our condition; thought it so comical and ludicrous the way the prisoners crowded the bank next the cook-house, looking over at the piles of bread, and compared us to wild men, and hungry dogs. A chicken belonging to the lieutenant flew up on the bank and was snatched off in short order, and to pay for it we are not to receive a mouthful of food to-day, making five or six thousand suffer for one man catching a little chicken.

Jan. 5.—Succeeded in getting Dr. Lewis into our tent; is rather under the weather, owing to exposure and hardship. Jimmy Devers spends the evenings with us and we have funny times talking over better days—and are nearly talked out. I have said all I can think, and am just beginning to talk it all over again. All our stories have been told from two, to three or four times, and are getting stale. We offer a reward for a good new story.

Jan. 6.—Still prisoners of war, without the remotest idea as to how long we are to remain so. Some of the paroled Yankees on the outside curse and treat the inside prisoners more cruel (when they have a chance,) than the rebels themselves. Blass, a Spaniard, who has been a prisoner over a year and refuses to be exchanged, is the lieutenant's right hand man. He tied up a man a few days ago for some misdemeanor and whipped him. He is afraid to come inside, knowing he would lose his life in a jiffy. He also raises the rebel flag at the island mornings, and lowers it at night.. It is a dirty rag, and the appearance of it ought to disgust any sensible person.

Jan. 7.—Rainy, cold and disagreeable weather. Henry Stilson, a fellow who was captured with me, was carried out dead this morning He was diseased when taken, and fell an easy prey to their cruelties. A good deal of raiding is going on among the men. One Captain Moseby commands a band of cut-throats who do nearly as they please, cheating, robbing and knocking down—operating principally upon new prisoners who are unacquainted with prison life. Moseby is named after the rebel guerrilla, his real name being something else. He is from New York City, and is a regular bummer.

Jan. 8.—All taken outside to-day to be squadded over—an all day job, and nothing to eat. The men being in hundreds and some dying off every day, leave vacancies in the squads of as many as die out of them, and in order to keep them filled up have to be squadded over every few days, thereby saving rations. Richmond papers are much alarmed for fear of a break among the prisoners confined within the city. It is said there are six hundred muskets secreted among the Belle Islanders. The citizens are frightened almost to death, double guards are placed over us, and very strict orders issued to them.

Jan. 9.—A signal light suspended over the island all last night for some reason unknown to the men confined here. We are cautioned against approaching within eight or ten feet from the bank. One of the raiders went through a man who lay near the bank and started to run after robbing him. A guard who saw the whole affair shot the villain dead and was applauded by all who knew of the affair. Fifteen or twenty carried out this morning dead and thirty or forty nearly so in blankets.

Jan. 10.—A brass band over to-day giving us a tune. Looks more like a wandering tribe of vagabonds than musicians. Discoursed sweet music, such as "Bonnie Blue Flag," "The Girl I Left Behind Me," and for their pains got three groans from their enemies in limbo. Dying off very fast on the island.

Jan. 11.—A steady rain for twenty-four hours, and have not been dry during the time. However it is a warm rain and get along very well. We are still issuing clothing but very slow. About one hundred per day get partly clothed up. No news of exchange. Abe Lincoln reported dead. Papers very bitter on Beast Butler, as they call him. Manage by a good deal of skirmishing to get the papers almost every day in which we read their rebel lies. A plan afoot for escape, but am afraid to say anything of the particulars for fear of my diary being taken away from me. As I came inside to-night with some bread in my haversack some fellows who were on the watch pitched into me and gobbled my saved up rations. I don't care for myself for I have been to supper, but the boys in the tent will have to go without anything to eat for this night. It don't matter much—they are all hungry and it did them as much good as it would our mess.

Jan. 12.—James River very high. A continual roar in our ears caused by the water falling over the cataract just above the island. Rebels fired a large shell over the prison to scare us.

Jan. 15.—Everything runs along about the same. Little excitements from day to day. The weather is fair, and taken all together thus far this winter has been very favorable to us as prisoners. Lieut. Bossieux lost his dog. Some Yanks snatched him into a tent and eat him up. Bossieux very mad and is anxious to know who the guilty ones are. All he can do is to keep all our rations from us one day, and he does it. Seems pretty rough when a man will eat a dog, but such is the case.

Jan. 18.—Too much exertion to even write in my diary. Talk of getting away by escaping, but find no feasible plan. Rebs very watchful. Some mail to-day but nothing for me. Saw some papers, and a new prisoner brought with him a New York paper, but not a word in it about "exchange." Am still outside most every day. Geo. Hendryx at work in the cook house cooking rations for the prisoners. Comes down where I am every day and hands me something to take inside for the boys. He tells the Lieut. he has a brother inside that he is feeding. Although it is against orders, Lieut. Bossieux pays no attention to it.

Jan. 20.—Rebel officers over to-day inspecting us Yanks. Some of the worst looking Arabs in shape of officers I ever saw. Jimmy Devers comes to our tent every night and sits with us until bed time. Is a jolly chap and keeps us all in good spirits with his sayings. Sergt. Robinson, I learned to-day, instead of being a sergeant is a lieutenant. His whole company being captured, he preferred to go with them and share their trials, than go with the officers. The men are very much attached to him and no wonder, as he is a fine fellow. His home is in Sterling, Whiteside Co., Illinois. Corp. McCartin is, as his name would indicate, an Irishman, and his home is Louisville, Ky. Is a shoemaker by trade. He is also a Mason, and I am going to write down wherein the fact of his being a Mason has brought good into the camp to-day. The boys feeling rather more hungry than usual were rather despondent, when the corporal gets up and says: "Boys, I'll go and get something to eat." Went out of the tent and in twenty minutes came back with three or four pounds of bacon and two loaves of corn bread. We were surprised and asked how he had performed the miracle. Told us then that he was a Mason, as also was the lieutenant in charge, from whom the food came. We decided then and there that the first opportunity that presented itself we would join the Masons. Can see the rebels drilling across the river.

Jan. 22.—Cold and clear weather. Nothing to write to-day. It's a task.

Jan. 24.—We are all troubled with heart-burn, sour stomach, &c. Drink weak lye made from ashes for it. Every day some new ones come inside, but they know nothing as to the prospects of our being exchanged. All are considerably surprised to find themselves in quite so bad a place, and the subject of prison life begins to interest them. Good deal of gambling going on among prisoners. Chuck-a-luck is the favorite game. You lay your ration of bread down on a figure on a board, and a fellow with a dice-box shakes it up a little, throws out the dice, and your bread is gone Don't understand the game myself. That's all I ever saw of the game. Lay down the bread and it's gone. Rather a one sided affair. Some men are very filthy, which makes it disagreeable for those of more cleanly habits. I believe that many, very many, who now die, would live if they adopted the rules that our mess has, and lived up to them. It is the only way to get along.

Jan. 25.—Being in this place brings out a man for just what he he is worth. Those whom we expect the most from in the way of braving hardships and dangers, prove to be nobody at all. And very often those whom we expect the least from prove to be heroes every inch of them. Notably one of these is George Hendryx, who is nothing but a good looking, effeminate boy, fit, you would say, to be going to school with a mother to look after him, and for not much else. But instead, he is brave. cheerful, smart, watching every chance to get the best of the Johnny Rebs. His position in the cook-house has given him a chance to feed, I presume, hundreds of men. Near the cook-house is a store-house, and in it are several hogsheads of hams. These hams were sent from the Sanitary Commission at the North for Union prisoners, but they for whom they were intended do not get them, and they are being eaten up by the rebels. Hendryx has managed to get up a board in the cook-house floor, where he can crawl fifteen or twenty feet under the store-house and up through that floor. By this Yankee trick he has stolen, I presume one hundred hams and gotten them inside where they belong. This is very risky on his part, for should he be discovered it would go very hard with him. He is about as unselfish a fellow as you can well find. This is only one of his plans to outwit the rebels for our benefit. His head is all the time, too, planning some way of escape. Well, we all hope he won't get caught. All shake in our boots for him. Was on guard last night, outside, over the clothing. There is so much clothing stole by the rebels that Bossieux put a guard of two over the boxes through the night, and if any of the Rebs. come around to steal we are instructed to wake up the lieutenant, who sleeps near by in a tent. I was on duty last night with Joe Myers, and Hendryx came where we were and unfolded a plan for escape which he has been working up. It is a risky affair, and had best be thought over pretty thorough before put into execution. Robinson has been found out as a lieutenant, and taken over to Richmond to be placed with the officers in Libby Prison. We are sorry that we must lose him.

Jan. 26.—Ninety-two squads of prisoners confined on less than six acres of ground—one hundred in a squad, making nine thousand and two hundred altogether. The lice are getting the upper hand of us. The ground is literally covered with them. Bean soup to-day and is made from the following recipe. (don't know from what cook book, some new edition): Beans are very wormy and musty. Hard work finding a bean without from one to three bugs in it. They are put into a large caldron kettle of river water and boiled for a couple of hours. No seasoning, not even salt put into them. It is then taken out and brought inside. Six pails full for each squad—about a pint per man, and not over a pint of beans in each bucket. The water is hardly colored and I could see clear through to the bottom and count every bean in the pail. The men drink it because it is warm. There is not enough strength or substance in it to do any good. We sometimes have very good bean soup when they have meat to boil with it.

Jan. 27.—More prisoners came to-day and say there is to be no general exchange during the war, and we are to be sent off into Georgia immediately. Stormy and disagreeable weather and everybody down-hearted. Very still among the men, owing to the bad news—hardly a word spoken by anybody. The least bit off anything encouraging would change the stillness into a perfect bedlam. This morning looked into a tent where there were seventeen men and started back frightened at the view inside. What a tableau for a New York theatre? They were all old prisoners nearly naked, very dirty and poor, some of them sick lying on the cold ground with nothing under or over them, and no fire; had just been talking over the prospect ahead and all looked the very picture of dispair, with their hollow eyes, sunken cheeks and haggard expression. I have before imagined such scenes but never before realized what they were until now. And such is but a fair sample of hundreds of men fully as bad.

Jan. 28.—No officers over from Libby for a few days past. Nearly all the clothing issued. A few days more will close up the clothing business, and then probably all the outsiders will be sent inside; and for fear such will be the case we have decided upon to-morrow night for the escape (which I have not said much about in my diary). The nights are dark and cloudy. Messrs. Mustard and Hendryx both sleep outside now, and I must manage to, both to-night and to-morrow night. I have been two weeks trying to get a map of Virginia, and have at last succeeded. A negro brought it to me from the city. It has cost over thirty dollars Confederate money—at the North would have cost twenty five cents. I would not take for it, unless I could get another one, one thousand dollars in gold. We are well rigged, have some food saved up to take along; in good health and determined to get away. Lieut. Bossieux suspects, and to-day took the pains to say in our hearing that he knew an escape among the outsiders was in view, and as sure as there was a God in heaven if we tried it and got caught, and we surely would be, he would first shoot all he could before catching us, and the balance would be tied up and whipped every day until he got tired, as long as we lived. We must expect trouble. It does not change us in the least; if anything, makes us the more determined to get away. To-night we are to start, and I will write down the plans we have, running the risk of the rebels getting hold of it. At a few moments past eleven and before midnight the guard will let us cross his beat and go to the water's edge. We all have rebel clothing which we are to wear, furnished partly by a negro, and partly by the guard who helps us off. We take the quarter-master's boat, which we unlock, and having been furnished the countersign give it to the picket who will pretend that he thinks we are rebel guards going over to the city, in case we are caught, which will screen him in a measure. Having passed him, we get into the boat and row across the river, give the countersign to the guards on the other side of the river, and talk with them a little, being ourselves posted on general information regarding the place. To quiet their suspicions if they have any, we then start up into the town and when out of sight of the guards take a turn to the left, and go straight to the Richmond jail; taking care to avoid patrols &c. We will then meet with a negro who will guide us ten miles up the river, and then leave us in charge of friendly blacks who will keep us through the next day and at night pilot us farther along toward our lives. If possible, I shall steal the rebel flag, which is kept nights in the lieutenant's tent, and a few other relics, to take along with me. The big bell in Richmond strikes six, and we close our diary, hoping never to look upon it again until we return to free our fellow prisoners, with the glorious army of the North. Now we leave our diary to finish preparations for the flight for freedom. May God aid us in this land of tyranny, where we have met nothing but suffering. Good bye, Belle Isle and Prison. Hail! Freedom, Home, Friends, and the

Grand Army of the Old Flag! What is in store for us in the future?

Feb. 5.—Have been reading over the last few pages of my diary. It sounds well, but the rebel flag still floats over Belle Isle. Our escapade was a grand fizzle, and all hands have been punished in more ways than one in the last few days. Bossieux suspected something going on among us and had us secretly watched, and long before we had made a move toward fulfilling our projected plans we were thrown into a guard house on the island; next morning taken out of it, and underwent a severe cross-questioning He found our rebel clothing, food we had packed, found the lock to the boat broke, and numerous other signs of an abandonment. Well, the result has been that we were bucked and gagged twice a day for an hour each time, and for four hours each of us carried a big stick of wood up and down in front of the gate, a guard to prick us with his bayonet if we walked too slow to suit him. Then Hendryx has been strung up by the thumbs. Nights we have been thrown into a damp, cold guard house to shiver all night. Every day now for six days we have walked with our sticks of wood so many hours per day, and last night were turned inside with all the prisoners to stay, Bossieux says, till we *rot*, he can place no dependence in us.

Feb. 6.—We have to laugh over our trials and tribulations. Where we had plenty a week ago, plenty of exercise, and many favors, we are now right where we were at first, fareing just as the rest, with no favors shown us. It's all right, we can stand it just as well as the rest. We have never belittled ourselves in the least in our dealings with the rebels. Bossieux told us himself, as we came inside, that he didn't blame us in the least for trying to get away, but he was obliged to punish us for the attempt. Hendryx says that he will be out again in three days.

Feb. 8.—Butler reported as commissioner on exchange and the rebels declare that they would never recognize him and would rather that we should all die here than negotiate with the Beast Congress still in session over in the city and we watch the papers eagerly for something relative to us. They Holy Sabbath day and the church bells ringing for morning service. Don't think I shall attend this morning; it is such a long walk and then I look so bad; have nothing fit to wear. A man stabbed a few minutes ago by his tent mate, killing him instantly. They had all along been the best friends until a dispute arose, and one of them drew a knife and killed his comrade. Strong talk of lynching the murderer. Have not heard the particulars. Corp. McCartin is missing from the island and am confident from what I have seen that he has escaped and by the help of Lieut. Bossieux. No endeavors are being made to look him up, still he offers a reward for his apprehension. They are both members of the secret craft.

Feb. 9.—Great news this morning. A raid is being made on Richmond by Kilpatrick, Rebels manning their forts in sight of us. All are at work, women, children, in fact everybody who can shovel. No cars running over the big bridge. Double guards placed over us and the greatest activity prevails among them. It is really amusing to see them flying around and many are the jokes at their expense. All business is suspended in Richmond; no papers issued, and everybody with their guns or working utensils. Brass bands are playing their best to encourage the broken down Confederacy. A portion of the congress came over this afternoon to take a look at us, among whom were Davis, Benjamin and Howell Cobb. They are a substantial looking set of men and of the regular southern cut The broad brim hats, gold headed canes and aristocratic toss of the head, alone would tell who they were. They are a proud, stern set of men and look as if they would like to brush us out of existence. Still we are not going to be brushed out so easy and they found men among us who were not afraid to stare, or hold our heads as high as their lordships. A band accompanied them and played the Bonnie Blue Flag, which was hissed and groaned at by the Yankees, and in return a thousand voices sang Yankee Doodle, very much to their discomfiture.

Feb. 10.—The hospital signal lights suspended over the island all night in order to direct the batteries where to aim their pieces in case of an outbreak which is greatly feared. Rockets sent up at intervals during the night over Richmond. Reported that there are six hundred muskets secreted among the prisoners and citizens very much alarmed and afraid of us. I hope there is but cannot believe it. It is impossible for me to sleep and I lay awake thinking how we are situated and wondering how long the play is to last.

Feb. 11.—Cold and pleasant. A good deal of fighting going on among us—a discontented set of beings; just like so many hungry wolves penned up together. Rebels still at work fortifying all around Richmond. A number of Yankees have been taken out on parole of honor to work building breastworks etc., but a very few will go and it is considered a great crime among us to work for them. Have they forgotten our existence at the North? It seems as if we were neglected by our government but will not judge them hastily until we know more. There are perhaps sufficient reasons for our remaining here. Very strongly guarded, nevertheless we talk of escape and are all the while building air castles.

Feb. 12.—Lieut. Bossieux has sent a squad of men from the island composed of runaways over to Castle Thunder to remain during the war as hostages, among whom were our friends Myres and Mustard. I never expect to see them again.

Feb. 13.—Very cold. The rebels are again settling down and getting over their scare. Not much to eat now and the men more disheartened than ever. A rebel preacher delivered us a sermon of two hours length from a dry goods box. He was listened to attentively and made the remark before closing that he didn't know as he was doing any good talking to us. It was like casting pearls before swine and he would close his remarks, to which a Yankee told him he might have stopped long ago if he had wanted to; no one would have made any objections. Was told that six hundred are to start for Georgia to-day and subsequently six hundred every day until all are removed from Richmond. Lieut. Bossieux says it is so but there is going to be an exchange of sick in a few days and all outside hands shall be sent north with them.

Feb 14.—Had quite an adventure last night with the raiders. One of Capt. Moseby's robbers was trying to steal a blanket from our tent by reaching through the tent opening when Dad (E. P. Sanders), who is always awake, threw a brick hitting him on the arm, breaking the brick, and as he jumped, halloed to us, "Come boys, let's catch the rascal," and out of the door he went. Dr. and myself nobly rushed to the rescue and reached the door just in time to see Dad turn a short corner way up the street and close on to the heels of Mr. Robber, but he slipped and fell and the thief got away. Were soon snugly ensconced in bed once more congratulating ourselves on losing nothing as we thought. But on getting up this morning I found my shoes gone and am barefoot in the middle of winter. However I can get more and have no fear on that score. Six hundred sent away to day, some say to our lines while others think to Georgia. Rebels say to our lines, and that a general exchange has been agreed upon. Great excitement among the men. Evening.—Lieut. Bossieux called me outside just before night and told me he was called upon to furnish some hostages to be sent to Charleston to be kept during the war, and had decided to send

Hendryx and myself, with some others. Said it was better to send those who were always trying to get away. Have succeeded in buying a pair of shoes, which, although about four sizes too large, are much better than none. Thanks to the Sanitary Commission I have good woolen stockings, under clothing complete, and am otherwise well dressed. Six hundred sent away this afternoon under a very strong guard. which does not look like an exchange.

Feb. 17.—Still on the island. Another squad taken out yesterday. It will not be our turn to go for some days, even if six hundred are taken out every day. Have not been sent for as hostages yet. Hendryx and myself have decided to flank out and go with the next that go, no matter where their destination may be. If we don't get away, with a ghost of a chance, then it will be funny.

Feb. 20.—All sorts of rumors afloat, but still we stay here. Strange officers come over and look at us. Bossieux away considerable, and something evidently up. Anything for a change. My health is good, and tough as a bear.

Feb. 23.—None have been taken away from the island for a number of days. Have heard that a box came for me, and is over in Richmond. Hope the rebel that eats the contents of that box will get choked to death. I wrote to the Governor of Michigan, Austin Blair, who is in Washington, D. C., some weeks ago. He has known me from boyhood. Always lived in the neighborhood at Jackson, Mich. Asked him to notify my father and brothers of my whereabouts. To-day I received a letter from him saying that he had done as requested, also that the Sanitary Commission had sent me some eatables. This is undoubtedly the box which I have heard from and is over in Richmond. Rebels are trying to get recruits from among us for their one-horse Confederacy. Believe that one or two have deserted our ranks and gone over. Bad luck to them.

PEMERTON BUILDING.

A GOOD-BYE TO BELLE ISLE—GOOD PLACE TO BE MOVED FROM—
ASTOR HOUSE MESS ON ITS TRAVELS—NEW SCENES—THE RAID ON
RICHMOND AND CONSEQUENT SCARE—ALL'S WELL IF IT ENDS WELL
—MEN SHOT, ETC., ETC.

PEMERTON BUILDING, Richmond, Va., Feb. 24.—We are confined on the third floor of the building, which is a large tobacco warehouse. Was removed from the island yesterday. Was a warm day and it was a long walk. Came across the "long bridge," and it is a long bridge. Was not sorry to bid adieu to Belle Isle. Were searched last night but our mess has lost nothing, owing to the following process we have of fooling them: One of the four manages to be in the front part of the crowd and is searched first, and is then put on the floor underneath and we let our traps down through a crack in the floor to him, and when our turn comes we have nothing about us worth taking away. The men so ravenous when the rations were brought in, that the boxes of bread and tubs of poor meat were raided upon before dividing, and consequently some had nothing to eat at all, while others had plenty. Our mess did not get a mouthful and have had nothing to eat since yesterday afternoon, and it is now nearly dark. The lice are very thick. You can see them all over the floors, walls, &c., in fact everything literally covered with them; they seem much larger than the stock on Belle Isle and a different species. We talk of escape night and day—and are nearly crazy on the subject. No more news about exchange. Papers state that Richmond is threatened, and that Kilpatrick's cavalry is making a raid on the place for the purpose of releasing us and burning the town. Unusual bustle among them.

George W. Hendryx.

Feb. 25.—We divide the night up into four watches and take turns standing guard while the other three sleep, to protect ourselves from Captain Moseby's gang of robbers. We are all armed with iron slats pulled off the window casings. They are afraid to pitch in to us, as we are a stout crowd and would fight well for our worldly goods. We expect to take it before long. They are eyeing us rather sharp, and I guess will make an attack to-night. Very long days and more lonesome than when on the island. Got rations to-day, and the allowance did not half satisfy our hunger.

Feb. 26.—Rather cold, almost spring. Guards unusually strict. Hendryx was standing near the window, and I close by him, looking at the high, ten story tobacco building, when the guard fired at us. The ball just grazed Hendryx's head and lodged in the ceiling above; all we could do to prevent Hendryx throwing a brick at the guard.

Feb. 27.—Organizing the militia; hauling artillery past the prison. Have a good view of all that is going on. Bought a compass from one of the guards for seven dollars, greenbacks; worth half a dollar at home. It is already rumored among the men that we have a compass, a map of Virginia, a preparation to put on our feet to prevent dogs from tracking us, and we are looked up to as if we were sons of Irish lords in disguise, and are quite noted personages. Cold last night, and we suffer much in not having blankets enough to keep us warm. The walls are cold and damp, making it disagreeable, and the stench nearly makes us sick. It is impossible for a person to imagine prison life until he has seen and realized it. No news of importance. Time passes much more drearily than when on Belle Isle. Were all searched again to-day but still keep my diary, although expecting to lose it every day; would be quite a loss, as the longer I write and remain a prisoner the more attached am I to my record of passing events. A man shot for putting his head out of the window. Men all say it served him right, for he had no business to thus expose himself against strict orders to the contrary. We are nearly opposite and not more than twenty rods from Libby Prison, which is a large tobacco warehouse. Can see plenty of union officers, which it is a treat to look at. Hendryx had a fight with the raiders—got licked. He ain't so pretty as he was before, but knows more. I am very wise about such matters, consequently retain my beauty.

Feb. 28.—Had the honor (?) of seeing Jefferson Davis again and part of his congress to-day. They visited Libby and we were allowed to look out of the windows to see them as they passed in and out of the building. Strut around like chickens with frozen feet. David Benjamin walked with the President and is a much better looking man. Prisoners were notified that if they made any insulting remarks they would be fired at. Have no more exalted opinion of them than before.

Feb. 29.—Excitement among the Johnnies—flying around as if the Yankee army were threatening Richmond. Cannot learn what the commotion is, but hope it is something that will benefit us. LATER: The occasion of the excitement among the rebels is that Dahlgreen is making a raid on Richmond, acting in conjunction with Kilpatrick, for the purpose of liberating prisoners. We are heavily guarded and not allowed to look out of the windows, nevertheless we manage to see about all there is going on.

Feb. 30.—Rebels in hot water all night and considerably agitated. Imagined we could hear firing during the night. This morning small squads of tired out union soldiers marched by our prison under guard, evidently captured through the night. Look as if they was completely played out. Go straggling by sometimes not more than half a dozen at a time. Would give something to hear the news. We are all excitement here. Negroes also go by in squads sometimes of hundreds in charge of overseers, and singing their quaint negro melodies. It is supposed by us that the negroes work on the fortifications, and are moved from one part of the city to another, for that purpose. Our troops have evidently been repulsed with considerable loss. We hear that Dahlgreen has been shot and killed. At the very first intimation that our troops were anywhere near, the prisoners would have made a break.

March 1.—Working along towards Spring slowly. A dead calm after the raid scare. We much prefer the open air imprisonment to confinement. Have considerable trouble with the thieves which disgrace the name of union soldier. Are the most contemptible rascals in existence. Often walk up to a man and coolly take his food and proceed to eat it before the owner. If the victim resists then a fight is the consequence, and the poor man not only loses his food but gets licked as well.

March 2.—The food we get here is poor, water very good, weather outside admirable, vermin still under control and the "Astor House Mess" flourishing. We are all in good health with the exception of Dr. Lewis, who is ailing. I was never tougher—

seems as if your humble servant was proof against the hardest rebel treatment. No exchange news. Trade and dicker with the guards and work ourselves into many luxuries, or rather work the luxuries into ourselves. Have become quite interested in a young soldier boy from Ohio named Bill Havens. Is sick with some kind of fever and is thoroughly bad off. Was tenderly brought up and well educated I should judge Says he ran away from home to become a drummer. Has been wounded twice, in numerous engagements, now a prisoner of war and sick. Will try and keep track of him. Every nationality is here represented and from every branch of the service, and from all parts of the world. There are smart men here and those that are not so smart, in fact a conglomeration of humanity—hash, as it were.

March 3.—The ham given us to-day was rotten, with those nameless little white things crawling around through it. Promptly threw it out of the window and was scolded for it by a fellow prisoner who wanted it himself Shall never become hungry enough to eat poor meat. Guards careless with their guns. An old man shot in the arm. Hendryx tried to pull a brick out of the casing to throw at the shooter. Barbarians these rebs.

March 4.—And now we are getting ready to move somewhere, the Lord only knows where. One good thing about their old prisons, we are always ready for a change. Have made many new acquaintances while here in Pemberton, and some agreeable ones; my boy Havens has fever and chills. Is rather better to-day. It is said we move to-night. Minnesota Indians confined here, and a number of sailors and marines. I am quite a hand to look at men, sometimes for hours, and study them over, then get to talking with them and see how near I was right in my conjectures. Its almost as good as reading books. The Astor House Mess is now composed of but four members, E. P. Sanders, F. L. Lewis, Geo. W. Hendryx and myself; we still adhere to our sanitary regulations and as a consequence are in better health than a majority of those here. Sanders may be said to be at the head of the mess, (we call him Dad,) while Lewis is a sort of moderator and advisor, with Hendryx and myself as the rank and file. Are quite attached to one another, and don't believe that either one would steal from the other. I certainly wouldn't take anything short of pumpkin pie or something of that sort. Of course a man would steal pie, at least we all say so, and Lewis even declares he would steal dough-cakes and pancakes such as his wife used to make. We are all well dressed, thanks to the Sanitary Commission and our own ingenuity in getting what was intended for us to have. False alarm of fire.

Routed at Midnight.

ON THE CARS, March 7, 1864.—We were roused from our gentle slumbers during the night, counted off and marched to the cars, loaded into them, which had evidently just had some cattle as occupants. Started southward to some portion of Georgia, as a guard told us. Passed through Petersburg, and other towns which I could not learn the names of. Cars run very slow, and being crowded, we are very uncomfortable—and hungry. Before leaving Richmond hard-tack was issued to us in good quantity for the Confederacy. Have not much chance to write. Bought some boiled sweet potatoes of the guard, which are boss. The country we pass through is a miserable one. Guards watch us close to see that none escape, and occasionally a Yank is shot, but not in our car. Seems as if we did not run over thirty or forty miles per day. Stop for hours on side tracks, waiting for other trains to pass us.

March 8.—Were unloaded last night and given a chance to straighten our limbs. Stayed all night in the woods, side of the track, under a heavy guard. Don't know where we are, as guards are very reticent.

March 10.—Still traveling, and unloaded nights to sleep by the track. Rebel citizens and women improve every opportunity to see live Yankees. Are fed passably well. Lewis feeling poorly. Watch a chance to escape but find none.

March 13.—Ran very slow through the night, and are in the vicininy of Macon, Ga. Will reach our prison to-night. Received a pone of corn bread apiece weighing about two pounds, which is liberal on their part. Two more days such riding as this would kill me. The lice are fairly eating us up alive, having had no chance to rid ourselves of them since leaving Richmond. One of the guards struck Hendryx during the night. We were talking on the all important subject, and the guard hearing us chatting away to ourselves struck over into the croud where the noise came from and hit George in the back part of the head. He didn't speak for a minute or two and I was afraid it had killed him, which happily proved to the contrary. As soon as it came daylight he showed the brute where he had struck him, and took the occasion to dress him down a little, whereupon the rebel threatened that if he said another word to him he would blow his head off. A drizzling rain has set in.

ANDERSONVILLE.

ARRIVAL AT THE WORST OF ALL PRISONS—BEGINNING OF A SUMMER THAT KILLED THIRTEEN THOUSAND MEN—BAD WATER, BAD FOOD, AND MOST INHUMAN TREATMENT—IN THE CLUTCHES OF WIRTZ AND HIS PICKED OUT REBEL AIDS—THE TRUTH AND NOTHING BUT THE TRUTH—A SEASON OF INTENSE SUFFERING.

CAMP SUMPTER, Andersonville, Ga., March 14.—Arrived at our destination at last and a dismal hole it is, too. We got off the cars at two o'clock this morning in a cold rain, and were marched into our pen between a strong guard carrying lighted pitch pine knots to prevent our crawling off in the dark. I could hardly walk have been cramped up so long, and feel as if I was a hundred years old. Have stood up ever since we came from the cars, and shivering with the cold The rain has wet us to the skin and we are worn out and miserable Nothing to eat to-day, and another dismal night just setting in.

March 15.—At about midnight I could stand up no longer, and lay down in the mud and water. Could hardly get up. Shall get food this morning, and after eating shall feel better. There is a good deal to write about here, but I must postpone it until some future time, for I can hardly hold a pencil now. LATER: Have drawn some rations which consisted of nearly a quart of corn meal, half a pound of beef, and some salt. This is splendid. I have just partaken of a delicious repast and feel like a different person. Dr. Lewis is discouraged and thinks he cannot live long in such a place as this.

March 16.—The prison is not yet entirely completed. One side is yet open, and through the opening two pieces of artillery are pointed. About 1800 Yankees are here now. Col. Piersons commands the prison, and rides in and talks with the men. Is quite sociable, and says we are all to be exchanged in a few weeks. He was informed that such talk would not go down any longer. We had been fooled enough, and paid no attention to what they told us. Our mess is gradually settling down. Have picked out our ground, rolled some big logs together, and are trying to make ourselves comfortable. I am in the best of spirits, and will live with them for some time to come if they will only give me one quarter enough to eat, and they are doing it now, and am in my glory. Weather cleared up, and very cold nights. We put on all our clothes nights and take them off day-times. The men do most of their sleeping through the day, and shiver through the long nights

March 17.—Get almost enough to eat, such as it is, but don't get it regularly; sometimes in the morning, and sometimes in the afternoon. Six hundred more prisoners came last night, and from Belle Isle, Va., our old home. Andersonville is situated on two hillsides, with a small stream of swampy water running through the center, and on both sides of the stream is a piece of swamp with two or three acres in it We have plenty of wood now, but it will not last long. They will undoubtedly furnish us with wood from the outside, when it is burned up on the inside. A very unhealthy climate. A good many are being poisoned by poisonous roots, and there is a thick green scum on the water All who drink freely are made sick, and their faces swell up so they cannot see.

March 18.—There are about fifteen acres of ground enclosed in the stockade and we have the freedom of the whole ground. Plenty of room, but they are filling it up. Six hundred new men coming each day from Richmond. Guards are perched upon top of the stockade; are very strict, and to-day one man was shot for approaching too near the wall. A little warm to-day Found W. B Rowe, from Jackson, Mich.; he is well and talks encouraging. We have no shelter of any kind whatever. Eighteen or twenty die per day. Cold and damp nights. The dews wet things through completely, and by morning all nearly chilled Wood getting scarce. On the outside it is a regular wilderness of pines. Railroad a mile off and can just see the cars as they go by, which is the only sign of civilization in sight. Rebels all the while at work making the prison stronger. Very poor meal, and not so much to day as formerly. My young friend Billy Havens was sent to the hospital about the time we left Richmond. Shall be glad to hear of his recovery. Prevailing conversation is food and exchange.

March 19—A good deal of fighting going on among us. A large number of sailors and marines are confined with us, and they are a quarrelsome set. I have a very sore hand, caused by cutting a hole through the car trying to get out. I have to write with my left hand. It is going to be an awful place during the summer months here, and thousands will die no doubt.

March 21.—Prison gradually filling up with forlorn looking creatures. Wood is being burned up gradually. Have taken in my old acquaintance and a member of my own company "A" 9th Mich. Cavalry, Wm. B. Rowe. Sergt. Rowe is a tall, straight, dark complexioned man, about thirty five years old. He was captured while carrying dispatches from Knoxville to Gen. Burnside. Has been a prisoner two or three months, and was in Pemerton Building until sent here. He is a tough, able-bodied man. Every day I find new Michigan men, some of them old acquaintances.

March 23.—Stockade all up, and we are penned in. Our mess is out of filthy lucre—otherwise, busted. Sold my overcoat to a guard, and for luxuries we are eating that up. My blanket keeps us all warm. There are two more in our mess. Daytimes the large spread is stretched three or four feet high on four sticks, and keeps off the sun, and at night taken down for a cover.

March 24.—Digging a tunnel to get out of this place. Prison getting filthy. Prisoners somewhat to blame for it. Good many dying, and they are those who take no care of themselves, drink poor water, etc.

March 25.—Lieut. Piersons is no longer in command of the prison, but instead a Capt. Wirtz. Came inside to-day and looked us over. Is not a very prepossessing looking chap. Is about thirty-five or forty years old, rather tall, and a little stoop shouldered; skin has a pale, white livered look, with thin lips. Has a sneering sort of cast of countenance. Makes a fellow feel as if he would like to go up and boot him. Should judge he was a Swede, or some such countryman. Hendryx thinks he could make it warm for him in short order if he only had a chance. Wirtz wears considerable jewelry on his person—long watch chain, something that looks like a diamond for a pin in his shirt, and wears patent leather boots or shoes. I asked him if he didn't think we would be exchanged soon. He said: Oh, yes, we would be exchanged soon. Somehow or other this assurance don't elate us much; perhaps it was his manner when saying it. Andersonville is getting to be a rather bad place as it grows warmer. Several sick with fevers and sores.

March 26.—Well, well, my birthday came six days ago, and how old do you think I am? Let me see. Appearances would seem to indicate that I am thirty or thereabouts, but as I was born on the 20th day of March, 1843, I must now be just twenty-one years of age, this being the year 1864 Of age and six days over. I thought that when a man became of age, he generally became free and his own master as well. If this ain't a burlesque on that old time-honored custom, then carry me out—but not feet foremost.

March 27.—We have issued to us once each day about a pint of beans, or more properly peas, (full of bugs), and three-quarters of a pint of meal, and nearly every day a piece of bacon the size of your two fingers, probably about three or four ounces. This is very good rations taken in comparison to what I have received before. The pine which we use in cooking is pitch pine, and a black smoke arises from it; consequently we are black as negroes. Prison gradually filling from day to day, and situation rather more unhealthy. Occasionally a squad comes in who have been lately captured, and they tell of our battles, sometimes victorious and sometimes otherwise. Sometimes we are hopeful and sometimes the reverse. Take all the exercise we can, drink no water, and try to get along. It is a sad sight to see the men die so fast. New prisoners die the quickest and are buried in the near vicinity, we are told in trenches without coffins. Sometimes we have visitors of citizens and women who come to look at us. There is sympathy in some of their faces and in some a lack of it. A dead line composed of slats of boards runs around on the inside of the wall, about twelve or fourteen feet from the wall, and we are not allowed to go near it on pain of being shot by the guard.

March 28.—We are squadded over to-day, and rations about to come in. It's a sickly dirty place. Seems as if the sun was not over a mile high, and has a particular grudge against us. Wirtz comes inside and has began to be very insolent. Is constantly watching for tunnels. He is a brute. We call him the "Flying Dutchman." Came across Sergt. Bullock, of my regiment, whom I last saw on Belle Isle From a fat, chubby young fellow, he is a perfect wreck. Lost his voice and can hardly speak aloud; nothing but skin and bone, and black and ragged. Never saw such a change in a human being Cannot possibly live, I don't think; still he is plucky and hates to die. Goes all around enquiring for news, and the least thing encouraging cheers him up. Capt. Moseby, of the raiders, is in the same squad with me. He is quite an intelligent fellow and often talks with us. We lend him our boiling cup which he returns with thanks. Better to keep on the right side of him, if we can without countenancing his murderous operations.

March 29.—Raiders getting more bold as the situation grows worse. Often rob a man now of all he has, in public, making no attempt at comcealment. In sticking up for the weaker party, our mess gets into trouble nearly every day, and particularly Hendryx, who will fight any time.

March 30.—The gate opens every little while letting some poor victims into this terrible place, which is already much worse than Belle Isle. Seems as if our government is at fault in not providing some way to get us out of here. The hot weather months must kill us all outright. Feel myself at times sick and feverish with no strength seemingly. Dr. Lewis worries, worries, all the day long, and it's all we can do to keep him from giving up entirely. Sergt. Rowe takes things as they come in dogged silence. Looks like a caged lion. Hendryx sputters around, scolding away, &c.

April 1.—This is an April Fool sure. Saw a fellow to-day from our regiment, named Casey. Says I was reported dead at the regiment, which is cheerful. Perhaps it is just as well though, for them to anticipate the event a few months. It is said that Wirtz shot some one this morning. Often hear the guards shoot and hear of men being killed. Am not ambitious to go near them. Have completely lost my desire to be on the outside working for extra rations. Prefer to stick it out where I am than to have anything to do with them. They are an ungodly crew, and should have the warmest corner in that place we sometimes hear mentioned.

April 2.—James Robins, an Indiana soldier, is in our close proximity. Was wounded and taken prisoner not long since. Wound, which is in the thigh, is in a terrible condition, and gangrene setting in. Although he was carried to the gate to-day, was refused admission to the hospital or medical attendance. Rebels say they have no medicine for us. Robins has been telling me about himself and family at home, and his case is only one of a great many good substantial men of families who must die in Southern prisons, as victims to mismanagement. The poorer the Confederacy, and the meaner they are, the more need that our government should get us away from here, and not put objectionable men at the head of exchange to prevent our being sent home or back to our commands.

April 3 —We have stopped wondering at suffering or being surprised at anything. Can't do the subject justice and so don't try. Walk around camp every morning looking for acquaintances, the sick, &c. Can see a dozen most any morning laying around dead A great many are terribly afflicted with diarrhea, and scurvy begins to take hold of some. Scurvy is a bad disease, and taken in connection with the former is sure death. Some have dropsy as well as scurvy, and the swollen limbs and body are sad to see. To think that these victims have people at home, mothers, wives and sisters, who are thinking of them and would do much for them if they had the chance, little dreaming of their condition.

April 4.—Same old story—coming in and being carried out; all have a feeling of lassitude which prevents much exertion. Have been digging in a tunnel for a day or two with a dozen others who are in the secret. It's hard work. A number of tunnels have been discovered. The water now is very warm and sickening.

April 5.—Dr. Lewis talks about nothing except his family. Is the bluest mortal here, and worries himself sick, let alone causes sufficient for that purpose. Is poorly adapted for hardships. For reading we have the "Pilgrim's Progress," donated to me by some one when on Belle Isle. Guess I can repeat nearly all the book by heart. Make new acquaintances every day "Scotty," a marine, just now is edifying our mess with his salt water yarns, and they are tough ones I tell him he may die here; still he declares they are true.

April 6 —John Smith is here and numerous of his family. So many go by nick-names, that seldom any go by their real names. Its "Minnesota," "Big Charlie," "Little Jim," "Marine Jack." "Indiana Feller," "Mopey," "Skinny," "Smarty," &c. Hendryx is known by the latter name, Sanders is called "Dad," Rowe is called the "Michigan Sergeant," Lewis is called plain "Doc." while I am called, for some unknown reason, "Bugler." I have heard it said that I looked just like a Dutch bugler, and perhaps that is the reason of my cognomen. Probably thirty die per day. The slightest news about exchange is told from one to the other, and gains every time repeated, until finally its grand good news and sure exchange immediately. The weak ones feed upon these reports and struggle along from day to day. One hour they are all hope and expectation and the next hour as bad the other way. The worst looking scallawags perched upon the stockade as guards, from boys just large enough to handle a gun, to old men who ought to have been dead years ago for the good of their country. Some prisoners nearly naked, the majority in rags and daily becoming more destitute. My clothes are good and kept clean, health fair although very poor in flesh   Man killed at the dead line.

April 7.—Capt. Wirtz prowls around the stockade with a rebel escort of guards, looking for tunnels. Is very suspicious of amateur wells which some have dug for water. It is useless to speak to him about our condition, as he will give us no satisfaction whatever. Says it is good enough for us —— yankees. I am deputized by half a dozen or so to speak to him as to the probabilities of a change, and whether we may not reasonably expect to be exchanged without passing the summer here. In his position he must know something in relation to our future. At the first favorable moment shall approach his highness. Prison is all the time being made stronger, more guards coming and artillery looking at us rather unpleasantly from many directions. Think it impossible for any to get away here, so far from our lines. The men too are not able to withstand the hardships attendant upon an escape, still fully one-half of all here are constantly on the alert for chances to get away. Foremost in all schemes for freedom is Hendryx, and we are engaging in a new tunnel enterprise. The yankee is a curious animal, never quiet until dead. There are some here who pray and try to preach. Very many too who have heretofore been religiously inclined, throw off all restraint and are about the worst. Tried and found wanting it seems to me. Those who find the least fault, make the best of things as they come and grin and bear it, get along the best. Weather getting warmer, water warmer and nastier, food worse and less in quantities, and more prisoners coming nearly every day.

April 8.—We are digging with an old fire shovel at our tunnel. The shovel is a prize; we also use half of canteens, pieces of boards, &c. Its laborious work. A dozen are engaged in it. Like going into a grave to go into a tunnel. Soil light and liable to cave in. Take turns in digging. Waste dirt carried to the stream in small quantities and thrown in. Not much faith in the enterprise, but work with the rest as a sort of duty. Raiders acting fearful. Was boiling my cup of meal to day and one of the raiders ran against it and over it went. Give him a whack side of the head that made him see stars I should judge, and in return he made me see the whole heavens. Battese, a big Indian, rather helped me out of the scrape. All of our mess came to my rescue. Came near being a big fight with dozens engaged. Battese is a large full blooded six foot Minnesota Indian, has quarters near is, and is a noble fellow. He and other Indians have been in our hundred for some weeks. They are quiet, attend to their own business, and won't stand much nonsense. Great deal of fighting. One Duffy, a New York rough, claims the light weight championship of Andersonville. Regular battles quite often. Remarkable how men will stand up and be pummeled. Dr. Lewis daily getting worse off. Is troubled with scurvy and dropsy. If he was at home would be considered dangerously ill and in bed, but he walks around slowly inquiring for news in a pitiful way. I have probably fifty acquaintances here that visit us each day to talk the situation over. Jimmy Devers, my Michigan friend whom I found on Belle Isle, Sergt. Bullock, of my regiment; Tom McGill, also of Michigan; Michael Hoare, a schoolmate of mine from earliest recollection, Dorr Blakeman, also a resident of Jackson, Michigan, a little fellow named Swan, who lived in Ypsylanti, Mich ; Burckhardt from near Lansing; Hub Dakin, from Dansville, Mich., and many others, meet often to compare notes, and we have many a hearty laugh in the midst of misery I dicker and trade and often make an extra ration. We sometimes draw small cow peas for rations, and being a printer by trade, I spread the peas out on a blanket and quickly pick them up one at a time, after the manner of picking up type. One drawback is the practice of unconsciously putting the beans into my mouth. In this way I often eat up the whole printing office. I have trials of skill with a fellow named Land, who is also a printer. There are no other typos here that I know of.

April 9 —See here Mr. Confederacy, this is going a little too far. You have no business to kill us off at this rate. About thirty or forty die daily. They have rigged up an excuse for a hospital on the outside, where the sick are taken. Admit none though who can walk or help themselves in any way Some of our men are detailed to help as nurses, but in a majority of cases those who go out on parole of honor are cut-throats and robbers, who abuse a sick prisoner. Still, there are exceptions to this rule. We hear stories of Capt. Wirtz's cruelty in punishing the men, but I hardly credit all the stories. More prisoners to-day. Some captured near Petersburg. Dont know anything about exchange. Scurvy and dropsy taking hold of the men. Many are blind as soon as it becomes night, and it is called moon blind. Caused, I suppose, by sleeping with the moon shining in the face. Talked with Michael Hoare, an old school fellow of mine. Mike was captured while we were in Pemerton Building, and was one of Dahlgreen's men Was taken right in the suburbs of Richmond. Has told me all the news of their failure on account of Kilpatrick failing to make a junction at some point. Mike is a great tall, slim fellow, and a good one. Said he heard my name called out in Richmond as having a box of eatables from the North. He also saw a man named Shaw claim the box with a written order from me. Shaw was one of our mess on Belle Isle. He was sent to Richmond while sick, from the island, knew of my expecting the box, and for ed an order to get it. Well, that was rough, still I probably wouldn't have got it any way. Better him than some rebel. Mike gave me a lot of black pepper which we put into our soup. which is a luxury. He has no end of talk at his tongue's end, and it is good to hear. Recounts how once when I was about eight or ten years old and he some older, I threw a base ball club and hit him on the shins. Then ran and he couldn't catch me. It was when we were both going to school to A. A. Henderson, in Jackson, Mich. Think I remember the incident, and am strongly under the impression that he caught me It is thus that old friends meet after many years. John McGuire is also here, another Jackson man. He has a family at home and is worried. Says he used to frequently see my brother George at Hilton Head, before being captured.

April 10.—Getting warmer and warmer. Can see the trees swaying back and forth on the outside, but inside not a breath of fresh air. Our wood is all gone, and we are now digging up stumps and roots for fuel to cook with. Some of the first prisoners here have passable huts made of logs, sticks, pieces of blankets, &c. Room about all taken up in here now. Rations not so large. Talk that they intend to make the meal into bread before sending it inside, which will be an improvement. Rations have settled down to less than a pint of meal per day, with occasionally a few peas, or an apology for a piece of bacon, for each man. Should judge that they have hounds on the outside to catch run-aways, from the noise. Wirtz don't come in as much as formerly. The men make it uncomfortable for him As Jimmy Devers says, "He is a terror." I have omitted to mention Jimmy's name of late, although he is with us all the time—not in our mess, but close by He has an old pack of cards with which we play to pass away the time. Many of the men have testaments, and "house-wives" which they have brought with them from home, and it is pitiful to see them look at these things while thinking of their loved ones at home.

    April 11.—Dr Lewis is very bad off with the scurvy and diarrhea. We don't think he can stand it much longer, but make out to him that he will stick it through. Our government must hear of our condition here and get us away before long. If they don't, its a poor government to tie to. Hendryx and myself are poor, as also are all the mess. Still in good health compared with the generality of the prisoners. Jimmy Devers has evidently sort of dried up, and it don't seem to make any difference whether he gets anything to eat or not. He has now been a prisoner of war nearly a year, and is in good health and very hopeful of getting away in time. Sticks up for our government and says there is some good reason for our continued imprisonment. I can see none. As many as 12,000 men here now, and crowded for room. Death rate is in the neighborhood of eighty per day. Hendryx prowls around all over the prison, bringing us what good news he can, which is not much. A very heavy dew nights, which is almost a rain Rebels very domineering. Many are tunneling to get out. Our tunnel has been abandoned, as the location was not practicable. Yank shot to-day near our quarters. Approached too near the dead line. Many of the men have dug down through the sand and reached water, but it is poor; no better than out of the creek.

    April 12.—Another beautiful but warm day with no news. Insects of all descriptions making their appearance, such as lizards, a worm four or five inches long, fleas, maggots &c. There is so much filth about the camp that it is terrible trying to live here. New prisoners are made sick the first hours of their arrival by the stench which pervades the prison. Old prisoners do not mind it so much, having become used to it. No visitors come near us any more. Everybody sick, almost, with scurvy—an awful disease. New cases every day. I am afraid some contagious disease will get among us, and if so every man will die. My blanket a perfect Godsend. Is large and furnishes shelter from the burning sun. Hendryx has a very sore arm which troubles him much. Even he begins to look and feel bad. James Gordan, or Gordenian, (I don't know which) was killed to-day by the guard. In crossing the creek on a small board crossway men are often shot. It runs very near the dead line, and guards take the occasion to shoot parties who put their hands on the dead line in going across. Some also reach up under the dead line to get purer water, and are shot Men seemingly reckless of their lives New prisoners coming in and are shocked at the sights.

April 13.—Jack Shannon, from Ann Arbor, died this morning. The raiders are the stronger party now, and do as they please; and we are in nearly as much danger now from our own men as from the rebels Capt. Moseby, of my own hundred, figures conspicuously among the robberies, and is a terrible villain. During the night some one stole my jacket. Have traded off all superfluous clothes, and with the loss of jacket have only pants, shirt, shoes, (no stockings,) and hat; yet I am well dressed in comparison with some others. many have nothing but an old pair of pants which reach, perhaps, to the knees, and perhaps not. Hendryx has two shirts, and should be mobbed. I do quite a business trading rations, making soup for the sick ones, taking in payment their raw food which they cannot eat Get many a little snack by so doing

April 14 —At least twenty fights among our own men this forenoon It beats all what a snarling crowd we are getting to be. The men are perfectly reckless, and had just as soon have their necks broken by fighting as anything else. New onions in camp. Very small, and sell for $2 a bunch of four or five Van Tassel, a Pennsylvanian, is about to die. Many give me parting injunctions relative to their families, in case I should live through Have half a dozen photographs of dead men's wives, with addresses on the back of them. Seems to be pretty generally conceded that if any get through, I will. Not a man here now is in good health An utter impossibility to remain well Signs of scurvy about my person. Still adhere to our sanitary rules. Lewis anxious to get to the hospital. Will die any way shortly, whether there or here. Jimmy Devers, the old prisoner, coming down Those who have stood it bravely begin to weaken.

April 15.—The hospital is a tough place to be in, from all accounts. the detailed Yankees as soon as they get a little authority are certain to use it for all it is worth. In some cases before a man is fairly dead, he is stripped of everything, coat, pants, shirt, finger rings (if he has any), and everything of value taken away. These the nurses trade to the guards. Does not seem possible but such is the case, sad to relate. Not very pleasant for a man just breathing his last, and perhaps thinking of loved ones at home who are all so unconscious of the condition of their soldier father or brother, to be suddenly jerked about and fought over, with the cursing and blaspheming he is apt to hear. The sick now, or a portion of them, are huddled up in one corner of the prison, to get as bad as they can before being admitted to the outside hospital. Every day I visit it, and come away sick at heart that human beings should be thus treated.

April 26 —Ten days since I wrote in my diary, and in those ten days was too much occupied in trying to dig a tunnel to escape out of, to write any. On the 21st the tunnel was opened and two fellows belonging to a Massachusetts regiment escaped to the outside. Hendryx and myself next went out. The night was very dark. Came up out of the ground away on the outside of the guard. We crawled along to gain the woods, and got by some pickets, and when forty or fifty rods from the stockade, a shot was fired at some one coming out of the hole. We immediately jumped up and ran for dear life, seemingly making more noise than a troop of cavalry. It was almost daylight and away we went. Found I could not run far and we slowed up, knowing we would be caught, but hoping to get to some house and get something to eat first. Found I was all broke up for any exertion. In an hour we had traveled perhaps three miles, were all covered with mud, and scratched up. I had fell, too, in getting over some logs, and it seemed to me broken all the ribs in my body. Just as it was coming light in the east we heard dogs after us. We expected it, and so armed ourselves with clubs and sat down on a log. In a few moments the hounds came up with us and began smelling of us. Pretty soon five mounted rebels arrived on the scene of action. They laughed to think we expected to get away. Started us back towards our charnel pen. Dogs did not offer to bite us, but guards told us that if we had offered resistance or started to run they would have torn us. Arrived at the prison and after waiting an hour Capt. Wirtz interviewed us. After cussing us a few minutes we were put in the chain gang, where we remained two days. This was not very fine, but contrary to expectation not so bad after all. We had more to eat than when inside, and we had shade to lay in, and although my ancles were made very sore, do not regret my escapade. Am not permanently hurt any. We had quite an allowance of bacon while out, and some spring water to drink. Also from the surgeon I got some elder berries to steep into a tea to drink for scurvy, which is beginning to take hold of me. Lewis is sick and can hardly walk around. His days are few. Have taken another into our mess, named Swan, from Ypsilanti, Michigan. Is a fresh looking boy for this place and looks like a girl.

April 27.—Well, I was out from under rebel guard for an hour or so any way. Hurt my side though, and caught a little cold. Am sore somewhat. Have given up the idea of escaping. Think if Hendryx had been alone he would have gotten away. Is tougher than I am. A man caught stealing from one of his comrades and stabbed with a knife and killed. To show how little such things are noticed here I will give the particulars as near as I could get them. There were five or six men stopping together in a sort of shanty. Two of them were speculators, and had some money, corn bread, &c., and would not divide with their comrades, who belonged to their own company and regiment. Some time in the night one of them got up and was stealing bread from a haversack belonging to his more prosperous neighbor, and during the operation woke up the owner, who seized a knife and stabbed the poor fellow dead. The one who did the murder spoke out and said: "Harry, I believe Bill is dead; he was just stealing from me and I run my knife into him." "Good enough for him," says Harry. The two men then got up and straightened out "Bill," and then both lay down and went to sleep. An occupant of the hut told me these particulars and they are true. This morning poor Bill lay in the hut until eight or nine o'clock, and was then carried outside. The man who did the killing made no secret of it, but told it to all who wanted to know the particulars, who were only a few, as the occurrence was not an unusual one.

April 28.—Dr. Lewis is still getting worse with scurvy and dropsy combined. Limbs swollen to double their usual size—just like puff-balls. Raiders do about as they please, and their crimes would fill more paper than I have at my disposal.

April 30.—Very small rations given to us now. Not more than one quarter what we want to eat and that of the poorest quality. Splendid weather, but too warm; occasional rains. The Flying Dutchman (Wirtz) offers to give any two at a time twelve hours the start, and if caught to take the punishment he has for runaways. The offer is made to intimidate those thinking to escape. Half the men would take the consequences with two hours start.

May 1.—Warm. Samuel Hutton, of the 9th Mich. Cavalry, died last night; also Peter Christiancy and Joseph Sargent, of Co. D, 9th Mich., have died within a few weeks. Last evening 700 of the 85th New York arrived here They were taken at Plymouth, N. C., with 1,400 others, making 2,100 in all. The balance are on the road to this place. Wrote a letter home to-day. Have not heard from the North for over six months. Dying off very fast.

May 2.—A crazy man was shot dead by the guard an hour ago. The guard dropped a piece of bread on the inside of the stockade, and the fellow went inside the dead line to get it and was killed. The bread wagon was raided upon as soon as it drove inside to-day and all the bread stolen, for which offense no more will be issued to-day. As I write Wirtz is walking about the prison revolver in hand, cursing and swearing The men yell out "Hang him up!" "Kill the Dutch louse!" "Buck and gag him!" "Stone him to death!" &c., and he all the time trying to find out who it is insulting him so. "I vish I find out who calls me such insulting vords, I kill the dam Yankee as soon I eat my supper!" And every few minutes a handful of dirt is thrown by some one. Wreaks his vengeance by keeping back rations from the whole camp.

May 3.—A rebel battery came to-day on the cars, and is being posted around the stockade. Ever since my introduction to Andersonville they have been constantly at work making their prison stronger, until now I believe it is impossible for a person to get away. Notwithstanding, there are men al the time at work in divers ways. Rebel officers now say that we are not going to be exchanged during the war, and as they can hold us now and no fear of escape, they had just as soon tell us the truth as not, and we must take things just as they see fit to give them to us. Tom McGill is well and hearty, and as black as any negro. Over 19,000 confined here now, and the death rate ninety or one hundred.

May 4.—Good weather. Gen. Howell Cobb and staff came among us to-day, and inspected the prison Wirtz accompanied them pointing out and explaining matters. Gen. Winder, who has charge of all the prisoners of war in the South, is here, but has not been inside. Gen. Cobb is a very large and pompous looking man. None of the men dare address his highness. Three men out of every hundred allowed to go out after wood under a strong guard.

May 5.—Cold nights and warm days. Very unhealthy, such extremes. Small-pox cases carried out, and much alarm felt lest it should spread.

May 6.—Six months a prisoner to-day. Longer than any six years of my previous life. It is wonderful how well I stand the hardships here. At home I was not very robust, in fact had a tendency to poor health; but there are not many in prison that stand it as well as I do. There are about eighty-five or ninety dying now per day, as near as I can find out. Of course there are stories to the effect that a hundred and fifty and two hundred die each day, but such is not the case. Have a code of reasoning that is pretty correct. Often wonder if I shall get home again, and come to the conclusion that I shall. My hopeful disposition does more for me than anything else. Sanders trades and dickers around and makes extra eatables for our mess. There is not a hog in the mess. Nearly every day some one is killed for some trifling offense, by the guards. Rather better food to-day than usual.

May 7.—A squad of Yankees taken outside to-day on parole of honor, for the purpose of baking meal into bread. George Hendryx is one of the number, and he will have enough to eat after this, which I am glad of. I could have gotten outside if I so chose, but curious to write down I don't want to go. George says he will try and send in something for us to eat, and I know he will, for a truer hearted fellow never lived.

May 8.—Awful warm and more sickly. About 3,500 have died since I came here, which is a good many, come to think of it—cooked rations of bread to-day. We get a quarter of a loaf of bread, weighing about six ounces, and four or five ounces of pork. These are small allowances, but being cooked it is better for us. Rebels are making promises of feeding us better, which we hope they will keep. There is nothing the matter with me now but lack of food. The scurvy symptoms which appeared a few weeks ago have all gone.

May 9.—Many rebels riding about camp on horseback. I listened to an animated conversation between an officer and two of our men. Mr. Rebel got talked all to pieces and hushed up entirely. He took it good naturedly, however, and for a wonder did not swear and curse us. It is a great treat to see a decent rebel. Am lonesome since Hendryx went outside. Men are continually going up to the dead line and getting shot. They do not get much sympathy, as they should know better.

May 10.—Capt. Wirtz very domineering and abusive. Is afraid to come into camp any more. There are a thousand men in here who would willingly die if they could kill him first. Certainly the worst man I ever saw. New prisoners coming in every day with good clothes, blankets, &c., and occasionally with considerable money. These are victims for the raiders who pitch into them for plunder. Very serious fights occur. Occasionally a party of new comers stick together and whip the raiders, who afterward rally their forces and the affair ends with the robbers victorious Stones, clubs, knives, slung shots, &c., are used on these occasions, and sometimes the camp gets so stirred up that the rebels, thinking a break is intended, fire into the crowds gathered, and many are killed before quiet is again restored. Then Wirtz writes out an order and sends inside, telling he is prepared for any break, etc., etc. No less than five have died within a radius of thirty feet in the last twenty-four hours. Hendryx has a sore arm and in turning over last night I hurt it He pitched in to me while I was in a sound sleep to pay me for it. Woke up in short order and we had it, rough and tumble. Tore down the tent poles—rolled around—scaring Lewis and all the rest. I am the stoutest, and soon get on top and hold him down, and keep him there until he quiets down, which is always in about five minutes. We have squabbles of this sort often, which don't do any particular harm. Always laugh, shake and make up afterwards. The "Astor House Mess," or the heads rather, have gently requested that we do our fighting by daylight, and Sanders very forcibly remarked that should another scene occur as happened last night, he will take a hand in the business and lick us both. Battese laughed, for about the first time this summer He has taken quite a shine to both Hendryx and myself. In the fore part of to-day's entry I should have stated that Hendryx has been sent inside, they not being quite ready for him at the cookhouse. He is a baker by trade.

May 11.—Rainy weather and cold nights. Men shiver and cry all night—groan and "holler." I lay awake sometimes for hours, listening to the guards yell out "Post number one; ten o'clock and all's well!" And then Post No. 2 takes up the refrain, and it goes all around the camp, every one with a different sounding voice, squeaky, coarse, and all sorts. Some of them drawl out "H-e-r-o-'s y-e-r m-u-l-e!" and such like changes, instead of "All's well." Rumors of hard fighting about Richmond, and the rebels getting whipped, which of course they deny.

May 12—Received a few lines from George Hendryx, who again went out to work on the outside last night. Wirtz with a squad of guards is about the camp looking for tunnels. Patrols also looking among the prisoners for deserters. A lame man, for telling of a tunnel, was pounded almost to death last night, and this morning they were chasing him to administer more punishment, when he ran inside the dead line claiming protection of the guard. The guard didn't protect worth a cent, but shot him through the head. A general hurrahing took place, as the rebel had only saved our men the trouble of killing him. More rumors of hard fighting about Richmond. Grant getting the best of it I reckon. Richmond surrounded and rebels evacuating the place. These are the rumors. Guards deny it.

May 13.—Rainy morning. We are guarded by an Alabama regiment, who are about to leave for the front. Georgia militia to take their places. Making preparations for a grand pic-nic outside, given by the citizens of the vicinity to the troops about to leave. I must here tell a funny affair that has happened to me, which, although funny is very annoying. Two or three days before I was captured I bought a pair of cavalry boots of a teamster named Carpenter. The boots were too small for him and just fitted me. Promised to pay him on "pay day," we not having been paid off in some time. We were both taken prisoners and have been in the same hundred ever since. Has dunned me now about 1,850 times, and has always been mad at not getting his pay Sold the boots stortly after being captured and gave him half the receipts, and since that have paid him in rations and money as I could get it, until about sixty cents remain unpaid, and that sum is a sticker He is my evil genius, and fairly haunts the life out of me. Whatever I may get trusted for in after life, it shall never be for a pair of boots. Carpenter is now sick with scurvy, and I am beginning to get the same disease hold of me again. Battese cut my hair which was about a foot long. Gay old cut. Many have long hair, which, being never combed, is matted together and full of vermin. With sunken eyes, blackened countenances from pitch pine smoke, rags and disease, the men look sickening The air reeks with nastiness, and it is wonder that we live at all. When will relief come to us?

May 14.—A band of music came from Macon yesterday to attend the pic-nic. A large crowd of women were present to grace the occasion. The grounds on which the festivities were held lay a mile off and in sight of all. In the evening a Bowery dance was one of the pleasures enjoyed. "The Girl I Left Behind Me," was about all they could play, and that very poorly.

May 15.—Sabbath day and hot. Would give anything for some shade to lay in. Even this luxury is denied us, and we are obliged to crawl around more dead than alive. Rumors that Sherman is marching towards Atlanta, and that place threatened. Kilpatrick said to be moving toward us for the purpose of effecting our release. Hope he will be more successful than in his attack on Richmond. Rebels have dug a deep ditch all around on the outside of the wall to prevent tunneling, and a guard walks in the bottom of the ditch. Banghart, of my Regiment, died to-day.

May 16 —Two men got away during the night and were brought back before noon. (Was going to say before dinner) The men are torn by the dogs, and one of them full of buck shot. A funny way of escape has just been discovered by Wirtz. A man pretends to be dead and is carried out on a stretcher and left with the row of dead. As soon as it gets dark, Mr. Dead-man jumps up and runs. Wirtz suspecting the trick took to watching, and discovered a 'dead man" running away. An examination now takes place by the surgeon before being permitted out from under guard. I hear a number of men have gotten away by this method, and it seems very probable, as dead men are so plenty that not much attention is paid to them.

May 17.—Had a funny dream last night. Thought the rebels were so hard up for mules that they hitched up a couple of gray-back lice to draw in the bread. Wirtz is watching out for Yankee tricks. Some one told him the other day that the Yankees were making a large balloon inside and some day would all rise up in the air and escape. He flew around as if mad, but could find no signs of a balloon. Says there is no telling what "te tam Yankee will do." Some prisoners came to-day who were captured at Dalton, and report the place in our possession, and the rebels driven six miles this side. Kilpatrick and Stoneman are both with Sherman and there are expectations of starting out on some mission soon. supposed to be for this place. Nineteen thousand confined here now and dying at the rate of ninety per day. Philo Lewis, of the 5th Michigan Cav , can live but a day or two. Talks continually of his wife and family in Ypsilanti, Mich. Has pictures of the whole family, which he has given me to take home to them, also a long letter addressed to his wife and children. Mr. Lewis used to be a teacher of singing in Ypsilanti. He is a fine looking man naturally, and a smart man, but he must go the way of thousands of others, and perhaps myelf One of his pupils is here confined. Philo Lewis must not be confounded with F. L. Lewis, the member of our mess The latter, however, cannot live but a short time unless relief comes. Fine weather but very warm. The sandy soil fairly alive with vermin. If this place is so bad at this time of the year, what must it be in July, August and September? Every man will die, in my estimation, but perhaps we may be relieved before then. We'll try and think so anyway. New prisoners die off the fastest.

May 18.—We have some good singers in camp, and strange as it may seem, a good deal of singing is indulged in. There are some men that are happy as long as they can breathe, and such men smoothe over many rough places here. God bless a man who can sing in this place. A priest comes inside praying and chanting. A good man to come to such a place. Performs his duty the same to small-pox patients as to any other. Shall try and find out his name. Some of the wells dug by the Yanks furnish passable water, an improvement anyway on swamp water. Well water in great demand and sells readily for such trinkets as the men have to dispose of. Rebels building forts on the outside Rebel officers inside trying to induce shoemakers, foundrymen, carpenters and wood choppers, to go out and work for the Confederacy. A very few accepted the offer. Well, life is sweet, and can hardly blame men for accepting the offer; still, I don't want to go, neither do ninety-nine out of every hundred. The soldiers here are loyal to the cause.

May 19.—Nearly twenty thousand men confined here now. New ones coming every day. Rations *very* small and *very* poor. The meal that the bread is made out of is ground, seemingly, cob and all, and it scourges the men fearfully. Things getting continually worse. Hundreds of cases of dropsy. Men puff out of human shape and are perfectly horrible to look at. Philo Lewis died today. Could not have weighed at the time of his death more than ninety pounds, and was originally a large man, weighing not less than one hundred and seventy. Jack Walker, of the 9th Mich. Cavalry, has received the appointment to assist in carrying out the dead, for which service he receives an extra ration of corn bread.

May 20.—Hendryx sent me in to-day from the outside a dozen small onions and some green tea No person, on suddenly being lifted from the lowest depths of misery to peace and plenty, and all that money could buy, could feel more joyous or grateful than myself for those things. As the articles were handed in through the gate a crowd saw the transaction, and it was soon known that I had a friend on the outside who sent me in extras. I learn that a conspiracy is being gotten up on the outside, in which Hendryx is at the head, and they will try and overpower the guard and release the prisoners. If Capt. Wirtz only knew it, he has a very dangerous man in George Hendryx. Cram full of adventure, he will be heard from wherever he is.

May 21.—Still good weather and hot, with damp nights. Dr. Lewis lingers along in a miserable state of existence, and scurvy and dropsy doing their worst. His old messmates at the 9th Michigan regimental head-quarters little think of their favorite, story-telling, good fellows' condition now. We take as good care of him as possible under the circumstances. Two men shot to-day by the barbarians, and one of them has lain all the afternoon where he fell.

May 22.—No news of importance. Same old story. Am now a gallant washer-man. Battese, the Minnesota Indian, learn't me in the way of his occupation, made me a wash board by cutting creases in a piece of board, and I am fully installed. We have a sign out, made by myself on a piece of shingle: "WASHING." We get small pieces of bread for our labors. some of the sick cannot eat their bread, and not being able to keep clean, give us a job Make probably a pound of bread two or three days in the week. Battese says: "I work, do me good; you do same." Have many applications for admission to the firm, and may enlarge the business.

May 23.—Rains very hard. Seems as if the windows of Heaven had opened up, in fact the windows out all together. It's a grand good thing for the camp, as it washes away the filth and purifies the air.

May 24.—Sherman coming this way, so said, towards Atlanta. It is thought the cavalry will make a break for us, but even if they do they cannot get us north. We are equal to no exertion. Men busy to day killing swallows that fly low; partly for amusement, but more particularly for food they furnish. Are eaten raw before hardly dead. No, thank you, I will take no swallow.

May 25.—One thousand new prisoners came to-day from near Petersburg, Va. They give us encouraging news as to the termination of the spring campaign. Gen. Burnside said in a speech to his men that Petersburg would be taken in less than a month or Mrs. Burnside would be a widow. Every one hopeful. Getting warmer after the rain. Our squad has a very good well, and about one quarter water enough, of something a trifle better than swamp water. Man killed by the raiders near where we slept. Head all pounded to pieces with a club. Murders an every day occurrence.

May 26.—For the last three days I have had nearly enough to eat such as it is. My washing business gives me extra food. Have taken in a partner, and the firm now is Battese, Ransom & Co. Think of taking in more partners, making Battese president, appointing vice presidents, secretaries, &c. We charge a ration of bread for admittance. Sand makes a very good soap. If we could get hold of a razor and open a barber shop in connection, our fortunes would be made. We are prolonging Lewis' life by trading for luxuries to give him. Occasionally a little real meat soup, with a piece of onion in it, etc. Am saving up capital to buy a pair of shears I know of. Molasses given us to-day, from two to four spoonfuls apiece, which is indeed a treat. Anything sweet or sour, or in the vegetable line, is the making of us. We have taken to mixing a little meal with water, putting in a little molasses and setting it in the sun to sour. Great trouble in the lack of vessels in which to keep it, and then too, after getting a dish partly well soured, some poor prisoner will deliberately walk up and before we can see him drink it all up. Men are fairly crazy for such things.

May 27.—We twist up pieces of tin, stovepipe, &c., for dishes. A favorite and common dish is half of a canteen. Our spoons are made of wood. Hardly one man in ten has a dish of any kind to put his rations of soup or molasses in, and often old shoes, dirty caps and the like are brought into requisition. Notwithstanding my prosperity in business the scurvy is taking right hold of me. All my old acquaintances visit us daily and we condole with one another. Fresh beef given us to-day, but in very small quantities with no wood or salt to put it into proper shape. No one can very well object to raw beef, however. Great trouble is in getting it to us before being tainted. I persistently let alone meat with even a suspicion of rottenness; makes no difference with nearly all here. We occasionally hear of the conspiracy of outside paroled Yankees. Time will tell if it amounts to anything.

May 28.—No more news. It really seems as if we're all to die here. My mouth getting sore from scurvy and teeth loose. New prisoners coming in every day and death rate increasing. I don't seem to get hardened to the situation and am shuddering all the time at the sights. Rainy weather.

May 29.—Sabbath day but not a pleasant one. Nearly a thousand just came in. Would seem to me that the rebels are victorious in their battles. New men are perfectly thunderstruck at the hole they have got into. A great many give right up and die in a few weeks, and some in a week. My limbs are badly swollen with scurvy and dropsy combined. Mouth also very sore. Battese digs for roots which he steeps up and I drink. Could give up and die in a short time but won't. Have got living reduced to a science.

May 30.—Another thousand came to day and from the eastern army. Prison crowded. Men who came are from Siegel's corps in the Shenandoah Valley. The poor deluded mortals never heard of Andersonville before. Well, they hear of it now. Charlie Hudson, from some part of Ohio, took his canteen an hour ago and went to the swamp for water. He has not returned for the very good reason that he was shot while reaching up under the dead line to get the freshest water. Some one has pulled the body out of the water on to dry land where it will stay until to-morrow, when it will be piled with perhaps forty others on the dead wagon, carted off and buried like a dog. And this is the last of poor Charlie, who has enlivened us many an evening with his songs and stories. The Astor House Mess is very sad to-night.

May 31.—A rebel came inside to-day and enquired for me, in the tenth squad, first mess. I responded, wondering and fearful as to what they should want with me. Was happily surprised on going to the gate to see Hendryx with something in his hand for me. Seemed thunderstruck at my appearance and said I was looking bad. He was looking better than when he went out. Had brought me luxuries in the shape of ginger bread, onions and tea, and am happy. Geo. is a brick. Says it is against orders to send anything inside but he talked them over. Was afraid the raiders would waylay me before reaching the mess but they did not.

June 1.—Reported that the 51st Virginia Regt. is here for the purpose of conducting us north for exchange. Believe nothing of the kind. Prisoners come daily. E. P. Sanders, Rowe and myself carried our old friend Dr. Lewis to the hospital. He was immediately admitted and we came away feeling very sad, knowing he would live but a short time. The sick are not admitted until they are near death, and then there is no hope for them. Rainy day.

June 2.—Another dark, stormy day. Raiders playing the very devil. Muddy and sticky.

Battese, the Minnesota Indian.

June 3.—New prisoners say that an armistice has been agreed upon for the purpose of effecting an exchange, and negotiating for peace. It may be so, and the authorities had good reasons for allowing us to stay here, but how can they pay for all the suffering? And now some negro prisoners brought inside. They belong to the 54th Massachusetts. Came with white prisoners Many of the negroes wounded, as, indeed, there are wounded among all who come here now. No news from Hendryx or Lewis. Quite a number going out after wood to cook with Hot and wet.

June 4.—Have not been dry for many days. Raining continually. Some men took occasion while out after wood, to overpower the guard and take to the pines. Not yet been brought back. Very small rations of poor molasses, corn bread and bug soup.

June 5.—Exchange rumors to the effect that transports are en-route for Savannah for the purpose of taking us home. Stick right to my washing however. A number of men taken out to be kept as hostages—so said. Raiders rule the prison. Am myself cross and feel like licking somebody, but Hendryx is gone and don't want to try to lick anybody else, fearing I might get licked myself. Some fun fighting him as it didn't make any difference which licked

June 6.—Eight months a prisoner to-day. A lifetime has been crowded into these eight months. No rations at all. Am now a hair cutter. Have *hired* the shears. Enough to eat but not the right kind. Scurvy putting in its work, and symptoms of dropsy. Saw Hendryx at the bake house up stairs window, looking over the camp. Probably looking to see if he can locate his old comrades among the sea of human beings. Wirtz comes inside no more, in fact, does very few rebels. The place is too bad for them.

June 7.—Heard to-day that Hendryx had been arrested and in irons for inciting a conspiracy. Not much alarmed for him. He will come out all right. Still rainy. Have hard work keeping my diary dry. Nearly all the old prisoners who were captured with me are dead. Don't know of over 50 or 60 alive out of 800.

FROM BAD TO WORSE.

THE ASTOR HOUSE MESS STILL HOLDS TOGETHER, ALTHOUGH DEPLETED—ALL MORE OR LESS DISEASED—AS THE WEATHER GETS WARMER THE DEATH RATE INCREASES—DYING OFF LIKE SHEEP—THE END IS NOT YET.

June 8.—More new prisoners. There are now over 23,000 confined here, and the death rate 100 to 130 per day, and I believe more than that. Rations worse.

June 9—It is said that a grand break will occur soon, and nearly the whole prison engaged in the plot. Spies inform the rebels of our intentions. Rains yet.

June 10.—The whole camp in a blaze of excitement. Plans for the outbreak known to Capt. Wirtz. Some traitor unfolded the plans to him Thirty or forty pieces of artillery pointed at us from the outside, and stockade covered with guards who shoot right and left. Thirty or forty outsiders sent inside, and they tell us how the affair was found out. A number of the ringleaders are undergoing punishment. Hendryx has made his escape, and not been heard of since yesterday. It is said he went away in full Confederate dress, armed, and furnished with a guide to conduct him. Dr. Lewis died to-day. Jack Walker told us about his death. Capt. Wirtz has posted up on the inside a notice for us to read. The following is the notice:

"NOTICE.

Not wishing to shed the blood of hundreds not connected with those who concocted a plan to force the stockade, and make in this way their escape. I hereby warn the leaders and those who formed themselves into a band to carry out this, that I am in possession of all the facts, and have made my arrangements accordingly, so to frustrate it. No choice would be left me but to open with grape and cannister on the stockade, and what effect this would have in this densely crowded place need not be told. Signed,

June 10, 1864. H. WIRTZ."

June 11.—And so has ended a really colossal attempt at escape. George Hendryx was one of the originators of the plan. He took advantage of the excitement consequent upon its discovery and made good his escape, and I hope will succeed in getting to our lines. It is the same old situation here only worse, and getting worse all the time. I am not very good at description, and find myself at fault in writing down the horrible condition we are in.

June 12.—Rained every day so far this month. A portion of the camp is a mud hole, and the men are obliged to lay down in it. Fort Pillow prisoners tell some hard stories against the Confederacy at the treatment they received after their capture. They came here nearly *starved to death*, and a good many were wounded after their surrender. They are mostly Tennesseans, and a "right smart sorry set." Battese has taken quite a fatherly interest in me. Keeps right on at the head of the washing and hair cutting business, paying no attention to anything outside of his work. Says: "We get out all right!"

June 13 —It is now as hot and sultry as it was ever my lot to witness. The cloudy weather and recent rains make everything damp and sticky. We don't any of us sweat though, particularly, as we are pretty well dried up. Laying on the ground so much has made sores on nearly every one here, and in many cases gangrene sets in and they are very bad off. Have many sores on my body, but am careful to keep away the poison. To-day saw a man with a bullet hole in his head over an inch deep, and you could look down in it and see maggots squirming around at the bottom. Such things are terrible, but of common occurrence. Andersonville seems to be head-quarters for all the little pests that ever originated—flies by the thousand millions. I have got into one bad scrape, and the one thing now is to get out of it. Can do nothing but take as good care of myself as possible, which I do. Battese works all the time at something. Has scrubbed his hands sore, using sand for soap.

June 14.—Mike Hoare stalks around, cheerful, black and hungry. We have long talks about our school days when little boys together. Mike is a mason by trade, and was solicited to go out and work for the rebels Told them he would work on nothing but vaults to bury them in. Is a loyal soldier and had rather die here than help them, as, indeed, would a majority of the prisoners. To tell the truth, we are so near death and see so much of it, that it is not dreaded as much as a person would suppose. We stay here day after day, week after week, and month after month, seemingly forgotten by all our friends at the North, and then our sufferings are such that death is a relief in the view of a great many, and not dreaded to any extent. By four o'clock each day the row of dead at the gate would scare the life out of me before coming here, while now it is nothing at all, but the same thing over and over

June 15.—I am sick; just able to drag around. My teeth are loose, mouth sore, with gums grown down in some places lower than the teeth and bloody, legs swollen up with dropsy and on the road to the trenches. Where there is so much to write about, I can hardly write anything. It's the same old story and must necessarily be repetition. Raiders now do just as they please, kill, plunder and steal in broad day light, with no one to molest them. Have been trying to organize a police force, but cannot do it. Raiders are the stronger party. Ground covered with maggots. Lice by the fourteen hundred thousand million infest Andersonville. A favorite game among the boys is to play at odd or even, by putting their hand inside some part of their clothing, pull out what they can conveniently get hold of and say "odd or even?" and then count up to see who beats. Think this is an original game here. never saw it at the North. Some of the men claim to have pet lice which they have trained. Am gradually growing worse. Nothing but the good care I have taken of myself has saved me thus far. I hope to last some time yet, and in the mean time relief may come. My diary about written through. It may end about the same time I do, which would be a fit ending.

June 16.—Old prisoners (some of them) will not credit the fact that there is plenty to eat at the North They think because we are starved here, that it is so all over. They are crazy (as you may say)

on the subject of food, and no wonder. In our dreams we see and eat bountiful repasts, and awake to the other extreme. Never could get a chance to talk with Capt. Wirtz, as he comes inside no more Probably just as well. Is a thoroughly bad man, without an atom of humanity about him. He will get killed, should we ever be released, as there are a great many here who would consider it a christian duty to rid the earth of his presence. Disease is taking right hold of me now. Battese is an angel; takes better care of me than of himself. Although not in our mess or tent, he is nearly all the time with us. It is wonderful the powers of endurance he has. I have always been blessed with friends, and friends, too, of the right sort. Had quite a talk with Dorr Blakeman, a Jackson, Mich., boy. Was not much acquainted with him at home but knew his people. Is a thoroughly good fellow, and a sensible one. It is a relief to see any one who does not lose his head.

June 17.—Must nurse my writing material. A New York *Herald* in camp, which says an exchange will commence the 7th of July. Gen. Winder is on a visit to Andersonville Is quite an aged man, and white haired. Very warm and almost suffocating. Seems as if the sun was right after us and belonged to the Confederacy. Chas. Humphrey, of Massachusetts, who has been in our hundred for months, has gone crazy; wanders about entirely naked, and not even a cap on his head. Many of the prisoners are crazy, and I only speak of those in our immediate proximity. Am in good spirits, notwithstanding my afflictions. Have never really thought yet that I was going to die in this place or in the Confederacy. Saw a new comer pounded to a jelly by the raiders. His cries for relief were *awful*, but none came. Must a few villains live at the expense of so many? God help us from these worse than rebels.

June 18.—Have now written two large books full; have another at hand. New prisoners who come here have diaries which they will sell for a piece of bread. No news to-day. Dying off as usual —more in numbers each day as the summer advances. Rebels say that they don't begin to have hot weather down here until about August. Well, it is plain to me that all will die. Old prisoners have stood it as long as they can, and are dropping off fast, while the new ones go anyhow. Some one stole my cap during the night. A dead neighbor furnished me with another, however. Fast as the men die they are stripped of their clothing so that those alive can be covered. Pretty hard, but the best we can do. Rebels are anxious to get hold of Yankee buttons. "Buttons with hens on," they enquire for. An insult to the American Eagle—but they don't know any better.

June 19—A young fellow named Conely tramps around the prison with ball and chain on. His crime was trying to get away. I say he tramps around, he tramps away from the gate with it on at nine in the morning, and as soon as out of sight of the rebels he takes it off, and only puts it on at nine o'clock the next morning to report at the gate duly ironed off. They think, of course, that he wears it all the time. Jimmy Devers looks and is in a very bad way. Too bad if the poor fellow should die now, after being a prisoner almost a year. Talks a great deal about his younger brother in Jackson, named Willie. Says if he should die to be sure and tell Willie not to drink, which has been one of Jimmy's failings, and he sees now what a foolish habit it is. Michael Hoare stands it well. When a man is shot now it is called being "parolled."

June 20.—All the mess slowly but none the less surely succumbing to the diseases incident here. We are not what you may call hungry. I have actually felt the pangs of hunger more when I was a boy going home from school to dinner. But we are sick and faint and all broken down, feverish &c. It is starvation and disease and exposure that is doing it Our stomachs have been so abused by the stuff called bread and soups, that they are diseased. The bread is coarse and musty. Believe that half in camp would die now if given rich food to eat.

June 21.—I am a fair writer, and am besieged by men to write letters to the rebel officers praying for release, and I do it, knowing it will do no good, but to please the sufferers. Some of these letters are directed to Capt Wirtz, some to Gen. Winder, Jeff Davis and other officers. As dictated by them some would bring tears from a stone. One goes on to say he has been a prisoner of war over a year, has a wife and three children destitute, how much he thinks of them, is dying with disease, etc., etc. All kinds of stories are narrated, and handed to the first rebel who comes within reach. Of course they are never heard from. It's pitiful to see the poor wretches who think their letters will get them out, watch the gate from day to day, and always disappointed. Some one has much to answer for.

June 22.—The washing business progresses and is prosperous. One great trouble is, it is run too loose and we often get no pay. Battese, while a good worker, is no business man, and will do anybody's washing on promises, which don't amount to much. Am not able to do much myself, principally hanging out the clothes; that is, laying the shirt on one of the tent poles and then watching it till dry. All day yesterday I lay under the "coverlid" in the shade, hanging on to a string which was tied to the washing. If I saw a suspicious looking chap hanging around with his eyes on the washed goods, then gave a quick jerk and in she comes out of harm's way. Battese has paid for three or four shirts lost in this way, and one pair of pants. Pays in bread. A great many Irish here, and as a class, they stand hardships well. Jimmy Devers losing heart and thinks he will die. Capt. Wirtz has issued another order, but don't know what it is—to the effect that raiding and killing must be stopped, I believe. Being unable to get around as I used to, do not hear the particulars of what is going on, only in a general way. New men coming in, and bodies carried out. Is there no end but dying?

June 23.—My coverlid nobly does duty, protecting us from the sun's hot rays by day and the heavy dews at night. Have no doubt but it has saved my life many times. Never have heard anything from Hendryx since his escape. Either got away to our lines or shot. Rebels recruiting among us for men to put in their ranks. None will go—yes, I believe one Duffy has gone with them. Much fighting. Men will fight as long as they can stand up. A father fights his own son not ten rods from us. Hardly any are strong enough to do much damage except the raiders, who get enough to eat and are in better condition than the rest. Four or five letters were delivered to their owners. Were from their homes. Remarkable, as I believe this is the first mail since our first coming here. Something wrong. Just shake in my boots—shoes, I mean, (plenty of room) when I think what July and August will do for us. Does not seem to me as if any can stand it After all, it's hard killing a man. Can stand most anything.

June 24.—Almost July 1st, when Jimmy Devers will have been a prisoner of war one year. Unless relief comes very soon he will die. I have read in my earlier years about prisoners in the revolutionary war, and other wars. It sounded noble and heroic to be a prisoner of war, and accounts of their adventures were quite romantic; but the romance has been knocked out of the prisoner of war business, higher than a kite. It's a fraud. All of the "Astor House Mess" now afflicted with scurvy and dropsy more or less, with the exception of Battese, and myself worst of any. Am fighting the disease, however, all the time, and the growth is but slight. Take exercise every morning and evening, when it is almost impossible for me to walk   Walk all over before the sun comes up, drink of Battese's medicine made of roots, keep clear of vermin, talk and even laugh, and if I do die, it will not be through neglect. Carpenter, the teamster who sold me the boots, is about gone, and thank the Lord he has received his sixty cents from me, in rations. Sorry for the poor fellow. Many who have all along stood it nobly now begin to go under   Wm. B Rowe, our tall mess-mate, is quite bad off, still, he has an iron constitution and will last some time yet.

June 25.—Another lead pencil wore down to less than an inch in length, and must skirmish around for another one   New men bring in writing material and pencils. To-day saw a New York *Herald* of date June 11th, nothing in it about exchange, however. That is all the news that particularly interests us, although accounts of recent battles are favorable to the Union side. Our guards are composed of the lowest element of the South—poor white trash Very ignorant, much more so than the negro. Some of them act as if they never saw a gun before. The rebel adjutant does quite a business selling vegetables to those of the prisoners who have money, and has established a sutler stand not very far from our mess. Hub Dakin, an old acquaintance, is a sort of clerk, and gets enough to eat thereby. Hot! Hot! Raiders kill some one now every day. No restraint in the least. Men who were no doubt respectable at home, are now the worst villains in the world. One of them was sneaking about our quarters during the night, and Sanders knocked him about ten feet with a board. Some one of us must keep awake all the time, and on the watch, fearing to loose what little we have.

June 26.—The same old story, only worse, worse. It seems all the time it was as bad as could be, but is not. They die now like sheep—fully a hundred each day. New prisoners come inside in squads of hundreds, and in a few weeks are *all dead*   The change is too great and sudden for them. Old prisoners stand it the best. Found a Jackson, Michigan man, who says I am reported dead there. Am not, however, and may appear to them yet. Jimmy Devers is very bad with the scurvy and dropsy and will probably die if relief does not come. Sergt. Rowe also is afflicted; in fact all the mess except Battese   He does all the cooking now. He has made me a cane to walk with, brings water from the well, and performs nearly all the manual labor for us. He is a jewel, but a rough one.

June 27.—Raiders going on worse than ever before. A perfect pandemonium. Something must be done, and that quickly. There is danger enough from disease, without being killed by raiders. Any moment fifty or a hundred of them are liable to pounce upon our mess, knock right and left and take the very clothing off our backs. No one is safe from them. It is hoped that the more peaceable sort will rise in their might and put them down. Our misery is certainly complete without this trouble added to it. We should die in peace anyway. Battese has called his Indian friends all together, and probably a hundred of us are banded together for self protection. The animal predominates. All restraint is thrown off and the very Old Harry is to pay. The farther advanced the summer, the death rate increases, until they die off by scores. I walk around to see friends of a few days ago and am told "dead." Men stand it nobly and are apparently ordinarily well, when all at once they go. Like a horse, that will stand up until he drops dead. Some of the most horrible sights that can possibly be, are common every day occurrances. See men laying all around in the last struggles.

June 28.—It seems to me as if three times as many as ever before are now going off, still I am told that about one hundred and thirty die per day. The reason it seems worse, is because no sick are being taken out now, and they all die here instead of at the hospital. Can see the dead wagon loaded up with twenty or thirty bodies at a time, two lengths, just like four foot wood is loaded on to a wagon at the North, and away they go to the grave yard on a trot. Perhaps one or two will fall off and get run over. No attention paid to that; they are picked up on the road back after more. Was ever before in this world anything so terrible happening? Many entirely naked.

June 29.—Capt. Wirtz sent inside a guard of fifteen or twenty to arrest and take out quite a number of prisoners. They had the names and would go right to their quarters and take them. Some tell-tale traitor has been informing on them, for attempting to escape or something. Wirtz punishes very hard now; so much worse than a few months ago. Has numerous instruments of torture just outside the gate. Sores afflict us now, and the Lord only knows what next. Scurvy and scurvy sores, dropsy, not the least thing to eat that can be called fit for any one, much less a sick man, water that to drink is poison, no shelter, and surrounded by raiders liable to cut our throats any time. Surely, this is a go. Have been reading over the diary, and find nothing but grumbling and growlings. Had best enumerate some of the better things of this life. I am able to walk around the prison, although quite lame. Have black pepper to put in our soups. Am as clean perhaps as any here, with good friends to talk cheerful to. Then, too, the raiders will let us alone until about the last, for some of them will get killed when they attack the "Astor House Mess." Am probably as well off as any here who are not raiders, and I should be thankful, and am thankful. Will live probably two or three months yet. "If t'weren't for hope the heart would break," and I am hopeful yet. A Pennsylvanian of German descent, named Van Tassel, and who has "sorter identified himself with us" for two or three months, died a few moments ago. The worst cases of the sick are again taken to the hospital—that is, a few of the worst cases. Many prefer to die among their friends inside. Henry Clayton also died to-day. Was at one time in charge of our Division, and an old prisoner. Mike Hoare still hangs on nobly, as also do many other of my friends and acquaintances. Dorr Blakeman stands it unusually well. Have had no meat now for ten days; nothing but one-third of a loaf of corn bread and half a pint of cow peas for each man, each day. Wood is entirely gone, and occasionally squads allowed to go and get some under guard. Rowe went out to-day, was not able to carry much, and that had to be divided between a hundred men. One of the most annoying things is being squadded over every few days, sick and all. It's an all day job, and have to stand out until we are all tired out, never getting any food on these days.

June 30.—A new prisoner fainted away on his entrance to Andersonville and is now crazy, a raving maniac. That is how our condition affected him. My pants are the worse for wear from repeated washings, my shirt sleeveless and feet stockingless; have a red cap without any front piece; shoes by some hocus-pocus are not mates, one considerable larger than the other. Wonder what they would think if I should suddenly appear on the streets in Jackson in this garb. Would be a circus; side show and all. But nights I have a grand old coverlid to keep off the wet. Raiders steal blankets and sell to the guards, which leaves all nearly destitute of that very necessary article. Often tell how I got my coverlid, to visitors. Have been peddling pea soup on the streets: "Ten cents in money or a dollar Confed for this rich soup! Who takes it?" And some wretch buys it. Anything in the way of food will sell, or water, if different from swamp water. Rebs making a pretense of fixing up sanitary privileges at the swamp, which amount to nothing. Strong talk of forming a police force to put down raiders and to enforce order. If successful it will prove of great benefit. Sanders, Rowe, Blakeman, Dakin and myself are among those who will take an active part, although the part I take cannot be very active. Half a dozen letters sent inside to prisoners, but no news in them that I can hear of. More hot and sultry, with occasional rains. The crazy man says nothing but "prayer" will save us He has been sucking a bone now for about two weeks and pays more attention to that than to prayer.

July 1.—Matters must approach a crisis pretty soon with the raiders. It is said that even the rebels are scared and think they will have no prisoners, should an exchange ever occur. John Bowen, a Corp. Christency, Hemmingway, Byron Goodsell and Pete Smith, old acquaintances, have all died within a few days. Jimmy Devers still lives, with wonderful tenacity to life To-morrow he will have been a prisoner of war a year. Mike Hoare still keeps very well, but the most comical looking genius in the whole prison. Could make a fortune out of him on exhibition at the North. He says I look worse however. That may be, but not so comical. It's tragedy with the most of us. New guards are taking the place of the old ones, and it is said that Wirtz is going away. Hope so. Never have heard one word from Hendryx since his getting away. Sanders is trying to get outside as a butcher. He understands the business. "Dad" has been to Australia, and has told us all about that country. Have also heard all about Ireland and Scotland. Should judge they were fine countries. Rowe has been telling me of the advantage of silk under clothing, and in addition to visiting all the foreign countries, we shall have silk under wear. Rowe once lived in Boston, and I shall likewise go there.

July 2.—Almost the Glorious Fourth of July. How shall we celebrate? Know of no way except to pound on the bake tin, which I shall do. Have taken to rubbing my limbs, which are gradually becoming more dropsical. Badly swollen. One of my teeth came out a few days ago, and all are loose. Mouth very sore. Battese says: "We get away yet." Works around and always busy. If any news, he merely listens and don't say a word. Even he is in poor health, but never mentions it. An acquaintance of his says he owns a good farm in Minnesota. Asked him if he was married—says: "Oh, yes." Any children? "Oh, yes." This is as far as we have got his history. Is very different from Indians in general. Some of them here are despisable cowards—worse than the negro. Probably one hundred negroes are here. Not so tough as the whites. Dead line being fixed up by the rebels. Got down in some places. Bought a piece of soap, first I have seen in many months. Swamp now in frightful condition from the filth of camp. Vermin and raiders have the best of it. Capt. Moseby still leads the villains.

THE RAIDERS PUT DOWN.

ANDERSONVILLE ON ITS METAL—LEADING RAIDERS ARRESTED, TRIED AND HUNG—GREAT EXCITEMENT FOR A FEW DAYS, FOLLOWED BY GOOD ORDER—DEATH RATE INCREASES, HOWEVER—THE ASTOR HOUSE MESS AS POLICEMEN.

July 3.—Three hundred and fifty new men from West Virginia were turned into this summer resort this morning. They brought good news as to successful termination of the war, and they also caused war after coming among us. As usual the raiders proceeded to rob them of their valuables and a fight occurred in which hundreds were engaged. The cut throats came out ahead. Complaints were made to Capt. Wirtz that this thing would be tolerated no longer, that these raiders must be put down or the men would rise in their might and break away if assistance was not given with which to preserve order. Wirtz flew around as if he had never thought of it before, issued an order to the effect that no more food would be given us until the leaders were arrested and taken outside for trial. The greatest possible excitement. Hundreds that have before been neutral and non-commital are now joining a police force. Captains are appointed to take charge of the squads which have been furnished with clubs by Wirtz. As I write, this middle of the afternoon, the battle rages. The police go right to raider headquarters knock right and left and make their arrests. Sometimes the police are whipped and have to retreat, but they rally their forces and again make a charge in which they are successful. Can lay in our shade and see the trouble go on. Must be killing some by the shouting. The raiders fight for their very life, and are only taken after being thoroughly whipped. The stockade is loaded with guards who are fearful of a break. I wish I could describe the scene to-day. A number killed. After each arrest a great cheering takes place. NIGHT.—Thirty or forty have been taken outside of the worst characters in camp, and still the good work goes on. No food to-day and don't want any. A big strapping fellow called Limber Jim heads the police. Grand old Michael Hoare is at the front and goes for a raider as quick as he would a rebel. Patrol the camp all the time and gradually quieting down. The orderly prisoners are feeling jolly.

July 4.—The men taken outside yesterday are under rebel guard and will be punished. The men are thoroughly aroused, and now that the matter has been taken in hand, it will be followed up to the letter. Other arrests are being made to-day, and occasionally a big fight. Little Terry, whom they could not find yesterday, was to-day taken. Had been hiding in an old well, or hole in the ground. Fought like a little tiger, but had to go. "Limber Jim" is a brick, and should be made a Major General if he ever reaches our lines. Mike Hoare is right up in rank, and true blue. Wm. B. Rowe also makes a good policeman, as does "Dad" Sanders. Battese says he "no time to fight, must wash." Jimmy Devers regrets that he cannot take a hand in, as he likes to fight, and especially with a club. The writer hereof does no fighting, being on the sick list. The excitement of looking on is most too much for me. Can hardly arrest the big graybacks crawling around. Capt. Moscby is one of the arrested ones. His right name is Collins and he has been in our hundred all the time since leaving Richmond.

Has got a good long neck to stretch. Another man whom I have seen a good deal of, one Curtiss, is also arrested. . I haven't mentioned poor little Bullock for months, seems to me. He was most dead when we first came to Andersonville, and is still alive and tottering around. Has lost his voice entirely and is nothing but a skeleton. Hardly enough of him for disease to get hold of. Would be one of the surprising things on record if he lives through it, and he seems no worse than months ago. It is said that a court will be formed of our own men to try the raiders. Any way, so they are punished. All have killed men, and they themselves should be killed. When arrested, the police had hard work to prevent their being lynched Police more thoroughly organizing all the time. An extra amount of food this P. M., and police get extra rations, and three out of our mess is doing pretty well, as they are all willing to divide. They tell us all the encounters they have, and much interesting talk. Mike has some queer experiences. Rebel flags at half mast for some of their great men. Just heard that the trial of raiders will begin to-morrow.

July 5.—Court is in session outside and raiders being tried by our own men. Wirtz has done one good thing, but it's a question whether he is entitled to any credit, as he had to be threatened with a break before he would assist us. Rations again to-day. I am quite bad off with my diseases, but still there are so many thousands so much worse off that I do not complain much, or try not to however

July 6.—Boiling hot, camp reeking with filth, and no sanitary privileges; men dying off over a hundred and forty per day. Stockade enlarged, taking in eight or ten more acres, giving us more room, and stumps to dig up for wood to cook with. Mike Hoare is in good health; not so Jimmy Devers. Jimmy has now been a prisoner over a year, and poor boy, will probably die soon. Have more mementoes than I can carry, from those who have died, to be given to their friends at home. At least a dozen have given me letters, pictures &c., to take North. Hope I shan't have to turn them over to some one else.

July 7.—The court was gotten up by our own men and from our own men; Judge, jury, counsel, &c. Had a fair trial, and were even defended, but to no purpose. It is reported that six have been sentenced to be hung, while a good many others are condemned to lighter punishment, such as setting in the stocks, strung up by the thumbs, thumb screws, head hanging, etc. The court has been severe, but just. Mike goes out to-morrow to take some part in the court proceedings. The prison seems a different place altogether; still, dread disease is here, and mowing down good and true men. Would seem to me that three or four hundred died each day, though officially but one hundred and forty odd is told. About twenty-seven thousand, I believe, are here now in all. No new ones for a few days. Rebel visitors, who look at us from a distance. It is said the stench keeps all away who have no business here and can keep away. Washing business good. Am negotiating for a pair of pants. Dislike fearfully to wear dead men's clothes, and haven't to any great extent.

July 8.—Oh, how hot, and oh, how miserable. The news that six have been sentenced to be hanged is true, and one of them is Moseby. The camp is thoroughly under control of the police now, and it is a heavenly boon. Of course there is some stealing and robbery, but not as before. Swan, of our mess, is sick with scurvy. I am gradually swelling up and growing weaker. But a few more pages in my diary. Over a hundred and fifty dying per day now, and twenty-six thousand in camp. Guards shoot now very often. Boys, as guards, are the most cruel. It is said that if they kill a Yankee, they are given a thirty days furlough. Guess they need them as soldiers too much to allow of this. The swamp now is fearful, water perfectly reeking with prison offal and poison. Still men drink it and die. Rumors that the six will be hung inside. Bread to-day and it is so coarse as to do more hurt than good to a majority of the prisoners. The place still gets worse. Tunneling is over with; no one engages in it now that I know of. The prison is a success as regards safety; no escape except by death, and very many take advantage of that way. A man who has preached to us (or tried to) is dead. Was a good man I verily believe, and from Pennsylvania. It's almost impossible for me to get correct names to note down; the last named man was called "the preacher," and I can find no other name for him. Our quartette of singers a few rods away is disbanded. One died, one nearly dead, one a policeman and the other cannot sing alone, and so where we used to hear and enjoy good music evenings, there is nothing to attract us from the groans of the dying. Having formed a habit of going to sleep as soon as the air got cooled off and before fairly dark, I wake up at two or three o'clock and stay awake. I then take in all the horrors of the situation. Thousands are groaning, moaning and crying, with no bustle of the daytime to drown it. Guards every half

Michael Hoare.

Now an inmate of the Home for Disabled Soldiers, Dayton, Ohio

hour call out the time and post, and there is often a shot to make one shiver as if with the ague. Must arrange my sleeping hours to miss getting owly in the morning. Have taken to building air castles of late, on being exchanged. Getting loony, I guess, same as all the rest.

July 9.—Battese brought me some onions, and if they ain't good then no matter; also a sweet potato. One half the men here would get well if they only had something in the vegetable line to eat, or acids. Scurvy is about the most loathsome disease, and when dropsy takes hold with the scurvy, it is terrible. I have both diseases but keep them in check, and it only grows worse slowly. My legs are swollen, but the cords are not contracted much, and I can still walk very well. Our mess all keep clean, in fact are obliged to or else turned adrift. We want none of the dirty sort in our mess. Sanders and Rowe enforce the rules, which is not much work, as all hands are composed of men who prefer to keep clean. I still do a little washing, but more particularly hair cutting, which is easier work. You should see one of my hair cuts. Nobby! Old prisoners have hair a foot long or more, and my business is to cut it off, which I do without regards to anything except to get it off. I should judge that there are one thousand rebel soldiers guarding us, and perpaps a few more, with the usual number of officers. A guard told me to-day that the yanks were "gittin licked," and they didn't want us exchanged; just as soon we should die here as not; a yank asked him if he knew what exchange meant; said he knew what shootin' meant, and as he began to swing around his old shooting iron we retreated in among the crowd. Heard that there were some new men belonging to my regiment in another part of the prison; have just returned from looking after them and am all tired out. Instead of belonging to the 9th Michigan Cavalry, they belong to the 9th Michigan Infantry. Had a good visit and quite cheered with their accounts of the war news. Some one stole Battese's wash board and he is mad; is looking for it—may bust up the business. Think Hub Dakin will give me a board to make another one. Sanders owns the jack-knife, of this mess, and he don't like to lend it either; borrow it to carve on roots for pipes. Actually take solid comfort "building castles in the air," a thing I have never been addicted to before. Better than getting blue and worrying myself to death. After all, we may get out of this dod-rotted hole Always an end of some sort to such things.

July 10.—Have bought of a new prisoner quite a large (thick I mean,) blank book so as to continue my diary. Although it's a tedious and tiresome task, am determined to keep it up. Don't know of another man in prison who is doing likewise. Wish I had the gift of description that I might describe this place. Know that I am not good at such things, and have more particularly kept track of the mess which was the "Astor House Mess" on Belle Isle, and is still called so here. Thought that Belle Isle was a very bad place, and used about the worst language I knew how to use in describing it, and so find myself at fault in depicting matters here as they are. At Belle Isle we had good water and plenty of it, and I believe it depends more upon water than food as regards health. We also had good pure air from up the James River. Here we have the very worst kind of water. Nothing can be worse or nastier than the stream drizzling its way through this camp. And for air to breathe, it is what arises from this foul place. On all four sides of us are high walls and tall trees, and there is apparently no wind or breeze to blow away the stench, and we are obliged to breathe and live in it. Dead bodies lay around all day in the broiling sun, by the dozen and even hundreds, and we must suffer and live in this atmosphere. It's too horrible for me to describe in fitting language. There was once a very profane man driving a team of horses attached to a wagon in which there were forty or fifty bushels of potatoes It was a big load and there was a long hill to go up. The very profane man got off the load of potatoes to lighten the weight, and started the team up the hill. It was hard work, but they finally reached the top and stopped to rest. The profane man looked behind him and saw that the end board of the wagon had slipped out just as he had started, and there the potatoes were, scattered all the way along up the hill. Did the man make the very air blue with profanity? No, he sat down on a log feeling that he couldn't do the subject justice and so he remarked: "No! it's no use, I can't do it justice." While I have no reason or desire to swear, I certainly cannot do this prison justice. It's too stupenduous an undertaking. Only those who are here will ever know what Andersonville is.

AN ACCOUNT OF THE HANGING.

July 11.—This morning lumber was brought into the prison by the rebels, and near the gate a *gallows* erected for the purpose of executing the six condemned Yankees. At about ten o'clock they were brought inside by Capt. Wirtz and some guards, and delivered over to the police force. Capt. Wirtz then said a few words about their having been tried by our own men and for us to do as we choose with them, that he washed his hands of the whole matter, or words to that effect. I could not catch the exact language, being some little distance away I have learned by enquiry, their names, which are as follows: John Sarsfield, 144th New York; William Collins, alias "Moseby," Co. D, 88th Pennsylvania; Charles Curtiss, Battery A, 5th Rhode Island Artillery; Pat Delaney, Co. E, 83d Pennsylvania; A. Munn, U. S. Navy, and W. R. Rickson of the U. S Navy. After Wirtz made his speech he withdrew his guards, leaving the condemned at the mercy of 28,000 enraged prisoners who had all been more or less wronged by these men. Their hands were tied behind them, and one by one they mounted the scaffold Curtiss, who was last, a big stout fellow, managed to get his hands loose and broke away and ran through the crowd and down toward the swamp. It was yelled out that he had a knife in his hand, and so a path was made for him. He reached the swamp and plunged in, trying to get over on the other side, presumably among his friends. It being very warm he over exerted himself, and when in the middle or thereabouts, collapsed and could go no farther. The police started after him, waded in and helped him out. He pleaded for water and it was given him. Then led back to the scaffold and helped to mount up. All were given a chance to talk. Munn, a good looking fellow in marine dress, said he came into the prison four months before perfectly honest, and as innocent of crime as any fellow in it Starvation, with evil companions, had made him what he was. He spoke of his mother and sisters in New York, that he cared nothing as far as he himself was concerned, but the news that would be carried home to his people made him want to curse God he had ever been born. Delaney said he would rather be hung than live here as the most of them lived, on their allowance of rations. If allowed to steal could get enough to eat, but as that was stopped had rather hang. Bid all good bye Said his name was not Delaney and that no one knew who he really was, therefore his friends would never know his fate, his Andersonville history dying with him. Curtiss said he didn't care a ——, only hurry up and not be talking about it all day; making too much fuss over a very small matter. William Collins, alias Moseby, said he was innocent of murder and ought not to be hung; he had stolen blankets and rations to preserve his own life, and begged the crowd not to see him hung as he had a wife and child at home, and for their sake to let him live. The excited crowd began to be impatient for the "show" to commence as they termed it. Sarsfield made quite a speech; he had studied for a lawyer; at the outbreak of the rebellion he had enlisted and served three years in the army, been wounded in battle, furloughed home, wound healed up, promoted to first sergeant and also commissioned; his commission as a lieutenant had arrived but had not been mustered in when he was taken prisoner; began by stealing parts of rations, gradually becoming hardened as he became familiar with the crimes practiced; evil associates had helped him to go down hill and here he was. The other did not care to say anything. While the men were talking they were interrupted by all kinds of questions and charges made by the crowd, such as "don't lay it on too thick, you villain," "get ready to jump off," "cut it short," "you was the cause of so and so's death," "less talk and more hanging," &c., &c. At about eleven o'clock they were all blindfolded, hands and feet tied, told to get ready, nooses adjusted and the plank knocked from under. Moseby's rope broke and he fell to the ground, with blood spurting from his ears, mouth and nose. As they was lifting him back to the swinging off place he revived and begged for his life, but no use, was soon dangling with the rest, and died very hard. Munn died easily, as also did Delaney, all the rest died hard and particularly Sarsfield who drew his knees nearly to his chin and then straightened them out with a jerk, the veins in his neck swelling out as if they would burst. It was an awful sight to see, still a necessity. Moseby, although he said he had never killed any one, and I don't believe he ever did deliberately kill a man, such as stabbing or pounding a victim to death, yet he has walked up to a poor sick prisoner on a cold night and robbed him of blanket, or perhaps his rations and if neccessary using all the force necessary to do it. These things were the same as life to the sick man, for he would invariably die. The result has been that many have died from his robbing propensities. It was right that he should hang, and he did hang most beautifully and Andersonville is the better off for it. None of the rest denied that they had killed men, and probably some had murdered dozens. It has been a good lesson; there are still bad ones in camp but we have the strong arm of the law to keep them in check. All during the hanging scene the stockade was covered with rebels, who were fearful a break would be made if the raiders should try and rescue them. Many citizens too were congregated on the outside in favorable positions for seeing. Artillery was pointed at us from all directions ready to blow us all into eternity in short order; Wirtz stood on a high platform in plain sight of the execution and says we are a hard crowd to kill our own men. After hanging for half an hour or so the six bodies were taken down and carried outside. In noting down the speeches made by the condemned men, have used my own language; in substance it is the same as told by them. I occupied a near position to the hanging and saw it all from first to last, and stood there until they were taken down and carried away. Was a strange sight to see and the first hanging I ever witnessed. The raiders had many friends who crowded around and denounced the whole affair and but for the police there would have been a riot; many both for and against the execution were knocked down. Some will talk and get into trouble thereby; as long as it does no good there is no use in loud talk and exciting arguments; is dangerous to advance any argument, men are so ready to quarrel. Have got back to my quarters thoroughly prostrated and worn out with fatigue and excitement, and only hope that to-day's lesson will right matters as regards raiding. Battese suspended washing long enough to look on and see them hang and grunted his approval. Have omitted to say that the good Catholic priest attended the condemned. Rebel negroes came inside and began to take down the scaffold; prisoners took hold to help them and resulted in its all being carried off to different parts of the prison to be used for kindling wood, and the rebels get none of it back and are mad. The ropes even have been gobbled up, and I suppose sometime may be exhibited at the north as mementoes of to-day's proceedings. Mike Hoare assisted at the hanging. Some fears are entertained that those who officiated will get killed by the friends of those hanged. The person who manipulated the "drop," has been taken outside on parole of honor, as his life would be in danger in here. Jimmy thanks God that he has lived to see justice done the raiders; he is about gone—nothing but skin and bone and can hardly move hand or foot; rest of the mess moderately well. The extra rations derived from our three mess-mates as policemen, helps wonderfully to prolong life. Once in a while some of them gets a chance to go outside on some duty and buy onions or sweet potatoes which is a great luxury.

July 12.—Good order has prevailed since the hanging. The men have settled right down to the business of dying, with no interruption. I keep thinking our situation can get no worse, but it does get worse every day and not less than one hundred and sixty die each twenty-four hours. Probably one-fourth or one-third of these die inside the stockade, the balance in the hospital outside. All day and up to four o'clock P. M., the dead are being gathered up and carried to the south gate and placed in a row inside the dead line. As the bodies are stripped of their clothing in most cases as soon as the breath leaves, and in some cases before, the row of dead presents a sickening appearance. Legs drawn up and in all shapes. They are black from pitch pine smoke and laying in the sun Some of them lay there for twenty hours or more, and by that time are in a horrible condition. At four o'clock a four or six mule wagon comes up to the gate and twenty or thirty bodies are loaded on to the wagon and they are carted off to be put in trenches, one hundred in each trench, in the cemetery, which is eighty or a hundred rods away. There must necessarily be a great many whose names are not taken. It is the orders to attach the name, company and regiment to each body, but it is not always done. I was invited to-day to dig in a tunnel, but had to decline. My digging days are over. Must dig now to keep out of the ground, I guess. It is with difficulty now that I can walk, and only with the help of two canes.

July 13.—Can see in the distance the cars go poking along by this station, with wheezing old engines, snorting along. As soon as night comes a great many are blind, caused by sleeping in the open air, with moon shining in the face. Many holes are dug and excavations made in camp. Near our quarters is a well about five or six feet deep, and the poor blind fellows fall into this pit hole. None seriously hurt, but must be quite shaken up. Half of the prisoners have no settled place for sleeping, wander and lay down wherever they can find room. Have two small gold rings on my finger, worn ever since I left home. Have also a small photograph album with eight photographs in. Relics of civilization. Should I get these things through to our lines they will have quite a history. When I am among the rebels I wind a rag around my finger to cover up the rings, or else take them and put in my pocket. Bad off as I have been, have never seen the time yet that I would part with them. Were presents to me, and the photographs have looked at about one-fourth of the time since imprisonment. One prisoner made some buttons here for his little boy at home, and gave them to me to deliver, as he was about to die. Have them sewed on to my pants for safe keeping.

July 14.—We have been too busy with the raiders of late to manufacture any exchange news, and now all hands are at work trying to see who can tell the biggest yarns. The weak are feeling well to-night over the story that we are all to be sent North this month, before the 20th. Have not learned that the news came from any reliable source. Rumors of midsummer battles with Union troops victorious. It's "bite dog, bite bear," with most of us prisoners; we don't care which licks, what we want is to get out of this pen. Of course, we all care and want our side to win, but it's tough on patriotism. A court is now held every day and offenders punished, principally by buck and gagging, for misdemeanors. The hanging has done worlds of good, still there is much stealing going on yet, but in a sly way, not openly. Hold my own as regards health. The dreaded month of July is half gone, almost, and a good many over one hundred and fifty die each day, but I do not know how many   Hardly any one cares enough about it to help me any in my inquiries. It is all self w th the most of them. A guard by accident shot himself. Have often said they didn't know enough to hold a gun. Bury a rebel guard every few days within sight of the prison   Saw some women in the distance. Quite a sight. Are feeling quite jolly to-night since the sun went down   Was visited by my new acquaintances of the 9th Michigan Infantry, who are comparatively new prisoners. Am learning them the way to live here   They are very hopeful fellows and declare the war will be over this coming fall, and tell their reasons very well for thinking so. We gird up our loins and decide that we will try to live it through. Rowe, although often given to despondency, is feeling good and cheerful   There are some noble fellows here. A man shows exactly what he is in Andersonville. No occasion to be any different from what you really are. Very often see a great big fellow in size, in reality a baby in action, actually sniveling and crying, and then again you will see some little runt, "not bigger than a pint of cider," tell the big fellow to "brace up" and be a man. Statue has nothing to do as regards nerve, still there are noble big fellows as well as noble little ones. A Sergt. Hill is judge and jury now, and dispenses justice to evil doers with impartiality. A farce is made of defending some of the arrested ones. Hill inquires all of the particulars of each case, and sometimes lets the offenders go as more sinned against than sinning. Four receiving punishment.

July 15.—Blank cartridges were this morning fired over the camp by the artillery, and immediately the greatest commotion outside. It seems that the signal in case a break is made, is cannon firing. And this was to show us how quick they could rally and get into shape In less time than it takes for me to write it, all were at their posts and in condition to open up and kill nine-tenths of all here. Sweltering hot Dying off one hundred and fifty-five each day. There are twenty-eight thousand confined here now.

July 16.—Well, who ever supposed that it could be any hotter; but to-day is more so than yesterday, and yesterday more than the day before. My coverlid has been rained on so much and burned in the sun, first one and then the other, that it is getting the worse for wear. It was originally a very nice one, and home made. Sun goes right through it now, and reaches down for us. Just like a bake oven. The rabbit mules that draw in the rations look as if they didn't get much more to eat than we do. Driven with one rope line, and harness patched up with ropes, strings, &c. Fit representation of the Confederacy. Not much like U S. Army teams. A joke on the rebel adjutant has happened. Some one broke into the shanty and tied the two or three sleeping there, and carried off all the goods. Tennessee Bill, (a fellow captured with me) had charge of the affair, and is in disgrace with the adjutant on account of it. Every one is glad of the robbery Probably there was not ten dollars worth of things in there, but they asked outrageous prices for everything. Adjt. very mad, but no good. Is a small, sputtering sort of fellow.

July 17.—Cords contracting in my legs and very difficult for me to walk—after going a little ways have to stop and rest and am faint. Am urged by some to go to the hospital but don't like to do it; mess say had better stay where I am, and Battese says shall not go, and that settles it. Jimmy Devers anxious to be taken to the hospital but is pursuaded to give it up. Tom McGill, another Irish friend, is past all recovery; is in another part of the prison. Many old prisoners are dropping off now this fearful hot weather; knew that July and August would thin us out; cannot keep track of them in my disabled condition. A fellow named Hubbard with whom I have conversed a good deal, is dead; a few days ago was in very good health, and its only a question of a few days now with any of us. Succeeded in getting four small onions about as large as hickory nuts, tops and all for two dollars Confederate money.

Battese furnished the money but won't eat an onion; ask him if he is afraid it will make his breath smell? It is said that two or three onions or a sweet potato eaten raw daily will cure the scurvy. What a shame that such things are denied us, being so plenty the world over. Never appreciated such things before but shall hereafter. Am talking as if I expected to get home again. I do.

July 18.—Time slowly dragging itself along. Cut some wretchs hair most every day. Have a sign out "Hair Cutting," as well as "Washing," and by the way, Battese has a new wash board made from a piece of the scaffold lumber. About half the time do the work for nothing, in fact not more than one in three or four pays anything—expenses not much though, don't have to pay any rent. All the mess keeps their hair cut short which is a very good advertisement. My eyes getting weak with other troubles. Can just hobble around. Death rate more than ever, reported one hundred and sixty-five per day; said by some to be more than that, but 165 is about the figure. Bad enough without making any worse than it really is. Jimmy Devers most dead and begs us to take him to the hospital and guess will have to. Every morning the sick are carried to the gate in blankets and on stretchers, and the worst cases admitted to the hospital. Probably out of five or six hundred half are admitted. Do not think any lives after being taken there; are past all human aid. Four out of every five prefer to stay inside and die with their friends rather than go to the hospital. Hard stories reach us of the treatment of the sick out there and I am sorry to say the cruelty emanates from our own men who act as nurses. These dead beats and bummer nurses are the same bounty jumpers the U. S. authorities have had so much trouble with. Do not mean to say that all the nurses are of that class but a great many of them are.

July 19.—There is no such thing as delicacy here. Nine out of ten would as soon eat with a corpse for a table as any other way. In the middle of last night I was awakened by being kicked by a dying man. He was soon dead. In his struggles he had floundered clear into our bed. Got up and moved the body off a few feet, and again went to sleep to dream of the hideous sights. I can never get used to it as some do. Often wake most scared to death, and shuddering from head to foot. Almost dread to go to sleep on this account. I am getting worse and worse, and prison ditto.

July 20.—Am troubled with poor sight together with scurvy and dropsy. My teeth are all loose and it is with difficulty I can eat.

Jimmy Devers was taken out to die to-day. I hear that McGill is also dead. John McGuire died last night, both were Jackson men and old acquaintances Mike Hoare is still policeman and is sorry for me. Does what he can. And so we have seen the last of Jimmy. A prisoner of war one year and eighteen days. Struggled hard to live through it, if ever any one did. Ever since I can remember have known him. John Maguire also, I have always known. Everybody in Jackson, Mich., will remember him, as living on the east side of the river near the wintergreen patch, and his father before him. They were one of the first families who settled that country. His people are well to do, with much property. Leaves a wife and one boy. Tom McGill is also a Jackson boy and a member of my own company. Thus you will see that three of my acquaintances died the same day, for Jimmy cannot live until night I don't think Not a person in the world but would have thought either one of them would kill me a dozen times enduring hardships Pretty hard to tell about such things. Small squad of poor deluded Yanks turned inside with us, captured at Petersburg. It is said they talk of winning recent battles. Battese has traded for an old watch and Mike will try to procure vegetables for it from the guard. That is what will save us if anything

July 21.—And rebels are still fortifying. Battese has his hands full. Takes care of me like a father. Hear that Kilpatrick is making a raid for this place. Troops (rebel) are arriving here by every train to defend it. Nothing but corn bread issued now and I cannot eat it any more.

July 22.—A petition is gotten up signed by all the sergeants in the prison, to be sent to Washington, D. C., *begging* to be released. Capt. Wirtz has consented to let three representatives go for that purpose. Rough that it should be necessary for us to *beg* to be protected by our government.

July 23.—Reports of an exchange in August. Can't stand it till that time. Will soon go up the spout.

July 24.—Have been trying to get into the hospital, but Battese won't let me go. Geo. W. Hutchins, brother of Charlie Hutchins of Jackson, Mich., died to-day—from our mess. Jimmy Devers is dead.

July 25.—Rowe getting very bad. Sanders ditto. Am myself much worse, and cannot walk, and with difficulty stand up. Legs drawn up like a triangle, mouth in terrible shape, and dropsy worse than all. A few more days. At my earnest solicitation was carried to the gate this morning, to be admitted to the hospital. Lay in the sun for some hours to be examined, and finally my turn came and I tried to stand up, but was so excited I fainted away. When I came to myself I lay along with the row of dead on the outside. Raised up and asked a rebel for a drink of water, and he said: "Here, you Yank, if you ain't dead, get inside there!" And with his help was put inside again. Told a man to go to our mess and tell them to come to the gate, and pretty soon Battese and Sanders came and carried me back to our quarters; and here I am, completely played out. Battese flying around to buy me something good to eat. Can't write much more. Exchange rumors.

July 26.—Ain't dead yet. Actually laugh when I think of the rebel who thought if I wasn't dead I had better get inside. Can't walk a step now. Shall try for the hospital no more. Had an onion.

July 27.—Sweltering hot. No worse than yesterday. Said that two hundred die now each day Rowe very bad and Sanders getting so. Swan dead, Gordon dead, Jack Withers dead, Scotty dead, a large Irishman who has been near us a long time is dead. These and scores of others died yesterday and day before. Hub Dakin came to see me and brought an onion. He is just able to crawl around himself.

July 28.—Taken a step forward toward the trenches since yesterday, and am worse Had a wash all over this morning. Battese took me to the creek; carries me without any trouble.

July 29.—Alive and kicking Drank some soured water made from meal and water.

July 30.—Hang on well, and no worse.

MOVED JUST IN TIME.

REMOVED FROM ANDERSONVILLE TO THE MARINE HOSPITAL, SAVANNAH—GETTING THROUGH THE GATE—BATTESE HAS SAVED US—VERY SICK BUT BY NO MEANS DEAD YET—BETTER AND HUMANE TREATMENT.

Aug. 1.—Just about the same. My Indian friend says: "We all get away."

Aug. 2.—Two hundred and twenty die each day. No more news of exchange.

Aug. 3.—Had some good soup, and feel better. All is done for me that can be done by my friends. Rowe and Sanders in almost as bad a condition as myself. Just about where I was two or three weeks ago. Seem to have come down all at once. August goes for them.

Aug. 4.—Storm threatened. Will cool the atmosphere. Hard work to write.

Aug. 5.—Severe storm. Could die in two hours if I wanted to, but don't.

Aug. 12.—Warm. Warm. Warm. If I only had some shade to lay in, and a glass of lemonade.

Aug. 13.—A nice spring of cold water has broken out in camp, enough to furnish nearly all here with drinking water. God has not forgotten us. Battese brings it to me to drink.

Aug. 14.—Battese very hopeful, as exchange rumors are afloat. Talks more about it than ever before.

Aug. 15.—The water is a God-send. Sanders better and Rowe worse.

Aug. 16.—Still in the land of the living. Capt. Wirtz is sick and a Lieut. Davis acting in his stead.

Aug. 17.—Hanging on yet. A good many more than two hundred and twenty-five die now in twenty-four hours. Messes that have stopped near us are all dead.

Aug. 18.—Exchange rumors.

Aug. 19 —Am still hoping for relief. Water is bracing some up, myself with others. Does not hurt us.

Aug. 20.—Some say three hundred now die each day No more new men coming. Reported that Wirtz is dead.

Aug. 21.—Sleep nearly all the time except when too hot to do so.

Aug. 22 —Exchange rumors.

Aug 23.—Terribly hot.

Aug. 24.—Had some soup. Not particularly worse, but Rowe is, and Sanders also.

Aug. 25.—In my exuberance of joy must write a few lines. Received a letter from my brother, George W. Ransom, from Hilton Head.† Contained only a few words.

Aug. 26.—Still am writing. The letter from my brother has done good and cheered me up. Eye sight very poor and writing tires me. Battese sticks by; such disinterested friendship is rare. Prison at its worst.

Aug. 27.—Have now written nearly through three large books, and still at it. The diary am confident will reach my people if I don't. There are many here who are interested and will see that it goes north.

Aug. 28.—No news and no worse; set up part of the time. Dying off a third faster than ever before.

Aug. 29.—Exchange rumors afloat. Any kind of a change would help me.

Aug. 30.—Am in no pain whatever, and no worse.

Aug. 31.—Still waiting for something to turn up. My Indian friend says: "good news yet." NIGHT.—The camp is full of exchange rumors.

---

†My brother supposed me dead, as I had been so reported; still, thinking it might not be so, every week or so he would write a letter and direct to me as a prisoner of war. This letter, very strangely, reached its destination.

Sept 1.—Sanders taken outside to butcher cattle. Is sick but goes all the same. Mike sick and no longer a policeman. Still rumors of exchange.

Sept. 2.—Just about the same; rumors afloat does me good Am the most hopeful chap on record.

Sept. 3.—Trade off my rations for some little luxury and manage to get up quite a soup. LATER.—Sanders sent in to us a quite large piece of fresh beef and a little salt; another God send.

Sept. 4.—Anything good to eat lifts me right up, and the beef soup has done it.

Sept. 4.—The beef critter is a noble animal. Very decided exchange rumors.

Sept. 5.—The nice spring of cold water still flows and furnishes drinking water for all; police guard it night and day so to be taken away only in small quantities. Three hundred said to be dying off each day.

Sept. 6.—Hurrah! Hurrah!! Hurrah!!! Can't holler except on paper. Good news. Seven detachments ordered to be ready to go at a moment's notice. LATER.—*All who cannot walk must stay behind.* If left behind shall die in twenty-four hours. Battese says *I shall go.* LATER.—Seven detachments are going out of the gate; all the sick are left behind. Ours is the tenth detachment and will go to-morrow so said. The greatest excitement; men wild with joy. Am worried fearful that I cannot go, but Battese says I shall.

Sept. 7.—Anxiously waiting the expected summons. Rebels say as soon as transportation comes, and so a car whistle is music to our ears. Hope is a good medicine and am sitting up and have been trying to stand up but can't do it; legs too crooked and with every attempt get faint. Men laugh at the idea of my going, as the rebels are very particular not to let any sick go, still Battese say I am going. MOST DARK.—Rebels say we go during the night when transportation comes. Battese grinned when this news come and can't get his face straightened out again.

MARINE HOSPITAL, Savannah, Ga., Sept. 15, 1864.—A great change has taken place since I last wrote in my diary. Am in heaven now compared with the past. At about midnight, September 7th, our detachment was ordered outside at Andersonville, and Battese picked me up and carried me to the gate. The men were being let outside in ranks of four, and counted as they went out. They were very strict about letting none go but the well ones, or those who could walk. The rebel adjutant stood upon a box by the gate, watching very close. Pitch pine knots were burning in the near vicinity to give light. As it came our turn to go Battese got me in the middle of the rank, stood me up as well as I could stand, and with himself on one side and Sergt. Rowe on the other began pushing our way through the gate. Could not help myself a particle, and was so faint that I hardly knew what was going on. As we were going through the gate the adjutant yells out: "Here, here! hold on there, that man can't go, hold on there!" and Battese crowding right along outside. The adjutant struck over the heads of the men and tried to stop us, but my noble Indian friend kept straight ahead, hallooing: "He all right, he well, he go!" And so I got outside, and adjutant having too much to look after to follow me. After we were outside, I was carried to the railroad in the same coverlid which I fooled the rebel out of when captured, and which I presume has saved my life a dozen times. We were crowded very thick into box cars. I was nearly dead, and hardly knew where we were or what was going on. We were two days in getting to Savannah. Arrived early in the morning. The railroads here run in the middle of very wide, handsome streets. We were unloaded, I should judge, near the middle of the city. The men as they were unloaded, fell into line and were marched away. Battese got me out of the car, and laid me on the pavement. They then obliged him to go with the rest, leaving me; would not let him take me. I lay there until noon with four or five others, without any guard. Three or four times negro servants came to us from houses near by, and gave us water, milk and food. With much difficulty I could set up, but was completely helpless. A little after noon a wagon came and *toted* us to a temporary hospital in the outskirts of the city, and near a prison pen they had just built for the well ones. Where I was taken it was merely an open piece of ground, having wall tents erected and a line of guards around it. I was put into a tent and lay on the coverlid. That night some gruel was given to me, and a nurse whom I had seen in Andersonville looked in, and my name was taken. The next morning, September 10th, I woke up and went to move my hands, and could not do it; could not move either limb so much as an inch. Could move my head with difficulty. Seemed to be paralyzed, but in no pain whatever. After a few hours a physician came to my tent, examined and gave me medicine, also left medicine, and one of the nurses fed me some soup or gruel. By night I could move my hands. Lay awake considerable through the night thinking. Was happy as a clam in high tide. Seemed so nice to be under a nice clean tent, and there was such cool pure air. The surroundings were so much better that I thought now would be a good time to die, and I didn't care one way or the other. Next morning the doctor came, and with him Sergt. Winn. Sergt Winn I had had a little acquaintance with at Andersonville Doctor said I was terribly reduced, but he thought I would improve. Told them to wash me. A nurse came and washed me, and Winn brought me a white cotton shirt, and an old but clean pair of pants; my old clothing, which was in rags, was taken away. Two or three times during the day I had gruel of some kind. I don't know what. Medicine was given me by the nurses. By night I could move my feet and legs a little. The cords in my feet and legs were contracted so, of course, that I couldn't straighten myself out. Kept thinking to myself, "am I really away from that place Andersonville?" It seemed too good to be true. On the morning of the 12th, ambulances moved all to the Marine Hospital, or rather an orchard in same yard with Marine Hospital, where thirty or forty nice new tents have been put up, with bunks about two feet from the ground, inside. Was put into a tent. By this time could move my arms considerable. We were given vinegar weakened with water, and also salt in it Had medicine. My legs began to get movable more each day, also my arms, and to day I am laying on my stomach and writing in my diary. Mike Hoare is also in this hospital. One of my tentmates is a man named Land, who is a printer, same as myself. I hear that Wm. B Rowe is here also, but haven't seen him.

Sept. 16 —How I do sleep; am tired out, and seems to me I can just sleep till doomsday.

Sept. 17.—Four in each tent. A nurse raises me up, sitting posture, and there I stay for hours, dozing and talking away. Whiskey given us in very small quantities, probably half a teaspoonful in half a glass of something, I don't know what. Actually makes me drunk. I am in no pain whatever.

Sept. 18.—Surgeon examined me very thoroughly to-day. Have some bad sores caused by laying down so much; put something on them that makes them ache. Sergt. Winn gave me a pair of socks.

Sept. 19.— A priest gave me some alum for my sore mouth. Had a piece of sweet potato, but couldn't eat it. Fearfully weak Soup is all I can eat, and don't always stay down

Sept. 20.—Too cool for me. The priest said he would come and see me often. Good man. My left hand got bruised in some way and rebel done it up. He is afraid gangrene will get in sore. Mike Hoare is quite sick.

Sept. 21. Don't feel as well as I did some days ago. Can't eat; still can use my limbs and arms more.

Sept. 22.—Good many sick brought here. Everybody is kind, rebels and all. Am now differently sick than at any other time. Take lots of medicine, eat nothing but gruel. Surgeons are very attentive. Man died in my tent. Oh, if I was away by myself, I would get well. Don't want to see a sick man. That makes me sick.

Sept. 23.—Shall write any way; have to watch nurses and rebels or will lose my diary. Vinegar reduced I drink and it is good; crave after acids and salt. Mouth appears to be actually sorer than ever before, but whether it is worse or not can't say. Sergt. Winn says the Doctor says that I must be very careful if I want to get well. How in the old Harry can I be careful? They are the ones that had better be careful and give me the right medicine and food. Gruel made out of a dish cloth to eat.

Sept 24.—Arrow root soup or whatever you may call it; don't like it; makes me sick. Priest spoke to me. Cross and peevish and they say that is a sure sign will get well. Ain't sure but shall be a Catholic yet. Every little while get out the old diary from under the blanket and write a sentence. Never was made to be sick— too uneasy. This will do for to-day.

HOSPITAL LIFE.

A GRADUAL IMPROVEMENT IN HEALTH—GOOD TREATMENT WHICH IS OPPORTUNE—PARTING WITH RELICS TO BUY LUXURIES—DALY, THE TEAMSTER AT ANDERSONVILLE, KILLED—A VISIT FROM BATTESE THE INDIAN, ETC., ETC.

Sept. 25—Can eat better—or drink rather; some rebel general dead and buried with honors outside. Had another wash and general clean up; ocean breezes severe for invalids. Am visited twice a day by the rebel surgeon who instructs nurses about treatment. Food principally arrow root; have a little whisky. Sleep great deal of the time. Land, my acquaintance and mess-mate, is lame from scurvy, but is not weak and sick as I am. When I think of anything, say: "Land, put her down," and he writes what I tell him. Everything clean here, but then any place is clean after summering in Andersonville Don't improve much and sometimes not at all; get blue sometimes; nature of the beast suppose; other sick in the tent worry and make me nervous.

Sept. 26—Am really getting better and hopeful. Battese has the two first books of my diary; would like to see him. Was mistaken about Rowe being in the hospital; he is not, but I hear is in the big stockade with bulk of prisoners. Say we were removed from Andersonville for the reason that our troops were moving that way. Well, thank heaven they moved that way. Mike Hoare, the irrepressible Irishman, is hobbling around and in our tent about half the time; is also getting well. Quite a number die here not having the constitution to rally. This is the first hospital I was ever in. My old coverlid was washed and fumigated the first day in hospital. Am given very little to eat five or six times a day; washed with real soap, an improvement on sand. Half a dozen rebel doctors prowling around, occasionally one that needs dressing down, but as a general thing are very kind. Can see from my bunk a large live oak tree which is a curiosity to me. Although it is hot weather the evenings are cool, in fact cold; ocean breezes. A discussion on the subject has set me down as weighing about ninety-five; I think about one hundred and five or ten pounds; weighed when captured one hundred and seventy-eight; boarding with the confederacy does not agree with me. The swelling about my body has all left me. Ser_t. Winn belongs to the 100th Ohio; he has charge of a ward in this hospital.

Sept. 27.—Getting so I can eat a little and like the gruel Have prided myself all during the imprisonment on keeping a stiff upper lip while I saw big strong men crying like children; cruelty and privations would never make me cry—always so mad, but now it is differen. and weaken a little sometimes all to myself. Land, my sick comrade, writes at my dictation.

Sept 28—Sent word to Battese by a convalescent who is being sent to the large prison, that I am getting well. Would like to see him. Am feeling better. Good many union men in Savannah. Three hundred sick here, with all kinds of diseases—gangrene, dropsy, scurvy, typhoid and other fevers, diarrhea, &c. Good care taken of me. Have medicine often, and gruel. Land does the writing.

Sept. 29.—Yes, I am better, but poor and weak. Feeling hungry more now, and can take nourishment quite often. Mike Hoare calls to see me. He is thinking of escape. Should think a person might escape from here when able. I shall get well now. Sweet potatoes for sale. Like to see such things, but cannot eat them. Rebel officer put his hand on my head a few minutes ago and said something; don't know what. It is said the Yankees can throw shell into Savannah from their gunboats down the river. Sergeant Winn comes to see me and cheers me up. Winn is a sutler as well as nurse, that is, he buys eatables from the guards and other rebels, and sells to our men. Number of marines and sailors in the building adjoining our hospital; also some Yankee officers sick. Winn makes quite a little money. They have soap here to wash with. The encouraging talk of ending the war soon helps me to get well.

Sept. 30.—Am decidedly better and getting quite an appetite but can get nothing but broth, gruel, &c. Mouth very bad. Two or three teeth have come out, and can't eat any hard food any way They give me quinine, at least I think it is quinine. Good many visitors come here to see the sick, and they look like union people. Savannah is a fine place from all accounts of it. Mike is getting entirely over his troubles and talks continually of getting away, there are a great many Irish about here, and they are principally union men. Mike wishes I was able to go with him. Nurses are mostly marines who have been sick and are convalescent. As a class they are good fellows, but some are rough ones. Are very profane. The cords in my legs loosening up a little. Whiskey and water given me to-day, also weakened vinegar and salt. Am all the time getting better. LATER—My faithful friend came to see me to-day. Was awful glad to see him. He is well. A guard came with him. Battese is quite a curiosity among the Savannah rebels Is a very large, broad shouldered Indian, rather ignorant, but full of common sense and very kind hearted. Is allowed many favors.

Oct. 1.—A prisoner of war nearly a year Have stood and went through the very worst kind of treatment. Am getting ravenously hungry, but they won't give me much to eat. Even Mike won't give me anything. Says the doctors forbid it. Well, I suppose it is so. One trouble with the men here who are sick, they are too indolent and discouraged, which counteracts the effect of medicines. A dozen or twenty die in the twenty-four hours. Have probably half tablespoonful of whiskey daily, and it is enough. Land is a good fellow. (I wrote this last sentence myself, and Land says he will scratch it out.—Ransom). A high garden wall surrounds us Wall is made of stone. Mike dug around the corners of the walls, and in out of the way places, and got together a mess of greens out of pusley. Offered me some and then wouldn't let me have it. Meaner than pusley. Have threatened to lick the whole crowd in a week.

Oct. 2.—Coming cool weather and it braces me right up. Sailors are going away to be exchanged. Ate some sweet potato to-day, and it beats everything how I am gaining. Drink lots of gruel, and the more I drink the more I want. Have vinegar and salt and water mixed together given me, also whiskey, and every little while I am taking something, either food or medicine, and the more I take the more I want. Am just crazy for anything, no matter what. Could eat a mule's ear. Eat rice and vegetable soup. All the talk that I hear is to the effect that the war is most over. Don't want to be disturbed at all until I am well, which will not be very long now. All say if I don't eat too much will soon be well. Mike lives high. Is an ingenious fellow and contrives to get many good things to eat. Gives me anything that he thinks won't hurt me. Setting up in my bunk. Have washed all over and feel fifty per cent. better. Just a jumping toward convalescence.

Oct 3.—The hospital is crowded now with sick; about thirty die now each day. Men who walked away from Andersonville, and come to get treatment, are too far gone to rally, and die. Heard Jeff. Davis' speech read to-day. He spoke of an exchange soon. I am better where I am for a few weeks yet. Number of sailors went to-day. Knaw onion, raw sweet potato. Battese here, will stay all day and go back to night. Says he is going with marines to be exchanged. Give him food, which he is loth to eat although hungry. Says he will come to see me after I get home to Michigan.

Oct. 4.—Am now living splendid; vegetable diet is driving off the scurvy and dropsy, in fact the dropsy has dropped out but the effect remains. Set up now part of the time and talk like a runaway horse until tired out and then collapse. Heard that all the prisoners are going to be sent to Millen, Ga. Wrote a few lines directed to my father in Michigan. Am now given more food but not much at a time. Two poor fellows in our tent do not get along as well as I do, although Land is doing well and is going to be a nurse. The hospital is not guarded very close and Mike Hoare cannot resist the temptation to escape. Well, joy go with him. Dosed with quinine and beastly to take. Battese on his last visit to me left the two first books of my diary which he had in his possession. There is no doubt but he has saved my life, although he will take no credit for it. It is said all were moved from Andersonville to different points; ten thousand went to Florence, ten thousand to Charleston and ten thousand to Savannah; but the dead stay there and will for all time to come. What a terrible place and what a narrow escape I had of it Seems to me that fifteen thousand died while I was there; an army almost and as many men as inhabit a city of fifty thousand population.

Oct. 5.—All in Andersonville will remember Daly, who used to drive the bread wagon into that place. He came to Savannah with us and was in this hospital; a few days ago he went away with some sailors to be exchanged. Soon after leaving Savannah he fell off the cars and was killed, and a few hours after leaving here was brought back and buried; it is said he had been drinking. Getting better every day, eat right smart. Mike waiting for a favorable chance to escape and in the meantime is getting well; heard that Battese has gone away with sailors to our lines Its wonderful the noticeable change of air here from that at Andersonville—wonder that any lived a month inhaling the poison. If some of those good fellows that died there, Jimmy Devers, Dr. Lewis, Swain, McGuire and scores of others, had lived through it to go home with me, should feel better. Have a disagreeable task to perform—that of going to see the relatives of fifteen or twenty who died and deliver messages. Rebel surgeons act as if the war was most over, and not like very bad enemies. Fresh beef issued to those able to eat it which is not me; can chew nothing hard, in fact cannot chew at all. Am all tired out and will stop for to-day.

Oct. 7 —Havn't time to write much; busy eating. Mouth getting better, cords in my legs loosening up. Battese has not gone; was here to-day and got a square meal. Don't much think that I have heretofore mentioned the fact that I have two small gold rings, which has been treasured carefully all during my imprisonment. They were presents to me before leaving home; it is needless to say they were from lady friends. Have worn them part of the time and part of the time they have been secreted about my clothes. Yankee rings are in great demand by the guards; crave delicacies and vegetables so much that think I may be pardoned for letting them go now, and as Mike says he can get a bushel of sweet potatoes for them, have told him to make the trade, and he says will do it. Sweet potatoes sliced up and put in a dish and cooked with a piece of beef and seasoned, make a delicious soup. There are grayback lice in the hospital, just enough for company's sake—should feel lonesome without them. Great many visitors come to look at us and from my bunk can see them come through the gate; yankees are a curiosity in this southern port, as none were ever kept here before; I hear that the citizens donate bread and food to the prisoners.

Oct. 8.—Talk of Millen, about ninety miles from here. Mike will trade off the rings to-night. Owe Sergt. Winn $12 for onions and sweet potatoes, confederate money however; a dollar confed. is only ten cents in money. Hub Dakin, from Dansville, Mich., is in this hospital. It is said Savannah will be in our hands in less than two months. Some Irish citizens told Mike so. Union army victorious everywhere. Going on twelve months a prisoner of war. Don't want to be exchanged now; could not stand the journey home; just want to be let alone one month and then home and friends. Saw myself in a looking glass for the first time in ten months and am the worst looking specimen—don't want to go home in twelve years unless I look different from this; almost inclined to disown myself. Pitch pine smoke is getting peeled off; need skinning. Eye sight improving with other troubles. Can't begin to read a newspaper and with difficulty write a little at a time Can hear big guns every morning from down the river; it is said to be yankee gunboats bidding the city of Savannah "good morning."

Oct. 9.—The reason we have not been exchanged is because if the exchange is made it will put all the men held by the union forces right into the rebel army, while the union prisoners of war held by the rebels are in no condition to do service; that would seem to me to be a very poor reason. Rowe and Bullock are in the main prison I hear, and well; it is one of the miracles that Bullock lived as he was ailing all through Andersonville. Brass buttons with hens on (eagles) are eagerly sought after by the guards. Mike still harping on escape, but I attend right to the business of getting enough to eat. Although can't eat much have the appetite all the same. The rebel M. D., by name Pendleton, or some such name, says if I am not careful will have a relapse, and is rather inclined to scold; says I get along all together too fast, and tells the nurse and Mike and Land, that I must not eat but little at a time and then only such food as he may direct, and if I don't do as he says, will put me in the main building away from my friends. Says it is suicide the way some act after a long imprisonment. Well, suppose he is right and I must go slow. Names of yankee officers marked on the tents that have occupied them as prisoner of war before us.

Oct. 10.—Mike traded off the gold rings for three pecks of sweet potatoes and half a dozen onions; am in clover. Make nice soup out of beef, potatoe, bread, onion and salt; can trade a sweet potatoe for most anything. Mike does the cooking and I do the eating; he won't eat my potatoes, some others do though and without my permission. 'Tis ever thus, wealth brings care and trouble. Battese came to-day to see me and gave him some sweet potatoes. He is going away soon the rebels having promised to send him with next batch of sailors; is a favorite with rebels. Mike baking bread to take with him in his flight. Set now at the door of the tent on a soap box; beautiful shade trees all over the place. Am in the 5th Ward, tent No. 12; coverlid still does me good service. Many die here but not from lack of attention or medicine. They haven't the vitality to rally after their sufferings at Andersonville. Sisters of Charity go from tent to tent looking after men of their own religion; also citizens come among us. Wheat bread we have quite often and is donated by citizens. Guards walk on the outside of the wall and only half a dozen or so on the inside, two being at the gate; not necessary to guard the sick very close. Should judge the place was some fine private residence before being transformed into the Marine Hospital. Have good water. What little hair I have is coming off; probably go home bald-headed.

Oct. 12.—Still getting better fast, and doctor says too fast. Now do nearly all the diary writing. Hardly seems possible that our own Yankee gunboats are so near us, so near that we can hear them fire off their guns, but such is the case. Reports have it that the Johnny Rebels are about worsted. Has been a hard war and cruel one. Mike does all my cooking now, although an invalid. He trades a sweet potato for vinegar, which tastes the best of anything, also have other things suitable for the sick, and this morning had an egg. My gold rings will put me in good health again. All the time medicine, that is, three or four times a day; and sores on my body are healing up now for the first time. Mouth, which was one mass of black bloody swellings on the inside, is now white and inflamation gone, teeth however, loose, and have lost four through scurvy, having come out themselves. My eyes, which had been trying to get in out of sight, are now coming out again and look more respectable. Battese was taken prisoner with eighteen other Indians; they all died but one beside himself.

Oct. 14.—Did not write any yesterday. A man named Hinton died in our tent at about two o'clock this morning, and his bunk is already filled by another sick man. None die through neglect here; all is done that could reasonably be expected. The pants with those buttons on to be taken North for a little boy whose father died in Andersonville, were taken away from me when first taken to the hospital. Have also lost nearly all the relics, pictures and letters given me to take North. For a week or ten days could take care of nothing. Winn took charge of the book that I am writing in now and Battese had the other two books, and now they are all together safe in my charge. Wonder if any one will ever have the patience or time to read it all? Not less than a thousand pages of finely written crow tracks, and some places blurred and unintelligable from being wet and damp. As I set up in my bunk my legs are just fitted for hanging down over the side, and have not been straightened for three or four months Rub the cords with an ointment furnished me by physician and can see a change for the better. Legs are blue, red and shiny and in some places the skin seems calloused to the bone

Oct. 15 —Richard is getting to be himself again. A very little satisfies me as regards the upward tendency to health and liberty. Some would think to look at me almost helpless and a prisoner of war, that I hadn't much to feel glad about. Well, let them go through what I have and then see. Citizens look on me with pity when I should be congratulated. Am probably the happiest mortal any where hereabouts. Shall appreciate life, health and enough to eat hereafter Am anxious for only one thing, and that is to get news home to Michigan of my safety. Have no doubt but I am given up for dead, as I heard I was so reported. Drizzling rain has set in. Birds chipper from among the trees. Hear bells ring about the city of Savannah. Very different from the city of Richmond; there it was all noise and bustle and clatter, every man for himself and the devil take the hindmost, while here it is quiet and pleasant and nice. Every one talks and treats you with courtesy and kindness. Don't seem as if they could both be cities of the Confederacy. Savannah has probably seen as little of real war or the consequence of war, as any city in the South.

Oct. 18.—Every day since last writing I have continued to improve, and no end to my appetite. Now walk a trifle with the aid of crutches Coming cool, and agrees with me. have fresh beef issued to us. Mike not yet gone. Battese went some days ago with others to our lines, at least it was supposed to our lines. Hope to see him sometime. Many have gangrene. Millen still talked of. See city papers every day, and they have a discouraged tone as if their cause were on its last legs. Mike goes to night for sure, he says. Think if I was in his place would not try to get away, we are so comfortable here. Still liberty is everything, and none know what it is except those deprived of it. It's a duty, we think, to escape if possible, and it seems possible to get away from here. Rebel guards that I sometimes come in contact with are marines who belong to rebel gunboats stationed in the mouth of Savannah

River and are on duty here for a change from boat life. They seem a kindly set, and I don't belive they would shoot a prisoner if they saw him trying to get away.

Oct. 19.—Last night I talked with a guard while Mike Hoare went out of his tunnel and got away safely from the hospital. The guard was on the inside and I hobbled to where he was and engaged him in conversation and Mike crawled away. It seems that Mike learned of some union Irish citizens in the city and his idea is to reach them which he may do, as there are scarcely any troops about the city, all being to the front. Now I am alone, best friends all gone one way or the other. The only acquaintances here now are Land and Sergt. Winn, with whom I became acquainted in Andersonville. Not like my other friends though. It is said there are half a dozen hospitals similar to this in Savannah which are filled with Andersonville wrecks. They have need to do something to redeem themselves from past conduct. Don't believe that it is the Confederacy that is taking such good care of us, but it is the city of Savannah; that is about the way it is as near as I can find out.

Oct. 22.—Lieut. Davis commands the prison in Savannah. Is the same individual who officiated at Andersonville during Wirtz's sickness last summer. He is a rough but not a bad man Probably does as well as he can. Papers state that they will commence to move the prisoners soon to Millen, to a Stockade similar to the one at Andersonville. I am hobbling about the hospital with the help of two crutches. Have not heard a word from old Mike, or Battese or any one that ever heard of before, for some days. Sweet potatoes building me up with the luxuries they are traded for. Had some rice in my soup. Terrible appetite, but for all that don't eat a great deal. Have three sticks propped up at the mouth of our tent, with a little fire under it, cooking food. Men in tent swear because smoke goes inside. Make it all straight by giving them some soup. Rebel surgeons all smoke, at least do while among us. Have seen prisoners who craved tobacco more than food, and said of the two would prefer tobacco. I never have used tobacco in any form.

Oct. 24.—Did not write yesterday Jumping right along toward health if not wealth. Discarded crutches and have now two canes. Get around considerable, a little at a time. It is said that they want Yankee printers who are prisoners of war to go and work in the printing offices in the city on parole of honor(?). Will not do it. Am all right where I am for a month yet, and by that time expect to go to our lines. Hub Dakin in hospital now. Priests still come and go. Convalescent shot and wounded by the guards, the first I have heard of being hurt since I came to this place. A small-pox case discovered in hospital and created great excitement. Was removed. Was loitering near the gate, when an Irish woman came through it with her arms full of wheat bread. All those able to rushed up to get some of it and forty hands were pleading for her favors. After picking her men and giving away half a dozen loaves her eyes lighted on me and I secured a large loaf. She was a jolly, good natured woman, and it is said that she keeps a bake shop   My bad looks stood me in well this time. As beautiful bread as I ever saw.

Oct. 25—Am feeling splendid and legs doing nobly, and even taking on fat. Am to be a gallant nurse as soon as able, so Sergt. Winn says. Most of the men as soon as convalescent are sent to big prison, but Winn has spoken a good word for me. Papers say the prison at Millen, Ga., is about ready for occupancy, and soon all will be sent there, sick and all. Nights cool and need more covering than we have. I am congratulated occasionally by prisoners who saw me in Andersonville. They wonder at my being alive. Rains

Oct. 26.—Time passes now fast; most a year since captured. When the Rebs once get hold of a fellow they hang on for dear life. Talk that all are to be vaccinated any way, whether they want to or not. Don't suppose it will do any harm if good matter is used. Vaccinate me if they want to. Walk better every day. Sometimes I overdo a little and feel bad in consequence. Land is "right smart," in fact, so smart that he will have to go to the big stockade pretty soon

Oct. 27.—A rebel physician (not a regular one), told me that it looked very dark for the Confederacy just now; that we need have no fears but we would get home very soon now, which is grand good news. I have no fears now but all will turn out well. Everything points to a not far away ending of the war, and all will rejoice, rebels and all.

Oct. 28.—Am feeling splendid, and legs most straight. Getting fat fast. Am to be a nurse soon. Reported that they are moving prisoners to Millen. Over a thousand went yesterday. About ten thousand of the Andersonville prisoners came to Savannah. ten thousand went to Florence and ten to Charleston, S. C. Only the sick were left behind there, and it is said they died like sheep after the well ones went away. Great excitement among the Gray-coats. Some bad army news for them, I reckon. Negroes at work fortifying about the city.

Oct. 29.—I suppose we must be moved again, from all reports. Savannah is threatened by Union troops, and we are to be sent to Millen, Ga. Am sorry, for while I remain a prisoner would like to stay here, am getting along so nicely and recovering my health. It is said, however, that Millen is a good place to go to, and we will have to take the consequences whatever they may be. Can eat now anything I can get hold of, provided it can be cooked up and made into the shape of soup. Mouth will not admit of hard food. This hospital is not far from the Savannah jail, and when the gate is open we can see it. It is said that some one was hung there not long ago. Papers referred to it and I asked a guard and he nodded "Yes." Have seen one "hanging bee," and never want to see another one. Last of my three pecks of sweet potatoes almost gone. For a dollar, Confed., bought two quarts of guber peas (pea-nuts), and now I have got them can't eat them. Sell them for a dollar per quart—two dollars for the lot. It is thus that the Yankee getteth wealth. Have loaned one cane to another convalescent and go around with the aid of one only. Every day a marked improvement. Ain't so tall as I "used to was." Some ladies visited the hospital to-day to see live Yankees, who crowded around. They were as much of a curiosity to us as we were to them.

Oct. 30.—It is said prisoners from main prison are being removed every day, and the sick will go last. Quite a batch of the nearest well ones were sent from here to-day to go with the others. Am to be a nurse pretty soon. Don't think I could nurse a sick cat, still it's policy to be one. Winn tells me that he has made money dickering at trade with the rebels and prisoners. He has trusted me to twelve dollars worth of things and says he don't expect or want pay. The twelve dollars amounts to only one dollar and twenty cents in our money. The surgeon who has had charge of us has been sent away to the front. It seems he had been wounded in battle and was doing home duty until able to again go to his command. Shall always remember him for his kind and skillful treatment. Came round and bid us all good bye, and sick sorry to lose him. Are now in charge of a hospital steward, who does very well. The atmosphere here makes gentlemen of everybody. Papers say that the city must be fortified, and it is being done. Considerable activity about the place. Trains run through at all hours of the

night, evidently shifting their troops to other localities. LATER --
Since the surgeon went away the rebels are drinking up our whiskey, and to-night are having a sort of carnival, with some of the favorite nurses joining in; singing songs, telling stories, and a good time generally. They are welcome to my share.

Oct. 31.—Reported that the well prisoners have all left this city for Millen and we go to-night or to-morrow. I am duly installed as nurse, and walk with only one cane. Legs still slightly drawn up. Hub Dakin, Land and myself now mess together. Am feeling very well. Will describe my appearance. Will interest me to read in after years, if no one else. Am writing this diary to please myself, now. I weigh one hundred and seventeen pounds, am dressed in rebel jacket, blue pants with one leg torn off and fringed about half way between my knee and good sized foot, the same old pair of miss matched shoes I wore in Andersonville, very good pair of stockings, a "biled" white shirt, and a hat which is a compromise between a clown's and the rebel white partially stiff hat; am poor as a tad-pole, in fact look just about like an East Tennesseean, of the poor white trash order. You might say that I am an "honery looking cuss" and not be far out of the way. My cheeks are sunken, eyes sunken, sores and blotches both outside and inside my mouth, and my right leg the whole length of it, red, black and blue and tender of touch. My eyes, too, are very weak, and in a bright sun I have to draw the slouch hat away down over them. Bad as this picture is, I am a beauty and picture of health in comparison to my appearance two months ago. When taken prisoner was fleshy, weighing about one hundred and seventy or seventy-five, round faced, in fact an overgrown, ordinary, green looking chap of twenty. Had never endured any hardships at all and was a spring chicken. As has been proven however, I had an iron constitution that has carried me through, and above all a disposition to make the best of everything no matter how bad, and considerable will power with the rest. When I think of the thousands and thousands of thorough-bred soldiers, tough and hearty and capable of marching thirty, forty, and even fifty miles in twenty-four hours and think nothing of it, I wonder and keep wondering that it can be so, that I am alive and gaining rapidly in health and strength. Believe now that no matter where we are moved to, I shall continue to improve, and get well. Succumbed only at the last in Andersonville, when no one could possibly keep well. With this general inventory of myself and the remark that I haven't a red cent, or even a Confederate shin-plaster, will put up my diary and get ready to go where ever they see fit to send us, as orders have come to get ready. LATER —We are on the Georgia Central Railroad, en-route for Millen, Ga., which is ninety miles from Savannah, and I believe north. Are in box cars and very crowded with sick prisoners. Two nurses, myself being one of them, have charge of about a hundred sick. There are, however, over six hundred on the train.

REMOVED TO MILLEN.

ANOTHER CHANGE AND NOT A BAD ONE—ALMOST A HOSTAGE OF WAR ELECTION DAY AND A VOTE FOR LITTLE MAC—ONE YEAR A PRISONER OF WAR, ETC., ETC.

CAMP LAWTON, Millen, Ga., Nov. 1 —Arrived at our destination not far from midnight, and it was a tedious journey. Two died in the car I was in. Were taken from the cars to this prison in what they call ambulances, but what I call lumber wagons. Are now congregated in the south-east corner of the stockade under hastily put up tents. This morning we have drawn rations, both the sick and the well, which are good and enough. The stockade is similar to that at Andersonville, but in a more settled country, the ground high and grassy, and through the prison runs a stream of good pure water, with no swamp at all. It is apparently a pleasant and healthy location. A portion of the prison is timber land, and the timber has been cut down and lays where it fell, and the men who arrived before us have been busily at work making shanties and places to sleep in. There are about six thousand prisoners here, and I should judge there was room for twelve or fifteen thousand. Men say they are given food twice each day, which consists of meal and fresh beef in rather small quantities, but good and wholesome. The rebel officer in command is a sociable and kindly disposed man, and the guards are not strict, that is, not cruelly so. We are told that our stay here will be short A number of our men have been detailed to cook the food for the sick, and their well being is looked to by the rebel surgeon as well as our own men. The same surgeon who for the last ten days had charge of us in Savannah has charge of us now He does not know over and above much but on the whole does very well. Barrels of molasses (nigger toe) have been rolled inside and it is being issued to the men, about one-fourth of a pint to each man, possibly a little more. Some of the men, luxuriantly, put their allowances together and make molasses candy of it. One serious drawback is the scarcity of dishes, and one man I saw draw his portion is his two hands, which held it until his comrade could find a receptacle for it.

Nov. 2.—Have seen many of my old comrades of Andersonville, among whom is my tried friend Sergt. Wm. B. Rowe; were heartily glad to see one onother; also little Bulluck who has improved wonderfully in appearance. Everyone is pleased with this place and are cheerful, hoping and expecting to be released before many weeks; they all report as having been well treated in Savannah and have pleasant recollections of that place; from what could be seen of the city by us prisoners it seems the handsomest one in America. Should judge it was a very wealthy place. My duties as nurse are hard, often too much so for my strength, yet the enforced exercise does me good and continue to improve all the time. A cane will be necessary to my locomotion for a long time as am afraid myself permanently injured; my cane is not a gold headed one; it is a round picket which has been pulled off some fence. Very cheering accounts of the war doings. All who want to can take the oath of allegiance to the confederacy and be released; am happy to say though that out of all here, but two or three has done so, and they are men who are a detriment to any army. The weather now is beautiful, air refreshing, water ditto; all happy and contented and await coming events with interest. Part of the brook, the lower part, is planked and sides boarded up for sanitary privileges; water has also been dammed up and a fall made which carries off the filth with force. Plenty of wood to do cooking with and the men putter around with their cooking utensils such as they have. Sort of prize fight going on now.

Nov. 3.—About a hundred convalescents were taken outside to-day to be sent away to our lines the officials told us. At a later hour the commander came inside and said he wanted twelve men to fall into line and they did so, myself being one of the twelve; he proceeded to glance us over and on looking at me said: "Step back out of the ranks, I want only able bodied men." I stepped down and out considerably chagrinned, as the general impression was that they were to go to our lines with the convalescents who had been taken outside before. He marched off the twelve men and it then leaked out that they were to be sent to some prison to be held as hostages until the end of the war. Then I felt better. It is said all the sick will be taken outside as soon as they get quarters fixed up to accommodate them. Think that I shall resign my position as nurse. Would rather stay with the "boys." Land is n longer with the sick but has been turned into the rank and file, also Dakin. Dakin, Rowe and Land are all together, and if the sick are taken outside I shall join my old comrades and mess with them. But few die now; quite a number died from the removal, but now all seem to be on the mend. I am called, contrary to my expectations, a good nurse; certainly have pity for the poor unfortunates, but lack the strength to take care of them. It needs good strong men to act as nurses.

Nov. 4.—The fine weather still continues. Just warm enough, and favorable for prisoners. Food now we get but once a day—not all we want, but three times as much as issued at Andersonville and of good quality The officer in command, as I have said before, is a kind hearted man, and on his appearance inside he was besieged by hundreds of applications for favors and for the privilege of going outside on parole of honor. He began granting such favors as he could, but has been besieged too much and now stays outside. Has, however, put up a letter box on the inside so that letters will reach him, and every day it is filled half full. Occasionally he takes to a letter and sends inside for the writer of it, and that one answered is the occasion of a fresh batch, until it is said that the poor man is harrassed about as much as the President of the United States is for fat offices As I have before remarked in my diary, the Yankee is a queer animal.

Nov 5.—Hostages taken out Everything is bright and pleasant and I see no cause to complain, therefore won't. To-morrow is election day at the North; wish I was there to vote—which I ain't. Will here say that I am a War Democrat to the backbone. Not a very stiff one, as my backbone is weak.

Nov. 6.—One year ago to-day captured. Presidential election at the North between Lincoln and McClellan. Some one fastened up a box, and all requested to vote, for the fun of the thing. Old prisoners haven't life enough to go and vote; new prisoners vote for present administration. I voted for McClellan with a hurrah, and another hurrah, and still another Had this election occurred while we were at Andersonville, four-fifths would have voted for McClellan. We think ourselves shamefully treated in being left so long as prisoners of war Abe Lincoln is a good man and a good president, but he is controlled by others who rule the exchange business as well as most other things. Of course our likes and dislikes make no difference to him or any one else. Yes, one year ago to-day captured. A year is a good while, even when pleasantly situated, but how much longer being imprisoned as we have been. It seems a lifetime, and I am twenty years older than a year ago. Little thought that I was to remain all this time in durance vile. Improving in health, disposition and everything else. If both breeches legs were of the same length should be supremely happy. Should make a bon-fire to-night if I wasn't afraid of celebrating a defeat. Had lots of fun hurrahing for "Little Mac."

Nov. 7.—A rather cold rain wets all who have not shelter. Many ladies come to see us; don't come through the gate, but look at us through that loophole. Any one with money can buy extras in the way of food, but, alas, we have no money. Am now quite a trader —that is, I make up a very thin dish of soup and sell it for ten cents, or trade it for something. Am ravenously hungry now and can't get enough to eat. The disease has left my system, the body demands food, and I have to exert my speculative genius to get it. am quite a hand at such things and well calculated to take care of myself. A man belonging to the Masonic order need not stay here an hour. It seems as if every rebel officer was of that craft, and a prisoner has but to make himself known to be taken care of. Pretty strong secret association that will stand the fortunes of war. That is another thing I must do when I get home—join the Masons. No end of things for me to do: visit all the foreign countries that prisoners told me about, and not forgetting to take in Boston by the way, wear silk underclothing, join the masons, and above all educate myself to keep out of rebel prisons. A person has plenty of time to think here, more so than in Andersonville; there it was business to keep alive. Small alligator killed at lower part of the stream.

Nov 8 —All eager for news. Seems as if we were on the eve of something. So quiet here that it must predict a storm. Once in a while some pesky rebel takes it upon himself to tell us a lot of lies to the effect that our armies are getting beaten; that England joins the Confederacy to whip out the North; that there is no prospect of ending the war; that we are not going to be exchanged at all, but remain prisoners, etc., etc. If he is a good talker and tells his story well it makes us all blue and down hearted. Then, pretty soon, we are told more joyful news which we are ready to believe, and again take heart and think of the good times coming. Would like to hear the election news. Wonder who is elected? Feel stronger every day, and have a little flesh on my bones. As the weather gets cool, we are made painfully aware of the fact that we are sadly deficient in clothing. Will freeze if compelled to stay through the winter. Coverlid still does duty although disabled by past experience, same as all of us. We talk over the many good traits of Battese and others who are separated from us by death and otherwise. The exploits of Hendryx we will never tire of narrating. What a meeting when we can get together in future years, and talk over the days we have lived and suffered together. Exchange rumors fill the air. One good sign—the rebels are making no more improvements about this prison; they say we are not to stay here long. We hear that our troops are marching all through the South Guess that is the reason why they think of moving us all the time All right, Johnny Rebels, hope we are an elephant on your hands. Jeff Davis denounced by the papers, which is a good sign. Occasionally get one in camp, and read it all up. No library here. Not a scrap of anything to read; principal occupation looking for stray news.

Nov. 9.—This diary would seem to treat of two things principally, that of food and exchange. Try to write of something else, but my thoughts invariably turn to these two subjects. Prisoners of war will know how to excuse me for thus writing. A dead line has also been fixed up in Camp Lawton, but thus far no one has been shot. Rebel doctors inside examining men who may be troubled with disease prison life might aggravate. Those selected are taken outside and either put in hospitals or sent to our lines. Yankee ingenuity is brought into play to magnify diseases, and ver often a thoroughly well man will make believe that he is going to die in less than a week unless taken away. Have laughed for an hour at the way a fellow by the name of Sawyer fooled them. The *modus operandi* will hardly bear writing in these pages, but will do to tell. Have made a raise of another pair of pants with both legs of the same length, and I discard the old ones to a "poor" prisoner. An advantage in the new pair is that there is plenty of room, too, from being three or four sizes too large, and the legs as long as the others were short. My one suspender has a partner now, and all runs smoothly. Although Bullock is fleshing up and getting better in health, he is a wreck and always will be. Seems to be a complete change in both body and mind. He was a favorite in our regiment, well known and well liked. Rowe is the same stiff, stern patrican as of old, calmly awaiting the next turn in the wheel of fortune.

Nov. 10.—Pleasant and rather cool. My hair is playing me pranks. It grows straight up in the air and only on the topmost part of my head. Where a man is generally bald, it's right the other way with me. If there is anything else that can happen to make me any more ridiculous, now is the time for it to appear. About all I lack now is to have an eye gouged out. A friend says that the reason my hair grows the way it does is because I have been scared so much, and it has stuck up straight so much, that it naturally has a tendency that way Perhaps that is it. If I thought we were to stay here for any length of time would open up a hair cutting shop; but should hate to get nicely started in business and a trade worked up, then have an exchange come along and knock the whole thing in the head. We are not far from the railroad track, and can listen to the cars going by Very often Confederate troops occupy them and they give the old familiar rebel yell. Once in a while the Yanks get up steam enough to give a good hurrah back to them. Seems to be a good deal of transferring troops now in the South I watch all the movements of the rebels and can draw conclusions, and am of the opinion that Mr. Confederacy is about whipped and will soon surrender. It certainly looks that way to me. Rumors that we are to be moved.

Nov. 11.—Very well fed. There it goes again. Had determined not to say anything more about how we were fed, and now I have done it. However, I was not grumbling about it any way. Will merely add that I have an appetite larger than an elephant. Will also say that there are rumors of exchange, for a change—a subject that has been spoken of before. Cannot possibly refrain from saying that I am feeling splendidly and worth a hundred dead men yet. Have two dollars in Confederate money and if I can sell this half canteen of dish-water soup shall have another dollar before dark. "Who takes it? Ah, here ye are! Sold again; business closed for to-night, gentlemen. Early in the morning shall have a fresh supply of this delicious soup, with real grease floating on top." Shutters put up and we settle down for the night without depositing in the bank. Shan't go to sleep until ten or eleven o'clock, but lay and think, and build those air castles that always fall with a crash and bury us in the debris. Often hear the baying of hounds from a distance, through the night—and such strange sounds to the Northern ear. Good night. In rather a sentimental mood. Wonder if she is married?

Nov. 12.—Everything quiet and running smoothly. Waiting for something. Have just heard the election news—Mr. Lincoln again elected, and "Little Mac" nowhere. Just about as I expected. Returns were rather slow in coming in, evidently waiting for the Camp Lawton vote. Well, did what I could for George; hurrahed until my throat was sore and stayed so for a week; know that I influenced twenty or thirty votes, and now can get no office because the political opponent was elected. 'Tis ever thus. Believe I would make a good postmaster for this place. There is none here and should have applied immediately, if my candidate had been elected. More sick taken away on the cars; rebels say to be exchanged Appears to be a sort of mystery of late, and can't make head nor tail of their movements. Would not be surprised at any hour to receive news to get ready for our lines. Don't know that I have felt so before since my imprisonment. Have lived rather high to day on capital made yesterday and early this morning. Just my way—make a fortune and then spend it.

Nov. 13.—To-day had an incident happen to me; hardly an incident, but a sort of an adventure. When I was nurse on one or two occasions helped the hospital steward make out his report to his superiors, and in that way got a sort of reputation for knowing how to do these things a little better than the ordinary run of people, and rebels in particular. A rebel sergeant came inside at just about nine o'clock this morning and looked me up and said I was wanted outside, and so went. Was taken to a house not far from the stockade, which proved to be the officers head-quarters. There introduced to three or four officers, whose names do not occur to me, and informed that they were in need of some one to do writing and assist in making out their army papers, and if I would undertake the job, they would see that I had plenty to eat, and I should be sent North at the first opportunity. I respectfully, gently and firmly declined the honor, and after partaking of quite a substantial meal, which they gave me thinking I would reconsider my decision, was escorted back inside. Many thought me very foolish for not taking up with the offer. My reasons for not doing so are these: I would be clearly working for the Confederacy; can see no real difference in it from actually entering their army. If I occupied that position it would relieve some rebel of that duty, and he could stay in the ranks and fight our men. That is one reason. Another is the fact that instead of their letting me go to our lines with the first that went, I would be the very last to go, as they would need me to do duty for them until the last moment. Was always willing to do extra duty for our own men, such as issuing clothing on Belle Isle, also my nursing the sick or in any way doing for them, but when it comes to working in any way for any rebel, I shall beg to be excused. Might have gone out and worked in the printing offices in Savannah had I so wished, as they were short of men all the time, in fact could hardly issue their papers on account of the scarcity of printers. And so I am still loyal to the Stars and Stripes and shall have no fears at looking my friends in the face when I do go home.

Nov. 14 —The kaleidoscope has taken another turn. Six hundred taken away this forenoon; don't know where to. As I was about the last to come to Millen, my turn will not come for some days if only six hundred are taken out each day. Rebels say they go straight to our lines, but their being heavily guarded and every possible precaution taken to prevent their escape, it does not look like our lines to me. Probably go to Charleston; that seems to be the jumping off place. Charleston, for some reason or other, seems a bad place to go to. Any city familiar with the war I want to avoid. Shall hang back as long as I can, content to let well enough alone. Some of my friends, of which Bullock is one, flanked out with those going off. What I mean by "flanked out" is crowding in when it is not their turn and going with the crowd. Hendryx and I did that when we left Belle Isle, and we brought up in Andersonville. Will let those do the flanking who want to, I don't.

Nov. 15.—At about six or seven o'clock last night six hundred men were taken away, making in all twelve hundred for the day;

another six hundred are ready to go at a moment's notice. I don't know what to think. Can hardly believe they go to our lines. Seems almost like a funeral procession to me, as they go through the gate. Rowe and Hub Dakin talk of going to day, if any go, having decided to flank. I have concluded to wait until it is my turn to go. If it is an exchange there is no danger but all will go, and if not an exchange would rather be here than any place I know of now. LATER —Eight hundred have gone, with Rowe and Dakin in the crowd, and I am here alone as regards personal friends. Could not be induced to go with them. Have a sort of presentiment that all is not right. STILL LATER —Six hundred more have gone, making 2,600 all together that have departed, all heavily guarded.

Nov. 16.—A decided thinness in our ranks this morning. Still house keeping goes right along as usual. Rebels not knowing how to figure give us just about the same for the whole prison as when all were here. Had a talk with a rebel sergeant for about an hour. Tried to find out our destination and could get no satisfaction, although he said we were going to our lines. Told him I was a mason, odd-fellow, had every kind of religion (in hopes to strike his), and flattered him until I was ashamed of myself. In a desultory sort of way he said he "reckoned we war goin' nawth." Well, I will write down the solution I have at last come to, and we will see how near right I am after a little. Our troops, Sherman or Kilpatrick or some of them, are raiding through the South, and we are not safe in Millen, as we were not safe in Andersonville, and as was plainly evident we were not safe in Savannah. There is the whole thing in a nutshell, and we will see. Six hundred gone to-day.

Nov. 17—It is now said that the prisoners are being moved down on the coast near Florida. That coincides with my own view, and I think it very probable. Will try and go about to-morrow. Hardly think I can go to-day. LATER.—The to-day's batch are going out of the gate. Makes me fairly crazy to wait, fearful I am missing it in not going. This lottery way of living is painful on the nerves. There are all kinds of rumors. Even have the story afloat that now the raid is over that drove us away from Andersonville, we are going back there to stay during the war. That would be a joke. However, I stick to my resolution that the rebels don't really know themselves where we are going. They move us because we are not safe here. They are bewildered. Believing this am in a comparatively easy state of mind. Still I worry. Haven't said a word in a week about my health. Well, I am convalescing all the time. Still lame, and always expect to be; can walk very well though, and feeling lively for an old man.

Nov. 18.—None being taken away to-day, I believe on account of not getting transportation. Notice that rebel troops are passing through on the railroad and immense activity among them. Am now well satisfied of the correctness of my views as regards this movement. Have decided now to stay here until the last. Am getting ready for action however. Believe we are going to have a warm time of it in the next few months. Thank fortune I am as well as I am. Can stand considerable now. Food given us in smaller quantities, and hurriedly so too. All appears to be in a hurry. Cloudy, and rather wet weather, and getting decidedly cooler. My noble old coverlid is kept rolled up and ready to accompany me on my travels at any moment. Have my lame and stiff leg in training. Walk all over the prison until tired out so as to strengthen myself. Recruiting officers among us trying to induce prisoners to enter their army. Say it is no exchange for during the war, and half a dozen desert and go with them. Even if we are not exchanged during the war, don't think we will remain prisoners long.

Nov. 19.—A car load went at about noon, and are pretty well thinned out. Over half gone—no one believes to our lines now; all hands afraid of going to Charleston. Believe I shall try and escape on the journey, although in no condition to rough it. Am going to engineer this thing to suit myself and have a little fun. Would like to be out from under rebel guard once more. When I can look around and not see a prison wall and a gun ready to shoot me, I shall rejoice. Have edged up to another comrade and we bunk together. Said comrade is Corporal Smith, belonging to an Indiana regiment. While he is no great guns, seems quite a sensible chap and a decided improvement on many here to mess with. The nights are cool, and a covering of great benefit. My being the owner of a good blanket makes me a very desirable comrade to mess with. Two or three together can keep much warmer than one alone. It is said that a number of outsiders have escaped and taken to the woods. Another load goes to-night or early in the morning. My turn will come pretty soon. Nothing new in our situation or the prospects ahead. Food scarce, but of good quality. More go and I go to-morrow.

Nov. 20.—None as yet gone to-day and it is already most night. My turn would not come until to-morrow, and if none go at all to-day I will probably not get away until about day after to-morrow. Shan't flank out, but await my turn and go where fate decrees. Had a falling out with my companion Smith, and am again alone walking about the prison with my coverlid on my shoulders. Am determined that this covering protects none but thoroughly good and square fellows. LATER—Going to be a decidedly cold night, and have "made up" with two fellows to sleep together. The going away is the all absorbing topic of conversation. Received for rations this day a very good allowance of hard tack and bacon. This is the first hard-tack received since the trip to Andersonville, and is quite a luxury. It is so hard that I have to tack around and soak mine up before I am able to eat it. There is a joke to this. Will again go to bed as I have done the last week, thinking every night would be the last at Camp Lawton.

Nov. 21.—Got up bright and early, went to the creek and had a good wash, came back, after a good walk over the prison, and ate my two large crackers and small piece of bacon left over from yesterday, and again ready for whatever may turn up. Lost my diminutive cake of soap in the water and must again take to sand to scrub with, until fortune again favors me. Men are very restless and reckless, uncertainty making them so. Try my very best not to have any words or trouble with them, but occasionally get drawn into it, as I did this morning. Came out solid however. Is pretty well understood that I can take care of myself. NOON.— Five hundred getting ready to go; my turn comes to-morrow, and then we will see what we will see. Decided rumors that Sherman has taken Atlanta and is marching toward Savannah, the heart of the Confederacy. All in good spirits for the first time in a week.

ESCAPE BUT NOT ESCAPE.

MOVED FROM CAMP LAWTON AFTER A SOJOURN OF TWENTY DAYS—DESTINATION BLACKSHEAR, GA.—JUMP OFF THE CARS AND OUT FROM REBEL GUARD FOR SIX DAYS—A HUNGRY TIME BUT A GOOD ONE—CAPTURED AND MAKE THE ACQUAINTANCE OF TWO OTHER RUNAWAYS WITH WHOM I CAST MY FORTUNES, ETC., ETC.

Nov. 22.—And now my turn has come, and I get off with the next load going to-day. My trunk is packed and baggage duly checked; shall try and get a "lay over" ticket, and rusticate on the road. Will see the conductor about it. A nice cool day with sun shining brightly—a fit one for an adventure and I am just the boy to have one Coverlid folded up and thrown across my shoulder, lower end tied as only a soldier knows how My three large books of written matter on the inside of my thick rebel jacket, and fastened in. Have a small book which I keep at hand to write in now. My old hat has been exchanged for a red zouave cap, and I look like a red headed woodpecker. Leg behaving beautifully. My latest comrades are James Ready and Bill Somebody. We have decided to go and keep together on the cars. One of them has an apology for a blanket, and the two acting in conjunction keep all three warm nights. LATER.—On the cars, in vicinity of Savannah en route for Blackshear, which is pretty well south and not far from the Florida line. Are very crowded in a close box car and fearfully warm. Try to get away to-night

IN THE WOODS NEAR DOCTORTOWN STATION, No. 5, Ga., Nov. 23.—A change has come over the spirit of my dreams During the night the cars ran very slow, and sometimes stopped for hours on side tracks. A very long, tedious night, and all suffered a great deal with just about standing room only. Impossible to get any sleep. Two guards at each side door, which were open about a foot. Guards were passably decent, although strict. Managed to get near the door, and during the night talked considerable with the two guards on the south side of the car. At about three o'clock this A. M., and after going over a long bridge which spanned the Altamaha River and in sight of Doctortown, I went through the open door like a flash and rolled down a high embankment. Almost broke my neck, but not quite. Guard fired a shot at me, but as the cars were going, though not very fast, did not hit me. Expected the cars to stop but they did not, and I had the inexpressible joy of seeing them move off out of sight. Then crossed the railroad track going north, went through a large open field and gained the woods, and am now sitting on the ground leaning up against a big pine tree *and out from under rebel guard!* The sun is beginning to show itself in the east and it promises to be a fine day. Hardly know what to do with myself. If those on the train notified Doctortown people of my escape they will be after me. Think it was at so early an hour that they might have gone right through without telling any one of the jump off. Am happy and hungry and considerably bruised and scratched up from the escape. The happiness of being here, however, overbalances everything else. If I had George Hendryx with me now would have a jolly time, and mean to have as it is. Sun is now up and it is warmer; birds chippering around, and chipmunks looking at me with curiosity. Can hear hallooing off a mile or so, which sounds like farmers calling cattle or hogs or something. All nature smiles—why should not I?—and I do. Keep my eyes peeled, however, and look all ways for Sunday. Must work farther back toward what I take to be a swamp a mile or so away. Am in a rather low country although apparently a pretty thickly settled one; most too thickly populated for me, judging from the signs of the times. It's now about dinner time, and I have traveled two or three miles from the railroad track, should judge and am in the edge of a swampy forest, although the piece of ground on which I have made my bed is dry and nice. Something to eat wouldn't be a bad thing. Not over sixty rods from where I lay is a path evidently travelled more or less by negroes going from one plantation to another. My hope of food lays by that road. Am watching for passers by. LATER.—

A negro boy too young to trust has gone by singing and whistling, and carrying a bundle and a tin pail evidently filled with somebody's dinner. In as much as I want to enjoy this out-door Gypsy life, I will not catch and take the dinner away from him. That would be the heighth of foolishness. Will lay for the next one traveling this way. The next one is a dog and he comes up and looks at me, gives a bark and scuds off. Can't eat a dog. Don't know how it will be to-morrow though. Might be well enough for him to come around later. Well, it is most dark and will get ready to try and sleep. Have broken off spruce boughs and made a soft bed. Have heard my father tell of sleeping on a bed of spruce, and it is healthy. Will try it. Not a crust to eat since yesterday forenoon. Am educated to this way of living though, and have been hungryer. Hope the pesky alligators will let me alone If they only knew it, I would make a poor meal for them. Thus closes my first day of freedom and it is *grand*. Only hope they may be many, although I can hardly hope to escape to our lines, not being in a condition to travel.

Nov. 24.—Another beautiful morning, a repetition of yesterday, opens up to me. It is particularly necessary that I procure sustenance wherewith life is prolonged, and will change my head-quarters to a little nearer civilization. Can hear some one chopping not a mile away. Here goes. LATER.—Found an old negro fixing up a dilapidated post and rail fence. Approached him and enquired the time of day. (My own watch having run down.) He didn't happen to have his gold watch with him, but reckoned it was nigh time for the horn. Seemed scared at the apparition that appeared to him, and no wonder. Forgave him on the spot. Thought it policy to tell him all about who and what I was, and did so. Was very timid and afraid, but finally said he would divide his dinner as soon as it should be sent to him, and for an hour I lay off a distance of twenty rods or so, waiting for that dinner. It finally came, brought by the same boy I saw go along yesterday. Boy sat down the pail and the old darkey told him to scamper off home—which he did Then we had dinner of rice, cold yams and fried bacon. It was a glorious repast, and I succeeded in getting quite well acquainted with him. We are on the Bowden plantation and he belongs to a family of that name. Is very fearful of helping me as his master is a strong Secesh., and he says would whip him within an inch of his life if it was known. Promise him not to be seen by any one and he has promised to get me something more to eat after it gets dark. LATER.—After my noonday meal went back toward the low ground and waited for my supper, which came half an hour ago and it is not yet dark. Had a good supper of boiled seasoned turnips, corn bread and sour milk, the first milk I have had in about a year. Begs me to go off in the morning, which I have promised to do. Says for me to go two or three miles on to another plantation owned by LeCleye, where there are good negroes who will feed me. Thanked the old fellow for his kindness. Says the war is about over and the Yanks expected to free them all soon. It's getting pretty dark now, and I go to bed filled to overflowing; in fact, most too much so.

Nov. 25.—This morning got up cold and stiff; not enough covering. Pushed off in the direction pointed out by the darkey of yesterday. Have come in the vicinity of negro shanties and laying in wait for some good benevolent colored brother. Most too many dogs yelping around to suit a runaway Yankee. Little nigs and the canines run together. If I can only attract their attention without scaring them to death, shall be all right. However, there is plenty of time, and won't rush things. Time is not valuable with me. Will go sure and careful. Don't appear to be any men folks around; more or less women of all shades of color. This is evidently a large plantation; has thirty or forty negro huts in three or four rows. They are all neat and clean to outward appearances. In the far distance and toward what I take to be the main road is the master's residence. Can just see a part of it. Has a cupola on top and is an ancient structure. Evidently a nice plantation. Lots of cactus grows wild all over, and is bad to tramp through. There is also worlds of palm leaves, such as five cent fans are made of. Hold on there, two or three negro men are coming from the direction of the big house to the huts. Don't look very inviting to trust your welfare with. Will still wait, McCawber like, for something to turn up. If they only knew the designs I have on them, they would turn pale. Shall be ravenous by night and go for them. I am near a spring of water, and lay down flat and drink. The "Astor House Mess" is moving around for a change; hope I won't make a mess of it. Lot of goats looking at me now, wondering, I suppose, what it is. Wonder if they butt? Shoo! Going to rain, and if so I must sleep in one of those shanties. Negroes all washing up and getting ready to eat, with doors open No, thank you; dined yesterday. Am reminded of the song: "What shall we do, when the war breaks the country up, and scatters us poor darkys all around." This getting away business is about the best investment I ever made. Just the friendliest fellow ever was. More than like a colored man, and will stick closer than a brother if they will only let me. Laugh when I think of the old darky of yesterday's experience, who liked me first rate only wanted me to go away. Have an eye on an isolated hut that looks friendly. Shall approach it at dark. People at the hut are a woman and two or three children, and a jolly looking and acting negro man. Being obliged to lay low in the shade feel the cold, as it is rather damp and moist. LATER.—Am in the hut and have eaten a good supper. Shall sleep here to-night. The negro man goes early in the morning, together with all the male darky population, to work on fortifications at Fort McAllister. Says the whole country is wild at the news of approaching Yankee army. Negro man named "Sam" and woman "Sady." Two or three negroes living here in these huts are not trustworthy, and I must keep very quiet and not be seen. Children perfectly awe struck at the sight of a Yankee. Negroes very kind but afraid. Criminal to assist me. Am five miles from Doctortown. Plenty of "gubers" and yams. Tell them all about my imprisonment. Regard the Yankees as their friends. Half a dozen neighbors come in by invitation, shake hands with me, scrape the floor with their feet, and rejoice most to death at the good times coming. "Bress de Lord," has been repeated hundreds of times in the two or three hours I have been here. Surely I have fallen among friends. All the visitors donate of their eatables, and although enough is before me to feed a dozen men, I give it a tussle. Thus ends the second day of my freedom, and it is glorious

Nov. 26.—An hour before daylight "Sam" awoke me and said I must go with him off a ways to stay through the day. Got up, and we started. Came about a mile to a safe hiding place, and here I am. Have plenty to eat and near good water. Sam will tell another trusty negro of my whereabouts, who will look after me, as he has to go away to work. The negroes are very kind, and I evidently am in good hands. Many of those who will not fight in the Confederate army are hid in these woods and swamps, and there are many small squads looking them up with dogs and guns to force them into the rebel ranks. All able bodied men are conscripted into the army in the South. It is possible I may be captured by some of these hunting parties. It is again most night and have eaten the last of my food. Can hear the baying of hounds and am skeery. Shall take in all the food that comes this way in the meantime. Sam gave me an old jack knife and I shall make a good bed to sleep on, and I also have an additional part of a blanket to keep me warm. In fine spirits and have hopes for the future. Expect an ambassador from my colored friends a little later. LATER.—The ambassador has come and gone in the shape of a woman. Brought food; a man told her to tell me to go off a distance of two miles or so, to the locality pointed out, before daylight, and wait there until called upon to-morrow. Rebel guards occupy the main roads, and very unsafe.

Nov. 27.—Before daylight came where I now am. Saw alligators—small ones This out in the woods life is doing me good. Main road three miles away, but there are paths running everywhere. Saw a white man an hour ago. Think he was a skulker hiding to keep out of the army, but afraid to hail him. Many of these stay in the woods day times, and at night go to their homes, getting food Am now away quite a distance from any habitation, and am afraid those who will look for me cannot find me. Occasionally hear shots fired; this is a dangerous locality. Have now been out four days and fared splendidly. Have hurt one of my ankles getting through the brush; sort of sprain, and difficult to travel at all. No water near by and must move as soon as possible. Wild hogs roam around through the woods, and can run like a deer. Palm leaves grow in great abundance, and are handsome to look at. Some of them very large. Occasionally see lizards and other reptiles, and am afraid of them. If I was a good traveler I could get along through the country and possibly to our lines. Must wander around and do the best I can however. Am armed with my good stout cane and the knife given me by the negro; have also some matches, but dare not make a fire lest it attract attention. Nights have to get up occasionally and stamp around to get warm. Clear, cool nights and pleasant. Most too light, however, for me to travel. The remnants of yesterday's food, have just eaten Will now go off in an easterly direction in hopes of seeing the messenger.

Nov. 28.—No one has come to me since day before yesterday. Watched and moved until most night of yesterday but could see or hear no one. Afraid I have lost communication. In the distance can see a habitation and will mog along that way. Most noon. LATER —As I was poking along through some light timber, almost ran into four Confederates with guns. Lay down close to the ground and they passed by me not more than twenty rods away. Think they have heard of my being in the vicinity and looking me up. This probably accounts for not receiving any visitor from the negroes Getting very hungry, and no water fit to drink. Must get out of this community as fast as I can. Wish to gracious I had two good legs. LATER.—It is now nearly dark and I have worked my way as near direct north as I know how. Am at least four miles from where I lay last night. Have seen negroes, and white men, but did not approach them. Am completely tired out and hungry, but on the edge of a nice little stream of water. The closing of the fifth day of my escape. Must speak to somebody to-morrow, or starve to death. Good deal of yelling in the woods. Am now in the rear of a hovel which is evidently a negro hut, but off quite a ways from it. Cleared ground all around the house so I can't approach it without being too much in sight. Small negro boy playing around the house. Too dark to write more

Nov 29.—The sixth day of freedom, and a hungry one. Still where I wrote last night, and watching the house. A woman goes out and in but cannot tell much about her from this distance. No men folks around. Two or three negro boys playing about. Must approach the house, but hate to. NOON.—Still right here. Hold my position. More than hungry. Three days since I have eaten anything, with the exception of a small pototoe and piece of bread eaten two days ago and left from the day before. That length of time would have been nothing in Andersonville, but now being in better health demand eatables, and it takes right hold of this wandering sinner. Shall go to the house towards night. A solitary woman lives there with some children. My ankle from the sprain and yesterday's walking is swollen and painful. Bathe it in water, which does it good. Chickens running around. Have serious meditations of getting hold of one or two of them after they go to roost, then go farther back into the wilderness, build a fire with my matches and cook them. That would be a royal feast. But if caught at it, it would go harder with me than if caught legitimately. Presume this is the habitation of some of the skulkers who return and stay home nights. Believe that chickens squawk when being taken from the roost. Will give that up and walk boldly up to the house.

RE-CAPTURED.

HOME GUARDS GOBBLE ME UP—WELL TREATED AND WELL FED—TAKEN TO DOCTORTOWN AND FROM THENCE TO BLACKSHEAR—THE TWO BUCK BOYS AS RUNAWAYS—RIDE ON A PASSENGER TRAIN—PROSPECTS AHEAD, ETC.

DOCTORTOWN STATION, No. 5, Nov. 5.—Ha! Ha! My boy, you are a prisoner of war again. Once more with a blasted rebel standing guard over me, and it all happened in this wise: Just before dark I went up to that house I spoke of in my writings yesterday. Walked boldly up and rapped at the door; and what was my complete astonishment when a white woman answered my rapping. Asked me what I wanted, and I told her something to eat. Told me to come in and set down. She was a dark looking woman and could easily be mistaken from my hiding place of the day for a negro. Began asking me questions. Told her I was a rebel soldier, had been in the hospital sick and was trying to reach home in the adjoining county. Was very talkative; told how her husband had been killed at Atlanta, &c. She would go out and in from a shanty kitchen in her preparation of my supper. I looked out through a window and saw a little darky riding away from the house, a few minutes after I went inside. Thought I had walked into a trap, and was very uneasy. Still the woman talked and worked, and I talked, telling as smoothe lies as I knew how. For a full hour and a half sat there, and she all the time getting supper. Made up my mind that I was the same as captured, and so put on a bold face and made the best of it. Was very well satisfied with my escapade anyway, if I could only get a whack at that supper before the circus commenced. Well, after a while heard some hounds coming through the woods and towards the house. Looked at the woman and her face pleaded guilty, just as if she had done something very mean. The back door of the house was open and pretty soon half a dozen large blood hounds bounded into the room and began snuffing me over; about this time the woman began to cry. Told her I understood the whole thing and she need not make a scene over it. Said she knew I was a yankee and had sent for some men at Doctortown. Then five horsemen surrounded the house, dismounted and four of them came in with guns cocked prepared for a desperate encounter. I said: "good evening, gentlemen." "Good evening," said the foremost, "we are looking for a runaway yankee prowling around here." Well," says I, "you needn't look any farther, you have found him." "Yes, I see," was the answer. They all sat down, and just then the woman said "supper is ready and to draw nigh." Drawed as nigh as I could to that supper and proceeded to take vengeance on the woman. The fellows proved to be home guards stationed here at Doctortown. The woman had mounted the negro boy on a horse just as soon as I made my appearance at the house and sent for them. They proved to be good fellows. Talked there at the house a full hour on the fortunes of war, &c. Told them of my long imprisonment and escape and all about myself. After a while we got ready to start for this place. One rebel rode in front, one on each side and two in the rear of me. Was informed that if I tried to run they would shoot me. Told them no danger of my running, as I could hardly walk. They soon saw that such was the case after going a little way, and sent back one of the men to borrow the woman's horse. Was put on the animal's back and we reached Doctortown not far from midnight. As we were leaving the house the woman gave me a bundle; said in it was a shirt and stockings. Told her she had injured me enough and I would take them. No false delicy will prevent my taking a shirt. And so my adventure has ended and have enjoyed it hugely. Had plenty to eat with the exception of the two days, and at the last had a horseback ride. How well I was reminded of my last ride when first taken prisoner and at the time I got the coverlid. In the bundle was a good white shirt, pair of stockings, and a chunk of dried beef of two pounds or so. One of the captors gave me ten dollars in Confederate money. Now am in an old vacant building and guarded and it is the middle of the afternoon. Many citizens have visited me and I tell the guard he ought to charge admission; money in it. Some of the callers bring food and are allowed to give it to me, and am stocked with more than can conveniently carry. Have had a good wash up, put on my clean white shirt with standing collar, and new stockings and am happy. Doctortown is a small village with probably six or eight hundred population, and nigger young ones by the scores. Am treated kindly and well, and judge from conversations that I hear, that the battles are very disastrous to the rebels and that the war is pretty well over. All the negroes are hard pressed, fortifying every available point to contest the advance of the Union Army. This is cheering news to me. My escape has given me comfidence in myself, and I shall try it again the first opportunity. A woman has just given me a bottle of milk and two dollars in money. Thanked her with my heart in my mouth. Having been captured and brought to this place, am here waiting for them to get instructions as to what they shall do with me. They say I will probably be sent to the prison at Blackshear, which is forty or fifty miles away. Think I should be content to stay here with plenty to eat. Am in a good clean room in a dwelling. Can talk with any one who chooses to come and see me. The room was locked during the night, and this morning was thrown open, and I can wander through three rooms. Guard is off a few rods where he can see all around the house. Occasionally I go out doors and am having a good time. LATER.—Have seen a Savannah paper which says Sherman and his hosts are marching toward that city, and for the citizens to rally to repel the invader. My swollen ankle is being rubbed to-day with ointment furnished by an old darky. I tell you there are humane people the world over, who will not see even an enemy suffer if they can help it. While I have seen some of the worst people in the South, I have also seen some of the very best, and those, too, who were purely southern people and rebels. There are many pleasant associations connected with my prison life, as well as some directly to the opposite.

Dec. 1.—Still at Doctortown, and the town is doctoring me up "right smart." There is also a joke to this, but a weak one. The whole town are exercised over the coming of the Yankee army, and I laugh in my sleeve. Once in a while some poor ignorant and bigoted fellow amuses himself cursing me and the whole U. S. army. Don't talk back much, having too much regard for my bodily comfort. Orders have come to put me on a train for Blackshear. Have made quite a number of friends here, who slyly talk to me encouragingly. There are many Union people all through the South, although they have not dared to express themselves as such, but now they are more decided in their expressions and actions. Had a canteen of milk, and many other luxuries. Darkys are profuse in their gifts of small things. Have now a comb, good jack knife, and many little nicknacks. One old negress brought me a chicken nicely roasted. Think of that, prisoners of war, roast chicken! Shall jump off the cars every twenty rods hereafter. Tried to get a paper of the guard, who was reading the latest, but he wouldn't let me see it. Looks rather blue himself, and I surmise there is something in it which he don't like. All right, old fellow, my turn will come some day. Young darky brought me a cane, which is an improvement on my old one. Walk now the length of my limit with an old fashioned crook cane and feel quite proud. LATER.—Got all ready to take a train due at 3:30, and it didn't stop. Must wait until morning. Hope they won't stop for a month.

BLACKSHEAR, GA., Dec. 2.—In with the same men whom I deserted on the cars. We are near the Florida line. Was put in a passenger train at Doctortown and rode in style to this place. On the train were two more Yanks named David and Eli S. Buck, who are Michigan men. They were runaways who had been out in the woods nearly three months and were in sight of our gunboats when recaptured. Belong to the 6th Michigan Cavalry. David Buck was one of Kilpatrick's scouts; a very smart and brave fellow, understands living in the woods, and thoroughly posted. We have mutually agreed to get away the first chance, and shall get to our lines. David Buck used to attend school at Leoni, Mich., and was educated for a preacher. They are cousins. We three Yankees were quite a curiosity to the passengers on the train that brought us to this place. Some of them had evidently never seen a Yankee before, and we were stared at for all we were worth. Some smarties were anxious to argue the point with us in a rather "we have got you" style. David Buck is a good talker, and satisfactorily held up our end of the war question; in fact, I thought talked them all out on their own grounds. The ladies in particular sneered and stared at us. Occasionally we saw some faces which looked as if they were Union, and we often got a kind word from some of them. The railroads are in a broken down condition, out of decent repair,

ANDERSONVILLE DIARY.

and trains run very slow. The Confederacy is most assuredly hard up, and will go to pieces some of these days. My out door life of the few days I roamed through the woods, was just jolly. Being out from under rebel guard made me the happiest chap imaginable. Knew that I couldn't escape to our lines, as I was not able to travel much, and my sole business was to remain a tramp as long as possible, and to get enough to eat, which I did The negroes, and especially the field hands, are all Union darkys, and fed me all I wanted as a general thing. Made a mistake in going to the house of a white woman for food.

Dec. 3.—Blackshear is an out-of-the-way place, and shouldn't think the Yankee army would ever find us here. The climate is delightful. Here it is December and at the North right in the middle of winter, and probably good sleighing, and cold; while here it is actually warm during the day time, and at night not uncomfortably cold. The Buck boys are jolly good fellows, and full of fun Seem to have taken a new lease of life myself. Both of them are in good health and fleshy, and open for an escape any hour. And we don't stay here but a few days, the guards say. Why not keep us on the cars and run us around the country all the time? There is no wall or anything around us here, only guards. Encamped right in the open air. Have food once a day, just whatever they have to give us. Last night had sweet potatoes. I am getting considerably heavier in weight, and must weigh one hundred and forty pounds or more. Still lame, however, and I fear permanently so. Teeth are firm in my mouth now, and can eat as well as ever, and oh! such an appetite. Would like to see the pile of food that I couldn't eat. Found Rowe and Bullock, and Hub Dakin. They are well, and all live in jolly expectancy of the next move. The old coverlid still protects my person. The Bucks have also each a good blanket, and we are comfortable. Some fresh beef given us to-day; not much, but suppose all they have got. Guard said he wished to God he was one of us prisoners instead of guarding us.

Dec. 4.—Another delightfully cool morning. There are not a great many guards here to watch over us, and it would be possible for all to break away without much trouble. The men, however, are so sure of liberty that they prefer to wait until given legitimately. Would like to have seen this guard hold us last summer at Andersonville. Fresh meat again to-day. Rebels go out to neighboring plantations and take cattle, drive them here, and butcher for us to eat. Rice is also given us to eat. Have plenty of wood to cook with. Have traded off the old missmated pair of brogans for a smaller and good pair, and feel quite like a dandy. Have some money to buy extras. Have plenty of food yet from that given me at Doctortown. Divide with the Bucks, or rather, it is all one common mess, and what any one owns belongs equally to the others. Rebels glum and cross, and sometimes we laugh at them, and then they swear and tell us to shut up or they will blow our heads off. Blackshear is a funny name and it is a funny town, if there is any, for as yet I haven't been able to see it. Probably a barn and a hen-coop comprise the place. Cars go thundering by as if the Yanks were after them About every train loaded with troops. Go first one way and then the other. Think they are trying to keep out of the way themselves.

Dec 5 —Guard said that orders were not to talk with any of the prisoners, and above all not to let us get hold of any newspapers. No citizens are allowed to come near us. That shows which way the wind blows. Half a dozen got away from here last night, and guards more strict to-day, with an increased force. Going to be moved, it is said, in a few days. Why don't they run us right into the ocean? That wouldn't do though, our gunboats are there. Well, keep us then, that is punishment enough. Do what you are a mind to. You dare not starve us now, for we would break away. In fact, although under guard, we are masters of the situation. Can see an old darky with an ox hitched to a cart with harness on, the cart loaded with sugar cane. This is quite a sugar country, it is said. On the road here saw the famous palmetto tree in groves. Live-oaks are scattered all over, and are a funny affair. Persimmon and pecan trees also abound here We are pretty well south now, spending the winter. But few die now; no more than would naturally die in any camp with the same numbers. It is said that some men get away every night, and it is probably so.

Dec. 6.—Thirteen months ago to-day captured —one year and one month. Must be something due me from Uncle Sam in wages, by this time. All come in a lump when it does come. No great loss without small gain, and while I have been suffering the long imprisonment my wages have been accumulating. Believe that we are also entitled to ration money while in prison. Pile it on, you can't pay us any too much for this business. This is the land of the blood hound. Are as common as the ordinary cur at the North. Are a noble looking dog except when they are after you, and then they are beastly. Should think that any one of them could whip a man; are very large, strong, and savage looking. Should think it would be hard for the negro to run away. See no horses about here at all—all mules and oxen, and even cows hitched up to draw loads. I walk the prison over forty times a day. Everybody knows me, and I hail and am hailed as I walk around, and am asked what I think of the situation. Tell them of my escape and the good time I had, which incites them to do likewise the first opportunity. Occasionally a man here who growls and grumbles, and says and thinks we will never get away, &c. Some would find fault if they were going to be hung. Should think they would compare their condition with that of six months ago and be contented.

Dec. 7.—Another day of smiling weather. Still call our mess the "Astor House Mess." It is composed of only three—the Bucks and myself. I am the only one of the original mess here, and it is still the most prosperous and best fed of any. We are all the time at work at something. Have a good piece of soap, and have washed our clothing throughout, and are clean and neat for prisoners of war. Eli S. Buck is a large fellow, and a farmer when at home. Both are young, and from the same neighborhood. As I have said before, are cousins, and think a great deal of one another, which is good to see. Relatives rarely get along together in prison as well as those who are not related. There were brothers in Andersonville who would not mess together. Seems funny, but such is the case. Should like to see myself throwing over a brother for any one else. Guards denounce Jeff Davis as the author of their misfortunes. We also denounce him as the author of ours, so we are agreed on one point. Going to move. The "mess" will escape *en masse* at the first move, just for the sake of roaming the woods. With the Bucks in company with me, shall have a good time, and we can undoubtedly soon reach our troops in as much as they are raiding through the South. Dave Buck is the acknowledged leader of us. He prays; think of that.

Dec. 8—There are many men of many minds here. That used to be a favorite copy at writing school in Jackson, Mich. "Many men of many minds, many birds of many kinds." How a person's thoughts go back to the old boyhood days in such a place as this. Happiest times of life are those of youth, but we didn't know it. Everybody told us so, but we didn't believe it; but now it is plain. Every one, I think, has that experience. We all see where we might have done different if we only had our lives to live over, but alas, it is not to be. A majority of the men here have about half enough to eat. Our mess has enough to eat, thanks to our own ingenuity. Now expect to go away from here every day. Have borrowed a needle, begged some thread, and have been sewing up my clothing; am well fixed up, as are also the Bucks. Am quite handy with the needle, and it is difficult to make some of them believe I am not a tailor by trade. If I always keep my ways mended as I do my clothes, I shall get along very well. Eli has come with four large yams bought of a guard and we will proceed to cook and eat a good supper, and then go to bed and perhaps dream of something pleasant to remember the next day. Rumors of all kinds in camp, and rebels say something is up that will interest us, but I can get no satisfaction as to what it is. Drew cuts for the extra potato, and Dave won, and he cut that article of food into three pieces and we all had a share. Good boy.

Dec. 9.—Still in Blackshear, and quiet. Many incidents happened when I was out in the wood, and I am just crazy to get there once more. Look at the tall trees in sight, and could hug them. My long sickness and the terrible place in which I was confined so long, and my recovering health, and the hope now of getting entirely well and recovering my liberty, has made a new man of me—a new lease of life, as it were. The Bucks are the best of fellows, and having money which they use for my benefit the same as their own, we get along swimmingly. One of these days my Northern friends and relatives will hear from me. Am getting over my lameness, and have an appetite for more than my supply of food. Certainly had a good constitution to stand all that has been passed through, during which time thousands and thousands died, of apparently better health than myself. Of all my many messmates and friends in prison, have lost track of them all; some died, in fact nearly all, and the balance scattered, the Lord only knows where. What stories we can talk over when we meet at the North. This Blackshear country is rather a nice section. Warm and pleasant, although rather low. Don't know where we are located, but must be not far from the coast.

Dec. 10.—The grand change has come and a car load of prisoners go away from here to-day. Although the Bucks and myself were the last in prison, we are determined to flank out and go with the first that go. Our destination is probably Charleston, from what I can learn. We three will escape on the road, or make a desperate effort to do so, anyway. Can walk much better now than ten days ago, and feel equal to the emergency. Fine weather and in good spirits, although many here are tired of being moved from place to place. More guards have come to take charge of us on the road, and it looks very discouraging for getting away, though "Dave" says we will make it all right. Place great reliance in him, as he has caution as well as the intention to escape. So like Hendryx, and added to it has more practical quiet common sense. Eli Buck and myself acknowledge him as leader in all things. Now comes the tug of war.

Dec. 11.—We flanked out this morning, or rather paid three fellows two dollars apiece for their turn to go. Are now thirty miles from Blackshear; have been unloaded from the cars and are encamped by the side of the railroad track for the night. Most dark. Rebel soldiers going by on the trains, with hoots and yells. We are strongly guarded, and it augurs not for us to get away to night. Our best hold is jumping from the cars. Ride on open platform cars with guards standing and sitting on the sides, six guards to each car. About sixty prisoners ride on each car, and there are thirty or forty cars. Were given rations yesterday, but none to-day. It is said we get nothing to eat to night, which is bad; more so for the other prisoners than ourselves. Low country we come through, and swampy. Bucks think we may get away before morning, but I doubt it. Rebs flying around lively, and Yanks going for them I guess.

Dec. 12.—Routed up at an early hour and loaded on to the cars, which stood upon a side track, and after being loaded have been here for six mortal hours. Small rations given us just before loading up. All are cramped up and mad. We will more than jump the first opportunity. We go to Charleston, via. Savannah. Wish they would hurry up their old vehicles for transportation. Being doubled up like a jack knife makes my legs stiff and sore, and difficult to use my limbs from cramped position. Worth four hundred dollars a day to see the rebel troops fly around. Would give something to know the exact position now of both armies. Guards are sleepy and tired out from doing double duty, and I think we can get away if they move us by night, which I am afraid they won't do. Bucks jubilant and confident, consequently so am I.

A SUCCESSFUL ESCAPE.

JUMP OFF THE CARS NEAR SAVANNAH—FIND FRIENDLY NEGROES—
TRAVEL BY NIGHT AND REST BY DAY—GOOD TIMES WITH MANY
ADVENTURES—A MORNING BATH—ALMOST RUN INTO REBEL PICK-
ETS, ETC., ETC.

IN THE WOODS, Dec 13.—How does that sound for a location to date from? Yesterday long toward night our train started from its abiding place and rolled slowly toward its destination, wherever that might be. When near Savannah, not more than a mile this side, David Buck jumped off the cars and rolled down the bank. I jumped next and Eli Buck came right after me. Hastily got up and joined one anotder, and hurried off in an easterly direction through the wet, swampy country. A number of shots were fired at us, but we were surprised and glad to find that none hit us, although my cap was knocked off by a bullet hitting the fore-piece. Eli Buck was also singed by a bullet. It seemed as if a dozen shots were fired. Train did not stop, and we ran until tired out. Knew that we were within a line of forts which encircle Savannah, going all the way around it and only twenty rods or so apart. It was dark when we jumped off, and we soon came in the vicinity of a school house in which was being held a negro prayer meeting. We peeked in at the windows, but dared not stop so near our jumping off place. Worked around until we were near the rail-road again and guided by the track going south—the same way we had come. It was very dark. Dave Buck went ahead, Eli next and myself last, going Indian file and very slow. All at once Dave stopped and whispered to us to keep still, which you may be sure we did. Had come within ten feet of a person who was going directly in the opposite direction and also stopped, at the same time we did. Dave Buck says: "Who comes there?" A negro woman says "it's me," and he walked up close to her and asked where she was going. She says: "Oh! I knows you; you are Yankees and has jumped off de cars." By this time we had come up even with Dave and the woman. Owned up to her that such was the case. She said we were her friends, and would not tell of us. Also said that not twenty rods ahead there was a rebel picket, and we were going right into them. I think if I ever wanted to kiss a woman, it was that poor, black, negro wench. She told us to go about thirty rods away and near an old shed, and she would send us her brother; he would know what to do. We went to the place designated and waited there an hour, and then we saw two dusky forms coming through the darkness, and between them a wooden tray of food consisting of boiled turnips, corn bread and smoked bacon. We lay there behind that old shed and ate and and talked, and talked and ate, for a full hour more. The negro, "Major," said he was working on the forts, putting them in order to oppose the coming of the Yankees, and he thought he could get us through the line before morning to a safe hiding place. If we all shook hands once we did fifty times, all around. The negroes were fairly jubilant at being able to help genuine Yankees. Were very smart colored people, knowing more than the ordinary run of their race. Major said that in all the forts was a reserve picket force, and between the forts the picket. He said pretty well south was a dilapidated fort which had not as yet been repaired any, and that was the one to go through or near, as he did not think there was any picket there. "Bress de Lord, for yo' safety." says the good woman. We ate all they brought us, and then started under the guidance of Major at somewhere near midnight. Walked slow and by a roundabout way to get to the fort and was a long time about it, going through a large turnip patch and over and through hedges. Major's own safety as much as ours depended upon the trip. Finally came near the fort and discovered there were rebels inside and a picket off but a few rods. Major left us and crawled slowly ahead to reconnoitre; returned in a few minutes and told us to follow. We all climbed over the side of the fort, which was very much out of repair. The reserve picket was asleep around a fire which had nearly gone out. Major piloted us through the fort, actually stepping over the sleeping rebels. After getting on the outside there was a wide ditch which we went through. Ditch was partially full of water. We then went way round near the railroad again, and started south, guided by the darky, who hurried us along at a rapid gait. By near day light we were five or six miles from Savannah, and then stopped for consultation and rest. Finally went a mile further, where we are now laying low in a swamp, pretty well tired out and muddy beyond recognition. Major left us at day light, saying he would find us a guide before night who would show us still further. He had to go back and work on the forts. And so I am again loose, a free man, with the same old feeling I had when in the woods before. We got out of a thick settled country safely, and again await developments. Heard drums'and bugles playing reveille this morning in many directions, and "We are all surrounded." David Buck is very confident of getting away to our lines. Eli thinks it is so if Dave says so, and I don't know, or care so very much. The main point with me is to stay out in the woods as long as I can. My old legs have had a hard time of it since last night and ache, and are very lame. It's another beautiful and cold day, this 13th of December. Biting frost nights, but warmer in the day time. Our plan is to work our way to the Ogechee River, and wait for the Stars and Stripes to come to us. Major said Sherman was marching right toward us all the time, driving the rebel army with no trouble at all. Told us to keep our ears open and we would hear cannon one of these days, possibly within a week. The excitement of the last twenty-four hours has worn me out, and I couldn't travel to-day if it was necessary. Have a plenty to eat, and for a wonder I ain't hungry for anything except things we haven't got. Dave is happy as an oyster, and wants to yell. Where they are so confident I am satisfied all will be well. As soon as it comes night we are going up to some negro huts less than a mile off, where we hope and expect that Major has posted the inmates in regard to us. The railroad is only a short distance off, and the river only three or four miles. As near as we know, are about twenty miles from the Atlantic coast. Tell the boys it may be necessary for me to stay here for two or three days to get recruited up, but they think three or four miles to-night will do me good. Don't like to burden them and shall try it.

Dec. 14.—We are now three miles from yesterday's resting place,

and near the Miller plantation. Soon as dark last night we went to the negro huts and found them expecting us. Had a jubilee. No whites near, but all away The Buck boys passed near here before when out in the woods, and knew of many darkys who befriended them. Had a surfeit of food. Stayed at the huts until after midnight, and then a woman brought us to this place. To-night we go to Jocko's hut, across the river. A darky will row us across the Little Ogechee to Jocco's hut, and then he will take us in tow. It is a rice country about here, with canals running every way. Negroes all tickled to death because Yankees coming. I am feeling better than yesterday, but difficult to travel. Tell the boys they had better leave me with the friendly blacks and go ahead to our lines, but they won't. Plenty to eat and milk to drink, which is just what I want. The whites now are all away from their homes and most of the negroes. Imagine we can hear the booming of cannon, but guess we are mistaken. Dave is very entertaining and good company. Don't get tired of him and his talk. Both of them are in rebel dress throughout, and can talk and act just like rebels. Know the commanders of different rebel regiments. They say that when out before they on different occasions mixed with the Southern army, without detection Said they didn't wonder the widow woman knew I was a Yankee. Ain't up to that kind of thing.

Dec. 15—Jocko's hut was not across the river as I supposed and wrote yesterday, but on the same side we were on. At about ten o'clock last night we went to his abiding place as directed and knocked. After a long time an old black head was stuck out of the window with a nightcap on. The owner of the head didn't know Jocko or anything about him; was short and crusty; said: "Go way from dar!" Kept talking to him and he scolding at being disturbed. Said he had rheumatics and couldn't get out to let us in. After a long time opened the door and we set down on the door step. Told him we were yankees and wanted help. Was the funniest darky we have met yet. Would give something for his picture as he was framed in his window in the moonlight talking to us, with the picturesque surroundings, and us yankees trying to win him over to aid us. Finally owned up that he was Jocko, but said he couldn't row us across the river. He was lame and could not walk, had no boat, and if he had the river was so swift he couldn't get us across, and if it wasn't swift, the rebels would catch him at it and hang him. Talked a long time and with much teasing. By degrees his scruples gave way, one at a time. Didn't know but he might row us across if he only had a boat, and finally didn't know but he could find a boat. To get thus far into his good graces took at least three hours. Went looking around and found an old scow, fixed up some old oars, and we got in; before doing so however, he had warmed up enough to give us some boiled sweet potatoes and cold baked fish. Rowed us way down the river and landed us on the noted Miller plantation and a mile in rear of the negro houses. Jocko, after we forced our acquaintance on him with all kind of argument, proved to be a smart able bodied old negro, but awful afraid of being caught halping runaways. Would give something for his picture as he appeared to us looking out of his cabin window. Just an old fashioned, genuine negro, and so black that charcoal would make a white mark on him. Took us probably three miles from his hut, two miles of water and one of land, and then started back home after shaking us a dozen times by the hand, and "God blessing us." Said "Ole Massa Miller's niggers all Union niggers," and to go up to the huts in broad day light and they would help us. No whites at home on the plantation. We arrived where Jocko left us an hour or so before daylight, and lay down to sleep until light. I woke up after a while feeling wet, and found the tide had risen and we were surrounded with water; woke up the boys and scrambled out of that in a hurry, going through two feet of water in some places. The spot where we had laid down was a higher piece of ground than that adjoining. Got on to dry land and proceeded to get dry. At about ten o'clock Dave went up to the negro huts and made himself known, which was hard work. The negroes are all afraid that we are rebels and tryin'; to get them into a scrape, but after we once get them thoroughly satisfied that we are genuine Yanks they are all right, and will do anything for us. The negroes have shown us the big house, there being no whites around, they having left to escape the coming Yankee army. We went up into the cupola and looked way off on the ocean, and saw our own noble gunboats. What would we give to be aboard of them? Their close proximity makes us discuss the feasibility of going down the river and out to them, but the negroes say there are chain boats across the river farther down, and picketed. Still it makes us anxious, our being so near, and we have decided to go down the river to night in a boat and see if we can't reach them. It is now the middle of the afternoon and we lay off from the huts eighty rods, and the negroes are about to bring us some dinner. During the night we traveled over oyster beds by the acre, artificial ones, and they cut our feet. Negroes say there are two other runaways hid a mile off and they are going to bring them to our abiding place. LATER.—Negroes have just fed us with corn bread and a kind of fish about the size of sardines, boiled by the kettle full, and they are nice. Fully as good as sardines. Think I know now where nearly all the imported sardines come from. Negroes catch them by the thousand, in nets, put them in kettles, and cook them a few minutes, when they are ready to eat. Scoop them out of the creeks. The two other runaways are here with us. They are out of the 3d Ohio Cavalry. Have been out in the woods for two weeks. Escaped from Blackshear and traveled this far. I used to know one of them in Savannah. We do not take to them at all, as they are not of our kind. Shall separate to night, they going their way and we going ours. Have secured a dug-out boat to go down the Ogechee River with to night. The negroes tell us of a Mr. Kimball, a white man, living up the country fifteen miles, who is a Union man, and helps runaways, or any one of Union proclivities. He lays up the river, and our gunboats lay down the river. Both have wonderful charms for us, and shall decide before night which route to take. Are on rice plantation, and a valuable one. Before the "wah" there were over fifteen hundred negroes on this place. Cotton is also part of the production. Have decided to go down the river and try to reach our gunboats. It's a very hazardous undertaking, and I have my doubts as to its successful termination.

Dec. 16.—Another adventure, and a red hot one. Started down the river in our dug-out boat somewhere near midnight. Ran down all right for an hour, frequently seeing rebel pickets and camp fires. Saw we were going right into the lion's mouth, as the farther down the more rebels. All at once our boat gave a lurch and landed in a tree top which was sticking out of the water, and there we were, swaying around in the cold water in the middle or near the middle of the Ogechee. Dave went ashore and to a negro hut, woke up the inmates, and narrated our troubles. A negro got up, and with another boat came to the rescue. Were about froze with the cold and wet. Said not more than a mile farther down we would have run right into a chain b at, with pickets posted on it. It really seems as if a Divine providence were guiding us. After getting a breakfast of good things started off toward the Big Ogechee River, and have traveled three or four miles. Are now encamped, or rather laying down, on a little hillock waiting for evening, to get out of this vicinity which is a dangerous one. In our river escapade lost many of our things, but still hang to my coverlid and diary. There are three or four houses in view, and principally white residences, those of the poor white trash order, and they are the very ones we must avoid. Have caught cold and am fearfully out of traveling condition, but must go it now. A mistake in coming down the river. Am resting up, preparatory to traveling all night up the country. No chance of getting out by the coast. Have enough food to last all day and night, and that is a good deal. Can't carry more than a day's supply. Have now been out in the woods, this is the fourth day, and every day has been fresh adventures thick and fast. If I could only travel like my comrades, would get along. Bucks praise me up and encourage me to work away, and I do. For breakfast had more of those imported sardines. Storm brewing of some sort and quite chilly. Saw rebel infantry marching along the highway not more than eighty rods off. Hugged the ground very close. Dogs came very near us, and if they had seen us would have attracted the rebels' attention. Am writing with a pencil less than an inch long. Shall print this diary and make my everlasting fortune, and when wealthy will visit this country and make every negro who has helped us millionaires. Could not move from here half a mile by daylight without being seen, and as a consequence we are feeling very sore on the situation. Don't know but I shall be so lame to-night that I cannot walk at all, and then the boys must leave me and go ahead for themselves. However, they say I am worth a hundred dead men yet, and will prod me along like a tired ox. Dave goes now bareheaded, or not quite so bad as that, as he has a handkerchief tied over his head. The programme now is to go as straight to Mr. Kimball's as we can. He is probably twenty miles away; is a white Union man I spoke of a day or so ago in this same diary. Wil stick to him like a brother. Can hear wagons go along the road toward Savannah, which is only thirteen or fourteen miles away. LATER—Most dark enough to travel and I have straightened up and am taking an inventory of myself. Find I can walk with the greatest difficulty. The boys argue that after I get warmed up I will go like a top, and we will see.

Dec. 17—And another day of vicissitudes. We traveled last night about four miles, piloted by a young negro. It was a terrible walk to me; slow and painful. Were fed, and have food for to-day.

Are now about three miles from a canal which we must cross before another morning. Negroes say "Sherman most here" and "Bress de Lord!" Mr. Kimball lives nine miles away and we must reach him some way, but it seems an impossibility for me to go so far. Are now in a high and fine country, but too open for us. Have to lay down all day in the bushes. David is a thorough scout. Goes crawling around on his hands and knees taking in his bearings. Troops are encamped on the main road. Every cross road has its pickets, and it is slow business to escape running into them. Eli S. Buck has a sore throat and is hoarse. Pretty good jaunt for him, tough as he is. Shall have no guide to-night, as Dave thinks he can engineer us all right in the right direction. Some thinks he will leave us both and reach Kimball's to-night, and then come back and see us through. Guess I will be on hand to go along however.

Dec. 18.—Six days of freedom and what a sight of hardship, sweetened by kind treatment and the satisfaction of being out from under guard. We traveled last night some four miles and now are in a very precarious position. When almost daylight we came to the canal, and found cavalry pickets all along the tow-path; walked along until we came to a lock. A cavalryman was riding his horse up and down by the lock. At the lock there was a smouldering fire. It was absolutely necessary that we get across before daylight. As the mounted picket turned his horse's head to go from us, Dave slid across the tow-path and went across the timbers which formed the lock, and by the time the picket turned around to come back Dave was hid on the opposite shore. At the next trip of the rebel Eli went the same as Dave. The third one to go was myself, and I expected to get caught, sure. Could not go as as quiet as the rest, and was slower. Thought the picket saw me when half way across but kept right on going, and for a wonder made it all right. Was thoroughly scared for the first time since jumping off the train. Am very nervous. All shook hands when the picket turned about to go back the fourth time. Getting light in the east and we must move on, as the country is very open. Dare not travel over half a mile, and here we are hid almost in a woman's door yard, not over thirty rods from her very door. Are in some evergreen bushes and shrubs, It's now most noon, and have seen a rather elderly lady go out and in the house a number of times. The intrepid Dave is going up to the house to interview the lady soon. LATER.—Dave crawled along from our hiding place until he came to the open ground, and then straightened boldly up and walked to the house. In fifteen minutes he came back with some bread and dried beef, and said the woman was a Union woman and would help us. Her daughter slept at her uncle's a mile off last night, and expected her back soon, and perhaps the uncle, who is a violent Secesh, with her. Said for us to lay low. LATER.—The daughter came home on horseback and alone. Could see the old lady telling the daughter about us and pointing our way. About the middle of the afternoon the old lady started out toward us. Behind her came a young darky, and behind the darky came another darky; then a dog, then a white boy, then a darky, and then the daughter. Old lady peeked in, and so did the rest except the grown up girl, who was too afraid. Finally came closer, and as she got a good view of us she says: "Why, mother, they look just like anybody else." She had never seen a Yankee before. Brought us some more food, and after dark will set a table for us to come to the house and eat. Her name is Mrs. Dickinson. They went back to the house and we proceeded to shake hands with one another. During the afternoon five rebel soldiers came to the house, one at a time. It is now most dark and we are about ready to go to the house and eat. Mr. Kimball lives only four miles away.

Dec. 19.—We are now less than half a mile from Mr. Kimball's. After dark last night we went to Mrs. Dickinson's house and partook of a splendid supper. I wrote a paper directed to the officer commanding the first Yankee troops that should arrive here telling what she had done for us runaway Yankees. She talked a great deal, and I thought was careless leaving the front door open. Three or four times I got up and shut that door. We had taken off our blankets and other wraps and left them in a sort of a kitchen, and were talking in the best room. I heard the gate click, and on looking out saw two rebel officers coming to the house and not six rods off. We jumped into the other room and out of the back door and behind a corn house, bare headed. The officers were asked into the front room by the daughter. They asked who the parties were who ran out of the back way. She said she reckoned no one. They kept at her and jokingly intimated that some of her skulking lovers had been to see her. See kept talking back and finally said: "Mother, did any one just go away?" And the old lady said: "Why, yes, brother Sam and his 'boy' just went off home." Them confounded rebels had come to see the girl and spend the evening, and we shivering out in the cold. Joked her for an hour and a half about her lovers and we hearing every word. Finally they got up and bid her good night, saying they would send back some men to guard the house and keep her lovers away. Just as soon as they were down the road a ways, the daughter came out very frightened and said for us to hurry off, as they would send back troops to look for us. Hurried into the house, got our things and some dried beef, and started off toward Mr. Kimball's house. Reached here just before daylight and lay down back of the house about eighty rods, in the corner of the fence, to sleep a little before morning. Just at break of day heard some one calling hogs. David got up and went toward an old man whom we knew was our friend Kimball. Came to us, and was glad to shake hands with genuine Yankees. Said one of his neighbors was coming over early to go with him to hunt some hogs, and for us to go farther off and stay until night, and he would think up during the day what to do with us. Did not want anything to eat. Came to this place where we now are, and feeling that our journey was most ended. Mr. Kimball said that Sherman was not over fifty miles off, and coming right along twenty miles per day, and our plan was to hide and await coming events. Mr. Kimball is an old man, probably sixty years old, white haired and stoop shouldered. He had five sons, all drafted into the rebel army. All refused to serve. Two have been shot by the rebels, one is in some prison for his Union proclivities, and two are refugees. The old man has been imprisoned time and again, his stock confiscated, property destroyed, and all together had a hard time of it. Still he is true blue, a Union man to the back bone. Really think our troubles coming to an end. Kimball said: "Glory to God, the old Stars and Stripes shall float over my house in less than a week!" It's a noble man who will stand out through all that he has, for his principles, when his interests are all here. Is not only willing, but glad to help us, and says anything he has is ours, if it will help us toward our escape. LATER.—Have been laying all day watching Kimball's house. Along in the morning the neighbor spoken of came to Kimball's, and they both went off on horseback to shoot hogs. The swine here roam over a large territory and become most wild, and when they want fresh pork they have to go after it with a gun. You may be sure the hunters did not come near us with Mr. Kimball for a guide. A negro boy went with them with a light wagon and mule attached. Near noon they returned with some killed hogs in the wagon. At three or four o'clock the old man came down where we were "to look after his boys," he said. Is in the best of spirits. Says we are to hide to-night where he tells us, and stay until our troops reach us. That is jolly good news for me, as I hate to travel. Said come to the house after dark and he would have a supper prepared for us, and has just left us. LATER.—Have just eaten a splendid supper at Kimball's and getting ready to travel three miles to a safe hiding place.

Dec. 20.—Well, we are just well fixed and happy. After partaking of a royal repast last night, served in an out-building near the main building of the Kimball home, we were directed to this place which is on the banks of the Big Ogechee river, in a most delightful spot. While we were at Kimball's he had negro sentinels stationed at different points on the plantation to announce the coming of any rebel soldiers or citizens that might see fit to come near. He gave us an axe, a quart of salt, a ham too big to carry conveniently, and all the sweet potatoes we could drag along; also a butcher knife. Went with us a mile as guide and then told us so we found the place pointed out. Also gave us some shelled corn to bait hogs and told Dave how to make a deadfall to catch them. We left the main road going directly West until we came to a fence, then turned to the left and followed the line of the fence, and when we had got to the end of it kept straight ahead going through a swampy low section. After a while came to higher and dry land and to the banks of the river. Is a sort of an island, and as I said before, a very pretty and pleasant spot. Out in the river grows tall canebrake which effectually hides us from any one going either up or down the river. Tall pines are here in abundance and nice grass plats, with as handsome palm clusters as ever I saw. Are going to build us a house to keep off the cold and rain. Have matches and a rousing fire cooked our breakfast of nice ham and sweet potatoes. We also roasted some corn and had corn coffee. Any quantity of hogs running around and Dave is already thinking of a trap to catch them. It will be necessary for we are making that ham look sick. Eat so much breakfast that we can hardly walk and don't know but will commit suicide by eating. Buzzards fly around attracted by the cooking. Are as large and look like turkeys. Our government should give to Mr. Kimball a fortune for his patriotism and sacrifices to the Union cause. About eight miles above is a long bridge across the river and there it is thought a big fight will take place when Sherman attempts to cross, and so we will know when they approach, as we could hear a battle that distance. NIGHT.—We have built the cosyest and nicest little house to lay in. Cut poles with the axe and made a frame, and then covered the top with palm leaves just like shingles on a house at the North, then fixed three sides the same way, each leaf overlapping the other, and the fourth side open to a fire and the river. The water is cold and clear and nice to drink; just like spring water. Have eaten the ham half up; ditto potatoes. The increased prosperity makes me feel well bodily, and mentally am more so. It is still the "Astor House Mess." We all cook, and we all eat. Dave prays to-night as he does every night and morning, and I ain't sure but all through the day. Is a thorough Christian if ever there was one. I also wrote a letter for Mr. Kimball to the commanding Union officer who may first approach these parts. In it I told how he had befriended us and others. We heard boats going by on the river to-day. At such times all we do is to keep still, as no one can see us. Rebels are too busy to look for us or any one else. All they can do now to take care of themselves. Eli is making up our bed, getting ready to turn in. I have just brought a tin pail of nice water and we all drink. Take off our shoes for the first time in some days. A beautiful night —clear and cold. And thus ends another day, and we are in safety.

Dec. 21.—Got up bright and early. Never slept better. Getting rested up. We talk continually. Both Bucks are great talkers, especially David. Cooked and ate our breakfast, and would you believe it the ham is all gone. Incredible, the amount of food we eat. Wonder it don't make us all sick. Sweet potatoes getting low. Dave fixing up his dead fall for hogs. Has rolled some heavy logs together forty rods away from our house, and fixed up a figure four spring trap, with the logs for weight to hold down the animal which may be enticed into it. Has scattered corn in and around the trap, and we wait for developments. Hogs are very shy of us and surroundings. Are apparently fat and in good order. Plenty of roots and shack which they eat, and thrive thereon. Buzzards are very curious in regard to us. They light on the limbs in the trees, and if their support is a dead limb it breaks and makes a great noise in the still woods. Two or three hundred all together make a terrible racket, and scare us sometimes. The weather is very fine, and this must be a healthy climate. Dave is going out to-day to look around. As I have said before, he is a scout and understands spying around, and won't get caught. If we had a fish hook and line or a net of some sort could catch fish to eat. That would be a grand sport as we can see nice large fish in the water. The main road is away about one and a half miles we think by the sound of the teams which occasionally rumble along. Often hear shouting on the road as if cattle were being driven along toward Savannah. Once in a while we hear guns fired off, but it is no doubt hogs being killed. We also hear folks going up and down the river, but cannot see them. After dark we have no fire as that would expose us, it is so much plainer to be seen in the night. The river is wide; should think a third of a mile, as we can view it from away up the stream. The cane that grows in the river is the same as we have for fish poles at the North, and are shipped from the South. Have added some repairs to the house and it is now water tight, we think. Made a bed of soft boughs, and with our three blankets have a good sleeping place. Dave got a tall cane and fastened up on the house, and for a flag fastened on a piece or black cloth—the best we could do. That means no quarter; and it is just about what we mean, too. Don't believe we would be taken very easy now. I am getting fat every day, yet lame, and have come to the conclusion that it will be a long time before I get over it. The cords have contracted so in my right leg that they don't seem to stretch out again to their original length. That scurvy business came very near killing me. LATER.—I also went out of our hiding place, and saw away out in a field what I took to be a mound where sweet potatoes were buried. Came back and got a pair of drawers, tied the bottom of the legs together, and sallied forth. The mound of potatoes was a good way back from the house, although in plain sight. I crawled up, and began digging into it with a piece of canteen. Very soon had a hole in, and found some of the nicest potatoes that you can imagine, of the red variety, which I believe are the genuine Southern yam. Filled the drawers cram full, filled my pockets and got all I could possibly carry, then closed up the hole and worked my way back to camp. Eli was alone, Dave not having returned from his scouting trip. Had a war dance around those potatoes. Believe there is a bushel of them, and like to have killed myself getting them here. After I got into the woods and out of the field, straightened up and got the drawers on my shoulders and picked the way to head-quarters. We don't any of us call any such thing as that stealing. It's one of the necessities of our lives that we should have food, and if we have not got it, must do the best we can. Now if we can catch a porker will be fixed all right for some days to come. Think it is about the time of year for butchering. We don't expect to be here more than two or three days at fartherest, although I shall hate to leave this beautiful spot, our nice house and all. Listen all the time for the expected battle at the bridge, and at any unusual sound of commotion in that direction we are all excitement. LATER.—Dave has returned. He went to the main road and saw a negro. Was lucky enough to get a Savannah paper three days old in which there was nothing we did not know in regard to Sherman's coming. The negro said yankee scouts had been seen just across the river near the bridge, and the main army is expected every day. The rebels will fall back across the river and contest the crossing. Fortifications are built all along clear to Savannah, and it may be reasonably expected that some hard fighting will take place. Savannah is the pride of the South and they will not easily give it up. Dave did not tell the negro that he was a yankee, but represented himself as a conscript hiding in the woods to keep from fighting in the rebel army. Was glad to see supply of potatoes and says I will do. Has freshly baited his trap for hogs and thinks before night we will have fresh pork to go with the potatoes. LATER.—We went around a drove of hogs and gradually and carefully worked them up to the trap. Pretty soon they began to pick up the corn and one of them went under the figure four, sprung it and down came the logs and such a squealing and scrambling of those not caught. The axe had been left near the trap standing up against a tree, and Dave ran up and grabbed it and struck the animal on the head and cut his throat. How we did laugh and dance around that defunct porker. Exciting sport this trapping for fresh pork. In half an hour Dave and Eli had the pig skinned and dressed. Is not a large one probably weighs ninety pounds or so, and is fat and nice. Have sliced up enough for about a dozen men and are now cooking it on sticks held up before the fire. Also frying some in a skillet which we are the possessor of. When the hogs run wild and eat acorns, roots and the like, the meat is tough and curly but is sweet and good. We fry out the grease and then slice up the potatoes and cook in it. Thanks to Mr. Kimball we have plenty of salt to season our meat with. The buzzards are after their share which will be small. And now it is most night again and the "Astor House" larder is full. Seems too bad to go to bed with anything to eat on hand, but must. That is the feeling with men who have been starved so long, cannot rest in peace with food laying around. My two comrades are not so bad about that as I am, having been well fed for a longer period. Have sat up three or four hours after dark, talking over what we will do when we get home, and will now turn in for a sound sleep. It's a clear moonlight night, and we can hear very plain a long distance. Can also see the light shining from camp fires in many directions, or what we take to be such.

Dec. 22.—As Dan Rice used to say in the circus ring: "Here we are again." Sleep so sound that all the battles in America could not wake me up. Are just going for that fresh pork to-day. Have three kinds of meat—fried pig, roast pork and broiled hog. Good any way you can fix it. Won't last us three days at this rate, and if we stay long enough will eat up all the hogs in these woods. Pretty hoggish on our part, and Dave says for gracious sake not to write down how much we eat, but as this diary is to be a record of what takes place, down it goes how much we eat.. Tell him that inasmuch as we have a preacher along with us, we ought to have a sermon occasionally. Says he will preach if I will sing, and I agree to that if Eli will take up a collection. One objection Eli and I have to his prayers is the fact that he wants the rebels saved with the rest, yet don't tell him so. Mutually agree that his prayers are that much too long. Asked him if he thought it stealing to get those potatoes as I did, and he says no, and that he will go next time. We begin to expect the Yankees along. It's about time. Don't know what I shall do when I again see Union soldiers with guns in their hands, and behold the Stars and Stripes. Probably go crazy, or daft, or something. This is a cloudy, chilly day, and we putter around gathering up pine knots for the fire, wash our duds and otherwise busy ourselves. Have saved the hog skin to make moccasins of, if the Union army is whipped and we have to stay here eight or ten years. The hair on our heads is getting long again, and we begin to look like wild men of the woods. One pocket comb does for the entire party; two jack knives and a butcher knife. I have four keys jingling away in my pocket to remind me of olden times. Eli has a testament and Dave has a bible, and the writer hereof has not. Still, I get scripture quoted at all hours, which will, perhaps, make up in a measure. Am at liberty to use either one of their books, and I do read more or less. Considerable travel on the highways, and going both ways as near at we can judge. Dave wants to go out to the road again but we discourage him in it, and he gives it up for to-day at least. Are afraid he will get caught, and then our main stay will be gone. Pitch pine knots make a great smoke which rises among the trees and we are a little afraid of the consequences; still, rebels have plenty to do now without looking us up. Many boats go up and down the river and can hear them talk perhaps fifty rods away. Rebel paper that Dave got spoke of Savannah being the point aimed at by Sherman, also of his repulses; still I notice that he keeps coming right along. Also quoted part of a speech by Jefferson Davis, and he is criticised unmercifully. Says nothing about any exchange of prisoners, and our old comrades are no doubt languishing in some prison. LATER.—Considerable firing up in vicinity of the bridge. Can hear volleys of musketry, and an occasional boom of cannon. Hurrah! It is now four o'clock by the sun and the battle is certainly taking place. LATER.—Go it Billy Sherman, we are listening and wishing you the best of success. Come right along and we will be with you. Give 'em another—that was a good one. We couldn't be more excited if we were right in the midst of it. Hurrah! It is now warm for the Johnnies. If we had guns would go out and fight in their rear; surround them, as it were. Troops going by to the front, and are cavalry, should think, also artillery. Can hear teamsters swearing away as they always do. LATER.—It is now long after dark and we have a good fire. Fighting has partially subsided up the river, but of course we don't know whether Yankee troops have crossed the river or not. Great deal of travel on the road, but can hardly tell which way they are going. Occasional firing. No sleep for us to-night. In the morning shall go out to the road and see how things look. Every little while when the battle raged the loudest, all of us three would hurrah as if mad, but we ain't mad a bit; are tickled most to death.

SAFE AND SOUND.

ONCE MORE SEE THE OLD FLAG AND THE BOYS IN BLUE—MR. KIMBALL AND MRS. DICKINSON RECOMPENSED—FIND THE NINTH MICHIGAN CAVALRY—INTERVIEWED BY GEN'L KILPATRICK—ALL RIGHT AT LAST.

Dec. 23.—It is not yet daylight in the morning, and are anxiously awaiting the hour to arrive when we may go out to the road. Slept hardly any during the night. More or less fighting all night, and could hear an army go by toward Savannah, also some shouting directly opposite us. Between the hours of about twelve and three all was quiet, and then again more travel. We conjecture that the rebel army has retreated or been driven back, and that the Yankees are now passing along following them up. Shall go out about nine o'clock. LATER.—Are eating breakfast before starting out to liberty and safety. Must be very careful now and make no mistake. If we run into a rebel squad now, might get shot. We are nervous, and so anxious can hardly eat. Will pick up what we really need and start. Perhaps good bye, little house on the banks of the Ogechee, we shall always remember just how you look, and what a happy time we have had on this little island. Dave says: "Pick up your blanket and that skillet, and come along." NIGHT.—Safe and sound among our own United States Army troops, after an imprisonment of nearly fourteen months. Will not attempt to describe my feelings now.

Could not do it. Staying with the 80th Ohio Infantry, and are pretty well tired out from our exertions of the day. At nine o'clock we started out toward the main road. When near it Eli and I stopped, and Dave went ahead to see who was passing. We waited probably fifteen minutes, and then heard Dave yell out: "Come on boys, all right! Hurry up!" Eli and I had a stream to cross on a log. The stream was some fifteen feet wide, and the log about two feet through. I tried to walk that log and fell in my excitement. Verily believe if the water had been a foot deeper I would have drowned. Was up to my arms, and I was so excited that I liked never to have got out. Lost the axe, which Dave had handed to me, and the old stand-by coverlid which had saved my life time and again floated off down the stream, and I went off without securing it—the more shame to me for it. Dave ran out of the woods swinging his arms and yelling like mad, and pretty soon Eli and myself appeared, whooping and yelling. The 80th Ohio was just going by, or a portion of it, however, and when they saw first one and then another and then the third coming toward them in rebel dress, with clubs which they mistook for guns, they wheeled into line, thinking, perhaps, that a whole regiment would appear next. Dave finally explained by signs, and we approached and satisfied them of our genuineness. Said we were hard looking soldiers, but when we came to tell them where we had been and all the particulars, they did not wonder. Went right along with them, and at noon had plenty to eat. Are the guests of Co. I, 80th Ohio. At three the 80th had a skirmish, we staying back a mile with some wagons, and this afternoon rode in a wagon. Only came about three or four miles to-day, and are near Kimball's, whom we shall call and see the first opportunity. The soldiers all look well and feel well, and say tle whole confederacy is about cleaned out. Rebels fall back without much fighting. Said there was not enough to call it a fight at the bridge. Where we thought it a battle, they thought it nothing worth speaking of. Believe ten or so were killed, and some wounded. Hear that some Michigan cavalry is with Kilpatrick off on another road, but they do not know whether it is the 9th Mich. Cav., or not. Say they see the cavalry every day nearly, and I must keep watch for my regiment. Soldiers forage on the plantations, and have the best of food; chickens, ducks, sweet potatoes, etc. The supply wagons carry nothing but hard-tack, coffee, sugar and such things. Tell you, coffee is a luxury, and makes one feel almost drunk. Officers come to interview us every five minutes, and we have talked ourselves most to death to-day. They say we probably will not be called upon to do any fighting during this war, as the thing is about settled. They have heard of Andersonville, and from the accounts of the place did not suppose that any lived at all. New York papers had pictures in, of the scenes there, and if such was the case it seems funny that measures were not taken to get us away from there. Many rebels are captured now, and we look at them from a different stand point than a short time since.

Dec. 24.—This diary must soon come to an end. Will fill the few remaining pages and then stop. Co. "I" boys are very kind. They have reduced soldiering to a science. All divided up into messes of from three to five each. Any mess is glad to have us in with them, and we pay them with accounts of our prison life. Know they think half we tell them is lies. I regret the most of anything, the loss of my blanket that stood by me so well. It's a singular fact that the first day of my imprisonment it came into my possession, and the very last day it took its departure, floating off away from me after having performed its mission. Should like to have taken it North to exhibit to my friends. The infantry move only a few miles each day, and I believe we stay here all day. Went and saw Mr. Kimball. The officers commanding knew him for a Union man, and none of his belongings were troubled. In fact, he has anything he wants now. Announces his intention of going with the army until the war closes. Our good old friend Mrs. Dickinson did not fare so well. The soldiers took everything she had on the place fit to eat; all her cattle, pork, potatoes, chickens, and left them entirely destitute. We went and saw them, and will go to headquarters to see what can be done. LATER.—We went to Gen. Smith, commanding 3d Brigade, 2d Divisiom, and told him the particulars. He sent out foraging wagons, and now she has potatoes, corn, bacon, cattle, mules, and everything she wants. Also received pay for burned fences and other damages. Now they are smiling and happy and declare the Yankees to be as good as she thought them bad this morning. The men being under little restraint on this raid were often destructive. Nearly every citizen declared their loyalty, so no distinction is made. Gen. Smith is a very kind man, and asked us a great many questions. Says the 9th Michigan Cavalry is near us and we may see them any hour. Gen. Haun also takes quite an interest in us, and was equally instrumental with Gen. Smith in seeing justice done to our friends the Kimballs and Dickinsons. They declare now that one of us must marry the daughter of Mrs. Dickinson, the chaplain performing the ceremony. Well, she is a good girl, and I should judge would make a good wife, but presume she would have something to say herself and will not pop the question to her. They are very grateful, and only afraid that after we all go away the rebel citizens and soldiers will retaliate on them. Many officers have read portions of my diary, and say such scenes as we have passed through seem incredible. Many inquire if we saw so and so of their friends who went to Andersonville, but of course there were so many there that we cannot remember them. This has been comparatively a day of rest for this portion of the Union army, after having successfully crossed the river. We hear the cavalry is doing some fighting on the right, in the direction of Fort McAllister. EVENING.—We marched about two or three miles and are again encamped for the night, with pickets out for miles around. Many refugees join the army prepared to go along with them, among whom are a great many negroes.

Dec. 25.—Christmas day and didn't hang up my stocking. No matter, it wouldn't have held anything. Last Christmas we spent on Belle Island, little thinking long imprisonment awaiting us. Us escaped men are to ride in a forage wagon. The army is getting ready to move. Are now twenty-four miles from Savannah and rebels falling back as we press ahead. NIGHT.—At about nine o'clock this morning as we sat in the forage wagon top of some corn riding in state, I saw some cavalry coming from the front. Soon recognized Col. Acker at the head of the 9th Michigan Cavalry. Jumped out of the wagon and began dancing and yelling in the middle of the road and in front of the troop. Col. Acker said: "Get out of the road you —— lunatic!" Soon made myself known and was like one arisen from the dead. Major Brockway said: Ransom, you want to start for home. We don't know you, you are dead. No such man as Ransom on the rolls for ten months." All remember me and are rejoiced to see me back again. Lieut. Col. Way, Surgeon, Adjutant, Sergeant-Major, all shake hands with me. My company "A" was in the rear of the column, and I stood by the road as they moved along, hailing those I recognized. In every case had to tell them who I was and then would go up and shake hands with them at the risk of getting stepped on by the horses. Pretty soon Co. "A" appeared, and wasn't they surprised to see me. The whole company were raised in Jackson, Mich., my home, and I had been regarded as dead for nearly a year. Could hardly believe it was myself that appeared to them. Every one trying to tell me the news at home all at the same time—how I was reported as having died in Richmond and funeral sermon preached. How so and so had been shot and killed, &c., &c. And then I had to tell them of who of our regiment had died in Andersonville—Dr. Lewis, Tom McGill and others. Although Jimmy Devers did not belong to our regiment, many in our company knew him, and I told them of his death. Should have said that as soon as I got to the company, was given Capt. Johnson's lead horse to ride, without saddle or bridle and nothing but a halter to hang on with. Not being used to riding, in rebel dress—two or three pails hanging to me—I made a spectacle for them all to laugh at. It was a time of rejoicing. The Buck boys did not get out of the wagon with me and so we became separated without even a good bye. Before I had been with the company half an hour Gen. Kilpatrick and staff came riding by from the rear, and says to Capt. Johnson: "Captain, I hear one of your company has just joined you after escaping from the enemy." Capt. Johnson said, "Yes, sir," and pointed to me as a Sergeant in his company. General Kilpatrick told me to follow him and started ahead at a break neck pace. Inasmuch as the highway was filled with troops, Gen. Kilpatrick and staff rode at the side, through the fields, and any way they could get over the ground. The horse I was on is a pacer and a very hard riding animal and it was all I could do to hang on. Horse would jump over logs and come down an all fours ker-chug, and I kept hoping the general would stop pretty soon; but he didn't. Having no saddle or anything to guide the brute, it was a terrible hard ride for me, and time and again if I had thought I could fall off without breaking my neck should have done so. The soldiers all along the line laughed and hooted at the spectacle and the staff had great sport, which was anything but sport for me. After a while and after riding five or six miles, Kilpatrick drew up in a grove by the side of the road and motioning me to him, asked me when I escaped, etc. Soon saw I was too tired and out of breath. After resting a few minutes I proceeded to tell him what I knew of Savannah, the line of forts around the city, and of other fortifications between us and the city, the location of the rivers, force of rebels, etc. Asked a great many questions and took down notes, or rather the chief of staff, Estes by name, did. After an extended conversation a dispatch was made up and sent to Gen. Sherman who was a few miles away, with the endorsement that an escaped prisoner had given the information and it was reliable. General Kilpatrick told me I would probably not be called upon to do any more duty as I had done good service as a prisoner of war.

Said he would sign a furlough and recommend that I go home as soon as communication was opened. Thanked me for information and dismissed me with congratulations on my escape. Then I waited until our company, "A," came up and joined them, and here I am encamped with the boys, who are engaged in getting supper. We are only twelve or fourteen miles from Savannah and the report in camp is to the effect that the city has been evacuated with no fight at all. Fort McAllister was taken to-day, which being the key to Savannah, leaves that city unprotected, hence the evacuation. Communication will now be opened with the gunboats on the coast and I will be sent home to Michigan. I mess with Capt. Johnson and there is peace and plenty among us. I go around from mess to mess this pleasant night talking with the boys, learning and telling the news. O. B. Driscoll, Al. Williams, Sergt. Smith, Mell Strickland, Sergt. Fletcher, Teddy Fox, Lieut. Ingraham and all the rest think of something new every few minutes, and I am full. Poor Robt. Strickland, a boy whom I enlisted, was shot since starting out on this march to the sea. Others too, whom I left well are now no more. The boys have had a long and tedious march, yet are all in good health and have enjoyed the trip. They never tire of telling about their fights and skirmishes, and anecdotes concerning Kilpatrick, who is well liked by all the soldiers. Am invited to eat with every mess in the company, also at regimental headquarters, in fact, anywhere I am a mind to, can fill. And now this Diary is finished and is full. Shall not write any more, though I hardly know how I shall get along, without a self-imposed task of some kind.

END OF DIARY.

THE FINIS.

A BRIEF DESCRIPTION OF WHAT BECAME OF THE BOYS—REFUSED PERMISSION TO GO HOME—A REFERENCE TO CAPT. WIRTZ—RETURN HOME AT THE END OF THE WAR.

In may interest some one to know more of many who have been mentioned at different times in this book, and I will proceed to enlighten them.

George W. Hendryx came to the regiment in March, 1865, when we were near Goldsboro, N. C. He says that after running away from Andersonville at the time of the discovery of a break in which all intended to get away in the summer of 1864, he traveled over one hundred and fifty miles and was finally re-taken by bushwhackers. He represented himself as an officer of the 17th Michigan Infantry, escaped from Columbia, S. C., and was sent to that place and put with officers in the prison there, changing his name so as not to be found out as having escaped from Andersonville. In due time he was exchanged with a batch of other officers and went home North. After a short time he joined his regiment and company for duty. He was both delighted and surprised to see me, as he supposed of course I had died in Andersonville, it having been so reported to him at the North. He did valiant service until the war was over, which soon happened. He went home with the regiment and was mustered out of service, since when I have never seen or heard of him for a certainty. Think that he went to California.

Sergt. Wm. B. Rowe was exchanged in March, 1865, but never

joined the regiment. His health was ruined to a certain extent from his long confinement. Is still alive, however, and resides at Dansville, Mich.

Sergt. Bullock was also exchanged at the same time, but never did service thereafter. He is now an inmate of a Michigan insane asylum, and has been for some years, whether from the effects of prison life I know not, but should presume it is due to his sufferings there. His was a particularly sad case. He was taken sick in the early days of Andersonville and was sick all the time while in that place, a mere walking and talking skeleton. There is no doubt in my mind that his insanity resulted from his long imprisonment.

E. P. Sanders arrived home in Michigan in April, 1865, and made me a visit at Jackson that Summer. He was the only one of all my comrades in prison that I came in contact with, who fully regained health, or apparently was in good health. He was a particularly strong and healthy man, and is now engaged in farming near Lansing, Michigan.

Lieut. Wm. H. Robinson, who was removed from Belle Isle, from our mess, it having been discovered that he was an officer instead of an orderly sergeant, was exchanged early in 1864, from Richmond, and immediately joined his regiment, doing duty all the time thereafter. Soon after my escape and while with company "A," a note was handed me from Capt. Robinson, my old friend, he having been promoted to a captaincy. The note informed me that he was only a few miles away, and asked me to come and see him that day. You may rest assured I was soon on the road, and that day had the pleasure of taking my dinner with him. He was on his general's staff, and I dined at head-quarters, much to my discomfiture, not being up with such distinguished company. We had a good visit, I remember, and I went to camp at night well satisfied with my ride. Told me that a pipe which I engraved and presented to him on Belle Isle was still in his possession, and always should be. Was a favorite with every one, and a fine looking officer. He is now a resident of Sterling, Whiteside Co., Ill. Is a banker, hardware dealer, one of the City Fathers, and withal a prominent citizen. It was lucky he was an officer and taken away from us on Belle Isle, for he would undoubtedly have died at Andersonville, being of rather a delicate frame and constitution.

My good old friend Battese, I regret to say, I have never seen or heard of since he last visited me in the Marine Hospital at Savannah.

Have written many letters and made many inquiries, but to no effect. He was so reticent while with us in the prison, that we did not learn enough of him to make inquiries since then effective. Although for many months I was in his immediate presence, he said nothing of where he lived, his circumstances, or anything else. I only know that his name was Battese, that he belonged to a Minnesota regiment and was a noble fellow. I don't know of a man in the world I would rather see to-day than him, and I hope some day when I have got rich out of this book (if that time should ever come,) to go to Minnesota and look him up. There are many Andersonville survivors who must remember the tall Indian, and certainly I shall, as long as life shall last.

Michael Hoare tells his own story farther along, in answer to a letter written him for information regarding his escape from the Savannah hospital. Mike, at the close of the war, re-enlisted in the regular army and went to the extreme west to fight Indians, and when his term of service expired again re-enlisted and remained in the service. In 1878 he was discharged on account of disability, and is now an inmate of the Disabled Soldier's Home, at Dayton, Ohio. From his letters to me he seems the same jolly, good natured hero as of old. I hope to see him before many months, for the first time since he shook me by the hand and passed in and out of his tunnel from the Marine Hospital and to freedom.

The two cousins Buck, David and Eli S., I last saw top of some corn in an army wagon I jumped from when I first encountered the 9th Mich. Cavalry. Little thought that would be the last time I should see them. Their command belonged to the Eastern Army in the region of the Potomac, and when communication was opened at Savannah they were sent there on transports. I afterward received letters from both of them, and David's picture; also his wife's whom he had just married. David's picture is reproduced in this book and I must say hardly does him justice as he was a good looking and active fellow. Presume Eli is a farmer if alive, and "Dave" probably preaching.

"Limber Jim," who was instrumental in putting down the raiders at Andersonville, was until recently a resident of Joliet, Illinois. He died last winter, in 1880, and it is said his health was always poor after his terrible summer of 1864. He was a hero in every sense of the word, and if our government did not amply repay him for valiant service done while a prisoner of war, then it is at fault.

Sergt. Winn of the 100th Ohio, who befriended me at Savannah, is, I think, a citizen of Cincinnati, Ohio, and a prosperous man. Any way, he was in 1870 or thereabouts. Was an upright man and good fellow.

Every one knows the fate of Capt. Wirtz, our prison commander at Andersonville, who was hung at Washington, D. C., in 1866, for his treatment of us Union prisoners of war. It was a righteous judgment, still I think there are others who deserved hanging fully as much. He was but the willing tool of those higher in command. Those who put him there knew his brutal disposition, and should have suffered the same disposition made of him. Although, I believe at this late day those who were in command and authority over Capt. Wirtz have successfully thrown the blame on his shoulders, it does not excuse them in the least so far as I am concerned. They are just as much to blame that thirteen thousand men died in a few months at that worst place the world has ever seen, as Capt. Wirtz, and should have suffered accordingly. I don't blame any of them for being rebels if they thought it right, but I do their inhuman treatment of prisoners of war.

Hub Dakin is now a resident of Dansville, Mich., the same village in which lives Wm. B. Rowe. He has been more or less disabled since the war, and I believe is now trying to get a pension from the government for disability contracted while in prison. It is very difficult for ex-prisoners of war to get pensions, owing to the almost impossibility of getting sufficient evidence. The existing pension laws require that an officer of the service shall have knowledge of the origin of disease, or else two comrades who may be enlisted men. At this late day it is impossible to remember with accuracy sufficient to come up to the requirements of the law. There is no doubt that all were more or less disabled, and the mere fact of their having spent the summer in Andersonville, should be evidence enough to procure assistance from the government.

And now a closing chapter in regard to myself. As soon as Savannah was occupied by our troops and communications opened with the North, a furlough was made out by Capt. Johnson, of our company, and signed by Assistant Surgeon Young, and then by Col. Acker. I then took the furlough to Gen. Kilpatrick, which he signed, and also endorsed on the back to the effect that he hoped Gen. Sherman would also sign and send me North. From Gen. Kilpatrick's headquarters I went to see Gen. Sherman at Savannah and was ushered into his presence. The Gen. looked the paper over and then said no men were being sent home now and no furloughs granted for any cause. If I was permanently disabled I could be sent to Northern hospitals, or if I had been an exchanged prisoner of war, could be sent North, but there was no provision made for escaped prisoners of war. Encouraged me with the hope, however, that the war was nearly over and it could not be long before we would all go home. Gave me a paper releasing me from all duty until such time as I saw fit to do duty, and said the first furlough granted should be mine, and he would retain it and send to me as soon as possible. Cannot say that I was very sadly disappointed, as I was having a good time with the company, and regaining my health and getting better every day, with the exception of my leg, which still troubled me. Stayed with the company until Lee surrendered, Lincoln assassinated and all the fighting over and then leaving Chapel Hill, North Carolina, in April, went to my home in Michigan. In a few weeks was followed by the regiment, when we were all mustered out of the service. As had been reported to me at the regiment, I had been regarded as dead, and funeral sermon preached.

It was my sad duty to call upon the relatives of quite a number who died in Andersonville, among whom were those of Dr. Lewis, John McGuire and Jimmy Devers. The relics which had been entrusted to my keeping were all lost with two exceptions, and through no fault of mine. At the time of my severe sickness when first taken to Savannah, and when I was helpless as a child, the things drifted away from me some way, and were lost. But for the fact that Battese had two of my diary books and Sergt. Winn the other, they also would have been lost.

I hope that this Diary may prove successful in its mission of truly portraying the scenes at Andersonville and elsewhere during the time of my imprisonment, and if so, the object of its author shall have been accomplished.

    Yours Very Respectfully,
        JOHN L. RANSOM,
        Late 1st Sergt. Co. A, 9th Mich. Cav.

John L. Ransom.

[From a photograph taken three months after escape.]

MICHAEL HOARE'S ESCAPE.

NATIONAL SOLDIERS' HOME, }
DAYTON, Ohio. May 5th, 1881. }

Comrade John L. Ransom,

DEAR FRIEND:— * * * * The night I left the stockade, going within twelve feet of a guard, I went down to the city. Had never been there before and did not know where to go, but wandered about the streets, dressed in an old suit of rebel clothes, until 12 o'clock that night. It was Oct. 18th, 1864, and I had been captured March 5th, in Col. Dahlgreen's raid, the object of which was to release the officers confined in Libby prison and the privates confined on Belle Island and Pemberton prisons. * * * * My whole uniform was disposed of * * * and I had to wear dirty rebel rags. They marched us to Stevensville. We remained there but a short time when we were marched about two miles and into the heart of a swamp. We did not know what the matter was but found out that Kilpatrick had turned back to look for us, the "forlorn hope," as we were called. If he had been one hour sooner, he would have released us; but fate would have it the other way. From the swamp we were marched to Richmond, surrounded by the mounted mob. They would not let us step out of the ranks even to quench our thirst, and we had to drink the muddy water from the middle of the road. Every little town we came to the rebels would assemble and yell at us, the women the worst. * * * * When we reached the headquarters of rebeldom the whole rebel city was out to meet us * * * * and the self-styled rebel ladies were the worst in their vim and foul language. They made a rush for us, but the guard kept them off until we were safely put in the third

story of the Pemberton building, where we were searched and stripped of everything we were not already robbed of. *   *   *   *
The next morning the Richmond people cried out for Jeff Davis to hang us, saying we were nothing but outlaws and robbers, on an errand of plunder and rapine. The press tried to excite hostility against us, and succeeded, in a measure. We were kept by ourselves and not allowed to mix with the other prisoners. A special guard was kept over us, and we were allowed but two-thirds the small rations issued to the other men. The windows were all out of the room we were in, and a cold March wind blowing and cutting through our starving, naked bodies.   *   *   *   *   In July we were going to get hanged in Castle Thunder. We were told the same story every day, and it was getting stale, so we paid no attention to it; but sure enough, we were called out one morning and thought our time had come. They marched us up Casey street toward Castle Thunder, and as we approached it some fairly shivered at their promised doom; but instead of stopping at that celebrated hotel, we were taken across the river and put in cattle cars. Where we were going none knew; but we started and the next day reached Dansville. We were removed from the cars and put into a tobacco warehouse and were kept there until the next morning, when we were put aboard the cars and started south again until we came to the world renowned hell-hole, Andersonville. When we arrived several men were dead in the cars, and the rebels would not let us remove them. The cars were packed like herring boxes, so you may imagine our situation.
*   *   *   * From there I was transferred to Savannah, and from the latter place I made my escape, as previously mentioned.

As I have said, I wandered about until 12 o'clock, and was then in a worn out condition. Not knowing where to turn or lay my head, I sat down under a tree to rest myself, and as I sat there, who should come along but a watchman. "Hello!" says he, "what are you doing here at this hour of the night?" I answered that I was one of the guards guarding the Yankees at the stockade, and that I had been down to Bryan street to see my sister. "All right," said he, "You fellows have a hard time guarding them d—d Yankees. Why don't you shoot more of 'em and get 'em out o' the way?" I passed on until I came to a place with a high board fence. I crawled over and looked around and found a small shed divided by a board partition. In one end they kept a cow and in the other some fodder. I went in where the fodder was and threw myself down and went to sleep, intending to be up before day; but what was my surprise when it proved to be broad daylight before I awoke. I lay there thinking what to do, when I heard the gate of the fence open. I jumped up and looked through a crack in the boards and saw an old man enter with a pail in his hand. Presently he came where I was in the fodder to get some for the cow. As he opened the door he started back with fright, saying, "Who are you and what brings you here?" I saw by his face and voice that he was an Irishman, and I made up my mind to tell him the truth. * * * He told me to remain where I was and he would try and get me something to eat. He went away and presently returned with a tin pan full of sweet potatoes and bacon. * * * * He told me the only way to get away was by the Isle of Hope, ten miles from the city on the Skidaway shell road. There was a picket post of twelve men right on the road, but I started off, and when I reached the picket put on a bold face and told them I belonged to Maxwell's battery, stationed at the Isle of Hope, and they let me pass. * * * I passed officers and soldiers on the road, but they never took any notice of me further than to return my kindly greeting. I finally reached the outpost on the road, about a mile from freedom. I had known, even before starting, that to pass that post I should have to have a pass signed by the commanding officer at Savannah; but there were swamps on both sides the road, and I thought I could swim in the marsh and flank the post. I took off my jacket and made the attempt, but had to return to the road. * * * * I saw there was no use trying to escape by the Isle of Hope. I could not pass the outpost, and besides, there was great danger that I should be hung as a spy. So I put back to Savannah that night. I had to wade the marsh to get by the post I first passed. I got safely back to my cowshed and laid there till woke up the next morning by my friend Gleason. When I told him where I had been he would hardly believe me. * * * He brought me something to eat and went away, but returned at night with two other men. Their names were Wall and Skelley and they belonged to the 3d Georgia artillery. They said they were northern men, but were in Savannah when the war broke out and had to join the rebel army. I told them the history of my adventure by the Isle of Hope and they were astonished. They said the only way was by the river to Fort Pulaski, fourteen miles from Savannah. The question was, where to get a boat. They were known in Savannah and their movements would be watched. They said they knew where there was a boat, but it was a government boat. I said that made it better, and if they would show me where the boat was, I would do the headwork. So they showed me and left me the management. I went when everything was ready, and muffled the oars and oarlocks, with a sentinel within twenty feet of me. The boat lay in the river, near the gashouse and a government storehouse, and the river was guarded by gunboats and the floating battery, and paved with torpedoes; but there is what is called "the back river," which flows into the Savannah above Smith Island. The mouth of this stream was guarded by a picket crew, sent from the battery every night; so when we left we had to lay in a rice sluice, where we ran the boat in about an eighth of a mile, and raised the grass as the boat passed along to conceal our tracks. We heard them searching the next morning, after the boat had been missed, but the search was at last given up. About this time Skelly began talking about being recaptured, as the shore was picketed all the way. He said there would be nothing done with me, if I was recaptured but to put me back in the stockade, while he and Wall would be shot as deserters. He proposed returning to Savannah at once. * * * * He began to win the other fellow over and I saw the game was up with me. Skelley was the only one of us who was armed and he had a Colt's revolver. * * * * I told him that his plan was the best and that I didn't want to be the means of getting him into trouble. I gained his confidence, but the thought of returning to Savannah never entered my head. I watched my chance, and at a favorable opportunity, snatched his pistol. * * * I rose to my feet with the pistol at full cock, pointed it at his breast and told him that one move towards returning to Savannah would end his career by a bullet from his own revolver. He turned all colors, but said nothing. I kept my distance, and at four o'clock in the afternoon told them to get into the boat. I then sat down in the stern and told them to pull out, which they did with a vim. Just as we passed the mouth, we heard the click of oars on the picket boat; but they were too late, and all the danger we had to encounter was the pickets on the shore which we had to hug on account of torpedoes in the channel. I don't know how we ever passed safely over the torpedoes and by the pickets, which latter were within forty yards of us all the way along until we reached Pulaski. All that saved us was that the pickets had fires lighted and were looking at them, and our oars and oarlocks being muffled, they did not hear or see us. It was very dark when we struck the mouth of the Savannah, and whereabouts Fort Pulaski lay we knew not; but we kept pulling until halted by a soldier of the 144th N. Y. Infantry, who was guarding the place at that time. We were ordered to pull in, which we did, and were taken up to the commanding officer and questioned. He said it was the most daring escape ever made, up to that time, considering the obstacles we had to encounter. We were kept in the guard house until my statement was confirmed by the war department, when I was released and sent to Washington, where I reported to the Adjutant-General who gave me a furlough and sent me to the hospital. I remained there until spring, when I rejoined my regiment and was mustered out at the close of the war. *　*　*　*　*

   I remain,
      Your true friend,
          MICHAEL HOARE.

REBEL TESTIMONY.

We cannot do better than copy into this book a very complete description of Andersonville Prison, by Joseph Jones, Surgeon P. A. C. S., Professor of Medical Chemistry in the Medical College of Georgia, at Augusta, Ga., as given at the Wirtz trial at Washington, D. C., he being a witness for the prosecution:

"Hearing of the unusual mortality among the prisoners confined at Andersonville, in the month of August, 1864, during a visit to Richmond, I expressed to the Surgeon General, S. P. Moore, Confederate States of America, a desire to visit Camp Sumpter, with the design of instituting a series of inquiries upon the nature and causes of the prevailing diseases. Small-pox had appeared among the prisoners, and I believed that this would prove an admirable field for the study of its characteristic lesions. The condition of Peyer's glands in this disease was considered as worthy a minute investigation. It was believed that a large portion of the men from the Northern portion of the United States, suddenly transported to a Southern climate, and confined upon a small portion of land, would furnish an excellent field for the investigation of the relations of typhus, typhoid, and malarial fevers.

The Surgeon General of the Confederate States of America furnished me with letters of introduction to the surgeon in charge of the Confederate States Military prison at Andersonville, Ga., and the following is my descriipton of that place:

The Confederate Military Prison at Andersonville, Ga., consists of a strong stockade, twenty feet in height, enclosing twenty-seven acres. The stockade is formed of strong pine logs, firmly planted in the ground. The main stockade is surrounded by two other similar rows of pine logs, the middle stockade being sixteen feet high, and the outer one twelve feet. These are intended for offense and defense. If the inner stockade should at any time be forced by the prisoners, the second forms another line of defense; while in case of an attempt to deliver the prisoners by a force operating upon the exterior, the outer line forms an admirable protection to the Confederate troops, and a most formidable obstacle to cavalry or infantry. The four angles of the outer line are strengthened by earthworks upon commanding eminences, from which the cannon, in case of an outbreak among the prisoners, may sweep the entire enclosure; and it was designed to connect these works by a line of rifle pits running zig-zag around the outer stockade; those rifle pits have never been completed. The ground enclosed by the innermost stockade lies in the form of a parallelogram, the larger diameter running almost due north and south. This space includes the northern and southern opposing sides of two hills, between which a stream of water runs from west to east. The surface soil of these two hills is composed chiefly of sand with varying mixtures of clay and oxide of iron. The clay is sufficiently tenacious to give a considerable degree of consistency to the soil. The internal structure of the hills, as revealed by the deep wells, is similar to that already described. The alternate layers of clay and sand, as well as the oxide of iron, which forms in its various combinations a cement to the sand, allows of extensive tunneling. The prisoners not only constructed numerous dirt houses with balls of clay and sand, taken from the wells which they had excavated all over these hills, but they have also, in some cases, tunneled extensively from these wells. The lower portion of these hills, bordering on the stream, are wet and boggy from the constant oozing of water. The stockade was built originally to accommodate ten thousand prisoners, and included at first seventeen acres. Near the close of the month of June the area was enlarged by the addition of ten acres. The ground added was situated on the northern slope of the largest hill.

Within the circumscribed area of the stockade the Federal prisoners were compelled to perform all the functions of life, cooking, washing, the calls of nature, exercise, and sleeping. During the month of March the prison was less crowded than at any subsequent time, and then the average space of ground to each prisoner was only 98.7 feet or less than eleven square yards. The Federal prisoners were gathered from all parts of the Confederate States east of the Mississippi, and crowded into the confined space, until, in the month of June the average number of square feet of ground to each prisoner was only 32.3 or less than four square yards. These figures represent the stockade in a better light even than it really was; for a considerable breadth of land along the stream flowing from west to east between the hills was low and boggy, and was covered with the excrements of the men and thus rendered wholly uninhabitable, and in fact useless for every purpose except that of defaction. The pines and other small trees and shrubs, which originally were scattered sparsely over these hills were in a short time cut down by the prisoners for firewood, and no shade tree was left in the entire enclosure of the stockade. With their characteristic industry and ingenuity, the Federals constructed for themselves small huts and caves, and attempted to shield themselves from the rain and sun, and night damps and dew. But few tents were distributed to the prisoners, and those were in most cases torn and rotten. In the location and arrangement of these huts no order appears to have been followed; in fact, regular streets appear to be out of the question on so crowded an area; especially, too, as large bodies of prisoners were from time to time added suddenly and without any preparations. The irregular arrangement of the huts and imperfect shelters was very unfavorable for the maintenance of a proper system of police.

The police and internal economy of the prison was left almost entirely in the hands of the prisoners themselves; the duties of the Confederate soldiers acting as guards being limited to the occupation of the boxes or lookouts ranged around the stockade at regular intervals, and to the manning of the batteries at the angles of the prison. Even judicial matters pertaining to the prisoners themselves, as the detection and punishment of such crimes as theft and murder appear to have been in a great measure abandoned to the prisoners.

The large number of men confined within the stockade soon, under a defective system of police, and with imperfect arrangements, covered the surface of the low ground with excrements. The sinks over the lower portions of the stream were imperfect in their plan and structure, and the excrements were in large measure deposited so near the borders of the stream as not to be washed away, or else accumulated upon the low boggy ground. The volume of water was not sufficient to wash away the feces, and they accumulated in such quantities as to form a mass of liquid excrement. Heavy rains caused the water of the stream to rise and as the arrangements for the passage of the increased amount of water out of the stockade were insufficient, the liquid feces overflowed the low grounds and covered them several inches after the subsidence of the waters. The action of the sun upon this putrefying mass of excrements and fragments of bread and meat and bones excited most rapid fermentation and developed a horrible stench. Improvements were projected for the removal of the filth and for the prevention of its accumulation, but they were only partially and imperfectly carried out. As the forces of the prisoners were reduced by confinement, want of exercise, improper diet, and by scurvy, diarrhea, and dysentary, they were unable to evacuate their bowels within the stream or along its banks; and the excrements were deposited at the very doors of their tents. The vast majority appeared to lose all repulsion of filth, and both sick and well disregarded all the laws of hygiene and personal cleanliness. The accommodations for the sick were imperfect and insufficient. From the organization of the prison, February 24, 1864, to May 22, the sick were treated within the stockade. In the crowded condition of the stockade, and with the tents and huts clustered thickly around the hospital, it was impossible to secure proper ventilation or to maintain the necessary police. The Federal prisoners also made frequent forays upon the hospital stores and carried off the food and clothing of the sick. The hospital was, on the 22d of May, removed to its present site without the stockade, and five acres of ground covered with oaks and pines appropriated to the use of the sick.

The supply of medical officers has been insufficient from the foundation of the prison.

The nurses and attendants upon the sick have been most generally Federal prisoners, who in too many cases appear to have been devoid of moral principle, and who not only neglected their duties, but were also engaged in extensive robberies of the sick.

From want of proper police and hygienic regulations alone it is not wonderful that from February 24 to September 21, 1864, nine thousand four hundred and seventy-nine deaths, nearly one-third the entire number of prisoners have been recorded.

At the time of my visit to Andersonville a large number of Federal prisoners had been removed to Millen, Savannah, Charleston, and other parts of the Confederacy, in anticipation of an advance of General Sherman's forces from Atlanta, with the design of liberating their captive bretheren; however, about fifteen thousand prisoners remained confined within the limits of the stockade and prison hospital.

In the stockade, with the exception of the damp lowlands bordering the small stream, the surface was covered with huts, and small ragged tents and parts of blankets and fragments of oil-cloth, coats, and blankets stretched upon sticks. The tents and huts were not arranged according to any order, and there was in most parts of the enclosure scarcely room for two men to walk abreast between the tents and huts.

If one might judge from the large pieces of corn bread scattered about in every direction on the ground the prisoners were either very lavishly supplied with this article of diet, or else this kind of food was not relished by them.

Each day the dead from the stockade were carried out by their fellow prisoners and deposited upon the ground under a bush arbor, just outside of the southwestern gate. From thence they were carried on carts to the burying ground, one-quarter of a mile northwest of the prison. The dead were buried without coffins, side by side, in trenches four feet deep.

The low grounds bordering the stream were covered with human excrements and filth of all kinds, which in many places seemed to be alive with working maggots. An indescribable sickening stench arose from these fermenting masses of human filth.

There were near five thousand seriously ill Federals in the stockade and the Confederate States Military Prison Hospital, and the deaths exceeded one hundred per day, and large numbers of the prisoners who were walking about, and who had not been entered upon the sick reports, were suffering incurable diarrhea, dysentery, and scurvy. The sick were attended almost entirely by their fellow prisoners, appointed as nurses, and as they received but little attention, they were compelled to exert themselves at all times to attend the calls of nature, and hence they retain the power of moving about to within a comparatively short period of the close of life. Owing to the slow progress of the diseases most prevalent, diarrhea and chronic dysentery, the corpses were as a general rule emaciated.

I visited two thousand sick within the stockade, laying under some long sheds which had been built at the northern portion for themselves. At this time only one medical officer was in attendance, whereas at least twenty medical officers should have been employed.

Scurvy, diarrhea, dysentary, and hospital gangrene were the prevailing diseases. I was surprised to find but few cases of malarial fever, and no well-marked cases either of typhus or typhoid fever. The absence of the different forms of malarial fever may be accounted for in the supposition that the artificial atmosphere of the stockade, crowded densely with human beings and loaded with animal exhalations, was unfavorable to the existence and action of the malarial poison. The absence of typhoid and typhus fevers amongst all the causes which are known to generate these diseases, appeared to be due to the fact that the great majority of these prisoners had been in captivity in Virginia, at Belle Isle, and in other parts of the Confederacy for months, and even as long as two years, and during this time they had been subjected to the same bad influences, and those who had not had these fevers before either had them during their confinement in Confederate prisons or else their systems, from long exposure, were proof against their action.

The effects of scurvy were manifest on every hand, and in all its various stages, from the muddy pale complexion, pale gums, feeble, languid muscular motions, lowness of spirits, and fetid breath, to the dusky, dirty, leaden complexion, swollen features, spongy, purple, livid, fungoid, bleeding gums, loose teeth, œdematous limbs, covered with livid vibices, and petechiæ spasmodically flexed, painful and hardened extremities, spontaneous hemorrhages from mucous canals, and large, ill-conditioned, spreading ulcers covered with a dark purplish fungus growth. I observed that in some of the cases of scurvy the parotid glands were greatly swollen, and in some instances to such an extent as to preclude entirely the power to articulate. In several cases of dropsy the abdomen and lower extremities supervening upon scurvy, the patients affirmed that previously to the appearance of the dropsy they had suffered with profuse and obstinate diarrhea, and that when this was checked by a change of diet, from Indian corn-bread baked with the husk, to boiled rice, the dropsy disappeared. The severe pains and livid patches were frequently associated with swellings in various parts, and especially in the lower extremities, accompanied with stiffness and contractions of the knee joints and ankles, and often with a brawny feel of those parts, as if lymph had been effused between the integuments and aponeuroses, preventing the motion of the skin over the swollen parts. Many of the prisoners believed that scurvy was contagious, and I saw men guarding their wells and springs, fearing lest some man suffering with scurvy might use the water and thus poison them. I observed also numerous cases of hospital gangrene, and of spreading scorbutic ulcers, which had supervened upon slight injuries. The scorbutic ulcers presented a dark, purple fungoid, elevated surface, with livid swollen edges, and exuded a thin, fetid, sanious fluid, instead of pus. Many ulcers which originated from the scorbutic condition of the system appeared to become truly gangrenous, assuming all the characteristics of hospital gangrene. From the crowded condition, filthy habits, bad diet, and dejected, depressed condition of the prisoners, their systems had become so disordered that the smallest abration of the skin, from the rubbing of a shoe, or from the effects of the sun, or from the prick of a splinter, or from scratching, or a musquito bite, in some cases, took on a rapid and frightful ulceration and gangrene. The long use of salt meat, oft-times imperfectly cured, as well as the most total deprivation of vegetables and fruit, appeared to be the chief causes of the scurvy. I carefully examined the bakery and the bread furnished the prisoners, and found that they were supplied almost entirely with corn-bread from which the husk had not been separated. This husk acted as an irritant to the alimentary canal, without adding any nutriment to the brian. As far as my examination extended no fault could be found with the mode in which the bread was baked; the difficulty lay in the failure to separate the husk from the corn-meal. I strongly urged the preparation of large quantities of soup from the cow and calves' head's, with the brains and tongues, to which a liberal supply of sweet potatoes and vegetables might have been advantageously added. The material existed in abundance for the preparation of such soup in large quantities with but little additional expense. Such aliment would have been not only highly nutricious, but it would also have acted as an efficient remedial agent for the removal of the scorbutic condition. The sick within the stockade lay under several long sheds which were originally built for barracks. These sheds covered two floors which were open on all sides. The sick lay upon the bare boards, or upon such ragged blankets as they possessed, without, as far as I observed, any bedding or even straw.

The haggard, distressed countenances of these miserable, complaining, dejected, living skeletons, crying for medical aid and food, and cursing their government for its refusal to exchange prisoners, and the ghastly corpses, with their glazed eye balls staring up into vacant space, with the flies swarming down their open and grinning mouths and over their ragged clothes, infested with lice, as they lay amongst the sick and dying, formed a picture of helpless, hopeless misery which it would be impossible to portray by words or by the brush.

A feeling of disappointment and even resentment on account of the United States Government upon the subject of the exchange of prisoners, appeared to be widespread, and the apparent hopeless nature of the negotiations for some general exchange of prisoners appeared to be a cause of universal regret and injurious despondency. I heard some of the prisoners go so far as to exonerate the Confederate Government from any charge of intentionally subjecting them to a protracted confinement, with its necessary and unavoidable sufferings, in a country cut off from all intercourse with foreign nations, and sorely pressed on all sides, whilst on the other hand they charged their prolonged captivity upon their own government, which was attempting to make the negro equal to the white man. Some hundred or more of the prisoners had been released from confinement in the stockade on parole, and filled various offices as druggists, clerks, carpenters, etc., in the various departments. These men were well clothed, and presented a stout and healthy appearance, and as a general rule they presented a more robust and healthy appearance than the Confederate troops guarding the prisoners.

The entire grounds are surrounded by a frail board fence, and are strictly guarded by Confederate soldiers, and no prisoner except the paroled attendants is allowed to leave the grounds except by a special permit from the commandant of the interior of the prison.

The patients and attendants, near two thousand in number, are crowded into this confined space and are but poorly supplied with old and ragged tents. Large numbers of them were without any bunks in their tents, and lay upon the ground, oft-times without even a blanket. No beds or straw appeared to have been furnished. The tents extend to within a few yards of the small stream, the eastern portion of which, as we have before said, is used as a privy and is loaded with excrements; and I observed a large pile of corn-bread, bones, and filth of all kinds, thirty feet in diameter and several feet high, swarming with myriads of flies, in a vacant space near the pots used for cooking. Millions of flies swarmed over everything, and covered the faces of the sleeping patients, and crawled down their open mouths, and deposited their maggots in the gangrenous wounds of the living, and in the mouths of the dead. Musquetos in great numbers also infest the tents, and many of the patients were so stung by these pestiferous insects, that they resembled those suffering from a slight attack of the measles.

The police hygiene of the hospital were defective in the extreme;

the attendants, who appeared in almost every instance to have been selected from the prisoners, seemed to have in many cases but little interest in the welfare of their fellow-captives. The accusation was made that the nurses in many cases robbed the sick of their clothing, money, and rations, and carried on a clandestine trade with the paroled prisoners and Confederate guards without the hospital enclosure, in the clothing, effects of the sick, dying, and dead Federals. They certainly appeared to neglect the comfort and cleanliness of the sick entrusted to their care in a most shameful manner, even after making due allowances for the difficulties of the situation. Many of the sick were literally encrusted with dirt and filth and covered with vermin. When a gangrenous wound needed washing, the limb was thrust out a little from the balnket, or board, or rags upon which the patient was lying, and water poured over it, and all the putrescent matter allowed to soak into the ground floor of the tent. The supply of rags for dressing wounds was said to be very scant, and I saw the most filthy rags which had been applied several times and imperfectly washed, used in dressing wounds. Where hospital gangrene was prevailing, it was impossible for any wound to escape contagion under these circumstances. The results of the treatment of wounds in the hospital were of the most unsatisfactory character, from this neglect of cleanliness, in the dressings and wounds themselves, as well as from various other causes which will be more fully considered. I saw several gangrenous wounds filled with maggots. I have frequently seen neglected wounds amongst the Confederate soldiers similarly affected; and as far as my experience extends, these worms destroy only the dead tissues and do not injure specially the well parts. I have even heard surgeons affirm that a gangrenous wound which had been thoroughly cleansed by maggots, healed more rapidly than if it had been left to itself. This want of cleanliness on the part of the nurses appeared to be the result of carelessness and inattention, rather than of malignant design, and the whole trouble can be traced to the want of the proper police and sanitary regulations, and to the absence of intelligent organization and division of labor. The abuses were in a large measure due to the almost total absence of system, government, and rigid, but wholesome sanitary regulations. In extenuation of these abuses it was alleged by the medical officers that the Confederate troops were barely sufficient to guard the prisoners, and that it was impossible to obtain any number of experienced nurses from the Confederate forces. In fact, the guard appeared to be too small, even for the regulation of the internal hygiene and police of the hospital.

The manner of disposing of the dead was also calculated to depress the already desponding spirits of these men, many of whom have been confined for months, and even for two years in Richmond and other places, and whose strength had been wasted by bad air, bad food, and neglect of personal cleanliness. The dead-house is merely a frame covered with old tent cloth and a few bushes, situated in the southwestern corner of the hospital grounds. When a patient dies, he is simply laid in the narrow street in front of his tent, until he is removed by Federal negroes detailed to carry off the dead; if a patient dies during the night, he lies there until the morning, and during the day even the dead were frequently allowed to remain for hours in these walks. In the dead-house the corpses lie upon the bare ground, and were in most cases covered with filth and vermin.

The cooking arrangements are of the most defective character. Five large iron pots similar to those used for boiling sugar cane, appeared to be the only cooking utensils furnished the hospital for the cooking of two thousand men; and the patients were dependent in a great measure upon their own miserable utensils. They were allowed to cook in the tent doors and in the lanes, and this was another source of filth, and another favorable condition for the generation and multiplication of flies and other vermin.

The air of the tents was foul and disagreeable in the extreme, and in fact the entire grounds emitted a most nauseous and disgusting smell. I entered nearly all the tents and carefully examined the cases of interest, and especially the cases of gangrene, upon numerous occasions, during the prosecution of my pathological inquiries at Andersonville, and therefore enjoyed every opportunity to judge correctly of the hygiene and police of the hospital.

There appeared to be almost absolute indifference and neglect of the part of the patient, of personal cleanliness; their persons and clothing in most instances, and especially those suffering with gangrene and scorbutic ulcers, were filthy in the extreme and covered with vermin. It was too often the case that the patients were received from the stockade in a most deplorable condition. I have seen men brought in from the stockade in a dying condition, begrimmed from head to foot with their own excrements, and so black from smoke and filth that they resembled negroes rather than white men. That this description of the stockade has not been overdrawn, will appear from the reports of the surgeon in charge.

We will first examine the consolidated report of the sick and wounded Federal prisoners. During six months, from the 1st of March to the 31st of August, forty-two thousand six hundred and eighty-six cases of sickness and wounds were reported. No classified record of the sick in the stockade was kept after the establishment of the hospital without the prison. This fact, in conjunction with those already presented relating to the insufficiency of medical officers and the extreme illness and even death of many prisoners in the tents in the stockade, without any medical attention or record beyond the bare number of the dead, demonstrates that these figures, large as they seem to be, are far below the truth.

As the number of prisoners varied greatly at different periods, the relations between those reported sick and well, as far as those statistics extend, can best be determined by a comparison of the statistics of each month.

During this period of six months no less than five hundred and sixty-five deaths are recorded under the head of morbi vauie. In other words, those men died without having received sufficient medical attention for the determination of even the name of the disease causing death.

During the month of August fifty-three cases and fifty-three deaths are recorded as due to marasmus. Surely this large number of deaths must have been due to some other morbid state than slow wasting. If they were due to improper and insufficient food, they should have been classed accordingly, and if to diarrhea or dysentary or scurvy, the classification in like manner should have been explicit.

We observe a progressive increase of the rate of mortality, from 3.11 per cent. in March to 9.09 per cent. of mean strength, sick and well, in August. The ratio of mortality continued to increase during September, for notwithstanding the removal of one-half the entire number of prisoners during the early portion of the month, one thousand seven hundred and sixty-seven (1,767) deaths are registered from September 1 to 21, and the largest number of deaths upon any one day occurred during this month, on the 16th, viz: one hundred and nineteen.

The entire number of Federal prisoners confined at Andersonville was about forty thousand six hundred and eleven; and during the period of near seven months, from February 24 to September 21, nine thousand four hundred and seventy-nine (9,479) deaths were recorded; that is, during this period near one-fourth, or more, exact ly one in 4.2, or 23.3 per cent. terminated fatally. This increase of mortality was due in great measure to the accumulation of the sources of disease, as the increase of excrements and filth of all kinds, and the concentration of noxious effluvia, and also to the progressive effects of salt diet, crowding, and the hot climate.

CONCLUSIONS.

1st. The great mortality among the Federal prisoners confined in the military prison at Andersonville was not referable to climatic causes, or to the nature of the soil and waters.

2d. The chief causes of death were scurvy and its results and bowel affections—chronic and acute diarrhea and dysentery. The bowel affections appear to have been due to the diet, and the habits of the patients, the depressed, dejected state of the nervous system and moral and intellectual powers, and to the effluvia arising from the decomposing animal and vegetable filth. The effects of salt meat, and the unvarying diet of corn-meal, with but few vegetables, and imperfect supplies of vinegar and sirup, were manifested in the great prevalence of scurvy. This disease, without doubt, was also influenced to an important extent in its origin and course by the foul animal emanations.

3d. From the sameness of the food and form, the action of the poisonous gasses in the densely crowded and filthy stockade and hospital, the blood was altered in its constitution, even before the manifestation of actual disease. In both the well and the sick the red corpuscles were diminished; and in all diseases uncomplicated with inflammation, the fibrous element was deficient. In cases of ulceration of the mucous membrane of the intestinal canal, the fibrous element of the blood was increased; while in simple diarrhea, uncomplicated with ulceration, it was either diminished or else remained stationary. Heart clots were very common, if not universally present in cases of ulceration of the intestinal mucous membrane, while in the uncomplicated cases of diarrhea and scurvy, the blood was fluid and did not coagulate readily, and the heart clots and fibrous concretions were almost universally absent. From the watery condition of the blood, there resulted various serous effusions into the pericardium, ventricles of the brain, and into the abdomen. In almost all the cases which I examined after death, even the most emaciated, there were more or less serous effusions into the abdominal cavity. In case of hospital gangrene of the extremities, and in case of gangrene of the intestines, heart clots and fibrous coagula were universally present. The presence of these clots in the cases of hospital gangrene, while they were absent in the cases in which there were no inflammatory symptoms, sustains the conclusion that hospital gangrene is a species of inflammation, imperfect and irregular though it may be in its progress, in which the fibrous element and coagulation of the blood are increased, even in those who are suffering from such a condition of the blood, and from such diseases as are naturally accompanied with a disease in the fibrous constituent.

4th. The fact that hospital gangrene appeared in the stockade first, and originated spontaneously without any previous contagion, and occurred sporadically all over the stockade and prison hospital, was proof positive that this disease will arise whenever the conditions of crowding, filth, foul air, and bad diet are present. The exhalations of the hospital and stockade appeared to exert their effects to a considerable distance outside of these localities. The origin of hospital gangrene among the prisoners appeared clearly to depend in great measure to the state of the general system induced by diet, and various external noxious influences. The rapidity of the appearance and action of the gangrene depended upon the powers and state of the constitution, as well as upon the intensity of the poison in the atmosphere, or upon the direct application of poisonous matter to the wounded surface. This was further illustrated by the important fact that hospital gangrene, or a disease resembling it in all essential respects, attacked the intestinal canal of patients laboring under ulceration of the bowels, although there were no local manifestations of gangrene upon the surface of the body. This mode of termination in case of dysentery was quite common in the foul atmosphere of the Confederate States Military Hospital, in the depressed, depraved condition of the system of these Federal prisoners.

5th. A scorbutic condition of the system appeared to favor the origin of foul ulcers, which frequently took on true hospital gangrene. Scurvy and hospital gangrene frequently existed in the same individual. In such cases vegetable diet, with vegetable acids would remove the scorbutic condition without curing the hospital gangrene. From the results of the existing war for the establishment of the independence of the Confederate States, as well as from the published observations of Dr. Trotter, Sir Gilbert Blane, and others of the English navy and army, it is evident that the scorbutic condition of the system, especially in crowded ships and camps, is most favorable to the origin and spread of foul ulcers and hospital gangrene. As in the present case of Andersonville, so also in past times when medical hygiene was almost entirely neglected, those two diseases were almost universally associated in crowded ships. In many cases it was very difficult to decide at first whether the ulcer was a simple result of scurvy or the action of the prison or hospital gangene, for there was great similarity in the appearance of the ulcers in the two diseases. So commonly have those two diseases been confined to their origin and action, that the description of scorbutic ulsers, by many authors, evidently includes also many of the prominent characteristics of hospital gangrene. This will be rendered evident by an examination of the observations of Dr. Lind and Sir Gilbert Blane upon scorbutic ulcers.

6th. Gangrenous spots followed by rapid destruction of the tissue appeared in some cases where there has been no known wound. Without such well established facts, it might be assumed that the disease was propagated from one patient to another. In such a filthy and crowded hospital as that of the Confederate States Military Prison at Andersonville, it was impossible to isolate the wounded from the sources of actual contact with gangrenous matter. The flies swarmed over the wounds and over filth of every kind, the filthy, imperfectly washed and scanty supplies of rags, and the limited supply of washing utensils, the same wash-bowl serving for scores of patients were sources of such constant circulation of the gangrenous matter that the disease might rapidly spread from a single gangrenous wound. The fact already stated, that a form of moist gangrene, resembling hospital gangrene, was quite common in this foul atmosphere, in cases of dysentery, both with and without the existance of the entire service, not only demonstrates the dependence of the disease upon the state of the constitution, but proves in the clearest manner that neither the contact of the poisonous matter of gangrene, nor the direst action of the poisonous atmosphere upon the ulcerated surface are necessary to the development of the disease.

7th. In this foul atmosphere amputation did not arrest hospital gangrene; the disease almost universally returned. Almost every amputation was followed finally by death, either from the effects of gangrene or from the prevailing diarrhea and dysentery. Nitric acid and escharoties generally in this crowded atmosphere, loaded with noxious effluvia, exerted only temporary effects; after their application to the diseased surfaces, the gangrene would frequently returned with redoubled energy; and even after the gangrene had been completely removed by local and constitutional treatment, it would frequently return and destroy the patient. As far as my observation extended, very few of the cases of amputation for gangrene recovered. The progress of these cases was frequently very deceptive. I have observed after death the most extensive disorganization of the stump, when during life there was but little swelling of the part, and the patient was apparently doing well. I endeavored to impress upon the medical officers the view that on this disease treatment was almost useless, without an abundance of pure, fresh air, nutricious food, and tonics and stimulants. Such changes, however, as would allow of the isolation of the cases of hospital gangrene appeared to be out of the power of the medical officers.

8th. The gangrenous mass was without true puss, and consisted chiefly of broken-down, disorganized structures. The reaction of the gangrenous matter in certain stages was alkaline.

9th. The best, and in truth the only means of protecting large armies and navies, as well as prisoners, from the ravages of hospital gangrene, is to furnish liberal supplies of well-cured meat, together with fresh beef and vegetables, and to enforce a rigid system of hygene.

10th. Finally, this gigantic mass of human misery calls loudly for relief, not only for the sake of suffering humanity, but also on account of our own brave soldiers now captive in the hands of the Federal Government. Strict justice to the gallant men of the Confederate armies, who have been or who may be, so unfortunate as to be compelled to surrender in battle, demands that the Confederate Government should adopt that course which will best secure their health and comfort in captivity; or at least leave their enemies without a shadow of an excuse for any violation of the rules of civilized warfare in the treatment of prisoners."

(END OF WITNESS'S TESTIMONY.)

SUMMARY.

The variation—from month to month—of the proportion of deaths to the whole number of living is singular and interesting. It supports the theory I have advanced above, as the following facts taken from the official report, will show:

In April one in every sixteen died.
In May one in every twenty-six died.
In June one in every twenty-two died.
In July one in every eighteen died.
In August one in eleven died.
In September one in every three died.
In October one in every two died.
In November one in every three died.

Does the reader fully understand that in September one-third of those in the pen died, that in October one-half of the remainder perished, and in November one-third of those who still survived, died? Let him pause for a moment and read this over carefully again, because its startling magnitude will hardly dawn upon him at first reading. It is true that the fearful disproportionate mortality of those months was largely due to the fact that it was mostly the sick that remained behind, but even this diminishes but little the frightfulness of the showing. Did anyone ever hear of an epidemic so fatal that one-third of those attacked by it in one month died; one-half of the remnant the next month, and one-third of the feeble remainder the next month? If he did his reading has been much more extensive than mine.

THE WAR'S DEAD.

---o---

The total number of deceased Union soldiers during and in consequence of the war, is 316,233. Of these, only 175,764 have been identified, and the rest will probably remain for ever unknown. Of the grand total, 36,868 are known to have been prisoners of war who died in captivity. There are seventy-two National Cemeteries for the dead of the Union armies, besides which there are 320 local and Post cemeteries. The largest of the Government grounds are: Arlington, Va., the former homestead of General Robert E. Lee, 15,547 graves; Fredericksburg, Va., 15,300 graves; Salisbury, N, C., 12,112 graves; Beaufort, S, C., 10,000 graves; Andersonville, Ga., 13,706 graves; Marietta, Ga., 10,000 graves; New Orleans, La., 12,230 graves; Vicksburg, Miss., 17,012 graves; Chattanooga, Tenn., 12,964 graves; Nashville, Tenn., 16,529 graves; Memphis, Tenn., 13,958 graves; Jefferson Barracks, near St. Louis, Mo., 8,601 graves. The National Cemetery near Richmond, Va. contains 6,276 graves, of which 5,450 are of unknown dead, mostly prisoners of war. The cemeteries are kept in good condition, and are generally well sodded and planted with ornamental trees.

EX-PRISONERS AND PENSIONERS.

---o---

The following is an Appeal to Congress in behalf of the ex-prisoners of war, issued by Felix LaBaume, President of the "National Ex-Prisoners of War Association," and I hope that the united efforts of every one of the survivors will be concentrated with an object in view which shall substantially benefit those who performed a most valuable service in putting down the rebellion, suffering horrors and privations that cannot fully be described, and for which privations and sufferings they have never been recognized in the existing pension laws.

APPEAL TO CONGRESS.

It is a historical fact that in the early part of 1864, shortly after the battles of the wilderness, certain high officials of the Federal government decided that it was more economical to stop the exchange of prisoners of war entirely.

The policy of non-exchange was understood to be based on the following facts:

That a soldier counted for more in the Confederate army then acting on the defensive; that many of the Andersonville prisoners were men whose term of service had already expired, that all of them were disabled by starvation and exposure, and unfit for further service, while every Confederate was able bodied and "in for the war" so that an exchange would have been a gratuitous strengthening of the armies of the Confederacy, which, at the same time, would have prevented the prisoners held in the South from falling into the hands of Sherman.

August 14th, 1864, General Grant telegraphed to General Butler: "It is hard on our men held in Southern prisons, not to exchange them, but it is humane to those left in the ranks to fight our battles. If we now commence a system of exchange which liberates all prisoners taken, we will have to fight on till the whole South is exterminated. If we hold those captured, they count for more than dead men."

In accordance with General Grant's opinion General Butler then wrote a letter in reply to General Ould's proposals of exchange.

In his famous Lowell speech, Butler said: "In this letter these questions were argued justly, as I think, not diplomatically, but obtrusively and demonstratively, not for the purpose of furthering an exchange of prisoners, but for the purpose of preventing and stopping the exchange, and furnishing a ground on which we could stand." The men who languished at Andersonville and other Confederate prisons, played, in their sufferings and death, an active part in the termination of the war.

This part was not so stirring as charging on guns or meeting in the clash of infantry lines. But as the victims of a policy, dictated by the emergency of a desperate condition of affairs, their enforced, long continued hardships and sufferings made it possible for the Union generals and their armies to decide the deplorable struggle so much sooner, and to terminate the existence of the Confederacy by the surrender at Appomatox. No soldier or seaman, in this or any other country, ever made such personal sacrifices or endured such hardships and privations as those who fell into the hands of the Confederates during the late war. The recital of their sufferings would be scarcely believed were they not corroborated by so large a number of unimpeachable witnesses on both sides.

Colonel C. T. Chandler's C. S. A. report on Andersonville, dated Aug. 5, 1864, in which he said: "It is difficult to describe the horrors of the prison, which is a disgrace to civilization," was endorsed by Col. R. H. Chilton, Inspector General C. S. A., as follows: "The condition of the prisoners at Andersonville is a reproach to us as a nation."

The sixty thousand graves filled by the poor victims of the several prisons, tells a story that cannot be denied or misunderstood. When we consider the hardships and privations to which these men were subjected, the wonder is not that so many died, but that any survived. We submit, it is hardly possible that any man who was subjected to the hardships and inhuman treatment of a Confederate prison for even two or three months only, could come out any other than permanently disabled. Statistics show that of those who were released, nearly five per cent. died before reaching home. In a few instances there was a roll kept of thirty to fifty of those men who, when released, were able to travel home alone, and it is now found that nearly three-fourths of the number have since died.

The roll of the Andersonville Survivors Association shows that during the year 1880, the number of deaths averaged sixteen and one-third per cent. of the total membership, showing an increase of five per cent. over the death rate of 1879.

But few of the most fortunate of these survivors will live to see the age of fifty, and probably within the next ten years the last of them will have passed away.

Congress has from time to time enacted laws most just and liberal (or that were intended to be so,) toward the men who were disabled in the late war, but a large majority of the prison survivors are excluded from a pension under these laws. This comes partly from the unfriendly spirit in which the pension department has been administered for the last six years, and partly from the peculiar circumstances surrounding their several cases.

Many paroled prisoners, on reaching the Union lines were at once sent home on furlough, without receiving any medical treatment. The most of these were afterwards discharged under General Order No. 77, dated War Department, Washington, D. C., April 28th, 1865, because physically unfit for service, and hence there is no official record whatever as to their disease.

If one of those men applies for a pension, he is called upon to furnish the affidavit of some army surgeon who treated him after his release and prior to discharge, showing that he then had the disease on which he now claims a pension. For reasons stated, this is impossible. The next thing is a call to furnish an affidavit from some doctor who treated the man while at home on furlough, or certainly immediately following his final discharge, showing that he was then afflicted with identical disease on which pension is now claimed. This is generally impossible, for many reasons.

In most cases the released prisoner felt it was not medicine he wanted, but the kindly nursing of mother or wife, and nourishing food. So no doctor was called, at least for some months after reaching home. In the instances where the doctor was called, not infrequently he cannot now be found, cannot swear that the soldier had any particular disease for the first six months after reaching home, as he was a mere skeleton from starvation, and it required months of careful nursing before he had vitality enough for a disease to manifest itself.

Then again in many cases the poor victim has never suffered from any particular disease, but rather from a combination of numerous ills, the sequence of a wrecked constitution commonly termed by physicians, "General Debility." But the commissioner refuses to grant a pension on disease save where the proof is clear and positive of the contracting of a particular disease while in the service, of its existence at date of final discharge, and of its continuous existence from year to year for each and every year, to present date.

In most cases it is impossible for a prison survivor to furnish any such proof, and hence his application is promptly rejected. Besides these, there are hundreds of other obstacles in the way of the surviving prisoner of war who applies for a pension. One thing is, he is called upon to prove by comrades who were in prison with him, the origin and nature of his disease, and his condition prior to and at the time of his release. This is generally impossible, as he was likely to have but few comrades in prison with whom he was on intimate terms, and these, if not now dead, cannot be found, they are men without sufficient knowledge of anatomy and physiology, and not one out of a hundred could conscientiously swear to the origin and diagnosis of the applicant's disease. Is it not ridiculous for the government to insist upon such preposterous evidence? Which, if produced in due form, is a rule drawn up by the applicant's physican, and sworn to by the witness—"*cum grano salis*,"—and in most cases amounts to perjury for charity's sake.

Hence, it will be seen the difficulties surrounding the prison survivor who is disabled and compelled to apply for a pension are so numerous and insurmountable as to shut out a very large majority of the most needy and deserving cases from the benefits of the general pension laws entirely.

We claim, therefore, that as an act of equal justice to these men, as compared with other soldiers, there ought to be a law passed admitting them to pensions on record or other proof of confinement in a confederate prison for a prescribed length of time—such as Bill 4495—introduced by the Hon. J. Warren Keifer, M. C., of Ohio provides for. And if this bill is to benefit these poor sufferers any, it must be passed speedily, as those who yet remain will, at best, survive but a few years longer.

This measure is not asked as a pecuniary compensation for the personal losses these men sustained, as silver and gold cannot be weighed as the price for untold sufferings, but it is asked that they may be partly relieved from abject want, and their sufferings alleviated to some extent by providing them with the necessaries of life, for nearly all of them are extremely poor, consequent on the wreck of their physical and mental powers.

LIST OF THE DEAD.

The following are those who died and were buried at Andersonville, with full name, Co., Regt, date of death and No. of grave in the Cemetery at that place, alphabetically arranged by States. The No. before each name is the same as marked at the head of the graves. The list will be found to be very accurate.

ALABAMA.

7524	Barton Wm	1 Cav	L	Sept	1 64
2111	Berry J M, S't	"	A	May	17
4622	Belle Robert	"	A	Aug	3
5505	Boobur Wm	"	E	Aug	13
8425	Brice J C	"	L	Sept	11
8147	Guthrie J	"	I	Sept	8
2514	Henry P	"	F	June	26
996	Jones Jno F	"	K	Mar	15
4715	Mitchell Jno D	1	A	Aug	4
5077	Ponders J	1 Cav	H	Aug	8
5763	Panter R	1	L	Aug	15
6886	Patterson W D	1	K	Aug	25
2504	Prett J R	1	F	June	3
10900	Redman W R	1 Cav	G	Oct	14
4731	Stubbs W	1	I	Aug	4

Total 15.

CONNECTICUT.

2380	Anderson A	14	K	June 23	64
3461	Batchelder Benj	16	C	July	17
3664	Baty John	16	C	July	19
7306	Brunkissell H	14	D	Aug	30
2833	Brennon M	14	B	July	3
3224	Burns Jno	7	I	July	12
10414	Blumly E	8	D	Oct	6
545	Bigelow Wm	7	B	Apr	14
11965	Bull H A	3	B	Nov	11
12089	Brookmeyer T W	8	H	Nov	18
12152	Burke H	16	D	Nov	24
12209	Bone A	1	E	Dec	1
10682	Burnham F, Cor	14	I	Oct	11
10690	Barlow O L	16	E	Oct	11
10876	Bennett N	18	H	Oct	13
5806	Brown C H	1	H	Aug	15
5919	Boyce Wm	7	B	Aug	17
6083	Bishop B H	1 Cav	I	Aug	18
6184	Bushnell Wm	14	D	Aug	19
1763	Bailey F	16	E	Sept	4
2054	Brewer G E	21	A	June	16
5596	Burns B	6	G	Aug	14
5632	Balcomb	11	B	Aug 14	64
5754	Beers James C	16	A	Aug	15
11636	Birdsell D	16	D	Oct	28
4296	Blakeslee H	1 Cav	L	July	30
3900	Bishop A	18	A	July	24
1493	Besannon Peter	14	B	June	2
2720	Babcock R	30	A	July	1
2818	Baldwin Thos	1 Cav	L	July	3
2256	Bosworth A M	16	D	June	21
5132	Bougin John	11	C	Aug	8
5152	Brooks Wm D Cor	16	F	Aug	9
5308	Bower John	16	E	Aug	11
5452	Bently F	6	H	Aug	12
5464	Bently James	1 Cav	I	Aug	12
4830	Blackman A Cor	2 Art	C	Aug	6
7742	Banning J F	16	E	Sept	3
8018	Ballentine Robert	16	A	Sept	6
12408	Bassett J B	11	B	Jan	6 65
12540	Bobine C	2	E	Jan	27
12620	Bennis Charles	7	K	Feb	8
3707	Chapin J L	16	A	July 21	64
3949	Cottrell P	7	C	July	25
3941	Clarkson	11	H	July	25
4367	Culler M	7	E	July	31
4449	Connor D	18	F	Aug	1
4848	Carrier D B	16	D	Aug	6
6000	Cook W H	1 Cav	G	Aug	18
6153	Clark H H	16	F	Aug	15
6846	Clark W	6	A	Aug	25
5799	Champlain H	10	F	Aug	15
336	Cane John	9	H	Apr	2
620	Christian A M	1	A	Apr	19
775	Crawford James	14	A	Apr	28
7316	Chapman M	16	E	Aug	30
7348	Cleary P	1 Cav	B	Aug	31
7395	Campbell Robert	7	E	Aug	31
7418	Culler M	16	K	Aug	31
7685	Carver John G	16	B	Sept	3
7780	Cain Thomas	14	G	Sept	4
9984	Crossley B	8	G	Sept	29
10272	Coltier W	16	B	Oct	3
11175	Callahan J	11	I	Oct	19

LIST OF THE DEAD.

No.	Name	Reg.	Co.	Date
11361	Candee D M	2 Art	A	Oct 23 64
25	Dowd F		I	Mar 8
7325	Davis W	1 Cav	L	Aug 30
1813	Davis W	10	E	July 3
3614	Damery John	6	A	July 20
7597	Dichenthal H	11	C	Sept 2
8568	Donoway J	1 Cav	A	Sept 12
8769	Dutton W H	16	K	Sept 14
5446	Dugan Charles	16	K	Aug 12
11339	Dean R	16	H	Oct 23
11481	Demmings G A	16	J	Oct 24
11889	Downer S	18	C	Nov 7
11991	Demming B J	16	G	Nov 13
3482	Emmonds A	16	K	July 17
4437	Easterly Thomas	14	G	July 31
4558	Earnest H C	6	I	Aug 2
7346	Ensworth John	16	C	Aug 31
7603	Edwards O J, Cor.	8	G	Sept 2
8368	Evans N L	16	I	Sept 10
11608	Emmett W	16	K	Oct 28
12442	Eaton W	6	F	Jan 12 65
186	Fluit C W	14	G	Mar 27 64
1277	Francell Otto	6	C	May 22
2612	Fry S	7	D	June 28
4444	Fibbles H	16	G	Aug 1
4465	Fisher H	1	E	Aug 1
5123	Florence J J, Cor,	16	C	Aug 8
5382	Fuller H S	24	H	Aug 11
5913	Frisbie Levi	1 Cav	G	Aug 17
5556	Fogg C S't	7	K	Aug 13
8028	Feely M	7	I	Sept 6
9089	Filby A	14	C	Sept 18
10255	Frederick John	7	A	Oct 3
12188	Fagan P D	11	A	Nov 28
3028	Gordon John	14	G	July 7
4096	Gray Pat	9	H	July 27
4974	Grammon Jas	1 Cav	K	July 7
4005	Gulterman J	Mus 1	E	July 26
5173	Gilmore J	16	C	Aug 9
7057	Gallagher P	16	D	Aug 28
7337	Gott G	Mus	18	Aug 30
7593	Goodrich J W	16	C	Sept 2
7646	Graigg W	16	B	Sept 3
9423	Guina H M	11	G	Sept 21
10300	Grady M	11	B	Oct 4
10397	Gladstone Wm	6	K	Oct 6
49	Holt Thomas	1 Cav	A	Mar 15
2336	Hughes Ed	14	D	June 22
3195	Hitchcock Wm A	16	C	July 12
3448	Hall Wm G	1	K	July 17
3559	Holcomb D	14	D	July 18
1350	Hilenthal Jas	14	C	May 25
5083	Haskins Jas	16	D	July 8
5029	Hollister A	1 Cav	L	Aug 8
5162	Hally Thomas	16	F	Aug 9
5352	Hanson F A	15	I	Aug 11
6695	Hodges Geo	1 Cav	H	Aug 24
4937	Harwood G	15	A	Aug 7
6964	Hoyt E S	17	B	Aug 27
7012	Hull M	16	E	Aug 27
7380	Holcomb A A	16	K	Aug 31
7642	Haley W	16	D	Sept 3
7757	Hubbard H D	16	D	Sept 4
8043	Haywood	18	E	Sept 11
8613	Heath I, S't	16	K	Sept 13
9129	Hall B	16	G	Sept 18
9369	Heart W	11	F	Sept 20
9981	Hurley R A	16	I	Sept 29 64
12086	Hibbard A	18	D	Nov 18
12117	Hancock W	14	G	Nov 22
12163	Hudson Chas	11	C	Nov 26
8148	Hubbard B	16	A	Nov 8
9340	Islay H	11		Sept 4
737	Jamieson Charles	7	D	April 26
5221	Johnson John	16	E	Aug 10
7083	Johnson G W	11	G	Aug 28
7365	Jamison J S, Q M	S 1 Cav		Aug 31
7570	Jones Jno J	16	B	Sept 2
7961	Jones James R	6	G	Sept 6
8502	Johnson F	1	D	Sept 12
11970	Johnson C S	16	E	Nov 12
12340	Johnson W	16	E	Dec 26
1590	Kingsbury C	14	K	June 3
5186	Klineland L	11	C	Aug 9
6374	Kempton B F	8	G	Aug 21
6705	Kershoff B	6	H	Aug 25
6748	Kelley F	14	I	Aug 25
7749	Kaltry J	1 Cav	L	Sept 3
8065	Kimball H H	7	H	Sept 7
8866	Kohlerburg C	7	D	Sept 15
10233	Kearn T	16	A	Oct 2
3401	Lenden H	16	D	July 16
5893	Lastry J	10	I	Aug 16
5499	Lewis J	8	E	Aug 12
6124	Leonard W	14	H	Aug 19
7912	Lavanaugh W O,	S't 16	C	Sept 5
7956	Linker C	8	G	Sept 6
9219	Lewis G H	7	G	Sept 19
10248	Lee. farrier	1 Cav	B	Oct 2
74	Mills W J		6	D	Mar 20
119	McCaulley Jas	14	D	Mar 20
2295	Miller Charles	14	I	June 21
3516	McCord P	16	G	July 18
3644	Miller A	14	D	July 19
3410	Mould James	11	E	July 16
3933	McGinnis J W	15	E	Aug 17
4079	Miller D	1 Cav	E	July 27
4417	Messenger A	16	G	July 31
4492	McLean Wm	11	F	Aug 1
4595	Marshalls B	8	H	Aug 3
5238	Mickallis F	16	F	Aug 10
7852	Miller F D	16	B	Sept
8150	Modger A	10	I	Sept 8
6902	Mape George	11	B	Aug 25
6240	Marshal L	8	H	July 20
7547	Moore A P, S't	1 Cav	H	Sept 2
8446	Mathews S J	16	K	Sept 11
8501	Myers L	1 Cav		Sept 12
9170	Mertis C	11	C	Sept 18
9321	Milor W, S't	14	F	Sept 20
5328	Miller H	16	A	Aug 11
6342	Malone John	16	B	Aug 22
6426	Messey M	7	E	Aug 22
6451	McGee Thomas	11	D	Aug 22
6570	McDavid James	1	K	Aug 23
6800	Meal John	11	D	Aug 25
10595	McCreieth A	14	H	Oct 10
10914	McKeon J	7	H	Oct 14
11487	Murphy W	16	C	Oct 26
11538	McDowell J	11	D	Oct 27
12134	Montjoy T	5	C	Nov 23
5044	Nichols C	16	G	Aug 8
6222	Northrop John	7	D	Aug 20
7331	North S S, S't	1 Cav	D	Aug 30

LIST OF THE DEAD.

No.	Name	Co.	Reg.	Date
10895	Nichols M	7	I	Oct 14 64
4565	Orton H C	6	I	Aug 9
7511	Olena R	1 Cav E		Sept 1
8276	Orr A	14	H	Sept 14
2960	Pendalton W	14	C	July 6
3808	Pompey C	14	B	July 24
4356	Parker S B	10	B	July 31
3803	Phelps S G	1	H	July 22
4934	Pimble A	16	I	Aug 7
5002	Plum James	11	G	Aug 8
5386	Patchey J	1 Cav	I	Aug 12
7487	Post C, S't	16	K	Sept 1
7688	Potache A	7	G	Sept 3
9248	Phillips J I	8	B	Sept 19
9444	Padfrey Sylvanus	8	H	Sept 21
9533	Painter N P	7	C	Sept 22
10676	Puritan O	1 Cav	L	Oct 11
11616	Peir A	7	D	Oct 28
2804	Ruther J. S't	1 Cav	E	July 3
2871	Reed H H	2 Art	H	July 4
3674	Risley E. S't	10	B	July 20
4636	Reins Wm	11	I	Aug 3
5902	Ross D	10	K	Aug 16
6400	Robinson H	21	K	Aug 21
7696	Ringwood R	14	I	Aug 25
8078	Reed John	7	B	Sept 7
8170	Richardson C S	16	E	Sept 9
8345	Ray A	11	G	Sept 10
7810	Reed Rob't K	7	A	Aug 30
8662	Roper H	16	G	Sept 13
10029	Robinson J W	18	D	Sept 29
10196	Richardson D T	16	G	Oct 2
10416	Reynolds E	1	E	Oct 6
12031	Rathbone B	2	A	Nov 15
4	Stone H I	1 Cav	A	Mar 3
234	Smith Horace	7	D	Mar 29
2405	Seward G H	14	A	June 24
2474	Stephens E W	1 Cav	L	June 25
3010	Scott W	14	D	July 7
3026	Sutcliff B	21	G	July 7
3041	Stuart J	7		July 8
3522	Smith J	14	I	July 18
3598	Sherwood D	1	D	July 18
4212	Smith C E, S't	1 Cav	L	July 27
4316	Stranbell L	11		July 30
4555	Straum James	2 Art	D	Aug 2
4722	Sullivan M	16	D	Aug 4
4892	Steel Sam	14	C	Aug 6
5385	Shults C T	14	I	Aug 12
5563	Stino P	16	K	Aug 13
5712	Steele Sam	16	C	Aug 15
5725	Smith S	7	B	Aug 15
6734	Steele James M	16	F	Aug 18
7070	Stephens B H	14		Aug 28
7975	Smith Henry	5	H	Sept 6
8088	Short L C	18	K	Sept 7
8235	Smally L	16	E	Sept 9
9304	Starkweather E M	1 Cav L		Sept 20
9435	Sutliff J	16	C	Sept 21
9648	See L	1	G	Sept 24
9987	Sling D	7	F	Sept 29
10138	Schubert K	16	K	Oct 1
10247	Sparring T	7	K	Oct 3
10476	Steele H	16	F	Oct 7
10787	Stauff J	1 Cav	L	Oct 12
12005	Swift J	1	K	Nov 14
12288	Smith J T	7	D	Dec 13
541	Taylor Moses	14	E	April 14 64
4443	Thompson Wm T	14	I	Aug 1
5427	Thompson F	14	A	Aug 12
5479	Tibbles Wm	16	G	Aug 12
7723	Tredway J H, S't	15	E	Aug 3
10035	Tisdale Ed F	1 Cav	B	Sept 29
10142	Taylor J	14	I	Oct 1
11089	Turner H	11	A	Oct 18
3107	Valter H	14	A	July 10
401	Winship J H	18	C	April 6
2158	Welden Henry	7	E	June 19
2601	Warner E	1 Cav	E	June 28
5543	Wickert Henry	14	C	Aug 13
5222	Wright C	16	B	Aug 10
4649	Wheely James	10	G	Aug 3
5675	Wenchell John L	16	E	Aug 14
6138	Way H C	16	K	Aug 19
6918	Wiggleworth M L	2 Art	H	Aug 26
8024	West Chas H	16	I	Sept 6
9028	Williams H D, S't	16	F	Sept 17
9265	Wheeler J	1 Cav	M	Sept 19
9512	Ward Gilbert, S't	11		Sept 22
10033	Weins John	6	K	Sept 29
12600	Ward G W	18	C	Feb 6 65
6394	Young C S, S't	16	C	Aug 21 64

TOTAL 290.

DELAWARE.

No.	Name	Co.	Reg.	Date
8812	Aiken Wm	7	G	Sept 15 64
5529	Boice J	4		Aug 13
7016	Frown J H	2	I	Aug 27
1709	Callihan Jno	1	B	June 7
2698	Conoway F	1	K	June 30
4394	Conley J H	2	F	July 31
12253	Connor G	1 Cav	D	Dec 9
10868	Conner C	2	F	Oct 13
11245	Cunningham K	1	F	Oct 13
6217	Donohue H	2	D	Aug 20
6677	Emmett W	1	K	Aug 24
2091	Field S	2	D	June 17
9004	Hanning H, Drum	2	F	Sept 17
8346	Hills W		2	K Sept 10
5504	Hobson W	1 Cav	E	Aug 13
9839	Hudson G W, S't	2		Sept 27
11634	Hussey J R	1 Cav	D	Oct 28
790	Joseph W C	1	E	April 28
5346	Jones H	2	B	Aug 11
11410	Kinney M	1	D	Oct 24
8292	Laughlin R M	1	C	Sept 9
483	Limpkins J H	2	D	April 9
5956	Maham Jas	2	C	Aug 17
8972	Moxworthy Geo	2	D	Sept 16
9580	Martin J	1	G	Sept 23
9043	Manner C	2	K	Sept 28
1671	McCracklin H	1	B	June 6
11570	McKinney J	1	F	Oct 27
12407	McBride	2	F	Jan 6 65
9450	Norris Clarence	1 Cav	L	Sept 21 64
6607	Peterson P	4	F	Aug 20
8743	Piffer W	2	F	Aug 14
7551	Reitter G	2	F	Sept 2
11534	Riddler H A	1	H	Oct 27
6618	Saurot John	2	E	Aug 23
6479	Sholder Ed	2	H	Aug 22
6593	Simble Wm	1 Cav	C	Aug 23
12707	Sill James	2	K	Feb 28 65
5764	Smith E E	2	E	Aug 15 64

276 Taylor Robert	1	G	Mch 31		64
8082 Thorn H I	2	D	Sept 8		
9324 Tilbrick E L	1 Cav	L	Sept 20		
11981 Warner G	2	K	Nov 13		
10902 Wilds J	2	K	Oct 4		
198 Wilburn Geo	2	G	Mch 27		
TOTAL 55.					

DISTRICT OF COLUMBIA.

8449 Boissonnault F M	1 Cav	H	Sept 11		64
1170 Clark Theodore	1 Cav	I	Oct 31		
11180 Farrell C	1 Cav	E	Oct 19		
5736 Gray G S	1 Cav	K	Aug 15		
9463 Pillman John	1 Cav	D	Sept 21		
6873 Ridley A C	1 Cav	M	Aug 26		
11716 Russel T	1 Cav	D	Nov 1		
6847 Stretch J	1 Cav	G	Aug 25		
8189 Sergeant L, S't	1 Cav	G	Sept 8		64
11742 Stanhope W H	1	"	I	Nov 2	
12457 Veasie F	1	"	K	Jan 15	65
8172 Winworth G	1	"	G	Sept 8	64
8807 Wiggins Nat	1	"	M	Sept 15	
10301 Wilson W	1	"	E	Oct 3	
TOTAL 14.					

ILLINOIS.

8402 Adams H F, S't	17	E	Sept 11	64
12430 Adder W	10	C	Jan 4	65
3840 Adlet John	119	K	July 23	64
8249 Adrian F	Cav 9	E	Sept 9	
5876 Akens C, S't	78	F	Aug 16	
8381 Albany D	22	D	Sept 10	
1264 Aldridge A	Cav 16	L	May 20	
8127 Alexander B	123	B	Sept 8	
1423 Allen R C	17	I	May 28	
10762 Alf H	89	A	Oct 12	
2400 Allison L J	21	B	June 24	
6710 Anderson A	19	K	Aug 24	
10242 Anderson A	98	E	Oct 3	
9946 Anderson W	89	C	Sept 28	
10271 Anthony E	3	E	Oct 3	
7339 Armstrong R	89	A	Aug 30	
12792 Arnold L	137	I	Mar 18	65
10979 Atkins E	6	C	Oct 15	64
9733 Atkinson Jas	Cav 14	D	Sept 25	
11777 Atwood A	23	G	Nov 3	
8046 Augustine J	100	I	Sept 6	
3709 Babbitt John	7	B	July 21	
2598 Babcock F	44	G	June 28	
3783 Bailey P, S't	38	B	July 22	
12530 Baker James	25	H	Jan 26	65
2892 Baker John	89	B	July 4	64
3308 Baker Thos	Cav 16	M	July 14	
1034 Bales Thomas	Art 2	M	May 11	
5848 Barber C F	112	I	Aug 16	
3829 Barclay P	42	I	July 23	
12758 Barnard W	14	F	Mar 12	65
10180 Barnes Thomas	135	F	Oct 7	64
8458 Barnett J	120	I	Sept 11	
8762 Barrett A, S't	25	A	Sept 14	
12687 Bass J	Cav 2	C	Feb 22	65
977 Basting C	47	B	May 9	64
3275 Bathrick J	Cav 1	A	July 14	
4618 Batsdorf M	93	F	Aug 3	
3603 Bayley Frank	Cav 16	E	July 19	

11917 Beaver M	29	B	Nov 8	64
11652 Beard J	14	K	Oct 30	
1870 Beal John	78		June 12	
6644 Bear D	93	B	Aug 28	
4573 Beck J	21	G	Aug 2	
411 Beliskey J	Cav 16	D	Apr 18	
1230 Bender George	12	C	May 20	
5242 Bennet A	16	B	Aug 10	
6412 Benning John	Cav 6	G	Aug 22	
3345 Benstill John	27	H	July 15	
10653 Benton C W	29	B	Oct 11	
8188 Berlizer B	Cav 16	F	Sept 8	
10681 Best William	88	E	Oct 11	
4815 Black John, S't,	31	A	July 30	
2904 Black J H	21	E	July 5	
1665 Blanchard L, S't	16 C	D	June 6	
1983 Bloss P		A	June 15	
11085 Bodkins E L	103	D	Oct 18	
2890 Bogley J E	21	D	July 4	
12456 Bohem J	Cav 14	B	Jan 14	65
9899 Boles William	89	C	Sept 27	64
10795 Bolton N P	100	B	Nov 4	
10791 Bowman J	108	D	Oct 12	
3008 Boorem O	64	B	July 7	
12621 Borem M	35	G	Feb 9	65
11921 Bonser G	89	F	Nov 8	64
5475 Bowden W		F	Aug 13	
5046 Bowen A O	113	C	Aug 8	
5943 Bowman E	123	F	Aug 17	
9328 Boyd B F	Cav 6	D	Sept 25	
11678 Boyd H P	14	I	Oct 31	
1971 Boyd J E	84	B	June 15	
10984 Boyer J, S't	14	H	Oct 16	
11729 Boyle F	4	B	Nov 1	
12840 Bradford D	85	C	Apr 25	65
4259 Branch J	38	C	July 29	64
1815 Brandiger F	24	K	June 9	
9570 Bridges W H	122	F	Sept 23	
1613 Bridewell H C	38	D	June 4	
2367 Brinkey M, S't	16 Cav	L	June 25	
3056 Britsnyder J	45	G	July 9	
2927 Brockhill J	Cav 4	M	July 5	
3717 Brookman J E	Cor 44	I	July 21	
8911 Brothers D	48	H	Sept 16	
9350 Brown A F, S't	73	C	Sept 20	
12450 Brown H	15	F	Jan 14	65
5978 Brown J	78	B	Aug 17	64
9011 Brown J H	12	F	Sept 17	
5924 Brown J M	29	B	Aug 17	
6836 Brown William	Cav 1	G	Aug 26	
8962 Brown William	16	C	Sept 16	
6256 Bryant Wm O	107	A	Aug 20	
10763 Briden E	35	E	Oct 12	
5785 Buck B F	30	I	Aug 15	
4963 Buchman	Cav 16	H	Aug 7	
10888 Buckmaster J	79	C	Oct 13	
12362 Buffington B	74	F	Dec 30	
5457 Burdes G	89	A	Aug 12	
4299 Burrows J	90	L	July 30	
7055 Burns John	100	K	Aug 28	
5936 Burns H, S't	Cav 16	D	Aug 17	

LIST OF THE DEAD.   197

No.	Name	Reg.	Co.	Date
526	Burr W B	112	E	Apr 13 64
1858	Burton O L	35	I	Nov 6
11858	Butler H J	89	D	Oct 10
10362	Butler N, S't	89	D	Oct 5
8776	Butler J	89	A	Sept 14
11668	Button A R	79	E	Oct 30
9824	Butts John	22	F	Sept 27
626	Byres George	65	B	Apr 19
12348	Cadding J C	89	B	Dec 27
6356	Callahan C	39	F	Aug 21
6505	Campbell J M	120	G	Aug 22
10026	Capell C	87	D	Sept 29
10257	Capsey J, S't	90	D	Oct 3
3556	Carl C C	38	H	July 18
666	Carrell J	3	H	Apr 22
7037	Carroll J Q, S't	78	I	Aug 27
3393	Carren O	38	H	July 16
6693	Caritt Robert	113	D	Aug 24
446	Caelt Albert	116	A	Apr 9
1844	Castle F	103	E	June 10
7502	Center E R	115	H	Sept 1
3907	Charles R J	5 Cav	M	July 24
6109	Chase E S	23	C	Aug 18
9095	Chattenay S'	82	H	Sept 18
10459	Chenly S	79	A	Oct 7
4319	Chitwood T C	16 Cav	H	July 30
3205	Chlunworth Wm	9	G	July 12
10551	Choate Wm	Cav 6	D	Oct 10
9935	Chunberg A	89	G	Sept 28
6935	Christiansen J	82	F	Aug 26
7868	Chuncey J W	38	E	Sept 5
504	Clark A E	Cav 16	M	Apr 12
7760	Clark C	51	K	Sept 4
9560	Clark C	29	B	Sept 23
8834	Clark F J	Cav 6	B	Sept 15
12672	Clark R	114	F	Feb 18 65
5143	Clark Wm	Cav 14	K	Aug 9 64
9925	Cleaver M	"	3	H	Sept 28
8750	Cleggett M, S't	36	I	Sept 14
5787	Cline John	Cav 12	I	Aug 15
12726	Cline M	14	B	Mar 4 65
12051	Cline T	15	E	Nov 16 64
2237	Clusterman	16 Cav	D	June 21
2048	Coalman H	16	"	June 15
2753	Colbern M	73	I	July 1
2214	Colburn Thos	16 Cav	G	June 20
5397	Colburn Wm	16	G	Aug 14
300	Cole John	112	E	Apr 1
7211	Cole W H	112	A	Aug 20
6971	Coller John	6	B	Aug 27
256	Collins Wm	93	G	Mar 30
1198	Coddington M J	93	G	May 18
11719	Compton H H	21	K	Nov 1
2933	Cooret D	78	F	July 5
4183	Carey J	38	I	Aug 4
2758	Corey O C	105	D	July 1
6738	Cornelius Jas	Cav 9	H	Aug 24
3856	Corwin J	Cav 7	K	July 24
3677	Corwin J V	Cav 6	L	July 20
6091	Cotton J, S't	100	H	Aug 18
9704	Craig G	23	B	Sept 25
9307	Craig J	38	I	Sept 20
12506	Craig J	Art 2	B	Jan 22 65
9704	Craig S	23	B	Sept 25 64
10087	Craig F	9	K	Sept 30
1374	Crandall W M	93	A	June 15
2329	Crane M	23	E	June 23
2253	Crawford Wm	Cav 16	K	June 21 64
10912	Crelley C W	29	B	Oct 14
4879	Cook G P	Cav 16	L	Aug 6
12433	Crosbey J	90	C	Jan 11 65
1417	Cross E	111	C	May 27 64
8859	Cross J D	Cav 14	I	Sept 15
7982	Cross J T	21	D	Sept 6
6744	Crouse J, S't	16	I	Aug 24
2032	Cruse J	79	D	June 15
2179	Creman George	24	C	June 19
10026	Cupell C	82	D	Sept 29
10257	Cupsay J, Cor	90	D	Oct 3
3887	Curtis A	16	D	July 24
8626	Dake G, Cor	100	D	Sept 13
4663	Dalby James	73	H	Aug 3
1826	Darling D W	93	B	June 10
10961	Darum J J	112	I	Oct 15
356	Davis And	112	A	Apr 2
8353	Davis C	112	E	Sept 12
10603	Davis J	113	D	Oct 10
4150	Davis W	Cav 16	M	July 28
4048	Davis H, S't	38	A	July 27
12311	Delancey L D	Art 2	F	Dec 9
7013	Day W H	111	H	Aug 27
9073	Decker C	Cav 7	M	Sept 17
4608	Decker J P	119	C	Aug 3
7150	Demos B F	78	F	Aug 29
2497	Denhart W	Cav 16	K	June 26
4422	Denior E, S't	79	B	July 31
7514	Deming Joseph	31	D	Sept 1
12660	Denton E. Cor	15	B	Feb 16 65
2231	Detreeman D, S't	44	E	June 20 64
5165	DePue J W	16	C	Aug 9
352	Deraus G W	21	B	Apr 2
2365	Dricks Henry	89	C	June 23
12547	Dilley A	15	E	Jan 28 65
1314	Dodson M, S't	Cav 3	H	May 23 64
8187	Dock C	"	9	H	Sept 8
3834	Dodd G W	21	F	July 23
4207	Dodson R B	Cav 6	B	July 29
2867	Dooley James	Cav 16	L	July 4
1441	Doran W H	78	I	May 28
1103	Donen C	6	I	May 15
1727	Dowd J W	38	G	June 8
1342	Dowdy John	16	K	May 24
10143	Dowell J W	112	K	Oct 1
10496	Downer A	24	H	Oct 8
12436	Doyle P	65	H	Jan 11 65
12476	Doyle J	112	I	Jan 17
15053	Drake R R	34	H	Aug 8
10332	Dresser C	24	G	Oct 4
9678	Drum G	89		Sept 24
3123	Dudley J W	89	F	July 10
2666	Dumond P	35	E	June 29
9947	Dunn Alexander	75	A	Sept 28
12496	Dunsing A	30	C	Jan 21
9037	Dyer J C	30	D	Sept 17 64
12686	Drew E	53	D	Feb 20 65
209	Eadley Levi	26	H	Mar 28 64
8045	Easinbeck M	100	D	Sept 6
10909	Easley W A, S't	21	G	Oct 14
5992	Eastman Wm	36	F	Aug 17
4962	Edwards C D	51	K	Aug 7
8084	Elliott Ed	92	B	Sept 7
9703	Ellis William	26	G	Sept 25
9731	Ellison W	Cav 14	F	Sept 25
2249	Elslin James	112	E	July 24

LIST OF THE DEAD.

No.	Name		Age/Co	Co	Date
4502	Emery J		22	K	Aug 1 64
4979	Emmerson J	Cav	16	L	Aug 7
9717	Erb J		9	C	Sept 27
12628	Ermains F	Cav	14	M	Feb 14 65
214	Errickson	Cav	16	M	Mch 28 64
2211	Esch W		29	H	June 20
11727	Enrow W	Cav	7	M	Nov 1
2996	Evans J		9	C	Sept 25
3373	Eydroner R		74	F	July 15
6368	Fagan O		23	G	Aug 20
2496	Fandish S	Art	1	A	June 25
2230	Farmer F		21	A	June 20
4991	Farnham C A		51	D	Aug 7
10740	Ferguson L Corpl		115	K	Oct 14
2512	File R		11	K	June 26
12628	Fermer J		14	M	Feb 20 65
3854	Finch F M		21	G	July 24 64
10097	Fink J P		53	F	Sept 30
11541	Fish J		65	G	Oct 27
9845	Fisher S F		123	F	Sept 27
2129	Fitzgerald H	Cav	16	I	June 18
9993	Flanagan J		42	H	Sept 29
6972	Floyd A		7	A	Aug 27
10881	Ford W J, S't		17	I	Oct 13
161	Folk A P		112	G	Mch 26
2564	Forncy D		93	G	June 27
8230	Foster A J	Cav	16	M	Sept 8
7720	Foster B B		112	G	Sept 12
12473	Foster E S. Corpl		9	A	Jan 17 65
531	Fowler John		14	D	April 13 64
1275	Frame W		120	E	Dec 17
12837	Francis J F		12	I	April 19 65
5938	Franklin H		81	F	Aug 17 64
432	Frass Louis		16	E	April 8
4381	Freeman D	Cav	11	L	July 26
2080	French J		129	B	June 17 63
2210	Fritz P S't		38	C	June 20 64
1055	Fremont James	Cav	7	B	May 13
497	Fuller Ira B		112	D	April 11
8114	Funk Wm		26	F	Sept 8
2021	Furlong H		23	B	June 15
9026	Gaines C		20	B	Sept 28
1347	Gallagher P		21	C	May 24
579	Garvin John, S't		59		Apr 16
12801	Gerlock D		30	C	Mar 30 65
1310	German P		24	G	May 24 64
1416	Gibson H D		93	K	May 27
4201	Gibson L F		78	I	July 29
4185	Gichma J, S't	Cav	16	G	Aug 1
1652	Giles J V		89	H	June 5
7988	Giles S P		112	A	Sept 6
5144	Gillespie J W		84	H	Aug 9
1499	Gillgrease J	Cav	16	I	May 30
1868	Gilmore J	"	16	E	June 12
13731	Gleason G M	"	14	A	Mar 4 65
1850	Glidwell F, Cor		73	K	June 11 64
2001	Goffinet P		51	D	June 15
10307	Goddard H		89	G	Oct 4
4203	Gooles H F, S't		47	B	July 29
12847	Gordon I		114	B	Apr 25 65
7953	Gore F		36	I	Sept 5 64
7761	Gore N		15	C	Sept 4
6111	Garrig J		78	F	Aug 18
12461	Gott H		39	C	Jan 15 65
9403	Graber J		24	H	Sept 21 64
9312	Graber J F		81	D	Sept 20
2164	Grace W		21	D	June 19
6617	Graham M J		41	E	Aug 23 64
10998	Gravel J		51	C	Oct 16
2942	Greadley H		20	A	July 6
4560	Greathouse J		6	I	Aug 2
783	Greaves George		16	K	Apr 28
12116	Green C		79	A	Nov 22
11155	Green John		23	H	Oct 19
7836	Green M		9	C	Sept 4
3111	Greenwall B	Cav	16	L	July 11
11778	Greer Geo, Cor		120	D	Nov 3
10594	Gress J		29	B	Oct 10
12834	Grimmins M A		42	H	Apr 17 65
4083	Griswold J P		79	E	July 27 64
2501	Grogan H		66	B	June 26
10466	Grower H		42	K	Oct 7
3730	Gulk P		79	B	July 21
5025	Guyen William		72	E	Aug 8
5961	Gonder H	Cav	16	E	Aug 17
5074	Hageman Jas	"	16	E	Aug 8
4094	Haggard E	"	16	K	July 27
11959	Haginis W		89	B	Nov 11
2825	Haines Theo	Cav	14	M	July 3
63	Haks William		16	E	Mar 19
11572	Hall G H	Cav	7	B	Oct 27
12314	Hall H C, Cor		41	D	Dec 20
7194	Hall J L		9	C	Aug 29
12223	Hall J L		89	G	Dec 4
11833	Hall Peter, Cor		103	D	Nov 5
10061	Haley C H		22	H	Sept 30
1241	Hallam Wm		82	H	May 20
2605	Hanna P		21	G	June 28
187	Hanna H, Cor		107	C	Mar 24
11188	Hansom D		39	E	Oct 19
318	Harken John		65	E	Apr 2
6684	Harlan J C		7	L	Aug 24
6113	Harrell G		120	K	Aug 19
2633	Harrington S M		112	A	June 29
11725	Harris E K		79	C	Nov 1
10447	Harris G W		9	G	Oct 7
8715	Harshman Peter		84	H	Sept 14
2677	Hart George	Cav	16	K	June 30
2202	Hart W	"	16	K	June 19
1980	Harney E		39	B	June 15
10606	Hathaway S	Cav	14	B	Oct 10
12791	Hanch L		15	D	Mar 18 65
8608	Hawkins J W		79	I	Sept 12 64
2326	Hayward W G, Cor		16	I	June 22
5192	Hayworth F	Cav	7	I	Aug 10
1852	Hegenberg W		24	F	June 11
8798	Helch S		77	K	Sept 15
6489	Hendson Geo B		31	C	Aug 22
1162	Henry Wm P		23	A	July 17
6035	Herdson Wm H		107	C	Aug 18
8428	Herrell Wm	Cav	14	K	Sept 11
2365	Hess H		84	G	June 27
1906	Hester John		38	G	June 13
7805	Hicks Geo W		65	F	Sept 5
8303	Hicks H		11	G	Sept 10
1102	Hicks W		85	D	May 15
12070	Highland C	Cav	14	C	Nov 17
725	Hilderbrand N		24	G	Apr 25
8830	Hill Aaron		115	C	Sept 15
67	Hill David, Cor		36	A	Mar 19
8721	Hill Henry		11		Sept 14
4189	Hill J	Cav	9	F	Aug 1
12683	Hinchcliff J		8	B	Feb 20 65
6117	Hoen Peter		112	H	Aug 19 64

LIST OF THE DEAD.

No.	Name	Regt.	Co.	Date
3825	Hoffman J	Cav 7	I	July 23 64
11847	Hofnian R	35	C	Nov 5
2098	Hook Jas J, S't	98	E	June 17
3255	Hoppock I	112	F	July 13
9880	Honeson A F	38	F	Sept 27
9214	Hormer J	38	F	Sept 19
12090	Horn T	86	A	Nov 18
89	Horseman W	Cav 16	I	Mar 21
5812	Howard D N, S't	79	E	Aug 16
10782	Howard G S, Cor	127	K	Nov 3
3211	Howell J W	78	F	July 12
11506	Hoye J	100	A	Oct 26
5741	Hude C	24	F	Aug 15
6085	Hudson W H	107	C	Aug 13
9062	Hughes D L	125	H	Sept 28
12755	Hulse A B	14	D	Mar 12 65
11140	Hungerford N	108	I	Oct 19 64
6085	Huntley R	89	F	Aug 18
1136	Hulburt D	84	C	May 16
1162	Hurry W B	23	A	May 16
5019	Hutchins S	104	A	Aug 8
4583	Hustand B F, S't	92	D	Aug 2
4091	Hyber John	Cav 6	A	July 27
3312	Iverson J S	Cav 16	I	July 14
4132	Jaccards S A, S't	29	E	July 28
2658	Jackson H	51	C	June 29
10287	Jackson M	123	F	Oct 4
12797	Janks J P	Cav 3	A	Mar 18 65
3686	Jarvis J	73	K	July 20 64
6783	Jenningsen G B	30	E	Aug 24
1845	Jenny E H, Cor	79	F	June 11
2135	Jewet F	14	A	June 18
1996	Johnson C W	Cav 7	F	June 15
9458	Johnson Joseph	125	K	Sept 21
1412	Johnson J S	7	C	May 27
5395	Johnson Samuel	100	B	Aug 12
9827	Jones G W	27	E	Sept 27
8971	Jones J	117	E	Sept 16
4880	Jones P	41	G	Aug 6
644	Jones Thomas	112	E	Apr 12
2567	Jones Thos	Cav 16	F	June 27
2990	Jones Wm	27	D	July 7
1764	Jordan B W	81	D	June 9
9153	Jordan M	38	C	Sept 18
2961	Joy B	16	I	July 6
2241	Joyce A	90	D	June 20
10513	Justice H	Cav 7	H	Oct 8
12052	Kane H	95	A	Nov 16
4308	Kappel H	29	H	July 30
4743	Keefe James P	Art 2	M	Aug 5
8348	Kelaze E	20	G	Sept 10
18	Kell M R, Cor	49	D	Mar 7
7183	Kelly John	75	F	Aug 29
6795	Kelley William	94	I	Aug 25
5518	Kennedy M	38	C	Aug 13
12488	Kent J	14	F	Jan 19 65
5707	Kerbey John	96	H	Aug 15 64
396	Kiger John	22	E	Apr 6
10520	Kilkreath J	42	A	Oct 8
82	Kimball Jas	Art 25	L	Mar 20
158	Kinkle John	16	C	Mar 25
696	Kinderman G	82	D	Apr 26
7807	Kingham J	38	G	Sept 4
685	Klinehaus D	65	D	Apr 23
4766	Kenigge A	113	C	Aug 5
4908	Knight J	9	H	Aug 6
11891	Knoble P	108	E	Nov 7
4700	Koahl J	Cav 16	H	Aug 4 64
2754	Krail J	"	16	I	July 1
12685	Kreiger J	14	E	Feb 20 65
652	Kaiber John	16	D	Apr 20 64
1809	Keyser John	32	I	June 10
7927	Lacost J M	89	E	Sept 5
7299	Ladien J	100	H	Aug 23
7105	Lambert C	38	D	Aug 20
10419	Lainsden W H	78	A	Oct 6
12044	Lance V	59	D	Nov 16
12270	Langley G	14	K	Dec 12
5906	Lanner W A	Cav 9	E	Aug 16
1233	Law Henry	93	G	May 20
9635	Lawrene L G	89	G	Sept 24
10179	Lape J	125	A	Oct 1
10896	Leatherman M	98	E	Oct 14
8164	Leach W	115	B	Sept 11
4172	Lee A	112	B	July 28
8524	Lee P, Corp	16	A	Sept 12
963	Lee Thomas	8	E	May 9
1297	Lee W E	Cav 16	I	May 23
11258	Lewis Charles	79	A	Oct 21
6238	Lewis Thomas	2	L	Aug 20
10148	Lickey J B, S't	96	F	Oct 1
8295	Liday J	113	I	Sept 9
6295	Liken John, S't	112	I	Aug 20
1085	Linday B	57	H	June 6
7768	Linderman H A	99	B	Sept 4
6414	Lindsay A	113	D	Aug 22
1818	Lin bergh I, Cor	16	F	June 10
11449	Linwood J	79	F	Oct 25
12358	Lipsey D, Cor	Cav 2	C	Dec 30
1405	Lord L B, Corpl	112	B	Oct 6
11222	Lorsam C	89	C	Oct 20
2268	London L	Cav 16	D	June 21
1017	Lowry Frank	35	E	May 11
2342	Lusk John	29	B	June 23
1456	Lutz John	23	H	May 29
8196	Lyman J	100	D	Sept 8
11497	Lynch V, Corpl	38	C	Oct 26
10849	Mack J	Cav 16	G	Oct 13
5390	Madden L	96	D	Aug 12
11358	Madoock J W, S't	79	A	Oct 23
10982	Madrill A	12	A	Aug 12
3935	Malcolm J R	38	K	July 25
2868	Manning A	215	A	July 4
953	Manty P, S't	Cav 16	E	May 8
2050	Markman Wm	Cav 16	K	June 16
6333	Marritt H	Cav 16	L	Aug 21
2762	Marshall A, Corpl	96	C	July 2
8444	Martin A	Cav 16	L	May 28
4071	Martin I	9	K	July 27
12757	Masman S	42	G	Mch 12 65
853	Mason Thos B	93	B	May 3 64
1428	Massey W H	111	D	May 28
746	Master Wm	12	A	April 26
429	Mathening A D, S't	79	I	April 8
12744	Mathews F M	32	G	Mch 7 65
1061	Maxem H C	19	H	May 13 64
3280	Maxwell S	Cav 8	C	July 13
10319	May M H	89	I	Sept 29
3100	McCampbell D	104	B	July 10
56	McCleary Thos	Cav 16	L	Mch 17
1315	McClusky Jas	Cav 16	K	May 27
4850	McCray A	103	A	Aug 6
1617	McCready Wm	96	C	June 4
6513	McCleary J	119	C	Aug 22

200 LIST OF THE DEAD.

No.	Name	Reg	Co	Date
5724	McCone R	Cav 16	K	Aug 15 64
3050	McCunne H	13	C	July 8
3470	McEntire L	Cav 16	K	July 17
5283	McGee Wm	30	D	Aug 11
11623	McGivens J	119	A	Oct 28
11952	McLarens B	89	A	Nov 10
1634	McLaughlin B	90	I	June 5
3109	McLing Benj, Cor	23	E	July 11
4725	McMahon M	93	E	Aug 4
1337	McMillan W B, Cor	112 E		May 24
9763	McMiller W B	78	D	Sept 25
692	McShaw B	80	B	April 23
9710	McWorthy W M	92	G	Sept 25
3279	Mead G	19	H	July 14
4648	Medler H	38	I	Aug 3
6266	Mee William	51	C	Aug 20
2177	Meher Charles	Cav 16	F	June 19
2049	Mercenner Charles	90	A	June 16
2637	Merritt F, S't	89	F	June 29
7464	Merg F	44	K	Sept 1
9145	Meyers A, Corpl	24	H	Sept 18
5608	Meyers J	24	K	Aug 14
2097	Meyers J K	116	C	June 17
5432	Myers Samuel	25	A	Aug 12
9188	Miller F Corpl	16	B	Sept 18
3139	Miller H	92	F	July 10
11721	Miller J	21	C	Nov 1
2257	Miller J M, S't	31	I	June 21
9795	Miller M	82	A	Sept 27
4515	Miller Mac	Cav 16	C	Aug 18
3 55	Mills N	11	K	July 25
10721	Mills S	Cav 14	F	Oct 14
7989	Mind D	8	D	Sept 6
381	Mitchan A	92	E	April 5
11617	Mitchell J R	89	G	Oct 27
9753	Mix C	22	C	Sept 25
4180	Mixwell L B	38	F	Aug 4
4526	Monecal J	21	G	Aug 2
2646	Morehead J	9	E	June 29
2539	Morley H	Cav 16	M	June 26
9187	Moran F	89	C	Sept 18
7428	Moran W	11	C	Aug 31
10845	Morbley B	48	H	Oct 11
6402	Mounty R	6	B	Aug 21
3263	Morris B	Cav 8	F	July 13
816	Morris J	15	H	April 30
1320	Morris James	66	K	May 23
12757	Nossman S	42	G	Mch 12 65
2993	Mulford W R, S't	23		July 7 64
2834	Mulkey D	89	D	July 3
11900	Munz P	14	I	Nov 7
50	Myers Charles	Cav 16	B	Mch 16
3080	Myers C H, Cor	24	F	July 9
5038	Myers F	Cav 16	L	Aug 8
1407	Myers P	24	F	May 27
438	Nashen Ed	65	A	April 8
283	Neal Joseph	16	K	April 1
7430	Needham L H, S't	42	K	Sept 1
9531	Nelson J, Cor	3	K	Sept 22
8166	Newberry H	22	F	Sept 8
299	Newberg Wm	Art 2	M	April 1
5778	Newby E	123	A	Aug 15
8129	Newian H	25	B	Sept 8
4894	Nicely F	82	A	Aug 6
6945	Nicholas L C	14	F	Aug 26
7847	Nicholsan R H	123	B	Sept 4
7085	Nugent T	108	E	Aug 28
12460	Nully C	120	A	Jan 15 65
6519	Obevre O B, Cor	112	C	Aug 22 64
10851	O'Brian D	89	C	Oct 13
11274	Ochley Wm	24	K	Oct 20
3847	O'Connor M	2	F	July 24
1921	O'Dean Thomas	78	F	June 14
1533	O'David J H	9	A	June 1
7751	O'Donnell	34	I	Sept 3
3109	Odom W	7	G	July 19
1502	Oglesby D	Cav 16	M	May 31
1214	O'Keefe M	Art 2	G	May 19
7856	Olderfield J R	Cav 6	B	Sept 5
9196	Oley O S, Cor	21	I	Sept 18
10042	Oleny A	108	K	Sept 29
9885	Olson J	112	K	Sept 27
6098	Olson J	89	D	Aug 18
30	O'Neil D	Cav 16	K	April 19
10469	Osborn J W	9	H	Oct 7
6774	Oss	89	D	Aug 25
4123	Ottway D	Cav 8	A	July 28
8414	Owens C	120		Sept 11
10279	O'Mine D J, Cor	Cav 9	E	Oct 3
5541	Pardon C	12	F	Aug 13
6095	Paine S	88	B	Aug 18
3408	Paisley F F	120	E	July 16
6301	Parshnil J M	114	A	Aug 20
12857	Parkhorst B	14	H	Dec 30
6308	Patridge W J, S't	30	F	Aug 30
12677	Patterson F J	14	F	Feb 19 65
393	Penny James	Cav 14	D	April 6 64
12707	Penny W	114	F	Feb 26 65
7700	Peeter H M	107	C	Sept 3 64
2621	Perkins A E	89	A	June 28
4853	Perry George	89	G	Aug 6
9343	Perry J	Cav 9	G	Sept 20
3953	Perry N	Cav 1	B	July 18
12,79	Peterson J B	112	I	Nov 27
188	Pettas Wm	65	I	June 6
5889	Pettijohn J	21	F	Aug 16
12594	Philbrook A, S't	Cav 17 F		Feb 5 65
440	Phillips W, Cor	Civ 16 L		April 6 64
4887	Pierce C, Cor	Cav 6	H	Aug 6
1505	Pierce W B	Cav 8	H	May 31
37 4	Place S	44	F	July 22
10050	Palmerly H	14	D	Sept 30
3 79	Porterlange Wm	24	K	July 24
1862	Pollard F	127	A	June 12
9 02	Post George	Cav 7	L	Sept 23
5784	Powell A	122	C	Aug 15
3058	Powell D	Cav 16	K	July 9
3422	Powers James	44	C	July 16
28	Preston C W	Cav 8	M	Mch 8
6007	Price J M	79	D	Aug 17
9350	Prickett F	30	E	Sept 17
12597	Pratt W	16	F	Feb 6 65
10893	Prime D	103	K	Oct 14 64
7972	Puck John	122	D	Sept 5
1143	Puhrer Fred	27	A	May 16
10412	Pyner T	89	D	Oct 6
10531	Quinn P	52	A	Oct 8
3139	Ralston John	79	I	July 8
1011	Ramsay J C	24	B	May 10
1765	Ramsay A B	45	K	June 9
12763	Ramsey T	79	A	Mch 12 65
10772	Randall C F	124	I	Oct 12 64
8578	Rankin W A, Cor	Cav 1	I	Sept 12
12680	Ransom J	Cav 4	B	Feb 19 65

LIST OF THE DEAD.

No.	Name	Reg.	Co.	Date
7604	Reany J H, S't	Cav 6	B	Sept 2 64
5968	Redmont John	112	H	Aug 17
8571	Reed A	98	I	Sept 12
3496	Reed D	26	H	July 18
12334	Richardson T	21	E	Dec 23
1616	Richards H	79	I	June 4
3809	Rickold W	16	G	July 23
2836	Rictor Charles	Cor 82	H	July 3
8032	Ripley J	9	B	Sept 13
7748	Riller D	Art 14	D	Sept 3
2074	Roberts W W	Cav 16	I	June 17
8410	Robinson E H	35	A	Sept 11
4400	Robinson H B, S't	Cav 6	B	Aug 1
6080	Robinson J B	79	A	Aug 18
10751	Roder F	Cav 16	G	Oct 12
2595	Rodenberger N	96	E	June 29
10184	Roferty J O	Cav 6	H	Oct 1
747	Rodgers O	12	A	April 25
1807	Rogers Silas	65	D	June 10
7228	Rogers Geo	Cav 16	G	June 29
528	Rolla E J	103	G	April 13
4389	Rosecrans H	113	A	July 31
11473	Poss J W	45	F	Oct 26
8495	Ross Thomas	113	K	Sept 11
305	Rudd Eras, S't	100	K	April 2
1294	Rudd F	Cav 16	L	May 23
2557	Ryan M	89	A	June 27
2000	Saddle M	27	G	June 15
9343	Saler J B, S't	14	F	Sept 20
10512	Sandler L Cor	19	D	Oct 8 65
11289	Sargeant M, S't	14	K	Oct 22 64
1902	Savage P P	13		June 13
9915	Sanin B	35	C	Sept 28
7558	Schrider D	23	A	Sept 2
7103	Schrider John	44	K	Aug 29
3493	Schaunoller C	24	H	July 17
10359	Schurtz	14	F	Oct 5
1573	Scituz Victor	Cav 16	L	June 3
11077	Scott H	28	G	Oct 17
4524	Scuyner N, Cor	64	G	Aug 2
12034	See S	11	G	Oct 15
1787	Seeley Charles	44	G	June 10
9325	Sern C	Cav 8	D	Sept 20
4872	Serens R B	112	I	Aug 6
1333	Setters Geo H	38	G	May 24
1287	Seward R	61	E	April 8 65
5350	Sebert A J	39	E	Aug 11 64
9322	Shadrach G H	Cav 7	C	Sept 20
16 1	Shaubick Ed	44	E	June 6
8861	Shark L F	113	D	Sept 15
12149	Sharp A	Cav 7	B	Nov 24
2579	Sharp A H	22	A	June 27
1899	Sharp E D T	89		June 13
2647	Shaw J	89	E	June 29
7325	Shaw Joseph	98	D	Aug 30
4135	Sheeby John, S't	12	G	July 28
8346	Sherwood J F	Cav 16	I	Sept 10
7270	Shields J A	"	6	E	Aug 30
12046	Siebert H C	"	7	M	Nov 16
10441	Siffle H	"	7	M	Oct 7
2430	Silkwood H M	89	D	June 24
1717	Silter John	Cav 16	I	June 9
12713	Simmons W D	42	H	Mar 1 65
7630	Simpson C	14	D	Sept 2 64
12334	Simmons M A	42	H	Apr 17 65
309	Sipple A	107	E	Apr 2 64
12890	Skinner H	14	C	Jan 4 65
10082	Skinner Wm	16	G	Sept 30 64
2585	Slasher H, Cor	96	E	June 28
10663	Slick P	9	E	Oct 11
9402	Smith C W	16	K	Sept 24
5860	Smith George	53	E	Aug 17
362	Smith Jno B	Cav 7	L	Apr 2
12566	Smith J S	115	D	Feb 1 65
10896	Smith N P	28	G	Oct 13 64
10975	Smith O	114	H	Oct 15
4659	Smith Wm	Cav 16	M	Aug 3
8223	Snyder B	"	6	B	Sept 8
8079	Sommers W	40	F	Sept 7
2165	Soms	82	A	June 19
4283	Spangler H J	Cav 16	L	July 30
9002	Spindler W	113	F	Sept 18
11359	Spurlock A	79	E	Oct 23
4598	Sprague W	Cav 8	K	Aug 3
1667	Springer M	112	E	Jan 6
12132	Steilhoult A	92	H	Nov 23
2532	Standsfield H	96	H	June 26
1718	Stark F	78	H	June 8
1018	Stegall J	Cav 16	L	May 11
10737	Stevens S	44	D	Oct 11
6292	Stewart F	78	I	Aug 20
4878	Stillwell F H	79	L	Aug 6
1640	Stillwell James	38	I	June 5
10824	Stine A	14	H	Oct 13
4724	Stopes S W	89	E	Aug 4
8451	Storem A	89	D	Sept 11
12190	Storem C	98	C	Nov 28
10440	Strand John	9	H	Oct 6
8549	Striker J	11	K	Sept 12
12822	Stringer P	15	B	Apr 5 65
9013	Strong S M	95	B	Sept 17 64
855	Stune S L	40	G	May 3
8615	Sullivan J	Cav 16	I	Sept 13
12482	Sullivan M	15	E	Jan 17 65
9525	Sunn C	Cav 8	D	Sept 20 64
11808	Suter B F	"	4	L	Nov 4
5515	Sutton M	"	9	M	Aug 13
4442	Swanson P	9	K	July 31
12725	Steinhaus J	15	B	Mar 3 65
6292	Stewart F	78	I	Aug 30 64
12557	Swarts E, Cor	24	G	Jan 30 65
6105	Swartz A	Cav 7	M	Aug 18 64
505	Sweet Wm	89	E	Apr 12
10515	Tanner A		A	Oct 8
502	Taylor Geo	Cav 16	M	Apr 12
10036	Taylor H, Cor	"	7	I	Sept 29
809	Taylor James	"	4	F	Apr 30
12526	Taylor M P	14	I	Jan 26 65
1825	Temple I	100	H	June 10 64
4466	Terry John	Cav 16	M	Aug 1
12137	Thayer D	64	E	Jan 12 65
2415	Thomas A	16	A	June 24 64
10411	Thompson D	24	K	Oct 6
6491	Thompson F	10	B	Aug 22
7128	Thompson G G	Cav 1	M	Aug 28 63
2453	Thompson John	" 16	I	June 25 64
6831	Thompson T	2	M	Aug 25
10347	Thornsburg N C	79	A	Oct 5
8863	Thorn J	Cav 16	K	Sept 15
9833	Thurmain J	84	E	Sept 27
46	Tuiler W	Cav 16	D	Mar 15
3064	Topp A	19	C	July 9
547	Trailer Van B	Cav 16	I	Apr 14
11550	Trask J J	"	7	B	Oct 27

201

LIST OF THE DEAD.

No.	Name	Co.	Regt.	Date
751	Trowbridge L	"	16	M Apr 26 64
1915	Trout E		21	F June 14
2502	Turnerholm S H		19	K June 26
3032	Tucker E		38	B July 8
12736	Tucker J		7	F Mar 6 65
10582	Tucker J P	Cav	8	G Oct 13 64
10088	Turner S		120	A Oct 16
11091	Underwood D		11	E Oct 18
5183	Vase	Cav	16	H Aug 9
1078	Vaugh James	"	16	L May 14
7765	Vincent L D	"	7	G Sept 4
1026	Voris Ross	"	16	I May 11
3271	Volter George		9	C July 13
2015	Yought Wm		24	H July 15
5638	Vox Wm		24	E Aug 14
6767	Waddle J, S't		112	C Aug 24
2964	Wahl M	Cav	16	I July 6
9218	Walker George		31	K Sept 19
12072	Ward R S		15	C Nov 18
11345	Ward G B	Cav	7	E Nov 23
2488	Ward W J	"	16	M June 26
12392	Wareck N		120	D Jan 4 65
7895	Warkwich J		93	C Sept 5 64
5898	Watts Wm	Cav	16	L Aug 16
11619	Waterman L		95	D Nov 28
6173	Weaver G	Cav	16	L Aug 19
9317	Weaver Alex		93	A Sept 20
742	Weeks Benj	Cav	16	L Apr 26
10785	Weedman J W, Cor		38	I Oct 12
4911	Weinmiller J, S't		56	G Aug 7
10001	Welch John		7	E Sept 29
11751	Welch L		24	F Nov 2
10085	Welch G, S't		95	A Sept 30
4358	Wentworth Chas		27	D July 31
7426	Westbrook B D	Cav	6	B Aug 31
3067	Whalin M		23	B July 9
3910	Wham T		21	G July 24
9184	Wheeler J		61	F Sept 18
92	Wheelock A		96	H May 10
1496	Whitmore B	Cav	16	D May 31
1699	Whitmore L		104	I June 7
5998	Whitney J F		89	G Aug 17
8713	Whipp Chas	Cav	9	E Sept 14
5613	Wildberger P	"	6	B Aug 14
5158	Wiley T		7	M May 15
12732	Wiley W P		32	C Mar 5 65
12671	Wilkes R		81	A Feb 18
7840	Wilhelm G A		9	C Sept 4 64
90	Will Gustavus	Cav	16	E Mar 21
9785	Will J		36	B Sept 26
8310	Williams A		22	H Sept 10
3254	Williams E		49	D July 13
10899	Williams G W	Bat	15	Oct 14
11497	Williams G B		15	B Oct 26
12760	Willis A P		84	A Mar 15 65
4737	Wilson A	Cav	16	M Aug 4 64
9531	Wilson J, Cor			K Sept 22
11712	Wilson W, S't		89	F Nov 15
1130	Wimmer G	Cav	16	I May 15
989	Wink Lewis	"	16	C May 10
8755	Winning D		125	C Sept 14
6079	Winters Wm		24	H Aug 18
3743	Wismer J, Cor		74	G July 21
2301	Wing John	Cav	7	H June 22
8815	Wood		21	G Sept 15
1042	Woodcock R	Cav	16	L May 12
3695	Workman James		7	G July 21
10582	Worthy A A		21	K Oct 10 64
2664	Wright J W		35	C June 28
5265	Wright M		59	E Aug 10
12309	Yates J		120	E Dec 19
10766	Yagle C		24	B Oct 12
2391	Zimmerman P	Art	1	June 24
72	Zoran Philip		44	I Mar 20

TOTAL 850.

INDIANA.

571	Allen Jesse, Cor		116	K Apr 15 64
1917	Adkins Geo	Cav	6	D June 14
3991	Andrews E L	"	6	K July 26
4270	Anderson D		76	E July 29
5680	Ault J W		40	D Aug 14
6921	Alexander S		93	D Aug 26
7124	Alexander J D	Cav	5	K Aug 28
9292	Auburn C		65	H Sept 19
9445	Atkins J F	Cav	2	H Sept 21
9584	Adams H		35	A Sept 23
9648	Allen D B, S't		29	Sept 24
9759	Alfred W J		117	K Sept 25
10473	Allyn D		88	K Oct 7
10793	Atland C		32	C Oct 12
11186	Albin I		89	D Oct 19
12183	Austin Alfred		5	K Nov 27
12513	Amick W		93	B Jan 23 65
313	Bash David		117	C Apr 2 64
576	Bee Thomas		Cav	Apr 16
596	Bock Samuel		75	I Apr 17
838	Brown T		66	D May 1
1514	Barry Henry		84	D May 31
1603	Boley A J		66	C June 4
1759	Barra John		65	H June 9
2016	Burnett Wm	Cav	6	G June 15
2191	Buckhart E		27	F June 19
2222	Brasier S, Mus		19	I June 20
2299	Bumgardner		44	D June 22
2458	Barrett E		42	I June 25
2874	Bowman John		42	C July 4
3044	Bruce J W	Cav	5	M July 8
3359	Broughton D		7	K July 15
3366	Bricker J		68	C July 15
4027	Barton J F		52	G July 26
4085	Ballinger Robert		39	I July 26
4251	Bonly James		81	C July 29
4479	Baker J		9	G Aug 1
4563	Baker D W		13	B Aug 2
4948	Bayer F		129	H Aug 7
5089	Brenton J W		29	I Aug 8
5093	Bowlin Wm		53	G Aug 8
5220	Barton E	Cav	2	G Aug 10
2275	Busick W A, Cor		101	F Aug 10
5442	Bryer P		81	K Aug 12
5590	Bohems Philip		79	A Aug 14
5690	Baker J P	Cav	7	H Aug 15
5794	Boom W P		31	F Aug 15
5981	Barton George		130	F Aug 17
6163	Brookers J M		112	E Aug 19
6410	Brown J M		66	F Aug 22
6518	Bartholomew I		99	A Aug 22
7370	Bamgroover J A		101	H Aug 31
7794	Barnes T M	Cav	5	C Sept 4
8314	Babbitt W H		29	I Sept 10
8397	Bassinger H		14	C Sept 10
8519	Boyd W F		125	F Sept 12
9008	Bortley S		88	I Sept 18

LIST OF THE DEAD.

No.	Name	Age	Co.	Date
9548	Bray T E	79	K	Sept 23 64
9708	Brown J, S't Cav	1	A	Sept 24
9777	Birch T A	58	L	Sept 26
9793	Bozell J F	40	B	Sept 26
9846	Bixter D	5	B	Sept 27
10350	Blackaber Wm H	42	I	Oct 5
10939	Benton L	30	H	Oct 14
11559	Bennett R N	72	D	Oct 27
11604	Bemis J M, S't	87	F	Oct 28
11919	Brown D	128	B	Nov 8
11930	Bailey George	72	A	Nov 8
12019	Bennet A	29	G	Nov 15
12128	Booth J	32	E	Nov 22
12294	Bennett C	6	H	Dec 15
12486	Barrey H	66	I	Jan 19 65
12504	Balstrum J	93	F	Jan 22
12596	Branson E	57	A	Feb 6
301	Charles James	6	G	Apr 1 64
625	Connell P Cav	6	M	Apr 19
634	Claycome S A, S't	66	G	Apr 20
1117	Cox Joseph, S't	2	B	May 15
1146	Carter Henry	2	C	May 16
1172	Curry J W	30	F	May 17
1463	Currier Wm	87	K	May 30
1523	Crest J D	31	F	May 31
2254	Carpenter O C, C.	29	D	June 21
2307	Cottrell M, S't Cav	6	G	June 22
2776	Cooley A	38	C	July 2
3043	Clark W	82	C	July 8
3922	Connolley D	9	I	July 25
4192	Cox S	66	E	July 28
4917	Clifford H C Cav	7	I	Aug 6
5262	Courtney J F	" 2	L	Aug 10
5654	Collar E	130	G	Aug 14
5660	Crews E M Cav	5	A	Aug 14
5901	Clark A	54	A	Aug 16
6208	Chrichfula S	93	A	Aug 19
6477	Croane J J	22	C	Aug 22
6646	Cornelius E	58	B	Aug 23
6926	Carnahan A W, S't	6	E	Aug 26
7383	Carpenter S	66	I	Aug 31
7726	Callings W	120	F	Sept 3
7737	Cramer A	30	H	Sept 3
7890	Cheny James Cav	7	I	Sept 5
8051	Crainton R	101	I	Sept 6
8108	Crazen J	53	G	Sept 7
8133	Crager J	13	C	Sept 8
8144	Cooper J	80	E	Sept 8
9294	Christman J E Cav	6	G	Sept 19
9535	Collins G	56	F	Sept 22
9980	Connett Daniel	130	F	Sept 28
10084	Conel J	13	D	Sept 30
10995	Callan M	35	B	Oct 13
11423	Cafer J H	87	K	Oct 24
11631	Cummings J W	93	F	Oct 28
12062	Clark M	101	B	Nov 17
12173	Cannon A	42	F	Nov 26
12213	Cregs Wm Cav	5	E	Dec 3
12415	Collins W A, S't	5	G	Jan 8 65
12559	Calvert G F Cav	8	I	Jan 30
4234	Curry W F	" 4	I	July 29 64
426	Dummond J H	65	F	Apr 7
508	Davis J M	66	I	Apr 12
964	Darker Wm	12	C	May 8
2205	Denny John	44	E	June 19
3157	Detrich C	29	K	July 11
3419	Dusan J	6	D	July 16
4021	Develin E	35	B	July 26 64
4029	Decer P	32	K	July 26
4124	Dill C P	42	F	July 27
5255	Davis K	13	D	Aug 10
5367	Dunben M	36	E	Aug 11
5420	Delup Z S	13	D	Aug 12
5681	Dallinger W C	38	E	Aug 14
6147	Denton Philip	81	D	Aug 19
6934	Downey S M	116	I	Aug 25
6944	Dowell W L	6	C	Aug 26
9638	Dunlap W	20	A	Sept 24
10010	Downs J R Cav	5	I	Sept 29
10435	Dane Andrew	36	I	Oct 6
10446	Dignon L	35	B	Oct 7
10916	Dawson L F	29	I	Oct 14
10954	Dial R	1	B	Oct 14
12087	Daffendall P H	58	D	Nov 18
12172	Davenport J Cav	6	I	Nov 24
12236	Delashment F, S't	14	B	Dec 6
12533	Duckworth J	85	F	Jan 27 65
12545	Dawley J	73	I	Jan 27
12580	Dawson J	124	D	Feb 3
9236	Diver O	19	F	Sept 19 64
916	Evans G H Cav	1	A	May 6
917	Edwards G H, Mus	6	G	May 7
1083	Ellis H C Cav	6	D	May 14
1279	Evans W	75	I	May 22
1346	Eskridge Oakley	29	D	May 24
1994	Edwards J W	38	G	June 15
2481	Esenthal F Cav	5	D	June 25
4075	Eaton W H	58	B	July 27
4953	Ecker J	39	I	Aug 17
5076	Evans J Cav	6	I	Aug 8
7917	Ells D	20	I	Sept 5
11320	Elston F	9	B	Oct 22
11429	Estelle E W, S't Cav	2	L	Oct 24
11712	Eldridge E	38		Nov 1
11774	Earl D, Cor Cav	2	B	Nov 3
12285	Emmons W	5	D	Dec 14
1482	Frecks F	35	D	May 30
1808	Fitter B	66	I	June 10
2143	Fike Tobias	30	D	June 18
3014	Fitzgerald I	30	D	July 7
3453	Fescher D	32	E	July 17
3637	Fuget W Cav	3	C	July 20
8379	Fields N	" 6	F	Sept 10
8547	Fenton I	72	D	Sept 12
8766	Forward S Cav	8	I	Sept 14
9847	Forshua W	25	H	Sept 27
10509	Farmingham W C	14	Cav K	Oct 8
11311	Fanier F Cav	6	I	Oct 22
11626	Fish C	" 2	H	Oct 26
12012	Falkerson J, S't	93	B	Nov 14
12144	Francis F, Mus	93		Nov 24 65
12320	Fross John, S't Cav	5	D	Dec 24 64
12728	Felnick H	10	F	Mar 4 65
98	Graham Wm	6	G	Mar 22 64
322	Gladman H	110	B	Apr 2
1048	Goodwin Wm Cav	2	M	May 12
1165	Grimes F O	66	I	May 17
1215	Garver John	29	F	May 19
1312	Gullsen Wm Cav	7	L	May 23
1594	Griffin William	" 6	I	June 3
2337	Gray D L	22	I	June 22
2386	Guthrie W B	80	C	June 24
2418	Gillard Wm	120	C	June 24
3573	Gibbons W T	128	I	July 19

LIST OF THE DEAD.

No.	Name		Age	Co.	Date
4179	Gould Wm		66	E	July 28 64
4273	Gilbert H A, S't	Cav 2		K	July 29
4847	Galliger Wm		7	B	July 31
4901	Gerard H		35	G	Aug 6
6189	Goodwin I		20	F	Aug 19
6398	Gordon W M		74	G	Aug 21
6493	Goodridge E, Cor	94		H	Aug 22
7298	Grass C		32	H	Aug 30
7321	Gray H F	Cav 2		H	Aug 30
7698	Gerber I		30	C	Sept 3
8546	Galliger P		58	C	Sept 12
8791	Gagham Wm		35	K	Sept 14
9112	Green S		72	E	Sept 18
9114	Gillan J		29	F	Sept 18
10782	Griswold Thomas		2	F	Oct 12
11409	Gordon J W		13	D	Oct 24
11581	Greenwood W		3	C	Oct 28
12216	Grant H G		5	G	Dec 3
12338	Garnet T		6	E	Jan 5 65
12483	Green Wm		39	E	Jan 19
680	Hollar John	Cav 5		I	Apr 19 64
879	Henick Wm		30	F	May 4
1953	Hall L S		117	C	June 14
2118	Hilliard J		116	D	June 17
2130	Hodges J		7	C	June 18
2379	Hustin James		74	B	June 23
2392	Hodges S		9	F	June 24
2629	Humphrey I		3	C	June 28
2768	Hendricks J	Cav 2		C	July 2
2768	Higgins M P	"	3	C	July 2
2793	Hodges W J		5	F	July 2
2812	Hillman H		65	G	July 3
2974	Hamilton James		7	K	July 7
3289	Hine S		68	A	July 14
3507	Hodgen J W		89	G	July 18
4487	Hanger L S		65	A	July 1
5362	Hart J R		88	H	Aug 11
5678	Hittle B	Cav 6		L	Aug 14
5995	Helville N C		29	F	Aug 15
5872	Heah Jacob		20	G	Aug 16
6076	Hearne John	Cav 5		F	Aug 18
6198	Hershton A		4	M	Aug 19
6491	Hendricks I		129	H	Aug 22
7031	Hartsock I		30	A	Aug 27
7790	Hunter J M		42	F	Sept 4
7837	Hammond G W, S't	65		D	Sept 4
7903	Halfree J A		32	A	Sept 5
7971	Hamilton P S		7	E	Sept 6
8031	Hughes W H, Cor	81		D	Sept 7
8347	Hart A		7	A	Sept 10
8511	Haff M	Bat 4			Sept 12
8581	Hunter H		42	F	Sept 13
8778	Haynes W		30	G	Sept 14
8836	Higgins J W	Cav 3		C	Sept 15
8897	Holloway J	"	5	M	Sept 16
9063	Hubbner F	"	4	E	Sept 18
9329	Hurst R V, Cor		36	B	Sept 20
9420	Higgins W E		53	H	Sept 21
9511	Haughton J		2	D	Sept 28
9533	Harrington O		30	I	Sept 28
10123	Hoffman J		80	C	Oct 1
10233	Hunstler W H, S't	38		E	Oct 4
10522	Hoagler N C		39	E	Oct 8
10513	Harris W C		13	D	Oct 10
10820	Hector E		13	D	Oct 12
11231	Haskins H		99	A	Oct 20
11243	Hasile J, Mus		1	F	Oct 21
11790	Hill R		14	D	Nov 4 64
12249	Hamilton D		13	B	Dec 9
12536	Hall H H		2	E	Jan 27 65
6444	Ihn C		129	B	Aug 22 64
8963	Igo T, Cor		4	E	Sept 16
670	Johnson Isaac		5	C	Apr 22
1931	Jennings C, Cor	Cav 6		I	June 14
2212	Jackson John		22	C	June 20
2353	Jones Wm M		63	D	June 23
3311	Jasper Wm		38	I	July 10
5245	Judd Henry, S't		2	D	Aug 10
6172	Julerso H	Cav 2		D	Aug 19
6811	Jones H C		5	C	Aug 20
7100	Jones A		88	I	Aug 28
9948	Johnson J	Cav 7		A	Sept 28
12517	Jones J		120	C	Jan 24 65
12799	Johnson H		40	C	Mar 19
417	Kistner George		42	B	Apr 7 64
618	Kinnan A		56	G	Apr 18
858	Ketchum G W, S't	Cav 5		I	May 3
2036	Kelly John, S't	Cav 5			June 15
2407	Kennedy Amos		2	H	June 24
1908	Keiso E O	Cav 3		C	June 13
2527	Kauga J		74	E	June 26
3017	Kennedy J W, Cor	3		I	July 8
4024	Keys Wm		72	E	July 26
5149	Keiler W J, S't	Cav 4		H	Aug 9
5253	Kocher T		29	I	Aug 10
5722	Kern W		25	H	Aug 15
6596	Kelly John		32	C	Aug 23
7085	Kames J		128	F	Aug 28
8621	King D		81	A	Sept 13
10689	Keller I		49	B	Oct 11
12278	Kuling I		79	A	Dec 12
12587	Keef P, Cor	Cav 10		C	Feb 4 65
1041	Lewis J		6	H	May 12 64
1239	Lawrence R J		30	G	May 20
1261	Lower N G		116	I	May 21
2615	Lewis James		65	F	June 28
2745	Luff C		58	F	July 1
3029	Lewis J	Cav 3		C	July 7
3767	Lannon J S		128	F	July 22
3890	Lawrence D		80	A	July 24
4548	Lyons Wm		35	A	Aug 2
5014	Lee John	Cav 3		C	Aug 8
5585	Lawson William		75	A	Aug 14
5616	Lawyer James		80	B	Aug 14
6775	Lyons Wm		1	E	Aug 25
7162	Lowery D	Cav 2		G	Aug 29
8607	Lunger A	"	7	M	Sept 12
9256	Liggett		52	G	Sept 10
10508	Lewis R	Cav 7		C	Oct 8
11152	Lash J		101	B	Oct 18
11715	Lakin A	Cav 7			Nov 1
12250	Lawrence B T		42	D	Dec 9
130	McCarty John		66	D	Mar 23
631	Mullen James	Cav 6		G	Apr 19
746	Masters Wm		65	G	Apr 26
841	Milton John		18	C	May 1
903	Mytinger Wm		117	F	May 5
954	Milburn J		6	K	May 8
1090	Moore Peter		6	I	May 14
1405	Miller Jacob		74	E	May 27
1516	Martin Geo, S't	Cav 3		C	May 31
1860	Merritt H		30	G	June 12
2240	Mitchell J J		30	D	June 20
2307	Milliken S L	Cav 1		G	June 24

LIST OF THE DEAD. 205

No.	Name	Co.	Date
2511	Moneyhon B	38 D	June 26 64
2608	Marsh J	88 D	June 28
5	Moodie Z	119 K	Mar 31
3387	Mank E	80 E	July 16
3633	Marlit J	80 H	July 20
3884	Mulchy J	35 A	July 24
4010	Mercer John	12 F	July 26
4388	Malsby F Cav	14 A	July 31
4959	McDall R	19 A	Aug 7
5562	Manihan J	38 D	Aug 13
5618	Mageson J Cav	7 A	Aug 14
5703	Mensome S, S't	42 E	Aug 15
5713	Monroe S	33 F	Aug 15
5767	Montgomery R	80 F	Aug 15
5863	Michael S	7 I	Aug 16
6461	Mitchell J H	30 I	Aug 22
6521	Monroe H J, S't	44 G	Aug 22
6566	Mathews M	42 K	Aug 23
7043	Milsker J	5 D	Aug 27
7253	Matheny N, S't	42 A	Aug 29
7272	McQueston J O	13 B	Aug 30
7510	Myers A	29 E	Sept 1
7820	Moore G, Cor	101 F	Sept 4
7973	Mine John N	2 H	Sept 6
8007	Miller W W	101 B	Sept 6
8176	McCoy W, S't	66 B	Sept 8
8389	Murphy J	9 E	Sept 10
8851	McElvain J	93 E	Sept 15
8925	Myers J	143 D	Sept 16
9575	Mortison J	4 B	Sept 23
9600	Miller J Cav	7 G	Sept 23
9856	Murgu A	35 D	Sept 27
10231	Monay G W	7 E	Oct 2
10245	McFarney J	93 B	Oct 3
10304	Maples H	29 H	Oct 6
10891	Murphy F	35 B	Oct 13
10995	McDonald I	74 B	Oct 16
11166	Mills Milton	56 D	Oct 18
11271	Mitchell I	7 K	Oct 21
11585	McCarty A	7 A	Oct 28
11665	McBeth I C	28 K	Oct 30
11680	Murphy F	35 C	Oct 31
11746	McCarty A	7 A	Nov 2
11857	McCarty I	6 A	Nov 6
11946	Miller F B	30 C	Nov 10
12548	Madlener L	12 K	Jan 27 65
12563	McFall I	30 A	Jan 31
12024	Manifold W Cav	6 I	Feb 9
12639	Montgomery W "	5 G	Feb 17
12709	Maloy I "	11 G	Feb 28
2007	Nossman G	117 G	June 15 64
3205	Newcomb George	22 A	July 12
3519	Nucha S Cav	3 I	July 18
4627	Napper W H, S't	6 I	Aug 3
6528	Norton N A	38 B	Aug 23
10187	Note John H	39 F	Oct 1
12226	Nichols J	38 G	Dec 5
9194	Newberry M Cav	7 L	Sept 21
342	Oniel Thomas	6 G	Apr 2
1874	Oliver John, Cor	42	June 12
2778	Oliver H H Cav	5 M	July 2
5226	Oliver J	120 K	Aug 10
5361	Osborn J	73 E	Aug 11
7863	Oliver J	19 D	Sept 5
7911	O'Conner Thos Cav	5 B	Sept 5
10940	Olinger E	65 A	Oct 14
12541	Ortell M	35 G	Jan 27
12590	Ousley W J	7 A	Feb 5 65
287	Leache Cyrus	66 D	Apr 1 64
559	Pashby John Cav	6 C	Apr 15
3434	Pavy W	123 A	July 17
3728	Palmer A	42 F	July 21
4068	Parker E, S't	29 A	July 27
4171	Park John	129 B	July 28
4551	Pettis H	53 C	Aug 2
4553	Pruitt H C Cav	7 K	Aug 2
5627	Prentice J M	22 K	Aug 14
6159	Penat Alexander	38 B	Aug 19
6278	Patterson E Cav	4 C	Aug 20
6874	Parten D R	65 F	Aug 26
7710	Plough J W, S't	89 D	Sept 3
8061	Palmer A	29 F	Sept 13
9196	Plumer A	2 D	Sept 18
9705	Pope I T, S't Cav	5 G	Sept 24
9709	Patterson N S	93 G	Sept 24
10128	Packett T C, S't	39 F	Oct 1
11880	Pangburn, S't	20 B	Nov 6
12572	Potts I	99 H	Feb 2 65
12588	Phepps A	30 D	Feb 4
1249	Packer Saml B Cav	6 G	May 20 64
872	Remy John	66 B	May 4
944	Reed R	57 F	May 7
1005	Remcett L	65 H	May 13
1558	Roll N C	117 F	June 2
1696	Reese L	116 I	June 7
2140	Robinson L	7 I	June 18
4039	Rogman	38 I	July 26
4165	Reiggs K N	39 K	July 28
4406	Richardson I	35 I	July 31
5180	Rawlings J W	117 F	Aug 9
5259	Rains G D	4 G	Aug 10
5454	Ritter Benjamin	29 K	Aug 12
5542	Ralph G	68 F	Aug 13
6247	Roundbush Daniel	6 B	Aug 20
6383	Redyard A	65 F	Aug 21
6754	Russell J	7 K	Aug 24
7677	Ringold I Cav	7 I	Sept 3
8488	Russmore E Cav	2 C	Sept 11
8577	Redman N E	80 F	Sept 12
9521	Richardson John	86 D	Sept 21
9547	Riggs L	19 E	Aug 23
10829	Reeves Wm	42 F	Oct 13
11416	Rierdon M D Bat	5	Oct 24
11451	Rutger W, Cor	44 D	Oct 25
11935	Russell W H	13 C	Nov 9
12454	Robinson R	8 G	Jan 14 65
12523	Richardson E	127 E	Jan 26
1440	Ryan Martin	35 B	May 28 64
6707	Rawlings E, S't	66 C	Aug 24
86	Smiley	65 I	Mar 21
129	Stein Thomas	66 D	Mar 23
205	Stonts ———	65 I	Mar 28
768	Sanderson H Cav	6 G	Apr 27
817	Sears I	65 I	Apr 30
901	Shick Eli	20 C	May 5
1039	Smith M C, Cor Bat	24	May 12
1331	Smith H	86 A	May 24
1400	Sapp A J	44 H	May 26
1430	Swindle T O, S't	82 A	May 28
1501	Smith L	116 A	May 31
1611	Schroder W	42 A	June 4
1690	Sparks L D	66 D	June 7
1732	Search C Cav	5 D	June 8
2079	Shigley T W	10 H	June 17

LIST OF THE DEAD.

No.	Name	Reg.	Co.	Date
2083	Stinit D	Cav 6	L	June 17 64
2218	Smudley W	5	E	June 20
2318	Swain J W	30	A	June 22
2420	Snow J	Cav 5	G	June 24
2447	Stafford J W	68	I	May 25
2740	Smith J	65	H	July 1
2799	Stanchley Wm	5	K	July 2
2823	Stofer L, S't	29	B	July 5
3416	Spencer M	80	K	July 16
4014	Shields J	128	F	July 26
4054	Smith J W	38	G	July 27
4062	Smith H	79	H	July 27
4088	Schneider S A	Cav 3		July 27
4229	Sollman C, S't	35	D	July 29
4418	Stevens M	Cav 6	M	July 31
4630	Snider D	117	K	Aug 3
4799	Summersvolt V	29	A	Aug 5
5254	Scott B	9	D	Aug 10
5418	Smith Samuel E	9	C	Aug 12
5513	Shoemaker E W	Cav 5	I	Aug 13
5514	Sims S	101	B	Aug 13
5571	Sackett J	Cav 6	G	Aug 14
5611	Stockman L M	68	E	Aug 14
5884	Standish M	66	B	Aug 16
5977	Stockhoff G	19	I	Aug 17
6044	Stout H	7	G	Aug 18
6736	Sipe J	82	A	Aug 24
6830	Strong L	9	F	Aug 25
7120	Spellman J	80	F	Aug 28
7264	Shaver F	129	I	Aug 30
7683	Snyder L	Cav 6	A	Sept 3
7822	Sanders D	7	I	Sept 4
8058	Suthien J H	66	E	Sept 7
8107	Starkey I	Cav 6	I	Sept 7
8262	Sizeman I	123	B	Sept 9
8313	Stagewald J M, S't	22	K	Sept 10
8823	Swillenger R	21	I	Sept 13
8666	Sylvanus J J	35	G	Sept 13
8727	Shoel J P	30	B	Sept 14
8910	Storm L M, S't	6	A	Sept 16
9093	Simmons J	84	I	Sept 18
9252	Sharp D M	13	E	Sept 19
9546	Sharpless W	43	G	Sept 23
9623	Smith S B	17	F	Sept 24
9807	Skeels W	65	A	Sept 26
10790	Smith George	131	D	Oct 12
10949	Smith I	39	I	Oct 14
11006	Sloat G W, S't	44	B	Oct 16
11187	Seigfred G H	Cav 4	I	Oct 19
11427	Sweitzer J	2	G	Oct 24
11842	Shaw W R	99	B	Nov 5
11969	Shoe G W	74	E	Nov 12
11984	Steamer F	29	F	Nov 13
12113	Scarff F	Cav 6	D	Nov 21
12381	Starke M S	93	D	Jan 2 65
12492	Salts H C	Cav 4	F	Jan 20
12582	Smith D H	" 12	H	Feb 3
12615	Sides G	66	A	Feb 8
12666	Smure C	Cav 2	G	Feb 17
12724	Stewart E B	38	E	Mar 3
12809	Staley G W	72	A	Mar 24
2625	Sattershwait A	82	I	June 28 64
518	Tenher James	117	I	Apr 13
3778	Tunblora B	65	B	July 22
3791	Thompson T	Cav 6	C	July 22
4733	Tooley G W	42	H	Aug 4
5065	Truman L H, S't	Cav 6	G	Aug 8
5403	Taylor N	63	I	Aug 12 64
6509	Tooley W R, Cor	42	H	Aug 22
6719	Todd T	6	B	Aug 24
7096	Thomas H D	42	I	Aug 28
7442	Taylor Geo H	Cav 4	M	Sept 1
8495	Trumble D A	30	A	Sept 11
8525	Taylor E	25	I	Sept 12
10438	Thomas M	Cav 2		Oct 6
12337	Tucer B, Cit			Nov 26
12609	Terhune C	Cav 9	A	Feb 7 65
10219	Tasnahet Chas, S't	33	E	Oct 2 64
10356	Underwood P	Cav 7	C	Sept 5
10760	Upton F M	52	A	Oct 12
1717	Voit T	Cav 6	K	June 8
5363	Venome James	30	K	Aug 11
6250	Vanose J	93	B	Aug 20
7691	Verhouse D	42	A	Sept 3
135	Windinger J	117	G	Mar 24
886	Walters J H, Cor	Cav 6	G	May 5
934	Williams A	6	G	May 7
1194	Wright Saml	Cav 6	I	May 18
1776	White P	"	6	C	June 9
1812	Wise Eli	88	D	June 10
1918	Warren E	65	H	June 14
2107	Williams F	38	F	June 17
2242	West E	Cav 7	H	June 20
2363	Woodward W W	29	A	June 23
2417	Wilson J N	75	G	June 24
2467	Warden I	44	B	June 25
2554	Warren E	37	I	June 27
2670	Ward J	79	F	June 29
2900	Wyn W E	13	D	July 5
2929	Wislake I	116	I	July 5
2984	Wicks L	Cav 6	H	July 6
4528	Whitehead J	29	I	Aug 2
4639	Winship James	36	K	Aug 4
4826	Witt T	125	D	Aug 5
5399	Wade C	81	K	Aug 12
5547	Waynin J H	Cav 4	I	Aug 13
6132	Washburn R H	"	6	A	Aug 19
6405	Winders A	120	I	Aug 21
6524	Wagner M	Cav 5	I	Aug 25
7184	Winters F W	84	C	Aug 29
7191	Wagoner E	42	A	Aug 29
7349	Witzgall John	2	D	Aug 31
8943	Weiber Charles	13	F	Sept 16
9228	White W	7	E	Sept 19
9316	Watkins J	81	A	Sept 20
6418	Wellington H	129	I	Sept 21
9501	Wilson J B	6	E	Sept 21
9998	Wagner F	7	D	Sept 29
10648	Ward J	29	G	Oct 11
11141	Whitehead N B	Cav 5	L	Oct 18
11424	White R B	6	D	Oct 24
11602	Walters J	5	I	Oct 28
12708	Winebrook P	35	B	Nov 18
12316	Werper J	32	E	Dec 20
12341	White J	7	A	Dec 26
12402	Wells J M	13	D	Jan 16 65
12497	What J	93	B	Jan 21
12737	Wade W	Cav 10	M	Mar 6
3837	Weltz Ira, S't	4	B	July 23 64
6000	West S N, Cor	7	B	Aug 17
9920	Williams J A, S't	38	C	Sept 28
5055	Younce Chas A	Cav 7	I	Aug 8
5838	Yorker Daniel	28	B	Aug 16
1540	Zuet J	65	H	June 1

TOTAL 593.

LIST OF THE DEAD.

IOWA.

No.	Name	Co.	Reg.	Date
5590	Allen N	3	K	Aug 13 64
8974	Ankobus L. Cor	6	I	Sept 17
9472	Ashford A W	11	C	Sept 21
11784	Alderman W W	31	F	Nov 4
11896	Austin Wm	Cav 3	A	Nov 7
1293	Bartche C P	5	K	May 23
1570	Bingman W H	39	H	June 3
5276	Blanchard A	7	A	Aug 10
6104	Bunsford M	7	F	Aug 19
7779	Baird J J	26	H	Sept 4
8265	Buckmaster F	15	K	Sept 9
9301	Buell J	4	D	Sept 20
9456	Boylan C	14	G	Sept 21
9691	Boles M B		I	Sept 24
10749	Bellings J	5	B	Oct 12
11334	Blakeley Geo	3	G	Oct 23
167	Collins Henry, S't	4	G	Mar 26
328	Chenworth Wm	4	K	April 2
4582	Cromwell G W	27	F	Aug 2
5101	Cooper S	5	B	Aug 9
5244	Cox E E, Cor	5	G	Aug 9
5020	Cox W A	5	G	Aug 14
5999	Coder E	31	E	Aug 17
6378	Cox H	5	I	Aug 21
6604	Clamson Henry	26	I	Aug 23
6848	Collins M	3	L	Aug 25
8062	Culbertson S, Cor	5	H	Sept 7
8352	Crow B	4	E	Sept 10
9784	Coles J W, S't	8	K	Sept 26
9820	Cobb E	Cav 3	C	Sept 26
10037	Cramer J M	" 5	B	Sept 29
10901	Chapman J	3	G	Oct 14
12230	Chamberlain J B. C	8	A	Dec 6
2903	Davis S	3	E	June 30
4206	Davis J	15	D	July 29
9229	Davis H	17	A	Sept 19
4675	Dermott L	5	G	Aug 4
6849	Discol S	26	I	Aug 25
9852	Dingman W	31	D	Sept 27
11098	Denoya W H	5	M	Oct 18
11753	Dutlin S	Cav 6	C	Nov 2
12245	Durochis Wm	12	H	Dec 8
12057	Derickson WW, Cor. C	8	M	Feb 15 65
262	Ennis Wm	4	B	Mar 31 64
11414	England G	9	F	Oct 24
3705	Field Jacob	5	K	July 21
4503	Farnsworth S	2	H	Aug 1
1316	Forney James M	10	K	May 23
7715	Frue J	10		Sept 3
7378	Frederick J A	16	C	Sept 5
8380	Frussell G W	6	D	Sept 10
10048	Fordson Michael	16	H	Sept 29
11078	Feuer J W	Cav 3	B	Oct 17
12701	Ferguson A W	15	A	Feb 28 65
750	Gain L	6	C	April 26 64
1484	Gender Jacob,	5	I	May 30
5004	Gentle G	4	G	Aug 8
5836	Gunshaw C	26		Aug 16
10511	Gray J	11	C	Oct 7
10306	Gothard J	4	G	Oct 11
5461	Harris J	Cav 8	H	Aug 13
8106	Hastings J, S't	11	B	Sept 7
9379	Hird D, Cor	3	G	Sept 20
9417	Hudson M	16	B	Sept 21
2168	Huffman R J	5	H	June 19
862	Heeler A	5	D	May 3 64
1633	Harper D	7	K	June 5
1816	Hurlay J	8	H	June 11
12749	Hubanks C, S't	17	H	Mar 8 65
10860	Ireland J S	Cav 5	H	Oct 5 64
4461	Jones C	4	B	Aug 1
8656	Jenks G A, S't	8	C	Sept 13
9401	Jones J	5	C	Sept 21
3204	Kolenbrander H	17	K	July 12
7	King Alexander	17	H	April 5
6464	King E	Cav 2	C	Aug 22
3560	Kesler F	4	B	July 18
11281	Knight J H, S't	9	I	Oct 22
892	Lambert Chas, Cor	39	K	May 5
2045	Littleton J	5		May 15
7959	Lord L	13	G	Sept 6
8263	Lanning A	13	I	Sept 9
9438	Lowdenbeck N	5	B	Sept 21
10224	LowelenbuckD R	5	B	Oct 2
10881	Layers W	5	E	Oct 14
11752	Luther J. Cor	9	B	Nov 2
12629	Littlejohn L D	Cav 4	B	Feb 10 65
257	Moore John	39	H	Mch 31 64
807	Myers M	4	K	April 2
450	Moon James	39	H	April 9
1192	McMullen James	4	C	May 18
1317	Miller F	5	H	May 23
1472	McCameron W	4	A	May 30
2027	McAllister A P	14	E	June 15
3423	McNeil J W	11	I	July 16
4804	Moore Wm	13	A	Aug 5
5445	Murray J J	17	I	Aug 12
6167	McCall Thomas	Cav 8	M	Aug 19
6815	Merchant Wm	13	G	Aug 25
6878	Maynard J D	4	B	Aug 26
7143	McDonald D B, S't	C 5	M	Aug 29
8120	McClure Z, S't	16	C	Sept 8
9274	Martin S S	11	G	Sept 19
9585	Mann J	16		Sept 23
10110	Miller H	5	D	Oct 1
10827	McCoy G B, Cor	5	G	Oct 13
10950	Mercer John	4	C	Oct 14
11745	Miller E. Cor	31	D	Nov 2
12484	Martin J B	5	B	Jan 19 65
12561	Macy C S	Cav 8	C	Jan 31
6959	O'Connor P	26	D	Aug 27 64
9500	O'Verturf P W	5	H	Sept 22
12160	Osborn F L	16	A	Nov 26
1972	Peterson J	76	E	June 15
2860	Palmer L H	9	D	July 4
6200	Phillpot C|P	31	B	Aug 19
9370	Putnam O	27	F	Aug 20
10270	Pitts J	16	I	Oct 3
10297	Pugh A. Cor	8	M	Oct 3
10413	Parker D	4	I	Oct 6
18	Rule Y A	10	A	April 12
1796	Ryan Charles	5	G	June 10
1820	Richardson John	C 5	I	June 11
1951	Ratcliff J	4	I	June 14
5878	Reed R	16	I	Aug 16
6572	Robinson D	13	G	Aug 23
7400	Rice H M, Sut's C'k	9		Aug 31
9413	Riley N	5	A	Sept 21
9483	Reeves S J	9	D	Sept 21
10015	Reed C	2	C	Sept 29
10017	Rogers L	4	F	Sept 29
12264	Russel E	4	G	Dec 12

LIST OF THE DEAD.

No.	Name	Co.	Rank	Date
12287	Raiser A	8	C	Dec 14 64
451	Stout John	5	A	April 9
599	Shuffleton J	5	H	April 17
641	Seeley Norman	9	B	April 20
2712	Smith R F, Cor	10	H	July 1
2845	Shutter J	20	K	July 3
3000	Sparks M J	5	K	July 9
4178	Sutton S	5	H	July 28
4773	Smith Charles, Cor	20	F	Aug 4
5410	Starr C F	30	H	Aug 12
5892	Sheddle G	16	C	Aug 16
7954	Seims Wm	3	D	Sept 6
8200	Smith J	13	A	Sept 8
9209	Smith O	5	D	Sept 19
9125	Sherman J W	3	I	Sept 17
9234	Spears J	Cav 5	H	Sept 19
9357	Smith D	Cav 3	B	Sept 20
11789	Shaw W W	5	H	Nov 4
12729	Smice W	16	E	Mch 4 65
10884	Sayres W	5	E	Oct 14 64
1981	Taiping Wm	5	K	June 16
3986	Thopson M	5	G	July 25
6687	Tivis C	5	A	Aug 24
9720	Tomme B	Cav	M	Sept 25
11703	Thier A F	3		Nov 1
10351	Voke John C, Cor	5	E	Oct 5
1674	Whitman O R, Cor	5	E	June 6
2162	Wells F, S't	5	I	June 19
2213	Witteśrick A K	9	K	June 20
2855	Wolf B F	8	E	July 4
4916	Wolfe J H	2	C	Aug 6
6934	Wheelan J, S't	26	D	Aug 26
8101	Walworth C. S't	5	K	Sept 17
8131	Woolston S P, S't	13	H	Sept 8
9221	Ward O R	3	E	Sept 29
9486	Wagner Joseph	13	E	Sept 21
9727	Wersbrod Y	31	A	Sept 25
10848	Wilson P D	10	G	Oct 13
10942	Woodward J, Sut	9		Oct 14
11114	Whiting J	2	H	Oct 18
11141	Whitehead N B	Cav 5	L	Oct 19
12741	Wen C	57	C	Mch 6 65

TOTAL 174.

KANSAS.

No.	Name	Co.	Rank	Date
1614	Freeman F J, S't	8	F	June 4 64
1935	Gensarde Thos	8	A	June 14
12127	Sweeney M	1	H	Nov 22
11139	Weidman W	8	B	Oct 19
1663	Williams C A	8	A	June 6

TOTAL 5.

KENTUCKY.

No.	Name	Co.	Rank	Date
329	Allen Sam'l S, Cor	13	F	April 2 64
674	Alford George	Cav 11	B	April 22
1575	Anderson S	Cav 11	D	May 3
3385	Adams J D	Cav 1	I	July 16
3759	Ashley J M	Cav 1	L	July 22
4723	Allen Wm, Cor	Cav 11	C	Aug 4
4894	Atkins A	Cav 39	H	Aug 6
6093	Anghlin J A, Cor C	18	B	Aug 18
6720	Arnett H S	Cav 13	A	Aug 24
10514	Adamson Wm	15	K	Oct 8
11759	Adams J L	27	G	Nov 3
12426	Arthur D	4	G	Jan 9 65
12528	Ayers E	52	A	Jan 26
12703	Ayers S	52	A	Jan 26
12593	Arnett T	Cav 4	F	Jan 5
193	Bow James	"	1	Mch 27 64
261	Burrows Wm	"	1	K	Mch 31
336	Eyesly Wm	"	11	E	April 2
379	Baker Isaac	"	1	H	April 5
413	Basham S	"	12	E	April 7
419	Button Ed	"	11	D	April 18
608	Burret B	"	6	D	April 18
600	Bloomer H	"	4	G	April 18
803	Baker A W	"	3	C	April 29
832	Boley Peter	"	12	L	May 1
891	Bird W T	Cav 11	H	May 5
957	Bailey A W	"	14	G	May 7
1167	Burton Tillman	Cav 1	F	May 17
1200	Butner L B, S't	"	6	I	May 18
1263	Bell P B	"	11	I	May 21
1352	Barnett James	"	8	H	May 25
1506	Baird Sam'l J	"	12	D	June 2
1780	Bishop D L	"	11	A	June 10
2022	Bowman G	"	11	D	June 15
2423	Bray H N, Cor	"	9	H	June 24
2520	Buchanan S	"	12	F	Jun 26
2760	Ball David	"	11	B	July 2
3087	Beard J C	"	1	C	July 9
3228	Brophy M	"	5	I	July 12
3433	Bailey F M	"	4	G	July 17
3309	Banner J	"	11	C	July 24
3398	Bridell S, Cor	"	3	F	July 26
4562	Booth Z, S't	"	16	E	Aug 2
4653	Barger George	"	5	I	Aug 3
4835	Baker Wm	"	3	I	Aug 6
4971	Bigler A	"	6	B	Aug 7
5471	Bailey J H	"	11	A	Aug 12
5644	Braman H	"	1	G	Aug 14
6556	Boston J	"	27	E	Aug 23
6737	Bottoms J M	"	11	H	Aug 24
9551	Linton W J, S't	"	11	C	Aug 23
9568	Barnett A	"	12	K	Sept 23
9628	Brown J	"	10	I	Sept 24
9740	Boyd M	"	13	A	Sept 25
10147	Batt W	5	G	Oct 1
10202	Byron H M, S't	C 1	I	Oct 2
10451	Bill B S	Cav 1	K	Oct 7
10816	Bodkins P, Cor	"	1	K	Oct 12
10859	Bagley T	"	11		Oct 13
11052	Brickey W L	4	F	Oct 17
12256	Baldwin J W	11	H	Oct 21
11303	Brown E W	4	F	Oct 22
11491	Barber T	Cav 4	H	Oct 26
12066	Brannon J	3	B	Nov 13
12304	Beatty R	5	B	Dec 18
12333	Barnes J	11	D	Dec 25
12360	Brodus O	Cav 11	A	Dec 30
12421	Britton J	45	F	Jan 9 65
5048	Bowman Henry	C 11	F	Aug 9 64
12777	Balson L	12	B	Mch 15
11483	Cranch J P	10	D	Oct 26
240	Conler Wm	14	I	Mch 30
484	Caldwell Wm	Cav 12	I	April 9
500	Cook Theo J	"	12	D	April 12
672	Colvin George	"	11	D	April 22
877	Christmas J	"	11	F	May 4
906	Collague M	"	12	E	May 8
1268	Cash Phillip	"	1	I	May 21
1600	Cole W C	"	1	C	June 4
1676	Christenburg R I	"	12	G	June 6

LIST OF THE DEAD.

No.	Name	Unit	Co.	Letter	Date	Yr
1087	Callihan Pat	Cav 11	A	June 6	64
1856	Clane H	" 11	E	June 12	
2152	Clinge W H	40	A	June 18	
2293	Cox A B	Cav 6	I	June 21	
2339	Chippendale C	" 1	B	June 22	
2446	Carlisle J	" 6	I	June 25	
2823	Cummings J	11	F	July 3	
2912	Cleming Thos	18	I	July 5	
3184	Carter W	Cav 11	H	July 11	
60	Cristian John	" 4	C	July 4	
4044	Clark A H	11	I	July 27	
4809	Chapman	11	H	Aug 5	
6387	Coulter M	23	B	Aug 21	
9835	Conrad R P	4	B	Sept 27	
11179	Clun W H	Cav 11	L	Oct 19	
11486	Chatsin W M	" 6	H	Oct 26	
12447	Carcanright	4	C	Jan 13	65
12700	Cook J P	4	G	Jan 26	
2223	Corbitt Thos	5	A	June 20	64
8113	Coyle C	Cav 11	I	Sept 7	
4740	Chance A J	" 1	C	Aug 5	
421	Dupon F	12	G	Apr 7	
1388	Delaney M	Cav 11	I	May 26	
1414	Dugean J R, S't	12	K	May 27	
1568	DeBarnes P M	11	C	June 2	
1027	Demody Thos	1	H	June 4	
1867	Drake J H	12	G	June 12	
2736	Davis B	5	C	July 1	
23	Duncan E	Cav 12	G	Apr 15	
3623	Dodson E	39	H	July 20	
27	Derine George	Cav 1	I	Apr 17	
3924	Davis G C	12	F	July 25	
3906	Derringer H	11	I	July 25	
4510	Dulrebeck H	11	E	Aug 1	
4556	Delaney H	Cav 4	H	Aug 2	
5088	Dounty P	5	F	Aug 8	
5899	Daniel R	9	F	Aug 16	
11405	Disque F, S't	Cav 6	G	Oct 24	
12280	Duland D W	3	K	Dec 13	
12623	Danmard W	4	D	Feb 9	65
12684	Dipple S	4	E	Feb 21	
1109	Dinsman H	Cav 4	E	May 15	64
2805	Davis J P	13	A	July 3	
2117	Davis C	Cav 6	D	June 30	
639	Eodus James	1	F	Apr 20	
1174	Edminston J W	11	A	May 17	
1439	Edwards H S, Cor	8	K	May 27	
2544	Emery J	10	G	June 27	
2341	Errbanks J	Cav 1	A	Aug 11	
12277	Esteff J	1	L	Oct 22	
1447	East R	1	G	May 29	
384	Falconburg I K	1	A	Apr 5	
2540	Fleming R	4	D	June 27	
3640	Forteen John	8	A	July 20	
4344	Fenkstine M	1	D	July 30	
6763	Featherstone J	6	C	Aug 25	
7068	Fritz J	Cav 4	G	Aug 28	
10280	Funk L	1	I	Oct 4	
11549	Frazier C R	23	H	Oct 27	
11720	Fletcher T	17	E	Nov 1	
1612	Gritton G	Cav 11	D	June 4	
1618	Graves G	18	C	June 4	
1841	Gritton M	Cav 11	B	June 11	
2583	Gibson John	6	L	June 27	
3680	Griffin B	11	E	July 20	
3663	Glassman P	Cav 4	B	July 20	
3888	Gonns J M	4	H	July 24	
4438	Gather M	Cav 4	F	July 31	64
5779	Gullett A	45	K	Aug 15	
7197	Green J B, S't	11	I	Aug 29	
7817	Grabul B	1	F	Sept 4	
8049	Gury J	4	H	Sept 6	
8003	Gray C D	20	G	Sept 18	
9318	Gett John, S't	40	G	Sept 20	
9950	Gill W J	Cav 11	H	Sept 28	
10053	Gower J C	13	A	Sept 30	
10650	Gibson A	Cav 8	K	Oct 10	
10831	Grulach J, S't	4	K	Oct 13	
11910	Grimstead J R	1	E	Nov 8	
12022	Griffin R	11	E	Nov 15	
1235	Gregory H	Cav 12	D	May 20	
81	Hauns J B	12	K	Mar 20	
237	Holloway Richard	4	I	Mar 29	
289	Harley Alfred	40	K	Apr 1	
292	Hood G	Cav 5	F	Apr 1	
348	Hammond J W	1	G	Apr 2	
376	Harper J	1	C	Apr 5	
402	Harlow Harvey	13	I	Apr 6	
614	Hess Wm F	Cav 12	M	Apr 18	
643	Hendree A, S't	11	F	Apr 20	
1026	Hillard Geo	11	D	May 11	
1127	Hoffman C	Cav 11	E	May 15	
1584	Hughes Thos, S't	9	G	June 3	
1790	Hennesey J	28	D	June 9	
1878	Hundley G W	Cav 4		June 12	
1956	Hazlewood J H	18	G	June 14	
1990	Hamner A	9	B	June 15	
2490	Huison J W, S't	9	B	June 26	
2705	Hillard S	Cav 1	I	June 30	
3239	Henderson J	18	B	July 12	
26	Hooper Saml	Cav 11	D	Apr 16	
3944	Hooper J	1	D	July 25	
3994	Hickworth J	45	D	July 26	
4313	Hall J H	Cav 1	C	July 30	
4420	Hammontius P	6	L	June 30	
4970	Hayner E	1	D	Aug 7	
5059	Haines J	12	D	Aug 8	
5091	Harrington C	15	K	Aug 8	
5793	Hatfield L	1	F	Aug 15	
6193	Hendrie Wm	Cav 11	F	Aug 19	
6801	Hardison G	23	I	Aug 25	
8032	Hise P	4	I	Sept 6	
8111	Hicks P	Cav 1	F	Sept 7	
8181	Heglen C	" 4	I	Sept 8	
9376	Hanker R	" 18	F	Sept 20	
9599	Hyrommus Jas	" 11	D	Sept 23	
10083	Halton S M	2	K	Oct 11	
11054	Halligan J	4	A	Oct 17	
11095	Hall F	Cav 1	F	Oct 18	
11132	Hazer John	11	I	Oct 18	
11251	Harter F	Cav 12	M	Oct 21	
12293	Hays J F	5	A	Dec 15	
12518	Hasting J	4	H	Jan 24	65
12638	Hudson B F	4	A	Feb 11	
5734	Inman John	24	A	Aug 15	64
9757	Isabell J M	3	H	Sept 25	
11392	Inman W	Cav 11	D	Oct 24	
12203	Isabel A	1	K	Dec 1	
649	Jackson John	45	D	Apr 20	
2679	Jeffries Wm	Cav 1	A	June 30	
5229	Jacobs John W	" 4	I	Aug 10	
7294	Johnson A	10	H	Aug 31	
7371	Jenkins S	Cav 6	A	Aug 31	
7594	Justin J	39	F	Sept 2	

LIST OF THE DEAD.

No.	Name				Date
7754	James W		5	K	Sept 4 64
9654	Jarvis W D		12	D	Sept 24
11000	Jordan J	Cav	5	B	Oct 16
11143	Jones D	"	1	L	Oct 18
12541	Jones J		16	E	Jan 27 65
87	Kennedy Jas	Cav	11	E	Mar 21 64
191	Knotts Fred	"	11	E	Mar 27
926	Kessmer John	"	12	I	May 7
1015	Kennedy S B		39	B	May 12
1173	Keiling M	Cav	11	D	May 17
3928	Keystone C		6	E	July 25
4921	Kennedy A, Cor	Cav 1	A	July 6
5558	Knapp Thos	"	6	M	July 13
5925	Kressler P	"	4	K	July 17
12265	Knapp J	"	5	B	Dec 12
48	Lenniert L		1	K	Mar 15
310	Lambert R	Cav	11	F	Apr 2
1135	Lay Wm	"	11	D	May 16
1726	Lossman A	"	4	E	June 8
1802	Larger W	"	1	L	June 10
1912	Ledford J A		16	B	June 13
2109	Little J		1	D	June 17
2852	Lonoey B	Cav	1	K	June 23
2668	Lasper Otto		15	H	June 29
837	Lublett M L		13	E	June 3
3340	Leville Thos		4	D	July 13
3398	Lee S	Cav	1	A	July 16
3658	Loy W B	"	8	L	July 20
3776	Lanhart J	"	6	G	July 22
3899	Lawry Jas W	"	12	G	July 23
6024	Lewis T	"	2	C	Aug 18
7132	Landers, Cor		26	I	Aug 28
7934	Luster W	Cav	1	B	Sept 5
8634	Little J F	"	12	D	Sept 13
11870	Lindusky G		11	G	Nov 6
12175	Ledwick A		7	C	Nov 27
9175	Lord Wm		20	G	Sept 18
271	McMannus Saml		11	D	Mar 31
369	Miller John		3	A	Apr 5
525	McDougal W C		14	K	Apr 13
796	Mills John		1	H	Apr 29
991	McClure P	Cav	11	C	May 10
1222	Marshall Wm	"	5	I	May 19
1380	Montgomery W A	" 5	H	May 26
1391	Moreland H	Cav	1	F	May 26
1969	Merix J	"	45	D	June 14
2024	Morton W	"	7	I	June 15
2137	Meldown D	"	11	E	June 18
2669	Miller W C	"	27	A	June 29
3152	Mitchell Jas	"	12	C	July 11
64	Mullins W W	"	1	H	Aug 8
3418	Morgan J	"	4	D	July 17
4513	Masters G	"	11	A	Aug 1
4550	McDonald J	"	4	I	Aug 2
4646	Mitchell R M	"	17	E	Aug 3
5691	Mooney Pat	"	11	G	Aug 15
7951	McCarty E	"	5	K	Sept 6
8455	McCarty John	"	6	K	Sept 9
8685	McCarter W	"	9	B	Sept 13
9239	Munch C	"	28	F	Sept 19
9498	Macary C	"	11	M	Sept 21
9711	Moore Wm	"	12	D	Sept 24
7336	Martin F P	"	12	D	Aug 30
10170	Marshall L	*	1	F	Oct 1
10460	Mills George	"	4	H	Oct 7
11455	Murphy W M	"	2	H	Oct 25
11478	Miller E	"	4	I	Oct 26
12456	Miller J	"	4	K	Jan 16 65
12491	Myers J	"	4	C	Jan 20
12720	Meach A J	"	1	A	Mar 3
12764	Morgan F, Cor		3	I	Mar 12
212	New Geo W	Cav	1	F	Mar 28 64
447	Neely B W	"	1	G	Apr 9
63	Nelson John	"	1	D	July 19
7693	Northcraft J	"	6	H	Sept 3
9230	Newton A, Cor	"	4	H	Sept 19
2499	O'Bannon Wm	"	11	B	June 20
2513	Oper L	"	4	B	June 26
11943	Owen W, Cor	"	1	L	Nov 9
1178	Pott J	"	7	C	May 17
1905	Porter J F	"	18		June 13
3654	Pulliam J		2		July 20
4220	Plyman Wm		39		July 27
5761	Pally S C, S't	Cav	12	B	Aug 15
6616	Phelps Wm E	"	6	F	Aug 23
6632	Pruils W H	"	1	F	Aug 23
7222	Pope Frank, Cor	"	5	B	Aug 29
8070	Pott Samuel	"	4	G	Sept 17
8207	Patterson J	"	2	B	Sept 8
9299	Phelps F M, S't	"	11	I	Sept 20
10249	Partis J R	"	1	F	Oct 3
12220	Pace John	"	3	G	Dec 4
12327	Purcell J	"	1	G	Dec 23
2144	Queata J	"	11	E	June 18
452	Rurves E, S't	"	4	F	Apr 9
577	Roberts R	"	12	H	Apr 16
590	Ramy Lester	"	39	H	Apr 17
637	Raberie Geo	"	1	A	Apr 20
825	Richardson M, Cor	3	H	May 1
1097	Ruus T	Cav	11	H	May 14
1193	Russell Jacob	"	12	B	May 18
1355	Ritter B B	"	6	L	May 25
1555	Rose R C, Cor	"	6	B	June 2
1571	Rogers W	"	1	F	June 3
2463	Reve F N	"	11	F	June 25
2751	Reilly Thos	"	1	D	July 1
4018	Ramsay Robert	"	45	A	July 26
4482	Robertson H	Cav	11	D	Aug 1
4549	Rodes James	"	1	F	Aug 2
4919	Rockwell W W, Cl C	1	C	Aug 6
5775	Roberts L	"	1	K	Aug 15
5067	Rieff R	Art	1		Aug 17
5976	Roberts A	Cav	1	K	Aug 17
6274	Readman W	"	11	I	Aug 20
7215	Rogers Henry	"	12	A	Aug 29
10124	Robny F	"	15	E	Oct 1
11369	Racine P	"	12	I	Oct 27
11583	Ryan W	"	1	I	Oct 28
11642	Riddle J H	"	1	I	Oct 30
11644	Rogers Wm	"	2	I	Oct 30
11873	Rusby J	"	2	F	Nov 6
12828	Rice P D, S't		3	I	Apr 9 65
1202	Ruble L, Cor	Cav	11	D	May 19 64
4106	Rankin J H, S't	"	18	G	July 27
213	Simpson W	"	1	C	Mar 28
277	Sims Geo, S't		40	I	Mar 31
567	Summers W H	Cav	11	D	Apr 15
797	Smith Geo	"	13	G	Apr 29
925	Sallac Geo, Cor	"	11	C	May 7
905	Smith Wm A	"	4	K	May 10
1003	Smith H	Cav	16	B	May 10
1101	Smith R C	"	1	I	May 14
1180	Schafer J E	"	4	A	May 18
1500	Stempf Lewis	"	12	G	May 31

LIST OF THE DEAD. 211

No.	Name	Rank	Co.	Reg.	Date
1659	Sutherland J E, S't	C 1	C		June 6 64
1681	Sebastian J W		45	C	June 6
1691	Sanders J S	Cav	12	E	June 7
1708	Stine C		4	K	June 7
1716	Sandfer Jno	"	11	B	June 8
1811	Summers Wm	"	11	D	June 10
1827	Sweeney M	"	5	I	June 11
1952	Shirley John	"	28	E	June 14
1954	Stanley C O	"	17	E	June 14
2033	Salmond P	"	18	H	June 16
2094	Shanks W L	"	6	B	June 17
2766	Show J	"	11	I	July 6
44	Smith John	"	2	I	May 13
51	Shaggs I P	"	11	G	June 2
3402	Shuman J	"	4	A	July 16
4258	Smith B, Cor	"	5	A	July 29
4829	Schmal And'w	"	4	B	Aug 6
4831	Schottsman F, Cor	C 1	D		Aug 6
4976	Snyder H M	Cav	10	B	Aug 7
5297	Smith W H, Cor		27	E	Aug 11
6260	Stevens P L, S't,	C 12	G		Aug 20
6280	Schransburg R,	C 1	K		Aug 20
8226	Stinnett J	Cav	6	K	Sept 9
8487	Sutton Thos	"	6	A	Sept 11
8827	Shulds J	"	2	K	Sept 15
10154	Sanders B	"	4	F	Oct 1
10673	Sheppard T L	"	5	H	Oct 11
11456	Sapp B	"	1	B	Oct 25
11898	Selors W H	"	1	C	Nov 7
12556	Stewart E	"	4	A	Jan 30 65
10197	Sawney Wm	"	5	H	Oct 2 64
2654	Sutherland H		32	G	June 29
253	Taylor Thos, Cor,	C 11	H		Mar 30
391	Thrope H	Cav	1	B	April 6
781	Tucker Wm	"	12	I	April 28
1009	Travis Geo	"	16	E	May 10
1628	Truncy J	"	11	C	June 4
2116	Tutune J, S't	"	11	A	June 17
2371	Tudor Ab'm, Cor	C 11	A		June 23
3701	Tullor G W	"	28	A	July 21
5424	Tabu Silas		27	D	Aug 12
6234	Templeton W H	C 11	B		Aug 20
6257	Tapp George	Cav	13	I	Aug 20
6508	Tracy James	"	11	L	Aug 22
6936	Thorp J	"	4	K	Aug 26
7205	Tucker Rob't	"	17	G	Aug 29
10028	Tucker J A	"	15	A	Sept 29
10398	Thornburg B	"	2	G	Oct 6
10588	Tussey E D	"	24	A	Oct 10
10809	Terry Wm	"	1	A	Oct 12
10892	Thomas W E, S't	C 11	G		Oct 14
10657	Vandevier J	Cav	11	C	Oct 11
278	West John C	"	11	E	Mar 31
494	White A	"	6	K	April 12
735	Wailar M R	"	16	C	April 24
1125	White John	"	11	D	May 15
1706	Westfall J	"	4	D	June 7
1734	Wickles John		40	K	June 8
1745	Walsh J E	Cav	6	L	June 8
1894	Wright Jno E	"	1		June 13
2199	Wheelan Jas	"	18	C	June 19
2584	White C	"	1	H	June 27
2901	Wiser R M	"	1	B	July 5
40	Ward F W	"	1	A	May 3
4374	Warren W P	"	34	K	July 30
4624	Wallace H	"	14	E	Aug 3
4697	West P H	"	6	K	Aug 3
15057	Webb J	"	6	F	Aug 8 64
5762	Welch T C	"	5	G	Aug 15
5790	Walsh John	"	6	H	Aug 15
6101	Winter H	"	11	E	Aug 18
6121	Winfries W S	"	3	A	Aug 19
6883	White S A	"	17	G	Aug 26
7038	Willser J	"	11	I	Aug 27
7694	Wells J W	"	12	C	Aug 3
8533	Wallace J, S't	"	11	K	Sept 12
9258	Warner D	"	12	A	Sept 19
9541	Wicog S	"	4	I	Sept 23
9636	Wagoner H, Cor	C 4	I		Sept 24
10770	Warner Thos	Cav	15	F	Oct 12
10898	Walton J J	"	8	A	Oct 14
11749	Willit M	"	4	I	Nov 2
12279	Weasett A	"	1	D	Nov 13
904	Yocombs H	"	11	D	May 5
1166	Yoam J	"	10	D	May 17
2089	Yeager L, S't	"	11	C	June 30
3757	Yeast R	"	1	I	July 22
5257	Zertes G	"	4	G	Aug 10

Total 436.

LOUISIANA.

| 6778 | Kimball Jas | Cav 2 | A | Aug 25 64 |

MAINE.

No.	Name	Rank	Co.	Reg.	Date
2604	Anderson John		19	I	June 28 64
3093	Allen A		32	K	July 10
7024	Arnold E W		17	G	Aug 27
22	Butler C A		3	K	Mar 7
269	Brown E M		5	G	Mar 31
3953	Buner A E		31	E	July 25
6211	Bachelor P, S't		3	K	Aug 19
9162	Baker James		17	H	Sept 18
10669	Ballast J		19	G	Oct 11
7663	Bartlett H		17	C	Sept 3
7255	Barney G S		32	I	Aug 30
6683	Bean G W		8	C	Aug 24
6603	Bennett L	Art	1		Aug 23
9007	Berry C H		6	H	Sept 18
7645	Bigelow C		19	H	Sept 3
5290	Blaizdell H		8	F	Aug 11
12055	Boren W		16	I	Nov 16
9408	Bowden ——		7	A	Sept 21
4776	Braley J		3	E	Aug 4
5015	Briggs J C		19	F	Aug 8
8542	Brinkerman L		9	D	Sept 11
8247	Broadstreet C B	C 1	B		Sept 9
6811	Brown J		8	G	Aug 25
11980	Bryant C D		16	E	Nov 13
5719	Bullsen E T, S't	C 5	B		Aug 15
5757	Bunker S A	Art	1	A	Aug 15
8474	Burgen A		4	I	Sept 11
7017	Cardor.ey C		17	G	Aug 27
7746	Carlen M	Cav	1	F	Sept 3
8374	Carr J		19	E	Sept 10
6246	Carlton J S		31	D	Aug 19
5989	Chase F W	Art	1	D	Aug 17
2316	Clark James	Cav	1	C	June 26
8143	Clark P M, S't	"	1	C	Sept 8
10376	Clark L		19	D	Oct 5
10421	Clayton E B		1	F	Oct 6
28	Cohan D		3	K	Mch 7
6950	Conder W H		16	G	Aug 26
8037	Conley W		5	F	Sept 6

LIST OF THE DEAD.

No.	Name	Reg.	Co.	Date
3943	Cook James	4	D	July 25 64
8433	Condon D H	20	K	Sept 11
425	Craw H	3	B	April 7
12061	Cressy N F	11	G	Nov 17
10936	Cromwell S R, Cor	A 1	M	Sept 14
11211	Cromwell W H	19	D	Oct 20
8625	Curtiss John	16	I	Sept 13
12367	Cutts O M	16	D	Jan 1 65
80	Cutler A	20	E	Mch 20 64
5171	Cross Noah Art	1	A	Aug 9
8581	Crosby W	4	A	Sept 12
8445	Davis D	3	C	Sept 11
227	Davis Wm L	20	E	Mch 29
5615	Dougherty Thos	8	G	Aug 14
6612	Donnell F	8	E	Aug 23
9624	Downes J	8	G	Sept 23
1359	Doyle Wm	6	D	May 25
5481	Drisdale F	1	H	Aug 13
4425	Duffy A	3	G	July 31
6415	Dugan D	32	A	Aug 21
6438	Dunning S P	29	G	Aug 21
7240	Dunnie G	5	G	Aug 29
6357	Dye John Cav	1	E	Aug 21
5035	Dutener H	20	A	Aug 8
10608	Eckhard H	7	C	Sept 10
7212	Edwards N S Cav	1	F	Aug 29
8538	Ellis A Art	2	H	Sept 11
1877	Emmerson H H	3		June 12
2628	Farewell E	31	E	June 28
8401	Ferrell P	6	H	Sept 10
4765	Fish Wm	7	A	Aug 5
5243	Flagg J B	5	K	Aug 10
69	Flanders L G	20	E	Mch 19
1989	Foley John	19	E	June 15
2362	Forrest Thos Cav	1	E	June 23
2482	Foster A, Cor	6	K	June 25
8145	Foster E R	16	C	Sept 8
7073	Foster Samuel C	16	K	Aug 28
6191	Frisble L	7	C	Aug 19
10957	Fitzgerald Joseph	8	E	Oct 14
5907	Gardner W H, S't	4		Aug 16
12515	Gibbs R	19	K	Jan 23 65
2906	Gilgan W	7	C	July 5 64
6107	Goodward A Art	1	I	Aug 18
5580	Goodwin M T	8	F	Aug 14
4141	Grant G Art	1	F	July 28
7391	Grant Frank	16	F	Aug 30
8392	Griffith S	8	G	Sept 10
9190	Gunney C	31	A	Sept 18
10031	Gunney J F, S't	1	I	Sept 29
11823	Gilgrist ——	31	E	Nov 5
8306	Hammond J	19	G	Sept 10
12343	Harris J S	1	F	Dec 26
3503	Hassen H	7	G	July 18
3274	Hatch J S	3	G	July 13
6112	Hatch S, S't	8	F	Aug 19
9,11	Heath B	3	F	Sept 20
4174	Heninger ——	19		July 28
12349	Hopes H	19	D	Dec 27
7474	Howard D H	17	D	Sept 1
3844	Howe Samuel W	1	K	July 23
7186	Hoyt A D	3	K	Aug 29
3237	Hudson W	17	E	July 12
8797	Hughes Wm	31	K	Sept 15
9652	Humphrey —— C	3	L	Sept 24
3484	Hunkey E B	1	L	July 17
4703	Henly D	8	G	Aug 4
5355	Ingols L	16	H	Aug 11 64
9389	Ingerson P	7	I	Sept 20
11489	Jackson A J	17	I	Oct 26
10619	Jackson R	7	B	Oct 10
10710	Jackson R W	7	D	Oct 11
12602	Jordan J	19	F	Feb 6 65
7385	Johnson B	7	K	Aug 30 64
5849	Jones Wm	19	E	Aug 16
10243	Jory G F	8	F	Oct 3
11586	Kellar J	19	J	Oct 28
8237	Kelley L	11	D	Sept 9
3313	Kennedy W	17	G	July 14
6169	Kilpatrick C	3	C	Aug 19
5366	Laud C	6	I	Aug 11
8350	Lamber W	17	K	Sept 10
11707	Levitt H	19	A	Nov 1
7967	Lincoln A	16	I	Sept 6
10931	Littlefield C Cav	1	F	Oct 14
6340	Lord Geo H	3	B	Aug 21
5549	Ludovice F	13	F	Aug 13
490	Lowell B	4	G	April 12
9426	Macon L	8	A	Sept 21
700	Malcolm H M	16	A	April 24
6606	Marshall B F	1	H	Aug 23
12122	Maston A	19	D	Nov 22
10392	Mathews James	32	F	Oct 14
12011	Maxwell J	8	E	Nov 14
3679	McFarland G	3	G	July 21
9538	McGinley J	7	A	Sept 22
2200	McKinney G	3	I	June 19
12084	McFarland E S	8	I	Nov 18
4391	Metcalf Oliver	8	H	July 31
12768	McFarland W, Cor	19	K	Mch 13
5200	Melgar J	7		Aug 10
5614	Messer C R	7	F	Aug 14
9399	Miller C J Cav	1	B	Sept 21
2002	Miller J O	2	D	June 15
7573	Mills M	1		Sept 2
2808	Moore Charles W	8	B	July 3
11042	Moore G	18	D	Oct 17
7273	Moore J D Cav	1	B	Aug 30
6940	Moore W C	7	A	Aug 26
8118	Moyes F	32	F	Sept 8
7046	Newton C	9	K	Aug 27
1507	Nickerson D	4	F	May 31
8020	Noltou H	7	B	Sept 6
2131	O'Brien W	16	A	June 18
6325	Opease S	19		Aug 21
143	Osborn A J	8		Mch 24
10866	Owens O H	10		Nov 6
3710	Parker A Cav	1	E	July 21
7979	Parsons James W	16	D	Sept 6
9362	Patrick F	14	F	Sept 20
2272	Peabody F S, S't	5	I	June 20
12543	Pequette P	4	G	Jan 28
1486	Perkins D Cav	1	I	May 31
5197	Perkins T	1	H	Aug 10
6011	Peters H	4	E	Aug 26
12056	Phillbrook F Art	1	A	Nov 17
2064	Phelps W H Cav	1	H	June 16
3436	Pinkham U W Art	1	A	July 17
1361	Pottle A E Cav	1		May 25
5698	Pratt A M "	1	L	Aug 15
8441	Pulerman G	16	D	Sept 11
12410	Prescott C	19	H	Jan 7 65
7785	Richardson C	31	L	Sept 4 64
6762	Richardson J K	8	G	Aug 24

LIST OF THE DEAD. 213

No.	Name		Co.	Reg.	Date
10465	Richardson W. Cor	C 1	B	Oct 7 64
5522	Ricker Wm Cor	C 1	D	Aug 13
8480	Ridlon N	7	D	Sept 11
900	Riseck R	3	I	May 5
3921	Roberts H	19	K	July 25
5236	Rowe L	1	A	Aug 10
166	Rosmer Frank	4	C	Mch 26
5796	Ruet H	2	H	Aug 15
8557	Russell G A Cav	1	E	Sept 12
5450	Sampson E	1	F	Aug 12
4532	Sawyer Enos Art	1	H	Aug 2
3182	Sawyer John	31	K	July 11
11462	Shorey S Cav	1	K	Oct 20
2243	Simmons G F	6	K	June 20
3159	Smith W	9	K	July 11
3331	Smith W A	6	F	July 14
1782	Snowdale F	4	C	June 10
9974	Snower S C	19	A	Sept 28
1998	Springer H W	36	A	June 15
4506	Steward G	20	H	Aug 3
11502	St Peter F	19	F	Oct 27
7001	Swaney P	19	F	Aug 27
199	Swan H B, Cor	3	F	Mch 28
1936	Swau F	3	F	June 14
8682	Thompson F	9	E	Sept 13
10455	Thompson John	3	E	Oct 7
621	Thorn E	9	I	April 19
10628	Toothache J	7	G	Oct 14
1106	Turner C C	4	E	May 15
5090	Tufts J	32	C	Aug 8
11875	Taylor G	9	C	Nov 16
12322	Tuttle D L	32	F	Dec 20
12196	Tuttle L S. Cor	32	F	Nov 30
12706	Thorndie WB,Cor	19	I	Mch 2 65
6245	Valley F	32	K	Aug 19 64
3335	Venill C	32	G	July 15
7226	Walker A B, Cor	1	K	Aug 29
3894	Walker M C	5	I	July 24
7722	Wall A Cav	1	K	Sept 4
5042	Walsh Thomas	20	H	Aug 17
6750	Watson B	7	K	Aug 24
10558	Webber Oliver	3	A	Oct 9
4559	Whiteman AM,Cor	5	I	Aug 2
1648	Whitcomb T O	4	F	June 5
6251	Whittier J K P	32	C	Aug 19
10445	Willard W	20	B	Oct 7
7711	Williams C	6	G	Sept 3
6900	Wilson George	32	C	Aug 26
3639	Wilson G W	16	H	July 20
3132	Willey D H	19	E	July 10
3860	Winslow E I	4	B	July 24
5512	Winslow N L	4	K	Aug 13
6372	Wyman A	32	C	Aug 21
2095	Wyman J	16	A	June 17
12470	Wyer R	3	K	Jan 16 65
12043	Wright C	1	G	Nov 16 64
178	Young E W, S't	3	H	Mar 26
6369	Young J	3	H	Aug 21
8140	Young J, Cor	8	I	Sept 8
	TOTAL, 233			

MARYLAND.

No.	Name		Co.	Reg.	Date
850	Allen W H	1	H	May 3 64
1028	Anderson Wm	2	C	May 11
1379	Aikens A Cav	1	I	May 26
1928	Adams Jas T	6	H	May 14
10288	Abbott D E	2	C	Oct 4
2325	Archer H	1	I	Dec 24 64
112	Babb Samuel	8	I	Mch 23
288	Berlin Jas Cav	2	F	April 1
472	Beltz W W	2	H	April 9
1086	Bowers A	1	I	May 14
1453	Brown Augustus	2	G	May 29
1487	Braddock Wm	2	D	May 30
1549	Buck H Cav	1	B	June 2
1644	Buckley Geo	9	B	June 5
2404	Bennett C B	1	D	June 24
3268	Brant D B	2	H	July 13
4602	Betson James Bat	1	A	Aug 3
5261	Ball J A	2	B	Aug 10
3525	Brown J C Art	1	B	Aug 23
6540	Brown E R	2	C	Aug 13
7797	Brown E	2	D	Sept 3
8975	Buckley A M	1	B	Sept 17
1184	Beale R Cav	1	D	Sept 19
11761	Buckner George	2	K	Nov 3
11620	Bell J R	8	D	Oct 28
12373	Bloom J, Cor	7	F	Jan 1 65
12679	Book C	8	G	Feb 19
54	Carpenter Wm Cav	2	I	Mch 17 64
304	Cook Lewis	9	E	April 1
469	Coombs E A	9	I	April 9
524	Carter Wm	2	C	April 13
728	Cary W H	9	F	April 25
1357	Carl J M	6	E	May 25
1371	Cabbage C H	2	H	May 25
2012	Cullin John	2	D	June 15
4182	Crasby M	1	G	July 28
4620	Carter John	2	C	Aug 3
5036	Carr Wm Cav	1	D	Aug 8]
5063	Childs G A	9	I	Aug 8
5826	Crisle J	6	G	Aug 16
8008	Crouse W A, Cole's	C	E	Sept 9
8035	Conway Wm E	4	E	Sept 6
8266	Crabb H	4	E	Sept 9
8357	Coon H S	1	E	Sept 10
8618	Crouse J A Cav	1	A	Sept 13
10600	Collins D	1	C	Sept 10
12395	Callahan P	1	F	Jan 4 65
181	Duff Chas, Cor	8	A	Mar 27 64
1410	Dunn John, Cor	9	H	May 27
2396	Davis Thomas	9		June 24
3912	Drew C	35	B	July 24
4138	Dennis Benj	2	A	July 28
4211	Davis G Cav	1	F	July 29
6510	Dickwall Wm	2	F	Aug 22
8199	Deller F	1	E	Sept 8
6788	Dennissen T	42	I	Aug 25
8428	Ellis C	4	D	Sept 12
10410	Eli W	7	C	Oct 6
3849	Fecker L	2	I	July 24
1321	Fairbanks J E	9	C	May 23
2559	Francis J. Cor	2	K	June 27
2600	Flage F J	2	H	June 28
2824	Farrass Jas	7	G	July 2
6016	Frantz F	2	H	Aug 17
7404	Fink L	2	H	Aug 31
9290	Frederick J E	9	I	Sept 19
12752	Freare W	8	A	Mar 10 65
1271	Gordon A B	9	E	May 22 64
2138	Gerard Fred Cav	1	B	June 18
3013	Green Thomas	2	D	July 7
3789	Gregg F	2	I	July 22

LIST OF THE DEAD.

No.	Name		Co.	Date	
6072	Gilson J E, S't	Cav 1	C	Aug 18	64
6731	Ganon J W	2	K	Aug 24	
12735	Goff John	1	I	Mar 6	65
1767	Houck J. Cor	2	H	April 27	64
826	Hickley John	9	G	May 1	
1625	Howell L H	Cav 1	M	June 4	
1720	Hoop H	2	I	June 8	
2657	Hickley J S	2	H	June 23	
2494	Hidderick H	1	I	June 26	
2978	Hite J E	2	I	July 7	
3864	Hering P, S't	2	C	July 24	
4767	Hank Thomas	Bat 1	D	Aug 5	
5292	Hilligar —	1	E	Aug 11	
5408	Hood John	8	C	Aug 12	
5017	Holmes L	2	H	Aug 17	
6484	Hour S	8	E	Aug 22	
6504	Harris J E	1	A	Aug 22	
7434	Hazel J	9	C	Sept 1	
8165	Himick F	Cav 1	E	Sept 8	
8398	Hall J	7	D	Sept 10	
9032	Holden J R	9	C	Sept 28	
11109	Hakaion F	2	K	Oct 18	
12422	Hoover J	Cav 2	C	Jan 9	65
2895	Isaac Henry	2	H	July 4	64
93	Jones David	Bat 1	A	Mar 22	
669	Jenkins M	2	A	April 22	
460	Keplinger J	2	H	April 9	
544	Keefe Lewis	7	F	April 14	
7242	Kirby J	9	F	Aug 29	
1019	Laird Corbin	Cav 1	F	May 11	
1056	Lees W H	2	C	May 13	
3913	Louis J, S't	2	B	July 24	
11385	Little D	Cav 2	K	Oct 24	
12361	Lebud J	Cav 1	D	Dec 30	
12067	Lambert W	1	I	Feb 17	65
206	McCarle James	Cav 1	B	Mar 28	64
471	Moland B	2	F	April 9	
896	Myers Noah	9	G	May 5	
1190	McGuigen S K	Bat 1	D	May 18	
1307	Myers L S	1	B	May 23	
1707	Moore Frank	9	A	June 10	
1898	Moffitt Thomas	6		June 13	
2059	Martz G H	2	H	June 16	
3429	Machler C S	Bat 1	A	July 17	
3797	McKinsay Jno	2	I	July 22	
4051	Miller F	6	C	July 27	
4146	Mathers F	8	G	July 28	
4881	Macomber John	C 1	B	Aug 6	
5179	Marvin J	2	H	Aug 9	
6757	Moon J J	1	D	Aug 25	
7281	McCullough J	1	I	Aug 30	
7327	McLamas J	7	C	Aug 30	
8043	Markell S	2	H	Sept 6	
10150	Munroe J, Cor	4	I	Oct 1	
10361	Markin W	1	F	Oct 13	
11547	Mathews J	8		Oct 27	
12608	McMiller J A	1	E	Feb 7	65
91	Nice Jacob	Cav 5	M	Mar 21	64
371	Nace Harrison	9	H	April 15	
9752	Norris N	1		Sept 25	
153	Pool Hanson	2	H	Mar 25	
7590	Porter G	1	I	Sept 2	
7981	Pindiville M	7	H	Sept 6	
5069	Papple P, Cor	2	H	Aug 8	
252	Rusk John	9	E	Mar 30	
918	Russell A P	2	C	May 6	
1606	Rodk Simon	9	E	June 4	
1901	Robinson J	9		June 13	64
2850	Rynedollar Wm C	1	D	June 23	
9590	Reed Thos P	Art 1	B	Aug 23	
155	Seberger F	9	F	Mar 25	
317	Scarboro Rob't	9	I	April 2	
478	Suffecol S	1	I	April 9	
718	Sinder John	2	H	April 24	
899	Snooks W	9	E	May 5	
1205	Spence Levi	9	D	May 19	
1272	Scarlett Jas	1	D	May 22	
1926	Smith Ed, S't	9	I	June 14	
2004	Stafford John	9	G	June 15	
2361	Shipley W	9	G	June 23	
2489	Schneder J	Bat 1	B	June 26	
5797	Smith John	Cav 1	B	Aug 15	
6751	Shelley B	2	F	Aug 24	
6816	Shiver G H, Cor	1	C	Aug 25	
6919	Stull G E	Cav 1	D	Aug 26	
7580	Shilling Wm	2	K	Sept 2	
7833	Stolz — —	7	K	Sept 4	
8296	Smitzer J	1	D	Sept 9	
8716	Segar Chas	6	F	Sept 14	
9309	Snyder F	2	K	Sept 20	
9151	Stratten J A	Art 1	C	Sept 21	
10215	Shafer J N	Cav 1	A	Oct 22	
11159	Samon L W	1	I	Oct 19	
11160	Speaker H	1	F	Oct 19	
12195	Spaulding J	4	C	Nov 29	
12704	Smith G C	1	I	Feb 26	65
149	Tyson J T	9	D	Mar 25	64
1022	Tysen J T	9	I	May 11	
677	Turner Wm F	Cav 1	D	April 22	
1029	Turner A	Cav 1	B	May 11	
1356	Tindle E. Cor	9	G	May 25	
1377	Turner C	9	E	May 26	
7872	Thompson J	13	I	Sept 5	
8689	Thompson John	2	S	Sept 14	
9246	Tucker —	2	D	Sept 19	
9335	Tindell Wm	11	B	Sept 20	
11450	Tilton J	Cav 1	F	Oct 25	
1583	Ulrich Daniel	9	I	June 3	
1305	Veach Jesse	2	H	May 23	
8269	Viscounts A J	Art 1	E	Sept 9	
78	Wise John	9	D	Mar 20	
21	White Wm	9	C	Mar 7	
553	Widdons D	1	E	April 14	
537	Webster Sam'l, Cor	9	G	April 17	
1171	Wharton Samuel	2	F	May 17	
2275	Worthen Wm	9	C	June 20	
4748	West M	4	D	Aug 5	
9409	Weaver George	1	B	Sept 2	
11578	Witman D	13	D	Sept 28	
12147	Wolfe H	1	B	Nov 24	
455	Yieldhan R	9	C	April 9	
1060	Zeck Wm J, Cor	7	E	May 13	
3223	Zimmerman C	9	E	July 12	

TOTAL, 194

MASSACHUSETTS.

No.	Name		Co.	Date	
11286	Adams I B	16	G	Oct 22	64
9561	Adams S B	18	G	Sept 23	
6360	Akers H H	2	I	Aug 21	
4290	Aldrich H	36	G	July 30	
10973	Aldrich H W	27	I	Oct 15	
5650	Alger W A, Cor	15	D	Aug 14	
8730	All n Francis	Art 1	M	Sept 14	
5334	Allen G H	2	E	Aug 11	

LIST OF THE DEAD. 215

No.	Name	Age	Co.	Date		No.	Name	Age	Co.	Date	
9748	Allen John	19	B	Sept 25	64	7440	Brown L	27	I	Sept 1	64
2286	Ames H	35	A	June 25		8780	Brown Samuel	56	E	Sept 14	
8349	Ames M L	32	G	Sept 10		5339	Brown Wm	Art 2	H	Aug 11	
8373	Analstine ——	54		Sept 10		6842	Brownell A G	58	B	Aug 25	
1084	Anchey J	61	F	May 4		6903	Bryant W A	Art 2	H	Aug 26	
8589	Armington H	13	C	Sept 12		7758	Buchanan J	27	A	Sept 4	
10693	Armstrong G	28	A	Oct 11		5775	Buldas L	56	I	Aug 9	
9781	Atmore C	Cav 2	A	Sept 25		10746	Bullen J W	60	C	Oct 11	
4065	Avery John W	Art 1	G	July 27		11517	Bubler J W	40	C	Oct 26	
5372	Avigron F	56	I	Aug 11		1734	Bullock W D	24	K	July 22	
10767	Baccy Wm	27	H	Oct 12		11154	Burns W H, Cor	Art 2	H	Oct 19	
7116	Baggard F	Art 1	B	Aug 28		2007	Burt C E	Art 2	K	July 5	
8338	Balce G A	27	G	Sept 10		7134	Burgan L	25	G	Aug 28	
6624	Barley R	20	A	Aug 23		3699	Burgess W F	16	H	July 21	
6785	Baker E E	34	C	Aug 25		5540	Burnhan J	12	I	Aug 13	
11435	Baldwin W	35	A	Oct 24		7777	Burton John	19	E	Sept 4	
9078	Banner M	20	B	Sept 17		2429	Butler A	72	H	June 24	
642	Burge Henry	20	E	April 20		4956	Buxton Thos	Art 1	G	Aug 7	
6974	Barnes L A	19	F	Aug 27		9868	Byerns I	Art 1	I	Sept 27	
1097	Barnes W L	Cav 2	M	June 7		7230	Callihan J	57	B	Aug 29	
7858	Barlen E F	18	E	Sept 5		3158	Callihan P	57	A	July 11	
3841	Barnsh John	17	H	July 28		12663	Campbell D A	15	G	Feb 16	65
6952	Barnett G H	25	G	Aug 26		4081	Carr Wm, Cor	Art 1	H	July 27	64
8848	Bassett B C	Art 1	I	Sept 15		456	Carroll J	Art 2	D	Aug 1	
4855	Batten Geo C, S't A 2		G	July 31		4366	Carroll O J	Art 2	G	July 31	
8603	Baxten H	Art 2	G	Sept 12		4168	Casey M	28	C	July 28	
2525	Bear G W	56	I	June 26		4509	Casey M	17	H	Aug 2	
6386	Beaupian Wm	Art 2	G	Aug 21		4226	Castle M	22	H	July 29	
6499	Beary Henry	59	B	Aug 22		6724	Caughlin B	56	E	Aug 24	
3801	Beels H	59	C	July 22		7070	Caswell James	18	F	Aug 18	
8110	Bell Wm	Cav 2	M	Sept 7		7313	Chase John	25	F	Aug 30	
8442	Bemis Albert	57	B	Sept 11		8086	Chase M M	Art 2	G	Sept 13	
11955	Berry George	18	K	Nov 10		6230	Child A F	Cav 1	E	Aug 20	
6403	Besson Wm	Cav 2	H	Aug 21		3344	Chiselson P	Cav 1	B	July 15	
8657	Biglow G	34	E	Sept 13		1684	Church W H	Cav 1	E	June 6	
5321	Biglow John	22	F	Aug 11		2416	Churchill F J	39	G	June 24	
2908	Black James	9	E	July 5		7674	Chute A M	23	B	June 11	
109	Blanchard Oscar	C 2	E	Mar 23		4516	Claflin F G	Art 1	F	Aug 1	
4067	Blanchard O S	52	G	July 27		11178	Claug J H	Art 1	E	Oct 19	
3357	Blair J W	27	C	July 15		3016	Clausky J, Cor	17	E	July 7	
3973	Blair D	27	B	July 25		10 99	Clark ——, Cor	27	A	Sept 30	
10753	Blake Wm	19	C	Oct 12		3648	Clark E	27	H	July 20	
7166	Blodgett A Z	34	A	Aug 29		4295	Clark George	16	I	July 30	
137	Blood T B	18	F	Mar 24		6492	Clark S	27	I	Aug 27	
470	Bodge S D	18	D	Aug 1		7928	Clemens J	19	B	Sept 5	
3030	Bosworth H	25	B	July 8		12825	Cloonan P	Art 1	E	April 7	65
7466	Bowler H A	Art 1	C	Sept 10		5315	Coffin A R	Cav 2	M	Aug 11	64
12013	Boyd F	18	A	Nov 10		11590	Cohash John	23	I	Oct 28	
1796	Boynton Henry	32	A	June 10		8099	Cole W H	16	K	Sept 7	
1857	Bracketts L	23	C	June 12		8	Coleman Leonard	C 1	A	Mar 5	
4059	Brackin Dennis	46		July 27		10773	Coalman C S	37	I	Oct 12	
6312	Bradford J	Cav 2	F	Aug 22		11853	Collins A J	Art 2	D	Nov 6	
3178	Brady F	27	G	July 11		6714	Collins C R	27	D	Aug 24	
11902	Bradish F	19	B	Nov 11		5109	Colt J	20	K	Aug 12	
12030	Brannagan C	Art 2	H	Nov 15		9081	Colyer B	Art 1	G	Sept 18	
4070	Brand S C	57	K	Oct 12		6062	Coney C W	Art 1	L	Aug 18	
2565	Briggs W	Art 2	G	July 2		6591	Congden E	Cav 2	C	Aug 25	
993	Briggs W W	36	H	May 10		9332	Connell J D	24	E	Sept 19	
8799	Bromley A	1	K	Sept 15		1848	Conner D	17	H	June 11	
465	Broadley James	17	A	April 9		6673	Connor John	11	F	Aug 24	
3587	Bronagan M	17	E	July 19		11892	Conner P	Cav 2	H	Nov 7	
11932	Brotherton W H, C	29	G	Aug 26		11575	Conner F	9	C	Oct 28	
2641	Brown A	56	D	June 29		4547	Conlin Tim	Art 1	L	Aug 2	
6057	Brown D	18	K	Aug 18		7593	Cook W H	37	H	Sept 2	
6177	Brown J	25	A	Aug 19		8841	Coombs Geo	Art 2		Sept 15	
9660	Brown J	11	E	Sept 24		1088	Coones J M	Cav 1	E	May 14	
10819	Brown John	Cor 57	E	Oct 12		11174	Copeland J	15	D	Oct 19	

LIST OF THE DEAD.

No.	Name		Co.	Date
7802	Corbet W M	Art 1	M	Sept 4 64
4210	Cox D O	59	F	July 29
687	Cox Joseph	7	G	May 23
11030	Cox P, S't	Art 1	G	Oct 16
4483	Crockett A W	17	K	Aug 1
174	Crofts E P	17	E	Mar 26
7619	Cromian John	Art 1	E	Sept 2
9026	Crowninshield T	37	I	Sept 17
6812	Crosby E	40	A	Aug 25
15	Cross Ira M	16	G	Mar 6
3592	Cross Geo W	Art 1	L	July 19
5248	Crosser E P	9	C	Aug 10
5150	Crossman E J	20	L	Aug 2
1290	Cummin'rs A B,S't	29	C	May 22
3746	Culligan Jos	Cav 2	A	July 22
574	Cunell H G	39	C	April 16
7853	Curren F	18	I	Sept 5
1869	Cushing C E	12		June 12
10172	Cutler C F	Art 2	G	Oct 1
3579	Dalber S A	17	B	July 19
787	Daly John	28	F	April 28
9421	Davis C	27	B	Sept 21
7180	Davis C A	58	I	Aug 29
1518	Davis Thomas	Cav 1	H	May 31
12037	Davidson W	27	H	Nov 16
7230	Day D B	25		Aug 29
2390	Decker C	Art 1	E	June 24
11763	Delano E	19	E	Nov 3
7848	Densmore Wm	9	F	Sept 4
6883	Dewry L A	27	C	Aug 26
4042	Dexter G	Cav 2	M	July 27
7069	Dill Z	58	A	Aug 28
10064	Dimmick Geo H	27	I	Oct 15
8130	Dodge Thos A	Cav 1	A	Sept 11
3059	Downing G	Bat 14		July 9
5501	Doggett L	22	L	Aug 13
9577	Dolan J	Cav 1	D	Sept 23
8732	Dole Charles H	10	H	Sept 4
6076	Dones S M	58	A	Aug 24
12004	Douglass B	10	H	Sept 14
1282	Dow H A, Cor	Art 1	E	April 10 65
3078	Dowlin J	27	H	July 20 64
1677	Downey Joel	Art 2	M	June 6
2676	Drake E C	67	E	June 3
12773	Drake T	4	D	Mar 14 65
7115	Dansfield John	19	E	Aug 28 64
5856	Drawn George	33	C	Aug 16
2717	Drickarm L	Cav 1	K	July 1
8294	Dromantle W	25	G	Sept 9
3570	Drum R	19	G	July 19
9251	Duff y J	Art 2	H	Sept 19
1512	Duffy James	13	A	May 31
4513	Dull W	Art 2	H	Aug 31
11666	Dunnett S	4	D	Oct 30
10360	Dunn J	Art 2	G	Oct 11
11319	Dunn I	20	H	Oct 22
4471	Dunn P	Art 2	H	Aug 1
4064	Dyer G W	Art 2	H	Aug 7
8212	Eaff N	56	H	Sept 8
8616	Earl G W. S't	Art 1	I	Sept 13
8157	Eastman D	35	I	Sept 8
10000	Eaton F W	5	D	Sept 29
7284	Edes W, Cor	11	F	Aug 20
11809	Edwards C	19	A	Nov 4
6374	Edwards C F	Art 2	H	Aug 21
171	Eagan Charles	17	K	Mar 26
10822	Eibers Henry	10		Oct 12
6994	Emerson G W	57	A	Aug 27 64
418	Emerson Wm	12	D	April 7
5619	Emery J	Art 1	F	Aug 14
5539	Emmerson F F	Art 1	B	Aug 13
3300	Empay Robert	25	E	July 14
10542	Emusin D G	21	B	Oct 8
5236	Evans H	Cav 1	K	Aug 10
2785	Evans J	17	H	July 2
7889	Ester W A	Art 1	A	Sept 5
4399	Evarts T P	Art 2	G	July 31
8556	Farmer G S, S't	Art 1	H	Sept 12
11908	Farralle G	19	K	Nov 7
9443	Farisdale H	Art 1	G	Sept 21
3926	Fearing J I	"	F	July 25
4987	Fearnley Wm	25	E	Aug 7
6450	Fegan John	Art 2	H	Aug 21
12812	Fellows H	15	E	Mar 19
7803	Felyer Wm	20	E	Sept 4
7611	Fenis J	Cav 1	C	Sept 2
5795	Fields E	37	F	Aug 15
11401	Finjay W	Cav 1	K	Oct 24
6723	Finigan B	19		Aug 24
3974	Fisher C B	Art 2	G	July 25
441	Fisher John	Cav 2	E	Apr 9
3451	Flanders Chas	Art 1	E	July 17
286	Fleming M	17	E	Apr 1
2476	Floyd Geo E	Art 2	H	June 25
4187	Forbs H	Art 1	B	July 28
70	Fosgate Henry S	17	K	Mar 19
5649	Fowler Saml	Art 1	M	Aug 14
10601	Frahar P	"	D	Oct 10
11135	Fraser L	20	F	Oct 18
3848	Fray Patrick	17	C	July 24
4267	Frederick C	20	A	July 29
8186	Frisby A	12	G	Sept 8
9502	Frost B	16	H	Sept 21
10205	Frost B	16	H	Oct 2
7170	Fuller A	Cav 2	G	Aug 29
12681	Fuller H	15	E	Feb 20 65
5467	Fuller S	57	D	Aug 13 64
7392	Fuller Geo A	Art 2	G	Aug 31
7154	Funold C G	23	G	Aug 29
9304	Gadkin G H	21	H	Sept 22
4333	Gaffering John	11	F	July 30
8027	Galligher F	18	B	Sept 19
2787	Galse I E, Cor	27	B	July 2
7569	Gardner D	25	E	Sept 2
12620	Garland W	Art 1	M	Feb 10 65
8882	Ganman E	"	2	Sept 16 64
11470	Gay C	Cav 1	K	Oct 6
7910	Gay Geo C	Art 2	G	Sept 5
8312	Gibson D E	33	F	Sept 10
8364	Gibson H H	25	B	Sept 10
4464	Gifford J	40	A	Aug 1
4250	Gilbert S	Art 2	H	July 29
159	Gilchrist J R, Cor	17	A	Mar 25
11157	Gilliland J	17	H	Oct 19
7110	Gilsby P	36	G	Aug 28
10918	Glancey P	59	A	Oct 18
9471	Goanney G	Art 2	G	Sept 21
2414	Godbold F A	29	K	June 24
3585	Gooding N	54	C	July 19
9202	Goodman J	25		Sept 18
5983	Goodman S	Art 2	B	Aug 17
9817	Goodridge G J	"	1	F	Sept 25
12844	Gonier D	4	D	Apr 23 65
179	Gordon Charles	17	C	Mar 26 64

LIST OF THE DEAD. 217

No.	Name	Rgt	Co.	Date
3486	Gordon W L	Art 2	H	July 17 64
10501	Goriche H	" 2	G	Oct 8
893	Gould Wm	17	G	May 5
8092	Core J	Art 4	G	Sept 7
8339	Gowen J	11	C	Sept 10
7885	Grant Geo W	Art 1	E	Sept 5
8277	Grant J	15	E	Sept 9
10491	Grant Wm	15	E	Oct 7
8898	Gray C	28	D	Sept 16
2018	Green John	18	A	June 15
9417	Gayson C W	25	I	Sept 21
3166	Guild C	Art 2	C	Aug 9
12568	Guilford J	" 1	I	Feb 1 65
10108	Gutherson G	" 1	B	Sept 30 64
3056	Haggert P, Cor	Cav 2	M	Sept 7
7408	Haley Wm	16	F	Aug 31
151	Halstead J W,	Cor C 2	M	Mar 25
11086	Hail G H	Art 1	E	Oct 18
1742	Hamlin H P	Cav 2	M	June 8
9342	Hammond G,	Cor 77	G	Sept 19
7374	Handy Geo	Art 1	K	Aug 31
10126	Handy Moses	59	A	Oct 1
8273	Hane J H	Art 1	I	Sept 9
8804	Hanks Nelson	98	D	Sept 15
6582	Hanley M	Cav 1	L	Aug 23
12276	Hare F	27	H	Dec 13
8697	Harding C	58	G	Sept 14
556	Harrison Henry	12	I	Apr 14
7626	Hainesworth F	27	A	Sept 2
3901	Harrington F	12	H	July 24
7957	Hart W	15	G	Sept 6
6923	Hartret M	34	I	Aug 26
766	Harty Jno, Cor	Cav 2	M	Apr 27
3505	Harvey S J	Art 2	G	July 7
10024	Hash Wm	" 1	H	Sept 29
3242	Hay Wm	" 2	H	July 13
5789	Haymouth N	Cav 2	M	Aug 15
4203	Haynes Chas E	Art 2	H	July 29
9904	Hayes P	37	A	Sept 23
3508	Heart John	28	G	July 18
7416	Hebban Thomas	28	B	Aug 31
3168	Henrie E W	17	H	July 14
5606	Henry D	16	H	Aug 14
4604	Henry J	Art 2	K	Aug 3
1093	Hermans John	11	G	May 24
7297	Hervey Geo W,	Cor 33	I	Aug 30
6242	Higgin A	23	B	Aug 20
4906	Hill F	9	I	Aug 6
1740	Hills J B	Cav 2	G	June 8
11762	Hillman G	16	H	Nov 3
6056	Hines S	59	C	Aug 10
9223	Hitchcock J C	27	C	Sept 19
6907	Hogan Pat	Art 2	G	Aug 26
6067	Hogan S	19	E	Aug 18
9260	Hoit D	19	B	Sept 19
4811	Hoitt J F	Art 2	D	Aug 5
6228	Holbrook Chas	" 2	H	Aug 20
6826	Holden Pat	" 2	G	Aug 25
1986	Holland P	17	I	June 15
905	Holland Pat	11	C	May 5
4816	Holmes S	12	I	Aug 5
8712	Holt E K	Art 1		Sept 14
6716	Holt T E	22	H	Aug 24
8575	Howard C	24	C	Sept 12
10864	Howard James	59	D	Oct 13
7025	Howe C H	36	G	Aug 27
222	Howe E H	36	H	May 29
3871	Howe John W	24	B	July 24 64
5973	Hubbard E	34	B	Aug 17
11045	Hubert G W	27	I	Oct 17
11960	Hunt J	84	D	Nov 11
4323	Hunting John W	25	I	July 30
12299	Hartshaw L E	56	A	Dec 16
6161	Hyde N L	Cav 2	B	Aug 19
5470	Hyde Richard	39	E	Aug 13
3487	Jackson N S	Art 1	K	July 17
3501	Jackson N S	17	K	July 17
8429	Jackson Wm R	Cav 2	B	Sept 11
5733	Jaquirions C	57	D	Aug 15
2308	Javnes H	59	G	June 22
10561	Jeff M	16	I	Oct 9
5915	Jeffrey A	58	B	Aug 17
9951	Jewett E	27	I	Sept 28
12820	Jewett G	4	A	Apr 11 65
5473	Johnson M	34	G	Aug 13 64
5850	Johnson R A	19	G	Aug 16
3684	Johnson Wm	Art 2	H	July 21
10702	Jones J	59	E	Oct 11
603	Jones John	Cav 2	M	Apr 18
8875	Jones N P	32	F	Sept 16
6054	Jones Thomas	11	A	Aug 18
6183	Kavanaugh Jas	32	K	Aug 19
8658	Kelly Chas	Art 3	C	Sept 13
6579	Kelley Henry	20	E	Aug 23
9083	Kelley M	Art 2	H	Sept 17
6275	Kelsey E	27	D	Aug 20
6712	Kempton E	Art 2	G	Aug 24
5708	Kennedy Wm	59	F	Aug 15
6529	Kenney J	Cav 3	G	Aug 23
8252	Kent S	27	H	Sept 9
12490	Kerr Wm, S't	56	D	Jan 20 65
6036	Keyes J C	Art 2	G	Aug 18 64
868	Kice Thomas	Cav 2	B	May 3
296	Kilan M, S't	17	I	Apr 1
4544	Kimball A	Art 1	B	Aug 2
1754	Kinnely F, S't	17	E	June 9
12813	Kluener F	27	A	Mar 25 65
554	Knapp David	Cav 2	M	Apr 14 64
3842	Knight ——	25	A	July 23
11119	Keephart M	Art 2	E	Oct 18
5037	Kuppy H	" 1	K	Aug 8
8648	Krote Huer	20	G	Sept 13
12549	Langley L F, S't	28	B	Jan 28 65
6735	Lain S	12	I	Aug 24 64
10885	Lane J H, S't	23		Oct 13
9738	Latham W	25	K	Sept 25
8835	Lathrop W O	58	C	Sept 15
2175	Laurens John	23	E	June 15
9621	Leach C W	20	I	Sept 23
2781	Leary D	Cav 2	A	July 2
7707	Leavey W H	12	A	Sept 3
7210	Lecraw W T	Art 1	G	Aug 29
7548	Leonard W E	59	H	Sept 2
7725	Leonard I G	Art 1	K	Sept 3
7798	Lewin Charles	19	E	Sept 3
2448	Lewis F	Art 2	G	June 25
10008	Lewis G C	" 2	G	Sept 30
4082	Lewis L	Cav 5	L	July 27
10750	Lewis L	Art 1	A	Oct 12
5401	Lindsay J	18	A	Aug 12
12413	Liswell L	27	F	Jan 8 65
8748	Livingston R	39	C	Sept 14 64
1156	Lochlen Joel	Cav 1	E	May 16
480	Lohem E D	18	H	Apr 9

218 LIST OF THE DEAD.

No.	Name	Age	Co.	Date	Yr
3163	Lombard B K	58	A	July 11	64
12256	Loring G	20	A	Dec 10	
10744	London Ed	22	G	Oct 11	
8437	Lovely Francis	25	I	Sept 11	
3217	Lovett A W	39	E	July 12	
3175	Lowell George	22	E	July 11	
9957	Lucier J	2	G	Sept 28	
4090	Lugby Z Art	2	G	July 27	
8593	Lyons E	27	I	Sept 12	
3683	Lynch John	56	K	July 21	
7521	Macey Charles	18	I	Sept 1	
4264	Macomber J	20	H	July 29	
4634	Mahan E	56	I	July 26	
3383	Marintine G H	18	I	July 16	
9940	Mann N C, Saddler	16	F	Sept 28	
6230	Mansfield D R	58	G	Aug 20	
503	Marden G O	17	I	Apr 12	
1350	Mariland W H	17	D	May 25	
7147	Marchet C	28	F	Aug 29	
8450	Martin C M Art	2	H	Sept 11	
6272	Maxwell M	"	1	I	Aug 20	
5060	McAllister J, Cor	17		Aug 8	
7823	McCaffrey J	27	E	Sept 4	
3835	McCloud J	56	K	July 23	
9942	McCord J G	32	H	Sept 28	
12176	McCorner J	19	F	Nov 27	
8905	McDarle J Art	2	M	Sept 15	
6162	McDermott J	"	2	B	Aug 19	
4409	McDevitt Wm	25	E	July 31	
9439	McDonald R	18	D	Sept 21	
430	McDonnell P	2	B	Apr 8	
7459	McDonough P, Cor	25	E	Sept 1	
1984	McGiven J	22	K	June 15	
6375	McGovern B	34	D	Aug 21	
2952	McGowen John Art	2	H	June 29	
5280	McGowen Wm	12	A	Aug 11	
4260	McGonegal R	16	K	July 29	
5121	McGuire A	58	D	Aug 9	
6460	McHenry Jas Art	2	G	Aug 21	
6544	McIntyre H	"	1	K	Aug 23	
11531	McKarren E	"	1	I	Oct 26	
11849	McKenny B	34	A	Nov 5	
6358	McKinzie George	27	I	Aug 5	
5223	McKnight B Cav	3	G	Aug 10	
3174	McLaughlin E, S't	9	C	July 11	
10030	Mc Masters —	57	A	Sept 29	
3675	Mc Millan Jos	24	B	July 20	
522	Mc Namara	17	I	April 13	
5185	Mc Naury R	27	I	Aug 9	
11381	Mc Nulty P Art	2	G	Oct 24	
5194	Mc Williams W	77	D	Aug 10	
7586	Medren W	20	G	Sept 2	
5808	Mehan B Art	2	H	Aug 16	
1434	Melan A	18	F	May 28	
9735	Melvin S Art	1	K	Sept 25	
2209	Merritt M	27	C	June 20	
1358	Merriman W H	17	D	May 25	
9117	Messrs W Art	1	B	Sept 18	
9597	Mesters E	34	H	Sept 23	
6286	Meyer — Cav	1	K	Aug 30	
8631	Miland John Art	2	H	Sept 13	
11514	Millard P S	19	G	Oct 26	
1219	Miller A	28	F	May 19	
4329	Miller J M	11	A	July 30	
10169	Miller L	20		Oct 1	
4050	Miller Jos, S't	57	C	July 27	
7178	Millrean MW,Cor C	2	E	Aug 29	
9539	Milton C	21	A	Sept 22	64
8506	Mitchell W C	23	A	Sept 11	
11867	Mitchell F	14	A	Nov 6	
11771	Mitchell John	19	C	Nov 3	
8343	Mittance L	20	G	Sept 10	
4053	Mixter G L Cav	1	E	July 27	
6235	Monroe J Art	2	M	Aug 20	
2436	Morgan C H	27	H	June 25	
8077	Morgan Pat	23	B	Sept 7	
3160	Moore A	56	C	July 11	
5490	Moore C A, Mus A	2	N	Aug 13	
10593	Moore M	57	A	Oct 10	
3411	Moore P	18	F	July 16	
3990	Morris N G Art	1		July 26	
1004	Morris R, S't	28	F	May 10	
9627	Mortimer L	19	E	Sept 24	
8272	Morton G H	42	C	Sept 9	
5360	Morton J	34	A	Aug 11	
6982	Moss Charles Art	2	H	Aug 27	
12516	Moulton H	15	F	Jan 23	65
12619	Murdock A B, Cor	27	D	Feb 8	
321	Murley D	9	D	April 2	64
7862	Murphy C	17	D	Sept 5	
5488	Murphy F	17	D	Aug 13	
1680	Murphy Michael	12	K	June 6	
12783	Murphy P	27	H	Mar 15	65
5041	Murray Thomas	19	A	Aug 8	64
9241	Needham J A Art	1	B	Sept 19	
9278	Nelson J	"	2		Sept 19	
7006	Newcomb J E	"	2	G	Aug 27	
9694	Nitchman A	19	B	Sept 24	
1282	Noble David	17	D	May 22	
12439	Norman E Art	1	E	Jan 12	65
350	Norton F F	39	H	April 14	64
10058	Nottage I L	2	F	Sept 30	
7193	O'Brien Jas Art	2	G	Aug 29	
2509	O'Brien John	36	K	June 26	
5117	O'Connell J	9	C	Aug 9	
12180	O'Connell J	15	H	Nov 28	
9780	O'Connell M	2	H	Sept 26	
11080	O'Conner Wm	29	K	Oct 17	
11493	O'Donnell W	11	G	Oct 26	
10592	Oliver J	39	E	Oct 10	
4640	Oliver S E	27	B	Aug 3	
7161	O'Neil Charles	25	B	Aug 29	
4884	O'Neil D	25	E	Aug 6	
4975	Osborn W	19	K	Aug 7	
5340	Packard N M	27	C	Aug 11	
6629	Page Wm	16	D	Aug 23	
598	Paisley Wm	17	D	April 17	
10695	Palmer T	59	E	Oct 11	
4714	Panier J M	17	K	Aug 4	
11059	Pantins A J	15	H	Oct 17	
6899	Pandes L Art	3	G	Aug 26	
7811	Parrish Chas Cav	1	C	Sept 4	
5380	Pains F Art	2	E	Aug 12	
1074	Parker D H	36	C	May 13	
2327	Parsons W D	23	E	June 22	
6860	Pasco J M	58	D	Aug 26	
1231	Patterson H W	33	G	May 20	
8868	Payne G A	57	H	Sept 16	
4067	Payne Wm A Art	1	M	Aug 7	
7556	Peabody W F	37		Sept 2	
6471	Peckham A P	15	B	Aug 21	
5441	Peeto A	36	A	Aug 12	
4003	Pennington R A A	1		July 26	
9603	Perry N Art	1	F	Sept 23	

LIST OF THE DEAD.   219

No.	Name		Age	Co.	Date
274	Perry Samuel K		39	D	Mar 31 64
4986	Pettie C	Art 2		H	Aug 7
7671	Phillbrook J E		56	F	Sept 3
7708	Phillips A		50	B	Sept 3
10383	Phillips L M, S't		17	D	Oct 5
6906	Phipps H B, Cor	A 1		B	Aug 20
4763	Phipps M M		27	C	Aug 4
11079	Pierson R, S't	Art 2		H	Oct 17
20	Pilhuton John		11	E	April 14
5128	Piper Charles		28	G	Aug 9
6740	Piper F		25	E	Aug 24
7080	Polshon F B		17	D	Aug 28
763	Poole Charles, Cor			G	April 23
6583	Pratt Daniel		27	I	Aug 27
12135	Pratt D W	Art 2		G	Nov 23
5742	Pratt Henry		23	C	Aug 15
2008	Price Edward	Art 2		M	June 15
12175	Prichard J, Cor		2	G	Jan 18 65
5404	Prior Michael		56	I	Aug 12 64
11975	Puffer E D		34	A	Nov 12
4218	Quinn James		15	M	July 29
12804	Quirk M J		1	D	Mar 20 65
12094	Ragan C, Cor		27	H	Nov 19 64
10156	Ramstell H		37	H	Oct 1
5500	Rand M	Art 2		G	Aug 13
3358	Randall J		2	F	July 15
54	Raymond C		20	I	June 12
8072	Reed Charles	Art 2		H	Sept 7
1725	Rensseller C N		54	C	June 8
6122	Rapp James		28	A	Aug 19
2970	Reynolds N A		36	C	July 7
3272	Rice C A J	Art 2		G	July 13
1285	Rich C		2	D	May 22
4233	Rich Samuel		27	B	July 29
4918	Richards G		16	I	Aug 6
3156	Richards James		27	C	July 11
11553	Richardson L	Art 1		G	Oct 27
4167	Richardson S R "		1	M	July 28
7546	Richards Thos		29	B	Sept 2
7199	Ridlaw James •		19	C	Aug 29
10638	Riley H J	Art 2		G	Oct 10
8642	Riley M		56	K	Sept 13
7200	Ripley M A		32	F	Aug 29
6650	Rippon Wm		58	G	Aug 23
6166	Roach J		35	F	Aug 19
11552	Roberts J H		18	I	Oct 27
9448	Roberts Joseph C		1	K	Sept 21
12505	Roberts L		13	F	Jan 22 65
11699	Robinson J		19	H	Oct 31 64
3833	Robinson R		27	F	July 23
5659	Roe Wm	Art 2		H	Aug 14
4875	Roferty John		2	K	Aug 6
12398	Rome R		1	I	Jan 4 65
4219	Rover F		4	E	July 29 64
6654	Rope A R		11	I	Aug 23
5396	Rowe Asa	Art		1	K	Aug 11
11521	Rowley Charles		19	K	Oct 26
3455	Russell		27	C	July 17
9349	Rustar R		27	A	Sept 19
5987	Ruth F		36	C	Aug 17
6036	Ryes J C	Art 2		G	Aug 18
5276	Sabines Edward		19	K	Aug 11
9465	Samlett P V		1	A	Sept 21
8074	Sanborn G B	Cav 2		B	Sept 7
10256	Smith C		27	D	Oct 3
8002	Smith C A	Art 1		C	Sept 6
4952	Smith D H		1	I	Aug 7
12499	Smith E		27	G	Jan 21 65
11804	Smith E M		1	D	Nov 4 64
7158	Smith H		57	D	Aug 29
7443	Smith J, Cor		20	E	Sept 1
967	Smith John		17	K	May 8
7538	Smith J P	Art 1		A	Sept 2
5780	Smith J H		19	G	Aug 15
8184	Smith W		23	B	Sept 8
154	Smith W H		12	I	Mar 25
2304	Smith Wm		54		June 22
12748	Smith V		57	K	Mar 6 65
3745	Snow W		16	E	July 21 64
12063	Somers F		19	G	Nov 17
5316	Switzer L		16	E	Aug 11
8280	Southworth J		18	G	Sept 9
2469	Southworth John		18	E	June 25
2188	Spalding J		2	E	June 19
12160	Spar H		19	H	Nov 25
10342	Spellman B F	Art 2			Oct 4
6179	Spence David		19	D	Aug 19
4153	Spooner C L		27	H	July 26
5600	Spooner E O		27	A	Aug 14
4652	Spooner F		18	A	Aug 3
3397	Stalder E P		17	H	July 16
9873	Stauf J		20	D	Sept 27
6501	Steadson W		16	G	Aug 22
5028	Stelle F	Art 1		J	Aug 8
7361	Stevens H		28	F	Sept 6
9183	Stevens N		1	E	Sept 18
392	Sanborn T		17	D	April 6
8281	Sanders F	Art 2		G	Sept 9
10637	Sandwich J		1	G	Oct 10
3405	Sanford J D		40	A	July 16
10406	Savin J H		34	C	Oct 6
11888	Sawer John		33	F	Nov 7
4180	Sawyer S F	Art 1		B	July 28
11203	Sayer G D		11	I	Oct 20
5834	Shalster S		25	G	Aug 16
5623	Seeley Chas H	A 2		G	Aug 14
11731	Sergeant J C		19	E	Nov 2
11338	Shamrock I		19	H	Oct 23
6782	Shaw Andrew		25	K	Aug 25
12303	Shaw C L, Cor		15	E	Dec 18
7827	Shea J	Art 2		H	Sept 4
7481	Shehan James	"	2	G	Sept 1
2324	Sherman P H		37	E	June 23
8822	Sherwood F		76	B	Sept 15
4950	Shindler Jno	Art 1		I	Aug 7
6602	Shore J J		1	F	Aug 23
10946	Short J		2	B	Oct 14
7735	Shults A M		23	B	Sept 3
10415	Shults George		28	H	Oct 6
1458	Simmonds E		17	D	May 29
6957	Simons A	Art 2		M	Aug 26
4186	Simpson D O		34	D	July 28
9842	Simpson W	Art 2		H	Sept 27
6141	Sinclair A		1	G	Aug 19
11189	Sloan S		20	K	Oct 19
8375	Small Z	Art 1		G	Sept 11
10404	Smalley J H		2	C	Oct 6
9	Smith Warren		12	F	Mar 5
2881	Stevens Thomas		2	H	July 4
1758	Stewart J		11	H	June 9
11291	Stewart E		52	D	Oct 22
12420	Stone F P		27	A	Jan 9 65
10181	Stone A	Art 2		H	Oct 1 64
5957	Sullivan Jno		16	A	Aug 17

LIST OF THE DEAD.

No.	Name	Co.	Age	Rank	Date
7401	Sullivan Jno		2	K	Aug 31 64
10890	Sullivan M		2	D	Oct 4
8203	Sullivan P		9		Sept 8
10792	Sullivan P		15	I	Oct 12
11671	Sullivan F		59	B	Oct 30
12788	Sylvester D		1	B	Mar 17 65
8325	Sylvester E	Art	2	H	Sept 10 64
12053	Sylvester J		4	A	Nov 16
11957	Tabor B		35	C	Nov 11
10697	Tabor F		16	E	Oct 11
2067	Taggerd John		17	E	June 19
3368	Taylor N		37	D	July 15
2515	Taylor Thos	Cav	2	G	June 26
8805	Teinerts T J		110	D	Sept 15
4386	Tenney Wm		3	G	July 31
3812	Thayer J		27	A	July 23
8612	Thomas J	Art	2	H	Sept 13
11123	Thomas J A		32	G	Oct 18
2421	Thomas J W		56	I	June 24
12527	Thompson C	Art	1	B	Jan 26 65
1890	Thompson Geo		16		June 13 64
4536	Thompson Geo		58	F	Aug 2
3908	Thompson J M		27	H	July 24
3596	Thompson W W		58	G	July 19
4634	Tibbett A		23	F	Aug 3
7468	Tiffany J		4	F	Sept 1
6549	Tilden A		27	B	Aug 23
3898	Tillson C E		20	E	July 24
3549	Toona Jno		28	E	July 18
407	Torey L		12	H	Apr 7
6019	Torrey C L		7	G	Aug 17
10131	Townley J J		1	F	Oct 1
9108	Travern W	Art	2	G	Sept 18
7860	Travis H C		59	C	Sept 5
7996	Trescutt W M		15	I	Sept 6
8132	Turner H		34	F	Sept 8
12161	Tuith F		20	F	Nov 25
5428	Twichell J		17	K	Aug 12
6332	Twichell —		36	C	Aug 21
9517	Usher Samuel		17	I	Sept 22
8466	Wade A D L	Art	2	G	Sept 11
5959	Waldon Wm		36	B	Aug 17
12444	Walker A		19	F	Jan 12 65
3377	Wallace P		57	B	July 16 64
11494	Walsh M		4	C	Oct 26
5191	Walton E A		57	H	Aug 10
8724	Walton Nat		59	E	Sept 14
8304	Wanderfelt —		6	C	Sept 10
1733	Wardin H		17	I	June 8
5217	Ware Sam		1	H	Aug 10
8864	Warffender J W		27	C	Sept 15
12131	Warner A F		19	D	Nov 22
6454	Washburne W E		27	I	Aug 21
4721	Weiden H		17	H	Aug 4
1066	Welsh Frank		17	B	May 13
6224	Weldon Chas	Art	1	D	Aug 20
11796	Wells S		1	A	Nov 14
5214	Wellington G W		2	G	Aug 10
3547	Welworth C W		18	D	July 18
3247	Werdier W		58	G	July 13
1334	West E		24	A	May 24
7002	West J G	Art	1	E	Aug 27
4577	White F		15	K	Aug 2
6807	White Joseph	Art	2	G	Aug 25
7188	White Joseph		2	G	Aug 29
7902	Whiting A		27	H	Sept 5
6867	Whitney F P		1	G	Aug 26
635	Whittaker S		17	D	Apr 20 64
1115	Wiggard Geo		22	A	May 15
6715	Wilber E		27	G	Aug 24
4539	Wilcox A	Art	14	C	Aug 2
5519	Wilder L E		2	G	Aug 13
7318	Wilkins S O		1	G	Aug 30
661	Williams Chas		27	G	Aug 24
668	Williams J		58	G	Sept 13
469	Willis C		17	K	July 17
7549	Wilson J	Art	2	H	Sept 2
769	Wilson Robert		34	A	Aug 25
6742	Wilson S	Art	2	G	Aug 24
10545	Wilson W		18	B	Oct 9
13	Witherill O		47	C	Aug 20
6483	Woodbury B		17	A	Aug 21
6564	Woodward W A		27	B	Aug 23
6368	Wright C E		27	B	Aug 21
6288	Wright M E		27	C	Aug 20
4923	Wyman H C	Art	2	H	Aug 6
3562	Wright W M	"	3	G	July 18
7152	Young N C		1	I	Aug 29
8882	Young E		2		Sept 16
6922	Young G W	Art	2	H	Aug 26

TOTAL, 758.

MICHIGAN.

No.	Name	Co.	Age	Rank	Date
2198	Ayres J B		22	C	June 17 64
2247	Acker J		22	K	June 20
2461	Atkinson P		22	C	June 22
2576	Anderson George		23	E	June 27
3257	Abbott C M		5	E	July 13
4947	Ammerman H H		23	A	Aug 7
5472	Aulger George		10	F	Aug 13
5601	Ackler W	Cav	3	C	Aug 14
6119	Austin D		8	C	Aug 19
6713	Allen A A		14	I	Aug 24
9156	Anderson F	Cav	1	G	Sept 18
12650	Arsnoe W		7	E	Dec 27
12571	Allen J		9	H	Feb 2 65
12606	Adams A		4	B	Feb 7
121	Brockway O		11	K	Mar 23 64
1154	Banghart J	Cav	9	G	May 16
1283	Broman C		4	H	May 22
1511	Beckwith E	Cav	6	I	May 31
1513	Bishop C		27	F	May 31
1664	Beard J		6	E	June 6
2004	Bostwick R S		2	F	June 15
2025	Bowerman R		22	H	June 17
2201	Bryant George	Cav	6	H	June 17
2271	Bush Thomas		8	A	June 20
2303	Brigham David		22	D	June 22
2381	Bowlin J		27	E	June 23
2478	Briggs I		6	E	June 25
2595	Berry Henry		15	E	June 28
2700	Broo F			A	June 30
2946	Bailey John	Cav	4	M	July 6
3149	Briggs W H		20	G	July 11
3215	Bibley J		3	C	July 12
3479	Brannock F		3	C	July 17
3517	Brush J		16	K	July 18
3531	Bradley Geo		17	B	July 18
3591	Built F	Art	3	A	July 19
3777	Bohnmiller J	Cav	10	H	July 22
3798	Beardslee M A		22	D	July 22
4109	Billiams Jno		2	K	July 27
4339	Binder Jno		2	A	Aug 30
4395	Brown G	Cav	4	E	July 31

LIST OF THE DEAD. 221

No.	Name		Co.	Date
4810	Baker A	Cav 5	F	Aug 5 64
5573	Betts P	1	C	Aug 14
8333	Brookiniger E	7	D	Sept 10
5950	Bertan I	Cav 8	B	Aug 16
5970	Burnett J	7	G	Aug 17
6013	Burkhart C	22	G	Aug 17
6065	Brower L F	17	H	Aug 18
6290	Billy Geo	9	E	Aug 20
6388	Burcham J	5	B	Aug 21
6590	Burdick Theo	Cav 6	I	Aug 27
7148	Beirs S	18	B	Aug 29
7227	Billingsby J	Bat 1		Aug 29
7536	Bradley B	Cav 9	E	Sept 1
7796	Blair Jno	7	E	Sept 4
7932	Barr W	Cav 8	L	Sept 5
8391	Brown H S	Cav 8	F	Sept 10
8505	Bradley E	11	K	Sept 12
8814	Blanchard Jas	7	G	Sept 15
8869	Brown A	3	G	Sept 15
9226	Beckley W	Cav 1	E	Sept 19
9240	Brown H	13	A	Sept 19
9305	Beebe Jno	1	A	Sept 20
9430	Baker Jno	Cav 1	H	Sept 21
9545	Birdsey J	7	D	Sept 23
9553	Barber J M	26	C	Sept 23
9637	Baxter S	Cav 6	L	Sept 24
9830	Batt W H	Cav 6	L	Sept 27
9834	Bunker R B	1	D	Sept 27
9853	Barnard G	Cav 7	M	Sept 27
9866	Beekley L	10	F	Sept 27
10044	Barney H	17	D	Sept 29
10340	Blackburn Jas	5	G	Oct 4
10490	Bentley H	24	I	Oct 7
10835	Bittman J	Cav 1	C	Oct 13
11275	Baldwin L A	24	B	Oct 22
12130	Beck G	Cav 1	H	Nov 23
12162	Bennett W L	26	G	Nov 26
12157	Barnett I	2	E	Nov 28
12745	Bearves M	15	G	Mar 7 65
34	Colan Fred	17	F	Feb 9 64
210	Chilcote Jas C	20	G	Feb 28
398	Chambers J R	Cav 5	K	Apr 5
439	Cowill Ed	" 8	G	Apr 8
593	Cowell John	" 10	H	Apr 15
1037	Conrad Edson	" 8	G	May 24
1077	Cripper G F	" 5	C	May 14
1164	Coastner J D	" 5	L	May 16
1330	Chapman H	" 5	E	May 24
1351	Cameron Jas	27	H	May 25
1505	Constank John	9	B	May 31
1692	Conkwrite John	22	K	June 7
1711	Cook J	Cav 4	D	June 7
1811	Churchward A R	9	C	June 10
1943	Clear James	22	F	June 14
2617	Cussick B	7	C	June 28
3071	Collins James	5	I	July 9
3462	Cartney A	Cav 2	E	July 17
3595	Cameron D	" 1	L	July 19
3800	Cummings W	2	F	July 22
3969	Clements Wm	S S 1	C	July 26
4032	Cook J	10	F	July 26
4620	Cronk Jas	Cav 5	G	Aug 3
4920	Cooper J	7	K	Aug 6
4956	Curtis M D	8	C	Aug 7
5201	Crunch J	Cav 1		Aug 10
5685	Cummings D	" 5	I	Aug 15
5686	Churchill G W	3	A	Aug 15
5905	Carr C B	25	K	Aug 16 64
6253	Coft Jas	20	F	Aug 20
6285	Cobb G	4	D	Aug 20
6446	Cook Geo	Cav 10	H	Aug 22
6604	Cahon W J	1	H	Aug 26
7904	Carp J S	1	K	Aug 28
7104	Caten M	Cav 7	E	Aug 29
7496	Cling Jacob	2	K	Sept 1
7534	Campbell S B	2	H	Sept 1
7883	Coldwell W	124	H	Sept 5
8406	Cope J B	17	A	Sept 11
8993	Cornice J D	7	F	Sept 17
9341	Carver J H	Cav 4		Sept 20
10644	Cooley G	3	A	Oct 9
10759	Clago S	7	C	Oct 12
10788	Crain R O	17	A	Oct 12
10871	Cooley Henry	34	G	Oct 13
11743	Collins C	2	K	Nov 2
11903	Clark G W	Art 1	C	Nov 7
12143	Cameron F	17	E	Nov 24
12258	Cook N	1	K	Dec 10
12391	Case S	Cav 5	L	Jan 4 65
12474	Coras E	" 6	C	Jan 17
12634	Chambers W	" 8	G	Feb 10
1345	Davis Wilson	8	A	May 24 64
43	Diets Jno	Cav 6	I	Feb 14
195	Dunay Jno	6	C	Feb 27
315	Deas Abe	Cav 7	L	April 2
716	Decker L	10	H	April 24
1270	Drummond Jno	27	E	May 21
1292	Dolf Sylvanus	27	G	May 23
1296	Denter W A	5	E	May 23
1683	Dougherty D	8	C	June 6
2090	Demerie D	Bat 1		June 17
2248	Dillingham W O	20	I	June 20
2383	Dennison H	Cav 5	G	June 30
2882	Dreal D	" 2	B	July 4
3207	Dusalt A	17	H	July 12
2314	Dyre Wm	17	B	July 14
3610	Davy R	22	C	July 19
3619	DeRealt F	5	C	July 20
4660	Decker G S	Cav 5	K	Aug 3
4669	Darct S	5	I	Aug 4
4670	Dugan D	21	I	Aug 4
5070	Dawson D	17	H	Aug 8
5351	Dalzell Wm	6	A	Aug 10
5666	Doyle S	8	B	Aug 14
6225	Duinz G W	Cav 3	I	Aug 20
6401	Denton G	5	E	Aug 21
7654	Derfly Wm	1	H	Sept 3
7769	Dumont W	36	H	Sept 4
8651	Daly A	Cav 7	E	Sept 13
9995	Dyer J	5	I	Sept 29
10161	Doass M	Cav 1	L	Oct 1
10922	Dixon Jno	" 5	L	Oct 14
11125	Dennis O	1	H	Oct 18
12124	Dunroe P	24	H	Oct 22
12574	Drake O	22	D	Feb 2 65
2850	Egsillim P H	22	K	July 4 64
5318	Eggleston Wm	Cav 7	E	Aug 10
3981	Elliot J	24	G	July 26
1210	Eaton R	22	H	May 19
1240	Ellis E	Cav 2	B	May 20
2788	Ensign J	11	A	July 2
7901	Edwards S	6	E	Sept 5
8255	Edmonds B	1	H	Sept 9
11065	English James	17	B	Oct 17

LIST OF THE DEAD.

No.	Name	Reg.	Co.	Date
5817	Everett J	77	K	Aug 16 64
890	Force F	27	D	May 5
1054	Fitzpatrick M	Cav 1	B	May 13
1367	Folk C	14	E	May 25
2197	Fitse T	Cav 1	C	June 19
2252	Fairbanks J	" 15	G	June 20
2343	Face W H	6		June 23
4194	Fisher F	23	G	June 29
5041	Farmer M	22	D	Aug 8
5861	Flanigan John	5	D	Aug 16
6135	Farnham A	5	A	Aug 19
6333	Fox James	8	H	Aug 21
6680	Fritchie M	22	G	Aug 24
6948	Fitzpatrick M	8	E	Aug 27
7027	Fox Charles	1	B	Aug 27
7030	Forsythe H	5	F	Aug 28
7171	Forbs C	Cav 1	B	Aug 27
8585	Fethton F	" 1	G	Sept 12
10275	Fliflin H	27	F	Oct 3
11500	Freeman B	S S 1		Oct 26
11703	Fredenburg F	7		Nov 1
12098	Findlater H	Cav 7	C	Feb 22 65
11845	Frederick G	9	G	April 23
8250	Face C	S S 1	B	Sept 9 64
11509	Fox W	22	E	Oct 26
145	Goodenough G M	23	K	Mch 25
506	Grover Jas	20	H	April 15
784	Grippman J	Cav 5	M	April 28
956	Graham Geo W	5	C	May 8
1049	Goodbold Wm	Cav 2	L	May 12
1131	Gorman E	13	H	May 16
1234	Garrett S H	Cav 2	G	May 20
1927	Grimley Jas	22	D	June 14
2192	Ganigan J	Cav 9	L	June 19
2614	Gorden Jas	1	D	June 28
2802	Gilbert F	3	K	July 3
2928	Gibbons M	6	C	July 5
3863	Goodman W	5	I	July 24
4092	Griffin G	11	H	July 27
4245	Green E	11	H	July 29
5716	Galvin M	23	I	Aug 15
6482	Greek C H	Cav 1	K	Aug 22
6806	Gillis Jno	Cav 4	F	Aug 26
7476	Gaines A	22	F	Sept 1
7518	Guilz H	1	A	Sept 1
7624	Griens G D	8	I	Sept 2
7659	Graff Jacob	17	H	Sept 3
7741	Gibson J	1	K	Sept 3
7968	Grant A H	7	D	Sept 6
8628	Gray Geo	Cav 1	E	Sept 13
10671	Gallitt L	22	F	Oct 9
10726	Gibbs J	7	B	Oct 11
11207	Gask I	Cav 8	C	Oct 20
11302	Gray James	Cav 6	A	Oct 22
11352	Groucher J	Cav 6	B	Oct 23
11647	Grabaugh J	5	G	Oct 30
12164	Gifford L	61		Nov 26
12443	Gowell N	19	F	Jan 12 65
12573	Goodel M	5	C	Feb 2
5818	Gurmane B S	77	K	Aug 16 67
4511	Grasman E	23	I	Aug 1 64
12207	Gabulison J	Cav 5	F	Dec 1
6	Hall William	Cav 2	M	Feb 5
339	Holton S M	1	B	April 20
367	Henry Jas	8	A	April 5
409	Hartsell Geo	Cav 7	B	April 6
818	Hutton S	Cav 9	G	April 30
830	Hood Jas D	22	H	May 3 64
947	Hart J R	6	E	May 7
1453	Hannah Jno	22	C	May 29
1519	Hunter F A	22	F	May 31
1656	Herriman D	22	D	June 6
1738	Huntley W	Cav 5	E	June 8
1813	Haines R	Cav 9	G	June 10
1904	Hough M	22		June 13
1910	Harty J S	16	F	June 13
2660	Hayes C	6	H	June 29
3015	Hardy Jno	4	H	July 7
3040	Hugney Jas	17	B	July 8
3206	Hopkins N	Cav 6	E	July 12
4	Halson David	Cav 8	A	Mar 27
3343	Heil H	9	G	July 15
3483	Honsigner W L	7	C	July 17
3889	Hance C, Bugler	7	D	July 24
3927	Hawkins George	12	H	July 25
4166	Hunter M W	22	D	July 28
4286	Herou Jno	5	F	July 30
4426	Heath M	21	C	July 31
4674	Hale S B	Cav 7	D	Aug 4
5332	Hollen Geo	Cav 1	L	Aug 11
5370	Haynes P	Cav 1	H	Aug 11
5376	Husted J	10	C	Aug 10
5536	Henrich J	3	C	Aug 13
5931	Hall W	26	I	Aug 17
6110	Holmes J F	42	H	Aug 18
6276	Hibler A	Cav 9	D	Aug 20
6992	Henny A	27	B	Aug 27
6998	Hungerford C	20	E	Aug 27
6999	Hunt L	2	C	Aug 27
8100	Holcomb J	Cav 6	K	Sept 7
8624	Harrington G	Cav 6	D	Sept 13
9233	Hawley C	4	F	Sept 19
9685	Hartman H	29	A	Sept 24
9958	Hinkley G C	20	F	Sept 28
10348	Hoag J M	20	H	Oct 5
11027	Hankins E	5	E	Oct 16
11057	Hayes Jas I		E	Oct 17
11070	Haywood J B	Cav 1	H	Oct 17
11260	Hamlin J H	S S 1	K	Oct 20
11335	Hoag J M	20	H	Oct 23
11412	Hill W	S S 1		Oct 24
11480	Howard F S	8	E	Oct 26
11593	Hawk H L	24	I	Oct 28
11757	Hodges M	22		Nov 3
11835	Hilmer C	Cav 6	M	Nov 5
12067	Howe J	Cav 7	F	Nov 17
12612	Hicks C	8	B	Feb 8 65
9718	Harper D	3	E	Sept 25 64
5141	Ingraham W L	Cav 5	B	Aug 9
1817	Jackson James	7	I	June 7
2576	Jones A	6	E	June 27
3564	Jaguet E B	Cav 7	C	July 19
3621	Jackson Geo G	22	F	July 20
4736	Johnson J H	7	G	Aug 4
6576	Johnson J	24	I	Aug 23
7520	Jump D O	1	A	Sept 1
7753	Johnson H	Cav 9	L	Sept 2
9746	Jackland C	Cav 8	E	Sept 25
12010	Jamieson H	Cav 5	H	Nov 14
12395	Jondro M	1	K	Jan 5 65
12463	Johnson A	5	C	Jan 16
338	King Leander	8	G	April 5 64
488	Keintzler R	Cav 5	F	April 12
705	Karl Wm	2	A	April 24

LIST OF THE DEAD.

No.	Name	Reg	Co	Date
4140	Klunder Chas	Cav 5	F	July 28 64
4397	Kennedy H	27	H	July 31
4424	Kinney John	17	H	July 31
4728	Kendall W	6	D	Aug 4
8229	Kessler F	11	G	Sept 9
10789	Kinsell George	Cav 5	B	Oct 12
10908	Kenkham H C	Cav 5	E	Oct 14
12431	Kenney C	Cav 5	H	Jan 11 65
1882	Lewis F L	Cav 2		June 12 64
253	Lossing John	Cav 8	B	Mar 29
960	Loring Jno	27	E	May 8
1187	Lewis P	5	D	May 18
1301	Lancreed M	14	B	May 23
37	Lumer Jno	17	F	Mar 28
3303	Lanning H B	22	H	July 14
3700	Lyon A D	Cav 5	G	July 21
4243	Lonsey L	Cav 1	L	July 29
4913	Luce F	Art 1	A	Aug 6
4992	Lu Duc Jas	17	G	Aug 7
5142	Larke J A	23	F	Aug 9
5216	Lowell Jas	Cav 7	E	Aug 10
5776	Laribee L	8	H	Aug 15
5923	Lofler E E	17	H	Aug 17
6967	Lord M	3	M	Aug 24
8085	Leamon G	Cav 8	H	Sept 7
9685	Lard H O	22	D	Sept 24
9700	Lund Jas	Cav 6	H	Sept 25
10877	Laidham G	1	D	Oct 13
11969	Lutz Wm	Cav 6	F	Nov 11
218	Mc Cartney H	Cav 6	K	Mar 29
268	Mc Guire Jno	20	A	Mar 31
542	Markham D	Cav 5	B	April 14
612	Mc Carter Jas	22	H	April 18
1059	Mum A F	27	F	May 13
1062	Miller Chas	Cav 5	D	May 13
1710	Miller J	3	C	June 7
2255	Maby Ep	Cav 8	K	June 20
2586	Mc Dowell J	"	8	F	June 28
2759	Mc Spoulding W	22	E	July 2
2828	Man aring Wm	22	D	July 3
2976	Man Thos G	5	A	July 7
3090	Marshall H E	27	B	July 9
3150	Morris A T	14	K	July 9
3537	Marvey Andrew	17	G	July 18
3697	Miller W E	2	K	July 21
3936	Mc Cabe F	22	H	July 25
3954	Morgan M	2	E	July 26
4078	Mc Fall H	17	E	July 27
4144	Miller G	5	I	July 28
4304	Monny Jno	Cav 5	L	July 30
4783	Monroe D	"	6	A	Aug 4
4942	Morgan E C	23	G	Aug 7
5153	Miller L	7	F	Aug 9
5630	Monch C	20	I	Aug 14
6249	Mc Carty Chas	20	I	Aug 20
6229	Meyers J	6	H	Aug 21
6820	Myer J	4	I	Aug 25
7114	Moore J	27	B	Aug 28
7269	Merrill S B	5	G	Aug 30
7279	Mc Laine Thos	1	I	Aug 30
7473	Mc Cloud A	21	I	Sept 1
7513	Mason F	Cav 7	L	Sept 1
7918	Martin Peter	17	H	Sept 5
7936	Musket J	Cav 4	K	Sept 5
7962	Miller F	22	G	Sept 6
8025	Munday E	17	G	Sept 6
8387	Mc Clure R	7	D	Sept 9
8518	Miles C S	Cav 1	F	Sept 12 64
8590	Mc Ginis P	16		Sept 12
8050	Mc Kay K	10		Sept 6
8876	Munson H C	30	E	Sept 16
8807	Morrison J	21	F	Sept 16
8994	Maher S L	Cav 7	I	Sept 17
9185	Marin Wm	22	E	Sept 18
9750	Mc Arthur W	Cav 7	D	Sept 25
9791	Moore John	"	6	G	Sept 26
10011	Moses C	"	5	I	Sept 29
10134	Moses A	"	6	M	Oct 1
10423	Migele J	9	A	Oct 6
10575	May Thomas	Cav 6	H	Oct 9
10958	Mc Millen Alex	"	5	M	Sept 14
11126	Miller John A	10	F	Oct 18
11536	Molash F	3	D	Oct 27
11548	Mc Mann W	17	A	Oct 27
11582	Mongby D	22	C	Oct 28
11798	Merrill C	4	K	Nov 4
12085	Miller H	9	A	Nov 18
12093	Magran J	S S 1		Nov 19
12252	Mc Came W	7	B	Dec 9
12458	Morton J	1	I	Jan 15 65
11511	Muckswarer W	S S 1	K	Oct 26 64
12674	Marshall G	4	M	Feb 19 65
12733	Mc Neill C	Cav 8	M	Mar 5
3790	Major Wm	22	D	July 22 64
7916	Monroe John	7	I	Sept 5
9791	Moore John	Cav 6	G	Sept 26
9965	Mc Clary W	"	7	H	Sept 28
513	Nicholson E	"	6	G	April 12
1209	Newbury James	"		A	May 19
2077	Nash Charles	22	H	June 17
3343	Nail	9	F	June 15
4102	Neck H	4	K	July 27
5092	Nirthhammer J	20	D	Aug 8
5400	Nagle C	11	G	Aug 11
5493	Narrane A	17	E	Aug 13
11011	Noyes James E	1		Oct 16
11911	Niland H	8	D	Nov 9
1005	Nurse H W	Cav 5	L	May 10
9812	Northam O H	6	M	Sept 26
285	O'Brien Austin	Cav 9	H	April 1
496	Oliver Alex	"	8	G	April 12
1180	Orrison Geo	"	9	M	May 18
2267	Olney G W	4	A	June 20
4384	Osborn S	27	B	July 31
4874	Overmeyer J F	Cav 6	E	Aug 6
5574	O'Neil J	22	K	Aug 14
5846	Orcutt C	3	F	Aug 16
8141	Ornig S W	20	C	Sept 8
8511	O'Brian W H	Cav 7	A	Sept 12
9011	Ogden E S	"	5	M	Sept 17
11040	O'Leary J	S S 1	H	Nov 9
11990	Osborn J L	6	E	Nov 13
12500	Oathart D	18	C	Jan 17 65
443	Parsons G	7	I	April 9 64
515	Pullman Geo	5	I	April 12
1038	Parker B C	Cav 8	C	May 12
1276	Perigo Jno	"	2	D	May 22
1374	Parish Thos	6	D	May 26
1892	Paisley A G	22		June 13
1997	Payne R H	17	E	June 15
2533	Piffer J	Cav 6	I	June 26
3546	Pierson Daniel	"	3	C	July 18
3594	Palmerly J	"	7	C	July 19
4100	Post R L	10	H	July 27

LIST OF THE DEAD.

No.	Name	Co.	Regt.	Date
4253	Pratt M		22 E	July 29 64
4486	Pelton A		21 A	Aug 1
4662	Philbrook F	Art	1	Aug 3
5056	Podroff D		13 D	Aug 8
5546	Peck J H	Cav	1 D	Aug 13
5612	Pond C		1 I	Aug 14
5745	Pettibone E E		7 D	Aug 15
4564	Porter L	S S	1 C	Aug 2
5760	Pentecost W G		18	Aug 15
5852	Palmer D		5 D	Aug 16
7389	Parks		7 C	Aug 31
7354	Perrin N	Cav	8 B	Aug 31
7960	Parks F	"	5 E	Sept 6
8195	Pearmell J		23 B	Sept 8
8636	Pike B H	Cav	2 C	Sept 13
8986	Plant Wm		16 G	Sept 16
9331	Pharrett Wm		22 D	Sept 20
11046	Platt R		22 A	Oct 17
11177	Palmer P		5 H	Oct 19
11986	Preston B		7 K	Nov 13
12273	Plins Wm	Cav	5 C	Dec 12
12409	Preston J		6 C	Jan 7 65
12578	Pratt L	Cav	8 C	Feb 3
12702	Parmalee C	"	8 M	Feb 12
77	Roloff Jno	"	5 E	Mar 20 64
324	Russell Peter		23 G	Apr 2
623	Rowland B		6 M	Apr 19
922	Robinson Wm		2 H	May 6
1804	Rhinehart D	Cav	5 C	June 10
2291	Rolland J		6 G	June 21
2402	Ruggles O		32 H	June 24
3296	Rassan A		28 I	July 14
3732	Riley Charles		6 I	July 21
3740	Riggs J		22 I	July 21
3876	Russ W J		22 C	July 24
5176	Rood C		22 C	Aug 9
5885	Roman John		5 C	Aug 16
6154	Relu A		17 G	Aug 19
5707	Ryan W		1 E	Sept 1
7750	Robinson H	Cav	5 L	Sept 2
7955	Rich A		11 B	Sept 6
8617	Riley Miles	Cav	7 F	Sept 13
9254	Rimer J C	"	1 C	Sept 19
9914	Ryan T		22 I	Sept 28
10136	Robinson T		27 F	Oct 1
10880	Randall H D		6 D	Oct 5
11151	Riley R		24 H	Oct 19
11457	Ramsay J		5 H	Oct 25
11675	Raley H	Cav	24 L	Oct 30
11705	Ricott S	S S	1 K	Nov. 1
12553	Richardson M B		1 L	Jan 29 65
12589	Rodgers W		26 G	Feb 5
12740	Robbins A	Cav	4 H	Mar 6
12745	Reaves M		15 G	Mar 8
134	Snyder E		17 F	Mar 24 64
172	Smith Wm	Cav	7 L	Mar 26
236	Soper Calvin		27 H	Mar 29
330	Sheldon H S		1 A	Apr 2
520	Shannon John		20 H	Apr 13
842	Smith W W	Cav	5 D	May 2
854	Stillman L D		6 M	May 3
1082	Stuck L H	Cav	2 B	May 14
1328	Schemerhorn J C		7 C	May 24
1406	Samborn H		22 K	May 27
1446	Snow Levi		20 H	May 28
1626	Smith A	Cav	1 L	June 4
1801	Smith S		17 C	June 10
1741	Stevens S		22 K	June 8 64
1948	Shafer W		22 G	June 14
1966	Strickland Thos		10 E	June 14
2299	Sanburn H		22 K	June 20
2507	Smith C	Art	1 E	June 26
2651	Sarmyes C		24 C	June 29
2664	Stevens L	Cav	6 M	June 29
2685	Stewart C A		7 F	June 30
2807	Sprague W B		11 I	July 3
2986	Shaw F N		2 K	July 7
3001	Steele E	Cav	2 C	July 7
3085	Sibley J E		1 G	July 9
3353	Stubbs J	Cav	9 L	July 15
3518	Simpson E T	Art	6 G	July 18
3224	Shultz C		5 B	July 18
3544	Shumnay Wm	C	8 L	July 18
3942	Shaw F F		7 D	July 25
3951	Sharp Jas		6	July 25
4103	Stines H		4 K	July 27
4311	Sprague B	Cav	7 E	July 30
4438	Sale Thos		17 G	July 31
4859	Smith Wm		17 H	Aug 6
5193	Swain D	Cav	6 H	Aug 10
5972	Stow Geo		10 C	Aug 17
6323	Simpson T		8 I	Aug 21
6506	Simons A		17 B	Aug 22
6686	Smoke H B		6 H	Aug 24
7014	Sullivan Jno		27 E	Aug 27
7303	Sherman Fred		22 G	Aug 30
7350	Sayrrer J M		1 G	Aug 31
7528	Schofield C		27 G	Sept 1
7676	Satterly H J	Cav	6 E	Sept 2
8000	Sutherland J		1 I	Sept 6
8580	Stanning G W	Art	5 G	Sept 12
9100	Suthphar H W		15 F	Sept 18
9469	Stewart F	Cav	6 E	Sept 21
9481	Stewart W V		5 E	Sept 21
9629	Snyder J	Cav	5 M	Sept 24
10080	Straut C A	"	5 F	Sept 30
10117	Spencer Geo		21 H	Oct 1
10254	Sammonds A		7 E	Oct 3
10285	Spencer John		2 I	Oct 3
10417	Skull Wm		7 B	Oct 6
10444	Simpson J P		22 A	Oct 7
11138	Swart M M		3 F	Oct 19
11148	Swester C		5 K	Oct 19
11234	Sutton H		22 I	Oct 21
11265	Strander A		6 G	Oct 21
11354	Stoddard S	Cav	5 F	Oct 23
11701	Steadman S		10 H	Oct 30
11717	Smith S		7 H	Nov 1
11773	Sickles M		14 I	Nov 3
12020	Seeley H	Cav	6 B	Nov 15
12225	Spondle C	"	1 C	Dec 5
12229	Sumner H		27 B	Dec 6
12281	Stedman S D		10 H	Dec 11
12300	South Peter	S S	1 K	Dec 19
12678	Smith C B	Cav	8 L	Feb 19 65
12803	Smith Geo		8 B	Mar 20
12254	Stickner J		16 D	Dec 10 64
11508	Sockem A	S S	1 K	Oct 26
11510	Springer J	Cav	7 K	Oct 26
1304	Turrell Henry		22 H	May 23
2945	Tubbs P		7 K	July 6
48	Tilt George	Cav	2 D	May 24
3498	Thatcher E H	"	6 F	July 18
6703	Tompkins N R		1 B	Aug 24

LIST OF THE DEAD.

No.	Name	Regt.	Co.	Date
7009	Tift H	Cav 5	M	Aug 27 64
7544	Thompson W	8	F	Sept 2
7509	Tracy D	Cav 7	K	Sept 2
7797	Thompson M C	C 5	I	Sept 4
9103	Taylor H	32	F	Sept 18
11118	Taylor J M	11	A	Oct 18
11148	Twesler C	5	K	Oct 19
3045	Udell W O	2	D	July 25
731	Vanderhoof Jas C	6	G	April 25
1126	Vangieson L	Cav 5	D	May 15
1467	Vogle Jacob	27	D	May 29
2270	Van Dyke Jno	Cav 6	D	June 20
2994	Van Brant W H C	9	E	July 7
3278	Vanlin C	6	F	July 14
6864	Vanshoten W H C	6	K	Aug 26
7595	Vansickle L	Cav 5	G	Sept 2
8958	Vanmake F	16	G	Sept 15
9536	York C	5	K	Sept 22
9936	Vleight A	22	D	Sept 28
12166	Vanallen C	27	K	Nov 25
12690	Vincient J	8	K	Feb 22 65
340	Whittaker J	7	B	April 2 64
733	Whipper G	4	A	April 25
741	Wilson Byron	Cav 5	D	April 26
749	Wright Wm A	7	K	April 26
957	Wilson J	22	K	May 8
2102	Wilson W	11	I	June 17
4961	Winegardner A S C	1	K	Aug 7
12723	White C	5	F	Mar 3 65
12796	Whitmore C	Cav 8	M	Mar 18
6781	Wiley E T	1	E	Aug 25 64
749	Wright Wm A	7	K	April 6
1089	Woolsey R	22	E	May 14
1701	Walker J	22	C	June 7
1920	Wolf F	13	E	June 14
3301	Wentdarbly —	5	G	July 14
2899	Whitlock M	2	B	July 5
3180	Wilet S	22	K	July 11
3269	Wright W	Cav 5	K	July 13
3437	Wolverton C	6	B	July 17
3992	Woodruff H	Cav 1	E	July 26
4419	Warren H	4	B	July 31
4860	Walker Geo	22	G	Aug 6
5051	Williams M	1	A	Aug 8
5786	Williams T	Cav 2	L	Aug 15
11323	Wolfinger J M	20	H	Oct 23
12307	Windlass S	Cav 8	K	Dec 18
5559	Warner C		F	Aug 13
11096	Warner J	Cav 5	K	Oct 18
9844	Wheeler E	24	A	Sept 27
5930	Wisner Jno	Cav 6	I	Aug 17
8831	Wood A O	Cav 8	M	Sept 10
8076	Wilder H S	23	K	Sept 7
6996	Wolverton J S	Cav 5	A	Aug 26
7362	Way F	7	C	Aug 31
7812	Whalen H	6	I	Sept 4
7882	Wells F	7	F	Sept 5
9022	Wing A	17	G	Sept 17
9525	Withworth W G C	6	A	Sept 2
2910	Yacht E	22	E	July 5
2026	Zett J	22	D	June 28
	Total, 638.			

MINNESOTA.

No.	Name	Regt.	Co.	Date
5964	Atkinson Geo	9	F	Mar 17 64
6567	Adcock Jas	9	B	Mar 23
11977	Abrian G	1	B	Nov 12
4294	Becker G	9	E	July 29 64
5715	Barnard H A	9	A	Aug 15
6630	Buyton M	9	H	Aug 23
7841	Brese D	9	E	Sept 4
7892	Brayton J M	9	B	Sept 5
8053	Buckley J F	9	G	Sept 7
8253	Burrows H	9	K	Sept 9
9474	Babcock L A	9	D	Sept 21
9800	Besgrove Isaac	9	E	Sept 26
12778	Baker J G	1	A	Mar 15 65
2747	Conner P	11	A	July 1 64
3575	Clabaugh J	9	D	July 19
4111	Conklin S	9	I	July 27
6970	Conklin E	9	C	July 27
10724	Cassady J	9	F	Oct 6
7692	Dnuham R H		K	Sept 3
10971	Davis E J	9	E	Oct 15
8517	Fitch W F	9	F	Sept 12
12656	Fuchs H	9	D	Feb 14 65
9905	Freeschelz F	9	F	Sept 27 64
3287	Geer O	9	F	July 14
10401	Goodfellow E C	9	D	Oct 6
10579	Goodwin G	9	A	Oct 9
4130	Gordon W C	17	I	July 28
6033	Higly M F	9	G	Aug 18
6064	Hill C J	9	K	Aug 18
6605	Handy J	9	I	Aug 23
9144	Heaway J E	9	K	Sept 18
4176	Holts A	9	F	July 28
7809	Johnson N	9	H	July 4
1211	Kerrick Sam	4	K	May 19
9127	Kloss L	9	H	Sept 18
5079	Lindley C	9	B	Aug 8
7795	Large M	9	G	Sept 4
12165	Lewis L	9	E	Nov 26
12510	Latimore W H	9	D	Jan 22 65
9312	Lenyer M	9	G	Aug 30 64
5460	Myers C	3	I	Aug 13
7288	Mander J W	9	A	Aug 30
8180	Mc Dougal J	9	A	Sept 8
9195	Montenary J	9	G	Sept 18
2829	Nichols John	15	A	July 3
7789	Ollman Wm	9	B	Sept 4
8384	Orcutt J	2	C	Sept 10
2841	Pitcher E	5	B	July 3
4813	Packett C	9	K	Aug 5
5506	Pericle J	0	H	Aug 13
5909	Pence Geo	9	H	Aug 16
8353	Poinder T	9	B	Sept 10
8823	Pettijohn S W	9	H	Sept 14
4277	Roberts J G	9	E	July 29
5588	Roovin J	1	H	Aug 14
10327	Robertson Jno	9	B	Oct 4
10715	Reers Wm	9	E	Oct 11
5941	Short M	9	K	Aug 17
6216	Spence C	9	G	Aug 20
6276	Sontor C	9	H	Aug 20
7185	Scheffer H	9	G	Aug 20
12058	Shiver F	9	E	Nov 17
12808	Sarf H	5	E	Mar 22 65
8408	Thompson W	9	A	Sept 11 64
10186	Tiltan N M	9	B	Oct 1
11603	Thomas W R	9	E	Oct 28
12106	Ulrici A	9	E	Nov 20
11505	Vanhouse B A	9	C	Oct 26
11568	Vittam E W	9	B	Oct 27
986	Wood A	2	B	May 9

LIST OF THE DEAD.

No.	Name	Reg.	Co.	Date
3867	Walrich P	1	C	July 24 64
4498	Wheeler A	9	C	Aug 1
4588	Woodbury J	9	C	Aug 2
5637	Wilson F C	9	E	Aug 14
8233	Walter G	9	H	Sept 9
8416	Whipple O C	9	F	Sept 11
8459	Westover J	9	E	Sept 9
8777	Warren E F (mus)	9	A	Sept 14
5006	Young D S	9	I	Aug 8

TOTAL, 79.

MISSOURI.

No.	Name	Reg.	Co.	Date
281	Burns Jno	17	I	April 1 64
1251	Burk J H	2	H	May 2
1464	Buel J	4	C	May 29
2217	Bishop P	15	I	June 20
2306	Bloomker Wm	2	F	June 22
4269	Broyer J	2	E	July 29
5855	Birley Peter	29	I	Aug 16
8664	Berger J	2	I	Sept 13
8772	Bitter H	29	F	Sept 14
11223	Bullard Jas	19	D	Oct 20
12795	Bates B	44	F	Mar 18 65
2861	Cling C	2	I	July 4 64
4328	Clements Jas	Cav 2	A	July 30
6533	Cornell Jas	Cav 9	H	Aug 23
12351	Coon F	15	K	Dec 28
12776	Chapman R	24	B	Mar 14 65
5260	Dicksen D	18		Aug 10 64
1641	Daley M	Cav 10	H	June 5
343	Eddington G W	29	A	April 2
3963	Engler Jno	15	B	July 25
6987	Fogg B F	Cav 1	H	Aug 27
8633	Folk L	18	C	Sept 13
11266	Fay J W	2	K	Sept 21
12805	Fry M	Cav 12	L	Mar 21 65
6914	Frick S	2	E	Aug 26 64
2770	Guffy R	18	E	July 2
3725	Gallegher F	2	G	July 21
226	Houston W E	18	E	Mar 29
4505	Hunter W	Cav 1	H	Aug 1
4568	Hartman V	29	G	Aug 2
4727	Huntsley A	22	H	Aug 4
7004	Haginey F	2	K	Aug 28
1552	Head B J	26	B	June 2
2655	Holtgen G	12	E	June 29
8026	Hasse Jno	Cav 14	L	Sept 6
9042	Hamilton W	31	A	Sept 17
11941	Hanahan A	29	D	Nov 9
4410	Isenhour J	9	I	July 31
5709	Keyan M	2	D	Aug 15
7414	Keller A	29	H	Aug 31
8178	Kline C S	2	F	Sept 8
10546	Kaunst H	18	G	Oct 9
12821	Keller I	40	H	April 65
7713	Kuhn Jacob	15	E	Sept 3 64
3249	Lowe Jno	18	E	July 13
4803	Lavilley Wm	29	K	Aug 5
7035	Lang C	Cav 10	B	Aug 27
12232	Litch J	4	A	Dec 6
5401	Lindsay J	18	A	Aug 12
7438	Miller W	Cav 4	E	Sept 1
8913	Morgan E	Cav 12	F	Sept 16
11035	Manning S H	30	A	Oct 16
12459	Menzt W	15	G	Jan 15 65
12706	Martin J	44	H	Feb 27
12754	McGuire O	Cav 2	I	Mar 12
12700	McDowell J	2	F	Mar 12 65
3456	Newkirk Chas	15	F	July 17 64
3539	Neclout W	2	E	July 18
4169	Nelson Jno	29	A	July 28
12774	O'Dell E	44	B	Mar 14 65
12823	Purcell J R	44	G	April 5
755	Phillips Pat	11	E	April 27 64
25	Payne Jos	29	A	April 16
4978	Perkins A H	29	L	Aug 7
6732	Plasmine A	26	D	Aug 24
10559	Plumer E D	24	B	Oct 8
1048	Reily P	29	B	May 25
3540	Riddle F	8	D	July 18
5110	Ritteman John	15	F	Aug 9
6915	Remers J	4	G	Aug 26
2422	Robertson J C	Cav 10	F	June 25
1424	Schenck Philip	15	B	May 26
1476	Seebel A	12	G	May 30
1023	Search Henry	15	D	June 4
2464	Stickle D	4	D	June 24
2480	Stofacke F	15	D	June 25
28	Stiner Gottlieb	29	A	April 17
5239	Stormn F	58	E	Aug 9
5667	Schmas G	15	G	Aug 14
6806	Segiu C	2	H	Aug 26
6030	Shuman Jos	1	B	Aug 26
7535	Sherman H	15	G	Sept 1
9821	Schaat D B	18	E	Sept 26
536	Trask Geo K	29	A	April 14
770	Terrill Christian	27	E	April 27
1509	Terrell J	12	A	May 31
5672	Tresler H W	4	I	Aug 14
12730	Turman D	44	B	Mar 4 65
2803	Vance H J	26	B	July 3 64
373	Walham H	4	C	April 5
678	Watson J J	18	A	April 22
3106	Wigan M	2	F	July 10
7494	Williams J M	31	H	Sept 1
10889	Weidam J	2	B	Oct 14
12550	Ware J B	40	K	Jan 29 65
12739	West J	40	K	Mar 6

TOTAL, 97.

NEW HAMPSHIRE.

No.	Name	Reg.	Co.	Date
26	Ames John C	2	F	Mar 18 64
29	Allen E S	2	H	Mar 9
4656	Allen S	9	C	Aug 3
4746	Abbott C	7	K	Aug 5
7130	Arches J L	9	A	Aug 28
9518	Atmore G W	3	C	Sept 22
9832	Anderson J N	7	E	Sept 24
11765	Avery J	Cav 1	H	Nov 3
5721	Austendalph J	3	D	Aug 15
833	Bushbey N	7	C	May 1
3346	Bailey A D	7	C	July 15
3380	Bush A	4	H	July 16
4447	Bachelor J R	1		Aug 1
4905	Baker Wm	4	H	Aug 7
4988	Babb Jas	7	D	Aug 7
6871	Brown W F	2	B	Aug 26
6765	Breakman A	12	I	Aug 25
7857	Baker D W	3	G	Sept 5
8463	Bell Geo	5	C	Sept 11
10294	Bond J	12	F	Oct 4
2228	Clark G M	7	C	May 20
3326	Combs John	7	B	July 14
4230	Coon Charles	7	G	July 29

LIST OF THE DEAD.

No.	Name	Reg	Co	Date
5137	Colbry John N	13	D	Aug 9 64
7072	Cooney Thomas	9	C	Aug 28
8551	Connelly M	4	C	Sept 12
2796	Chadwick C E	7	H	July 2
11192	Carr P	1	H	Oct 20
1870	Downs E	7	I	May 25
2986	Doer S	7	D	June 17
3008	Dodge C F	7	K	July 20
5577	Drake Chas C Cav	1	B	Aug 14
3506	Eschoymer H Cav	1	B	July 19
5337	Estey E E	4	C	Aug 10
8426	Edwards John	9	H	Sept 11
12841	Elliott A	7	I	April 21 65
1396	Fuller George	7	B	May 26 64
5240	Faucett J	7	C	Aug 10
6078	Flanders O	9	F	Aug 24
6894	Ford W	7	K	Aug 26
9400	Faggerty Jackson C	1	A	Sept 21
12440	Felch G P	7	H	Jan 12 65
2588	Guinguelett H	2	E	July 3 64
4413	Gill N	7	A	July 31
4087	Gooley J	7	G	Aug 4
11905	Goodwin A	1	I	Nov 7
9071	Gardiner A	4	C	Sept 24
6516	Gray G H	4	E	Aug 22
6143	Hunter C	4	K	Aug 19
6875	Hurd Wm	6	I	Aug 26
7609	Hartford H	4	A	Sept 5
8537	Hally H	7	C	Sept 12
10269	Huse W	11	H	Oct 3
11156	Hamlin G W Cav	1	I	Oct 19
11439	Holmes J	7		Oct 24
11468	Holmes J	7		Oct 26
7783	Janes J B	9	K	Sept 3
9198	Johnson O O	5	F	Sept 18
11216	Juutplute F	12	E	Oct 20
11758	Johnson P	9	E	Nov 3
4314	Keyes C Cav	1	K	July 30
5114	Kemp C H	7	A	Aug 9
5151	Kingsbury H R	9	R	Aug 9
5444	Karson H B	2	C	Aug 12
7394	Kreaser M	4	I	Aug 31
11877	Klinsmith J	10	I	Nov 6
11994	Kingsbury J H Cav	1	A	Nov 13
6144	Lawrence A	" 1	C	Aug 19
6787	Lenert D	9	K	Aug 25
8048	Libby A G	4	H	Sept 6
11415	Leport J Cav	3	I	Oct 24
1484	Lucht P	5	C	Oct 26
2637	Mumford A	12	A	June 30
3652	Mantove J	4	H	June 20
4284	Miller F	11	G	July 30
4629	Miller R	11	H	Aug 3
7203	Milliot P	5	I	Aug 29
7423	Morrison O P	9	C	Aug 31
7918	Morten J	4	C	Sept 6
8573	McCann M	9	G	Sept 12
9921	Matheson F	7	B	Sept 28
11207	McCann O	13	E	Oct 20
12234	Montyan P	35	F	Dec 6
1658	O'Brien Chas	7	I	June 6
11698	Osmore J Cav	1	C	Oct 31
6185	Patch John	3	T	Aug 19
819	Poore Samuel	2	H	April 30
3260	Puny J	3	G	July 13
4764	Place I K	7	F	Aug 5
7011	Patterson N	9	I	Aug 27 64
11121	Parsons Samuel	5	H	Oct 18
11828	Perven H A	7	A	Nov 5
11837	Phelps M F	9	D	Nov 5
5383	Paschal E	7	E	Aug 12
1572	Reed F K	2	H	June 3
2771	Ramsay Wm	7	G	July 2
3406	Richards W R	7	C	July 16
11000	Ringer I K, S't Mj	11		Oct 22
1336	Smith John		7	K	May 24
2330	Sanburn W	7	H	June 22
2505	Sanlay E	9	E	June 26
2708	Simms S	9	C	June 30
2925	Searle I R	7	E	July 5
3472	Smith L F	13	C	July 17
4779	Steward George	10	A	Aug 5
5140	Smith J	7	B	Aug 9
5198	Schean W	7	A	Aug 9
5405	Shorey Ed	1	C	Aug 12
5438	Salsbur I	4	K	Aug 12
5621	Stanley John	9	A	Aug 14
6547	Smith I	11	E	Aug 23
7040	Swain C	7	D	Aug 27
8629	Smith C	3	F	Sept 13
8652	Stark S	15	A	Sept 13
8980	Smith John	3	T	Sept 17
9412	Smith L	12	B	Sept 21
10503	Shantz I	11	G	Oct 8
11887	Spaulding T C	4	K	Nov 7
3396	Taylor A B	5	H	July 16
3431	Tobine T	6	A	July 17
4072	Tilton D B	7	G	July 26
8098	Thompson A	9	K	Sept 8
10734	Tittou L G	11	B	Oct 11
10493	Upkins A Cav	1	B	Oct 7
5491	Valley John	10	K	Aug 12
794	Woodward L A	7	K	April 29
1991	Williams I	7	I	June 15
2345	Woodbury A	7	H	June 23
2545	Whipple A	7	H	June 23
4156	Webster I	6	I	July 28
2710	Welson W	4	F	July 1
4104	Whalen M	9	H	July 27
4750	Weston W W	8	A	Aug 5
4749	Welch Jes	7	I	Aug 5
5702	Wagner John	7	H	Aug 15
7559	Welsh F	7	C	Sept 2
7834	Wolf John D	3	F	Sept 4
8083	Wultramsen F	9	I	Sept 7
11278	Williams P	3	H	Oct 22
11472	Wingerd D	3	G	Oct 26
11768	Wilson I	11	I	Nov 3
11878	Warren E Cav	1	H	Nov 6
12734	Whitman G E	" 1	B	Mch 6 65
8736	York Charles	" 1	B	Sept 14 64

Total 144.

NEW JERSEY.

No.	Name	Reg	Co	Date
3347	Aaron Thos	2	B	July 15 64
3354	Aney G	1	K	July 15
4098	Austin D B	2	I	July 27
7138	Anderson T	2	E	Aug 28
8513	Albright — Cav	3	C	Sept 12
11389	Alexander W L	" 3	C	Oct 24
12646	Amps C	33	I	Feb 13 65
909	Broderick I S	2	A	May 5 64

LIST OF THE DEAD.

No.	Name	Reg.	Co.	Date		No.	Name	Reg.	Co.	Date	
1548	Beach I H	11	E	June	1 64	12416	Hook J M	Cav 2	D	Jan	8 65
2181	Brannin Pat	11	B	June	19	5252	Jennings G H	" 2	A	Aug 10	64
2260	Bells I H	2	H	June	21	9519	Jone A	" 1	A	Sept	22
2577	Buckley John	1	G	June	27	11117	Jay H	5	K	Oct	18
2980	Bloon Adam	2	I	July	4	11399	Jomson G W	6	G	Oct	24
3099	Buffman A C	Art 1	B	July	10	12344	Johnson A F	9	D	Dec	26
5761	Baily L	7	A	Aug	9	3762	Kronk Peter	Cav 2	H	July	22
5272	Brann Geo	Cav 1	B	Aug	10	5085	Kuhn R	9	A	Aug	8
5357	Burns P	" 3	C	Aug	11	8649	Kitchell S	7	K	Sept	13
5379	Baker Wm	" 1	K	Aug	12	12023	King C	15	G	Nov	15
5483	Blanchard G	7	K	Aug	13	1985	Lyous D	Cav 1	K	June	15
5934	Bennet C	14	B	Aug	17	795	Layton Stephen	11	A	April	29
11682	Brant Chas	1	E	Oct	31	1769	Lindsley Samuel	10	H	June	9
12238	Buver A	6	I	Dec	7	3622	Lewis S	Cav 3		July	20
12640	Brewer W H	10	D	Feb 12	65	4095	Leadbeater J H	6	B	July	27
715	Corley Daniel	11	A	April 24	64	5944	Leighton Wm	5	H	Aug	17
1437	Creamer E	35	A	May	28	6157	Luney Ed	8	G	Aug	19
6929	Creamer E	10	B	Aug	26	12102	Larime C	15	C	Nov	20
3209	Chamberlain R	Cav 1	D	July	12	2019	Menner Jacob	11	H	June	15
5730	Clark C H	2	C	Aug	15	2852	Miller J	Cav 1	K	July	4
8240	Coonan J	2	C	Sept	9	3323	McIntire R	8	I	July	14
10552	Collar H	2	D	Sept	9	3548	Marks Chas	Cav 2	G	July	18
11990	Clayton L	10	B	Nov	13	4594	Mulrainy I	4	B	Aug	3
3476	Curtis W O	Cav 1	L	July	17	4645	Miller S S	Cav 2	G	Aug	3
8041	Coykendall D	15	K	Sept	6	5250	Morell A	5	K	Aug	10
335	Disbrow J P	14	K	April	2	5832	Mahler Jno	35	I	Aug	16
2473	Davenport J	7	I	June	25	6986	Munn Chas	4	K	Aug	27
3444	Davis H	12	F	July	17	8019	McElroy E	10	I	Sept	6
4926	Dayton C	2	C	Aug	6	8332	Mount C H	9	D	Sept	10
5148	Dorland A H	10	I	Aug	9	8592	Miller J	7	K	Sept	13
6306	Dewinger J	2	G	Aug	20	10959	Mullan A	39	B	Oct	14
7076	Dunham L	35	H	Aug	28	12252	Mills F	2	I	Oct	21
7804	Dilan Edward	9	G	Aug	30	11564	Millington J	Cav 1	H	Oct	27
7469	Dermer J L	9	G	Sept	1	6780	Noll M	9	A	Aug	25
7734	Doremus C	Cav 2	A	Sept	3	4983	Nichols J	S S 1	C	Aug	7
7804	Duncan H P	2	G	Sept	4	7131	Osborne E	14	E	Aug	28
8440	Doyle H	16	C	Sept	11	10463	Osborn J M	9	H	Oct	7
10533	Dunn G	1	F	Sept	18	1071	Pratt J F	1	M	May	13
1426	Ebner Chas	Cav 1	K	May	28	1072	Purdee Chas	11	C	May	13
1715	Egbert Jas	15	B	June	8	5206	Peterson Henry	Cav 3	H	Aug	10
4303	Esligh Jacob	10	D	July	13	6298	Peer T	9	K	Aug	20
1522	Farrell J H	5	G	May	31	6962	Pelger M	10	G	Aug	27
3938	Foliand M	Cav 1	K	July	25	7451	Peterson G	12	I	Sept	1
4693	Fitch F	35	F	Aug	4	8017	Post G	H	I	Sept	6
5327	Fry Jno	9	G	Aug	4	9990	Parker W	2	I	Sept	29
6737	Fisher Wm	9	C	Aug	24	12221	Prink J	2		Dec	4
7285	Farran J	3		Aug	30	2145	Rooks H	5	H	June	18
9912	Fairbrother H	35	D	Sept	28	2821	Riley M	Cav 1	L	July	3
11584	Ford A	7	K	Oct	28	4066	Robinson Jacob	" 1	B	July	27
7338	Fisher N O	9	I	Aug	0	4858	Radford Wm	18	B	Aug	6
5900	Gade B	9	D	Aug	16	8282	Reed A	9	D	Sept	9
7089	Galloway F C	12	K	Aug	27	10461	Ray J	10	A	Oct	7
11165	Glenn C H	4	I	Oct	19	10708	Regan D O	8	C	Oct	11
11120	Guier G	7	D	Oct	20	11292	Reevis F	2	I	Oct	21
1508	Hallman H	6	C	May	31	2548	Starr N	5	H	June	27
3072	Hemis Daniel	Cav 1	D	July	9	5087	Simonds J	9	K	Aug	8
3819	Hick James	9	G	July	23	5807	Shauahan W	9	C	Aug	16
4151	Hegamann J	14	K	July	28	7364	Stout L	2	C	Aug	21
4189	Hammle A	Cav 1		July	28	7565	Street John J	9	D	Sept	2
4544	Huber C	9	G	Aug	5	7577	Stiffin H	3	M	Sept	2
4862	Herbert J S	Cav 2	I	Aug	6	7729	Skell C W	Cav 2	M	Sept	3
4911	Halman M	" 1	A	Aug	6	8687	Swetser P	9	G	Sept	13
821	Hull Alex	7	C	Sept	4	8751	Stevenson W	Cav 2	M	Sept	14
7870	Howell J	1	K	Sept	5	9328	Shay H H	7	I	Sept	19
7900	Hilgard P F	10	A	Sept	5	10846	Smith A	5	G	Oct	13
10,61	Hatter W	3	I	Oct	12	10615	Sutton T	12	K	Oct	28
12302	Humes E M	2	M	Dec	17	11653	Stimmell I	5	A	Oct	30

LIST OF THE DEAD.

No.	Name	Co.	Regt.	Date
11793	Sullivan I	8	C	Nov 8 64
11882	Steele George	2	B	Nov 6
10882	Sweet B F	10	K	Oct 13
1853	Tindel E	1	B	June 11
5112	Taylor Peter	9		Aug 9
6131	Townsend J	35	I	Aug 19
7937	Turner B	4	G	Sept 5
9398	Townsend F	10	C	Sept 21
11364	Thompson S	4	I	Oct 21
12451	Thatcher J	8	H	Jan 14 65
12705	Toy J	7	G	Feb 27
10212	Thomas Henry	10	B	Oct 2 64
6448	Traittman Jas	9	D	Aug 22
3634	Utter Stephen	Art 1	B	June 29
12100	Vallett W	" 5	A	Nov 19
1955	Weed Wm	15	I	June 14
2246	Wood W J	12	E	June 20
4643	Widder W	5	G	Aug 3
4998	Wainwright	9	C	Aug 7
5031	Wolverton	1	I	Aug 8
5099	Warner A	4	A	Aug 9
5333	Willey J	Cav 2	M	Aug 10
6168	Winard Wm	2	I	Aug 19
7560	Willis A	35	I	Sept 2
8142	Wright S M	7	K	Sept 8
8307	Ward J	Cav 1	H	Sept 10
12157	Williams W	1	D	Nov 20
12658	Wells G	10	C	Feb 15 65

TOTAL 170

NEW YORK.

No.	Name	Regt.	Co.	Date
2038	Abbey O	174		June 15 64
2141	Abbey W H	85	E	June 18
4719	Abel C	Art 15	C	Aug 4
4612	Aber J	104	I	Aug 3
5626	Ackerman Saml	97	K	Aug 14
64	Ackheart David	20	A	Mar 19
8497	Adams H	98	G	Sept 11
4581	Adams J A	10	F	Aug 2
6467	Adams O	61	C	Aug 22
8559	Adams S	100		Sept 12
3226	Adams T R	85	H	July 12
1700	Ades Ed	Cav 8	C	June 7
5047	Adeler A	8	D	Aug 8
6575	Adney F	85	K	Aug 23
4382	Ahearn Daniel	170		July 31
3349	Aiken J W	85	H	July 15
8001	Akerman M	Art 7	L	Sept 6
7062	Albarson J	42	C	Aug 28
6608	Albert Wm	Bat 24		Aug 24
7007	Alderman F	Cav 15	F	Aug 27
1755	Alexander J	125	C	June 9
11212	Alford B C	152	F	Oct 20
3293	Allen A W	Art 14		July 14
12452	Allen J I	82	A	Jan 14 65
5568	Allen W	Cav 1	H	Aug 13 64
5844	Allenburger J	39	B	Aug 16
7478	Allenberens E	39	D	Sept 1
11497	Allinger L	48	I	Oct 26
7587	Allman Chas	Art 7	C	Sept 2
6941	Almy F	111	K	Aug 26
5938	Alphord J	75	G	Aug 17
7739	Alsaver S	47	H	Sept 3
800	Ambler Fred	47	H	Apr 29
2344	Ambrose Jacob	C 2	C	June 23
10642	Ames Henry	Art 2		Oct 10
4654	Ames J R	Art 14	I	Aug 3

No.	Name	Regt.	Co.	Date
7743	Amgere G	47	E	Sept 3 64
1954	Amigh A	162	K	June 14
3739	Anderson A	100	I	July 21
4890	Anderson A	99	F	Aug 6
537	Anderson H	Cav 20	M	Apr 14
8819	Anderson J	39	E	Sept 15
4110	Anderson L	14	D	July 27
1389	Andrews G	111	I	May 26
7593	Andrews W	85	K	Sept 1
8717	Ansom Robt	Cav 1	K	Sept 14
6548	Answell J	" 15	A	Aug 23
8220	Antisdale Geo	" 5		Sept 4
6976	Appleby S W	85	K	Aug 27
9741	Argt C	6		Sept 25
11172	Armond W	7	F	Oct 19
9475	Armstrong H	140	G	Sept 21
10818	Armstrong J	164	C	Oct 12
11571	Armstrong W	Bat 24		Oct 27
7470	Arnold R B	Art 7	L	Sept 1
6551	Arnott C	47	C	Aug 26
1580	Asley C G	146	G	June 3
12202	Auster F	39	B	Dec 1
12622	Ashley S, Citizen			Feb 9 65
5544	Ashton ———	10	I	Aug 13 64
7207	Atwood G S, Bat	24		Aug 29
950	Aubray K	14	A	May 8
11748	Augh J	66	D	Nov 2
5027	Augustine F	52	A	Aug 8
1736	Austin A	147	H	June 8
3094	Austin J	Art 7	M	July 10
8218	Austin G	147	H	Sept 3
12830	Ayers G S	147	G	Mar 29 65
12347	Babcock J M	140	I	Dec 27 64
1712	Babcock H	111	G	May 7
3066	Babcock J	72	E	July 9
5335	Babcock J	55	E	Aug 11
4638	Babcock J S	140	D	Aug 3
4893	Babcock R	9	L	Aug 9
11831	Babcock W H	Cav 13	L	Nov 5
5692	Babst M	9	D	Aug 15
754	Bacon E P	154	B	Apr 27
9101	Bacon J	154	E	Sept 18
2870	Bacchus A	169	A	July 4
11272	Bacchus E R	Art 15	F	Oct 22
3447	Bachelder B F	Bat 24		July 17
3115	Backley C	" 24		July 10
3771	Badger P	47	E	July 22
7890	Bailey A	5	K	Sept 5
10163	Bailey C	76	K	Oct 1
5697	Bailey G W	154	G	Aug 15
7403	Bailey Jno	Cav 12	A	Sept 1
8215	Baker J	Bat 24		Sept 8
10636	Baker A	9	B	Oct 10
4468	Baker Chas	52	G	Aug 1
3550	Baker E	85	E	July 18
12376	Baker Geo	40	H	Jan 1 65
8759	Baker H	146	F	Sept 14 64
8052	Baker Ira	85	H	Sept 8
11848	Baker J	24	F	Nov 9
11660	Baker J	Cav 16	K	Oct 31
61	Baker Wm	7	D	Mar 18
7591	Baldwin C	Cav 24	M	Sept 2
6853	Baldwin G	154	C	Aug 25
4457	Ballard Robt B	85	C	Aug 1
4364	Barnard Wm	85	K	July 31
5347	Bancroff A H	85		Aug 11
8592	Barrett G M	184	E	Sept 8

LIST OF THE DEAD.

No.	Name	Regt	Co.	Date
11605	Banigan A	82	A	Oct 28 64
5536	Banker J M	118	K	Aug 13
9819	Banker J T	152	G	Sept 26
8443	Bannan H	39	H	Sept 11
11056	Bannyer F	126	K	Oct 17
12315	Barber H	96	D	Dec 20
1689	Barge H	120	A	June 6
3748	Barnes J	Cav 12	F	July 22
6771	Barnes J S	" 10	K	Aug 25
11343	Barnes M	115	F	Oct 23
6963	Barnes A C	85	D	Aug 27
8821	Barnes R W	Bat 24		Sept 15
10418	Barnes Thos	76	B	Oct 6
1835	Barrett J	132	C	June 11
8361	Barnum H	39	H	Sept 10
7877	Barklett H	Bat 24		Sept 5
8192	Barrett G M	184	A	Sept 8
10153	Barratt G	22	A	Oct 1
588	Barrett D	13	H	Apr 16
9979	Barron C L	Bat 12		Sept 28
3580	Barrows M	14	G	July 19
11612	Bartill R	164	F	Oct 28
4769	Bartlett L	118	I	Aug 5
8409	Barton D	85	I	Sept 11
6552	Bass Chas	Art 7	B	Aug 23
8217	Bass Geo, Teamster	63		Sept 8
8097	Bassford J	Cav 12	G	Sept 7
5555	Bates G	5	A	Aug 13
530	Bates J	97	A	Apr 13
3845	Bates Jno	14	I	July 24
1069	Bates Lester	97	A	May 13
10556	Baters W	139	G	Oct 9
10999	Baty A	132	K	Oct 16
61	Bayne Daniel	57	D	July 4
9380	Baywood J	Cav 1	I	Sept 20
6021	Beam B	" 2	M	Aug 17
4302	Beck John	97	H	July 30
6034	Beckham F B	Cav 10	A	Aug 18
9216	Beckshire J	" 12	F	Sept 19
8472	Beckwith C	Art 14	D	Sept 11
5012	Bee George	119	F	Aug 8
8992	Beebe J E	11		Sept 17
3843	Beekmam J	43	A	July 23
11933	Beers W	82	B	Nov 8
8010	Belden Wm	82	E	Sept 6
3267	Bell D S, State Mil	20	D	July 13
9136	Bell J	6	B	Sept 18
11124	Bell J C	120	D	Oct 18
8942	Bell Wm	39	K	Sept 16
11694	Bellvea C	179	F	Oct 28
3089	Bennett J H	85	E	July 9
3138	Bennett ——	146	B	July 10
5045	Bentley C	Cav 22	L	Aug 17
6670	Bentner Josh	100	I	Aug 24
6979	Benway C	Art 6	K	Aug 27
10955	Berges E	146	B	Oct 14
6598	Benall M L	125	A	Aug 23
5749	Beat Isaac	42	G	Aug 15
6039	Bertin F	69	G	Aug 18
6137	Besrha John	Art 15	B	Aug 19
8234	Buell J	85	B	Sept 9
5230	Beyers H	24	K	Aug 10
351	Bidon S	52	A	Apr 2
10635	Bidwell J	Cav 5	D	Oct 10
3232	Bigelow L	85	D	July 12
10555	Billings J	Cav 2	M	Oct 8
601	Billings W W	52	G	Apr 17
10945	Bings G	Art 5	B	Oct 14 64
10005	Bingham C E	Cav 5	D	Sept 29
12831	Bird M	Art 7	K	Apr 14 65
4780	Bird P	" 7	K	Aug 5 64
6590	Bishop C	" 7	M	Aug 23
5786	Bissell J S	85	D	Aug 15
11018	Black J	42	G	Oct 16
2574	Black L	9	A	June 27
11971	Black H C	42	F	Nov 12
1885	Blackman J	85		June 13
4076	Blackwood W	115	G	July 27
7989	Blair D	15	C	Sept 5
12469	Blair Jas	Cav 8	K	Jan 16 65
498	Blaize H	Art 3	H	Apr 12 64
3236	Blake W D	Bat 24		July 22
2439	Blake Geo	100	I	June 25
6129	Blanchard E	Cav 12	F	Aug 19
8340	Blanchard L	100	K	Sept 10
10083	Blancolt Wm	95	B	Sept 30
1861	Blank J M	95	A	June 12
4933	Bliss Jas H*	Cav 22	I	Aug 7
8959	Block J P	100	F	Sept 16
7206	Blood L	7	C	Aug 29
2777	Blyme S	85	G	July 2
12521	Boaman J	Cav 1	D	Jan 25 65
6371	Boares A	178	D	Aug 21 64
5285	Bode A	85	B	Aug 11
2989	Bodishay J	7	F	July 7
474	Boermaster J	14	A	Apr 9
3073	Bohl H	Cav 10	E	July 9
6018	Bolan E	35	F	Aug 17
11718	Bolby O	Art 14	D	Nov 1
8267	Boles J	Cav 22	D	Sept 9
3606	Bomsteel S A	20	G	July 19
5269	Borst J	Cav 5	B	Aug 10
4401	Bodler D	7	D	July 31
51	Boughton H	77	A	Mar 16
7627	Boulton T	43	G	Sept 2
10066	Bowden P	Cav 16	M	Oct 17
6744	Bowen J H	65	D	Aug 24
4601	Bowin J	Cav 7	K	Aug 3
11944	Bowman H	84	K	Nov 10
12521	Bowman I	Cav 1	D	Jan 25 65
3635	Bowman S	147	H	July 20 64
1275	Box G	111	D	May 22
9728	Boyce A	Cav 3	I	Sept 25
2673	Boyce R	" 6	M	June 30
10	Boyle Pat	63	A	Mar 5
8912	Boyle Pat	48	F	Sept 16
11974	Boyle I	16	D	Nov 12
4365	Bradford D B	Art 7	B	July 31
5232	Bradley Jno	69	K	Aug 10
6685	Bradshaw R	120	E	Aug 24
12219	Brady J	140	E	Dec 4
3979	Bragg J C	Cav 2	E	July 26
12263	Brain Wm	Art 5	B	Dec 12
7704	Brandon O	" 15	A	Sept 3
1800	Breny Jas	178	K	June 10
5134	Brewer Fred	39	C	Aug 9
11685	Brewer Henry	Cav 2	E	Oct 31
10221	Brewer J S	6	B	Oct 2
1365	Brewer S	15	K	May 25
519	Brewer Thos	111	F	Apr 13
9690	Bryant L A	146	B	Sept 24
8116	Bright ——	104	C	Sept 8
11627	Brightman E	7	D	Oct 28
8415	Brill C	140	F	Sept 11

LIST OF THE DEAD.

No.	Name	Regt.	Co.	Date
6953	Brink C	109	K	Aug 26 64
9787	Britansky J	52	E	Sept 26
2997	Brobst J	52	B	July 7
9148	Brock W	76	F	Sept 18
6882	Broder H	76	F	Aug 26
12002	Brogan J M	85	B	Nov 14
1324	Brooks W	Cav 10	E	May 24
1221	Brott A	" 1	K	May 19
9838	Broscang C	150	C	Sept 27
7517	Brought Chas	Art 14	I	Sept 1
51	Broughten H	77	H	Mar 16
10608	Brown A	140	K	Oct 11
5538	Brown B M	85	I	Aug 13
4112	Brown C	103	C	July 27
9356	Brown C	66	K	Sept 23
11953	Brown C	39	H	Nov 10
11928	Brown C	Cav 1	M	Nov 8
6623	Brown Chas	97	F	Aug 23
7501	Brown D	118	B	Sept 1
3659	Brown E G	Art 7	L	July 20
9674	Brown G H	" 85	H	Sept 24
7985	Brown G H	63	C	Sept 6
2465	Brown H	72	C	June 25
1879	Brown H	Cav 12		June 12
7266	Brown H	39	F	Aug 30
1887	Brown J	125		June 13
7658	Brown J	16		Sept 3
6655	Brown James	Cav 4	E	Aug 24
6691	Brown James	170	K	Aug 24
7526	Brown John	66		Sept 1
7615	Brown Wm	5	D	Sept 2
552	Brown Warren	120	K	Apr 14
428	Brown Wm	42	A	Apr 8
7390	Broxmire Thos	15	E	Aug 31
1559	Brumaghin T	125	E	June 2
4475	Bryant D	179	B	Aug 1
7248	Bryant H	82	F	Aug 30
7668	Bryan Wm	Cav 1	I	Sept 3
3814	Buck	24	H	July 23
9975	Buckbier J	Art 7	F	Sept 28
10585	Buckley Wm	122	D	Oct 10
5714	Buel G W	115	E	Aug 15
331	Buel S	42	B	Apr 2
12417	Buffman L	100	K	Jan 8 65
7567	Buckley E A	97	E	Sept 2 64
12509	Burfield C	Citizen		Jan 22 65
5953	Bullier Wm	Cav 23	B	Aug 17 64
9642	Bullock E	85	E	Sept 24
4137	Bundy Josh	Art 7	B	July 28
540	Bunn W H	132	F	Apr 14
9870	Bunnell W	59	C	Sept 27
6452	Burbanks J	85	D	Aug 22
10924	Burdick A	85	C	Oct 14
978	Burdick C	47	F	May 9
2134	Burdick Sam'l	125	A	June 18
7838	Burdock L	Cav 22	L	Sept 1
10016	Burleigh L	Art 5	E	Sept 29
12389	Burley C	3	B	Jan 4 65
619	Burns E J	Cav 13	D	Apr 19 64
477	Burns Jno	40	I	Apr 9
924	Burns Jno	99	H	May 6
11881	Burns J	118	F	Nov 6
8745	Burns W	Cav 3	C	Sept 14
5991	Burns Daniel	Art 5	D	Aug 17
7247	Burr H	59	C	Aug 30
6171	Bursha Thos	Art 2	M	Aug 19
3165	Burshen F	54	C	July 11
2875	Burt J	Cav 2	A	July 4 64
7214	Burton G E	85	K	Aug 29
217	Burton Henry	140		Mar 29
5847	Buserman E	97	E	Aug 16
6457	Bush E	20	D	Aug 22
1415	Bushnell A	65	D	May 27
487	Buthan J R	132	G	Apr 11
11366	Bushley Wm	Art 5	A	Oct 23
1360	Buskirk A	47	A	May 25
2047	Buskirt O	13		June 15
721	Butler Thos	132	G	Apr 25
4183	Butler W	43	D	July 28
12651	Butoff R	124	C	Feb 13 65
10848	Butler Jas	Cav 2	D	Oct 13 64
9235	Butter P	126	D	Sept 19
5805	Button Jas	Art 24	B	Aug 16
3446	Butts A	111	C	July 17
9790	Byron J	69	A	Sept 26
1224	Burke W H	120	I	May 19
5196	Burk Jno	69	K	Aug 10
1073	Brower Jno	A Art 5	D	Oct 17
12190	Cademus C	48	A	June 19
10765	Cady Geo	66	G	Oct 12
2377	Cady J	77	E	June 23
10721	Cady J J	14	H	Oct 11
3062	Cane M	132	E	July 9
2136	Cale J	85	G	June 18
9040	Caldham L C	Cav 8	L	Sept 17
11807	Caldwell A	42	A	Nov 4
1530	Caling Ed	7	H	Oct 26
9706	Calkins S V	120	D	Sept 25
8411	Callbrook J	147	B	Sept 11
2848	Cameron Jno	Cav 1	H	July 4
1770	Camp H	" 2	F	June 9
1238	Campbell D	" 8	H	May 20
7236	Campbell J	99	I	Aug 29
946	Campbell L R	104	B	May 7
8793	Campbell M	169	K	Sept 15
11294	Campbell W	2	C	Oct 22
7378	Campbell Wm	76	B	Aug 31
12178	Card A	152	C	Nov 27
5034	Card G	109	F	Aug 8
8136	Carboines W	39	C	Sept 8
6433	Cardon E	115	A	Aug 22
7555	Carey D	57	A	Sept 2
11512	Carey F	65	E	Oct 26
372	Carl Josh	14	A	Apr 5
5545	Carl L	120	G	Aug 13
12339	Carle ——	Cav 1	D	Dec 26
12268	Carmac F	2	D	Dec 12
7655	Carmer A	85	B	Sept 3
11640	Carney M	Cav 9	L	Oct 30
8470	Carnehan Chas	B 24		Sept 11
5258	Carney D J	132	G	Aug 10
9879	Carney Francis	A 2	C	Sept 27
3102	Carnes P	Cav 13	B	July 10
10806	Carpenter Frank	A 7	D	Oct 12
8854	Carpenter G	7	D	Sept 15
4632	Carpenter H A	Art 2	A	Aug 3
3916	Carpenter L	" 2	B	July 25
3977	Carpenter M B	85	B	July 26
6743	Carr Andrew	22		Aug 24
3859	Carr D	25	B	July 24
581	Carr F	Art 3	K	Apr 16
6470	Carr Geo A	" 3	K	Aug 22
5673	Carr Wm	125	K	Aug 14
6304	Carr Wm	97	E	Aug 20

232 LIST OF THE DEAD.

No.	Name	Reg.	Co.	Date
4139	Carroll James	69	A	July 28 64
10293	Carroll P	95	E	Oct 4
2061	Carroll F	132	F	June 15
12015	Carroll W	42	D	Nov 15
8563	Carson J G	100	B	Sept 12
8023	Cart M A	118	F	Sept 6
1987	Carter A	146	E	June 15
5212	Carter Ed	Art 7	A	Aug 10
6433	Carson E	115	A	Aug 22
11640	Carney M	Cav 9	L	Oct 30
8479	Case A F	" 8	A	Sept 11
8377	Case E	" 8	M	Sept 10
6296	Case H J	" 12	A	Aug 20
3832	Casey J	100	G	July 23
5271	Casey P	174	A	Aug 10
8241	Cassells Sam'l	52	D	Sept 11
2643	Cassine Jno S	Bat 24		June 29
1177	Castano J	104	H	May 16
10482	Cashel C	Art 7	I	Oct 7
1785	Castle J W	147	H	June 10
6128	Castle Wm	Art 1	E	Aug 19
1534	Cavenaugh John	146	H	June 1
5971	Cæsar D	Art 7	B	July 7
1466	Centre A	16	A	May 29
9682	Chaffe R A	Cav 5	H	Sept 24
11101	Chambers J	140	F	Oct 18
6557	Chambers J	147	E	Aug 23
5890	Chamberlain C	154	D	Aug 16
4768	Champlin W	85	E	Aug 5
4726	Chapel A	85	D	Aug 4
5478	Chapel R	Cav 6	A	Aug 13
5831	Chappell A	39	E	Aug 16
10748	Chappell E	76	K	Oct 12
3222	Chapin F	Cav 24	A	July 12
3286	Chapman J	85	K	July 14
1593	Chase A	111	H	June 3
4856	Chase D	98	I	Aug 6
5469	Chase N F	85	K	Aug 13
7450	Chase S M	Art 4	D	Sept 1
2157	Chatbrim H	Bat 23		June 18
8033	Chatman C	Art 6	I	Sept 6
6353	Chatman S M	2	F	Aug 23
9019	Chatterton J	95	B	Sept 28
7865	Chagnon E	Cav 12	F	Sept 25
7189	Chesley P S	" 10	G	Aug 29
7539	Chestey Jno	174	G	Sept 2
10680	Chickchester C H	57	I	Oct 11
6317	Childs A	85	I	Aug 20
4141	Childs Wm	73	A	July 28
11555	Chile H	47	E	Oct 27
10612	Christey J	Drag 1	I	Oct 10
5824	Church C L	Cav 5	C	Aug 16
5413	Church F M	" 2	D	Aug 12
4257	Churchill C	99	I	July 29
3449	Cluncey Robb	164	E	July 17
2114	Clark A	85	E	June 17
5167	Clark Chas	Cav 12	F	Aug 10
2947	Clark F	" 8	B	July 6
12114	Clark J	" 8	K	Nov 21
12403	Clark J B	Art 7	L	Jan 6 65
2154	Clark Jno	48	D	June 18 64
11304	Clark L	100	G	Oct 22
10611	Clark P	42	B	Oct 10
5802	Clemens A	Cav 15	F	Aug 15
6909	Clements H	65	F	Aug 26
11028	Cleaver W	43	F	Oct 16
813	Clifford Chas	16	B	Apr 30
740	Cufford Geo	132	K	Apr 26 64
6494	Cline B	85	K	Aug 22
11437	Cline J W	85	K	Oct 24
12021	Cline S M	Drag 1	H	Nov 15
9721	Cline W	76	F	Sept 25
6243	Clingman J	150	L	Aug 20
12471	Clinton R	102	D	Jan 17 65
1497	Clute H V	Bat 24		May 31 64
5955	Clyen J P	147	B	Aug 17
7343	Coanas W	73	D	Aug 31
5365	Coburn C	122	E	Aug 11
10129	Coburn A	116	H	Oct 1
933	Coddington W	99	H	May 7
7992	Cochran Jno	126	K	Sept 6
11775	Cochran M	42	A	Nov 3
9237	Cochson J	140	C	Sept 19
10651	Cogger M	125	B	Oct 11
3715	Cogswell L	Art 6	M	July 21
10062	Cole E B	" 14	B	Sept 30
8456	Cole Geo	Cav 12	A	Sept 11
6241	Cole Jno J	" 5	M	Aug 20
5890	Cole M	Art 15	M	Aug 16
4142	Cole R S	152	H	July 28
11589	Cole F	109	K	Oct 28
4519	Cole Wm	61	H	Aug 2
7855	Coleby A	Cav 1	M	Sept 5
10553	Coleman I	Art 2	I	Oct 9
3070	Collins A	98	B	July 9
7557	Colwell D C	Art 2	F	Sept 2
5743	Colwell J	120	A	Aug 15
6969	Comstock G E	Art 2	A	Aug 27
3509	Condon Thos	Cav 22	F	July 18
4320	Cone R	8	A	July 30
9619	Conely John	125	K	Sept 23
5528	Conely Pat	164	G	Aug 13
8019	Conger James	49	A	Sept 16
11347	Corvier Chas	Cav 1	C	Oct 25
2160	Conkin A	69	A	June 19
10699	Conlin Daniel	5	A	Oct 11
11513	Conell T	139	C	Oct 26
2033	Connelly F	52		June 15
10006	Coners E	43	D	Sept 20
4025	Connor Henry	52	D	July 26
936	Conners John	99	D	May 7
7842	Cosgrove F	76	H	Sept 4
11093	Cook C H	Cav 6	E	Oct 18
11240	Cook Geo		E	Oct 21
7485	Cook G W	146	E	Sept 1
5228	Coombs B	69	A	Aug 10
10626	Coombs J	96	I	Oct 10
2195	Coons F	52	B	June 19
11418	Coom Geo F	65	K	Oct 24
3692	Cooney F	14	G	July 21
10723	Cooney T	82	E	Oct 11
5816	Cooper Jas	Cav 22	G	Aug 16
12274	Cooper N	" 22	F	Dec 13
1150	Copeland J	106	I	May 16
1778	Corbit B F	Bat 24		June 9
10329	Corbit John	24	C	Oct 8
6662	Corless R	Art 7	E	Aug 24
7182	Cornelius J	Cav 12	F	Aug 29
1995	Corry P	99	A	June 15
6729	Correll O B	Cav 1	D	Aug 24
11331	Cornell P	100	C	Oct 23
11347	Corrier Chas	Cav 1	C	Oct 23
7471	Castin J	" 22	C	Sept 1
12767	Corselman G	152	K	Mar 13 65

LIST OF THE DEAD. 233

No.	Name	Rank/Unit	Co.	Date
7786	Cottin Z T	85	E	Sept 4 64
5329	Countryman ——	120	A	Aug 11
3899	Courtney W	Cav 12	A	July 24
8976	Cowen J	4	I	Sept 7
7058	Cox D	Cav 1	H	Aug 28
7675	Coy Jno H	" 1	L	Sept 3
11158	Coyne M	98	H	Oct 19
7274	Cozin J	82	E	Aug 30
3601	Craft B	48	D	July 21
8221	Craig J	139	H	Sept 8
8328	Crandall D	85	E	Sept 10
8399	Crandall J	85	C	Sept 10
2950	Crandall R	115	I	July 6
3061	Crandle J F	120	K	July 9
334	Craven J	134	E	Apr 2
3432	Crawford Jno	61	B	July 17
12649	Cripman S	2	K	Feb 13 65
8783	Crissman Josh	140	F	Sept 14 64
11471	Crine C	Cav 6	C	Oct 26
2311	Criswell J	" 12	F	June 22
2882	Crocker J	93	E	July 3
5886	Cromark J	77	B	Aug 16
2644	Crompter Jas	14	F	June 20
8695	Cromwell T	Art 6		Sept 14
3624	Crosby M	Bat 24		July 14
2273	Crouse Geo	" 24		June 21
11297	Crowley S	2	B	Oct 22
5893	Cuff S	14	E	Aug 17
7159	Culbert Wm	39	D	Aug 29
4119	Culver N L	Bat 24		July 28
8960	Cunnings ——	22	D	Sept 16
11269	Cron F	115	D	Oct 21
5476	Cunningham J	170	E	Aug 13
6721	Cunningham J	41	I	Aug 24
1447	Cunningham Wm	45	B	May 29
1204	Curley P	125	E	May 19
3627	Currey John	146	B	July 20
4458	Custerman F	47	G	Aug 1
9540	Cate A	Cav 8	A	Sept 22
9611	Cuter C F	2	G	Sept 23
12434	Cutler J P	99	B	Jan 11 65
4846	Cutler Wm	59	B	Aug 6 64
8493	Daher G	66	D	Sept 8
8650	Daley V	42	I	Sept 13
10741	Damon J D	Art 7	K	Oct 11
3577	Dailey Wm	Cav 5	I	July 19
11122	Daniels W O	76	K	Oct 18
5599	Daratt Louis	111	G	Aug 14
1480	Daly Jno	99		May 30
6641	Dawson J	47	K	Aug 23
8095	Darley J	Art 14	D	Sept 7
6726	Darling G H	Cav 18	F	Aug 24
5083	Darling J	" 4	C	Aug 8
7562	Dart Chas W	85	C	Sept 2
6404	Davidson M	Cav 15	M	Aug 21
6391	Davis D	164	G	Aug 21
6037	Davis G	1	H	Aug 18
1383	Davis H	85	I	May 26
7670	Davis H	Art 1	D	Sept 3
8080	Davis H J	85	C	Sept 7
961	Davis H R	99	I	May 8
12652	Davis H T	Cav 5	G	Feb 14 65
5120	Davis J	85	H	Aug 9 64
7894	Davis J J	43	B	Sept 5
11017	Davis Jno	47	E	Nov 5
10241	Davis P	94	I	Oct 3
10018	Davy J J	Cav 2	A	Sept 29
5838	Day J W	32	D	Aug 11 64
3866	Dean	43	E	July 24
9400	Dean J	Cav 3	G	Sept 21
2305	Dean Jno	Art 6	K	June 22
10523	Debrass J	9	A	Oct 8
9058	Decker A	82	I	Sept 28
3660	Deckman J G	104	B	July 20
7505	Declercy W E	C 22	E	Sept 1
10555	Dedrich P	9	K	Oct 9
12320	Deman W	26	E	Dec 22
7059	Dessotell J	98	D	Aug 28
7935	Deet F	90	D	Sept 5
4400	Deffer Louis	40	H	July 31
4014	Degammo J	48	E	Aug 6
6283	Degroff C	115	H	Aug 20
12074	Degroot W	Art 7	I	Nov 18
12238	Devit Chas	" 7	G	Dec 5
7261	Delane M	111	C	Aug 30
11206	Delany C	52	H	Oct 20
12271	Demara Jno	108	M	Dec 12
5669	Demeres D	5	A	Aug 15
10163	Demerest H H	Cav 2	M	Sept 30
8761	Demhart W	111	F	Sept 14
9592	Demming F M	85	H	Sept 23
7278	Dempsey Jno	85	B	Aug 30
7623	Demming L	85	D	Sept 2
9930	Dennis A A	106	H	Sept 28
1489	Dennis Thos	132	G	May 31
4090	Dennison J	Cav 12	A	July 27
12257	Dennison J	155	I	Dec 10
7461	Dennison W	Art 14	M	Sept 1
3259	Denorf F	147	B	July 13
2320	Densamore S F	115	G	June 22
6324	Densmore E	85	K	Aug 21
12603	Desmond D	82	C	Feb 6 65
1799	Deveny H	99	I	June 10 64
7598	Devlin A	Art 1	M	Sept 2
5502	Devlin J	Cav 12	F	Aug 13
10077	Dewise Dennis	7	E	Sept 30
2839	De Witt S C	120	E	July 3
9334	Dewitt J S	48	H	Sept 20
9855	Dickinson N	152	K	Sept 27
10597	Dickerman W B	A 6	A	Oct 10
11854	Difendorf R	Art 2	L	Nov 6
2234	Dykeman F	47	C	June 20
10089	Dingle J	122	G	Sept 30
1821	Dingley C	Cav 5	A	June 10
8588	Dighard F	" 15	B	Sept 12
8245	Doan A	85	C	Sept 9
3773	Dodson E	85	C	July 22
2959	Dolan J	48	E	June 14
11805	Dolan M	Cav 6	F	Nov 4
5658	Dolan P	30	I	Aug 14
11884	Domick E	Art 4	E	Nov 6
4886	Donaghen J	16	A	Aug 6
2809	Doud Daniel	155	I	July 3
6149	Dondall B	111	G	Aug 19
11357	Donely M	10	F	Oct 23
3081	Donovan J	Art 14		July 9
229	Donley E J M	Rifles 2	K	Mar 29
12718	Donnell W	Art 4	A	Mar 2 65
655	Donnelly Jas	C C 2	D	Apr 21 64
10102	Doolittle W	76	D	Sept 30
3533	Dorchester H S, V S	C 12		July 18
12715	Dormity M	Citizen		Mar 1 65
10320	Dotsey J	139	E	Oct 4 64
9416	Dougherty E S	85	I	Sept 21

LIST OF THE DEAD.

No.	Name	Reg.	Co.	Date
4650	Dougherty J	9	C	Aug 3 64
2052	Dougherty O	99	I	June 16
10992	Doughty E S	48	A	Oct 16
9298	Downey H	11	I	Sept 19
5735	Downey J A	85	H	Aug 15
7275	Douglas M	48	D	Aug 30
10356	Douglas P	147	C	Oct 5
6149	Dondall B	111	G	Aug 19
2561	Doyle Jno	Cav 5	G	June 27
4827	Doyle Jas	120	H	Aug 5
9142	Doyle W	Art 7	I	Sept 18
9318	Dow M	125	H	Sept 20
3929	Drake D W	Art 2	H	July 25
2317	Drake D B	158	F	June 23
699	Driscoll ——	52	B	Apr 23
2826	Drum A	155	A	July 3
9357	Druse I	Art 15	D	Sept 20
394	Derfee Jas	99	H	Apr 6
3063	Dumfray Dennis	100	I	July 9
3490	Dudley J C	Cav 10	H	July 17
3957	Duell R	Art 6	F	July 25
5264	Dumond A	85	E	Aug 10
5810	Dumond C	120	A	Aug 16
6773	Dumond S	5	B	Aug 25
10144	Dumond F	146	A	Oct 1
9116	Dunlap C	85	B	Sept 18
8669	Duane T	95	E	Sept 13
8453	Dritman Wm	42	C	Sept 11
6905	Duble Henry	61	F	Aug 26
6087	Dule Levi	5	B	Aug 18
10948	Duger P	67	A	Oct 14
11104	Dunham R	Art 14	G	Oct 18
7621	Dunn J	40	G	Sept 2
8244	Dunn L H	Eng 50	E	Sept 9
5732	Dunn Jas	88	D	Aug 15
1695	Dunn J H	99	I	June 7
10948	Devine P	67	A	Oct 14
123	Dunbar Thos	2	F	Mar 23
3234	Dunn M	99	I	July 12
919	Dunn Owen	126	H	May 6
1033	Dunn Pat	149	A	May 11
3584	Dunning Wm	132	G	July 19
2972	Dunsham Abr	120	C	July 7
7554	Durand H	82	K	Sept 2
4832	Durand Jas E	C 10	E	Aug 6
9616	Dyer S	Art 7	D	July 24
4086	Dyer Jno S	Cav 10	M	Sept 25
3574	Dykeman D	" 22	F	July 9
12274	Dunaram Jno	108	F	Dec 12
9033	Earl C	85	D	Sept 17
2443	Earl H	174	H	June 25
3203	Eastern Thos	Cav 5	L	July 12
3019	Eastman Wm	10	C	July 25
4239	Easton E E	52	F	July 29
4410	Eastwood E	Bat 24		July 31
7440	Eber Jas	76	B	Sept 1
3552	Edmonds L	Cav 5	M	July 18
4288	Edwards S	52	F	July 30
7309	Edson John	64	D	Aug 30
7850	Edson W	105	E	Sept 5
2728	Egan John	125	D	July 1
9454	Egerton H	Art 14	L	Sept 20
2319	Elberson J	Cav 10	E	June 21
7420	Eldeny B	146	E	Aug 31
6407	Eldred H	125	K	Aug 22
3597	Eldred I	76	F	July 19
0339	Ellis J	2	H	Oct 4
12071	Ellis P M	2	E	Nov 17 64
9736	Ellis C	85	G	Sept 25
7204	Ellis R H	76	F	Aug 29
8960	Elliott F P	76	B	Sept 16
8163	Elliott L	Cav 3	I	Sept 8
1107	Ellis Wm	119	F	May 15
3526	Ells Perry	106	I	Nov 18
8274	Ellison W	95	F	Sept 9
6343	Elster James	Art 7	E	Aug 21
9564	Elwell W	47	B	Sept 23
8152	Emery C Z	48	G	Sept 8
6096	Engal W	39	B	Aug 18
9086	English G	Cav 7	I	Sept 18
9961	Eagh John	Art 7	E	Sept 28
2454	Easley W H	Cav 2	H	June 25
10375	Erst J	51	H	Oct 4
2731	Ethear J	Cav 13	E	July 1
9459	Evans Franklin	140	D	Sept 21
12365	Evans L	Art 7	I	Dec 31
6786	Evens B	66	B	Aug 25
6429	Everett J	58	K	Aug 22
11263	Everly G	108	I	Oct 21
11362	Faggerty C	Cav 2	C	Oct 23
1622	Fallam Pat	Art 3	K	June 3
11576	Famcle E	43	D	Oct 28
7666	Fairfax Chas	111	A	Sept 3
12091	Farland T	6	I	Nov 19
11247	Farley W	Art 14	F	Oct 21
10259	Farrell Jas	100	C	Oct 3
5840	Farn C	169	G	Aug 16
5946	Fairman H B	Art 6	M	Aug 17
6995	Fawry Jno	" 2	C	Aug 27
7415	Face J	115	E	Aug 31
10057	Fareclough R	2	F	Sept 20
9609	Ferris C	100	E	Sept 23
8439	Ferris Robt	Art 14	I	Sept 3
3452	Ferris Jno	5	E	July 17
4760	Felter F	69	C	Aug 5
7260	Ferguson H C	14	C	Aug 30
7498	Ferguson M	39	G	Sept 1
7412	Felton Geo	164	C	Aug 31
8407	Feasel H	Art 7	F	Sept 3
9779	Ferguson J M	Cav 15	G	Sept 26
12507	Finnerty P	155	G	Jan 22 65
247	Fich Jno	8	M	Mar 30 64
3869	Fincucum Jno	96	E	July 24
6192	Fields F	Art 2	L	Aug 19
6656	Finch Henry	Cav 22	L	Aug 24
8699	Finch Jas	" 22	L	Sept 14
10072	Findley Andrew	70	D	Sept 20
11482	Finlay A	Art 7	D	Oct 26
6215	Fish L V	" 7	B	Aug 20
4412	Fish H	179	A	July 31
5752	Fish F	52	K	Aug 15
9723	Fish J W	Cav 12	C	Sept 25
279	Fish Wm	17	H	Apr 1
11651	Fisher C P	124	C	Oct 30
10049	Fisher Conrad	Cav 1	E	Sept 29
5104	Fisher Daniel	45	F	Aug 9
2389	Fisher D	125	K	June 22
12542	Fisher H	59	K	Jan 27 65
10966	Fisher L	39	D	Oct 15 64
10171	Fitch A	3	F	Oct 1
4819	Fitch C	Bat 24		Aug 5
3569	Fitzgerald N	111	C	July 19
6453	Fitzgerald Thos	Bat 24		Aug 22
12400	Fitzpatrick	Cav 10	G	Jan 5 65

LIST OF THE DEAD.

No.	Name	Unit	Co.	Date
6961	Fitzpatrick O	100	E	Aug 27 64
6500	Flagler Wm	Art 7	M	Aug 22
7452	Flanigan Ed	" 7	C	Sept 1
5558	Flenigan P	40	D	Aug 13
8583	Fleming P	Cav 22	E	Sept 12
190	Fletcher Wm	Cav 13	G	Mar 27
12537	Flintkoff F	102	E	Jan 27 65
774	Florence B	99	H	Apr 28 64
7690	Fluke J	76	K	Sept 3
8379	Flynn J	Bat 24		Sept 10
11958	Flynn J	13	K	Nov 11
9242	Flynn Wm	71	E	Sept 19
9283	Fohnsbelly C	169	A	Sept 19
8042	Folden H	Art 7	B	Sept 6
3987	Folet D	Cav 1	A	July 26
10841	Follard Jas	" 1	I	Oct 13
4807	Foulke Peter	100	F	Aug 5
175	Ford E B	112	K	Mar 26
7344	Foreber A	Cav 13	F	Aug 31
11736	Foley F	77	B	Nov 2
1589	Forget G H	85	K	June 3
2470	Foster H	Cav 1	B	June 25
759	Foster J	" 5	G	Apr 27
408	Foster James	" 2	D	Apr 6
6115	Fox A	49	K	Aug 19
11173	Fox D	152	A	Oct 19
2630	Fox M	Art 15	K	July 3
9432	Frahworth F	57	I	Sept 21
8393	Frake S	11	G	Sept 10
2863	Francis P L	Cav 2	H	July 4
9997	Franklin J	39	I	Sept 28
4227	Franklin J C	Cav 2	L	July 29
10484	Fraser J H	73	C	Oct 7
11353	Freilander C	Cav 2	B	Oct 23
4820	Freburg E	52	F	Aug 5
6619	Fredinburg Jas	85	H	Aug 23
6668	Free C	30	B	Aug 24
11363	French J	Cav 2	H	Oct 23
10968	French James	" 22	G	Oct 15
6998	French John C	" 5	H	Aug 27
1395	Freiser John	111	K	May 2
5125	Frisby W L	111	B	Aug 9
11421	Frositer F	Cav 16	L	Oct 24
3806	Fuller A	49	K	July 22
11638	Fuller C	52	H	Oct 30
3713	Fuller J B	85	F	July 21
1050	Fuller N	18	C	Oct 17
10295	Fuller W	122	A	Oct 4
10328	Funday F	39	B	Oct 4
10140	Fricks A	62	L	Oct 1
2472	Gagan Thos	85	C	June 25
5773	Gale George	2	A	Aug 15
1148	Gallagher G	Cav 3	D	May 16
6106	Gallagher P	47	D	Aug 18
4699	Gallewin Thos	Art 20	F	Aug 4
10489	Galush W	Cav 5	D	Aug 15
7678	Gandley J	" 3	F	Sept 3
6993	Gannon S	Art 7	E	Aug 27
385	Gansey ——	94	B	Apr 5
1153	Gardner H	52	A	Oct 19
5251	Gardner R	155	K	Aug 10
982	Gardner H	132	E	May 9
1313	Gardner O	104	C	May 24
9206	Gardner Wm	Cav 7	I	Sept 18
7926	Garlock Jno	46	B	Sept 5
8982	Gaman J	126	H	Sept 17
8383	Garney C	40	A	Sept 10
7033	Garry Jas	95	C	Aug 27 64
2688	Garrison J	65	H	June 30
7216	Gartill H	Cav 22	L	Aug 29
7044	Gartland ——	169		Aug 27
94	Garbey Jno	32	K	Mar 22
10539	Gatiff H	82	D	Oct 8
5270	Garette C	134	G	Aug 10
6868	Gear Jas	142	A	Aug 26
7120	Gees A	95	I	Aug 28
7930	Geiser Chas	39	D	Sept 5
8878	Gemminge J	Art 6		Sept 16
7650	Gesler Jas	65	E	Sept 3
6728	Glan Benj	11		Aug 24
10967	Gibbs Chas	Art 4	B	Oct 15
6259	Gibbs M H	Cav 22	E	Aug 20
3218	Gibson J	170	A	July 12
12017	Gibson J	82	I	Nov 15
6942	Giddings J	115	H	Aug 26
2042	Gifford H N	111		June 15
4185	Gilbert E	43	D	July 28
10925	Gilbert E	Cav 22	B	Oct 14
1834	Gilbert J	111	K	June 11
11270	Gillis G	85	G	Oct 21
10160	Gill Jno F	Cav 1	B	Oct 1
2413	Gill Jas	111	K	June 24
3339	Gillen M	107	E	July 15
7898	Gillett Wm	85	F	Sept 5
12345	Gilmore M	17	B	Dec 27
3106	Gimrich P, Bugler	C 2	K	July 10
1678	Gleick Wm	Cav 1	A	June 6
3946	Gleason Thos	97	D	July 25
10336	Goaner F	16	K	Oct 4
2553	Goffney J	104	D	June 27
8639	Goldsmith Wm	2	F	Sept 13
2962	Gond E	104	C	July 6
7088	Goodbread J F	147	B	Aug 28
12529	Goodell F	122	K	Jan 26 6
4145	Goodenough Jas	140	D	July 28 64
7342	Goodman J A	154	A	Aug 31
3042	Goodrich F	154	B	July 8
4561	Goodrich Geo	Cav 2	D	Aug 2
1415	Gorman G	Art 3	K	June 17
8228	Goodnow J	64	I	Sept 9
12604	Golt C	49	D	Feb 7 65
2203	Goss Jas	132	G	June 19 64
3322	Gould Richard	61	D	July 14
11985	Gough H	146	B	Nov 13
3765	Gower J	147	B	July 22
10499	Graff F	Cav 14	M	Oct 8
9347	Graham J	" 15	L	Sept 20
7089	Graham Wm	" 12	F	Aug 28
10093	Grampy M J	52	D	Sept 30
2640	Grandine D S	111	E	June 29
3638	Granger A	98	I	July 20
5798	Granger John	107	H	Aug 15
4131	Granner H	62	I	July 28
3212	Grant C	96	B	July 12
3875	Grant James	125	K	July 24
6449	Grant J K	9	D	Aug 22
9511	Grass H	42	G	Sept 22
12200	Graves E	Cav 2	I	Dec 1
4787	Graves W F	2	H	Aug 5
5354	Gray John	Art 6	H	Aug 11
1342	Green E	85	C	May 24
12522	Green H W	146	E	Jan 26 65
10277	Green J H	109	K	Oct 3 64
6863	Greer John	76	B	Aug 26

LIST OF THE DEAD.

No.	Name	Reg.	Co.	Date
5202	Green O	154	G	Aug 10 64
2184	Greenman J S	Cav 2	D	June 19
7634	Gregory A D L	120	E	Sept 2
4322	Gregory John	61	E	July 30
7492	Gregory L	Art 7	M	Sept 1
7201	Grenals H	70	F	Aug 29
11502	Griffin J B	Cav 7	D	Oct 26
3816	Griffin John	40	H	July 23
5766	Griffin N	52	F	Aug 15
3101	Griffith A	Bat 24		July 10
11185	Griffith E P	85	D	Oct 19
8351	Gilmartin A	60		Sept 10
3815	Griswold B F	109	F	July 23
1220	Gronely M	47	E	May 19
10944	Gross C	68	E	Oct 14
9553	Gross J	140	I	Sept 24
9981	Gross J	151	B	Sept 29
3092	Groven Josh	49	F	July 10
10997	Grundy R J	73	G	Oct 16
10813	Gunan Wm	Cav 8	D	Oct 12
5867	Gundaloch F	95	A	Aug 16
1459	Gunn Calvin	Cav 12	G	May 29
6651	Gunnahan J	85	G	Aug 23
9372	Gunnell Jno	Cav 2	B	Sept 20
8317	Guile A L	154	C	Sept 10
12145	Guyer F	Art 15	A	Nov 24
12328	Gwin Chas	69	H	Dec 24
6495	Hack J	12	K	Aug 22
10194	Hackett C	43	C	Oct 2
2623	Hackett ——	Cav 12	F	June 28
7113	Hackett J	Art 7	D	Aug 28
6876	Hagate Jacob	Cav 10	F	Aug 26
4677	Hager ——	52	H	Aug 4
3646	Hager J	59	B	July 20
6869	Hagerty Wm	147	E	Aug 26
8275	Hadden C	20		Sept 9
473	Haddish T	14	A	Apr 9
7721	Hadsell F	Art 2	L	Sept 3
8924	Haight J E	" 8	H	Sept 16
2887	Hair G	89	A	July 4
11036	Halbert A H	85	D	Oct 16
3342	Halbert L	1	D	July 15
170	Haline Gotfred	C 12	K	Mch 26
11310	Hall C	Drag 1	H	Oct 28
2214	Hall Chas	Cav 12	K	June 20
5003	Hall Chas	109	G	Aug 8
12370	Hall C W	40	I	Jan 1 65
870	Hall Ed	111	C	May 3 64
2846	Hall Jas	Cav 9	E	July 3
4459	Hall Jno	109	E	Aug 1
9661	Hall S	Cav 14	L	Sept 24
7731	Hall W C	Cav 8	K	Sept 3
7819	Hall William	2	K	Sept 8
10865	Hallembeck S	145	B	Oct 13
4173	Halloway J	146	D	July 28
9253	Halpin P	68		Sept 19
11049	Harper Jno	134	F	Oct 17
8213	Hamilton H	132	D	Sept 8
12405	Hamiton J	111	G	Jan 6 65
10032	Hamilton Jno	Art 6	L	Sept 29 64
6601	Hamilton Thos	Art 6	L	Aug 23
5634	Hammond M	66	G	Aug 14
1104	Hand L	Cav 5	C	May 15
9862	Hanlon Thos	180	F	Sept 27
11076	Hand H S	169	A	Oct 17
3589	Hanks J	Cav 1	L	July 19
3857	Hanley D	22	B	July 24
12448	Hanley Wm	29	D	Jan 13 65
6009	Hancock R	Cav 2	D	Aug 17 64
1207	Hanor Frank	12	G	May 19
6432	Hansom C	67	F	Aug 22
11149	Hardy J	95	C	Oct 19
9363	Hardy J	Cav 5	I	Sept 20
10101	Hardy W	95	E	Sept 30
7929	Hannom Jno	164	I	Sept 5
1411	Haines Philip	85	I	May 27
2383	Harp M	95	I	June 23
8323	Harper J	126	G	Sept 10
10115	Hauen F J	52	C	Oct 1
5550	Harris C	63	E	Aug 13
5482	Haynes H	Cav 5	I	Aug 13
6784	Harris Thos	85	C	Aug 25
4056	Harris V S	Cav 8	M	July 27
1378	Harrington Pat	71	D	May 26
10384	Harrison Henry	76	K	Oct 5
8362	Harrison O	14	K	Sept 10
2726	Harry A	143	K	June 26
4705	Hart D R	109	D	Aug 4
5148	Hart J	Cav 12	F	Aug 15
11524	Hart J	Art 7	K	Oct 21
8287	Hart S	146	B	Sept 9
8337	Hart S	Cav 22	M	Sept 10
7432	Hartman J N	40	H	Aug 31
766	Harty John	Cav 2	M	April 27
10812	Hasket A	39	I	Oct 12
8758	Hasler M	119	C	Sept 14
11947	Hass J F	49	F	Nov 10
1891	Hathaway Chas	Bat 24		June 13
10878	Hanse John	Cav 1	L	Oct 13
2262	Haveland H	Art 6		June 21
11461	Havens Geo	22	G	Oct 25
3826	Havens H	141	A	July 23
4814	Havens S	104	A	Aug 5
8523	Haverslight H	66	E	July 18
11629	Hawley W L	Cav 2	D	Oct 28
10646	Hawley F	76	E	Oct 11
5355	Hayatt L P	Cav 1	A	Aug 11
11786	Hayes C	2	F	Nov 4
8022	Hayes Edward	69	G	Sept 6
9080	Hayes J	6	A	Sept 18
10904	Hayes James	39	E	Oct 14
1264	Hayes P	35	H	Oct 21
9134	Head Thos	Art 6	A	Sept 18
3394	Haynes W C	Art 6	K	July 16
10220	Hayner L	125	H	Oct 2
10662	Hencock R	66	H	Oct 11
3581	Hecker C	47	C	July 19
6181	Heddle Wm	Cav 5	M	Aug 19
3155	Hefferman D	132	C	July 11
8135	Helafsattau J	63	K	Sept 8
11382	Helf J C	Cav 1	G	Oct 24
6828	Heller D	Art 14		Aug 25
7330	Henderson N J	85	K	Aug 30
10206	Hendfest J B	100	K	Oct 2
11380	Henertes B	15	I	Oct 24
11733	Hilbert G	5	E	Nov 2
8336	Hennesy M	Art 3	K	Sept 10
7196	Henyon W	85	H	Aug 29
10870	Heratage Thos	8	C	Oct 13
196	Herget Jno	111	A	Mch 27
3119	Hermance F C	Stm 20	A	July 10
11996	Hermance J	100	C	Nov 13
4496	Herrick Chas	39	M	Aug 1
6027	Henning C	140	I	Aug 23

LIST OF THE DEAD.

No.	Name	Reg.	Co.	Date
10506	Hestolate Jno	69		Oct 9 64
12104	Hewes J	Cav 1	A	Nov 20
11193	Hewes R	100	C	Oct 20
7605	Hicks W H	99	I	Sept 2
99	Hietzel C	52	B	Mch 22
9937	Higgins J	43	G	Sept 28
888	Higgins Wm	99	B	May 4
4058	Higley Geo	85	F	July 27
7652	Hildreth H	85	K	Sept 3
5698	Hildreth L C	88	D	July 21
777	Hill A A	44	G	April 28
8643	Hill A J	2	F	Sept 13
8970	Hill Frank	Cav 2	K	July 25
11998	Hill L	22	B	Nov 13
11912	Hill Wm	Cav 24	E	Nov 8
3316	Hillman Geo	85	B	July 14
4454	Hines J	126	G	Aug 1
9060	Hingman A	140	G	Sept 17
31	Hinkley B	Cav 9	B	Mch 9
6255	Hinkley D	" 1	E	Aug 20
5331	Hinton J	Art 14	B	Aug 11
2967	Hinton Thos	Cav 12	E	July 6
7192	Hoag I	196	A	Aug 29
395	Hoag Jno A	Cav 21	L	April 6
11670	Hoar H J	120	I	Oct 30
1085	Hobbs J	8	H	June 17
2984	Hobson Wm	Cav 14	F	July 7
6556	Hodge Jno	" 22	A	Aug 23
6977	Hodgekiss A	" 8	M	Aug 27
1027	Hofland Jno	132	E	May 11
5010	Hoffman Fred	48	B	Aug 8
3811	Hoffman H	47	E	July 23
4932	Hoffman H	Art 7	L	Aug 7
6248	Hoffman N	Cav 5	F	Aug 20
7718	Hofyenneck T	" 21	I	Sept 3
11317	Hogan J	63	F	Oct 22
5449	Hogan Jno J	Art 6	M	Aug 13
162	Horsenton E L	94	B	Mch 26
6465	Holbrook G	76	K	Aug 22
6327	Holbrook J E	85	E	Aug 21
5013	Holcomb M D	95	F	Aug 8
2204	Holcomb Theo	40	K	June 19
11662	Holfe J	48	E	Oct 30
6475	Holiday S	85	E	Aug 22
2510	Hollands H	115	E	June 26
7218	Hollen M	152	A	Aug 29
2573	Hollendeck H J	120	G	June 27
7051	Holliday S	85	K	Aug 28
10624	Holmen J	50	C	Oct 10
7952	Holmes C	85	A	Sept 6
7104	Holmes E	Art 7	K	Aug 28
5531	Holmes Henry	99	H	Aug 13
12467	Holmes J	22	K	Jan 16 t5
1504	Holstenstein H	48	E	May 31 64
12298	Holtcaup B	96	F	Dec 16
7826	Homvighausen F	140	B	Sept 4
7117	Hooker T	111	D	Aug 28
5369	Hoover A	Art 15	H	Aug 11
514	Hoppock A	Art 15	H	April 12
4040	Homstead H	22	A	Sept 6
6114	Hose R	Cav 15	L	Aug 19
2445	Hosford W F	Bat 24		June 25
6094	Houghdalinger M	129	D	Aug 18
10817	Houghteling C	Art 5	A	Oct 12
5652	Hour Jas	119	E	Aug 14
7457	Hous A R	96	C	Sept 1
11099	Houslin E	95	G	Oct 18
11093	Howard A	Art 2	M	Oct 31 64
8477	Howard J	Cav 12	F	Sept 11
4387	Howard Wm	39	A	July 31
10114	Howe Geo	Cav 16	M	Oct 1
12292	Howe S	59	C	Dec 15
11064	Howell C R	Cav 2	C	Oct 17
6622	Hoye J	Art 9	I	Aug 23
7301	Hubbard A	76	B	Aug 30
10066	Hudson J A	148	A	Oct 11
9562	Hudson S R	Cav 15	L	Sept 23
9387	Hull J E	" 24	E	Sept 20
1462	Huff W S	140	C	May 29
7931	Huganer A	85	K	Sept 5
16	Huganer D M	64	I	Mch 6
7805	Hughes Jno	93	K	Sept 4
11191	Hughes M	82	K	Oct 20
7287	Hughes Thos	61	G	Aug 30
2562	Hulet W	Cav 22	L	June 27
7584	Hulee G	99	I	Sept 2
1474	Hulse W S	47	G	May 30
7113	Humphrey H	85	F	Aug 29
2618	Humphrey Jas	155	I	June 28
2898	Hunnell J	100	A	July 5
476	Hunt F J	46	D	April 9
3365	Hunter E	Bat 24		July 15
10978	Hunter J	115		Oct 15
9802	Hanlon Thos	180	F	Sept 27
5841	Huntsmore G	66	E	Aug 16
5497	Hurlburt S B	100	F	Aug 13
4430	Hurley Jno	52	A	July 31
12014	Hurrell J	Cav 10	E	Feb 8 65
11851	Hutchings H W	" 1	D	Nov 1 64
3112	Hutchings S A	" 5	B	July 10
5024	Hutchings Wm	Art 6	G	Aug 8
898	Hutchinson T	Cav 13	D	May 4
8585	Hutchinson J	82	A	Sept 12
10019	Hutchinson M	52	G	Oct 16
9173	Huleson Wm E	Art 2	B	Sept 18
8055	Hyde C	14	F	Sept 16
11083	Hyde G	42	C	Oct 18
8770	Hyde J F	76	B	Sept 14
7625	Hyland O	5	D	Sept 2
2106	Hyman J	45	E	June 17
2187	Imhoff R	Cav 2	G	June 19
4019	Imlay E	95	A	July 26
4359	Imman J P	Cav 1	A	July 31
10549	Ingerson S	Art 14	G	Oct 9
4685	Ingraham C B	85	B	Aug 4
3428	Inner I	Cav 1	H	July 16
4588	Irish G	85	C	Aug 2
11781	Ivespack W	Cav 15	E	Nov 3
8159	Jaquays R	9	L	Sept 8
7590	Jack J W	95	H	Sept 2
6558	Jackson A	Cav 5	E	Aug 23
9048	Jackson J	43	K	Sept 17
11391	Jackson T A	122	E	Oct 24
5402	Jackson John S	109	F	Aug 12
7253	Jackson Wm	85	F	Aug 30
6966	Jarmine Jas	115	I	Aug 27
4795	Jamison A	51	A	Aug 5
3645	Jarvis E	106	H	July 20
11704	Jasper C	Art 7	D	Oct 31
6071	Jay John	" 8		Aug 24
9389	Jay John	" 2	G	Sept 20
3984	Jeffrey B	" 9	D	July 26
1120	Jelley John	99	K	May 15
29	Jenner Henry	Art 3	K	April 19

LIST OF THE DEAD.

No.	Name	Reg.	Co.	Date
10757	Jennings C	140	K	Oct 12 64
744	Jewell J R	Art 3	K	April 26
9934	Johnson A	74	C	Sept 28
11182	Johnson A	Art 7	A	Oct 19
12121	Johnson B	63	D	Nov 22
12477	Johnson B F	82	H	Jan 17 65
10118	Johnson H S	85	B	Oct 1 64
5916	Johnson H	115	I	Aug 17
6232	Johnson H	Cav 10	C	Aug 20
7712	Johnson J	89	I	Sept 3
12346	Johnson J	146	A	Jan 27 65
10043	Johnson L W	Art 14	C	Sept 29 64
5985	Johnson M	96	H	Aug 17
9495	Johnson P B	Bat 24		Sept 21
8054	Johnson R	111	A	Sept 7
3427	Johnson R	120	I	July 16
4047	Joice Thos	22	C	July 27
7413	Jolley F	93	E	Aug 31
5980	Jones C N	Cav 10	C	Aug 17
6898	Jones David	85	H	Aug 26
10769	Jones E C	147	E	Oct 12
3650	Jones E	134	F	July 20
4373	Jones G C	20		July 31
3282	Jones G W	47	F	July 14
3758	Jones H	Cav 10	I	Aug 15
5582	Jones Jno	76	K	Aug 14
11855	Jones Jno	Cav 6	A	Nov 6
2487	Jones R	99	B	June 26
4403	Jones Thos	116	B	July 31
5042	Jones Wm	52	B	Aug 8
8367	Jones Wm, Far	C	5	Sept 15
8771	Jones J B	22	F	Sept 14
9528	Jourdan Barney	Art 7	E	Sept 22
4188	Jule H	51	E	July 28
9107	Jump O	Cav 8		Sept 18
5198	Kahbaum E	Cav 12	F	Aug 10
12170	Kane H	82	A	Nov 26
792	Kane Peter	Cav 20		April 28
8868	Kanope C	49		Sept 15
9194	Kapp D	100	F	Sept 18
10222	Kearney W	Cav 16	A	Oct 2
8452	Keating M	146	A	Sept 11
4434	Keating Thos	83	L	Aug 1
11075	Kean W	47	I	Oct 17
7387	Keers M	49	A	Aug 31
11756	Kehoe T	155	A	Nov 3
10341	Kelley M	Art 2	L	Oct 4
10049	Kellar Jno	140	E	Oct 4
6739	Kelley D	45	C	Aug 24
11100	Kelley J	Art 4	K	Oct 18
10675	Kelley Jas	146	K	Oct 11
6997	Kelley Jas	40	F	Aug 27
10388	Kelley M	63		Oct 5
9676	Kelley P	106	D	Sept 24
12209	Kelley T	82	F	Dec 2
10960	Kenarm Alfred	70	K	Oct 14
11425	Kennedy M E	82	K	Oct 24
9865	Kennedy W	132	D	Sept 27
11244	Kennien F	8	H	Oct 21
3572	Kenney A W	85	D	July 19
1250	Kenney G W	Bat 24		May 21
3671	Kenney M	2	F	July 30
4398	Kent E L	33	I	July 31
7403	Kenwell R	Cav 5	D	Aug 31
1079	Keogh Peter	132	C	May 14
5952	Kerritt Jacob	132	D	Aug 17
5310	Kerr C L	85	B	Aug 11
2484	Kerr H	Cav 2	L	June 25 64
3915	Kertser T	178	K	July 25
2797	Kester Chas	141	F	July 2
1622	Kettle Sol	Art 2	K	Oct 28
9015	Keys R	95	C	Sept 17
650	Keyes O S	Cav 5	E	April 20
1932	Kidd Owen	126	K	June 14
4606	Killner Sanford	125	F	Aug 3
1864	Kilmer J	5	I	June 12
10514	Kilson J	115	E	Oct 10
10026	Kimball S	Art 7	F	Nov 15
3262	Kimberly C	76	B	July 13
7999	King ——	99	I	Sept 6
9816	King N	Cav 21	G	Sept 26
8738	King Sylvanus	Bat 24		Sept 14
3787	King Richard	99	H	July 22
3095	Kinsley D	Cav 12	H	July 10
9089	Kinsley Jas	Cav 5		Sept 24
239	Kinney Lucas	99	H	Mar 30
11558	Kinney M	42	C	Oct 27
8400	Kinnie J	76	F	Sept 10
564	Kinsey B B	132	K	April 15
7977	Kinsman JnoE	Art 14	I	Sept 6
12869	Kinsman W S	86	I	April 20 65
4287	Kirby Chas	Cav 12	F	July 30 64
7087	Kirkland I	Art 2	D	Aug 28
12742	Kirkpatrick ——	C 12	D	Mar 6 65
5589	Kittle E N	125	E	Aug 14 64
8873	Kizer G W	76	B	Sept 15
4525	Knapp Henry	Cav 24	A	Aug 2
5233	Knapp Philip	Cav 10	C	Aug 10
2604	Knabe F	48	C	June 28
7949	Knight Wm	142	C	Sept 6
12818	Knowl H	66	C	Dec 21
11976	Kossuth W	54	F	Nov 12
8860	Krasipars K	65	L	Sept 15
9211	Krantz H	54	E	Sept 19
12115	Kreit J K	Cav 1	L	Nov 21
11948	Krelar A	Bat 13		Nov 10
3892	Kroom C E	64	G	July 24
1208	Krouger G R	178	K	May 19
8956	Lahey P	1	D	Sept 16
8447	Lacey P	Cav 12	F	Sept 11
3001	Lacey Wm	85	K	July 19
10736	Lackley P I	Cav 1		Oct 11
10879	Lacks Lee	22	G	Oct 13
8372	Lacoster H	85		Sept 10
10527	Lader A	9	E	Oct 26
7156	Lagay Frank	118	B	Aug 29
41	Lahey Daniel	82	I	Mar 13
12775	Lahiff D	42	K	Mar 14 65
12100	Lake Wm	146	K	Nov 21 64
6487	Laman C	39	H	Aug 22
6381	Lamareux J	76	K	Aug 21
11893	Lambright A	Art 7	K	Nov 7
11599	Lambly J	1	I	Oct 28
11318	Lampman W S	Art 6	M	Oct 22
11213	Lampert R	98	D	Oct 20
9886	Larrabee E	15	D	Sept 27
3283	Landers C	Art 7		July 14
12214	Lane C	146	E	Dec 3
7462	Lane Chas	Cav 3	E	Sept 1
2678	Lane G W	85	C	June 30
11499	Lane J W	Cav 15	M	Oct 26
2288	Lang A	85	F	June 21
13	Lang Wm W	Drag 1		Mar 6
8236	Langdon A M	85	B	Sept 9

LIST OF THE DEAD.

No.	Name	Unit	Age	Co.	Date
4375	Lansing Wm	Cav 12	B		July 31 64
3788	Lansop J		85	D	July 22
10096	Langen A		39	I	Sept 30
4871	Lampan L H	Bat 24			Aug 6
8087	Larcks G		85	F	Sept 7
6631	Larkins M C		100	A	Aug 23
14	Lasar Benj	Cav 6		F	Mar 6
8956	Latey P		1	D	Sept 19
851	Lattaratta J	Cav 1		A	May 3
4107	Laugha W	Art 1		M	July 27
8162	Lawton J		69	E	Sept 8
10095	Lawrence J	Art 7		G	Sept 30
4101	Lawson John	Cuv 2		D	July 27
6434	Layman C		120	K	Aug 22
2374	Leubrook John		157	B	June 23
2119	Leach S	Cav 10		E	June 17
1737	Lean W H	Cav 21		C	June 8
7142	Ledderer Wm		132	G	Aug 29
1944	Lee A	Bat 24			June 14
2169	Lee F		15	F	June 19
2572	Lee P	Art 2		A	June 27
9696	Lee Wm	Cav 6		L	Sept 24
8514	Legrist W		11	E	Sept 10
6399	Leichinger J	Cav 3		D	Aug 21
3565	Leiner A		39	B	July 19
11697	Lenot V		47	I	Oct 31
2686	Lent A	Bat 24			June 30
7499	Leonard A		52	B	Sept 1
12076	Leonard C H	Art 7		A	Nov 18
8987	Leonard J W		85	K	Sept 17
10065	Lestraff C	Art 7		A	Sept 30
6150	Letch John	Cav 5		C	Aug 19
8774	Levalley C		140	A	Sept 14
9045	Lewis C		85	F	Sept 17
3727	Lewis C F		52	E	July 21
1329	Lewis F A		9	G	May 24
11515	Lewis G W		146	G	Nov 8
8297	Lewis J	Art 1		E	Sept 9
5115	Lewis P W		85	B	Aug 9
10365	Lickley P	Cav 1		E	Oct 5
11551	Limbach S		7	D	Oct 27
8419	Linch J H		76	I	Sept 11
5845	Linchler F	Cav 1		E	Aug 15
10559	Lindlay D		147	E	Oct 9
7815	Lineham Thos		125	C	Sept 4
6759	Ling Jno	Art 4		F	Aug 25
38	Link Gotlib		54	K	Mar 12
10073	Little C		76	F	Sept 30
10933	Livingstone A	Cav 1		C	Oct 14
4543	Locher Conrad	Art 15			Aug 2
5565	Lock A		98	B	Aug 13
2162	Lodge T		12	A	June 18
8246	Loftern H	Cav 10		F	Sept 9
9722	Loftus M	Cav 11		E	Sept 24
7010	Longs R	Art 2		A	Aug 27
11591	Long J		75	A	Oct 28
7924	Long L		40	I	Sept 5
4514	Longle Wm	Art 4		B	Aug 1
5464	Loomis Jno	Art 14		M	Aug 12
9712	Loony C		48	A	Sept 25
9088	Lorzbran J		64	E	Sept 29
11906	Louis C	Cav 16		C	Nov 7
12329	Love J		125	A	Dec 24
7146	Lovejoy F	Cav 1		I	Aug 29
10248	Lovering F	Art 14		I	Oct 3
12313	Lowery G		7	A	Dec 20
2568	Lowery Jas F		140	A	June 27

No.	Name	Unit	Age	Co.	Date
9663	Laws H	Cav 22		E	Sept 24 64
8395	Lloyd S		47	D	Sept 10
9854	Luce V		140	D	Sept 20
10311	Lucia A		95	H	Oct 4
7268	Lurcock E	Art 14		M	Aug 30
9002	Lutton O	Art 14		H	Sept 17
5772	Lynch D		164	A	Aug 15
6895	Lynch F		43	K	Aug 26
931	Lynch Pat		99	H	May 7
12683	Lyons Chas	Cav 2		M	Feb 10 65
1427	Lyons Michael		99	E	May 28 64
8419	Luch J H		76	I	Sept 11
6151	Lucha Jno	Cav 5		C	Sept 19
8342	Lyons J H	Art 5			Sept 10
6156	Lyons Thos	Art 6		G	Aug 19
7913	Lyons W		47	A	Sept 5
37	Mace Jeff		134	I	Mar 12
6665	Mace L		48	H	Aug 24
10850	Mack J		39	D	Oct 13
5016	Mackin Wm		85	F	Aug 8
3933	Mudder P		155	E	July 25
10506	Madden F		122	E	Oct 8
4822	Madden ——	Cav 1		D	Aug 5
11257	Madezau Jno		125	B	Oct 21
9798	Madison D		75	D	Sept 26
11714	Magrath G H		61	D	Nov 1
4028	Mahon E		170	G	July 26
122	Mahon Jas		132	K	Mar 23
1422	Mahon Thos		120	C	May 28
5842	Mailer J R		134	B	Aug 16
11679	Maine F O		85	A	Oct 31
11580	Mainhart F		39	B	Oct 28
12669	Makay J		5	E	Nov 17
7942	Mallock M	Cav 6		D	Sept 5
9427	Malley S S		16	K	Sept 21
9457	Maloue Pat		123	F	Sept 20
3234	Maloney C		6	C	July 14
11417	Maloney J		73	G	Oct 25
7600	Mandeville Wm		85	F	Sept 2
2802	Mangin F	Art 7		F	July 3
10023	Manning ——		33		Oct 9
7139	Manning M	Art 6		D	Aug 28
10540	Manning Thos		125	B	Oct 8
2952	Mannilly J		74	C	July 6
2856	March J	Cav 22		C	July 4
4000	Marley John	Mus 53		E	July 26
1123	Maron J		99	I	May 15
11764	Martaugh J	Cav 6		A	Sept 3
3824	Marsh Ira	Art 6		M	July 23
5407	Marsh J		104	D	Aug 12
11997	Marston A		65	G	Nov 13
3441	Martin A	Cav 12		F	July 17
435	Martin C	Cav 10		A	Apr 8
6543	Martin Chas		42	G	Aug 23
11600	Martin E A	Cav 5		C	Oct 28
12208	Martin J		39	G	Dec 2
4321	Martin H		76	H	July 30
5086	Martin J C	Bat 24			Aug 8
9164	Martin P		99	H	Sept 18
6293	Martin John	Cav 16		L	Aug 20
1256	Martin Peter		40	I	May 21
8003	Martin W		142	F	Sept 6
3939	Martin W B		12	I	July 25
8746	Martin W H	Art 24		M	Sept 14
1073	Martin Wm	Cav 13		D	May 13
676	Marvoney James		132	G	Apr 22
10483	Mason F	Art 14		I	Oct 7

LIST OF THE DEAD.

No.	Name		Co./Reg.	Age	Co.	Date
2315	Martin Samuel			85	I	June 22 64
11290	Masterson E			2	D	Oct 22
11296	Massen H L			86	C	Oct 22
10498	Maxwell J			85	D	Oct 8
1477	Maxwell Robt			43	D	May 30
11788	Matthews W			155	I	Nov 4
4472	Matthews H	Cav	12		M	Aug 1
2100	Mattice H C			134	E	June 17
5651	Mattison R			85	D	Aug 14
4946	Maxum S G	Cav	12		A	Aug 7
10519	McAllister J			125	I	Oct 8
7995	McBride ——			52	K	Sept 6
4508	McCabe Jas			88	D	Aug 1
2517	McCabe P	Cav	12		F	June 26
732	McCabe Peter	"		2	E	Apr 25
2196	McCabe J			44	C	June 19
8324	McCafferty W			100	D	Sept 10
10716	McCain L			18	C	Oct 11
9864	McCardell W	Cav	15		H	Sept 27
7620	McCarten L	Art	9		B	Sept 2
3413	McCarty D			155	G	July 16
4480	McCarty Deni	Art	2		D	Aug 1
5122	McCarty I			99	H	Aug 9
9633	McCarty I	M R	2		K	Sept 24
4759	McCarty Jno			69	K	Aug 5
6136	McCarty Jno			104	E	Aug 19
1035	McCarty P			132	K	May 11
2065	McCarty S			99	C	July 6
6227	McCarty W	Cav	9		L	Aug 20
8242	McClusky F			173	E	Sept 9
1344	McColigan Pat			99	F	May 24
9266	McCauly J H			47	G	Sept 19
6440	McCloud Jno			97	A	Aug 22
4416	McConnell E	Art	9			July 31
6012	McCord H	"	7		G	Aug 17
11110	McCormick M			93	K	Oct 18
6697	McCormick H			69	K	Aug 29
9018	McCormick H			178	F	Sept 17
3629	McCormick J			155	H	July 20
6203	McCormick J	Bat	24			Aug 19
7441	McCormick J			43	F	Sept 1
10258	McCormick P			43	D	Oct 3
1433	McCormick Peter			39	I	May 28
5203	McCormick W			2	I	Aug 10
7730	McCraker B	Art	7		B	Sept 3
8644	McCrass J			148		Sept 13
2279	McCrember M			85	I	June 21
8507	McCullen D			57	F	Sept 12
10778	McDavid J			5	D	Oct 12
6912	McDermott P			164	H	Aug 26
8969	McDonald A	Bat	24			Sept 16
7745	McDonald A H			85	E	Sept 3
7140	McDonald B			52	D	Aug 20
4013	McDonald Jno			164	E	July 26
12138	McDonald F	Cav	16		L	Nov 28
10002	McDonald F			95	A	Sept 29
7250	McDonnell Wm	Art	14		D	Aug 30
8126	McDurie C			71		Sept 8
4089	McElray Jno				I	July 27
9581	McErmany P	Art	7		G	Sept 23
338	McFarland A			72	I	Apr 2
12478	McGiben I			170	B	Jan 17 65
11116	McGowan Wm	Art	6		L	Oct 18 64
4001	McFadden Jas			39	F	July 26
2065	McGain I			99	H	June 29
354	McGeatte			52	D	Apr 2
3551	McGibney H			85	E	July 18
2756	McGiven Wm			158	B	July 1 64
8225	McGowan F			170	H	Sept 9
248	McGowan Jno			132	K	Mar 30
1112	McGrath M	Cav	12		E	May 15
4709	McGucker A	Cav	1		C	Aug 4
4995	McGuire P			140	C	Aug 7
6827	McGuire P			10	C	Aug 25
3220	McGuire Pat			101	F	July 12
8354	McHarty M			69	A	Sept 10
3233	McKabe J	Cav	12		F	July 12
1168	McKenley J			99	I	May 16
12664	McKenna H			12	F	Feb 16 65
5359	McKerchay J H			85	F	Aug 11 64
9390	McKinney John			82	D	Sept 20
10392	McLain R			42	F	Oct 6
10055	McLaughlin O			9	F	Sept 30
4268	McLorens R	Cav	20		M	July 29
6850	McLaughlin J			63	D	Aug 25
3611	McMahon C L	Cav	3		E	July 19
6814	McMurrier Wm	"	2		L	Aug 25
9969	McNamara Wm	Art	2		L	Sept 28
10728	McNamirin B F			14	A	Oct 11
5406	McNulty ——			85	E	Aug 12
3724	McPeak W	Cav	2		B	July 21
7271	McPherson Wm	Art	14		M	Aug 30
5868	McQuillen A	Art	6		L	Aug 16
8889	McSorley G W			20	M	Sept 16
3127	Mead P	Art	1		C	July 10
150	Megrame W H			99	E	Mar 25
10599	Melin A	Art	14		L	Oct 10
11167	Melins W			82	B	Oct 10
2068	Menzie A	Art	3		K	June 16
6042	Merritt H D			76	F	Aug 18
9353	Merkle J			15	A	Sept 20
12204	Merwin A	Cav	2		A	Oct 20
11214	Merz F A			5	I	Oct 20
8906	Messing I			39	A	Sept 16
10116	Messinger C	Cav	1		L	Oct 1
6462	Messirie J M	"	1		A	Aug 22
2523	Metcalf A			85	G	June 26
3134	Meyers F			45	G	July 10
8852	Meyer H			66	F	Sept 10
11723	Meyers I			57	F	Nov 1
2896	Meyers W			54	C	July 5
4520	Michael ——			66	A	Aug 2
11780	Michells W	Cav	2		B	Nov 3
3750	Midlaw F	"		12	A	July 22
2709	Migner H			54	D	June 30
6202	Millard F J	Cav	12		A	Aug 19
168	Millens Adam			125	E	Mar 26
5520	Miller A W			52	D	Aug 13
4647	Miller C			111	I	Aug 3
6469	Miller Chas B	Cav	24		E	Aug 22
3221	Miller F			182	D	July 18
5155	Miller F			99		Aug 9
6865	Miller F	Art	15		D	Aug 26
11516	Miller G A			152	C	Oct 26
6585	Milen Geo			61	F	Aug 23
11522	Miller Geo			1	G	Oct 26
3131	Miller H	Cav	1		L	July 10
10627	Miller H W			96	E	Oct 10
8278	Miller J			95	E	Sept 9
5521	Miller Jacob			39	I	Aug 13
628	Miller J E, Bugler	C	2		M	Apr 19
9505	Miller Jno			12	A	Sept 22
708	Miller O			126	G	Apr 24
9986	Miller Wm	Art	2		C	Sept 29

LIST OF THE DEAD. 241

No.	Name	Unit	#	Co.	Date		No.	Name	Unit	#	Co.	Date
8063	Millerman G	Cav 22		B	Sept 7 64		7672	Mortimer Wm	Art 5		A	Sept 3 64
8862	Mills J J		85		Sept 15		7079	Mosher E	"	9	D	Aug 28
2844	Mills S	Cav 12		A	July 3		10152	Mosier E	"	9	E	Oct 1
4854	Millspaugh F	Art 6		A	Aug 6		11016	Mosier M W		4	G	Oct 16
79	Miline Jno		95	G	Mar 20		2872	Moses L		85	E	July 4
1889	Mindler Peter	Cav 1			June 13		12008	Motts C	Bat 24			Nov 14
4771	Miner J G	Bat 24			Aug 5		8711	Moss W S	Art	7		Sept 14
3618	Minie F		99	F	July 20		11406	Mulcady W		42	E	Oct 26
8080	Mitchell J		125	E	Sept 7		7997	Molcohy D D		76	F	Sept 6
9939	Mitchell Jno		120	I	Sept 28		11368	Mulgrave Jas		2	C	Oct 23
7396	Milty Sam'l	Cav 12		L	Aug 30		12240	Mullen Chas	Art	7	I	Dec 7
2486	Moe Jno		120	I	June 25		11324	Muller P		7	H	Oct 23
4121	Moffat J	Art	7	C	July 28		6985	Mulligan J		34	H	Aug 27
5720	Monaghan		66	D	Aug 15		11485	Mulish R		48	A	Oct 26
4441	Monihan J		85	C	July 31		12155	Mullin J		82	G	Nov 25
4392	Monohan J		73	D	July 31		4720	Mullington C	Art	6	H	Aug 4
11537	Monahan P		88	D	Oct 27		8370	Munger D	"	2	C	Sept 10
4658	Monroe J R		111	G	Aug 3		8404	Murchison D	Cav 4		D	Sept 11
11961	Monroe A J		22	G	Nov 11		146	Murphy Jno		99	H	Mar 24
7453	Morgan M		76	B	Sept 1		5894	Murphy F		61	B	Aug 16
8241	Monschitz J		65	D	Sept 9		5918	Murphy L		170	E	Aug 17
1933	Monson Wm		11	G	June 14		6550	Murphy W S		40	K	Aug 28
7830	Monson Geo		6		Sept 4		11803	Murphy R		85	E	Nov 4
5635	Monta Henry		52	B	Aug 14		10200	Murphy Martin	C 2		D	Oct 2
3512	Montag Geo		39	B	July 18		12118	Murray J	Cav 23		F	Nov 22
11650	Moran D G		40	G	Oct 30		11273	Murray J		47	I	Oct 22
6565	Moran Thos		85	A	Aug 23		3389	Murry A		118	C	July 16
7732	Moram M J	Cav	3		Sept 3		8947	Murry J		39	C	Sept 16
11621	Morearty I		1	M	Oct 28		11519	Murry M John		63	F	Oct 26
10308	Morgraff Wm		64	H	Oct 4		6218	Murny ——	Bat 11			Aug 20
8461	Moody C R		100	B	Sept 11		11954	Murrey M		98	D	Nov 10
6423	Moody Thos		147	B	Aug 22		1560	Murville S		1	C	June 2
3108	Moony P	Art	3	K	July 10		12494	Muselman J		2	K	Jan 20 65
3451	Moony I		188	D	July 20		1384	Myers E		154	D	May 26 64
8417	Mooney J		52	D	Sept 11		4958	Myers H		47	A	Aug 7
10886	Mooney Thos		139	F	Oct 14		9913	Myers H	Cav	2	G	Sept 28
2766	Moore A. Bugler	C 22		E	July 12		5000	Myers H L		147	H	Aug 7
7656	Mooore C C	Cav	1	B	Sept 3		8970	Myers J	Cav 20		M	Sept 16
11829	Moore C	Art	2	B	Nov 5		6221	Myers James		66	K	Aug 20
658	Moore Martin		74	C	Apr 21		8073	Neal J		22	E	Sept 16
1694	Moore S		46	H	June 7		10587	Nedden J		82	A	Oct 10
442	Moore T H	Cav	5	M	Apr 9		7922	Nellman A		66	I	Sept 4
457	Moore W H		125	F	Apr 9		2541	Nelson B		39	A	June 27
7767	Moore Jno		39	H	Sept 4		6051	Nelson John		82	D	Aug 18
9778	Moore W S		85	D	Sept 26		11002	Nelson John	Art 2		D	Oct 17
10781	Morgan E	Art	14		Oct 12		3922	Nevens C		100	F	July 7
7563	Morgan E J		179	C	Sept 2		2985	Newton L C	Art	14	I	July 7
10831	Mortross D H	Art	7	L	Oct 10		4469	Newton R J	Bat 24			Aug 1
624	Moriand H	Cav 21		H	Apr 19		4943	Newton Samuel	D 85		G	Aug 7
4086	Morris E	Art	7	K	Aug 4		5227	Newton C W		85	K	Aug 10
9314	Morris T		65	C	Sept 28		2258	Nichols A S		2	C	June 20
3780	Morris H		71	F	July 22		5109	Nichols D A		125	D	Aug 9
8031	Morris J			D	Sept 6		7050	Nichols F E	Art	7	F	Aug 27
11226	Morris J	Cav	5				9017	Nobles E		14	A	Sept 17
5866	Morris J A	Art	7	G	Aug 16		11533	Nolan M		5	I	Oct 26
6069	Morris Jno		70	B	Aug 18		11356	Nolan Pat		88	D	Oct 28
12387	Morris R		66	G	Jan 3 65		5050	Nooman E	Cav 16		L	Aug 8
9073	Morris L R		85	B	Sept 20 64		4633	Norman J	Art 15		H	Aug 3
7703	Morris T A		111	E	Sept 3		633	Northrop D		125	H	Apr 10
4880	Morris Wm		102	G	Aug 6		5228	Northrop V		10	G	Aug 17
8638	Morrison W		5	I	Sept 13		17	Norton Alonzo		154	A	Mar 7
9371	Morrison W	Cav	5	I	Sept 20		4451	Norwood D F		85	E	Aug 1
7358	Morse E		"	5	L	Sept 6		4735	Nostrand C	Art 2		I	Aug 4
12511	Morse I		1	L	Jan 23 65		12241	Nott S A	Cav 15		E	Dec 7
617	Martin Chas		47	A	Apr 18 64		2549	Nutt M		126	D	June 27
10625	Martin G H	Art	7	L	Oct 10		11681	Nutterville W		8	G	Oct 31
3181	Martin Henry		61	C	July 11		5439	O'Brien D		63	F	Aug 12

LIST OF THE DEAD.

No.	Name	Unit	Co.	Date
9765	O'Brien M	Cav 1	A	Sept 25 64
8036	O'Brien S	" 5	L	Sept 6
1553	O'Brien W	" 8	A	June 2
6270	O'Carrell F	69	A	Aug 20
7356	Och S	46	D	Aug 31
3530	O'Connell Thos	72	B	July 18
2755	O'Dougherty J	51		July 1
12397	O'Kay Peter	110	E	Jan 5 65
9737	O'Keif C	146	C	Sept 25 64
9616	Olahan A	65	F	Sept 28
10069	Olmstead F H	Art 2	I	Sept 30
6435	Older W M	Cav 16	L	Aug 22
1448	Omat M	178	B	May 28
12150	Omma Jas	Art 7	B	Nov 24
11404	O'Neil J	39	H	Oct 24
1988	Ostenhal L	73	C	June 15
12	Osterstuck W	154	I	Mar 5
6456	Osborne R H	22	E	Aug 22
2714	Osterhardt B S	120	C	July 1
12269	Ostrander J	86	A	Dec 12
108	Ostrander J H	120	F	Mar 23
6326	Otis Jno	94	A	Aug 21
8768	Otto Chas	100	F	Sept 14
656	Otto Jas L	Cav 12	E	Apr 21
5447	Owens Ed	47	G	Aug 12
12227	Owens Wm	49	I	Dec 5
7504	O'Reilly Philip	Art 2	I	Sept 1
1819	Page O D	146	F	Sept 20
2825	Palmer P H	85	D	June 22
2582	Palmer F	17	F	June 27
6753	Pallette D	Cav 15	K	Aug 24
20	Palmiter R	86	D	Mar 7
5958	Pamperin Wm	71	H	Aug 17
3350	Pardy E	85	K	July 15
5710	Parish D	146	E	Aug 15
12180	Parker F	125	C	Nov 27
2092	Parker I	85	I	June 17
2819	Parker Isaac	124	G	July 3
1392	Parker J	80	I	May 26
2953	Parker J	154	G	July 6
3886	Parker J	Cav 15	F	July 16
4732	Parkinson A	Art 4	C	Aug 4
11956	Parks Wm	109	K	Nov 11
11218	Parsons W	64	E	Oct 20
9487	Patterson D	76	D	Sept 21
5880	Patterson E	Art 6	M	Aug 16
3440	Patterson G W	" 15	M	July 17
6105	Patterson H	Cav 1		Aug 19
5279	Patterson I H	85	F	Aug 11
4703	Patterson J H	85	G	Aug 4
10368	Paul P	39	L	Oct 8
6696	Pease Martin	Cav 2	C	Aug 24
2166	Peck J G	" 22	F	June 19
11630	Peckins L	" 2	A	Oct 28
11673	Pedro Francis	" 12	B	Oct 30
1542	Pellet Ed	" 15	I	June 1
3781	Pen R	" 2	F	July 22
2763	Pinablin Jno	69	F	July 12
11348	Pen Chas	Art 6	D	Oct 23
7398	Perkey D	85	B	Aug 31
7172	Perkins J P	Bat 24		Aug 29
10502	Perry A	39	G	Oct 9
4527	Perry Jno	84	D	Aug 2
7866	Perry W	Cav 2	B	Sept 5
3721	Perry Wm	99	E	July 21
12182	Perry Wm	79	A	Nov 27
4517	Person A	61	H	Aug 2
3082	Persons W B	64	B	July 9 64
5224	Peters Fritz	52	C	Aug 10
3914	Peters J	114	F	July 25
5684	Peterson C	178	I	Aug 15
9120	Peterson H	48	B	Sept 18
3302	Pettis L P	100	F	July 14
5727	Petrie Josh	81	I	Aug 13
480	Phelps Martin	132	G	Apr 9
4235	Phillips Geo A	85	B	July 29
12461	Phillips I	Cav 6	E	Jan 17 65
7637	Phillips H	100	H	Sept 2 64
3318	Phillips R	85	B	July 14
4152	Pierce Albert	Art 2	M	July 28
2459	Pierce Chas	73	F	June 25
5371	Pierce H	85	B	Aug 11
6027	Pierce J	85	D	Aug 18
11663	Pierce J H	Cav 8		Oct 30
6005	Pierson J	76	B	Aug 17
9422	Pilseck E	61	I	Sept 21
1532	Pinmon John	99	I	May 31
9994	Pitts G	97	K	Sept 29
11441	Pivant M	61	D	Oct 25
6086	Place E	47	F	Aug 18
815	Plass H	120	G	Apr 30
11379	Plunkett J	146	A	Oct 24
9549	Polock J	85	C	Sept 23
4432	Pollock R	Cav 16	L	July 31
1843	Pomroy C	" 21	G	June 11
4531	Pouteis G	" 16	K	Aug 2
1830	Popple W G	85	B	June 11
11120	Pope Jas E	Art 15	A	Oct 18
12291	Post H E	125	G	Oct 15
12425	Post J A	94	E	Jan 10 65
6385	Potter H	48	E	Aug 21 64
1582	Potter W H	85	F	June 3
5116	Powell Geo	Art 7	H	Aug 9
2948	Powers F	Cav 24	H	July 6
3367	Powers J	10	K	July 15
6890	Powers O	Art 6	I	Aug 21
5435	Pratt B F	146	G	Aug 12
1394	Presselman C	Cav 4	M	May 26
5523	Preston H G	9	G	Aug 13
1096	Price David	154	A	May 14
12346	Price J, Citizen			Dec 27
6455	Pratt P	Bat 24		Aug 22
1651	Priest W	132	E	June 5
1479	Pratt G B	Cav 10	D	May 30
7964	Pringler Thos W	118	A	Sept 6
6914	Prow Jno	Art 14	L	Aug 26
9668	Prowman S H	149	H	Sept 24
9937	Puff I	Art 15		Sept 28
2321	Puley Daniel	115	I	June 22
729	Pullers U H	132	E	Apr 25
2395	Putnam A	Art 14	L	June 24
1515	Purkey Jacob	84	B	May 31
4063	Purstle S	49	A	July 27
11432	Prunan L	147	H	Oct 24
9046	Quackenbuss P	11	K	Sept 17
8227	Quigley J	99	I	Sept 9
8064	Quinn Edser	Cav 10	B	Sept 27
4305	Randolph ——	9	E	July 30
11648	Rafbrun W	59	C	Oct 30
512	Rafferty M	132	G	Apr 12
2534	Rafferty P	Cav 5	M	June 26
11330	Rafferty T	Art 5	B	Oct 23
4593	Raker L	Cav 1	E	Aug 3
3751	Ranch J	100	D	July 22

LIST OF THE DEAD. 243

No.	Name	Reg.	Co.	Date	No.	Name	Reg.	Co.	Date
10875	Randall Jno	99	A	Oct 13 64	11195	Roberson C A	122	B	Oct 20 64
6503	Ralinger J	47	B	Aug 22	2346	Robertson W H	134	B	June 23
6794	Rangneart Jno	100	A	Aug 25	8554	Robertson W M	96	B	Sept 12
7778	Rasterfer Jno	100	A	Sept 4	9970	Robinson H	39	K	Sept 28
4216	Rattery Jno	104	I	July 26	7607	Robinson A	111	I	Sept 2
10937	Ray C	Cav 3	B	Oct 14	3880	Robinson H C	95	I	July 21
10246	Ray R S	154	A	Oct 3	6419	Robinson Jno	115	A	Aug 22
4336	Raynard F	125		July 30	27	Robins L	154	K	Mar 8
3435	Rattersboon J	Art 3	K	July 17	7663	Roberts A	173	C	Sept 3
2880	Ramsay Isaac	86	I	July 4	7585	Rockwell N C	A 14	D	Sept 2
1265	Ramsay Hiram	31	K	May 21	8318	Rockfeller R E	85	D	July 23
2186	Reamer W C	111	B	June 19	11342	Rockfeller H	Art 15	M	Oct 23
2820	Rodman J	Art 3	K	July 3	3959	Rock F	"	G	July 25
11695	Reddo D V	Cav 8	M	Oct 31	4350	Rogers A	"	7	I	July 31
7232	Reed F A	64	E	Aug 30	6059	Rogers A	125	H	Aug 18
8574	Reed J	140	H	Sept 12	5791	Rogers G	Mus 85	F	Aug 15
406	Reed S G	13	B	Apr 6	3011	Rogers Jas	132	H	July 7
6041	Reed W D	146	H	Aug 18	4287	Rogers H C	85	C	July 30
10232	Reed W J	41	I	Oct 2	8369	Rogers H J	Art 2	E	Sept 10
8492	Reed Wm	Art 14	I	Sept 11	4912	Rogers M	43	D	Aug 6
7369	Reetz Jno	52	A	Aug 31	7208	Rogers O S	85	C	Aug 29
5694	Reeve G	152	C	Aug 5	6824	Rogers Thos	12	F	Aug 25
1680	Reeves Jno	57	H	June 6	11772	Romer F	9	A	Nov 3
10467	Redmond J	43	C	Oct 7	8468	Rook G	Art 6	E	Sept 11
10911	Regler W H	Cav 22	M	Oct 14	9663	Rooney Jno	152	G	Sept 28
9122	Reiley P O	164	B	Sept 18	9102	Rooney M	132	F	Sept 18
7195	Reuback C	29		Aug 29	8922	Rooney P	Art 2	C	Sept 16
12455	Rebman J	59	C	Jan 15 65	5669	Root A N	85	C	Aug 14
8431	Rencermane J R	C 5	B	Sept 11 64	2998	Roots W T	120	H	July 7
9320	Randall A B	76	F	Sept 20	1735	Root Legrand	Bat 24		June 8
3352	Remson F	Cav 2	M	July 15	10278	Rose A	16	L	Oct 2
8209	Reynolds O	155	E	Sept 8	9550	Rosecrans J E	125	H	Sept 23
6799	Reynolds O S	85	E	Aug 25	8171	Ross C	Cav 23	A	Sept 8
10265	Reynolds Samuel	92	H	Oct 3	3874	Ross E F	111	I	July 24
6350	Reynolds Wm	140	l	Aug 21	5591	Ross David	27	D	Aug 14
6546	Reidy J D	65	I	Aug 23	6741	Ross G	76	K	Aug 24
4318	Rice F	39	I	July 30	9751	Ross A	Cav 1	M	Sept 25
3077	Rich T D	Bat 24		July 9	11963	Ross J H	121	G	Nov 11
12289	Rich J	82	C	Dec 15	5929	Rosenbarger Jno	4	D	Aug 17
3561	Richey R	66	C	July 18	3616	Rosser Lewis	84	A	July 20
2427	Rider E	178	E	June 24	2924	Rosenburg J	30	A	July 5
8005	Rhenebault R H	21	B	Sept 6	8737	Rosson Chas	Cav 24	E	Sept 14
11904	Rehn W	Art 7	C	Nov 7	12259	Roswell J	93	K	Dec 10
3891	Richistine C	132	D	July 24	727	Ross Jacob	151	A	Apr 25
5317	Richards A	52	D	Aug 11	1940	Row W J	120	B	June 14
5674	Richards A	41	E	Aug 14	5097	Roth Louis	39	D	Aug 9
12243	Richards A	9	C	Dec 7	8504	Rothwell M	Cav 20	M	Sept 12
3682	Richards H	47	E	July 21	3720	Rouge Wm, Bug	C 12	F	July 21
7578	Richards N J	146	C	Sept 2	7709	Rowbotham R	C 11	L	Sept 3
4240	Richardson HM	C 20	M	July 29	5857	Rowell J E	70	G	Aug 16
12193	Ricker M	Art 2	M	Nov 29	3492	Rowell L N	99	H	July 17
8155	Rickhor J	85	E	Sept 8	59	Roberts A B	Cav 8	B	Mar 18
415	Rikel Robert	125	G	Apr 7	2609	Ruddin C	120	H	June 28
12382	Riley I	73	E	Jan 2 65	867	Rudler Wm	120	M	May 3
2885	Riley J	99	C	July 4 64	40	Rue Newton	Cav 5	A	Mar 13
5021	Riley John	176	C	Aug 8	8667	Runey F	69	H	Sept 13
6347	Riley John	39	D	Aug 21	12635	Russ Jno	2	K	Feb 10 65
11163	Ripley F A	152	C	Oct 19	8856	Russell J	Art 7	A	Sept 15 64
11760	Ripp W	42	B	Nov 3	5094	Ryan D	106	D	Aug 8
3514	Rising C	75	B	July 18	8599	Ryan J	95	E	Sept 12
10610	Risley Geo W	46	G	Oct 4	8741	Ryan J	Cav 22	E	Sept 14
2558	Ritcher F	132	D	June 27	7258	Ryan Owen	12	A	Aug 30
7245	Ritson S	Cav 18	E	Aug 29	4762	Ryonch Jno	66	I	Aug 5
9224	Ritzmiller Jno	115		Sept 19	6413	Ryson Jno	Art 7	L	Aug 22
1775	Roach F	99	F	June 9	6206	Ryne J M	39	E	Aug 9
1842	Roach Chas	85	E	June 11	684	Rush Jno	111	E	Apr 23
2354	Robberger P H	46	B	June 23	7234	Sackett R S	85	G	Aug 29

LIST OF THE DEAD.

No.	Name	Reg.	Co.	Date	Grave
1920	Sadley M		77	H June 14	64
1880	Safford B J	Bat	24	June 12	
11870	Salsbury H	Art	1	M Nov 6	
10652	Salisbury E		16	D Oct 11	
10023	Samlett ——	Cav	13	I Oct 14	
10880	Samet W		15	H Oct 13	
3769	Sampson J		106	K July 22	
346	Sanders Chas	Mil	9	A Apr 2	
3618	Sanders J		99	C July 23	
9857	Sanders J	Cav	12	A Sept 27	
4423	Sandford P O	Art	7	L July 31	
2341	Saughin J	Cav	12	F June 23	
7740	Sawyer J	"	2	L Sept 3	
11232	Sayles A	"	22	E Oct 21	
3612	Seaman A		85	H July 19	
10856	Seaman A	Art	2	Oct 13	
1372	Sears F	Cav	2	H May 25	
6120	Seagher J		8	M Aug 19	
4325	See Henry		11	K July 30	
8824	Seeley A J		140	A Sept 15	
11374	Seeley C B		15	H Oct 24	
4256	Seeley Thos		100	F July 29	
10027	Segum Ed	Cav	5	K Sept 29	
4204	Seigler Geo		10	July 29	
7458	Seigle John R		120	K Sept 1	
11886	Selson H		59	C Nov 6	
3457	Serrier R		40	C July 17	
1746	Serine C	Cav	4	M June 8	
629	Settle Henry		99	H Apr 19	
9828	Seyman F	Cav	1	A Sept 27	
5951	Seard Louis		77	E Aug 17	
6688	Schayler J W	Cav	21	M Aug 26	
10794	Schadt Theo		160	A Oct 12	
3557	Scheck B	Cav	2	G July 18	
3190	Schemerhorn H		120	G July 12	
11965	Schempp M	Art	7	F Nov 11	
2795	Schermashie B		170	A July 2	
1325	Schlotesser J		91	H May 24	
11515	Schlotesser J		1	L Oct 26	
9578	Schmaker Jno		30	B Sept 23	
10291	Schmaley J		1	G Oct 16	
10550	Schmeager A		39	A Oct 9	
5311	Schneider Chas		39	A Aug 11	
8595	Shockney T T	Bat	24	Sept 12	
8796	Schofield J		7	H Sept 15	
2441	Scholl Jno		54	D June 25	
11422	Schriber H		59	I Oct 24	
7814	Schroeder G	Art	7	E Sept 4	
8550	Schrum J	"	14	K Sept 12	
1070	Schrimer Wm		20	B May 13	
4280	Schware F	Cav	12	K July 20	
6613	Schwick A		66	G Aug 23	
4849	Scott J C		85	K Aug 6	
6857	Scott P C	Cav	14	G Aug 26	
8622	Scott W W	"	2	F Sept 13	
8290	Sibble E		148	G Sept 9	
4362	Sick R E			July 31	
4557	Sickler E	Art	7	E Aug 2	
3210	Sickles A		120	D July 12	
11950	Siddell G		40	Nov 10	
12284	Simmons A	Art	8	H Dec 13	
6364	Simmons C G		85	B Aug 21	
8316	Simon H		116	B Sept 10	
6284	Simons H L		85	E Aug 20	
142	Simondinger B		155	I Mar 24	
242	Simpson D		99	H Mar 30	
6345	Sisson P V	Art	22	M Aug 21	
10067	Shaab J		50	A Sept 30	64
201	Shea Pat, drum'r		61	M Mar 28	
4801	Shaffer M	Art	7	Aug 5	
4584	Shaffer J		66	E Aug 2	
782	Shafer II		103	F Apr 28	
6747	Shaughnessey J	C	6	A Aug 24	
4446	Shannan E	Art	6	H Aug 1	
5645	Shenk S W	Bat	24	Aug 14	
290	Shaw Alex	Art	3	K Apr 1	
9667	Shaw T I	Cav	15	M Sept 24	
12814	Shaw W	Art	7	F Mar 25	65
7660	Shay John		69	B Sept 3	64
3360	Sheldon M	Art	7	B July 15	
4247	Shepardson L	Cav	22	E July 29	
5474	Shaw J	"	2	E Aug 13	
7798	Shuler Chas		52	G Sept 4	
8335	Shaw M		76	D Sept 10	
9924	Sheppard W H		9	F Sept 28	
8205	Sherer H	Cav	5	Sept 8	
109 0	Sherridan J	"	2	Oct 14	
4676	Sherwood J E		76	G Aug 4	
720	Shields Richard		132	F Apr 25	
701	Shilts E		52	K Apr 23	
10495	Shidler Geo		97	F Oct 8	
8206	Shindler J	Art	15	E Sept 8	
7437	Shirlock R		85	K Sept 1	
5837	Shippey F		85	D Aug 16	
2430	Shirley P	Bat	24	June 23	
2151	Shats C		111	F June 18	
5755	Shortey Robert		164	B Aug 15	
5343	Shotliff J	Art	7	L Aug 11	
2975	Shults Jno		118	F July 7	
6633	Shultz F		76	F Aug 23	
12194	Shultz Wm	Art	7	C Nov 29	
11822	Shultz C		66	F Nov 5	
11813	Shumaker P		100	K Nov 4	
11280	Shuhps P D		125	K Oct 22	
2462	Shuster ——		54	C June 26	
2922	Slater F		48	F July 5	
700	Slater Jno		120	H Apr 23	
12534	Slater Jas		7	K Jan 27	65
11162	Slater Richard		2	E Oct 19	64
12811	Sleight C		32	I Mar 24	65
10377	Sloat Wm		140	E Oct 5	64
6819	Sloates F		76	F Aug 25	
10125	Slimp W		146	A Oct 11	
7028	Smades W		9	D Sept 2	
12083	Small S		53	F Nov 18	
7783	Smarty Jno	Cav	22	G Sept 4	
7406	Smead L	Art	18	D Aug 31	
762	Smalley Geo		140	H Apr 27	
12503	Smith A	Art	7	F Jan 21	65
11371	Smith A		9	A Oct 23	64
7326	Smith A J		85	D Aug 30	
802	Smith Bernard		132	B Apr 29	
1310	Smith Benjamin	C	2	H May 23	
2659	Smith Chas		61	A June 29	
3735	Smith Chas		52	E July 21	
4534	Smith Chas		100	B Aug 2	
7612	Smith Chas	Art	15	K Sept 30	
10052	Smith Chas		9	G Sept 30	
11283	Smith E		61	D Oct 22	
1819	Smith F		48	F June 10	
1246	Smith Frank		99	I May 20	
11839	Smith G R	Cav	2	H Nov 5	
3872	Smith N	"	9	C July 15	
1247	Smith Henry		132	C May 20	

LIST OF THE DEAD. 245

No.	Name	Regt.	Co.	Date
3238	Smith J	Cav 5		July 12 64
3504	Smith J	" 4	B	July 18
4834	Smith J	115	G	Aug 6
9300	Smith J	52	A	Sept 20
10456	Smith J	Cav 13	D	Oct 7
12627	Smith J	46	E	Feb 10 65
1245	Smith Jas	Cav 20	M	May 20 64
7004	Smith Jas	6	A	Aug 27
11787	Smith Jas	57	B	Nov 4
7610	Smith Jackson	85	I	Sept 2
11210	Smith J	52	A	Oct 20
305	Smith Jno	71	C	April 1
534	Smith Jno	Cav 3	F	April 14
5496	Smith Jno	41	E	Aug 13
5602	Smith Jno	66	F	Aug 14
6428	Smith Jno	95	D	Aug 22
10547	Smith Jno	69	G	Oct 9
5482	Smith Jno J	109	C	Aug 16
11454	Smith J M	59	A	Oct 25
10079	Smith K	Cav 22	K	Sept 30
5009	Smith L A	115	F	Aug 8
9973	Smith Levi	125	B	Sept 28
7706	Smith John C	48	E	Sept 3
2780	Smith S	11	I	July 2
5854	Smith S A	132	F	Aug 16
6709	Smith T	147	E	Aug 24
6361	Smith Thos	47	C	Aug 21
9499	Smith T R	2	E	Sept 21
139	Smith Wm	99	H	Mar 24
325	Smith Wm	Art 3	K	April 2
532	Smith Wm	104	A	April 14
812	Smith Wm	106	B	April 30
7550	Smith Wm	2	L	Sept 2
10164	Smith Wm	76	K	Oct 1
12394	Smith H	7	C	Jan 5 65
3708	Snedegar A J	111	D	July 21 64
7173	Snyder A	25	E	Aug 29
4148	Snyder B	2	B	Aug 1
10076	Snyder Wm	Drag 1	E	Sept 30
1319	Sombeck Geo	52	I	May 23
5169	Somers John	2	E	Aug 9
2773	Sopher James	132	F	July 2
2103	Sopher S	102	K	June 24
4352	Sotter J M	47	C	July 31
3534	Southard H	Cav 5	C	July 18
10526	Southard N	2	H	Oct 8
11346	Southard W A	18	I	Oct 23
2877	Souther Henry	69	K	July 4
8124	Southworth R	Cav 22	E	Sept 8
10188	Skall S	Art 7	L	Oct 7
12029	Skeeley T	66	H	Nov 15
9954	Spark G	Art 16	C	Sept 28
6975	Sparks E	10	B	Aug 27
5421	Spaulding H	Cav 1	F	Aug 12
5567	Spellman John	66	B	Aug 13
12712	Spencer A	93	D	Feb 28 65
10989	Sperry A	51	F	Oct 16 64
3532	Span Jas	147	H	July 18
5982	Spanbury S	Art 14	C	Aug 17
5821	Sprague E I	Bat 10		Aug 16
3593	Sprague J	85	I	July 19
10730	Sprig Jas A	Cav 24	E	Oct 11
4877	Sprink A	146	F	Aug 6
9035	Strata Jno	15	I	Sept 17
889	Stacey Jno	99	I	May 4
4574	Stadler J	39	A	Aug 2
10078	Stancliff A B	106	H	Sept 30
2570	Stanton H H	22	E	June 27 64
5187	Stark J D	100	A	Aug 9
11740	Starkweather L	146	E	Nov 2
12050	Star C	15	D	Feb 13 65
7381	Stanton L H	Art 7	K	Aug 31 64
2520	Stark J H	121	A	June 26
1698	Stanley J C	85	C	June 7
10200	St Dennis L	16	F	Oct 4
9903	Stewart Peter	5	B	Sept 27
7636	Stevens E	120	C	Sept 2
95	Stevenson Wm	132	G	Mar 22
3782	Sternhoff A	Art 15	C	July 22
4678	Stevens Jno S	100	F	Aug 4
5530	Steiner C	Art 7	M	Aug 13
7028	Stevens Wm	99	I	Aug 27
2546	Stead J	115	F	June 27
6531	Stebins C	85	C	Aug 23
3872	Stevenson W	10	F	July 24
6443	Stead J	15	D	Aug 22
2034	Stewart Jno	89		June 15
1863	Stebbins H	85	B	June 12
6049	Stelrocht D	Cav 22	C	Aug 18
10149	Stickler E	169	A	Oct 1
11755	Stivers R	111	F	Nov 2
7075	Still D	132	D	Aug 28
6102	Stump W	6	K	Aug 18
4193	Still Jas	164	E	July 29
4385	Stillwell S	Art 2	E	July 31
915	Stone Jno Mus	Cav 5	C	May 16
11043	Stoddard J	111	F	Oct 17
6722	Stone L	24	E	Aug 24
2053	Stoup J	15	A	June 16
3415	Strue G A	Art 1	B	July 16
3997	Storing A	54	B	July 26
8520	Strain A W	Cav 2	I	Sept 12
3905	Streeter F	76	F	July 24
4665	Storms A N	Art 7	I	Aug 4
4798	Strale J	178	B	Aug 5
5342	Strater Geo	85	K	Aug 11
6988	Stratton J H	140	H	Aug 27
11967	Strip W	42	E	Nov 11
116	Streight Lewis	127	A	Mar 23
2401	Stratten Chas	125	K	June 24
7845	Sturdevant G	Cav 5	I	Sept 4
5994	Stutzman P	39	D	Aug 17
6102	Stump W	60	K	Aug 18
11832	Styler G W	Art 7	I	Nov 5
9953	Sughem I	H A	B	Sept 28
640	Sullivan Ed	69	A	April 20
6048	Sullivan M	69	K	Aug 18
1492	Sullivan Pat	99	H	May 31
7728	Sullivan P C	155	E	Sept 3
5440	Susear Fred	39	I	Aug 12
10661	Sutliff E	Cav 15	M	Oct 11
1	Swarner J H	Cav 2	H	Feb 27
4005	Swarner J, Bu.	Cav 2	H	July 26
6466	Swartz M	Cav 2	M	Aug 22
12267	Swager G	103	F	Dec 12
2322	Sweeney Jas	155	I	June 22
5835	Sweeney M	122	C	Aug 16
3527	Sweet E	93	F	July 18
2921	Sweet L	Art 4	M	July 5
4960	Sylurs S	140	E	Aug 7
12765	Swancent J	2	A	Mar 13 65
10559	Stratton E	76	E	Oct 10 64
1934	Taylor A	Cav 2	F	June 14
4867	Taylor C	115	F	Aug 6

LIST OF THE DEAD.

No.	Name	Unit	Co.	Date
551	Taylor Chas	B	154	April 14 64
11321	Taylor D		149	D Oct 22
2742	Taylor R H		125	F July 1
403	Taylor Thos	B Cav 10		E April 11
9993	Taylor L B		147	K Sept 29
12200	Taylor W	Cav	12	A Dec 15
12480	Taylor W		42	B Jan 17 65
10370	Taylor W H	Art	7	C Oct 5 64
10738	Taylor W H	Cav	7	C Oct 11
10157	Taylor Wm	Cav	22	C Oct 1
8961	Taylor W W		2	I Sept 16
8988	Tarvis G W	Drag	1	K Sept 17
9480	Tare W		115	D Sept 21
3681	Tambrick A	Cav	16	A July 21
3976	Tanner M		1	E July 25
4326	Tanschivit Ed	Art	15	E July 30
7019	Tell Wm		59	C Aug 27
9143	Thompson A		9	D Sept 18
133	Terry Aaron		12	K Mar 24
9064	Teneyck M	Art	14	E Sept 17
4909	Tewey J		99	H Aug 6
6445	Terwilliger D R		85	D Aug 22
10352	Thomas J	Cav	2	D Oct 5
3598	Thomas H		88	D July 19
3711	Thomas W		3	H July 21
4619	Thomas J		85	G Aug 3
10361	Thearer J	Bat	1	Oct 5
8161	Thompson C W		85	K Sept 8
4781	Thompson J		39	H Aug 5
5510	Thompkins Ira	Art	6	Aug 13
5524	Thompson P		10	E Aug 13
6730	Thompson N B		146	A Aug 24
5784	Thompson J		104	G Aug 15
2613	Thompson T	Cav	12	F June 28
320	Thompson Daniel		142	E April 2
3538	Thresh G	Cav	5	K July 18
5147	Thurston N E		85	C Aug 9
11235	Thornton J	Art	14	I Oct 21
6309	Thorpe W C		82	I Aug 20
4303	Thurston G W		85	E July 31
12843	Thayer G		70	E April 22 65
679	Thierbach P M		39	D April 22 64
11230	Tilton H	Art	24	Oct 20
8283	Tillitson N P		51	A Sept 9
8849	Timerson Wm	Art	2	I Sept 15
2680	Timmish —		85	C June 30
659	Tiner David		79	E April 21
10422	Townsend W		111	B Oct 6
8068	Townsend L	Cav	22	G Sept 7
3883	Townsend Jno		52	A July 24
535	Townsend Geo M		111	F April 14
9050	Thornson E		22	Sept 17
4774	Toney L		100	D Aug 5
10727	Tolal Pat		164	K Oct 11
5833	Towner L	Cav	5	G Aug 16
6047	Tobias A		120	G Aug 18
2112	Toomey J F		85	I June 17
12465	Tourney P		99	B Jan 16 65
12636	Toedt H		1	K Feb 10
12708	Tomlinson W F		22	G Feb 28
3193	Tripp Ira		77	B July 12 64
10442	Tripp O S	Art	3	K Oct 7
9507	Truman A M	Art	2	D Sept 22
7629	Trueman R	Art	7	G Sept 2
8544	Tremor M		76	F Sept 12
7317	Trumpp E	Cav	22	F Aug 30
3382	Trumbull H		115	I July 24
7187	Travis T	Cav	8	G Aug 29 64
4052	Truesdale W J		85	H July 27
3425	Trompter F		140	B July 16
100	Tracey Pat		99	I Mar 22
707	Turner Wm	Cav	5	G April 24
7970	Turner Jno		49	A Sept 5
11376	Turner J	Cav	22	M Oct 24
1688	Turner Thos	Cav	16	B June 6
2120	Turner J B		85	C June 17
10535	Tutbill C	Cav	22	G Oct 8
9687	Tuthill S D	Art	2	M Sept 24
10604	Tuft E		29	C Oct 10
7915	Turden E S	Cav	15	D Sept 5
7421	Turton W F	Art	2	I Aug 31
3796	Tubbs W H		85	D July 22
3084	Tupple H		154	H July 9
3129	Tucker L		120	D July 10
2893	Tuttle W		48	K July 4
10494	Tyrrell J	Cav	22	A Oct 8
4217	Uncer Jas		15	H July 29
416	Uber Chas		14	A April 7
12401	Udell J	Art	7	H Jan 5 65
10887	Ulmer H	Art	15	K Oct 14 64
2317	Underburg L W		77	G June 22
254	Underhill H		47	E Mar 30
1495	Underwriter A		62	F May 21
1091	Van Clarke Wm		106	D May 14
9087	Van Allen C		7	E Sept 18
1025	Van Buren J W	Art	3	K May 11
664	Van Buren H	Art	3	K April 21
10071	Van Bethysen H	Art	7	I Sept 30
12539	Van Bramin T		71	K Jan 27 65
1511	Van Derbreck A		132	B June 3 64
3463	Van Dugen ——	C	24	M July 17
6560	Van Hosen C		95	A Aug 23
10656	Van Housen B	Bat	12	Oct 11
3371	Van Haughton J		124	C July 15
1418	Vanderbrogart W		104	F May 27
8957	Vanarsdale P		1	G Sept 16
8782	Vanalstine H		152	A Sept 14
8806	Vanclack F		5	D Sept 15
7564	Vanvelzer J M		85	I Sept 2
7635	Vanburen J	Cav	15	B Sept 2
11446	Vanscott L		59	C Oct 25
11596	Vanarnum J	Cav	8	E Oct 28
7054	Vanwagner C	Art	2	F Aug 28
7244	Vanesse M	Cav	2	K Aug 29
7252	Vanzart Wm	Art	7	E Aug 30
6472	Varney C		169	E Aug 22
6634	Vanalstine C	Art	7	C Aug 23
3333	Vanest J H	Art	14	B July 15
83	Vanvelsen J		120	A Mch 21
2089	Vaughan W H	Cav	8	K June 17
937	Vespers Jas W		85	D May 9
7506	Van Osten C		52	H Sept 1
5661	Fencot L	Cav	2	H Aug 14
4196	Veil Wm	Art	6	F July 27
1539	Vernon S	Cav	2	M June 1
7846	Vincent R		178	I Sept 4
2782	Vincent Richard ●		1	K July 2
2879	Vinsant G M	Art	14	I July 4
2715	Vish O		178	E July 1
6525	Vibbard Geo	Cav	22	E Aug 22
10023	Voerling H	Art	15	C Sept 29
4623	Vogle Anton		10	C Aug 3
5503	Voorhies A H	Cav	1	H Aug 13
11507	Voorhies E R		85	C Oct 26

LIST OF THE DEAD. 247

No.	Name	Unit	Co.	Date
6682	Voorhies Geo	85	C	Aug 23 64
1184	Walls Peter	Cav 4	D	May 18
5001	Wall Jas	15	G	Aug 7
1398	Wallace Jno	Cav 11	B	May 26
10211	Watt H	" 12	A	Oct 2
9977	Watts C	6	C	Sept 28
0313	Waters A L	Cav 8	F	Oct 4
0477	Warner Chas L	" 2	D	Oct 7
4026	Warren L	95	I	July 26
7351	Warner P P	Art 14	M	Aug 31
7444	Warner A J	76	F	Sept 1
12449	Warner Luther	Cav 12	A	Jan 9 65
10543	Ward Patrick	88	C	Oct 8 64
5127	Ward J	99	G	Aug 9
10920	Ward J	40	H	Oct 14
2238	Ward H	95	I	June 20
400	Ward W A	99	B	April 6
12816	Warden H B	5	B	Mch 25 65
9858	Walters D	125	E	Sept 27 64
1557	Walters Nelson	120	K	June 2
3381	Walterhouse Ed	9	I	July 16
2827	Wallace J	Cav 2	M	July 3
8339	Watson G	Art 6	C	Sept 16
10965	Watson Jas	Art 15	M	Oct 15
6947	Watson T	99	I	Aug 26
9356	Wade M	Art 14	D	Sept 20
8146	Walker J	Art 2	D	Sept 8
8198	Wall J	64	I	Sept 8
7276	Warhurst Sam'l	Art 7	I	Aug 30
3731	Washington I	76	G	July 21
56"9	Washburn H	Cav 5	D	Aug 14
2023	Wagner C	39	E	June 15
10686	Wagner C	93	K	Oct 11
11001	Warren P	Art 7	C	Oct 16
16537	Warren E	Cav 22	L	Aug 23
4120	Warren Geo R	2	F	July 28
11082	Warrell E C	57	I	Oct 17
11945	Waterman S	169	K	Nov 10
6978	Waldron N	146	A	Aug 27
7249	Walz M	Art 14	I	Aug 30
6425	Walling Geo	76	B	Aug 22
6046	Watchler J	119	G	Aug 18
4060	Wails C H	109	K	July 27
3336	Walser Jno	Art 15	D	July 15
1564	Walcott G P	67	D	June 2
2294	Wales J	85	D	June 22
1537	West Jas	Art 3	H	June 1
9572	West T	Cav 13	F	Sept 23
3964	West Wm	152	E	July 25
739	West Jas	Cav 2	E	Apr 25
10303	Weston L	115	F	Oct 4
9731	Webster G	29	C	Sept 25
5593	Webster E	76	E	Aug 14
1598	Webster James	137	C	June 4
9889	Wendle John	Art 7	E	Sept 27
9941	Wellstraff C	100	D	Sept 28
10013	Welch W	76	G	Sept 29
5030	Welch C	Cav 3	B	Aug 8
8555	Welber E G	120	K	Sept 15
8308	Weil E C	164	B	Sept 8
7561	Welson Jas H	74	K	Sept 2
8177	Welch C	39	H	Sept 8
5181	Welch E	Bat 24		Aug 9
6092	Welch J	Cav 5	K	Aug 24
2310	Welsh L	146	B	June 22
8855	Welber E G	120	K	Sept 15
9428	Weaver J	Cav 1	E	Sept 21
7078	Weaver B S	96	I	Aug 28 64
9448	Webber C H	85	C	Sept 21
9506	Westerfield P S	Art 7	B	Sept 22
8731	Werting John	52	D	Sept 14
7987	Wellington G R	C 12	A	Sept 6
8204	Weeks J	7	G	Sept 8
7472	Wells Jeff	1	H	Sept 1
12036	Wells E	69	K	Nov 16
7667	Weismere H	32	I	Sept 3
4915	Wedder N C	184	E	Aug 6
11061	Wellder C M	Cav 22	G	Oct 17
11397	Westbrook D	155	H	Oct 24
6927	Weafer Chas	115	A	Aug 26
7256	Wertz Jas	Cav 12	I	Aug 30
6370	Webb M E	Art 14	F	Aug 21
11127	Welch J	Cav 5	D	Oct 18
6002	Weiber J	Art 6	E	Aug 17
4272	Weller W H	85	E	July 29
3285	Westfall Jno	151	H	July 12
265	Weldon Edson	C 20	M	Mar 31
507	Westhrop H	125	B	April 12
6755	Webster H	Cav 22	A	Aug 24
10303	Weston L	115	F	Oct 4
7543	Whitmore D	140	I	Sept 2
10423	Wharton J R	Cav 5	L	Oct 6
9743	Whittle J C	85	E	Sept 25
9878	Whertmore M	Art 15	M	Sept 13
8611	Whipple M	Cav 22	D	Sept 13
8680	White Jas	Drag 1	D	Sept 13
11879	White L	Art 8	G	Nov 6
3034	White E	Cav 10	D	July 8
8792	Whiting M	85	D	Sept 15
7417	Whitney John	39	K	Aug 31
5207	Whitney J	104	E	Aug 10
10972	Whitman I	16	H	Oct 15
12049	Whitmans P	66	E	Nov 16
11724	Whifbeck J	20	D	Nov 1
6611	Wheeler D	147	H	Aug 23
5770	Whitmore O B	40	A	Aug 15
4155	Whitlock Wm	Art 14	I	July 28
1133	Wilson James	132	K	May 16
5757	Wilson John	95	A	July 22
0832	Wilson M	Art 2	H	Aug 25
11983	Wilson W	155	H	Nov 13
5870	Wilson A	57	A	Aug 16
1645	Wilson D	48	H	June 5
6233	Windness A	Art 15	C	Aug 20
4080	Williams F	125	A	July 27
4522	Williams Ed	42	A	Aug 2
11130	Williams H	Cav 2	M	Oct 18
12697	Williams S	94	I	Feb 23 65
9516	Williams L D	85	G	Sept 22 64
8478	Wilcox T E	85	B	Sept 11
7945	Williams Jas	63	G	Sept 5
4603	Williams Geo	Cav 1	K	Aug 3
4701	Williams John	52	K	Aug 4
3947	Williams O	Bat 24		July 25
1567	Williams H	9	A	June 2
6861	Williams L	16	A	Aug 26
7112	Williams I B	Cav 24	C	Aug 28
6219	Williams C R	85	E	Aug 20
3069	Wiron P	Cav 20	M	July 9
3273	Wicks D	63	D	July 13
1938	Wilcox Geo	Cav 12	F	June 14
2044	Wilcox R	14		June 15
9496	Wilcox W	43	G	Sept 21
3576	Wilcox J	85	D	July 19

248 LIST OF THE DEAD.

No.	Name	Reg.	Co.	Date
11111	Wilcox H R	55	C	Oct 18 64
11428	Wilcox C	Cav 5	G	Oct 24
12607	Wiley I	59	B	Feb 7 65
10122	Willis I	121	G	Oct 1 64
9057	Willsey D	7		Sept 17
8729	Wiggins James	52	D	Sept 14
7980	Winn James	Art 7	I	Sept 6
8208	Will E C	164	B	Sept 8
7622	Wiley W	115	G	Sept 2
3728	Wilkey S	8	B	July 21
10977	Wilkinson I N	42	A	Oct 15
5663	Wicks Frank	Art 1	K	Aug 14
11474	Winney G A	100	D	Oct 25
11520	Winter G	Cav 10	L	Oct 26
11689	Wilds I	154	B	Oct 31
7122	Winser I	117	I	Aug 28
7581	Wood E G	Bat 24		Sept 2
3607	Wood F	Cav 5	I	July 19
9874	Wood H	115	G	Sept 27
10063	Wood H	15	B	Sept 30
9715	Wood J	Cav 10	H	Sept 25
7686	Wood John	97	D	Sept 3
3881	Wood M	111	H	July 24
5039	Wood J S	Art 6	A	Aug 8
9132	Woodmancy D M	C 3	H	Sept 18
10141	Wood W J	95	H	Oct 1
8382	Woodworth B	56	D	Sept 10
7884	Woodland H	1	F	Sept 5
5696	Woodhull D T	8	E	Aug 15
12356	Wooley G C	Art 7	K	Dec 30
11821	Wolf T	88	D	Nov 5
11031	Wolf W	Art 2	H	Oct 16
6130	Wood Fred	Cav 24	E	Aug 19
591	Wolpan A	52	C	April 16
4847	Wright Chas S	118	E	Aug 6
10941	Wright D	43	G	Oct 14
5126	Wright I I	148	I	Aug 9
4281	Wang C	39	E	July 30
7784	Wulslager John	85	G	Sept 4
4589	Wyatt James	147	G	Aug 2
7334	Wyncoop G	Cav 12	H	Aug 30
2104	Winegardener L	18	G	June 17
7433	Yales W G	71	H	Sept 1
4984	Yencer I D	Bat 24		Aug 7
12501	Yeomand G	7	A	Jan 21 65
6539	Young C	41	D	Aug 23 64
5598	Young Chas	15	C	Aug 14
8224	Young E	Art 2	I	Sept 8
1306	Young Fugene	111	G	May 23
8733	Young George	22	H	Sept 14
6946	Young J	Cav 1	B	Aug 26
7411	Young T B	148	A	Aug 31
10481	Yonker W	Art 10	B	Oct 7
7480	Zaphan H P	Art 7	E	Sept 1
12204	Zolber F W	40	D	Dec 1
12617	Zegler S	145	G	Feb 9 65

TOTAL, 2571.

NORTH CAROLINA.

No.	Name	Reg.	Co.	Date
1596	Barker J	2	F	June 3 64
849	Briggs Wilson	1	A	May 3
275	Callowhill B	2	F	Mar 31
475	Cox William C	2	F	Apr 9
864	Check W F	2	F	May 8
144	Dunbar Alex	2	F	Mar 22
1057	Miller J, Drum	2	D	May 13

No.	Name	Reg.	Co.	Date
10705	Macey Henry	7		Oct 11 64
11844	Moss Wm	1	F	Nov 5
8690	Norfield Warren	1	G	Sept 14
370	Stone Jno A	2	F	Apr 5
2636	Smith Jas	2	F	June 29
4809	Smith George	2	E	Aug 5
333	Turner F	2	I	Apr 2
798	Turner H, Colored	2	I	Apr 29
204	Weeks Nathan	2	F	Mar 28
712	Williams Thos	2	D	Apr 24

TOTAL, 17.

OHIO.

No.	Name	Reg.	Co.	Date
12846	Akers J W	4	B	Apr 24 65
251	Arthur George	7	B	Mar 30 64
789	Arrowsmith W R	45	K	Apr 28
1118	Ames George	100	K	May 15
1550	Allen W	45	B	June 1
1569	Alinger D	51	C	June 2
1724	Anderson D	111	B	June 8
1779	Augustus T	89	K	June 9
1805	Akers A A	94	F	June 10
2040	Aldridge C W	33		June 15
2935	Adam Miller	103	I	July 5
3046	Anderson R	93	C	July 8
3197	Aldbrook C W	60		July 12
3485	Arthur I C	89	A	July 17
3852	Armebrish A	21	A	July 24
3932	Almond A	72	A	July 25
4529	Arnold Chas	Cav 9	G	Aug 2
4990	Ailes T G	20	I	Aug 7
5048	Andrews Sam'l G			Aug 8
6422	Adams E	Cav 2	C	Aug 22
7429	Allen A B	121	C	Aug 31
7482	Alward A	135	B	Sept 1
7436	Arthur J	69	I	Sept 3
7843	Arne I	64	D	Sept 4
9818	Alown A	34	D	Sept 26
10393	Andrews I R	63	K	Oct 6
10425	Adams I	122	I	Oct 6
10874	Allen James C	91	F	Oct 13
11198	Andermill John	24	K	Oct 20
12495	Allen J W	1	G	Jan 20 65
188	Baiel W T	45	F	Mar 27 64
207	Bodin Thomas S	44		Mar 28
691	Beaver George F	111	B	Apr 23
829	Beeman Richard	125	E	May 1
861	Biddinger M, Mus	94	K	May 3
952	Branigan James	82	F	May 8
1094	Blangy S	70	B	May 14
1212	Botkins A S	45	G	May 19
1226	Black G W	99	F	May 20
1366	Bates L B	Cav 1	A	May 25
1368	Bodkin W	45	K	May 25
1376	Baldwin N	Cav 9	T	May 26
1385	Bowers James	89	A	May 26
1468	Boyd H I	7	H	May 30
1602	Boman John	2	C	June 4
1609	Bryan R	16	C	June 4
1781	Balcomb D	19	F	June 9
1919	Brownles John	7	I	June 14
1937	Brooks J	135	I	June 14
1970	Bothin W J	45	F	June 15
1993	Bartholomew EW	205	C	June 15
2065	Belding F	105	D	June 16
2067	Brookheart W	45	I	June 16
2087	Benor H	100	E	June 17

LIST OF THE DEAD. 249

No.	Name	Reg.	Co.	Date
2110	Bishop S	49	K	June 17 64
2170	Berry J C	90	E	June 19
2254	Beers A	45	A	June 20
2292	Barnham W Art	1	K	June 21
2415	Bird I	45	A	June 24
2492	Bratt G	21	G	June 26
2599	Broughfman I	39	C	June 28
2696	Brandon John	15	F	June 30
3053	Barnes V H	92	H	July 9
3245	Brown Charles	23	D	July 13
3299	Burns M G	111	B	July 13
3608	Brackneck H Cav	7	A	July 19
3656	Bogart John	9	G	July 20
3706	Bontrell C	6	G	July 21
3756	Butch O	45	I	July 22
3881	Bowman S	51	K	July 23
4073	Brockway M Art	2	D	July 27
4279	Boyle W H	11	H	July 30
4684	Britton B H	125	H	Aug 4
4908	Berdy M J	45	D	Aug 7
5138	Buckle J J	126	E	Aug 9
5219	Brabham Geo Cav	9	B	Aug 10
5498	Baldwin Geo "	9	G	Aug 13
5653	Bonestine W H	107	I	Aug 14
5656	Burns J M	121	K	Aug 14
5758	Balmet J	19	I	Aug 15
5771	Brutch E Cav	10	I	Aug 15
5819	Bond S T	123	B	Aug 16
5825	Boyle H	130	B	Aug 16
5937	Bower F	61	I	Aug 17
5985	Birch L T	31	H	Aug 17
6003	Bowman A	104	E	Aug 17
6020	Bright N	6	E	July 17
6152	Brown G S	111	F	Aug 18
6239	Buren T J	89	A	Aug 25
7280	Barrett S C	26	F	Aug 30
7283	Bell A	70	B	Aug 30
7484	Baxter P D	121	D	Sept 1
7490	Brenning C	14	G	Sept 1
7529	Brown W	26	G	Sept 1
7806	Bear E	33	A	Sept 4
7983	Bender C	54	C	Sept 6
7993	Brown M	110	F	Sept 6
7994	Barnes T S	31	B	Sept 6
8365	Benear W A	135	F	Sept 10
8376	Barston G H	135	F	Sept 10
8476	Brenner N	60	F	Sept 11
8496	Barnes A	36	G	Sept 11
8508	Blythe C	1	I	Sept 12
8509	Brinhomer J	65	C	Sept 12
8676	Brown H H	41	A	Sept 13
8693	Bell James	135	B	Sept 14
8872	Buckley J G	126	A	Sept 15
8939	Blessing C	9	F	Sept 16
9247	Baker W C	94		Sept 19
9446	Brookover Geo	135	B	Sept 21
9473	Briace J R	122	C	Sept 21
9625	Bradley A	101	A	Sept 24
9679	Blackman S	72	G	Sept 24
9897	Birchfield Eli	14		Sept 27
9949	Beant H T	34	D	Sept 28
10120	Brewer D C	43	K	Oct 1
10199	Brown E N	21	E	Oct 2
10281	Brum W H	20	B	Oct 4
10591	Briggs F	17	G	Oct 10
11072	Baymher L G	153	A	Oct 17
11307	Boles G	112	H	Oct 22
11308	Bunker J	11	K	Oct 22 64
11313	Burns M	12	K	Oct 22
11626	Bricker J J	126	H	Oct 28
11920	Bumgardner Joel	3	C	Nov 8
11939	Barber B Cav	10	D	Nov 9
12296	Bissel J	2	E	Dec 16
12383	Beckley G	102	F	Jan 3 65
12524	Barnes E H	2	D	Jan 26
12641	Bower A	37	F	Feb 12
517	Blackwood I H	92	I	Apr 12 64
12772	Bowens W	100	A	Mar 13 65
5	Carpenter W	92	D	Mar 4 64
458	Copeland C	1	A	Apr 9
561	Coates Geo Cav	7	I	Apr 15
563	Campbell Jas "	7	H	Apr 15
723	Callaway Wm "	7	F	Apr 25
763	Coleman G	101	A	Apr 27
911	Chapman G	75	A	May 1
928	Crosser M	111	B	May 7
965	Corby W C	111	B	May 8
1269	Cruat Wm	89	C	May 21
1291	Collins Thos	21	G	May 22
1521	Capeheart H	70	I	May 31
1587	Clark H S	62	E	June 3
1631	Conklin W	121	B	June 5
1679	Clark D V	111	B	June 6
1900	Childers Wm	89	B	June 13
1945	Crocker Geo Art	1	A	June 14
1992	Christy W	89	K	June 15
2017	Curtis N	45	D	June 15
2025	Careahan G M	65	F	June 15
2101	Caldwell J	15	D	June 17
2162	Cornelius L C	89	C	June 19
2207	Cochrane James	22	G	June 20
2468	Church E	2	G	June 25
2578	Combston J Cav	7	I	June 27
2963	Cameron H	69	B	July 6
3002	Callahan H	34	C	July 7
3241	Caynee Geo M	89	D	July 13
3307	Canard J Q A	14	G	July 13
3356	Cruer J W	60	B	July 15
3541	Cole B	82	A	July 18
3578	Collins T	15	I	July 19
3604	Cook L B Cav	2	C	July 19
3617	Clark J C	31	H	July 20
3774	Clayton D J Cav	9	D	July 22
3937	Cover L	49	B	July 25
4128	Clayton J	89	G	July 28
4342	Conway J	103	A	July 30
4493	Cordray J J	89	G	Aug 1
4865	Cahill J N	90	C	Aug 6
5105	Charles F	10	A	Aug 9
5451	Collyer J	11	G	Aug 12
5548	Chandler M	124	E	Aug 13
5922	Clark James	89	I	Aug 17
6022	Cline K	111	B	Aug 17
6108	Church Geo E	14	C	Aug 18
6188	Chambers R S	89	A	Aug 19
6258	Copir S A	33	C	Aug 20
6281	Conklin J R	45	I	Aug 20
6562	Craig D	2	D	Aug 23
7483	Caswell G	21	C	Sept 1
7486	Coons David	57	C	Sept 1
7495	Crooks J M	92	K	Sept 1
7695	Chard C W	2	H	Sept 3
7800	Cregg I	49	K	Sept 4
7835	Cline M	2	E	Sept 4

LIST OF THE DEAD.

No.	Name	Age	Co.	Date		No.	Name	Age	Co.	Date	
7919	Clark George	60	D	Sept	5 64	7479	Drake M	59	D	Sept	1 64
7998	Clokir J W, S Maj	49		Sept	6	7500	Doran James	60	A	Sept	1
8430	Cummings W S	35	I	Sept	8	7609	Ditto John	51	A	Sept	2
8454	Cattlehock T	35	A	Sept	14	7631	DeMastoris J	54	B	Sept	2
8457	Campbell W C	5	I	Sept	11	8034	Davison P S	21	K	Sept	6
8694	Chapin Jas	135	F	Sept	14	8483	Donley M	59	G	Sept	11
8701	Crooke W B	135	B	Sept	14	8498	Drake J F	135	C	Sept	11
8810	Clarke J R	135	F	Sept	15	8779	Diver J	4		Sept	14
9243	Constein W	98	C	Sept	19	8820	Davere J	49	D	Sept	15
9288	Cramblet A J	123	H	Sept	19	9293	Diver J	123	H	Sept	19
9452	Campbell Sam'l	74	G	Sept	21	9605	Decker S	12	C	Sept	23
9476	Cadwell A T	3	E	Sept	21	9702	Dobson J R	99	H	Sept	25
9491	Clay O	122	D	Sept	21	9849	Duffy G	45	C	Sept	27
9662	Cort W	11	D	Sept	24	10112	Dunbar J	122	F	Oct	1
9770	Cummings A Cav	6	E	Sept	25	10113	Diven J	135	F	Oct	1
9772	Clark S	24	H	Sept	26	10130	Duncan A	49	K	Oct	1
9895	Conner J B Cav	9	G	Sept	27	10190	Dunhand Jas Cav	8	H	Oct	1
9971	Castable I	51	A	Sept	28	10424	Dewit Joseph	65	G	Oct	6
10381	Cotes Rufus Cav	2		Oct	5	10596	Dibble F	101	H	Oct	10
10796	Colts R E	2	C	Oct	12	11017	Diper O	128	I	Oct	16
10834	Cepp J	14	I	Oct	13	11102	Danton W H	105	E	Oct	18
10968	Cary A	21	E	Oct	16	12159	Donahue P	72	K	Oct	25
11103	Oarter J B	89	I	Oct	18	12224	Drith C	33	K	Dec	4
11224	Craven A J	15	C	Oct	20	12675	Dunken T	20	K	Feb	19
11262	Cromwell W H	59	H	Oct	21	12738	Deputy W	21	H	Feb	6 65
11403	Cutsdaghner W J	95	D	Oct	24	7431	Davis G W	21	G	Aug	31
11540	Crominberger J C	23	I	Oct	27	1629	DeRush Sam'l	94	F	June	5 64
11567	Cantwright L	51	F	Oct	27	327	Elijah Baker	45	B	Apr	2
11587	Chapin J A	135	F	Oct	28	341	Evalt E J	10	M	Apr	12
11618	Clark H M	21	A	Oct	28	1047	Eppart Samuel	9	B	May	12
11641	Clingan A P	26	K	Oct	30	2221	Earles Wm Cav	4	G	June	20
11766	Cohven J H	6	K	Nov	3	3376	Ellis Chas	29	B	July	16
12082	Cahill Wm	51	A	Nov	18	4504	Elliott W	20	F	Aug	1
12385	Calvington R	72	C	Jan	3 65	5304	Evans Sam'l	33	C	Aug	11
12435	Chambers J C	15	C	Jan	11	5349	Eastman J	18	C	Aug	11
12691	Crampton A	79	C	Feb	22	5717	Evans Chas Art	1	D	Aug	15
12798	Conover S	175	B	Mar	19	5887	Ensly William	135	T	Aug	16
690	Davis Wm E	7	H	Apr	23 64	6015	Eckhart J	2	B	Aug	17
930	Downing George	45	C	May	7	7438	Elmann A	28	F	Sept	1
981	Dumar R	45	D	May	9	8981	Entulin B C	104	K	Sept	17
1267	Dugan Thos Cav	1	B	May	21	11051	Evans W	51	I	Oct	17
1748	Davis I	7	T	June	9	11169	Evans E M	20	I	Oct	19
2251	Decker B F	111	B	June	21	11542	Elha D	8	A	Oct	25
2296	Dumas J P	2	H	June	21	11654	Ewing D	135	D	Oct	30
2351	Douglass W	24	F	June	23	12321	Ellerman N	59	K	Dec	22
2674	Davis B	22	B	June	30	75	Falman A	82	H	Mar	20
2909	Davis G H	45	E	July	5	176	Fairbanks Alph	45	A	Mar	26
2973	Dandelion T Ind Cav	3		July	7	246	Ferris Joseph Cav	2	H	Mar	30
3703	Dodson L Cav	7	H	July	21	311	Foster A M	100	A	Apr	2
3802	Dille Chas	23	I	July	22	572	Frayer Daniel	99	I	Apr	5
4455	Dodge ——	2	I	Aug	1	636	Facer Wm	111	K	Apr	20
4501	Diecy C	26	C	Aug	1	830	Fisher Chas Cav	3	C	May	1
4772	Denton John Cav	7	E	Aug	5	1054	Free M Bat	22		May	13
5020	Desselbem M	1	I	Aug	8	1381	Freenough Geo C	3		May	26
5208	Dorson L	12	I	Aug	10	1786	Frasier James	2	E	June	10
5299	Doty E E	41	H	Aug	11	2457	Fry W L	123	H	June	25
5368	Dyke F Cav	5	K	Aug	11	2479	Fenton J M	35	I	June	25
5465	Donley James "	1	F	Aug	13	2761	Finlan Jas	18	K	July	2
5620	Davis W H	33	D	Aug	14	4231	Fry Jacob	99	I	July	29
6043	Decker J	111	B	Aug	18	4317	Fitch E P	40	G	July	30
6223	Durant B	95	D	Aug	20	4337	Fulkinson H	2	I	July	30
6312	Downer A P	52	B	Aug	20	4651	Fife J	33	E	Aug	3
6708	Dougherty W H	15	H	Aug	24	4868	Fling T I	27	A	Aug	6
7229	Dildine J	33	K	Aug	29	5249	Ferce R S	2	C	Aug	10
7376	Deming W	111	B	Aug	31	5626	Falk W	82	D	Aug	14
7419	Daley S	33	D	Aug	31	5864	Fullerston W	18	K	Aug	16
7427	Dick Chas	53	G	Aug	31	6212	Foreman A	64	E	Aug	19

LIST OF THE DEAD. 251

No.	Name	Reg.	Co.	Date
6308	Fisher D	80	I	Aug 20 64
6891	Futers John H	82	F	Aug 26
7873	Franks R L	122	E	Sept 5
7976	Forney W O	123	D	Sept 6
9158	Firman V	Cav		Sept 18
9225	Ferguson H	" 3	D	Sept 19
9530	Fowler C	100	A	Sept 22
9357	Finch C		B	Sept 23
9976	Franklinburg C	72	G	Sept 28
10045	Farshay A	116	F	Sept 29
10915	Freely P	10	G	Sept 14
11819	Flowers W T	116	D	Nov 5
11914	Forest Wm	21	K	Nov 8
12108	Fargrove M B	135	F	Nov 21
12637	Fusselman J	20	H	Feb 11 65
12781	Foults M	183	D	Mar 15
12427	Fike W P	95	H	Jan 9
197	Griling Daniel	13	A	Mar 27 64
245	Gardner A	100	H	Mar 30
386	Grescanst S	Cav 6	G	Apr 2
611	Gillinghar B	" 7	I	Apr 18
681	Godfrey Amos	45	C	Apr 23
693	Greek Samuel	100	C	Apr 23
906	Gibson Collins	40	H	May 5
1465	Greer R J	Cav 6	C	May 29
2452	Gillanni J	35	K	June 27
2926	Garner C	Cav 1	K	July 5
3130	Goff P E	19	K	July 10
3251	Gaunt Wm	14	I	July 13
3327	Gibson R	40	B	July 15
3962	Ginging P S	21	E	July 25
4037	Gillett G W	6	G	July 26
4242	Gilbert J	19	B	July 29
4301	Grafton D	118	D	July 30
4383	Graham J W	31	C	July 31
4445	Goffy P	113	G	Aug 1
4055	Gragrer H	125	H	Aug 3
4802	Greer G G	49	D	Aug 5
4902	Granbaugh	85	E	Aug 6
6023	Gordon Wm	45	B	Aug 17
6075	Gallagher James	30	F	Aug 18
6207	Green E	Cav 4	D	Aug 19
6346	Gordon W	10	G	Aug 21
6408	Greff A J	13	E	Aug 22
6486	Gates H	13	G	Aug 22
6821	Grooves L	12	C	Aug 25
7111	Gilland A	27	F	Aug 28
8330	Goodrich J S	9	A	Sept 10
8367	Ganold L	60	A	Sept 10
9566	Gould J M	124	A	Sept 23
9813	Graft P	Bat 20		Sept 26
9927	Galbraith J S	Cav 6	H	Sept 28
11218	Gaither J	60	B	Oct 20
11850	Gardner G	1	K	Nov 5
12033	Glissin A	Cav 2	M	Nov 15
12064	Gillinbuck I	77	E	Nov 17
12109	Goodbrath C	28	G	Nov 21
12560	Griffith J H	58	C	Jan 31 65
12842	Gassler P	64	A	Apr 22
35	Hall J W	4	A	Mar 9 64
295	Hochenburg N	45	C	Apr 1
420	Hanney W T	45	A	Apr 7
424	Hill J	Cav 7	I	Apr 7
437	Henry Jas	" 7	I	Apr 8
464	Haner Jacob	45	B	Apr 9
527	Hickcox M R	Cav 3	B	Apr 13
580	Holdman F	Bat 1	D	Apr 16
748	Hanning Mark	Cav 7	I	Apr 26 64
758	Harvey Chas	76	E	Apr 26
875	Henry G W	95	E	May 4
949	Hawkins W W	103	G	May 3
1129	Hudsonpilfer R L C 7		I	May 15
1354	Hind George	103	H	May 25
1390	Holloway G W	1	C	May 28
1524	Harrison J	21	I	May 31
1666	Hazlett Wm	2	K	June 6
1822	Hull S	21	E	June 10
1979	Harris E D	99	I	June 15
2029	Hengle John	Cav 1	C	June 15
2185	Humphreys W	45	C	June 19
2263	Hanley C	15	F	June 20
2300	Henderson S W	40	H	June 22
2369	Howard J, Mus	70	D	June 23
2424	Hayford A E	125	C	June 24
2997	Harrington S J	103	I	June 28
2671	Hurles I	126	C	June 30
2775	Hurlburt O	14	H	July 2
2842	Hadison J	111	B	July 3
3185	Hall T	2	H	July 11
31	Heaton Amos	45	T	Apr 20
3388	Hudsen Wm	74	G	July 16
3420	Hunt W H	113	G	July 16
3736	Harman L	9	F	July 21
4030	Hansbury E A	6	G	July 26
4408	Hindershot John	45	D	July 31
4411	Harris J	1	E	July 31
4506	Hartman H	73	K	Aug 1
4599	Harrison J M	105	H	Aug 3
4993	Hendrickson O	19	F	Aug 7
5293	Holibaugh J A	23	E	Aug 11
5296	Hatfield G W	126	K	Aug 11
5396	Holman A	68	K	Aug 12
5554	Honnihill T R	9	G	Aug 13
5636	Hany B T	89	C	Aug 14
5813	Hicks F	40	H	Aug 16
5853	Hibbett Wm	21	D	Aug 19
5858	Hoit P	116	B	Aug 16
6058	Hamm E J		K	Aug 18
6123	Higgins I W	14	C	Aug 18
6774	Houser W R	89	K	Aug 18
6522	Hicks I	11	D	Aug 23
6625	Hughes Henry	33	A	Aug 23
6639	Henricks E	34	H	Aug 23
6647	Hartman I	2	K	Aug 23
6793	Herrig N	Cav 7	D	Aug 25
6802	Hine T E	" 2	D	Aug 25
7022	Hull O	89	B	Aug 27
7388	Hubbell W A	23	A	Aug 31
7446	Hurdnell O	72	C	Sept 1
7825	Holley V H	100	B	Sept 4
7946	Hughes I	12	E	Sept 5
8060	Herbolt Dan'l	115	T	Sept 7
8067	Harper I H	60	I	Sept 7
8284	Halshult A	12	C	Sept 9
8481	Hechler John	36	G	Sept 11
8696	Hitchcock G	34	G	Sept 14
8725	Hifner G	86	C	Sept 14
9189	Hoyt R	7	K	Sept 18
9210	Hart E	10	H	Sept 19
9538	Hall S	126	F	Sept 20
9413	Hood F	13	F	Sept 21
9510	Hamilton J	13	A	Sept 22
9582	Hoover J	18	K	Sept 23
9622	Hurley J C	124	C	Sept 23

252 LIST OF THE DEAD.

No.	Name	Reg.	Co.	Date
10094	Holmes Wesley	135	F	Sept 30 64
10207	Harrison J	Cav 2	A	Oct 2
10208	Holcomb L	7	I	Oct 2
10225	Harkins M	60	D	Oct 2
10390	Hinton Wm	72	A	Oct 5
10492	Hererlin B	32		Oct 7
10518	Herbert Wm	4	I	Oct 8
10524	Homich C	110	D	Oct 8
10647	Herman R	135	F	Oct 11
11029	Hilyard J	98	F	Oct 16
11032	Hubber D	5	A	Oct 16
11053	Heymers B	2	G	Oct 17
11209	Hanard J B	123	C	Oct 20
11288	Hoyt W B	29	A	Oct 20
11335	Henderson D	122	H	Oct 23
11588	Hintz D	1	B	Oct 28
11592	Hutchins G W	135	A	Oct 28
11696	Hutchins I W	153	A	Oct 31
11856	Hayner B	135	A	Nov 6
11938	Hatfield A G	114	E	Nov 9
12353	Hume J A	32	F	Dec 29
12371	Haines N S	72	E	Jan 1 65
12404	Hill W L	54	A	Jan 6
12446	Hill E P	89	G	Jan 13
12512	Hagerman R	33	B	Jan 23
12569	Hart H C	2	C	Feb 1
12611	Hagerly D G	72	E	Feb 7
12743	Holtz W	101	I	Mar 7
1129	Hudson R L	Cav 7	I	May 15 64
1132	Hank George B	7	I	May 16
2607	Hander L C	92	E	June 28
1280	Irving Ester	114	H	May 22
1967	Ingler Wm	31	C	June 14
7489	Imboden J	44	E	Sept 1
8744	Irwin A	1	I	Sept 14
10700	Idold A	Cav 7	C	Oct 11
12579	Isham D	89	G	Feb 3 65
354	Justice G W	45	B	Apr 2 64
1637	Johnson J H	98	D	June 5
3590	Jacobs P O	45	E	July 19
3751	Jones R	45	C	July 22
3903	Jones S	111	B	July 24
4381	Jewell I	99	F	July 31
5120	Johnston J W	89	H	Aug 9
5508	Johnson M	126	C	Aug 13
5583	Jones H	40	G	Aug 14
5624	Jewell W A	126	G	Aug 14
5839	Jolly G	21	K	Aug 16
6265	Jeffries H	36	I	Aug 20
6810	Jones John	40	G	Aug 25
7308	Johnson E	124	I	Aug 30
7861	Jones R W	118	F	Sept 5
8647	Jenkins Wm	Bat 3		Sept 13
8757	Johnson D	43	B	Sept 14
8760	Johnson I	51	A	Sept 14
9306	Jordan A	103	G	Sept 20
9700	Jones I B	3	M	Sept 25
9744	Johnson I B	2	C	Sept 25
9850	Jones Wm	84	B	Sept 27
11014	Jones S D	135	F	Oct 16
11203	Jennings Jno	24	K	Oct 20
11942	Jones G L	105	G	Nov 9
12126	Jarvitt W	15	A	Nov 22
12231	Johnson A S	45	I	Dec 6
12335	Jones W H	2	C	Dec 26
12428	Jackson S	72	E	Jan 10 65
7947	Jacobs H	26	F	Sept 6 64
836	Kelley Josiah	45	C	May 1 64
4615	Kimble S	98	A	Aug 1
4715	Knight J	21	E	Aug 4
5381	Kelly E	21	D	Aug 12
5448	Knidler J W	33	H	Aug 12
5576	Kelly H	1	I	Aug 14
6195	Kelsey Jno	3	I	Aug 19
7177	Kennedy S J B	45	E	Aug 29
7424	Kelly G	15	E	Oct 31
9377	Kelly Wm	46	C	Sept 20
9436	Kerr J H	122	C	Sept 21
9680	Knapp J	54	E	Sept 24
10139	Killar J	15	D	Oct 1
10607	Kirby A	Cav 4	A	Oct 10
10853	Keanshoff L	28	I	Oct 13
11055	Kerr A	13	I	Oct 17
11732	Kingkade S	18	C	Nov 2
12661	Kennedy J	70	K	Jan 16 65
12746	Kaler J	72	B	Mar 8
12802	Karch J	183	B	Mar 20
765	Kinney Jno	67	E	Apr 27 64
2406	Knowlton E	Cav 6	B	June 24
13	Kiger J H	45	E	Apr 9
834	Lowry Jas	49	I	May 1
935	Lewis Frank	103	D	May 7
1286	Larme Chas	45	K	May 22
1364	Larkin Jos	Art 1		May 25
1470	Logan Frank	89	F	May 30
1615	Logan H	Cav 6	E	June 4
1828	Leonard Jno	21	A	June 11
2173	Lever H B	2	C	June 19
2372	Lisure Samuel	7	A	June 23
2426	Lemons M	89	E	June 24
3495	Lutz M	11	C	July 18
3497	Love John	96	E	July 18
3649	Linsay J	21	D	July 20
4097	Lyon L L	Art 1	E	July 27
4354	Law S S	124	I	July 31
4262	Lawson J	2	E	July 29
4641	Lucas J	89	H	Aug 3
4628	Legrand D	111	B	Aug 3
4692	Long John	45	H	Aug 4
5195	Lightfoot Wm	Cav 9	G	Aug 10
5246	Latta W H	89	H	Aug 10
5449	Lehigh W	22	B	Aug 12
5665	Lamphare G W	125	K	Aug 14
5676	Larison A	63	D	Aug 14
6066	Lowe G H	72	C	Aug 18
6344	Leasure Isaac	122	K	Aug 21
7123	Leasure F	45	K	Aug 28
7744	Linway J	2	H	Sept 3
8016	Lambert Jas	89	A	Sept 6
8739	Lickliter Henry	135	B	Sept 14
8874	Lindsley A K	99	K	Sept 16
9336	Leonard T M	12	H	Sept 20
9358	Lovely John	100	K	Sept 20
9361	Lawyer J B	89	L	Sept 20
7419	Lefarer W E, Cit Gard'r, Athen Co			
10039	Laley ——	28		Sept 29 64
11161	Lepe A	7	K	Oct 19
11196	Lantz A W	45	A	Oct 20
11344	Lochner M	72	E	Oct 23
11440	Laughlin M W	1	I	Oct 24
11490	Lips F	2	H	Oct 26
11816	Lane D	91	D	Nov 4
12007	Lay John	123	K	Nov 19
12201	Lohmeyer H	35	K	Nov 30

LIST OF THE DEAD.

12297	Livingood C B	35	G	Dec 16 64
12525	Longstreet W F	31	A	Jan 26 65
12698	Lewis D	7	A	Jan 23
12826	Little Wm	175	D	Apr 7
06	Metcalf Milo R	100	E	Mar 19 64
96	Malsbray Asa Cav	40	A	Mar 22
113	Moore T J	2	D	Mar 23
141	McKeever Jas	8	G	Mar 24
165	Mickey Samuel	45	E	Mar 26
215	Murphy Jno Cav	7	B	Mar 28
412	Mitchell J	120	F	Apr 7
444	McKindry M	7	I	Apr 9
575	Malone R J	40	H	Apr 16
880	McCormick J W E	33	B	May 4
984	Musser D	45	B	May 9
998	Meek David	111	K	May 10
1262	McKnight H	11	G	May 21
1283	McMunny Geo	21	G	May 22
1630	Moore Chas	19	H	June 5
1849	Masters Samuel	17	I	June 11
1930	Martin G	105	F	June 14
2075	McCling B Cav	7	I	June 17
2139	Maloney A	4	H	June 18
2150	Mitchell W H	31	D	June 18
2290	Massey J C	33	A	June 21
2471	Mullin J	65	K	June 25
2667	McCloud A	35	G	June 29
2682	Miller T Cav	7	A	June 30
2743	McFarland L	2	I	July 1
2806	McInnes A	45	B	July 3
2873	Moriatt Joseph	5	K	July 4
2991	Mitchell Jas	17	D	July 7
3104	Malone L B Cav	7	L	July 10
3122	Mitchell C	1	K	July 10
3137	Minchell R	45	C	July 10
3290	Mahin B	51	I	July 13
3491	Master J	13	A	July 17
3718	Miller E	4	E	July 21
4040	Marshall T	21	G	July 26
4199	Myer C	21	I	July 29
4252	Meek J	19	E	July 29
4298	McKell M J	89	D	July 30
4361	Mooney Jas	50	D	July 31
4421	Morris C E	11	H	July 31
4501	McCann A	33	C	Aug 3
4657	Maher P	7	E	Aug 3
4789	Martin D Cav	3	L	Aug 5
5738	McCabe H	12	C	Aug 15
5777	Manson W	9	G	Aug 15
5888	McIntosh D	50	D	Aug 16
6026	Manahan Thos	21	D	Aug 18
6040	McKee Jas	51	A	Aug 18
6055	McHugh W S	2	D	Aug 18
6063	McClair P M	27	A	Aug 18
6478	McCabe J	66	C	Aug 22
6841	McCormick W P	2	G	Aug 25
6855	McSorley D	49	F	Aug 26
6862	McCoy J B	98	A	Aug 26
6920	McDell Wm	89	K	Aug 26
7108	McDonald J	99	H	Aug 28
7133	Mason J	45	D	Aug 28
7136	More Jno H	60	D	Aug 28
7515	Myers L H	135	B	Sept 1
7896	Morris J	105	A	Sept 5
8021	Meek Robert	111	K	Sept 6
8044	Myers A	51	I	Sept 6
8385	Maymer R	68	D	Sept 10
8408	McCabe J	70	C	Sept 11 64
8482	Morens H	51	A	Sept 11
8688	Moore T H	59	C	Sept 13
8726	Miller Samuel	135	F	Sept 14
8838	Mackrill R	50	I	Sept 15
8885	Manlig S	60	A	Sept 16
9039	Miller C	28	I	Sept 17
9096	McMillan J F	123	A	Sept 18
9241	McComb J S	14	K	Sept 19
9348	Maxwell P	12	A	Sept 20
8236	Moor D D	2	A	Sept 9
9659	Manly J	7	M	Sept 24
9867	Mitchell R C Cav	10		Sept 27
10064	Morgan R O	" 12	H	Sept 30
10081	McIntosh Wm	23	I	Sept 30
10106	Morais Wm	135	F	Sept 30
10517	Montgomery J	2	G	Oct 8
10563	Myer L, Blacksmith	1	A	Oct 9
10936	Martin F Cav	10	A	Oct 14
11156	McElroy Jno	92	B	Oct 18
11200	Martin W	15	A	Oct 20
11341	McQuilken F	1	I	Oct 23
11400	Mark J	135	B	Oct 24
11811	Miller J	135	I	Nov 4
12050	Moore R F	101	C	Nov 16
12054	Mills G W	60	F	Nov 16
12184	Morrison J H	21	H	Nov 28
12535	McDonald H H, Cit			Jan 27 65
12717	Milholland R	183	B	Mar 1
12872	McGrath D	115	G	Mar 15
12875	Martin M	135	B	Mar 16
983	Neal Jno	45	C	May 9 64
2328	Nash C D	45	B	May 22
4994	Nelson J Cav	1	K	Aug 7
5897	Neff B	95	H	Aug 16
7103	Nelson Thos Cav	1		Aug 28
10584	Nelder S	89	G	Oct 10
11012	Nott J	153	H	Oct 16
11448	Norman G L	135	B	Oct 25
12815	Norris E J	102	K	Mar 25 65
2183	Niver Edward Cav	3	I	June 19 64
2245	Ostrander E W	100	A	June 20
2442	Ott C	51	C	June 25
4352	O'Neil Jas	126	F	Aug 2
12024	O'Connor F	103	F	Nov 15
12247	Oliver J	122	C	Dec 8
12429	Olinger J	63	F	Dec 10
12835	Ornig J B	101	I	Apr 17 65
11349	O'Brien Jno	2	D	Oct 23 64
65	Pusey Jas	45	H	Mar 19
724	Parker Wm E	45	H	Apr 25
913	Penny A	59	C	May 6
1326	Prouty Wm Cav	9	L	May 24
2692	Phenix A H	21	H	June 20
9	Price Barney	45	I	Apr 5
3391	Pile Wilson	33	F	July 16
3555	Pierce H	100	A	July 18
4020	Perkins W B	89	G	July 26
5190	Piffer G	123	A	Aug 9
5377	Parker W	124	H	Aug 11
5426	Perrin N	72	A	Aug 12
6463	Parlice Geo W	94		Aug 22
6589	Potter H	72	E	Aug 23
6690	Pullen Sam'l	33	B	Aug 24
6717	Post J Art	1	D	Aug 24
6984	Palmer Sam'l	135	I	Aug 27
7021	Pease G E Cav	10	I	Aug 27

LIST OF THE DEAD.

No.	Name		Reg.	Co.	Date
7157	Plunket M		124	E	Aug 29 64
7329	Pelterson F		113	G	Aug 30
7368	Purcell Jno		72	D	Aug 31
7384	Pierson J		125	B	Aug 31
7399	Palmer F G	Cav	2	D	Aug 31
7519	Patten W		21	D	Sept 1
7644	Pierce Wm		75	H	Sept 3
7701	Pruser H		1	B	Sept 3
7724	Payne J		89	E	Sept 3
8109	Potts Jas		122	E	Sept 7
8288	Phillips H		33	I	Sept 9
8534	Powell F		9	G	Sept 12
8597	Pror A M	Cav	135	B	Sept 12
8620	Pinert F		21	C	Sept 13
8753	Parker Z		124	E	Sept 14
9111	Parks J W	Cav	6	G	Sept 18
9327	Parker J		40	H	Sept 20
9470	Perrin G		3	B	Sept 21
9768	Pipenbring Geo		13	K	Sept 25
9822	Preston Wm	M I	34	B	Sept 27
10056	Parks E F		36	D	Sept 30
11221	Piper E A		23	B	Oct 20
11453	Patterson F	Cav	28	F	Oct 25
11676	Prouse P I		1	I	Oct 30
11779	Preshall J A		116	C	Nov 3
12088	Peasly. J		65	H	Nov 16
12040	Porter W C		40	H	Nov 16
12352	Powers J		21	K	Dec 28
12551	Poistan J		183	F	Jan 29 65
12645	Piper I		64	F	Feb 13
344	Ricker Henry	Cav	2	E	April 2 64
908	Rush D		107	H	May 5
1642	Radabaugh W H		33	A	June 5
2030	Ralston W J		89	C	June 15
2124	Rawlings S		45	E	June 17
2156	Rancey A K		111	B	June 18
2281	Rickards W V		33	B	June 20
2410	Rowe A		124	F	June 24
2878	Rees Thos		98	C	July 4
3074	Rix Wm		2	K	July 9
49	Reed Harmon		103	E	May 25
3400	Rogers T		51	C	July 16
3426	Ralston J M		89	C	July 16
3613	Russell L F		111	B	July 20
3802	Regman O		2	D	July 24
3961	Robinson H H		110	H	July 25
4061	Reiggs H		21	F	July 27
4335	Rex J W	Cav	3	K	July 30
4777	Robbins A	"	6	D	Aug 5
5570	Reichardson G		82	G	Aug 14
5631	Russell J G		116	C	Aug 14
5639	Read Geo H		21	H	Aug 14
5641	Redder G		45	G	Aug 14
6488	Robbins D B		89	I	Aug 22
6511	Ross J		59	A	Aug 22
6835	Ridgeway Jno		23	D	Aug 25
6948	Redd C		122	H	Aug 26
7174	Ross A		45	H	Aug 29
7353	Roberts Ed		75	K	Aug 31
7639	Rutain E B		44	E	Sept 2
7844	Russell Jas		9	E	Sept 4
8521	Khotin W		2	C	Sept 12
8747	Riley W M		89	B	Sept 14
8818	Robertson R		120	D	Sept 15
9614	Robinson J		65	D	Sept 23
9617	Rose Jno		72	H	Sept 23
10165	Riper O H		110	G	Oct 1
10354	Rogers C		13	H	Oct 5 64
10558	Rocheile Jno		135	F	Oct 11
11279	Romain J		59	H	Oct 21
11360	Reese A		80	C	Oct 23
11413	Reese R		59	D	Oct 24
11646	Rapp N		10	A	Oct 30
11657	Robbins P		122	H	Oct 30
11672	Robinson C	Cav	2	E	Oct 30
11859	Rourk J		6	G	Nov 6
12366	Repau A		47	A	Dec 31
12047	Rapp D C		2	C	Feb 13 65
12692	Ramsbottom A F		99	D	Feb 22
1763	Rei J		124	K	June 6 64
33	Smith J E	Cav	7	C	Mar 9
44	Smith H B		82	B	Mar 14
58	Strill Michael		100	K	Mar 18
231	Sears Samuel	Cav	2	F	Mar 29
260	Stephen H		100	B	Mar 31
263	Smelus Geo	Cav	7	L	Mar 31
284	Saughessy Jno		45	B	April 1
481	Steele Abraham		80	H	April 9
594	Sweuch W		45	A	April 16
653	Snyder Lewis		89	C	April 20
726	Sweeny Sam	Cav	7	G	April 25
771	Shannon Chas		45	I	April 28
804	Starbuck F		62	E	April 29
937	Storer Jno		17	A	May 7
962	Smith Jno	Cav	7	F	May 8
994	Smith Wm		103	E	May 10
1100	Samse Wm		14	H	May 17
1179	Smith Conrad		100	A	May 18
1183	Smith Wm		2	G	May 18
1229	Spangler A		45	E	May 20
1281	Swineheart J W		111	B	May 22
1404	Seyman Aaron		89	D	May 27
1672	Sprague W L	Cav	6	K	June 6
1773	Simmons Jno	Bat	22		June 9
2220	Shannon E		35	A	June 20
2230	Stanett J		45	C	June 20
2370	Stiver J		93	C	June 23
2524	Smith G W		11	K	June 26
2575	Sampson C		89	D	June 27
2638	Stuits P		45	F	June 29
2783	Snyver L		31	B	July 2
2792	Smith N H		1	H	July 2
3116	Smith G		21	I	July 10
42	Sabine Alonzo		100	A	May 11
3252	Short Jas	Cav	4	A	July 13
3288	Smith D		7	H	July 13
3361	Saffle J		2	E	July 15
3536	Steward C S		33	K	July 18
3602	Stevenson D		111	B	July 19
3298	Squires Thos		49	C	July 20
3744	Snyder Thos		9	G	July 21
3770	Smith D		2	I	July 22
3794	Sever H H		2	C	July 22
4249	Shephard J H		2	E	July 29
4275	Smith J B		1	B	July 29
4294	Steward J		2	K	July 30
4745	Steiner J M		72	F	Aug 5
5018	Smock A		93	D	Aug 8
5054	Smarz A		93	E	Aug 8
5066	Shipple John	Cav	6	A	Aug 8
5133	Scott S E		4	I	Aug 9
5287	Stevenson John		111	B	Aug 11
5330	Spegle F		14	D	Aug 11

LIST OF THE DEAD.

No.	Name	Reg.	Co.	Date
5373	Schem J	101	K	Aug 11 64
5455	Stevens G W	101	K	Aug 12
5596	Sullivan W	78	D	Aug 16
6610	Staley G	89	A	Aug 17
6032	Smith Wm	Cav 2	G	Aug 18
6178	Simpson W J	32	F	Aug 19
6199	Sheddy G	2	K	Aug 19
6214	Shaw Geo W	105	A	Aug 20
6253	Shoulder E	24	F	Aug 20
6779	Soper P	72	G	Aug 25
6870	Scarberry O	89	D	Aug 26
7034	Satton J	4	A	Aug 27
7065	Shoemaker J	47	E	Aug 28
7436	Stinchear F E	101	A	Sept 1
7475	Shafer J	9	G	Sept 1
7540	Sell Adam	125	E	Sept 2
7788	Stewart John S	19	B	Sept 4
7597	Smith H H	Cav 2	A	Sept 5
7986	Seib Jacob	28		Sept 6
8014	Shriver Geo	45	K	Sept 6
8015	Snider Jas	4	C	Sept 6
8156	Sturtevant W	72	A	Sept 8
8197	Shrouds J	Bat 6		Sept 8
8200	Stroufe A	7	E	Sept 8
8229	Shaw W	15	I	Sept 9
8300	Smith N	121	H	Sept 9
8319	Sheldon W	49	E	Sept 10
8422	Sullivan Jno	135	F	Sept 11
8728	Sisson P B	18	H	Sept 14
8752	Sickles J	51	I	Sept 14
8914	Simmonds S P	1	A	Sept 16
8931	Stull G	15	G	Sept 16
9009	Sharp F S	63	K	Sept 17
9244	Schmall J D	12	E	Sept 19
9386	Smith L	158	H	Sept 20
9645	Scott J H	33	H	Sept 24
9649	Skiver J	114	H	Sept 24
10250	Sheets W	81	A	Oct 3
10312	Spencer S M	89	E	Oct 4
10434	Shingle D	Cav 2	L	Oct 6
10437	Stanford P W	Cav 2	A	Oct 6
10576	Stonchecks J D	51	F	Oct 9
10618	Schafer P	101	I	Oct 10
10703	Stout Samson	2	F	Oct 11
10833	Sheppard Jno	34	D	Oct 13
11139	Snark H	72	F	Oct 17
11146	Smith G A	45	F	Oct 19
11249	Sullivan F	76	C	Oct 21
11433	Swaney E	124	A	Oct 24
11579	Smith P	69	I	Oct 28
11395	Sapp W N	20	E	Oct 28
11711	Spiker J	122		Nov 1
11797	Shaler F	72	E	Nov 4
12105	Sly F	89	G	Nov 20
12281	Singer J	6	G	Dec 13
12305	Sweet M	49	F	Dec 18
12441	Shoemaker C	8	F	Jan 12 65
12538	Stewart A F	2	D	Jan 27
12562	Sponcerlar Geo	71	B	Jan 31
12608	Shorter W	89	K	Feb 17
12709	Sloan L	123	D	Mar 13
12789	Stroup S	50	B	Mar 17
12793	Seeley N	132	D	Mar 18
12810	Scott R	75	G	Mar 24
730	Tweedy R	Cav 1	A	April 25 64
743	Trescott Samuel	2	C	April 26
999	Trimmer Wm	40	H	May 10
1196	Turney U S	Cav 2	G	May 18 64
1496	Thomas Wm	Cav 10	M	May 30
4784	Thompson J	2	E	Aug 5
4951	Toroman W R	13	E	Aug 7
5356	Tierney W	Art 1	L	Aug 11
5552	Tinsley M	90	B	Aug 13
5608	Terilliger N	12	C	Aug 14
6330	Tanner A	32	G	Aug 21
7224	Thompson V B	26	C	Aug 29
7246	Turner S B	45	B	Aug 30
7640	Thomas Jas	44	C	Sept 2
8850	Talbert R	135	F	Sept 15
9774	Thomas N	103	B	Sept 26
9945	Townsend J	26	C	Sept 28
10471	Tattman B	153	C	Oct 7
10800	Tinway P	93		Oct 12
11820	Townsley E M	89	B	Nov 5
12577	Tensdale T H	Cav 2	E	Feb 3 65
12251	Uehre S	12	E	Dec 9 64
2194	Vining W H H	45	G	June 19
3902	Valentine C	123	H	July 24
4450	Vaugh B	125	F	Aug 1
4497	Vaugrider H	103	H	Aug 1
5203	Vatier J F	Cav 6		Aug 10
6170	Vail Jno L	17	C	Aug 19
6859	Vauaman M	21	E	Aug 26
6985	Vanderveer A	6	H	Aug 27
7756	Victor H	Art 1	D	Sept 4
9576	Volis J	34	H	Sept 23
10252	Vail N	12	K	Oct 3
10389	Vail G M	7	D	Oct 5
10472	Van Fleet H	14	I	Oct 7
11095	Van Kirk G	135	B	Oct 18
11097	Van Malley J	M 89	G	Oct 18
12554	Vanhorn S	Cav 9	C	Jan 30 65
7	Wiley Samuel	82	A	Mch 5 64
185	Wickman Wm	111	B	Mch 27
779	Wooley Jno	45	B	April 28
807	Werts Louis	45	D	April 30
1085	Wood Wm	89	A	May 14
1449	Wentling Joseph	100	K	May 29
1604	Wood Joseph	15	B	June 4
1836	Wilkinson W	89	D	June 11
1913	Wilson Jas	93	I	June 13
2020	Way Jno	44	I	June 13
2041	Windgrove S R	15		June 15
2172	Webb E	45	A	June 19
2358	Walters F	9	E	June 23
2536	Wing	Cav 2	M	June 26
2815	Willis A	89	A	July 3
2840	Wroten L	89	H	July 3
3188	Williams D	90	A	July 12
34	Wright Wm	7	H	April 24
3310	White H	15	A	July 15
3325	Whitten G	75	K	July 14
4214	West J B	89	B	July 29
4681	Witt Jno T	93	G	Aug 4
4688	Won J	111	B	Aug 4
4695	Wile A	33	D	Aug 4
5121	Winder I	70	D	Aug 9
5211	Wood N L	Cav 4	L	Aug 10
5726	Winters Geo	145	K	Aug 15
6314	Wainwright S G	89	G	Aug 20
6318	Wisser F J	35	A	Aug 20
6362	Wistman N	9	A	Aug 21
6397	Wilson E	4	A	Aug 21
6700	Watson G	21	A	Aug 24

LIST OF THE DEAD.

No.	Name	Reg.	Co.	Date
6761	Wood S	123	A	Aug 22 64
7056	Wool W H	59	E	Aug 28
7373	Wyatt J	90	B	Aug 31
7582	Wentworth L	72	A	Sept 1
8298	Wright J S	89	E	Sept 9
8306	Warner T	14	C	Sept 10
8907	Wyckmann D	73	G	Sept 16
9384	Worte J	116		Sept 20
9527	Woodruff J M	135	F	Sept 22
9691	Wagner J	93	F	Sept 24
10007	Whitney E	21	K	Sept 29
10230	Williams Orland	C 7	K	Oct 2
10309	Weaver M	72	H	Oct 4
10402	Ward Francis	21	H	Oct 6
10464	Whitehead A B	33	E	Oct 7
10528	Wiley A	26	I	Oct 8
10733	White I	73	E	Oct 11
10844	Westbrook R L	135	F	Oct 13
11013	Walker C	65	I	Oct 16
11034	Waldron H	14	A	Oct 16
11417	Williams S M	60	F	Oct 24
11770	Worthen D	122	B	Nov 3
11874	Weason J	35	F	Nov 6
12042	Wickham J	14	H	Nov 16
12073	White R M	15	D	Nov 18
12158	Warner B F	35	E	Nov 25
12584	Whitaker E	72	A	Feb 4 65
12722	Wella E	57	A	Mch 3
12759	Winklet T, McL's Sqn			Mch 12
12786	Warner M	102	G	Mch 16
4833	Webricks Josh H	9	G	Aug 6 64
638	Yuterler W A	45	E	April 20
5477	Younker S	80	F	Aug 13
6068	Young Jno	7	E	Aug 18
7816	Yeager Jno	Cav 2	B	Sept 4
7876	Young J	9	F	Sept 5
10583	Young W	6	G	Oct 10
12659	Young W	15	A	Feb 16 65
3225	Zubers J M	100	B	July 12 64
11253	Zink A J	72	E	Oct 21

TOTAL 1031.

PENNSYLVANIA.

No.	Name	Reg.	Co.	Date
224	Attwood Abr'm	C 18	I	Mch 29 64
250	Armidster M	Cav 4	A	Mch 30
468	Ackerman C	8	B	April 9
758	Arb Simon	Cav 4	C	April 27
846	Ailbeck G B	52	F	May 3
975	Algert H K	54	F	May 9
1282	Arble Thos	Cav 13	A	May 26
1837	Ait M	21	K	June 11
2348	Akers Geo	90	H	June 23
2398	Allison E	55	K	June 24
2547	Anderson D	103	K	June 27
2648	Able J	54	F	June 20
2956	Amagart Eli	103	F	July 6
3018	Ackley G B	Art 3	B	July 7
3917	Alexander M	Cav 1	F	July 14
3967	Ardray J F	13	F	July 25
4055	Anderson J	79	I	July 27
4143	Aches T J	7	H	July 28
4149	Alcorn Geo W	145	F	July 28
4495	Archart H	51	C	July 29
4673	Allen C	Cav 8	K	Aug 4
4973	Andertin J	Cav 4	L	Aug 7
5286	Aler B	103	D	Aug 11
5511	Ault J L	101	C	Aug 13
5862	Armstrong C	Cav 4	C	Aug 16 64
6029	Anersen Jno	91	C	Aug 18
7163	Arnold Daniel	184	C	Aug 29
7887	Angstedt Geo W	1	F	Sept 5
8185	Allen J L	101	I	Sept 8
8232	Ambler C	Cav 13	D	Sept 9
8388	Alexander W	Res 2	I	Sept 10
8653	Armstrong A	7	K	Sept 13
8655	Arnold L	73	A	Sept 13
8765	Altimus Wm	7	E	Sept 14
1743	Ainley Wm	Cav 3	E	June 8
9150	Alcorn J W	" 18	D	Sept 18
9896	Allison D B	55	K	Sept 27
10487	Anderson A	135	F	Oct 7
10570	Allen D	126	A	Oct 9
10823	Allin S	Cav 7	H	Oct 13
11419	Applebay T M	149	K	Oct 24
11607	Antill J	61	I	Oct 28
11710	Anger W	118		Nov 1
11852	Affleck T	2	F	Nov 6
11810	Amandt J	184	D	Nov 6
12520	Atchinson W P	142	F	Jan 25 65
228	Bull Frank	Cav 4	H	Mar 29 64
249	Burton Lafayette	C 18	D	Mar 30
332	Briggs Andrew	C 13	H	April 2
427	Begler A	27	C	April 8
543	Breel Jacob	27	H	April 14
569	Black Jus A	Cav 14	D	April 15
661	Bradley Alex	" 3	F	April 21
671	Burns Sam	73	K	April 22
673	Barra J	54	F	April 22
822	Bayne Wm	145	I	May 1
874	Bradley M	Art 3	A	May 4
897	Brown Henry	90	H	May 5
938	Brown D	4	C	May 7
974	Batting Isaac	Cav 8	H	May 9
1046	Baker J D	57	F	May 12
1188	Butler Wm	90	B	May 18
1300	Boyd Thomas	9	D	May 23
1309	Bryson J	Cav 2	D	May 23
1327	Brining J	" 13	B	May 24
1375	Burney J	" 13	G	May 26
1393	Brown J B	" 4	K	May 26
1576	Boman Sam'l	Art 3	B	June 3
1601	Berfert R	103	B	June 4
1654	Brumley Geo	Cav 4	I	June 5
1790	Butler J F	76	B	June 10
1859	Berkhawn H	73	G	June 12
1872	Brooks D S	79		June 12
1923	Brian Chas	183	F	June 14
1999	Bixter R	73	C	June 15
2026	Burns Owen	Cav 13	C	June 15
2046	Bigler M	" 4		June 15
2127	Brown C	" 3	B	June 17
2134	Buckhannan W	Art 3	B	June 18
2180	Ball L	26	K	June 19
2236	Barr J T	Cav 4	K	June 20
2323	Baker Henry	" 18	I	June 22
2483	Bisel Jno	" 18	K	June 25
2539	Balsley Wm	" 20	F	June 26
2610	Brown M	" 14	C	June 28
2727	Brenn J	73	K	July 1
2733	Bolt J H	Cav 18	E	July 1
2741	Beam Jno	76	E	July 1
2816	Burns Jno	Cav 13	A	July 3
2913	Bish J	108	F	July 5
2918	Belford Jno	115	F	July 5

LIST OF THE DEAD.

No.	Name	Reg.	Co.	Date
3005	Bryan P	Art 3	A	July 7 64
3019	Barr S	103	G	July 7
3027	Braney J	48	E	July 7
3051	Barnes W	101	H	July 8
3097	Butler L J	118	E	July 10
3100	Brunt A	110	G	July 10
3216	Beraine A A	101	B	July 12
3294	Burns Jas	103	F	July 14
3442	Brinton J	157	D	July 17
3477	Baker Wm	103	F	July 17
3535	Burnside J	57	H	July 18
3600	Black W O	103	G	July 19
3693	Billig J L	Cav 3	H	July 21
3716	Breninger W R	" 4	D	July 21
3808	Butter C P	148	A	July 22
3824	Batchell D	55	D	July 23
3917	Bright E	90	I	July 23
3988	Bradford L	10	I	July 26
4002	Berkley M	50	I	July 26
4084	Backner Adam	116	G	July 27
4330	Barrett J	6	K	July 30
4360	Brown J	53	G	July 31
4402	Butler D	53	G	July 31
4494	Barton Jas	Cav 4	B	Aug 1
4500	Burke J	90	A	Aug 1
4610	Baker E	4	K	Aug 3
4667	Behreus A	7	E	Aug 4
4752	Bennett Geo	55	D	Aug 5
4989	Bowers J	Art 2	I	Aug 7
5040	Bammratta	—	73	D	Aug 8
5071	Barber C	6	D	Aug 8
5084	Buck B F	Cav 2	K	Aug 8
5113	Brown M	50	D	Aug 9
5324	Burlingame A J	141	K	Aug 11
5391	Bear Jno	79	D	Aug 12
5416	Bruce Jno	101	C	Aug 12
5526	Bower Benj	Cav 6	L	Aug 13
5587	Burnham H	143	F	Aug 14
5592	Broadbuck A	Cav 11	A	Aug 14
5662	Buck B F	" 2	K	Aug 14
5877	Browning Thos	103	A	Aug 16
5948	Bohnaberger A	115	G	Aug 17
5969	Boyer F	43	E	Aug 17
6061	Baker Jas	101	C	Aug 18
6074	Bower G W	103	K	Aug 18
6099	Baily J F	18	D	Aug 18
6127	Benhand J A	103	D	Aug 19
6229	Bear Sam'l	55	G	Aug 20
6244	Boles M S	Cav 4	K	Aug 20
6279	Bower C	101	C	Aug 20
6319	Birney J	Cav 4	C	Aug 20
6359	Bennett A	67	K	Aug 21
6542	Blackman W	18	D	Aug 23
6551	Bannon P	7	A	Aug 23
6554	Baldwin C H	Cav 2	K	Aug 23
6604	Barnett E T	149	I	Aug 23
6621	Bell Thos	11	E	Aug 23
6660	Blair Jno G	46	F	Aug 24
6663	Breckinridge W	73	K	Aug 24
6688	Bowman A	63	B	Aug 24
6701	Boyd J W	101	C	Aug 24
6704	Beemer Wm	145	K	Aug 24
6887	Brown T	Cav 11	I	Aug 26
6928	Bryan L	106	F	Aug 26
7125	Bridaham H W	55	H	Aug 28
7181	Bemer S	184	E	Aug 29
7347	Ball P	49	H	Aug 31
7460	Barnes W	119	G	Sept 1 64
7477	Bennett J	55	D	Sept 1
7541	Barnett M	145	K	Sept 2
7684	Black J	143	I	Sept 3
7747	Blair J G	49	E	Sept 3
7775	Brink F	Cav 11	M	Sept 4
7940	Browers J A	184	F	Sept 5
7963	Brumley Fred'k	54	K	Sept 6
8073	Bright Adam	101	K	Sept 7
8073	Boland	183	I	Sept 7
8256	Barr P	103	C	Sept 9
8286	Brown L	Cav 8	C	Sept 9
8356	Brown A	101	H	Sept 10
8358	Brickenstaff W	101	I	Sept 10
8363	Bruce J B	101	F	Sept 10
8413	Blosser Jonas	Res 7	H	Sept 11
8434	Bowsteak T D	106	H	Sept 11
8499	Bicklet E H	57	K	Sept 11
8606	Boots E N	101	H	Sept 12
8719	Beattie Robert	95	D	Sept 14
8769	Boyer J M	Cav 7	F	Sept 14
8795	Bentley T	54	H	Sept 14
8794	Brown P	55	A	Sept 15
8902	Baker J	184	C	Sept 16
8917	Baker Wm	Cav 11		Sept 16
9147	Blake E	69	K	Sept 18
9520	Boyler Jas	7	E	Sept 22
9632	Baldwin A	51	K	Sept 24
9745	Bowers F	Cav 5	A	Sept 25
9809	Bonewell W W	" 14	C	Sept 26
9952	Blair Geo	Art 7		Sept 28
10201	Burdge H	Cav 3	D	Oct 2
10226	Byers J	22	E	Oct 2
10260	Burns J	103	E	Oct 3
10292	Brown G M	10	I	Oct 4
10357	Burgess H	27	C	Oct 5
10534	Buck D C	Cav 2	L	Oct 8
10577	Ballinger Geo	87	D	Oct 9
10674	Blackman W	84	A	Oct 11
10758	Beightel J F	51	G	Oct 12
10779	Boice J N	145	G	Oct 12
10783	Bowling J	3	A	Oct 12
10943	Barthart I	116	H	Oct 14
10980	Baney Geo	4	I	Oct 15
10983	Bowyer J S	55	E	Oct 15
11024	Bunker F	55	K	Oct 16
11087	Bowman G	149	E	Oct 18
11322	Bissel B	142	F	Oct 22
11329	Bruce A	11	I	Oct 23
11434	Berk G	51	A	Oct 24
11445	Ball J	19	K	Oct 25
14504	Bain G	183	G	Oct 26
11528	Baney I	Cav 4	I	Oct 26
11556	Baker B H	148	B	Oct 27
11563	Brock C	46	A	Oct 27
11569	Beighley W	103	C	Oct 27
11597	Blair Jno	106	H	Oct 28
11611	Boyer T	11	F	Oct 28
11635	Burr E	145	K	Oct 28
11674	Bolinger G	87	D	Oct 30
11818	Bayley H	66	K	Nov 4
11894	Burch W	Art 2	F	Nov 7
11920	Burke J D	Cav 22	D	Nov 9
11972	Bupp L	149	G	Nov 12
12039	Bailey J J	Art 2	F	Nov 16
12059	Bogar David	184	C	Nov 17
12079	Bond C C	20	K	Nov 18

LIST OF THE DEAD.

No.	Name	Reg.	Co.	Date
12006	Brady N	Cav 5	M	Nov 19 64
12108	Brubaker B P	79	D	Nov 26
12177	Braddock T	77	C	Nov 27
12418	Barrens J	Cav 5	G	Jan 9 65
12812	Barnett J	6	D	Mar 25
2917	Brin Jas	56	I	July 5 64
12665	Bennett J	184	E	Feb 16 65
45	Carter Wm	139	H	Mar 14 64
97	Chase Wm B	Cav 15	C	Mar 22
156	Compsey Jas	" 14	H	Mar 25
355	Carman F H	54	F	Apr 2
445	Coyle P	45	A	Apr 9
466	Crouch Levi	40	I	Apr 9
479	Croghan Jno	Cav 3	A	Apr 9
548	Case Daniel	" 8	M	Apr 14
734	Conner Andrus	C 4	L	Apr 25
837	Cravener S P	Cav 14	K	May 1
869	Curry A	119	E	May 3
1015	Campbell Wm	Cav 8	E	May 10
1099	Case Silas	" 2	L	May 14
1138	Carmichael G	" 18	K	May 16
1186	Crisholm J H	150	H	May 18
1206	Caldwell S A	Cav 14	E	May 19
1232	Coburg M C	" 6	L	May 20
1490	Coon J H	" 18	K	May 31
1498	Campbell H B	103	E	May 31
1530	Clatter F	Cav 18	C	May 31
1702	Calihan Thos	" 14	H	June 7
1781	Cephas L	145	I	June 8
1829	Carter Wm	101	K	June 11
1832	Calvert R R	6	B	June 11
1871	Coombs Jno	Art 3		June 12
1873	Cox J A	Cav 113		June 12
2069	Cooper T	" 18	K	June 16
2349	Curry R	73	F	June 23
2399	Coyle H	Cav 8	F	June 24
2455	Crouse E	141	A	June 25
2695	Copple F	54	H	June 30
2713	Chapman J	7	H	July 1
2849	Carron Jas	Cav 4	C	July 4
2884	Calean Sam'l	103	K	July 4
2995	Coleman J	Cav 18	F	July 7
3320	Chase F M	72	G	July 14
3362	Clark N	Cav 8	D	July 15
3417	Caton W T	49	D	July 16
3430	Couch Benj	50	H	July 17
3948	Coyle Ed	58	E	July 25
3993	Curtey L	10	I	July 26
4045	Carpenter L	12	K	July 27
4117	Cantrill M	6	B	July 28
4263	Conklin N	90	K	July 29
4331	Chapman J	Art 3	B	July 30
4353	Crawford M	Cav 14	G	July 31
4357	Cox Jas	103	A	July 31
4369	Claybaugh G W	A 2	F	July 31
4512	Crock H	45	A	Aug 1
4682	Croup W S	103	L	Aug 4
4729	Cochran C	103	I	Aug 4
4903	Chew Jno	18	F	Aug 6
5177	Cranes E	Cav 4	M	Aug 9
5375	Campbell Jas	" 3	F	Aug 11
5417	Cregg J G	54	I	Aug 12
5423	Cumberland T	C 14	B	Aug 12
5484	Conahan M	115	B	Aug 13
5578	Carpenter W C	145	G	Aug 14
5584	Campbell R D	11	E	Aug 14
5623	Cox H	Cav 7	B	Aug 14
5828	Cummings Benj	3	A	Aug 16 64
5979	Conor J N	184	C	Aug 17
6237	Corbin W	49	C	Aug 20
6269	Campbell R G	11	C	Aug 20
6320	Coon George	2	F	Aug 21
6336	Cameron Wm	101	A	Aug 21
6395	Connelly Wm	55	C	Aug 21
6430	Conner J	6	D	Aug 22
6502	Cline J	3	H	Aug 22
6615	Crawford J	77	E	Aug 23
6645	Coleman C	19	E	Aug 23
6746	Conly Jno	101	A	Aug 24
6913	Craft A	90	G	Aug 26
7045	Cobert F C	Cav 11	L	Aug 27
7095	Carr J	51	G	Aug 28
7116	Cathcart Robt	103	H	Aug 29
7209	Crain J	Cav 4	H	Aug 29
7456	Craig Wm	103	D	Sept 1
7463	Clay Henry	184	A	Sept 1
7617	Curry S	140	C	Sept 2
7632	Carroll A	Cav 2	A	Sept 2
7669	Campbell G T	Art 3	A	Sept 3
7696	Criser M	54	F	Sept 3
8117	Crawford J A	103	B	Sept 8
8121	Collins M	101	K	Sept 8
8169	Cole J C	118	K	Sept 8
8260	Chapman ——	18	A	Sept 9
8512	Coyle M	79	B	Sept 12
8594	Culver J	69		Sept 12
8665	Clutler L	11	C	Sept 13
8700	Cavender J L	119	E	Sept 14
8884	Cysey A	Heavy A 3		Sept 15
9034	Coffman Wm	13	F	Sept 18
9131	Cramer E	55	F	Sept 18
9141	Church C H	45	B	Sept 18
9269	Clark J	101		Sept 19
9396	Coats S R	135	C	Sept 20
9410	Combs S	1	H	Sept 21
9508	Clonay J	145	F	Sept 22
9554	Crum C	149	G	Sept 23
9639	Cline J	118	A	Sept 24
9773	Coulter G	45	K	Sept 25
9823	Cummings R	65	K	Sept 27
9886	Callahan M	52	D	Sept 27
9931	Conrad W	Cav 14	M	Sept 28
10104	Campbell Wm	" 13	D	Sept 30
10120	Coats L R	139	H	Oct 1
10274	Crawford Geo	1	F	Oct 3
10276	Cantler J L	13	A	Oct 3
10283	Cromich F	7	H	Oct 4
10386	Cornelius Wm	Cav 7		Oct 5
10399	Cullingford P	55	C	Oct 6
10443	Clark W	Cav 5	K	Oct 7
10462	Canby G C	" 2	E	Oct 7
10497	Coperhewer Wm	1	D	Oct 8
10541	Culberton Louis	73	B	Oct 9
10842	Corbin M	184	D	Oct 13
10847	Clark G	Cav 1	H	Oct 13
11005	Coe Geo W	145	E	Oct 16
11025	Clark J	3	D	Oct 16
11250	Clark H	184	F	Oct 21
11309	Clark E B	101	B	Oct 22
11370	Carrol W	145	B	Oct 23
11436	Crawford L	184	R	Oct 24
11438	Cole H O	Cav 2	L	Oct 24
11477	Campbell C A	" 11	C	Oct 26
11565	Creagan G	" 1	F	Oct 27

LIST OF THE DEAD.

ID	Name	Unit	Reg	Co	Date
11614	Crawford M		14	K	Oct 28 64
11656	Coyle H		54	K	Oct 30
11659	Craney Geo	Cav	20	L	Oct 30
11800	Cregger W H	"	5	G	Nov 4
11815	Chacon A W		106	B	Nov 4
11826	Colebaugh W		60	K	Nov 5
11876	Crandall L		145	I	Nov 6
11922	Cleaveland E	Cav	10	I	Nov 8
11993	Crampton A B		143	B	Nov 13
12120	Cullen T I		31	I	Nov 22
12141	Conway C C	Art	2	A	Nov 23
12255	Crompton F G		71	F	Dec 10
12295	Cone S		115	E	Dec 16
12301	Culp P K		138	B	Dec 17
12368	Connor S		112	H	Jan 1 65
12424	Clark J		89	D	Jan 9
12487	Collins G		118	E	Jan 19
12599	Cassell D		20	E	Feb 6
12672	Clark F D		7	C	Feb 20
12818	Copeland B	Cav	14	D	Mar 29
1961	Culbertson Jno	"	13	B	June 14 64
152	Davidson H		57	I	Mar 25
866	Dorr Phineas		119	K	May 3
1020	Doran McK		63	D	May 11
1161	Duntler Henry		51	K	May 16
1338	Dooner M		2	K	May 24
1463	Davis Richard	Cav	3	L	May 29
1541	Deamott J K		45	C	June 1
1545	Davis Isaac	Cav	8	H	June 1
2630	Dun R B		101	B	June 29
2657	Donovan J		139	K	June 29
2716	Deily Wm		53	H	July 1
2938	Davis M	Cav	22	B	July 6
3338	Degret N	"	15	M	July 15
3363	Davidson Chas		100	M	July 15
3741	Dallin Jas	Cav	8	H	July 21
3795	Davis J		103	A	July 22
3873	Davis M H		103	E	July 24
3985	Dougherty J		7	E	July 26
4087	Deron Robt		149	B	July 29
4202	Drenkle J A		79	K	July 29
5232	Dechmann Jno		184	G	July 29
4481	Dodrick Louis		50	I	Aug 1
4491	Denton M	Cav	9	B	Aug 1
4497	Day Wm		97	A	Aug 1
4625	Davis J		101	E	Aug 3
4711	Dort C R	Cav	4	H	Aug 4
4786	Dondle Robt		101	A	Aug 5
4792	Davy H		68	K	Aug 5
4806	Davenbrook J J		101	G	Aug 5
4885	Delaney J		101	A	Aug 6
4897	Dunbar Jno	Cav	14	M	Aug 6
4910	Dean J		148	F	Aug 6
5023	Dawlin		110	D	Aug 8
5256	Ditztell L		73	I	Aug 10
5431	Davidson Geo		57	C	Aug 12
5468	Dougherty		101	I	Aug 13
5664	Decker J		45	B	Aug 14
5740	Day And H	Cav	2	H	Aug 15
5746	Doran P		99	I	Aug 15
6017	Deal F		63	A	Aug 17
6045	Degroot H	Cav	13	A	Aug 18
6176	Defrec Jas		15	G	Aug 19
6226	Dodd J		18	F	Aug 20
6316	Davis Wm		153	A	Aug 20
6568	Dawney Geo		148	B	Aug 23
9679	Donavan D		90	B	Aug 24
6678	Dunn Johnes		69	F	Aug 25 64
6797	Dailey M		7	I	Aug 25
6879	Dunn Jno		184	A	Aug 26
7053	Dakenfelt J		55	D	Aug 28
7077	Deets R		3	A	Aug 28
7282	Day S		13	A	Aug 30
7360	Dively J		110	C	Aug 31
7488	Dilks C		1	K	Sept 1
7651	Dewell Samuel		50	G	Sept 3
7828	Dougherty J		184	D	Sept 4
8211	Dixon J		105	B	Sept 8
8334	Doherty J		73	F	Sept 10
8569	Duff J	Cav	4	B	Sept 12
8579	Dougherty F		90	C	Sept 12
8718	Durharse B	Cav	11	G	Sept 14
8828	Donnelly J		97	H	Sept 15
8887	Dean R	Cav	2	M	Sept 16
9109	Davidson C		90	G	Sept 18
9146	Driscoll N C		26	I	Sept 18
9191	Duffie J		52	F	Sept 18
9289	Delancy E		7	G	Sept 19
10004	Davidson G		12	K	Sept 29
10193	Dougherty M	Cav	3	D	Oct 2
10436	Durkale Jno	"	1	F	Oct 6
10917	Dalzell J G		139	I	Oct 14
11295	Derry Frederick		20	C	Oct 22
11350	Dichell Espy		55	D	Oct 23
11394	Dewitt M	Cav	1	E	Oct 24
11628	Davidson S		184	A	Oct 28
11988	Dickens Chas	Art	2	A	Oct 13
12136	Dalrysuffle J E		145	K	Oct 23
12399	Donley P		120	G	Jan 5 65
12575	Deeds J	Cav	13	H	Feb 2
11181	Dixon H		145	K	Oct 19 64
972	Ellers Henry	Cav	13	H	May 9
1081	Eisley Jno	"	18	K	May 14
1436	Engle Peter	"	14	K	May 28
2105	Elliott Jno	"	13	F	June 17
2794	Elliott J		69	D	July 2
3038	Erwin C		78	D	July 8
3052	Epsey Jas		145	H	July 9
3295	Elliott J P		103	D	July 14
3823	Ebright Benj	Cav	9	A	July 23
4278	Eaton Nat	Rifle	1	E	July 30
4761	Ellenberger P		145	D	Aug 5
5087	Ennies Andrew		145	K	Aug 15
6424	Ewetts Jas		103	G	Aug 22
6607	Ellis F		53	B	Aug 23
6872	Eckles E		77	E	Aug 26
6889	Ensley C		184	A	Aug 26
7300	Ellis H H	Cav	18	I	Aug 30
7657	Egan Jno		55	C	Sept 3
8006	Exline Jacob		55	K	Sept 7
8543	Eichnor C		143	F	Sept 12
8964	Earhman J		7	K	Sept 16
10009	Elfrey B S		7	K	Sept 29
10694	Elliott Jno H		83	D	Oct 11
10731	Erdibach C	Cav	5	B	Oct 11
10799	Ervingfelts Jacob		187	D	Oct 12
11834	Edgar W H		7	G	Nov 5
11838	Erebedier J		5	B	Nov 5
12001	Etters D		145	D	Nov 14
12673	Ebhart J		87	E	Feb 18 65
9490	English J C		100	K	Sept 21 64
200	Fluher Jno		73	D	Mar 28
511	Fich Jno		83	B	Apr 12
791	Fry L	Cav	4	D	Apr 28

260 LIST OF THE DEAD.

No.	Name		Reg.	Co.	Date
1010	Fuller H	"	13	H	May 10 64
1098	Fifer Chas		27	I	May 14
1431	Fry Alex	Cav	4	B	May 28
1728	Fink Peter		73	C	June 8
1937	Freeman W M	Art	2	A	June 14
2078	Fulton Thos A		103	H	June 17
2099	Friday S D		101	H	June 17
2147	Fish Chas W		101	B	June 18
2155	Farley Jas		54	F	June 18
2261	Fox Geo		78	E	June 21
2477	Flay L		26	G	June 25
2530	Funkhanna Jas		101	C	June 26
2537	Fatleam A		50	D	June 26
2594	Fagartus T		90	K	June 28
2853	Fancy Geo	Cav	13	F	July 4
3088	Ford M		53	K	July 19
3258	Fisher B M		101	H	July 13
3582	French A	Art	2	G	July 19
3742	Forsyth J	Cav	18	H	July 21
3870	Fingley Jno	Cav	14	D	July 24
4307	Flick L		184	G	July 30
4439	Filey J H		53	E	July 31
4452	Foreman G S	Cav	1	B	Aug 1
4521	Flashorse B	"	12	A	Aug 2
4586	Flynn M	"	13	B	Aug 2
4642	Fewer E		87	H	Aug 3
4668	File C		145	D	Aug 4
5062	Fish J		85		Aug 8
5172	Fleming W		97	E	Aug 9
5586	Flickinger Jno		50	B	Aug 14
5788	Ferry W		79	A	Aug 15
5873	Fee Geo M		103	G	Aug 16
6092	Faiss A		145	E	Aug 18
6134	Farman E		57	E	Aug 19
6155	Feltharsen		145	G	Aug 19
6180	Fatlenger F		53	K	Aug 19
6365	Fanen J F Reserve		7	G	Aug 21
6396	Finlaugh S	Cav	14	G	Aug 21
6649	Fox R		155	H	Aug 23
6675	Fritzman J W		18	K	Aug 24
6694	Finlin Thos		143	G	Aug 24
6681	Fuller G	Cav	2	A	Aug 26
6884	Frederick L		148	B	Aug 26
6890	French Jas		101	H	Aug 26
6892	Ford Thos		7	I	Aug 26
7041	Fullerton E		99	E	Aug 27
7097	Fester Jno		103	B	Aug 28
7169	Fisher W		54	I	Aug 29
7198	Fry		101	E	Aug 29
7375	Fitzgerald M		145	K	Sept 2
7588	Fahy Jno	Cav	13	B	Sept 2
7776	Fritz D	"	18	K	Sept 4
8006	Felter H M	"	13	K	Sept 6
8149	Fullerton J		118	I	Sept 8
8175	Fetterman J		48	H	Sept 8
8321	Francis N		69	G	Sept 10
8631	Fagan R		118	B	Sept 13
9062	Fisher C	Cav	4		Sept 17
9099	Floyd B		67	K	Sept 18
9232	Farr J C		107	H	Sept 19
9869	Faith Alex		183	C	Sept 27
10176	Fessenden N E		149	F	Oct 1
10408	Fingley S		14	B	Oct 6
10639	Fisher W		101	E	Oct 10
10667	Flynn S		76	C	Oct 11
10688	Free J		145	H	Oct 11
11026	Flemming J		97	E	Oct 16
11112	Flanney J		106	K	Oct 18 64
11164	Ferguson J R	Cav	11	D	Oct 19
11367	Fox M	"	8	H	Oct 23
11378	Frill D		55	C	Oct 24
11601	Ferguson Jno		134	A	Oct 28
11802	Frish H		115	E	Nov 4
11916	Freed S		53	B	Nov 8
11962	Fairbanks E		140	A	Nov 11
12000	Fagley C	Cav	14	I	Nov 14
12025	Forest S L		149	I	Nov 15
12207	Foster C W		76	B	Dec 1
12244	Falkenstine F		148	C	Dec 8
12336	Fruce J		52	A	Dec 26
12445	Fisk J		67	H	Jan 13 65
12605	Faile W D	Cav	20	A	Feb 7
71	Goodman Robt	"	13	M	Mar 19 64
131	Gesse Christian		54	F	Mar 23
314	Graffell Wm		73	B	Apr 2
529	Guley J		145	G	Apr 12
573	Green Wm	Cav	3	A	Apr 16
968	Garman B	"	18	E	Apr 9
1001	Greer J A	"	3	E	May 10
1008	Graham W J		4	C	May 10
1063	Goodman Henry		27	I	May 13
1302	Gray M		7	B	May 23
1373	Gilbert Jno		29	G	May 25
1399	Gilroy Berney		73	F	May 26
1528	Getts B		84	G	May 31
1649	Griffil G W	Cav	13	L	June 5
1761	Geest J W		57	I	June 9
1793	Gardner (negro)		8	F	June 10
1930	Gensle Jno	Cav	19	F	June 13
1939	Goerlt E		73	H	June 14
2060	Galliger F	Cav	13	B	June 16
2084	Gilmore Jas		110	E	June 17
2297	Gunn Alex	Cav	4	D	June 21
2356	Greenwald G		27	H	June 23
2531	Gumbert A		103	B	June 26
2587	Gettings J H	Rifle	1	C	June 28
2944	Gross Sam'l		51	E	July 6
2955	Gotwalt H		55	D	July 6
2988	Griffin J		103	I	July 7
2992	George A		149	G	July 7
2996	Gists H		103	H	July 7
3037	Gilleland Wm	Cav	14	B	July 8
3528	Gorsuch M A		110	B	July 18
3599	Gibbs E	Cav	18	K	July 19
4944	Gost W H	Cav	5	K	Aug 7
5422	Gregg T		139	K	Aug 12
5655	Gross Jno		62	K	Aug 14
5735	Gregg D		142	A	Aug 15
5737	Graham Wm		103	F	Aug 15
5803	Graham D	Cav	4	K	Aug 16
5881	Grouse G		145	C	Aug 16
5888	Gettenher D M		103	I	Aug 16
6006	Geand C	Cav	4	M	Aug 17
5288	Gladen A		21	C	Aug 11
6140	Garrett Jas		51	K	Aug 19
6158	Gunn J W		101	H	Aug 19
6384	Gamble O J		77	A	Aug 21
6389	Gallagher E		48	A	Aug 21
6897	Green J C	Cav	13	D	Aug 26
7223	Gibson D		56	A	Aug 29
7320	Graham J		56	B	Aug 30
7840	Geary D		184	G	Aug 30
7357	Groves A T		45	A	Aug 31

LIST OF THE DEAD.

No.	Name		Reg.	Co.	Date
7352	Glass Wm		55	C	Aug 31 64
7527	Griffith A		54	F	Sept 1
7589	Granger E H		55	C	Sept 2
7679	Geslin E H		4	G	Sept 3
7773	Giles C		7	K	Sept 4
7839	Gross G W		79	A	Sept 4
8109	Galbraith C		11	K	Sept 6
8311	Garrison W		8	K	Sept 10
8448	Gallagher Wm	Cav	5	F	Sept 11
8735	Griffin J C	"	5	D	Sept 14
9005	Gearhan S		142	C	Sept 17
9210	Griffin D		11	E	Sept 19
9326	Gilbert H		53	F	Sept 20
9437	Gorbay F J	Cav	19	M	Sept 21
9503	Goodman F		55	H	Sept 21
9764	Grubbs J		103	F	Sept 25
9776	Gibson J		11	D	Sept 26
9792	Glenn Wm		101	C	Sept 26
9811	Grear R		73	H	Sept 26
9966	Gilbert D		138	B	Sept 28
9989	Garrett F		139	G	Sept 29
10051	Gibson D G	Cav	16	A	Sept 30
10127	Gemperling Wm		79	A	Oct 1
10468	Grant M	Cav	18	I	Oct 7
10615	Griffin J		56	A	Oct 10
10706	Gimberling I		184	F	Oct 11
11060	Greathouse E		14	B	Oct 17
11197	Grabb M P		83	H	Oct 20
11299	Gilbert A F	Cav	14	F	Oct 20
11496	Grant J		6	E	Oct 26
11573	Ganse R		22	B	Oct 27
11806	Gordon R		65	F	Nov 4
11901	Green W S		12	I	Nov 7
12181	Giher P		73	H	Nov 27
12237	George F	Cav	19	D	Dec 6
12337	Garrety Thos		106	C	Jan 2 65
12411	Gates J	Cav	11	E	Jan
12432	Grunnell Jno		26	H	Jan 11
5843	Gillespie J		11	A	Aug 16 64
5118	Gibbons Wm		11	H	Aug 9
6228	Gallagher T		101	A	Aug 21
5971	Gray L		163	D	Aug 17
423	Hanson T R		119	E	April 7
470	Herbert Otto		73	A	April 9
555	Hoffmaster L		16	H	April 14
654	Hamilton J G	Cav	4	L	April 20
711	Hall J (negro)		8	E	April 24
769	Hessimer P		73	E	April 27
988	Hammons J	Art	3	A	May 10
990	Heager J		4	B	May 10
1080	Huff Arthur		54	F	May 14
1113	Hates Chas		2	H	May 15
1225	Henderson R	Cav	18	D	May 20
1311	Heckley M	"	2	M	May 23
1420	Hill H C		18	K	May 28
1483	Holtenstein G W C		18	I	May 30
1562	Henen Pat		145	E	June 2
1650	Hendricks N	Cav	4	D	June 5
1768	Holmes Rob't	"	12	H	June 9
2011	Hannah Thos	"	4	D	June 15
2153	Hammer P C	"	18	D	June 18
2189	Harts Jno		51	H	June 19
2387	Hooks T		103	D	June 24
2450	Hiler H		50	C	June 25
2551	Hammer Jno		73	G	June 27
2707	Howard Jas		83	I	June 30
2723	Henderson A		58	F	July 1
2786	Hollibaugh W		57	C	July 2 64
2800	Hastings J		118	D	July 2
2916	Homer D	Cav	13	F	July 5
3020	Holley E F		57	A	July 7
3201	Harrington Jno		55	C	July 12
2	Headley J D		18	G	Mar 15
3379	Height S C		55	H	July 16
3439	Hughes Jno		118	A	July 17
3525	Heenann Jno	Cav	14	F	July 18
3554	Hazlet J	"	4	G	July 18
3663	Hester I P		7	H	July 18
3626	Heth R		2	A	July 20
3785	Harrington J W	C	3	A	July 22
3792	Haller Peter		139	K	July 22
3836	Harvey P D		57	B	July 23
3853	Hollenbeck J A		55	B	July 24
3920	Hall Henry		53	H	July 25
3953	Haller A		73	A	July 25
4105	Hartlick C		99	E	July 27
4136	Hiffefinger V		14	K	July 28
4147	Hobbs A		141	H	July 28
4154	Hill P		101	B	July 28
4222	Hoover Jno	Cav	18	E	July 29
4332	Holland J		143	I	July 31
4370	Hilt Jno		73	I	July 31
4379	Hardinger W		147	B	July 31
4431	Hill Thos		18	L	July 31
4474	Hans Jno		116	K	Aug 1
4790	Haflinger J		91	C	Aug 5
4921	Hick G		12	G	Aug 6
5045	Haber C	Cav	14	B	Aug 8
5080	Hall		149	I	Aug 8
5082	Hunter L		63	C	Aug 8
5131	Hardis J L		11	A	Aug 9
5178	Harden M. Res Hme Gds			F	Aug 9
5281	Huffman Chas	Cav	7	K	Aug 11
5284	Hickey D C	"	3	C	Aug 11
5289	Hanson J		76	B	Aug 11
5486	Harder ——		184	C	Aug 13
5575	Hoffmaster G		20	F	Aug 14
5688	Heinbeck S		116	H	Aug 15
5954	Holinbeck D		101	E	Aug 17
6175	Honigan C		55	C	Aug 19
6302	Henry R W		4	H	Aug 20
6367	Hill J E	Cav	2	L	Aug 21
6481	Hollingworth J (neg)		8	A	Aug 22
6597	Hofmaster L		73	I	Aug 23
6635	Hazenfflucey J	Bat	26		Aug 23
6711	Hoch Jno		103	K	Aug 24
6752	Haden R		119	A	Aug 24
6792	Hogan Thos		103	K	Aug 25
6845	Hurling A		57	F	Aug 25
6910	Hammer Jno	Art	3	B	Aug 26
7000	Hoy J		101	F	Aug 27
7102	Houseman G		118	I	Aug 28
7286	Holloman Wm		102	G	Aug 30
7328	Hopes W	Art	2	A	Aug 30
7422	Havert B		52	I	Aug 31
7491	Halliger C		63	D	Sept 1
7531	Hill E		110		Sept 1
7537	Henry A B		103	E	Sept 2
7568	Hobson B F		7	G	Sept 2
7571	Harman Jno		14	H	Sept 2
7588	Harris A	Cav	2	K	Sept 2
7613	Homiker J		119	H	Sept 2
7661	Hockenbroch J	Art	2	F	Sept 3
7661	Hughes J	Cav	11	B	Sept 3

LIST OF THE DEAD.

No.	Name	Regt.	Co.	Date
7682	Hoover S P	7	H	Sept 3 64
7687	Hunter Chas	3	A	Sept 3
7881	Holmes S	140	B	Sept 5
7965	Hutton Jas	118	I	Sept 6
7990	Hazel Geo	Cav 2	D	Sept 6
8254	H cker G Reserves	6	C	Sept 9
8162	Henry O H	Cav 2	L	Sept 11
8326	Heselport J F	68	G	Sept 12
8532	Hopkins —	50	K	Sept 12
9088	Hensey —	90	C	Sept 18
9118	Hooker Wm	8	G	Sept 18
9123	Holdhaus C	63	E	Sept 18
9404	Houghbough J	143	D	Sept 21
9434	Hanks J	1	A	Sept 21
9433	Hartzel J	7	I	Sept 21
9532	Houston D	4	B	Sept 22
9579	Harmony J	109	H	Sept 23
9843	Heninshalt W	149	E	Sept 27
9884	Hibbane J	99	H	Sept 27
9934	Hughly Jno	69	D	Sept 27
10022	Hamilton B	183		Sept 29
10070	Holden Isaac	7	G	Sept 30
10109	Harper R	103	B	Sept 30
10239	Hicks J F	Cav 4	A	Oct 2
10349	Hammond J	10	D	Oct 5
10385	Hill S M	14	D	Oct 5
10430	Haldwell P	Cav 7	E	Oct 6
10448	Hiller S	64	D	Oct 7
10474	Howe M A	Cav 12	B	Oct 7
10538	Hand H	58		Oct 8
10571	Holden P	Cav 12	B	Oct 9
10574	Hayes J	"	15	G	Oct 9
10640	Hands J	106	A	Oct 10
10670	Hull Ed	77	G	Oct 11
10804	Hennessy P	49	H	Oct 12
10814	Hushbach J	116	G	Oct 12
10862	Hoberg A J	Cav 2	M	Oct 13
10903	Hannesay A	55	I	Oct 14
10906	Hall A	118	E	Oct 14
10952	Hoover S	79	G	Oct 14
10962	Huffman S	64	C	Oct 15
11033	Happy G	101	K	Oct 16
11092	Harty Jas	148	I	Oct 18
11113	Horton S	106	I	Oct 18
11183	Hess G	118	D	Oct 19
11194	Hepsey M	73	K	Oct 20
11383	Hunter T	Cav 5	M	Oct 24
11431	Hart J	7	I	Oct 26
11219	Hunter J	Cav 14	M	Oct 26
11495	Hardinwick J	2	C	Oct 28
11609	Hosaflock H A	Cav 6	E	Oct 28
11643	Hacket J	30	D	Oct 30
11702	Hoover J	90	A	Oct 31
11799	Hagerty W R	7	G	Nov 4
11897	Hart M	11	K	Nov 7
12215	Hyatt J F	118	F	Dec 3
12260	Healy J B	100	M	Dec 11
12306	Hammond W	20	K	Dec 18
12610	Heneman E L	5	C	Feb 7 65
12632	Healey J	143	K	Feb 10
12719	Hummell J	87	B	Mar 2 64
7020	Hazen M J	101	H	Aug 22
3474	Hall B	105	F	July 17
10227	Haman I	118	E	Oct 1
124	Isheart N	Cav 18	G	Mar 23
1491	Illy Tobias	27	C	May 27
10405	Irvin T	Cav 15	M	Oct 8
10316	Ireton S R	138	I	Oct 10 64
11560	Irwin W	184	A	Oct 27
831	Ingersoll Sam	3	D	May 1
233	Johnson Jno J	45	I	Mar 29
463	Johnson Chas	90	C	Apr 1 9
565	Johnson Jno	Cav 2	G	April 15
570	Jacobs Jacob	"	2	M	April 9
1308	Jones Wm	145	A	May 23
1595	Jones J	147	C	June 3
1840	Jones Wm	26	C	June 11
2108	Jones O	Cav 4	D	June 17
2312	Johnston Wm Art	3	A	June 22
2593	Jones R	103	D	June 28
2914	Jordan D W	108	B	July 5
3199	Johnson D	45	I	July 18
3510	Jennings H	45	G	July 18
3885	Jones Wm	55	C	July 24
4037	John Thomas	54	E	July 27
4093	Jones J	79	A	July 27
4540	Johnson J W	50	G	Aug 2
4590	Jamesou Wm	103	H	Aug 3
4817	Johns Rob't	101	I	Aug 5
5295	Johnson H	Art 2	I	Aug 11
5516	Jacobs B G	150	F	Aug 13
5871	Jones Rob't	100	A	Aug 16
6197	Jones T	101	I	Aug 19
6200	Jones W E	27	B	Aug 19
6317	Jones S	49	G	Aug 22
6760	Joslin J	145	I	Aug 25
6817	Jober J	77	B	Aug 25
6931	Jurmter C	7	A	Aug 26
7566	Johnson Chas	53	G	Sept 2
8318	Johnson J	45	I	Sept 10
8853	Jolly Jas	101	H	Sept 15
9303	Jones P	63	F	Sept 20
9351	Jordan J M	149	D	Sept 20
9378	Jacobs J S	Cav 6	F	Sept 20
9982	Jeffries C	4	B	Sept 29
9999	Jones T	101	B	Sept 29
10735	Jabin Jas	55	E	Oct 11
10987	Jones A	27	D	Oct 16
11058	Johnson Wm	184	D	Oct 17
11430	Jordan Thos	148		Oct 24
11539	Jenks J C	115	H	Oct 27
12007	Johnson L	118	C	Nov 4
12331	Jack J P	7	E	Dec 24
2880	Johnson A G	103	I	July 4
2	Kelly Chas H	71	H	Mch 1
238	Kelly H S	Cav 13	H	Mar 30
266	Kuntzelman J	63	E	Mar 31
1024	Kenny Wm	12	F	May 11
1824	Kyle Wm	5	H	June 10
1875	Kelly Peter	73		June 12
2076	Knight Jno	Cav 7	K	June 17
2335	Kehoe Moses	8	H	June 22
2639	Kenoan M A	Cav 14	L	June 29
3048	King C	6	C	July 8
3187	Kiech N	54	A	July 12
3265	Klink A	101	C	July 13
3471	Kemp E	103	A	July 17
3634	Keeston E	103	I	July 20
4162	Kagman J T	45	B	July 28
4293	Kuffman S D	45	E	July 30
4545	Kauf J	Art 2	B	Aug 2
4895	Kelley O F	148	B	Aug 6
5058	Kock H	21	H	Aug 8
5145	Kawell Jno	Cav 18	E	Aug 9

LIST OF THE DEAD. 263

No.	Name	Reg	Co	Date
5154	Keyes Alex C	Cav 16	H	Aug 9 64
5208	Kester L	149	F	Aug 10
5443	Kelley T	Cav 13	H	Aug 12
5851	Kahn R	96	K	Aug 13
5718	Keister Jno M	103	A	Aug 15
5744	Keeley Wm	Cav 13	A	Aug 15
6028	Kauffman B F	45	K	Aug 18
6084	Kemper J	73	D	Aug 18
6459	Kiger Wm	Cav 3	C	Aug 22
6197	Kenter A W	67	B	Aug 22
6344	Kniver S	184	F	Aug 22
6338	Krigle H	11	K	Aug 23
6985	Krader W O	55	H	Aug 27
7005	King M	Cav 3	A	Aug 27
7372	Koller A	9	M	Aug 31
7753	Keller M	105	G	Sept 1
7781	Kyle Wm	118	F	Sept 7
8210	Kinsman F P	184	F	Sept 8
8734	Kanford Jno C S m C 5			Sept 14
8799	Kaufman J	45	E	Sept 17
9139	Kipp W	Cav 12	D	Sept 18
9563	Kinmick T	145	K	Sept 23
9630	Kearney L	50	F	Sept 24
10335	Kerr B	149	B	Oct 4
10307	Kirby J A	101	E	Oct 5
10439	Kline Ross	184	F	Oct 6
10502	Kennedy J	152	A	Oct 8
10698	King M	11	K	Oct 11
10747	Kirkwood H	101	C	Oct 11
10926	Knieper C	89	F	Oct 14
11238	Kurtz J	55	K	Oct 21
11332	King J R	55	K	Oct 23
11381	Kelley E	Cav 7	F	Oct 24
11463	King R	6	E	Oct 25
11645	Kramer Geo	116	G	Oct 30
12695	Knox J	184	A	Feb 23 65
8676	Kerer H N	63	E	July 20 64
88	Liesen Lewis	Cav 13	A	Mch 21
243	Lancaster E	14	F	Mch 30
297	Luck W	11	H	April 1
549	Lynch Adam	6	L	April 14
1403	Levy Frank	3	H	May 27
1429	Liesine Wm	13	E	May 28
1579	Lindline J	Art 3	A	June 3
1588	Little M	106	F	June 3
1621	Luhaus Melter	145	A	June 4
2250	Lackey Jas	182	D	June 21
2379	Leach J	Cav 3	D	June 23
3031	Larimer J	11	E	July 9
3734	Ladbeater Jas	7	K	July 21
3305	Link P	98	H	July 14
3306	Long A	118	H	July 14
3363	Linigan N	Cav 13	L	July 15
3403	Lewis Ed	101	I	July 16
3448	Leonard Geo	49	G	July 17
3489	Logan B	90	B	July 17
3545	Lee Jas	Cav 13	B	July 18
4312	Long D F B	101	I	July 30
4434	Lambert W	Cav 4	K	July 31
4606	Larrison Wallace C 14		C	Aug 4
4818	Lewis A	Cav 3	D	Aug 5
4857	Laughlin J	101	E	Aug 6
4907	Lahman C	73	C	Aug 6
4929	Livingston J K	2	B	Aug 6
5199	Long Augustus	55	H	Aug 10
5225	Loudin H N	14	H	Aug 10
5314	Lacock H gh	116	E	Aug 11
6252	Lodiss H	90	A	Aug 20 64
6636	Leach Jas	49	E	Aug 23
6783	Light S	143	H	Aug 25
7145	LaBelt J	21	F	Aug 29
7938	Lemon Jno E	Cav 4	I	Sept 6
7950	Lockhard J	145	B	Sept 8
8415	Lepley Chas	103	E	Sept 10
8754	Layman F	49	B	Sept 10
8823	Laughlin J L	1	H	Sept 15
8895	Lester W H	Cav 7	I	Sept 16
8904	Lippoch J	5	E	Sept 16
9085	Logne S	26	A	Sept 18
9291	Leery C	83	K	Sept 19
9647	Loden J	Cav 4	C	Sept 24
10046	Laytin P	110	D	Sept 30
10086	Lutz P M	21	G	Sept 30
10091	Lebos C	116	D	Sept 30
10273	Limar W	140		Oct 3
10298	Long W	67	G	Oct 4
10372	Long P	Cav 11	C	Oct 5
10548	Lancaster C	119	B	Oct 8
10572	Lynch W J	Cav 3	I	Oct 9
10580	Labor R	7	F	Oct 10
10687	Luchford R	143	F	Oct 11
10873	Lang I	110	C	Oct 13
11604	Leuchlier J	5		Oct 16
11255	Lantz Wm	7	C	Oct 21
11465	Lewis J	Cav 4	L	Oct 26
11728	Luther I	4	L	Nov 1
11869	Lego Geo	12	A	Nov 6
11907	Ladd A	53	M	Nov 7
12192	Lape J	18	K	Nov 28
12210	Lewis D S	53	K	Dec 2
12489	Linsey D	77	G	Jan 19 65
5699	Ledwick F M	139	C	Aug 15 64
7084	Latchem David	Cav 4	K	Aug 25
7307	Lochery A	14	E	Aug 30
5985	Logan W	97	A	Aug 17
6030	Loudon S	101	A	Aug 18
5055	Luyton Samuel	181	A	Aug 18
6071	Lamb C	71	B	Aug 18
6282	Lane Amos	Cav 6	E	Aug 18
6152	Lehnich Jno	Art 2	F	Aug 19
753	Lenard M	Cav 13	D	April 24
761	Lord G W	141	E	April 27
871	Loudon Samuel	2	F	May 4
183	Maynard Jno	105	G	Mar 27
208	Missile Val	47	C	Mar 28
225	Miller Daniel	Cav 13	H	Mar 29
361	Martin J F	14	K	April 2
461	McEntre W	51	F	April 9
538	Mine Josh	54	F	April 14
586	Marple S L	14	A	April 17
605	McKissick Jno	23	F	April 18
667	Myers G	Cav 1	E	April 22
736	McKeever E L	71	F	April 25
773	McDonald R	24	C	April 28
780	McCarthy Jas	Cav 18	E	April 28
969	McQueeny W	79	B	May 9
1006	Meyer Jno	Cav 2	E	May 10
1128	McKey J	1	E	May 15
1139	McMahon J	73	F	May 16
1147	McKnight J E	57	B	May 16
1151	McHale J	Cav 14	D	May 16
1185	Moser Jno	13	B	May 18
1273	McCollen W	4	L	May 22
1287	Midgau J	61	F	May 22

LIST OF THE DEAD.

1308	McCartney M		73	B	May 23 64	5704	Miller Jno		101	G Aug 15 64
1460	Murray Jno	Cav	13	E	May 29	5723	McCann Jno	Art	3	A Aug 15
1586	Miles Lewis	"	4	I	June 3	5781	Miller S		143	B Aug 15
1643	Myers J R	"	13	M	June 5	5809	Montgomery R		62	A Aug 16
1722	Marshall M M		78	E	June 8	5868	McQuillen A	Art	6	L Aug 16
1748	Moyer Thos		103	E	June 9	5893	McCuller S	Cav	4	B Aug 16
1792	Miller M		118	A	June 10	5926	Mulchey J A		50	D Aug 17
1858	McHose J	Cav	4	E	June 12	5988	Mann Jas		119	G Aug 17
1907	Miller Henry		8	G	June 13	6014	McPherson D		103	F Aug 17
1982	Muchollans J		101	K	June 15	6088	Moore C		103	G Aug 18
2056	Monny W H	Cav	3	A	June 16	6148	McCracker J		53	K Aug 19
2058	Matchell J J		101	K	June 16	6294	McLaughlin Jas	C	4	A Aug 20
2159	Monan J		101	C	June 19	6441	McWilliams H		92	I Aug 22
2265	McCutchen J	Cav	4	C	June 21	5480	Martin Jno		103	D Aug 22
2278	Milton Wm	"	19	H	June 21	6532	McGan J	Cav	18	Aug 23
2333	Myers F		27	H	June 22	6664	McKee —		144	C Aug 24
2364	Myers Peter		76	G	June 23	6689	Manner M		73	K Aug 24
2388	Morton T		79	I	June 24	6910	McGlann H		143	B Aug 26
2409	McCabe J	Cav	3	L	June 24	6925	McGuigan H	C	7	K Aug 26
2411	McKay M J		103	B	June 24	7026	Marks P		143	B Aug 27
2493	Mrry Jas		67	E	June 26	7061	Moore M J		107	Aug 28
2509	Martin A J	Cav	4	E	June 26	7107	Moyer Wm H		55	H Aug 28
2508	Morris J	"	18	A	June 26	7119	Miller Jno L		53	K Aug 28
2653	McManes —		77	B	June 29	7127	McAffee Jas		72	F Aug 28
2684	Mipes J		101	B	June 30	7175	Moore Thos		69	D Aug 29
2690	Morris G		77	G	June 30	7263	Martin Jno		77	C Aug 30
2798	Marsh D		50	D	July 2	7265	Musser Juo		77	D Aug 30
2831	McCane Chas		14	C	July 3	7305	Moser S		103	E Aug 30
3017	McRath J		48	C	July 7	7333	Morris Jno		183	G Aug 30
3065	Morris Calvin		53	D	July 9	7407	Marchin Wm		50	E Aug 31
3133	McCalasky J E	Cav	4	K	July 10	7512	Millinger Jno H		7	C Sept 1
3151	Mattiser B		57	F	July 11	7602	Moorhead J S		103	D Sept 2
3172	Madden Daniel		149	G	July 11	7719	Myers H		9	A Sept 3
3250	Myers M		103	E	July 13	7875	Mayer W		8	M Sept 5
3374	Mink H	Art	3	A	July 16	7925	Mays N J		103	H Sept 5
3467	Meaker E N		155	H	July 17	8027	Murphy A	Cav	13	I Sept 6
3481	McKeon Jno		101	H	July 17	8047	McKnight J	Cav	18	I Sept 6
3488	Mihan J		138	D	July 17	8122	Miller J		101	C Sept 8
3939	Maroney Jno	Cav	1	D	July 20	8123	Mullings W		145	G Sept 8
3690	McCarron J	Cav	4	A	July 21	8128	Munager W	Cav	13	L Sept 8
3766	Myers Jno		116	D	July 22	8134	Mehaffey J M	Cav	16	B Sept 8
3971	Murtin G		45	I	July 25	8153	McCantley W	Art	2	A Sept 8
4016	McDermott J M		70	F	July 26	8158	McLane T		12	E Sept 8
4123	McGee Jas		103	I	July 28	8194	McKink J		119	D Sept 8
4197	Moore M G	Art	1	A	July 29	8216	Mansfield J		101	K Sept 8
4141	Marquet M		6	M	July 30	8322	Myers A		118	I Sept 10
4407	McKever Jno		100	A	July 31	8469	Magill H		103	I Sept 11
4414	McFarland Jas		55	E	July 31	8596	Morrison J		146	E Sept 12
4546	Moan Jas		101	K	Aug 2	8627	McKinney D		90	C Sept 13
4607	Martin Bryant		7	F	Aug 3	8691	Moritze A		118	D Sept 14
4635	McKeral Jas		14	K	Aug 3	8802	McCullogh —		101	E Sept 15
4710	Mathews C W		145	B	Aug 4	9071	Maynard A	Art	3	Sept 17
4734	Moore		71	I	Aug 4	9090	McCall Wm	Cav	22	B Sept 18
4796	McDevitt J	Art	3	D	Aug 5	9228	McCullough S		138	K Sept 19
4824	Miller H	Cav	14	I	Aug 5	9270	Mayhan F	Cav	20	Sept 19
4876	Mills Wm		150	G	Aug 6	9315	Marsh W		149	K Sept 20
4898	Muldany M		96	K	Aug 6	9339	Meyers J A		138	C Sept 20
5068	Martain Jno		103	E	Aug 8	9526	McQuigley Jno		101	C Sept 22
5069	Mensler Jas		103	E	Aug 8	9583	Mead H J		184	B Sept 23
5139	McCaffrey Jno. h s	Art	3 A	Aug 9		9598	Martin J	Cav	17	C Sept 23
5159	Martin C	Cav	8	A	Aug 9	9644	Morris J		54	I Sept 24
5266	Marcy H F		103	F	Aug 10	9646	Morgan J E		2	A Sept 24
5291	Mohr J R		14	G	Aug 11	9651	McCook B		118	A Sept 24
5415	McCarty Dennis		101	K	Aug 12	9761	McMurray Wm	C	1	I Sept 25
5433	McGee J		14	H	Aug 12	9871	Mason Jno		112	A Sept 27
5595	Mickelson B	Cav	16	B	Aug 14	4578	McKerner S		73	E Aug 2
5642	McClough L C		18	C	Aug 14	10050	Mesin Jas		90	F Sept 30

LIST OF THE DEAD.

No.	Name	Regt.	Co.	Date
10060	Morgan C	45	A	Sept 30 64
10119	Mc Clany J	101	C	Oct 1
10154	Mc Elroy Wm	Cav 13	L	Oct 1
10306	Meese J	48	A	Oct 4
10396	Mc Graw Jno	Art 3	A	Oct 6
10407	Miller H	79	K	Oct 6
10486	Miller Wash'gton	C 18	C	Oct 7
10610	Mc Kearney J W	118	K	Oct 10
10620	Mc Clief Wm	7	A	Oct 10
10641	Marker W H	118	D	Oct 10
10678	Martin J P	7	I	Oct 11
10684	Miller Jas	7	I	Oct 11
10803	Mattis Aaron	138		Oct 12
10825	Moore C H	Cav 13	C	Oct 13
10929	Martin Geo H	108	I	Oct 14
10981	Maxwell S	Cav 14	B	Oct 15
10991	Moses W	16	H	Oct 16
10993	Mc Knight Jas	118	K	Oct 16
11081	Mitchell J O	55	H	Oct 18
11142	Mansfield Geo	101	I	Oct 19
11229	Mc Clay J H	Cav 11	D	Oct 20
11305	Mc Bride —	2	H	Oct 22
11326	Marshall L	184	A	Oct 23
11387	Moore S	101	F	Oct 24
11459	Moore J	Cav 13	B	Oct 25
11461	Mc Nelse J H	100	E	Oct 26
11512	Miller F	54	K	Oct 27
11655	Midz J	Cav 20	A	Oct 30
11658	Menk W	12	F	Oct 30
11683	Morrow J C, S't Maj	101	E	Oct 31
11684	Mc Cann J	Cav 11	L	Oct 31
11686	Moore W	184	B	Oct 31
11692	Mulligan J	7	H	Oct 31
11909	Mc Cune J	67	E	Nov 8
11913	Mc Clush N	97	E	Nov 8
11982	Manee M	53	H	Nov 13
12006	Mc Cray J	145	A	Nov 14
12088	Maher D	118	E	Nov 18
12103	Miller W	31	I	Nov 22
12248	Murray W	Cav 14	H	Dec 8
12326	Mc Intire J	55	C	Dec 24
12334	Myers A D	52	A	Dec 26
12554	Matthews J	Cav 6	F	Jan 30 65
12595	Maloy J M	184	D	Feb 5
12625	Mc Genger J	20	C	Feb 9
12696	Myers H	87	E	Feb 23
12771	Mc Donald —	9	G	Mar 13
12806	Mc Garrett R W	103	F	Feb 21
1134	Nicholson Jno	Cav 3	H	May 16 64
1298	Nelson Wm	76	H	May 23
2832	Nolti Wm	6	F	July 3
3653	Newell G S	183	A	July 20
4246	Nicholson W	Cav 1	H	July 29
4489	Nelson Geo	2	K	Aug 1
4936	Naylor G W	Cav 13	L	Aug 7
5109	Nichols D A	125	D	Aug 9
6001	Neal H G	90	B	Aug 17
6011	Nickle C	37	G	Aug 17
6702	Nickem Jas	77	G	Aug 24
8154	Naylor S	Cav 20	H	Sept 8
8907	Noble J	73	D	Sept 16
9424	Nice Isaac	11	L	Sept 21
9468	Neff J	Cav 4	D	Sept 21
10146	Nelson G	55	A	Oct 1
10286	Nelson J A	145	G	Oct 4
10764	Newberry Jno	Cav 20	A	Oct 12
11107	Nelson A	160	E	Oct 18
11254	Noble Thos	Cav 19	G	Oct 21 64
11776	Nichols G	20	C	Nov 3
414	Osbourne S K	4	K	April 7
622	Oglesby J	Cav 4	K	April 19
1318	O'Brien P	13	A	May 23
1409	Ottinger I	Cav 8	I	May 27
1817	O'Neil Jno		69	June 12
2589	Oswald Stephen	55	G	June 28
3161	O'Conor —	83		July 11
3199	O'Neil J	63	I	July 12
3704	Olmar H	Cav 2	H	July 21
3861	O'Counor H	49	E	July 24
4161	Owens G H	7	A	July 28
5119	Offlebach Z	90	K	Aug 9
5184	Oliver W	103	D	Aug 9
5939	O'Hara M	101	E	Aug 17
6254	O'Connell Wm	183	G	Aug 20
6535	O'Hara Jno	150	E	Aug 23
6658	Oiler Sam	103	G	Aug 24
6908	O'Rourke Chas	109	C	Aug 26
7105	Otto Jno	Cav 5	B	Aug 28
9330	Owens E	50	D	Aug 20
10805	Osborn E	Cav 11	A	Oct 13
30	Peck Albert	57	K	Mar 9
62	Patterson Rob	Res 2	E	Mar 18
125	Parker Jas M	76	B	Mar 23
500	Petrisky H	54	F	April 12
1110	Patterson T	Cav 3	A	May 15
1119	Patent Thos	73	G	May 15
1258	Powell Wm	Cav 14	D	May 21
1556	Powers Jno	26	I	June 2
1750	Preso Thos	26	E	June 9
1884	Powell Frank	18		June 12
2566	Page J	183	G	June 27
2500	Porter David	101	H	June 28
2903	Parsons J T	103	D	July 5
3197	Painter J G	26	F	July 11
3445	Painter S	63	A	July 17
4019	Patterson R	101	H	July 27
4157	Pickett J C	Cav 3	A	July 28
4177	Pratt F	14	I	July 28
4191	Plymeer W	20	B	July 28
4415	Page Jno	112	A	July 31
4473	Powell H	102	H	Aug 1
5323	Prosser J	63		Aug 11
5579	Pyers Isaac	72	G	Aug 14
5610	Phillips Jas B	101	I	Aug 14
5947	Parish J A	184		Aug 17
6341	Preans H	149	K	Aug 21
6439	Palmer H	140	D	Aug 22
6527	Poole G	52	B	Aug 22
6536	Pifer M	13	G	Aug 23
6574	Phillips J W	Cav 1	F	Aug 23
6843	Peterson G	103	D	Aug 23
6841	Penn Jno	Cav 5	E	Aug 25
6885	Patten H W	Art 2	F	Aug 26
7118	Potts Edw	183	H	Aug 28
7232	Perkins N	103	D	Aug 29
8030	Powell A T	149	C	Sept 6
8100	Pricht F	87	H	Sept 8
8763	Peck C W	145	H	Sept 14
8877	Perrill Frederick	101		Sept 15
9220	Palmer A	143	D	Sept 19
9684	Perego W	143	G	Sept 24
9754	Phipps J H	57	E	Sept 26
10074	Price G	106	H	Sept 30
10573	Penstock A	144	B	Oct 9

LIST OF THE DEAD.

No.	Name	Regt.	Co.	Date
10358	Powell I	101	I	Oct 13 64
11168	Price O	109	C	Oct 19
11261	Phay M	60	C	Oct 21
11637	Phillins F	61	K	Oct 28
11737	Pees M T	145	H	Nov 2
11833	Penn J	Cav 18	I	Nov 6
11918	Phelps W	" 4	G	Nov 8
11328	Porterfield J K	" 5	M	Oct 23
12075	Pencer W	18	C	Nov 18
12191	Pryor Wm	11	C	Nov 28
12359	Poleman H	Cav 1	F	Dec 30
12378	Perry H	121	C	Jan 2 65
12338	Pritchett J	72	C	Jan 8
12479	Potter B F	148	I	Jan 17
6756	Quinby L C	76	E	Aug 24 64
47	Reed Sam	Cav 4	D	Mar 15
126	Robertson J	119	K	Mar 23
132	Rosenburg Henry	49	G	Mar 24
171	Reign Jno	83	K	Mar 26
308	Richpder A	13	B	April 2
610	Ray Wm	Cav 8	F	April 18
817	Rhinehart J	" 3	D	May 3
895	Russell F	4	D	May 3
907	Rhinebolt J	Cav 18	I	May 5
940	Robinson C W	150	E	May 7
1152	Rendall H	Cav 4	H	May 16
1218	Rigney Chas	" 4	G	May 19
1151	Raleigh A	51	G	May 29
1485	Rudolph S	Cav 13	K	May 30
1599	Rhine Geo	63	I	June 4
1624	Rosenburg H	Cav 13	H	June 4
1719	Raymond Jno	" 18	H	June 8
1803	Rheems A	73	I	June 10
1833	Ramsay J D	103	F	June 11
1922	Rush S	18	G	June 14
1942	Robinson Wm	77	D	June 14
2225	Roush Peter	101	E	June 20
2538	Rupert F	Cav 2	H	June 26
2602	Roat J	54	F	June 28
2735	Rhoades F	79	E	July 1
2911	Rock J E	5	M	July 5
2979	Cogart Jno	Cav 13	E	July 7
2103	Ray A	77	E	July 17
3024	Rugh M J	103	D	July 7
3270	Robins R	69	B	July 13
3458	Ransom H	148	I	July 17
3927	Rinner L	Cav 5	A	July 23
4074	Ringwalk J F	79	H	July 27
4241	Roger L	115	L	July 29
4309	Rogers C	73	C	July 30
4476	Ray Jas R	184	B	Aug 1
4507	Riese S	103	B	Aug 1
4841	Richie Jas	103	B	Aug 6
4940	Ruther J	Art 2	F	Aug 7
5319	Rice Sam'l	101	K	Aug 11
5389	Ross David	103	B	Aug 12
5430	Robinson John	99	D	Aug 12
5537	Rose B	13	I	Aug 13
5800	Robins J	Cav 2	M	Aug 15
5879	Rider H	" 7	L	Aug 16
5894	Richards E	143	E	Aug 16
5912	Reese Jacob	103	B	Aug 17
5940	Richards Jno	Cav 1	G	Aug 17
6321	Robbins G	106	G	Aug 21
6373	Roger Jno L	110	H	Aug 21
6520	Reynolds J	14	H	Aug 22
6725	Rowe E	103	A	Aug 24
6777	Rangardener J	149	H	Aug 25 64
6789	Richards G	Cav 13	A	Aug 25
6790	Runels Jno	" 6	L	Aug 25
6822	Rum A	188	C	Aug 25
6838	Reese D	148	K	Aug 25
6896	Raiff T	1	A	Aug 26
6933	Richardson —	61		Aug 26
7067	Reese D	143	F	Aug 28
7202	Ruff J	103	F	Aug 29
7292	Redmire H	98	B	Aug 30
7293	Robins Geo	62	A	Aug 30
7410	Richardson H	103	K	Aug 31
7467	Richard D	Cav 18	D	Sept 1
7716	Rice E	7	B	Sept 3
7738	Roads Frederick	101	E	Sept 3
8139	Rathburn K	2	F	Sept 8
8540	Russell S A	79	A	Sept 12
8545	Ray A	149	D	Sept 12
8602	Richards J	106	H	Sept 12
8635	Rhangmen G	138	D	Sept 13
8742	Root D	48	B	Sept 14
9019	Ret Geo	18	A	Sept 17
9272	Ramsay J I	149		Sept 19
9585	Richie H	11	F	Sept 3
9599	Renamer W E	87	H	Sept 23
9612	Richards Jno	113	D	Sept 23
9653	Reed R	103	A	Sept 24
9706	Ramsay R	84	D	Sept 25
9882	Richards J	53	K	Sept 27
10174	Reed J	55	A	Oct 1
10863	Ramsay Wm	87	B	Oct 13
1 622	Reedy E T	87	B	Oct 10
10935	Roundabush H B	51	A	Oct 14
10947	Rockwell A	Cav 2	L	Oct 14
11071	Raoff J B	72	E	Oct 17
11115	Rinkle Jno A	20	A	Oct 18
11293	Rolston J	18	F	Oct 22
11147	Rudy J	13	F	Oct 19
11444	Rifle S G	189	C	Oct 25
11566	Richardson A	144	E	Oct 27
11808	Rowland N	111	F	Nov 6
12008	Rapp A E	Cav 18	I	Nov 15
12048	Ruth B S	23	I	Nov 16
12206	Rothe C	101	A	Dec 1
12355	Reese D	7	A	Dec 29
12372	Reed W S	128	H	Jan 1 65
377	Smith M D	18	B	April 5 64
788	Smith Geo	Cav 5	H	April 28
881	Smith Wm	4	A	May 4
882	Smith T	19	G	May 4
921	Steffler W J	Cav 12	G	May 6
1011	Serend H	" 4	D	May 10
1030	Shebert Gotlieb	73	C	May 11
1058	Spilyfiter A	51	F	May 13
1105	Sullivan D	101	K	May 15
1114	Shindle S R	140	K	May 15
1155	Stearnes E K	Cav 14	A	May 16
1169	Sloat D	76	I	May 16
1175	Scott Wm	4	B	May 16
1216	Severn C	139	A	May 19
1256	Sammoris B	Cav 2	B	May 21
1349	Smith Chas	26	A	May 24
1453	Schlerbough C	Cav 4	G	May 29
1508	Smith Martin	" 18	H	May 31
1535	Stone Samuel	26	F	June 1
1543	Shoemaker M	Cav 13	H	June 1
1605	Swearer G	13	H	June 4

LIST OF THE DEAD.

No.	Name	Regt.	Co.	Date
1620	Schiefeit Jacob	54	F	June 4 64
1632	Schmar R	45	F	June 5
1963	Smith D	Cav 11	H	June 14
2039	Slough H	53		June 15
2070	Stevens A	Cav 13	M	June 16
2121	Sherwood C H	" 4	M	June 17
2123	Stall Sam'l	75	D	June 17
2126	Say J R	Cav 4	K	June 17
2163	Steele J S	" 7	F	June 19
2259	Scoles M	27	K	June 21
2331	Sims B	Cav 14	G	June 22
2412	Shop Jacob	2	M	June 24
2622	Springer Jno	101	E	June 28
2650	Stewart J B	103	A	June 29
2725	Scott Allen	150	H	July 1
2738	Schingert J	73	G	July 1
2791	Shimer J A	Cav 13	A	July 2
2864	Scott Wm. (negro)	8	D	July 4
2905	Stump A	11	I	July 5
2941	Smith Jacob	51	H	July 6
2982	Shaw W	140	B	July 7
2999	Smulley Jno	112	K	July 7
3057	Sutton R M	103	I	July 9
3113	Sweet H	57	K	July 10
3136	Shoemaker M	148	G	July 10
3154	Sillers Wm	77	D	July 11
3214	Stone W F	53	G	July 12
3480	Swelser J	103	D	July 17
3567	Smalley L	58	K	July 19
3568	Stevens S G	150	H	July 19
3586	Sickles Daniel	116	K	July 19
3632	Serders J S	142	K	July 20
3670	Stopper Wm	16	B	July 20
3763	Stillenberger F	172	F	July 22
3775	Stance D	11	H	July 22
3855	Smith J	79	F	July 24
3906	Smith O C	77	G	July 24
3956	Seik A	141	D	July 25
3960	Sullivan T	77	F	July 25
4006	Smith F	64	K	July 26
4000	Shafer J H	81	E	July 26
4012	Shapley Geo	103	G	July 26
4043	Strickley C	53	H	July 27
4064	Shriveley E S	Cav 19	M	July 27
4113	Sheppard E	145	G	July 28
4164	Smith S W	101	B	July 28
4213	Shaffer Peter	52	F	July 29
4223	Shister F	Cav 3	A	July 29
4228	Stein J	7	G	July 29
4274	Sloan J	11	E	July 29
4285	Shone P	Cav 4	D	July 30
4345	Stobbs W W	101	E	July 30
4348	Scott A	22	F	July 31
4351	Scundler J	67	A	July 31
4372	Smith P	72	C	July 31
4566	Sale Thos	15	M	Aug 2
4775	Shink Jas	81	F	Aug 5
4791	Sullivan Ed	67	H	Aug 5
4797	Sear C	Cav 14	L	Aug 5
4845	Shember Jno	" 11	D	Aug 6
4928	Slicker J	77	D	Aug 6
4931	Sheit P	61	G	Aug 7
4945	Swartz P	27	I	Aug 7
5160	Stiner Jno	Cav 22	G	Aug 9
5189	Striker F	" 14	C	Aug 9
5215	Sworeland Wm	184	A	Aug 10
5232	Speck A	118	A	Aug 10
5411	Shaffer Daniel	Cav 13	F	Aug 12 64
5529	Spangrost A	103	D	Aug 12
5437	Shears J S	149	K	Aug 12
5463	Stibbs W	56	H	Aug 13
5494	Shape F	Cav 18	A	Aug 13
5603	Somerfield W	69	E	Aug 14
5700	St'nebach A	150	C	Aug 15
5750	Spears W M	Cav 2	K	Aug 15
5874	Sheppard N	79	F	Aug 16
5965	Shultz F	Cav 13	K	Aug 17
6205	Shoop G	103	K	Aug 19
6289	Smith H	26	K	Aug 20
6337	Smith W	Cav 18	B	Aug 21
6382	Swager M	101	F	Aug 21
6436	Spain Thos	118	H	Aug 22
6523	Stover J	49	F	Aug 22
6526	Stahler S	149	G	Aug 22
6534	Snyder Jno	118	C	Aug 23
6584	Sloate E	50	D	Aug 23
6595	Shirley Henry	105	I	Aug 23
6669	Sherwood P	84	I	Aug 24
6776	Shellito R	150	C	Aug 25
6823	Spain Richard	118	H	Aug 25
6829	Sturgess W A	79	G	Aug 25
6880	Stuler D	Cav 4	A	Aug 26
7029	Strickler J W	11	F	Aug 27
7106	Smith Jno F	55	C	Aug 28
7137	Sloan J M	Cav 18	D	Aug 28
7141	Springer J	113	F	Aug 29
7262	Shriver B	Cav 18	K	Aug 30
7302	Singer J	Art 2	A	Aug 30
7358	Scoleton J	53	F	Aug 31
7363	Sweeney D	Cav 14	E	Aug 31
7379	Scott W B	" 4	D	Aug 31
7631	Streetman J	7	E	Sept 2
7638	Steele J	62	M	Sept 2
7648	Spencer Geo	20	C	Sept 3
7662	Snyder M S	183	A	Sept 3
7705	Swartz Geo	Cav 5	A	Sept 3
7770	Stockhouse D	" 18	I	Sept 4
7905	Sellers H	149	G	Sept 5
7939	Shultz Jno	Cav 4	I	Sept 5
7960	Smith A C	7	F	Sept 6
8038	Simpson T	53	K	Sept 6
8103	Stump J	105	I	Sept 7
8112	Slade E	150	H	Sept 7
8444	Shirk M B	142	A	Sept 11
8567	Simons Wm H	76	K	Sept 12
8659	Spould E	90	E	Sept 13
8773	Smith Wm	2	K	Sept 14
8795	Stella J F	1	B	Sept 15
9296	Signall ——	79	H	Sept 19
9012	Steadman W	54	F	Sept 17
9123	Schably J	54	A	Sept 18
9138	Shoup S	Cav 16	B	Sept 18
9310	Smith Chas	7	H	Sept 20
9365	Stebbins Z	7	H	Sept 20
9411	Scott D	149	G	Sept 21
9567	Snyder A	148	I	Sept 23
9593	Sternholt Wm	38		Sept 23
9742	Supple C M	63	B	Sept 25
9780	Surplus W	Cav 13	L	Sept 26
9890	Siherk Christian	145		Sept 27
9898	Sweeny W P	Cav 13		Sept 27
9912	Sanford C	69	H	Sept 28
9985	Sheppard C	118	E	Sept 29
10088	Sloan P	115	A	Sept 30

LIST OF THE DEAD.

No.	Name	Reg.	Co.	Date
10132	Smith J S	Cav 22	B	Oct 1 64
10299	Strong H	55	E	Oct 4
10323	Smith E	10	H	Oct 4
10516	Snyder Wm	54	H	Oct 8
10525	Stones T	121	K	Oct 8
10530	Smallwood C	7	F	Oct 8
10609	Small H	101	H	Oct 10
10720	Smallman J W	63	A	Oct 11
10808	Steele F F	Cav 20	A	Oct 12
10837	Shank A	184	C	Oct 13
11044	Smith Andrew	C 22	B	Oct 17
11069	Stevens C P	11	A	Oct 17
11233	Smith H W	53	B	Oct 21
11246	Smith Jas	57	E	Oct 21
11355	Silvy David	Cav 18	I	Oct 23
11368	Seyoff H	81	C	Oct 23
11488	Sunderland E	11	D	Oct 26
11529	Stevenson Jno	111	I	Oct 26
11661	Speck Olive	67	H	Oct 30
11741	Smith H	183	D	Nov 2
11785	Snodgrass R J	145	H	Nov 4
11792	Sellentine M	145	C	Nov 4
11825	Seltzer D	20	K	Nov 5
11885	Smith W B	Cav 14	B	Nov 6
11890	Shure J P	184	F	Nov 7
11895	Snively G W	Cav 20	F	Nov 7
11926	Scover J H	79	G	Nov 8
11951	Sheffley W	118	G	Nov 9
12057	Stitzer G	2	E	Nov 16
12081	Stensley D	184	A	Nov 18
12217	Smith J S	118	F	Dec 3
12218	Skinner S O	77	A	Dec 4
12282	Shafer T	184	E	Dec 13
12308	Stafford W	67	H	Dec 19
12384	Sourbeer J E	20	A	Jan 3 65
12590	Sipe F	87	C	Feb 5
12598	Stauffer J	1	K	Feb 6
12648	Stain G W	Cav 20	K	Feb 13
12669	Slough E B	" 1	D	Feb 17
12670	Scott A J	14	D	Feb 17
12676	Sheridan M	103	F	Feb 19
12817	Sharks J N	14	D	Mar 27
12824	Shultz H H	87	A	Apr 5
778	Thistlewood J	73	E	Apr 28 64
785	Tolland D	Cav 13	D	Apr 28
1144	Taylor J F	13	E	May 16
1145	Tull D	4	D	May 16
1153	Toner Peter	10	A	May 16
1814	Thompson H	57	C	June 10
2182	Thompson A, Mus	C 4	C	June 19
2302	Townsend D	Cav 18	D	June 22
2335	Tyser L	145	D	June 29
2897	Terwilliger E	103	H	July 5
3003	Thompson R	103	F	July 7
47	Taylor C W	84	D	May 24
3329	Titus W	171	D	July 14
3473	Todd Wm	103	K	July 17
3571	Thompson J S	183	H	July 19
3768	Terrell A	Cav 12	B	July 22
3968	Trumbull H	3	E	July 25
4116	Thompson Jas	C 18	G	July 28
4160	Tinsdale ——	149	E	July 28
4713	Thompson J	Art 3	A	Aug 4
5179	Thompson W W	101	E	Aug 9
5345	Thomas F	7	F	Aug 11
5996	Thompson J B	100	H	Aug 17
6146	Thompson F A B	69	I	Aug 19
6447	Tubbs E	143	I	Aug 23 64
6476	Toll Wm	Res 11	I	Aug 22
6791	Turner Jno	118	H	Aug 25
7250	Thomas E	23	F	Aug 30
7409	Thorpe L	61	E	Aug 31
7904	Trash Seth	81	A	Sept 6
8231	Truman E W	9	G	Sept 9
8531	Tilt W	115	A	Sept 12
8619	Tutor C	184	A	Sept 13
9027	Tits P		C	Sept 17
9212	Thorpe D	18	D	Sept 19
9302	Thompson H	Cav 18	I	Sept 20
9726	Tonson J	99	B	Sept 25
9775	Thuck I	7	C	Sept 26
9981	Tones E	145	F	Sept 26
10008	Thompson J	90	H	Sept 29
10725	Tibbels Geo	69	K	Oct 11
11002	Thatcher R	14	C	Oct 16
11407	Thompson J	Cav 12	E	Oct 24
11754	Trespan P	67	H	Nov 2
12080	Townsend C	103	E	Nov 18
971	Ulrick Jno	17	E	May 9
4184	Urndragh W	4	B	July 28
12133	Utter Wm	45	H	Nov 23
1369	Ventler Chas	75	G	May 25
7739	Vogel L	150	A	June 8
2428	Vernon S	7	K	June 24
4265	Vanholt T	13	A	July 29
5392	Vandeby B	7	A	Aug 12
6877	Vanderpool F	57	B	Aug 26
7716	Vancampments G	52	I	Sept 4
8270	Vail G B	77	G	Sept 9
8791	Vaughan J	108	A	Sept 15
8948	Varndale J	112	A	Sept 16
9688	Vandier Wm, Phila			Sept 24
57	Wilkins A	Cav 12	L	Mar 17
128	Waterman Jno	88	B	Mar 23
193	Wise Isaac	18	G	Mar 27
496	Wheeler J	110	I	Apr 12
516	Warren J	76	A	Apr 12
587	Weed A B	4	K	Apr 17
657	Wentworth Jas	83	G	Apr 21
665	Watson F F	2	B	Apr 22
686	Wahl Jno	73	C	Apr 23
764	Wilson Jno	Cav 14	H	Apr 27
852	Williams S	" 18	I	May 3
941	Wolf J H	" 13	H	May 7
1021	Wright J	" 12	B	May 11
1067	Whitton Robt	145	C	May 13
1093	Wright Wm	Cav 16	A	May 14
1386	Wymans Jas	150	C	May 26
1387	Wilson Jas	Cav 13	D	May 26
1443	Williams F	" 3	B	May 28
1494	Williams Fred	101	K	May 30
1525	Wallace H	Cav 13	H	May 31
1563	Waltermeyer H	76	H	June 2
1721	Whitney W	83	A	June 8
1749	Woodsides W I	18	E	June 9
1791	Wolf Samuel	77	A	June 10
1903	Woodward G W	Cav 3		June 13
1977	Wyant H	103	G	June 15
2338	Walters C	73	B	June 22
2616	Williams J	83	F	June 28
2699	Wike A	96	B	June 30
2790	Whitaker (negro)			July 2
2937	Winsinger S	96	E	July 6
3023	Weider L	50	H	July 7

LIST OF THE DEAD.

No.	Name	Rank/Co.	Regt.	Co.	Date
3135	Wallace A		116	I	July 10 64
3277	Wright W A	Cav	20	G	July 14
3384	Woodruff W D		103	B	July 16
3392	Wait Geo	Cav	1	G	July 16
3605	Walker E		7	A	July 19
3694	White E D	Cav	2	H	July 21
4181	Wisel M		18	K	July 28
4338	Ward Daniel		138	E	July 30
3880	White M		7	C	July 24
3822	Wilson Andrew		103	H	July 23
4069	Wolf A		146	D	July 27
4046	Winegardner A		73	G	July 27
3921	Wilson Wm		43		July 25
4428	Williams Geo		54	H	July 31
4702	Willebough E		148	I	Aug 4
4828	Ward P		103	B	Aug 6
4966	Wetherholt C		54	F	Aug 7
4981	Waserun G	Cav	4	I	Aug 7
4996	White S		14	B	Aug 7
5106	Weaver Jas		90	K	Aug 9
5353	Wilks S		77	G	Aug 11
5458	Wilson Wm		7	K	Aug 12
5677	Weeks D		53	G	Aug 14
6050	Williams		4	A	Aug 18
6052	Waterhouse W	C	3	L	Aug 18
6133	Workman A		118	D	Aug 19
6305	Whipple H, Cor		18	B	Aug 20
6427	Wart C		143	E	Aug 22
6530	Winerman Jas		77	A	Aug 23
6563	Wible Paul		57	A	Aug 23
6626	Walker S A		103	I	Aug 23
6808	Wick R C		103	E	Aug 25
6980	Woolslaer WH, Cor		77	C	Aug 27
6981	White Jas P		149	D	Aug 27
7023	Woodford J A		101	E	Aug 27
7277	White Ed		103	K	Aug 30
7382	Webb J S		69	K	Aug 31
7386	Walton A, Ser	Cav	4	A	Aug 31
7680	Wallwork T		118	D	Sept 3
7714	Warner L	Cav	5	C	Sept 3
7799	Wynn H		101	F	Sept 4
7809	Wiggins D	Art	2	D	Sept 5
7914	Weekland F		101	K	Sept 5
7933	Wade Geo W		118	E	Sept 5
8081	Weber W		116	F	Sept 7
8300	White D	Art	2	F	Sept 10
8879	Wheeler J		7	C	Sept 15
9091	Wheeler C C	Cav	14	M	Sept 18
9343	Williams W		20		Sept 20
9434	Wilson W H		3	I	Sept 21
9534	Woolman H	Cav	18	A	Sept 23
9573	Wingert C		111	I	Sept 23
9634	Wismer J		100	A	Sept 24
9657	Wilson G M	Cav	7	M	Sept 24
9825	Walke G		4	K	Sept 27
9909	Wentley J		155	G	Sept 28
10092	Watson Wm		99	I	Sept 30
10217	Weeks C		76	F	Oct 2
10229	Waltz J		7	H	Oct 2
10236	Weekly John		14	A	Oct 2
10253	Weeks C		76	F	Oct 3
10315	Wolfhope J		184	A	Oct 4
10400	Wilson G		55	C	Oct 6
10426	Wilson J		118	D	Oct 6
10521	Williams W		46	K	Oct 8
10568	Walk W		87	E	Oct 9
10632	Welsy Jno M, Cor		116	E	Oct 10
10659	Watts A J	Cav	12	I	Oct 11 64
10729	White J M		21	G	Oct 11
10797	Walker Wm		148	B	Oct 12
9464	Warner Cyrus W		184	B	Oct 21
10840	Wright Wm		16	I	Oct 13
10902	Wolford D		54	K	Oct 14
10974	Watson C		184	E	Oct 15
11048	Wilderman E		14	D	Oct 17
11108	Walker A		45	D	Oct 18
11120	Wilson G		140	F	Oct 18
11498	Warrington J H		106	H	Oct 26
11503	Waiter W		184	F	Oct 26
11557	Wood J, Ser		19	C	Oct 27
11722	Woodburn D J		7	G	Nov 1
11750	Wyncoop F P		7	I	Nov 2
11899	Webster J, Ser	C	20	L	Nov 7
11978	Wilkinson C, Ser		104	I	Nov 12
11987	Weaver J		53	K	Nov 13
12095	Walder John	Cav	5	L	Nov 19
12098	Wider N H		184	F	Nov 19
12123	Weatherald H W		7	H	Nov 22
12129	Webb C M, Ser		101	H	Nov 23
12222	Williams J		145	A	Dec 4
12187	Wood J M		2	A	Nov 23
12380	Watson H		184	A	Jan 2 65
12485	Williams B		75	B	Jan 19
12493	Walker N C		87	B	Jan 20
10158	Van Dyke D L		103	A	Oct 1 64
11810	Vanmarkes D		6	E	Nov 4
12154	Vanhatterman I		4	G	Nov 25
3958	Vogle V		78	D	July 25
3799	Yocumbs W B		93	B	July 22
4900	Yocum D	Cav	1	M	Aug 6
6103	Yinghing E		78	E	Aug 18
6545	Yeager Samuel		158	D	Aug 23
10204	Young J B		49	G	Oct 2
11040	Young W H		145	F	Oct 17
11512	Yeager J		49	C	Nov 6
1806	Zerphy J		79	E	June 10
4255	Zimmerman B		148	B	July 29
6573	Zane Wm		19	K	Aug 23
4818	Zerl S		103	F	Aug 25
11327	Zane W		118	E	Oct 23

Total, 1808.

RHODE ISLAND.

No.	Name	Rank/Co.	Regt.	Co.	Date
3206	Austin J A, S't	Cav	1	H	July 13 64
6331	Allen Chas	"	1	D	Aug 21
1744	Boneley Wm	"	1	M	June 8
1958	Bidmead Jas	"	1	G	June 14
2521	Blake J F	"	1	M	June 26
3647	Burk Jas		1	C	July 20
4261	Bether J		2	C.	July 29
4576	Baine H		5	A	Aug 2
1339	Carpenter P	Cav	1	E	May 24
1413	Carson B F	"	1	K	May 27
3810	Callihan Jas	Bat			July 23
7966	Calvin E O, Cor	Art	5	A	Sept 6
12832	Collins J H	Cav	1	A	Apr 16 65
651	Delanah E B, S't	"	1	G	Apr 20 64
1217	Dix Geo	"	1	M	May 19
1435	Dickinson J, S't	"	1	K	May 28
3036	Dearborn G	"	1		July 8
4742	Durden Robert	"	1	F	Aug 5
4927	Doolittle G S	Art	2	B	Aug 6
5670	Doyle Jas		5	A	Aug 14
827	Eustace Geo C	Cav	1	M	May 1

LIST OF THE DEAD.

```
10203 Eaton A         Art 5   A  Oct   1 64
  939 Freelove H      Cav 1   H  May   7
 4538 Farrell Jas F   Art 1   A  Aug   2
 4672 Fay John            2   G  Aug   4
 7356 Fay A           Art 5   A  Aug  31
 1866 Goudy John       "  5   A  June 12
 4866 Gallagher C         5   A  Aug   6
 5361 Garvey Wm       Art 5   A  Aug  13
 8308 Green R             2   B  Sept 10
 9978 Green Daniel        2   H  Sept 29
 1075 Henry T         Cav 1   F  May  13
 2656 Healy A          "  1   D  June 29
 2746 Hunt C W         "  1   A  July  1
 3904 Hampstead J     Art 5   F  July 24
 7032 Hooker A        Cav 1   G  Aug  27
11843 Hawkins D F         5   A  Nov   5
12016 Hanley T        Art 5   A  Nov  15
 1962 Ide S R         Cav 1   H  June 14
 3049 Johnson A G     Art 5   A  July  8
 2968 Kettell Jas     Cav 1   B  July  6
 3096 Kiney J             2   B  July 20
 4215 Lewis Edward    Art 5   A  July 29
 5827 Littlebridge, Cor" 5   A  Aug  16
 6798 Lee Cornelius    "  5   A  Aug  25
 7849 Leach L D       Cav 1   F  Sept  5
11688 Livingston J, Mus A 5  A  Oct  31
 1750 Miner S         Cav 1   D  June  9
 7333 McKay Thos          2   F  Aug  31
 8306 McKenna J       Art 3      Sept 10
 3192 Northrop E      Cav 1   H  July 12
 7904 Navoo G             5   K  Sept  5
  607 Peterson John       1   D  Apr  18
 7219 Rathburn J      Cav 1   A  Aug  29
 2382 Sweet M          "  1   D  June 28
 2563 Spink J          "  1   H  June 27
 2859 Slocum Geo T, 2 Lt C 1 A July  4
 4158 Smith P         Cav 1   A  July 28
 4949 Staford J       Bat 1   A  Aug   7
 6186 Sisson Chas T   Art 5   A  Aug  19
 6187 Seymour H        "  5   A  Aug  19
 6351 Sullivan J       "  5   A  Aug  21
 7129 Sanders Chas     "  5   A  Aug  28
 7425 Slocum C A, Cor" 5   A  Aug  31
 3075 Turner Chas         7   E  July  9
 8522 Thomas J            5      Sept 12
   19 Wright Moses Cav    2   A  Mar   7
 1788 West H              1   A  June 10
 3173 Wallace Wm      Art 5   A  July 11
 5908 Wood J B            5   A  Aug  16
 6222 West J          Cav 2   A  Aug  21
 6766 Wayne S          "  1   A  Aug  25
 7831 Wilson J            5   A  Sept  4
 9273 Witham B, Lieut A 1          19
      TOTAL, 74.

             TENNESSEE.

  883 Allen James W       11  B  May   4 64
  987 Amos F G             2  C  May  10
 2313 Allison B F    Cav  13  D  June 22
 2631 Andrewson Joseph 2    C  June 29
 3167 Anderson S     Cav   8  B  July 11
 3194 Aber J                2  A  July 12
 3334 Anglon Wm       "    7  A  July 15
 4004 Athens J H    East   2  C  July 26
 6411 Aikin Geo W, Cor 7   K  Aug  22
 6474 Ashby J F       Cav  7  B  Aug  22
 6541 Antoine P       "   13  H  Aug  23

 7372 Aspray Wm, S't     13  B  Sept  2 64
 7907 Anderson C S, S't  10  D  Sept  5
 9151 Achley A            3  A  Sept 18
 9910 Atkins L            2  D  Sept 28
 1895 Arrowood Jas Cav   8      June 13
 8493 Alexander P S  "  13  D  Sept 11
12710 Allen G W           7  I  Feb  28 65
  539 Bowling Wm         11  E  Apr  14 64
  585 Blason Benj         2  E  Apr  17
  663 Bond Jas J T        2  F  Apr  21
  695 Baker T K      Cav  5      Apr  23
  705 Batey W H           2  B  Apr  24
  772 Burton Wm      Art  1  A  Apr  28
  808 Brannin Ellis       2  F  Apr  30
  845 Browden H V         2  K  May   1
  859 Byerly W H          1  A  May   3
  920 Brewer M            2  E  May   6
 1053 Boyden A L          2  B  May  13
 1137 Beatty Thomas       2  B  May  16
 1242 Bryant Jas A        8  I  May  20
 1244 Barnard W H         2  A  May  20
 1248 Boyd A D, Cor       2  F  May  20
 1527 Butler J J, S't     7  B  May  31
 1538 Bradshaw A G        2  B  June  1
 1610 Browning J          2  F  June  4
 1635 Brown J        Cav 13  E  June  5
 1847 Branon Wm           2  F  June 11
 1876 Birket W D, Cor     7      June 12
 1883 Burchfield W R      2      June 12
 1976 Berger W            2  B  June 15
 2037 Berger W M          2  B  June 15
 2555 Bontwright A, S't   7  A  June 27
 2744 Brewer W T     Cav  7  A  June 27
 2939 Bibbs Alex      "   7  D  July  6
 2983 Bright John         8  G  July  7
 3176 Blalock H           2  D  July 11
 3198 Brown J B, S't      2  F  July 12
    6 Brandon C           4  D  Apr   4
   16 Burke John          2  D  Apr  12
   52 Brummell A D        2  H  June  3
   57 Broits S            4  F  June 20
   58 Beeler Daniel       5  D  June 25
 3328 Barton F F     Cav 13  A  July 14
 3330 Bynom J W       "  13  C  July 14
 3414 Brennan James       2  I  July 16
 3636 Burris D B         13  B  July 20
 3643 Brannan J           2  A  July 20
 3726 Billings W          6  I  July 21
 3786 Bowman J       Cav  7  C  July 22
 3934 Boles H            13  C  July 25
 4108 Boyd W H       Cav  9  C  July 27
 4221 Barnes A C         15  H  July 29
 4770 Bryant Wm           2  D  Aug   5
 5017 Butler W W     Cav  7  B  Aug   8
 4371 Bradfield E L       7  C  July 31
 5279 Brummetti B        11  C  Aug   8
 5277 Barnhart D F        7  B  Aug  11
 5294 Baker Isaac        13  B  Aug  11
 5313 Blackwood G W      11  B  Aug  11
 5583 Boles G W      Cav 13  B  Aug  13
 5617 Baker M A       "  13  E  Aug  14
 6003 Boles W G       "  13  B  Aug  17
 6142 Boyles K            2  C  Aug  19
 6194 Burnett S H         6  H  Aug  19
 6287 Butler W J          7  B  Aug  20
 6569 Barnes Wm      Cav  7  M  Aug  23
 6672 Bishop W        "   7  H  Aug  23
```

LIST OF THE DEAD. 271

No.	Name		Co.		Date	
7130	Brewer J		2	D	Aug 31	64
7664	Bales Henry		2	K	Sept 2	
7943	Boyer D		15	D	Sept 5	
8222	Bird S H	Cav	13	D	Sept 8	
8998	Blackner Thos	"	7	L	Sept 17	
9023	Bill F		5	I	Sept 17	
9079	Boyle R C	Cav	7	I	Sept 17	
9149	Bean C S	"	3	E	Sept 18	
9478	Bowlen C F		13	B	Sept 21	
9543	Bromley H, S't		7		Sept 23	
4888	Brannon L		2	A	Aug 6	
10098	Byerly James E C		1	A	Sept 30	
10452	Bible W		8	D	Oct 7	
10617	Blackney B		7	E	Oct 10	
10826	Bartholomew J	Cav	7	H	Oct 13	
11015	Bosworth W H	"	7	E	Oct 16	
11298	Brogan John, Cor		2	C	Oct 22	
11372	Brown J B, Cor		2	K	Oct 23	
12171	Bradford H A		7	E	Oct 26	
12565	Brown J W		13	B	Jan 31	65
12613	Barnhart G		7	C	Feb 8	
12662	Barnes F B	Cav	7	D	Feb 16	
462	Bell E S		4	C	Apr 9	64
4782	Barnes G		10	D	Aug 5	
189	Cardwell W C		6	C	Mar 27	
216	Conaster Philip		2	D	Mar 28	
230	Chinney Jesse, S't		2	A	Mar 29	
375	Colwell J H		2	C	Apr 5	
436	Crosswell Samuel		2	K	Apr 8	
459	Childers J M		2	D	Apr 19	
482	Clark Lewis	Cav	2	B	Apr 9	
615	Covington A		2	K	Apr 18	
717	Chitwood J H		2	G	Apr 24	
811	Carden Robert		2	C	Apr 30	
840	Cardwell W C		6	G	May 2	
1050	Cooper C		2	B	May 12	
1213	Clark Alexander		2	C	May 19	
1425	Cross M C		2	F	May 28	
1574	Childers J		13	A	June 3	
1636	Clemens J D	Cav	7	D	June 5	
1751	Campbell W		2	A	June 9	
1839	Carden A K	Cav	7	E	June 11	
2031	Covington J B		2	K	June 15	
2062	Carwin James		1		June 16	
2071	Crow J, S't		2	F	June 16	
2289	Crawford A	Cav	13	B	June 21	
2466	Childers Thomas L		2	G	June 25	
2632	Cooper E		1	A	June 30	
2789	Cook W P E		2	A	July 1	
2858	Cooper G W		7	B	July 4	
2886	Collins W		2	H	July 4	
2940	Carter H C	Cav	13	E	July 6	
3687	Cross N		2	H	July 21	
3983	Corwine J East Tenn		G		July 26	
4601	Cornish A	Cav	13	C	Aug 4	
5298	Chase A P	"	7	I	Aug 11	
5829	Collins R	"	7	K	Aug 16	
5893	Clyne E T, S't	"	11	E	Aug 16	
6310	Crews G	Cav	7	B	Aug 20	
7523	Childers E		13	E	Sept 1	
7525	Clark James		13	A	Sept 1	
7001	Cunise E	Cav	7	I	Sept 2	
7702	Childers W E	"	7	E	Sept 3	
7857	Cotbrain S		13	E	Sept 5	
7871	Camp W W		7	K	Sept 5	
7880	Cotterell G W		7	C	Sept 5	
8219	Creesy S P	Cav	7	K	Sept 8	
9021	Crum A		4	F	Sept 17	64
9503	Cooley J	Cav	7	L	Sept 18	
9698	Chadwick M		16	I	Sept 24	
10137	Cole Geo M, S't		9	C	Oct 1	
10208	Clay H		13	H	Oct 3	
10403	Cleaver W		7	G	Oct 6	
10654	Churchill E		13	A	Oct 11	
11239	Check R	Cav	6	D	Oct 20	
11312	Carter W B		11	E	Oct 22	
12643	Camway H		6	K	Feb 13	65
202	Dodd Benjamin		2	D	April 1	64
399	Doss J W		2	C	April 6	
485	Dudley Sam	Cav	1	A	April 9	
645	Dutrow Irdell		2	G	April 20	
759	Duncan G W, Cor		2	B	April 27	
856	Doak I V		2	F	May 3	
894	Davis Leroy		7	K	May 5	
1016	Diggs J G		2	C	May 9	
43	Dykes Pleasant		2	K	May 11	
1182	Duff I W		16	B	May 18	
1581	Davis J W		2	C	June 3	
2266	Dabney B		1	A	June 20	
2306	Daniel Suttrell		2	K	June 23	
2449	Diggs Jno G East		2	C	June 25	
3513	Deer H		7	M	July 18	
3667	Davis J		3	A	July 20	
5398	Disney E W, S't C		11	C	Aug 12	
6261	Dunn R		19	I	Aug 20	
6991	Dyn Wm	Cav	7	K	Aug 27	
4821	Diaan R H		10	I	Aug 5	
8423	Davis Levi	Cav	7	K	Sept 11	
7219	Davis James		7	C	Aug 30	
7608	Diel S F, S't	Cav	7	B	Sept 2	
8329	Dyer W	"	7	K	Sept 10	
9373	Dodd Chas, Citizen Dec				Sept 20	
9453	Dort R		7	G	Sept 21	
9701	Duke Wm		7	E	Sept 25	
10014	Dyer H	Cav	4	A	Sept 29	
10244	Davis Wm		7	D	Oct 3	
12119	Dodd J A	Cav	1	M	Nov 22	
12379	Dykes L		2	K	Jan 2	65
12498	Delf E		8	C	Jan 21	
12794	Doty I, Citizen				Jan 18	
293	Edwards I		5	B	April 1	64
360	Everitt A T		2	A	April 2	
510	Evans S D		8	C	April 12	
557	Everitte John		2	G	April 14	
648	Evans W, S't		7	C	May 3	
873	Edwards C S		5	B	May 4	
950	Evans J M		7	M	May 9	
979	Etler Valentine		11	D	May 9	
1836	Emmert J C, S't		4		June 14	
55	Eddes James C		2	E	June 16	
3761	Ellison Isaac, East		2	F	July 22	
4785	Ellis C O	Cav	13	C	Aug 5	
5904	Ethridge Wm		13	B	Aug 16	
7402	Elder P		2	F	Aug 31	
9075	Escue H, Cor Cav		6		Sept 17	
10560	Elliott Wm		4	A	Oct 9	
10985	Easton J	Cav	13	B	Oct 16	
11639	Ellington J	"	13	B	Oct 30	
353	Fairchilds Jesse		2	B	April 2	
683	Fryer W L, S't		2	H	April 23	
697	Fagen Parker		8	I	April 23	
1145	Fannon G H, Tenn St Gd				April 28	
2408	Fisher C N		2	K	June 24	
2506	Francisco R	Cav	7	B	June 26	

LIST OF THE DEAD.

62	Friar John		2	H	July 9 64	1159	Heatherby John	1	C	May 19 64
2835	Fox E, Tenn St Gd				July 3	1491	Hickson Daniel	2	F	May 31
5820	Firestone ——	Cav	1	M	Aug 11	1551	Hopkins A Art	1	A	June 2
5997	Frazier John		8	H	Aug 17	1554	Hunt J	2	B	June 2
6299	Flowers W P, S't C		13	B	Aug 20	1766	Harrison Wm	8	I	June 9
7244	Franks W W		2	B	Aug 29	1774	Hodges I M	2	F	June 9
7782	Fields R G		1		Sept 4	1846	Hartman A B	4	A	June 11
8555	Finch A	Cav	7	L	Sept 12	1925	Hendson J S	2	K	June 14
10133	Finch J B		7	B	Oct 1	1950	Hickerman T Cav	9	B	June 14
12502	Franshier J D		8	K	Jan 21 65	2276	Hilton A F, S't	2	H	June 20
3005	Fowler (		4	A	July 7 64	2375	Hugely C W Cav	13	D	June 23
3733	Finch H	Cav	7	I	July 21	2491	Hawa E A	2	B	June 26
578	Goddard John		2	B	April 16	2642	Hale R H	3	F	June 29
1831	German P		2	C	June 11	2851	Hall B A	2	A	July 4
2043	Gorman James		6		June 15	2949	Hudson J A Cav	8	F	July 9
2571	Graham J D	Cav	7	D	June 27	3012	Haines J A	13	E	July 7
2891	Gooding James		2	D	July 4	4855	Hall J J Cav	13	E	Aug 6
3	Guild James		11	B	Mar 18	4836	Hermsen Wm "	13	B	Aug 6
15	Graves Henry		2	E	April 11	4805	Haywood J G	7	I	Aug 5
59	Gray John W		2	I	June 29	3098	Hawkins S D	3	E	July 10
3291	Gorman F		6	B	July 14	3121	Hodgen ——	7	K	July 10
3357	Grays L		12	F	July 15	3248	Hopson Thos Cav	3	E	July 13
9238	Gamon I A	Cav	7	A	Sept 19	3421	Howard A	2	F	July 16
3620	Grundee Alex		4	D	July 20	3672	Heckman Wm, Cor	2	G	July 20
3719	Grier J O, Cor		7	B	July 21	3712	Henderson J R	6	B	July 21
3887	Gilson C G		1	B	July 24	3729	Hendlay J	9	A	July 21
4531	Grevett S P	Cav	7	C	Aug 1	3807	Hayes J C Cav	7	C	July 22
5182	Given I A		9	I	Aug 9	4535	Henry Wm	7	C	Aug 1
5146	Griswell T J	Cav	7	H	Aug 9	5278	Hudson John	55	I	Aug 11
5374	Garrett M T	"	7	L	Aug 11	5526	Harvey Morgan	2	F	Aug 11
5398	Green S G	"	7	I	Aug 12	5535	Hensley James M	3	E	Aug 13
6376	Grims Wm		2	A	Aug 21	5604	Hicks M	2	I	Aug 14
6400	Graves J C		2	E	Aug 21	5607	Hasborough J H C	13	E	Aug 14
6496	Grisson C		8	B	Aug 22	6393	Haines G Cav	13	A	Aug 21
7221	Green J C		7	I	Aug 29	6553	Hughes Wm	2	K	Aug 23
7454	Gunter R C, S't		13	A	Sept 4	6581	Hibbrath M H Cav	7	I	Aug 27
7905	Griswold W H Cav		7	K	Sept 5	6648	Harris A G	5	E	Aug 23
8012	Gibbs J A	"	7	L	Sept 6	6681	Horton W C Cav	7	H	Aug 24
8003	Griffin W A	"	2	C	Sept 7	7808	Hinson John "	7	H	Sept 4
8016	Gill G W	"	1	L	Sept 16	8094	Hallford J A	13	A	Sept 7
9271	Gaff R	"	1	C	Sept 19	8115	Hicks E	9	F	Sept 7
9875	Gibson James	"	13		Sept 27	8486	Hale Ira Cav	7	C	Sept 11
10334	Gardner H	"	14	C	Oct 4	8529	Haywood A J, Ser	7	I	Sept 12
10590	Garrison A, Cor		7	E	Oct 10	9044	Henderson A G	13	C	Sept 13
11063	Galbraith G W Cav		7	E	Oct 17	9788	Hodges John	13	E	Sept 26
11632	Grier J		7	B	Oct 28	9797	Herbs D Cav	1	D	Sept 26
11925	Giles M C		7	I	Nov 8	9805	Haney H "	7	A	Sept 26
12402	Ganon T	Cav	4	I	Jan 6 65	9802	Hanks A, Ser	11	D	Sept 27
12438	Gilbert Wm	"	7	C	Jan 12	10003	Hall W R	2	D	Sept 29
12464	Golden J H	"	7	C	Jan 18	10145	Haliwarke ——	7	E	Oct 10
1000	Gray Thomas		11	E	May 19 64	10329	Hooks John L Cav	7	A	Oct 4
433	Graves James		2	E	April 8	10810	Holler W "	6	E	Oct 12
58	Hampton I A		8	D	Mar 16	10956	Holloway H B	2	G	Oct 14
85	Henniger Peter		11	I	Mar 21	11377	Herman H	4	K	Oct 23
163	Hoover Samuel		2	B	Mar 26	11791	Hickman D	2	I	Nov 4
316	Huff Benjamin		2	K	April 2	11801	Howard ——	16		Nov 4
357	Huckleby Thomas		2	C	April 2	11861	Higgs L	7	D	Nov 6
407	Hickson George		11	E	April 9	12028	Hazzle Wm	7	C	Nov 13
616	Hurd Wm		2	B	April 18	12146	Hall J M	1	A	Nov 24
660	Head Wm	Cav	12	B	April 21	12212	Hanley T	2	E	Dec 2
682	Hixton John		2	F	April 23	12423	Hoag B F	7	E	Jan 9 65
714	Henderson Robert		2	B	April 24	12655	Huffaker J	2	K	Feb 14
805	Hayes J		7	E	April 29	12603	Hanbuck J	7	K	Feb 22
844	Hughes E		2	I	May 2	1941	Israel S	21	B	June 14 64
958	Hickley Thomas		2	K	May 8	9515	Irwin P P	49	F	Sept 22
1036	Hickson Henry		2	I	May 12	52	Jones Rufus	2	I	Mar 16
1124	Hall John		2	B	May 15	291	Jones Warren T	11	C	Apr 1

LIST OF THE DEAD.

No.	Name	Reg.	Co.	Date
358	Jeffers J	2	C	Apr 2 61
584	Jack Benjamin S	2	B	Apr 17
668	Jones H D	4	F	Apr 22
1181	Johnson E A, Ser	2	A	May 18
1227	Johnson S L	2	A	May 19
1536	Jones John J Cav	13	C	June 1
3805	Jones H	2	H	July 22
3980	Johnson A	10	C	July 26
4571	Jones D	6	C	Aug 2
5517	Johnson C F	7	K	Aug 13
5921	Jones J M	2	K	Aug 17
7447	Jones Alb't, Ser C	13	B	Sept 1
8013	Joiner J M Cav	7	B	Sept 6
8503	Jones J	" 13	B	Sept 12
8560	Johnson J Cor East	3		Sept 12
8764	Johnson C M		K	Sept 14
9552	Jones D	11	E	Sept 23
9618	Jones Wm T, CorC	11		Sept 23
10479	Johnson M Cav	13	G	Oct 7
12319	Johnson E W "	7	C	Dec 21
12702	Johnson W	13	D	Feb 26 65
32	Kirby James		M	Mar 11 64
434	Kilpatrick R	2	E	Apr 8
595	Kelsey John, Ser	2	A	Apr 17
600	Kenizler Henry	2	G	Apr 17
35	King James T	2	D	Apr 25
3702	Kirk B J Cav	7	B	July 21
3749	Keene Hoza "	7	C	July 22
7367	Keen J S "	7	C	Aug 31
7641	Kirk J P	3	D	Sept 2
8183	Kingsley S	2	D	Sept 8
8714	Kenser Jos Cav	2		Sept 14
9407	Kelley J W, S't		E	Sept 21
11241	Kissinger F	7	I	Oct 21
12570	Kidwell J	4	C	Feb 2 65
1157	Kuncr E B	3	E	May 16 64
627	Long Jonathan	2	H	April 19
688	Lane L E	2	I	April 23
713	Lofty R J	2	I	April 24
1223	Lovette W T Cav	13	A	May 19
1252	Langley E G	11	B	May 21
1352	Long C C	2	C	May 25
1597	Long John	2	C	June 3
2193	Looper E	2	D	June 19
8	Lanen Thomas	2	H	April 5
45	Lingo James	2	C	May 17
53	Levi J N	2	I	June 3
3696	Lamphey J Cav		C	July 21
3700	Little E D	7	A	July 22
3830	Lemmar J E, S't C	13	A	July 23
4114	Lawrence J C Cav	13	I	July 28
4292	Lewis R Bat	1	B	July 30
4575	Long John	13	H	Aug 2
8640	Lawson M	8	H	Sept 13
8926	Lawson H G	8	I	Sept 14
9594	Lester James Cav	7	M	Sept 23
9641	Lewis J	3	G	Sept 24
11827	Laprint J	11	K	Nov 5
1352	Long C C	2	C	May 25
11979	Leonard J	7	C	Nov 12
388	McCune Robert	2	E	April 5
405	Meyers W J	12	F	April 6
558	Miller W H	2	F	April 15
562	Macklin John	2	H	April 15
583	Malcolm S A	4	B	April 16
722	Maines Wm	1	D	April 27
801	McCart Wm	2	B	April 29
845	McDowell G I	2	D	April 26 64
1051	Mynck Eli	2	A	May 12
1176	May W	10	C	May 16
1289	Meyers D	2	H	May 22
1402	Martin F A	2	A	May 27
1451	McLane H C East Tenn	21		May 29
1561	Massie Eli	2	C	June 1
1668	Myers John. Cor	2	H	June 6
1703	Moulden Wm	2	A	June 7
1723	McCart J	2	B	June 8
1960	McDonald L M, S't	2	G	June 14
2050	Meyers Wm, S't		H	June 16
2171	Matheney D C	7	D	June 19
2224	Melterberger M	2	G	June 20
2277	Morris J, Cor Cav	2	E	June 20
2475	Mitchiner H	13	H	June 25
2500	Mackin W Cav	7	K	June 26
2516	Moss J	2	A	June 26
3124	McAllister W H C	4	H	July 10
24	Mayes William	2	E	April 15
38	Mee Thomas	2	F	April 29
46	Mergen H S	2	G	May 18
3243	McGee Wm Cav	7	B	July 3
3642	Maynard W J	13	A	July 20
4567	Miller J W Cav	8	G	Aug 2
4523	McLean A G	3	C	Aug 1
3897	McCoy W C	2	G	July 24
4236	McDover H	2	C	July 29
4237	Montgomery Wm	4	C	July 29
4751	McGwin M Cav	7	C	Aug 5
4905	Mussurgo M Cav	9	H	Aug 6
4496	Mulanox A C, Cor	2	B	Aug 1
5008	Myers A Cav	13	C	Aug 8
5064	Miles Samuel	2	A	Aug 8
5282	Morris H S Cav	13	C	Aug 11
5594	Mitchell Jas "	7	K	Aug 14
5782	Miflin Wm	13	B	Aug 15
6555	Maddro Jas	2	C	Aug 23
7435	Melford J, Cor Cav	8	C	Sept 1
7574	Moore Jas	13		Sept 2
7764	McGee A	13	B	Sept 4
8059	Mayher J W	2	E	Sept 7
8174	Martin J S Cav	7	H	Sept 8
8954	Mackey S		D	Sept 16
9140	McNeese Sam'l Cav	8	G	Sept 17
9542	McDonald W	7	E	Sept 23
9559	Montgomery C F C	1	L	Sept 23
9783	Metheney V V C	13	A	Sept 26
9861	Macart R	2	B	Sept 27
10795	Martin S Cav	7	G	Oct 12
10976	Meare J H "	7	I	Oct 15
11532	May S L "	9	A	Oct 26
11544	McCaslin M C	7	D	Oct 27
11649	Myracle C	7	C	Oct 30
11667	Morris Wm Cav	7	I	Oct 30
11845	Moore Wm P	11	D	Nov 5
11277	McNearly W Cav	7	C	Dec 3
12338	Moore T "	7	I	Dec 26
7497	Norton J	10	K	Sept 1
160	Newman Jesse	2	K	Mar 25
828	Norris Thomas	2	D	May 1
1237	Norman J, Cor C	13	C	May 20
3191	Newport H Cav	13	E	July 12
50	Nicely A		H	June 2
6262	Nichols W T Cav	7	A	Aug 20
7818	Newman T A, S't	4		Sept 4
9068	Norwood Wm Cav	7	I	Sept 17

LIST OF THE DEAD.

No.	Name	Reg.	Co.	Date	Year
9447	Norris P W	Cav 7	B	Sept 21	64
9640	Needham F	13	C	Sept 24	
9996	Neighbour M	7	E	Sept 29	
10223	Norris W	2	D	Oct 2	
12642	Neighbor A	7	B	Feb 13	65
4689	Odorn John, S't	8	B	Aug 4	64
1758	Owen A	2	D	June 9	
10743	Oliver L	13	C	Oct 11	
923	Ollenger John	2	I	May 6	
2097	Overton J S	2	C	June 30	
689	Palmer Wm	2	K	April 23	
806	Perkins G W, S't	7	M	April 29	
1141	Penix John	5	G	May 16	
1363	Perry Jas	Cav 6	L	May 25	
1517	Proffett Jas	13	C	May 31	
1638	Powers H, S't	Cav 7	A	June 5	
2146	Parder E H	11	K	June 18	
2748	Perry Thomas	13	B	July 1	
2767	Pursley W B, S't	C 13	C	July 2	
3170	Pankey A J	13	B	July 11	
506	Pilot Joseph	2	K	April 12	
4592	Piscall J B	13	B	Aug 3	
4572	Powell A N, S't	7	K	Aug 2	
8005	Pavies S	Cav 7	C	Sept 12	
1	Polivar Martin	2	E	Mar 12	
10	Phillips N	2	H	April 5	
32	Parker Wiley	3	B	April 25	
4041	Parmer E	7	I	July 26	
4380	Palmer D P	Cav 7	I	July 31	
6190	Parks R T	'' 7	I	Aug 19	
6335	Prison E T	7	B	Aug 21	
6485	Princes Nelson	15	B	Aug 22	
6000	Phillips T	2	G	Aug 23	
7290	Park Jas	Cav 7	E	Aug 30	
9020	Penn W H	2	E	Sept 17	
9121	Paddock D W, Cor	C 2	I	Sept 17	
9606	Pennington G W, Cor	11		Sept 23	
10304	Pegram W	7	A	Oct 4	
10318	Powers H M, Cor	7	A	Oct 4	
10364	Poster N P, S't	13	E	Oct 4	
10655	Pomeroy John	7	K	Oct 11	
10852	Pierce Wm	8	A	Oct 13	
10907	Parkham W	7	K	Oct 14	
11285	Pickering E	Cav 4	G	Oct 22	
11400	Pinkley J	7	B	Oct 24	
11501	Powers J	Cav 7	A	Oct 26	
12644	Powers R	'' 7	H	Feb 13	65
675	Perry Wesley	2	I	April 22	64
1978	Pope F	Cav 7	D	June 15	
2232	Quiller T	'' 7	D	June 20	
271	Ragan J	2	B	Mar 28	
380	Ronden Wm	2	A	April 5	
382	Reynolds Henry	C 11	L	April 5	
454	Ru-sell R	2	K	April 9	
4644	Roberts John	2	F	Aug 3	
5815	Ronser A, Cor	1	A	Aug 16	
2519	Reed John C	7	A	June 26	
523	Robinson Jas M	3	A	April 13	
646	Robinson Isaac	3	A	April 20	
951	Robinson Wm	1	G	May 8	
1438	Rayle F	Art 1	C	May 28	
1450	Reice James	13	C	May 29	
1783	Ralph J F	13	E	June 10	
1924	Reed G W	7	A	June 14	
2005	Ringoland W H	2	D	June 15	
2006	Rabb G W	13	A	June 15	
2093	Ryan Wm	3	K	June 17	
2219	Robinson J C	2	B	June 20	64
2314	Roberts T	2	H	June 22	
2691	Riley J M	6	G	June 30	
2750	Ryan C P	2	G	July 1	
17	Riddle Robert	2	F	April 12	
3752	Ritter John	3	C	July 22	
2755	Robbins T	2	D	July 22	
3772	Reeves Geo W	4	F	July 22	
4086	Robinson A	2	B	July 27	
4254	Renshaw H G	Cav 7	C	July 29	
4368	Rainwater A	7	F	July 31	
5974	Riter Henry	Cav 7	E	Aug 17	
4616	Roberts Chas	7	A	Aug 3	
6267	Reeves A	Cav 11	B	Aug 20	
6409	Rider W R, S't	13	C	Aug 22	
6837	Rogers A G	Cav 7	B	Aug 25	
7082	Russell J S	7	E	Aug 28	
7090	Ross John	Cav 7	B	Aug 28	
7099	Roach J W	'' 7	K	Aug 28	
7190	Riter John	7	E	Aug 29	
7774	Reynolds W	3	G	Sept 4	
7978	Reagan Geo W	3	G	Sept 6	
8137	Rose M L	East 2	A	Sept 8	
8523	Ramsay W A			Sept 12	
9513	Renmeger Jeff	Cav 13	E	Sept 22	
10107	Richardson R	'' 13	E	Sept 30	
10869	Rushing W R	7	B	Oct 13	
11995	Roberts J G	7	I	Nov 18	
12101	Risley J	6	E	Nov 20	
12753	Robins W	7	B	Mar 12	65
8968	Reeder C, Sutler	51		Sept 16	64
298	Stinger A E	2	K	April 1	
319	Sanc Joseph	8	B	April 2	
874	Sukirk J F	2	B	April 15	
390	Smith John	Cav 2	I	April 16	
776	Scott R S	2		April 28	
985	Smithpater Eli	11	K	May 9	
1140	Seals John	2	D	May 16	
1191	Stepp Preston	2	D	May 18	
1254	Stafford Wm	Cav 13	C	May 21	
1278	Sisson James	2	E	May 22	
1284	Smith T A	2	C	May 22	
1313	Short L H	Cav 7	C	May 23	
1353	Smith C	2	B	May 25	
1408	Simpkins Thomas	9	A	May 27	
1475	Smith Joel	2	A	May 30	
1481	Stansberry A	8	A	May 30	
1488	Sutton John	2	I	May 31	
1526	Stover A	2	C	May 31	
1670	Smith Wm	2	D	June 6	
2280	Stevens R	2	D	June 20	
2284	Smith J	Cav 13	E	June 21	
2958	Smith J B	20	I	July 6	
11	Stanton W	4	E	April 5	
12	Sutton Thomas	2	I	April 8	
39	Sandusky G	2	B	April 29	
56	Stout D D	2	F	June 18	
3035	Scarbrough S N	13	E	July 8	
3276	Shrop J B	East 2	E	July 14	
3298	Sells W	East Cav 2	D	July 14	
3322	Swappola O B	4	A	July 15	
3520	Slaver A	Cav 11	C	July 18	
3865	Smith John M	12	M	July 24	
4038	Sapper S	8	H	July 26	
4170	Snow W	Cav 7	M	July 28	
5462	Smith L	13	L	Aug 13	
5625	Sutton Andrew	C 13	E	Aug 14	

LIST OF THE DEAD.

No.	Name		Co.	Date	Yr
5850	Swan John	2	D	Aug 16	64
5962	Scott John	13	8	Aug 17	
6643	Sutton D	Cav 1	H	Aug 23	
7056	Smith J	6	M	Aug 23	
7296	Stewart J W	Cav 13	B	Aug 30	
7314	Smidney E	1	E	Aug 30	
7787	Scobey L A H	13	B	Sept 2	
7923	Sarret Jas D	Tenn St Gd	Sept 5	
8637	Smith J	Cav 3	E	Sept 13	
9192	Smith T A	13	C	Sept 18	
9381	Southerland J	Cav 13	C	Sept 20	
9395	Stewart E	13	D	Sept 20	
9555	Smith W H	7	B	Sept 23	
9719	Swatzell W L	Cav 8	E	Sept 25	
9803	Stratten J L	7	M	Sept 25	
10109	Stafford S	13	A	Oct 6	
10454	Shouall John	13	C	Oct 7	
11594	Shay D	11	E	Oct 28	
12558	Smith H	2	E	Jan 30	65
12749	Stevens J F	Cav 2	E	Mch 8	
12756	Smith J D	4	C	Mch 12	
12784	Stewart R H	7	C	Mch 15	
12800	Shook N A	7	B	Mch 19	
12836	Smith George	2	B	April 18	
36	Stiner W H	2	E	April 28	64
3095	Slorer A W	2	C	July 26	
211	Tompkins T B	2	F	Mch 28	
258	Thompson W D	2	F	Mch 31	
793	Thompson Charles	2		April 29	
932	Thomas W H	2	K	May 7	
1057	Tomlin A	Cav 7	M	June 6	
1704	Thanton S A	Art 1	H	June 7	
2229	Tice S J	7	B	June 20	
2718	Tipton W H	2	I	July 1	
3400	Taylor J	13	D	July 17	
4122	Tyffle John	Cav 1	A	June 28	
4778	Templeton G W	2	C	Aug 5	
5046	Tite W S	13	C	Aug 14	
7052	Thomas W H	Cav 7	A	Aug 28	
9203	Tolley D	8	H	Sept 19	
9375	Terry D	Cav 9	D	Sept 20	
10780	Thinn R A	7	B	Oct 12	
12694	Tidwell T	13	D	Feb 22	65
4825	Tidwell J W	13	C	Aug 5	64
2592	Usley T R	2	A	June 23	
4518	Undergrate A	2	I	Aug 2	
885	Vaugh I	8	H	May 5	
1203	Vanhorn J	2	H	May 19	
2915	Varner T W	Cav 11	E	July 5	
7217	Vanhook J M, Cor C	11	H	July 29	
4530	Vaughry Frederick	2	D	Aug 1	
60	Wolfe John		11	E	Mch 18
259	Woolen I		2	A	Mch 31
339	Webb Robert		2	B	April 2
359	Wuas M		2	I	April 2
501	Watts C C		2	A	April 12
570	Ward Jordan		2	A	April 15
810	White John		2	B	April 30
902	William C		7	B	May 5
1052	Ward A		3	I	May 12
1756	Watts J W		7	M	June 9
1794	White I		2	D	June 10
1865	Wallace L	East 2		C	June 12
2057	Ward C		2	H	June 14
2066	Watts T, Cor		2	I	June 16
2132	Wray Samuel		13	C	June 18
2496	Wilson A	Cav 8			June 26
2764	Winningham J	2	B	July 2	64
2810	Wells E	8	H	July 3	
3021	Watkins J M	4	I	July 7	
3031	Woods nd T	7	K	July 8	
3189	Webb D	Cav 8	G	July 12	
21	Winchester J D	1	E	April 15	
19	Weaver P		2	D	April 13
4551	West W F		2	H	Aug 2
4869	Ward John, Citizen			Aug 6	
22	Whitby R B	2	C	April 15	
33	Weese W	2	I	April 23	
3297	Weir I	Cav 1	B	July 14	
3304	Wilson H	2	B	July 14	
3319	Wo f A	10	C	July 14	
3458	Williams A	Cav 3	E	July 17	
3615	Willis James	Tenn S Gds	July 20
3714	Webbe J	2	B	July 21	
3737	Wilson J	12	F	July 21	
3982	Wilson S L	2	D	July 26	
4033	Walford W	7	A	July 26	
4704	Wallace L	2	C	Aug 4	
5267	Wright J W	Cav 7	B	Aug 10	
5572	Withyde S	1	A	Aug 14	
6108	Wood P D	3	B	Aug 19	
6580	Webb Robert	2	B	Aug 23	
6604	Wortell H H	Cav 7	I	Aug 23	
7618	White R O M	13	B	Sept 2	
8740	Whicks N	7	H	Sept 14	
7231	Wood J	7	C	Aug 29	
9193	Woolsey J	2	F	Sept 18	
9479	Walker John	Cav 13	C	Sept 21	
9658	Williams C S	9	B	Sept 24	
9670	Whittle H W	7	C	Sept 24	
9730	Webb T	6	G	Sept 25	
9929	White L S	Cav 11	D	Sept 28	
10337	Wiggins G W	11	C	Oct 4	
10338	White H S't	7	A	Oct 4	
10739	Warrell J W, Cor C 7			Oct 11	
10003	Webb W	3	A	Oct 10	
11386	Warden J W, S't	7	E	Oct 24	
12107	Winelug J	7	M	Nov 21	
12125	White Wm M	11	D	Nov 22	
12139	Watson I C	Cav 7	C	Nov 23	
12576	Walker C H	6	H	Feb 3	65
12699	Woodruff J	Cav 4	B	Feb 24	
12779	Woods Thomas	13	B	Mch 15	
8190	White J, S't	Cav 7	A	Sept 8	64
5669	Wilson Wm A	6	A	Aug 14	
4717	Westbrook J H	Cav 6	A	Aug 4	
4793	Wilson J M	13	D	Aug 5	
383	Yarber Wiley	5	I	April 5	
878	Young James	2	D	May 4	
1142	Young James	2	F	May 16	
14	Yeront Samuel	3	E	April 10	
5682	Yarnell J E	3	E	Aug 14	

TOTAL 736.

VERMONT.

3975	Averill T E	9	I	July 25	64
4579	Adams Dan'l	Cav 1	L	Aug 2	
8301	Albee S, S't	11	G	Sept 9	
9960	Atwood A	1	C	Sept 28	
10664	Aldrich L E, S't	11	A	Oct 11	
11259	Aldrich H B	Art 1	A	Oct 21	
12092	Aiken M A	1	A	Nov 19	
12766	Avery B F	3	C	Mar 13	65

LIST OF THE DEAD.

No.	Name		Reg.	Co.	Date	
2035	Bloomer J	Bat	2		June 15	64
3166	Bailey James		2	A	July 11	
4036	Brown George		10	B	July 20	
4173	Bailey S P	Cav	1	H	July 28	
4200	Beadle H H		9	G	July 29	
4509	Bucker James		1	M	Aug 1	
4637	Boyd A M	Cav	1	L	Aug 3	
4954	Bently M W		6	A	Aug 7	
5671	Bacon A M		8	G	Aug 14	
5728	Bliss J H	Cav	1	L	Aug 15	
6334	Burchard C		11	L	Aug 21	
6349	Benson A		1	C	Aug 21	
6416	Bennvills J		4	D	Aug 22	
6594	Barnes W	Cav	1	F	Aug 23	
7886	Barton W		11	K	Sept 5	
8029	Beady Wm		9	I	Sept 6	
8086	Barker F	Art	1	A	Aug 7	
8315	Burrows H		11	F	Sept 10	
8591	Brainard J B	Cav	1	L	Aug 12	
10305	Brown G		9	D	Oct 4	
10371	Bowles L H		7	A	Oct 5	
10431	Burton C		4	A	Oct 6	
10743	Barker C		4	D	Oct 11	
11068	Brown J B		1	A	Oct 17	
11225	Batch B F		4	C	Oct 20	
11375	Bohamar J		9	I	Oct 24	
11469	Baker John		11	E	Oct 26	
11747	Bonlon A		2	B	Nov 2	
11841	Babcock T		1	K	Nov 5	
12055	Barber W H		1	C	Nov 16	
12185	Burns J		7	B	Nov 28	
12230	Butler A F	Art	1	L	Dec 7	
12106	Baxter G		4	A	Jan 6	65
12412	Bishop E		11	E	Jan 8	
12585	Bailey E		4	B	Feb 4	
1041	Corey C A	Cav	1	F	May 12	64
1170	Clifford Jas		4	F	May 17	
1228	Chatfield Wm, Cor	10	F	May 20	
1973	Collit Jas	Cav	1	H	June 15	
2675	Caswell F		9		June 30	
2694	Clough B		9	A	June 30	
2811	Chase M		6	H	July 3	
3354	Cole A H		9	H	July 15	
3817	Crocker D		5	D	July 23	
3918	Clough John D		11	A	July 24	
4205	Chamberlain —		6	A	July 29	
4883	Crouse N		5	C	Aug 6	
5103	Chester A		11	K	Aug 9	
5480	Carey Thomas	Art	1		Aug 13	
6806	Carmine P	"	1	L	Aug 25	
6932	Conner W A, S't		4	A	Aug 26	
7345	Clark M L		11	F	Aug 31	
7361	Clark John	Art	11	M	Aug 31	
7698	Cunningham J	Cav	1	F	Sept 3	
8320	Cook J J, Cor	"	1	I	Sept 10	
8923	Chase E L	Art	1	C	Sept 16	
9724	Crowley D		11	F	Sept 25	
11738	Cross E F		11	L	Nov 2	
11769	Carter J		11	A	Nov 3	
10330	Colborn W	Art	1	M	Oct 4	
3068	Drew F	Cav	1	F	July 9	
5927	Donohoe P	"	1	D	Aug 17	
6104	Dunn G E, Cor		1	G	Aug 18	
6338	Doying F W	Art	1	F	Aug 21	
6840	Darcy F		4	D	Aug 25	
7974	Day Geo		11	H	Sept 6	
8271	Davis O F		9	I	Sept 9	
10420	Dunn W W	Cav	1	G	Oct 6	64
10458	Day J D	"	1	A	Oct 7	
12375	Dragoon N	"	1	G	Jan 1	65
6353	Ennison G		11	A	Aug 21	64
10316	Eliot C		4	F	Oct 4	
821	Farmer E L		14	H	May 1	
3464	Freeman C R		9	H	July 17	
4077	Farnsworth M		1	B	July 26	
5851	Farnham L B	Art	1	A	Aug 16	
5914	Foster A		17	K	Aug 17	
6758	Fuller W	Cav	1	G	Aug 25	
7165	Forrest S		3	I	Aug 29	
8096	Fox W		11	K	Sept 7	
8201	Foster H B		11	L	Sept 8	
10784	Feast Geo	Art	1	K	Oct 12	
10969	Fisk W P		4	K	Oct 15	
11314	Farrell J H		4	D	Oct 22	
11351	Flint O B		4	D	Oct 23	
11453	Foster H C	Art	1	D	Oct 25	
12317	Ferand A	Art	1	B	Dec 21	
12322	Ferrett J		1	K	Dec 23	
12065	Fairchild G L	Art	1	A	Nov 17	
6264	Farnham L D, S't	11	A	Nov 20	
1730	Gelo A		3	B	June 8	
5273	Green E	Bat	2		Aug 10	
8572	Gleason C W	Art	1	H	Sept 12	
9739	Gillman S A		4	G	Sept 26	
11598	Graves J		11	E	Oct 28	
12531	Gerry E B, Cor		4	H	Jan 26	65
2176	Hubbard F	Bat	2		June 19	64
3851	Humphrey J	Cav	1	A	July 14	
5218	Hall Benj		11	A	Aug 10	
6145	Hyde E, Cor		11	L	Aug 18	
6657	Havens E W		9	H	Aug 24	
7394	Hazen W		9	H	Aug 31	
10824	Hines L		11	A	Oct 13	
10843	Hart S L		2		Oct 13	
10910	Hudson J B		11	A	Oct 14	
10996	Hudson J M		11	A	Oct 16	
11442	Howard J	Cav	1	K	Oct 25	
11730	Holmes Joseph	Art	1	K	Nov 2	
11814	Howard J		11	A	Nov 4	
1206	Hall C A		1	A	Nov 17	
12300	Hodges J	Cav	1	H	Dec 17	
3309	Jones H L		6	B	July 14	
3858	Joslin H		1	B	July 24	
3886	Jordan A E		17	A	July 24	
4690	Johnson D W		11	H	Aug 4	
10183	Johnson John	Art	1	K	Oct 1	
4007	Knapp L		1	G	July 25	
6968	Kelsey L C	Art	1	F	Aug 27	
7762	Kingsley S		1	D	Sept 4	
8901	Knowles C W		4	H	Sept 16	
6239	Knight Chas	Art	1	K	Aug 26	
4597	LaBoney H		1	M	Aug 3	
4664	Larraway H		5	A	Aug 3	
7653	Lapcam A	Cav	1		Sept 3	
7891	Laddenbush J		17	A	Sept 5	
8355	Leoport C		11	L	Sept 10	
10180	Lungershaw W C	Cav	1	F	Oct 1	
11074	Lacker H		11	A	Oct 17	
12916	Lumsden C	Cav	4	D	Feb 8	65
1335	Mitchell Jacob	Bat	2		May 24	64
1544	Moscy A	Cav		K	June 1	
2088	McIntyre John		7	F	June 17	
2394	Manian P		9		June 24	
4617	Morse W		1	F	Aug 3	

LIST OF THE DEAD. 277

5073	Martin Jas		1	M	Aug 8 64	5833	Tatro Alfred		9	F	Aug 16 64
5949	Mills Wm		1	E	Aug 17	6587	Taylor H C	Art	1	L	Aug 23
7324	Merrill B J		1	B	Aug 30	6659	Trow H		17	D	Aug 24
8475	Mayhim J		6	C	Sept 11	9374	Tanner H, Cor		11	I	Sept 20
8965	Manchester J M C		1	I	Sept 16	9574	Tolman W C, S't		11	F	Sept 23
9352	McGager J		2	G	Sept 20	11171	Taylor J W	Art	1	A	Oct 19
9405	Montgomery O A		10	A	Sept 21	11220	Thompson W A "		1	I	Oct 20
11227	McAllister W B		3	I	Oct 20	5693	Varnum E G J		11	F	Aug 15
11735	Martin M	Art	1	A	Nov 2	3177	Weller D		9	B	July 11
12631	Monroe A	"	11	L	Feb 10 65	4376	Whitehall Geo		6	B	July 31
9001	Morgan Chas	"	11	M	Sept 27 64	4485	Wilson A		6	B	July 31
4478	McCrillis Edw	Cav	1	C	Aug 1	4585	Wilder L F		11	H	Aug 2
7289	Milcher Wm		9	F	Aug 30	5075	Whitney A		9	D	Aug 8
6559	Nownes Geo H Cav		1	C	Aug 23	5307	Warner Geo O		10	E	Aug 11
11067	Nichols H	Art	1	A	Oct 17	5751	Woodworth S P	Art	1	H	Aug 15
12283	Nelson S H	"	4	I	Dec 13	7063	Wells Geo A		4	F	Aug 28
704	O'Brien Wm		1	H	Apr 23	7322	Wright E S	Art	11	A	Aug 30
4300	O'Neil J M		10	A	July 30	7689	Witt T	Cav	1	F	Sept 3
3183	Plude John	Bat	2		July 11	7920	Ward Alfred		11	A	Sept 5
3243	Pev Jas		17	D	July 12	8239	Watkins G C		1	C	Sept 9
4981	Preston F	Art	1		Aug 7	9264	Woodmance G		11	F	Sept 9
5135	Phelps H W		9	H	Aug 9	9178	Welles C		11	H	Sept 18
5605	Poppins Frank		3	I	Aug 14	10510	White A		11	A	Oct 8
6586	Parmor E		4	C	Aug 23	10741	Webster W A, S't		4	A	Oct 11
7290	Park James	Cav	7	E	Aug 30	11289	Wakefield J W		4	H	Oct 22
10040	Pillsbury F	"	4	C	Sept 29	11398	Woods J M		1	F	Oct 24
10237	Paul John C	"	4	G	Oct 2	11783	Wheeler B		11	K	Nov 3
11041	Page E		4	I	Oct 17	11840	Warden G		3	B	Nov 5
11307	Powers A		4	H	Oct 22	11865	Worthers S T	Cav	1	D	Nov 6
11992	Packard M G, Cor	A	1	A	Nov 13	12156	Willey J S	Art	1	A	Nov 25
12198	Pike N N		4	I	Nov 30	4533	Washburn Tru	Cav	1	D	Aug 2
12721	Perry A B		4	H	Mar 3 65		TOTAL 240.				
1888	Reed D W	Cav	1		June 13 64						
6699	Ransom Geo W	Art	1	L	Aug 24		VIRGINIA.				
7697	Roscoe C		11	H	Sept 3	824	Anderson A		2	H	May 1 64
8138	Roberts J M		11	K	Sept 8	876	Armstrong, St	Mil	8	C	May 4
8173	Richards J	Cav	1	L	Sept 8	942	Ayers S V		11	C	May 7
9462	Raynor Louis	"	4	C	Sept 21	1908	Armstrong G B		8	C	June 14
9894	Ross H E	Bat	11	K	Sept 27	2760	Arinhalt W H, Cor		10	I	July 1
11009	Reynolds F		11	F	Oct 15	5011	Armstrong J		3	C	Aug 8
11426	Raney A		4	A	Oct 24	5341	Arbogast C W	Art	1	C	Aug 11
11691	Rice F W		14	F	Oct 13	8863	Abercrombie W H		12	C	Sept 15
12519	Rouncervee E T		9	D	Jan 25 65	11525	Allison G		1	F	Oct 26
648	Spoore W O	Cav	1	B	Apr 20 64	221	Burns S A, S't		8	C	Mar 29
2943	Smith J C		1	H	July 6	255	Brooks Samuel F		10	I	Mar 30
3382	St John A		11	A	July 17	448	Boone Jas	Cav	1	L	Apr 9
4580	Seward O		5	C	Aug 2	756	Bennett L J		11	C	Apr 27
5707	Skinner F A		4	H	Aug 15	943	Brake J, S't		6	C	May 7
5963	Stone Jas A	Art	1	H	Aug 17	980	Blackburn Geo		10	I	May 9
6640	Simons L		1	G	Aug 23	1705	Bates T E		11	F	June 7
7509	Seaton T B			F	Sept 1	2518	Brown M		14	E	June 26
7810	Sweeney Henry		11	C	Sept 4	2627	Bowermaster S R	C	3	D	June 28
7813	Sprout A		17	F	Sept 4	3407	Bateman D P		2	B	July 16
8444	Stockwell A		11	H	Sept 11	4427	Barber Jas	Cav	1	F	July 31
10696	Sanburn H		4	G	Sept 11	5495	Bishop J C		3	C	Aug 12
10811	Styles A B, Cor		4	K	Sept 12	6706	Bearer P		10	I	Aug 24
10897	Sheldon H	Cav	1	M	Sept 14	10297	Boutwell O		4	F	Oct 3
11282	Sarlett L		1	M	Oct 22	7126	Beasldy P		9	G	Aug 28
11476	Swaddle W		4	G	Oct 26	7909	Bogard Jno R, Cor		14	A	Sept 5
11966	Sanborn M L	Art	1	A	Nov 11	8539	Batt M		18	E	Sept 12
12266	Scott R O		4	F	Dec 12	9796	Butcher Peter		14	F	Sept 26
12514	Shay J	Cav	1	K	Jan 23 65	10198	Broom J	Cav	1	B	Oct 2
12552	Sheldon G		1	K	Jan 29	11000	Blessing P		15	K	Oct 18
12567	Stewart E W		11	A	Feb 1	11337	Bush H H		14	B	Oct 23
5911	Scott Geo W	Cav	1	C	Aug 17 64	11411	Burton W B	Cav	6	A	Oct 24
8436	Suppes T E	"	1	K	Sept 11	11669	Barnett J	"	6	K	Oct 30
3784	Tuttle C S	"	1	F	July 22	11924	Beach J F		14	K	Nov 8

LIST OF THE DEAD.

No.	Name		Co.	Date
12045	Boggs H C, Cor	C 6	E	Nov 16 64
12414	Burton N	Cav 3	B	Jan 8 65
110	Corbett L B W, Va Mil		C	Mar 23 64
403	Carr Wm	8	B	Apr 6
835	Clendeman C L	C 4	D	May 1
1032	Caste Jesse	8	E	May 11
1100	Coon Nathan	14	K	May 14
2013	Carrington Jas	2	A	June 15
2235	Coffman F	Cav 3	A	June 20
2560	Cunderson ——	8	D	June 27
2661	Carnes H	10	E	June 29
2817	Conrad P	3	F	July 3
2930	Cunningham J	8	E	July 5
3315	Cox T A, S't	Cav 3	A	July 14
4363	Cool J B, Cor	" 3	H	July 31
4741	Crook E H, S't	7	I	Aug 5
5174	Cuppett J	3	H	Aug 9
5384	Covil Wm	3	I	Aug 12
6674	Clements L	Cav 3	A	Aug 24
6809	Curtin B	" 4	B	Aug 25
7091	Clark ——	7	E	Aug 28
7179	Cremones D	9	D	Aug 29
8990	Cook J	Cav 7	I	Sept 17
9406	Campbell O H	14	F	Sept 21
9755	Christian J	15	C	Sept 25
9702	Catnill L	9	B	Sept 25
9967	Cobin J M	14	B	Sept 28
10598	Childs S P	Cav 1	C	Oct 10
11561	Castle C H	1	A	Oct 27
11830	Cooper A H, Cor	C 7	I	Nov 5
12174	Campbell B	12	I	Nov 26
24	Deboard H A	5	G	Mar 8
202	Douglas Geo	8	C	Mar 28
317	Dean Samuel	5	H	Apr 2
632	Defibaugh W R, Cor A 1		G	Apr 19
647	Davis S	3	D	Apr 20
843	Duncan J M	5	D	May 2
2081	Daly Jas	Cav 3	A	June 17
3105	Duckworth W B	14	A	July 10
3246	Dyer James	10	I	July 13
3507	Drake Samuel	9	B	Aug 13
5588	Dorsey A L	15	K	Aug 23
6745	Daner J	10	I	Aug 24
6936	Darsey M	9	L	Aug 26
6949	Dodd S, S't	9	F	Aug 26
7092	Dunberger Geo	9	C	Aug 28
8248	Divers G	15	D	Sept 9
8467	Dant Jno M	Cav 7	H	Sept 10
8582	Dason N	" 8	L	Sept 12
9159	Dunn I	2	K	Sept 18
12235	Duncan Wm	Cav 6	C	Dec 6
12807	Donohue S	9	C	Mar 21 65
12508	Doty John	Cav 6	A	Jan 23
10975	Estuff Jno	" 1	L	Oct 12 64
117	Fuller Irwin	Militia		Mar 23
613	Foster Charles K	9	H	Apr 18
935	Fox H C, Cor	1	D	May 8
5765	Fawkes Wm	14	D	Aug 15
7203	Foster S	8	A	Aug 29
7941	Feather J B	14	B	Sept 5
8698	Fensley Leu	Art 1		Sept 14
8723	Fusner J E	Cav 6	D	Sept 14
10206	Freeborn R L, Ser 14		B	Oct 2
10709	Furr E	10	K	Oct 11
11022	Fleming W W	Cav 6	A	Oct 16
10314	Forth R	8	D	Sept 3
2485	Grey P	Va 3	A	June 25
2649	Greshoe M	11	C	June 29 64
2712	Golden J	Cav 2	G	July 1
4738	Gordon S	2	G	Aug 4
6348	Guenant A	2	I	Aug 21
10581	Garton Wm, Cor	2	I	Oct 10
11574	Gluck A E	10	D	Oct 28
11864	Gibson A	1	A	Nov 6
84	Hollingshead S	1	G	Mar 8
294	Harrison D	10	I	Apr 1
365	Henry Robert O	8	C	Apr 2
398	Hunter G W	8	A	Apr 6
568	Heller Wm, Cor	3	D	Apr 15
839	Halpin Jno	2	D	May 2
997	Hoffman G W	8	E	May 10
1013	Hess J	11	C	May 10
1421	Hatfield J	1	B	May 28
1854	Harkins H	2	F	June 11
2702	Hoover W H	3	A	June 30
2902	Howell A	14	E	July 5
2957	Howe S	2	I	July 5
3980	Horant E A	3	C	July 25
4739	Hine Wm	2	A	Aug 5
5061	Hammer S	Cav 3	G	Aug 8
5412	Hartley Isaac	3	I	Aug 12
5649	Hall Henry	10	F	Aug 14
6538	Harper W	8	H	Aug 23
8061	Hushman W	10	I	Sept 7
8268	Hardway D B	9	G	Sept 9
8341	Harden G W	Cav 6	A	Sept 10
8344	Hutson J	14	A	Sept 10
9166	Hanslan B	Cav 6		Sept 18
9537	Hudgins J	14	B	Sept 22
9794	Handland H	1	H	Sept 26
10990	Hollinbeck W H, Cor C 1		B	Oct 14
11316	Hubert W C	12	G	Oct 22
11396	Hendershot F F	7	E	Oct 24
11739	Hurn R	8	E	Nov 2
12014	Hartzel S	1	D	Nov 15
12153	Hickman E	11	B	Nov 24
312	Johns E K	Mil 8	C	Apr 2
3045	Jake A R	8	I	July 8
3969	Jackson S E	2	E	July 25
6098	Jones G	Cav 2	D	Aug 18
7681	Johnston I A	" 1	D	Sept 3
8371	Jenkins W	Art 1		Sept 10
323	Kane J	Cav 4	L	Apr 2
5822	Kimball Jno	14	K	Aug 16
589	Ludihing W	2	A	Apr 17
1565	Langstan N H	Cav 1	A	June 2
1592	Lanham Henry	8	C	June 3
1949	Logger J	Cav 3	B	June 14
2734	Lyshon Wm	2	I	July 1
2730	Loud Geo	9	D	July 1
6924	Lansbury W, Ser 15		E	Aug 26
7237	Lough H	Cav 1	L	Aug 29
10564	Liston David	" 6	C	Oct 9
10569	Lowe /	9	C	Oct 9
11021	Lowe W G	13	G	Oct 16
11325	Layman W F	14	C	Oct 23
11624	Laughlin D, Cor	9	E	Oct 31
11980	Lucas J	9	D	Nov 13
12262	Loring J	Art 1	D	Dec 12
41	Maddons W L	Cav 4	K	May 3
280	Mason Peter	10	G	Apr 1
387	Magnher J	Cav 3	A	Apr 5
422	McNeily Jas	" 3	A	Apr 7
582	McCormick R		F	Apr 16

LIST OF THE DEAD.

No.	Name		Co.	Date
786	McConnaughy D	11	F	Apr 28 64
820	McGitton J	6	G	May 1
1068	Morris J M	Cav 3	E	May 13
1419	Murphy J	8	D	May 28
1675	Moore M	14	K	June 6
2932	Millum Jas	8	I	July 5
3955	Mokie R	Cav 7		July 20
6960	Miller C W	2	C	Aug 27
7018	Meiner H	12	I	Aug 27
9699	Mencar L B	14	B	Sept 24
9767	Morris G	14	A	Sept 25
9955	Miller D	14	C	Sept 28
10567	Moody R W	Cav 6	E	Oct 9
10578	McKinney Wm	C 1	L	Oct 9
10834	McConkey A, Cor	C 6	B	Oct 14
10970	McLaughlin R	Art 1	D	Oct 15
11546	Monsen J F	14	C	Oct 27
12099	Matt Henry	12	E	Nov 19
12272	McCausland R	1	G	Dec 12
9488	McGregor P	1	E	Sept 21
13068	McWilson J	14	F	Nov 17
2857	Norman H	2	I	July 4
3395	Newman A	Cav 1	B	July 16
6442	Nichols L D	9	F	Aug 22
12472	Nicholson J	Cav 3	B	Jan 17 65
241	Oxley Robert	14	C	Mar 30 64
1767	Osborne Thos		H	June 9
39	Packard Myron	C, C 2	I	Mar 13
1707	Peterfield Jno	4	F	June 7
2433	Porrellson C D	10	I	June 24
2645	Patney J	8	G	June 29
2737	Painter C, Ser	9	F	July 1
3055	Petit J, Cor	Cav 1	L	July 9
4707	Paine M, Cor	8	F	Aug 3
5004	Pugh L	3	I	Aug 8
5213	Pollend Jno	10	I	Aug 10
6004	Polley J	8	C	Aug 17
6196	Perkins James A	12	K	Aug 19
11267	Palmer Jno, Ser	C 1	L	Oct 21
349	Reakes Wm	Mil 8	C	Apr 2
521	Rice A	Cav	G	Apr 13
560	Randall Jas A	9	K	Apr 15
959	Rinker F A	Cav 3	A	May 8
1040	Robb M	2	A	May 12
1916	Richards G L	14	D	June 14
3459	Rummer L	5	A	July 17
3465	Read J	12	B	July 17
3641	Redden J	9	F	July 20
4163	Ronsey Wm	9	C	July 29
7257	Rutroff Jacob	7	H	July 30
8082	Reush Jas	7	B	Sept 7
10527	Reed J M, Cor	12	B	Oct 7
11518	Rock J H	12		Oct 26
11794	Raleigh S	Cav 1	I	Nov 4
7005	Richardson W	14	K	Aug 27
273	Sayre Michael	14	I	Mar 31
680	Sprague Geo	11	F	Apr 23
927	Stackleford S	Cav 3	A	May 7
1510	Scott Z, Ser	8	D	May 31
2226	Steward C	Cav 2	I	June 20
2359	Stagg Wm	10	I	June 23
2437	Stutter J N	Cav 3	B	June 25
2931	Skillington G	"	4	D	July 5
3321	Stephenson A	"	1	B	July 16
3588	Shilber C A	3	A	July 19
3747	Shaub F	2	E	July 22
3895	Simons C E	8	C	July 24
3865	Stewart Wm A	14	I	July 25 64
4463	Steele A	Cav 2	C	Aug 1
4812	Snider S	3	K	Aug 5
4935	Sturn E E	12	F	Aug 7
5180	Smith ——		2	F	Aug 8
5237	Simmons E	8	C	Aug 10
5727	Sprouse A	11	F	Aug 15
5975	Smith J W	8	G	Aug 17
6473	Sprouse W	11	F	Aug 22
6610	Squares Sam'l	Cav 6	D	Aug 23
7091	Stratton B B	Art 1	F	Aug 28
7944	Stoker S	Cav 3	C	Sept 5
8011	Sands Wm	10	F	Sept 6
8164	Scritchfield W	6	F	Sept 18
8390	Stuck H M	14	B	Sept 10
8516	Smith B	9	H	Sept 12
8646	Sturgiss W T, D'm	14	B	Sept 12
9217	Smith G H	Cav 7	G	Sept 19
9714	Sullivan E	2	A	Sept 25
9786	Snyder J V, Ser	3	D	Sept 26
9872	Semeir G S	Cav 4		Sept 27
9906	Sands G W	1		Sept 28
10151	Smith J	14	B	Oct 1
11276	Smith J A	9	B	Oct 22
11625	Slee R, Ser	Cav 1	D	Oct 25
11824	Spaulding F	"	1	A	Nov 5
11836	Stockwell C H	3	B	Nov 5
7291	Saylor C M	9	B	Aug 30
1108	Thatcher J P	2	A	Apr 15
3404	Trobridge S	6	B	July 16
5136	Tyom T	8	H	Aug 8
6379	Thurston C C	1	I	Aug 21
8663	Taylor J	8	G	Sept 13
12332	Thorpe S S	3	I	Dec 26
3846	Tomlinson S, Ser	3	I	July 24
8119	Tatro L	11	B	Sept 8
244	Vincent Jas	8	C	Mar 30
814	Very W	Cav 1	C	Apr 30
1149	Vanscoy A, Cor	"	3	E	May 16
1322	Virts R	"	3	A	May 23
945	Wilson Walter	11	F	May 7
1757	Weaver M	Cav 1	C	June 7
2854	Warp J	3	F	July 6
3723	Wich J	Cav 1	L	July 21
3825	Whitney W A	8	F	July 25
3996	Whit A	5	F	July 25
7542	Wilson J	3	B	Sept 2
7832	Warwicke E	2	D	Sept 4
8598	Wells E	7	F	Sept 12
9026	Wolfe C	14	B	Sept 24
10854	White J N	Cav 6	C	Oct 13
148	Young A	8	C	Mar 25
456	Young A B	8	C	Apr 9
694	Young Ed	8	C	Apr 23

TOTAL, 288.

WISCONSIN.

2113	Allwise J R	24	E	June 17 64
4477	Austin Isaac	25	G	Aug 1
5241	Abbott A, Ser	21	D	Aug 10
5453	Allen C P	2	G	Aug 12
8692	Adams A F	36	F	Sept 14
10830	Adams P	10	A	Oct 13
11492	Aultin E V, Cor	13	E	Oct 26
12728	Antone C	31	D	Mar 4 65
1341	Bower H	1	A	May 24 64

LIST OF THE DEAD.

No.	Name	Reg	Co	Date
1838	Burk O	15	B	June 11 64
2009	Bawgarder B	2	K	June 15
2055	Ball A	7	A	June 16
2123	Bowhan H A, Ser	10	F	June 18
2334	Brooks E Cav	1	H	June 22
2451	Broomer B F, Cor	10	I	June 25
2681	Brown O	15	G	June 30
3253	Brown J	4	H	July 13
3673	Bruce H	24	H	July 20
4870	Brumsted G, Ser	15	A	Aug 6
5026	Briggs H	1	L	Aug 8
5100	Budson John "	1	L	Aug 9
5164	Bemis H	10	C	Aug 9
5322	Briggs E Cav	1		Aug 11
5564	Bailey W, Cor	25	E	Aug 13
6304	Banick S	17	I	Aug 19
7295	Bailey J	36	I	Aug 30
7323	Burk J Cav	10	E	Aug 30
7755	Borden E, Cor	21	K	Sept 3
7759	Boyle P	25	D	Sept 4
8576	Batchelder J	1	I	Sept 12
8641	Bushell C C	2	B	Sept 13
9607	Brinkman J	2	A	Sept 23
10686	Britton H, S't	15	I	Oct 11
10919	Bohnsen N	15	I	Oct 14
11751	Butler M	10	K	Nov 2
12032	Blakeley R	7	F	Nov 15
11610	Batterson L	10	K	Oct 28
2360	Church A	7	H	June 23
2663	Chapman J	2	G	June 29
2969	Cowles D	10	B	July 6
3392	Cummings S	21	A	July 14
3828	Crane R, Drummer	7	D	July 23
4390	Chapel C	1	E	July 31
5102	Cavanaugh John	C 1	H	Aug 9
8105	Chase F M, Cor	1	A	Sept 7
9418	Currier C C	21	F	Aug 22
9169	Carlintyre G	23		Sept 18
19752	Castle C Cav	1	C	Oct 12
11020	Cofam W	10	A	Oct 16
11088	Chusterson F	15	E	Oct 18
11585	Chamberlain J	21	I	Oct 27
11741	Clark W C	10	E	Nov 2
10316	Crommings H	7	C	Oct 5
1591	Duffey E	1	L	June 3
2522	Damhocker E	26	I	June 26
3244	Daggo John Cav	1	L	July 13
5830	Destler Fred	26	G	July 16
6967	Dick Benjamin	36	G	Aug 27
7455	Davis J	36	B	Sept 1
8530	Decker G, S't	Bat	F	Sept 12
8587	Depas A	21	A	Sept 12
8900	Doryson W	7	C	Sept 15
9739	Dacy G	12	I	Sept 25
10771	Davis John	1	B	Oct 12
12750	David D P	25	B	Mar 8 65
2419	Enger E	15	K	June 24 64
5247	Egan John	7	A	
6160	Erickson C	15	B	Aug 19
8601	Ellwood S, S't	10	C	Aug 13
9337	Erricson S	50	D	Sept 20
11687	Ellenger P	21	K	Oct 31
12286	Enkhart H	36	G	Dec 14
36	Fordway G W	7	E	Mar 12
1260	Fuller C W, Cor	7	E	May 21
2283	Fountain W F	10	A	June 20
5007	Forslay W K	8	K	Aug 8
5759	Flenis Oscar Cav	1	H	Aug 15 64
5811	Fisk J B, S't "	1	H	Aug 16
6097	Fischnor D, S't	36	H	Aug 18
6236	Fanon Wm	1	A	Aug 20
8400	Farnham M B	4	K	Sept 11
9664	Ferguson I	15	G	Sept 24
10234	Fagan M	15	G	Oct 2
12618	Frost A	7	B	Feb 2 65
12653	Ferguson W R	24	D	Feb 14
1529	Gilbert I	16	K	May 31 64
2392	Grush Fred	15	I	June 24
3164	Guth H	1	D	July 11
3390	Greenman D	21	K	July 16
5557	Greenwall M Cav	1	C	Aug 16
7355	Grunds L	15	I	Aug 31
8326	Groupe D	4	F	Sept 10
10691	Gunduson H	15	I	Oct 11
6614	Goon Jno E	36		Aug 23
303	Helt Carl	26	E	Apr 1
710	Hale A C	21	I	Apr 24
1062	Haskins J	1	E	May 10
1655	Hoffland --, 1 S't	15	K	June 5
1673	Harvey D M	1	I	June 6
2984	Hanson J	15	K	June 23
2556	Hough B J	10	K	June 27
3720	Henderson O	15	F	July 24
4542	Hewick Nelson	10	B	Aug 2
4570	Halts S	26	C	Aug 2
5312	Howard F B	10	K	Aug 11
5628	Holenback A	25	D	Aug 14
6468	Hall A W	21	I	Aug 22
7081	Hanley T Art	3	D	Aug 28
7149	Hutchins B Cav	1	E	Aug 29
7849	Hanson L	15	B	Sept 3
7791	Harding W F	21	C	Sept 4
8584	High M	25	E	Sept 12
9333	Halter D	22	D	Sept 20
10427	Hans P	10	D	Oct 6
11443	Holenbeck C	13	A	Oct 25
11927	Hanson	1	B	Nov 8
12167	Harris N	12	D	Nov 26
12586	Hardy F L	6	E	Jan 4 65
12848	Hanson R L	1	F	Apr 28
12468	Hand G	10	D	Jan 16
8614	Ingham J	10	K	Sept 13 64
9808	Irwin A	25	C	Sept 26
2003	Jacobson O	15	D	June 15
3281	Jackson T	4	H	July 13
3478	Jillett J	7	H	July 17
6938	Jennings J R	45	G	Aug 5
11284	Johnson W H	6	H	Oct 22
1165	Kemmett J	1	H	May 17
2498	Kundson J	15	E	June 26
4133	Kellett Jno B	21	B	July 27
4405	Kull L	24	C	July 31
4614	Klepps C H Cav	1	E	Aug 3
8592	Kendall W	32		Sept 12
9063	Keeroger Wm	36	G	Sept 17
10536	Kane F	26	E	Oct 8
10692	Knowles H	21	D	Oct 11
8299	Kinds M O	21	A	Sept 9
3009	Lack Peter	7	A	July 7
5397	Livingston J H Art	3	E	Aug 12
6642	Lansing G	10	A	Aug 23
7235	Lowe F	16	G	Aug 29
7522	Lawson M	15	B	Sept 1
8044	Laich F	26	K	Sept 16

LIST OF THE DEAD. 281

9997	Latgen E	15	A	Sept 29	64
8977	Laich F	26	K	Sept 17	
1752	Manger Jas	24	H	June 9	
1896	Mulligan J	1	I	June 13	
2732	McMann W Bat	3		July 1	
2954	McCormick E Cav	1	L	July 6	
2981	McKenzie J	1	F	July 7	
3625	McLaulin C	36	I	July 20	
4925	Mathison E N	2	E	Aug 6	
5043	Many J	24	D	Aug 8	
5163	McFadden H Cav	1	F	Aug 9	
5683	Mortes B	10	D	Aug 15	
5739	Main Henry	30	F	Aug 15	
6231	McClury A	10	I	Aug 20	
6377	Messer F	5	B	Aug 21	
10249	Myers S	15	G	Oct 4	
11936	Mulasky E	21	B	Nov 9	
4299	Nelson R	15	K	July 30	
4980	Northam S R	10	C	Aug 7	
6030	Nichols Wm	10	I	Aug 18	
10369	Neff Wm	33	I	Oct 6	
3162	Olson O	15	B	July 11	
11545	Ochle F	26	E	Oct 27	
11931	Olston M	15	B	Nov 7	
604	Palmer Jno	7	C	Apr 18	
2535	Plum A Cav	4	K	June 26	
2847	Peterson A	15	K	July 4	
3511	Picket T B	1	F	July 18	
4340	Purdy M	10	E	July 30	
6406	Pirisis J	17	F	Aug 22	
7530	Purdee J	10	I	Sept 1	
7893	Peterson S	15	K	Sept 5	
8515	Pillsbury A J Cav	H	H	Sept 12	
8654	Patterson J	21	A	Sept 13	
9014	Painter H	10	F	Sept 17	
9902	Patterson S	15	I	Sept 27	
9461	Peterson C	15	I	Sept 21	
2028	Roach A	21	F	June 15	
3624	Renscler H	2	G	July 20	
3665	Reynolers F S	10	K	July 20	
4997	Reed G	6	K	Aug 7	
5792	Rasmusson A Cav	1	L	Aug 15	
6088	Robinson Will	10	C	Aug 18	
9860	Rice J	7	C	Aug 27	
11812	Randles J	25	D	Nov 4	
12233	Richmond B Cav	1	L	Dec 6	
12242	Randell P B "	1	K	Dec 7	
68	Schleassen J J	7	F	Mar 19	
440	Shrigley H	10	G	Apr 8	
2418	Stiffus R	15	F	July 3	
3078	Sirbirth F	24	E	July 9	
3503	Shoop W	1	G	July 18	
3583	Sutton J	10	B	July 19	
4343	Sharp J W	2	G	July 30	
4378	Smith W F	10	B	July 31	
4436	Shun J	24	H	July 31	
4708	Scott E G	21	D	Aug 5	
4882	Slingerland Jno Cav	1	B	Aug 6	
6943	Starr E	16	F	Aug 26	
7614	Seaman M	21	D	Sept 2	
8168	Smith L Cav	4	K	Sept 8	
9693	Snyder M	26	E	Sept 24	
11037	Smith S M	21	F	Oct 17	
11047	Sales A D	4	K	Oct 17	
2148	Tung S W	21	D	June 18	
2385	Tay S	1	K	June 24	
2588	Tomlinson Robert	6	B	June 28	
3120	Thompson D D	36	B	June 10	64
3375	Tyler J	10	A	July 16	
3661	Tucker C P	1	L	July 20	
4467	Taylor A L	25	E	Aug 1	
6858	Taylor I	6	E	Aug 26	
7160	Thorn P C Cav	1	L	Aug 29	
8500	Troutman A	2		Sept 12	
11236	Thurber D	36	G	Oct 21	
11420	Tyler E P	10	F	Oct 24	
11473	Thorson P	24	G	Oct 26	
12374	Thompson O	15	K	Jan 1	65
2309	Updell J S	15	B	June 22	64
2954	Vohoss O H	1	L	July 6	
3076	Vitter J	6	F	July 9	
8359	Vancoster H Cav	1	C	Sept 10	
8427	Vanderbilt J	36	D	Sept 11	
11390	Voelee F	10	E	Oct 24	
929	Webster A C	7	E	May 7	
884	Winleis P	1	M	May 5	
1007	Wilder Jno Cav	1	F	May 10	
1520	Welcome E D "	1	L	May 31	
1693	Walter S P	21	G	June 7	
1909	Welton M S Cav	1	L	June 13	
2591	Winchester Geo	21	I	June 28	
2894	Weaver H	10	F	July 4	
3378	Wens Chas	7	B	July 16	
4706	Wakefield D	25	K	Aug 4	
9484	Woodward W B	1		Sept 21	
9938	Wick A Cav	1	H	Sept 28	
10213	Willis E	7	E	Oct 2	
10395	Winchell S	1	D	Oct 6	
12111	Whalen W	12	B	Oct 21	
12363	Ward A Cav	1	C	Dec 31	
12626	Yessen A	24	A	Feb 10	65

TOTAL, 244.

UNITED STATES ARMY.

1798	Anderson A	16	C	June 10	64
3666	Atwell Thos Cav	6	M	July 20	
4349	Allen Chas	18	H	July 31	
4537	Aschley D B	16	C	Aug 2	
6077	Arnold H	18	H	Aug 18	
6089	Adams G	14	C	Aug 18	
8069	Austin Jas Cav	4	K	Sept 7	
11523	Annis Chas (col'd)	8	I	Oct 26	
9250	Alfka A H Cav	2	D	Sept 19	
102	Blossom Chas "	8	E	Mar 22	
1122	Boughton M	15	E	May 15	
1158	Bailey Andrew	16	K	May 16	
1199	Britner A	16	K	May 18	
1201	Banks E E	17	C	May 19	
1266	Burton Geo (col'd)	8	I	May 21	
1397	Bardon Chas S	15	C	May 26	
1442	Beal H	15	C	May 28	
1461	Becker L	2	B	May 29	
1762	Brown C	16	D	June 9	
2122	Bates E L Cav	5	E	June 17	
2434	Brannagan J	18	D	June 24	
2436	Bigler N M Cav	2	B	June 25	
2749	Bradshaw H Mar Corps			July 1	
3370	Bush W	15	E	July 15	
4861	Baldwin G	19	A	Aug 6	
4669	Baker F, Signal Corps			Aug 7	
5657	Boyd S	4	C	Aug 14	
5774	Breen A	2	F	Aug 15	
6126	Boyd John B	4	K	Aug 19	

LIST OF THE DEAD.

No.	Name		Co.	Regt.	Date
6628	Bradman A M	Cav	6	M	Aug 23 64
6652	Burd W H		6	E	Aug 23
6937	Bowers J		4	K	Aug 26
7717	Burk Jas		1	K	Sept 3
7921	Brossessault M	Art	2	M	Sept 5
9909	Banvall J		4	F	Sept 16
9477	Bartlett E K	S S	2	D	Sept 21
9631	Burstow J		18	D	Sept 24
9848	Barrett J		18	D	Sept 27
10321	Britzer L B		15	C	Oct 10
11577	Brown J		12	H	Oct 28
11706	Brickley H		1	K	Nov 1
12077	Ball W		12	C	Nov 18
12112	Boyer J	Cav	1	K	Nov 21
12564	Bromley J		18	G	Jan 31 65
760	Chisholm J M	M Corps			Apr 27 64
1947	Clemens D'		6	L	June 14
2174	Clemburg J		16	D	June 19
2216	Cassman A	M Corps			June 20
2726	Carter Thos		15	H	July 1
3126	Cavanaugh P		16	A	July 10
3500	Conden H		12	A	July 18
3911	Crookey S		15	H	July 24
4346	Chase V		16	C	July 30
4930	Campbell S L		15	C	Aug 7
5107	Croy J		18	B	Aug 9
5156	Cussey Jas		15	A	Aug 9
5234	Casey J		15	A	Aug 10
5436	Champney P A	Sig Corps			Aug 12
6420	Cammell J		12	H	Aug 22
7532	Coolidge M		17	B	Sept 1
7722	Connor H		15	H	Sept 3
7906	Corst Jas		14	D	Sept 5
8161	Conuell J		14	D	Sept 8
8243	Chamberlain C		17	B	Sept 9
8570	Collins M	Cav	4	H	Sept 12
8767	Carter C A		1	B	Sept 14
9034	Clifford J	Cav	6	B	Sept 17
9113	Chase L		10	C	Sept 18
9186	Carroll L	Cav	2	G	Sept 18
9395	Congreve E		5	A	Sept 19
9482	Cuyler W		16	B	Sept 21
9814	Crocker Chas		2	A	Sept 26
10210	Corgill C		12	F	Oct 2
10557	Clark R W	S S	2		Oct 9
11176	Casey Jno		19	A	Oct 19
11201	Childs G		16	B	Oct 20
11633	Cramer A		19	C	Oct 28
914	Dunn Jno		6	A	May 6
910	Dangler W G		5	M	May 5
1255	Doney J W	Cav	6	D	May 21
1653	Dunn Wm		19	F	June 5
2274	Dunn Jno		18	H	June 20
2495	Donalan M	Cav	2	L	June 26
3025	Deyer H		18	D	July 7
4377	Darwin W W	S S	2	B	July 31
4490	Dinslow B F		12	G	Aug 1
4626	Delaney Jacob	Art	5	F	Aug 3
5348	Doll R		14	O	Aug 11
5459	Dolan P		19	F	Aug 12
5756	Davis G		19	A	Aug 15
6025	Decker Jas		10		Aug 18
6210	Davis J W		15	E	Aug 19
6297	Doran J M		19	E	Aug 20
6770	Doughty D B	Art	3	C	Aug 25
6805	Davidson J H		15	C	Aug 25
6955	Delaney E		19	F	Aug 26
7049	Davis G		15	F	Aug 27 64
7241	Delaney J		2	F	Aug 29
7792	Dean Samuel	Cav	4	B	Sept 3
8214	Downing M		10	D	Sept 8
8832	Donle J		10	D	Sept 15
10235	Davis Clarke	Bat	1	K	Oct 2
10883	Draper L		14	F	Oct 14
11554	Davy H		18	G	Oct 27
11613	Diller O M	Cav	5	I	Oct 28
12140	Drummond J		18	F	Nov 23
12591	Dunn C		15	C	Feb 4 65
5648	Evans T		14	F	Aug 14 64
6813	Edwards Wm (neg)		8	A	Aug 25
7576	Erick J		2	K	Sept 2
7616	Ellerton N		16	D	Sept 2
12689	Emmich S S		5	C	Feb 22 65
42	Ferguson J	Cav	6	E	Mar 15 64
1243	Fitzgibbons Thos		2	C	May 20
1509	Ferrell J		12	A	May 31
2355	Fifley H		18	E	May 23
2888	French Geo, 1st Lt		37		July 3
3007	Feed G	Cav	6	D	July 7
3256	Frenchy D		2	F	July 13
3543	Fielding A		13	E	July 18
5487	Fliestine S		16	C	Aug 13
6804	Felps Dan'l (negro)		8	H	Aug 25
7167	Flanigan M		2	I	Aug 29
8536	Faunton H		14	F	Sept 12
9154	Flanery M	Cav	1	H	Sept 18
9725	Frum E	"	3	C	Sept 25
9983	Flarety O		16		Sept 29
10655	Fenall J		14	G	Oct 11
10839	Flanagan P	Cav	14	D	Oct 13
11402	Fritz A		19	A	Oct 24
12312	Foster J			H	Dec 19
272	Gilligan Mat		1	I	Mar 31
1639	Gardener C	Sig Corps			June 5
2801	Gutterman S		16	D	July 2
4977	Gray Wm		18	C	Aug 7
6182	Gale Walter		11	F	Aug 19
7220	Gulvere David		4	C	Aug 29
8057	Griffith S		11	F	Sept 7
8571	Gunter Jno	Cav	4		Sept 13
8857	Grace Thos		1	B	Sept 15
9851	Gilbert A		5	K	Sept 27
12066	Getts F		19	E	Nov 16
7335	Golton R		76	B	Aug 30
397	Hatch T C		11	A	Apr 6
533	Halbert F		2	H	Apr 13
1547	Halpin P	Art	5	H	June 1
1585	Haney H		16	D	June 3
1608	Hurman J H	Cav	4	E	June 4
2096	Hendricks J		16	D	June 17
2209	Hogan M		16	A	June 20
2706	Henry Wm		2	B	June 30
2730	Hurley D, Marine Corps				July 1
2987	Hulit Wm		16	D	July 7
3753	Hill Geo		17	H	July 22
3893	Hopkins W (neg)		17	C	July 24
4429	Hill D S (negro)		16	C	July 31
7238	Heddington W		15	F	Aug 29
7405	Horsham J R		15	G	Aug 31
8004	Halley J		13	B	Sept 6
9104	Hook H		19	F	Sept 18
9155	Heir J		14	A	Sept 18
9565	Hildreth Jas		12		Sept 24
9918	Haney J		12	C	Sept 28

LIST OF THE DEAD.

No.	Name	Co.	Reg.	Date
10054	Hasler C	13	M	Sept 20 64
10430	Hirchfield G	M Corps		Oct 7
10857	Harman J	15	E	Oct 14
11136	Hamilton S	S S 2	D	Oct 19
12369	Hill M A	2	G	Jan 1 65
12601	Hoit E (negro)	35	H	Feb 6
10322	Hamman W H	15	F	Oct 3 64
5532	Imhoff I	15	E	Aug 13
7647	Ireland Geo	14	E	Sept 3
10472	Ireson I	Cav 4	A	Oct 11
8125	Johnson P	Bat 2		Sept 8
8366	Jones W	Art 1	K	Sept 10
10319	Jones C B	Cav 1	H	Oct 3
11923	Jerald W H	18	F	Nov 8
495	Kingeny J	1	K	Apr 12
912	Kelly Jno	16	C	May 5
1662	Kain P F	15	A	June 6
3256	Kenley D	2	F	July 13
3341	Kerkney F	18	F	July 15
3685	Kilbride J	15	F	July 21
4245	Kane Wm	18	H	July 29
4266	Kalkrath C	3	I	July 29
4271	Kelly D	4	H	July 29
4694	Kester J	15	F	Aug 4
5640	Kay Robert	4	F	Aug 14
5643	Kelly J	M Corps		Aug 14
6271	Kochel J	19	G	Aug 20
6577	Kelly Wm	9	I	Aug 23
6764	King I	7	K	Aug 25
7465	Kinney G W	Bat 1	D	Sept 1
8261	Kilnty H	Art 1	K	Sept 9
8490	Kricks F	14	C	Sept 11
8527	Kripp J	16	D	Sept 12
9082	Knapp C	11	A	Sept 18
11208	Kain Pat	15	A	Oct 21
11767	Kelly J S	2	D	Nov 3
11949	Kennedy J	12	A	Nov 10
12205	Kahl Chas	Art 2	M	Dec 1
12532	Kemp J W	2	K	Jan 27 65
55	Lore Wm	6	F	Mar 17 64
2282	Larreby G	16	D	June 20
2774	Little J	19	E	July 21
3999	Lackey J	16	B	July 26
4453	Langstaff R	10	F	Aug 1
5711	Lake Horace	Cav 4	K	Aug 15
5891	Lynch B	18	E	Aug 16
6116	Lattin E	12	A	Aug 19
6300	Lawrence C	11	E	Aug 20
6352	Lyons E	Signal Corps		Aug 21
6561	Little R	19	F	Aug 23
9732	Larqdell Wm	14	A	Sept 25
10317	Lonby O	Cav 4	H	Oct 3
10379	Lockwood H (neg)	8	D	Oct 5
11038	Lyons R	Cav 1	E	Oct 17
11543	Lyman O S	18	A	Oct 27
11973	Lewis Wm P	8	B	Nov 12
180	Mc Coy Augustus	6	M	Mar 26
267	Mc Clellan J	Cav 6	D	Mar 31
828	Mason C H	12	I	May 1
948	Murphy D	12	B	May 8
1012	Mc Evers T L	13	C	May 10
1043	Mc Guire J	3	C	May 12
1332	Murray Thos	Art 1	I	May 24
1471	Mulhall Peter	M Corps		May 30
1823	Marze Jas	12	D	June 10
1946	Mc Laughlin J	2	H	June 14
1965	Mc Conaghy P	M Corps		June 14
2444	Meadow Jno	Cav 6	E	June 25 64
3054	Muller J	M Corps		June 30
2920	Miller C H	Cav 6	E	July 5
3054	Mc Kinney J	M Corps		July 9
308	Maloney B	19	B	July 9
3950	Merkili Peter	14	H	July 25
4712	Murch Wm	11	C	Aug 4
4823	Mc Clintock J S	18	H	Aug 5
4863	Martin M	Mar Corps		Aug 6
5303	Martin J	Cav 1	K	Aug 11
5364	Mc Cann B	12	B	Aug 11
5476	Nichols R	Cav 1	K	Aug 12
5781	Mc Lean P	17	C	Aug 14
5769	Mc Coslin Robt	Art 1	B	Aug 15
6073	Mc Donald	Cav 4	E	Aug 18
6081	Mc Clair R	11	G	Aug 18
6313	Munson C	12	D	Aug 20
6407	Mulhern C	Cav 4	C	Aug 22
6515	Mantle J M	15	F	Aug 22
6851	Marston B	S S 51	G	Aug 25
6973	Mc Kinley E W	Mar Cor		Aug 27
7341	Mc Guire J	12	D	Aug 30
8293	Munn W	18	H	Sept 9
8473	Mc Ginnis A	Art 4	E	Sept 11
9110	Montgomery C	13	G	Sept 18
9231	Mc Coy J M, M Brigade			Sept 19
9368	Miller H	Art 2		Sept 20
9472	Morris G J	18	I	Sept 21
9830	Mc Dermott H	18	E	Sept 22
10135	Man'ing J	15	A	Oct 1
10321	Mc Coy J	4	F	Oct 3
10457	Mills A	15	G	Oct 7
10554	Mc Cord G	14	E	Oct 9
10855	Mc Gee P	2		Oct 13
11008	Murray Jas	17	G	Oct 16
12148	Mizner W	1 Sig Cor	K	Nov 24
12151	Moran J	4	F	Nov 24
7341	Mc Guire J	12	D	Aug 31
12361	Mc Gorren J	17	C	Dec 31
2876	Northrup H E	4	H	July 3
6803	Newcombe Jno	18	G	Aug 20
6954	Nichols H	12	A	Aug 26
10210	North Jacob	15	A	Oct 3
12386	Ne'se J	6	F	Jan 2 65
12833	Naff ——, Bugler, Art 1		B	Apr 16
12790	Newel L	18	G	Mch 17
2368	O'Reilly Theodore	3	K	June 23 64
7036	Ott Jno	10	A	Aug 27
11846	Osrans J	Cav 4	I	Nov 5
492	Partridge J W, Sig Corps			Apr 12
1607	Pace J F	18	C	June 4
1803	Pulliam Wm	Cav 1		June 13
3219	Pigot J	M Corps		July 12
3669	Ponter ——	Art 1	I	July 18
4631	Pearson S C	40	C	Aug 3
5309	Pratt C E	Art 1	M	Aug 11
5729	Pike Wm	Cav 5	G	Aug 15
5731	Poulton Henry	19	A	Aug 15
6392	Page J E	18	B	Aug 21
7008	Phillips C	14	D	Aug 27
7267	Pruet Jas M	19	A	Aug 30
7311	Plummer G	S S 2	D	Aug 30
2611	Preston Jno, Marine Cor			June 28
7752	Pratt J	3	B	Sept 3
9571	Post A	Art 1	F	Sept 23
10951	Palmer Wm E	15	F	Oct 14
11170	Pattit J S	11	F	Oct 19

LIST OF THE DEAD.

No.	Name	Age	Co.	Date
12142	Puck C	15	G	Nov 24 64
4022	Quinback J	18	G	July 26
11	Ross ——	19	A	Mch 5
194	Rooney Mark	14	F	Mch 27
404	Reardon D	13	G	April 6
702	Reynolds Edwd M Cor			April 23
3355	Roney F J	18	E	July 15
3820	Ritzer Geo A Cav	5	H	July 23
4276	Ro:ison W R "	6	H	July 30
4957	Rhodes A	18	B	Aug 7
5210	Rinkle Geo Cav	2	G	Aug 10
5934	Ronke J	10	D	Aug 17
7151	Richards Theo Cav	2	D	Aug 29
8438	Rogers Wm	18	G	Sept 14
9268	Reynolds D Cav	4	C	Sept 19
10792	Reilly J	3	B	Oct 2
2701	Rawson J	16	K	June 30
363	Striff Jno	2	F	April 2
123	Shelton C	8	F	May 20
1251	Spaulding Wm Cav	3	B	May 21
1295	Scripter C E "	5	D	May 23
1617	Sweitzer M	19	H	June 5
1714	Smith H W	15	C	June 7
2073	Stoltz ——	16	C	June 17
2082	Smith Jas	16	D	June 17
2298	Styles J N	13	A	June 22
2550	Sumser J	19	G	June 27
3110	Spaulding Jas	13	B	July 10
3114	Skinner L	13	C	July 10
3838	Smartkash C	15	C	July 23
3978	Somers P Cav	4	C	July 26
4238	Seybert J S S S	1	H	July 29
4310	Smith Allen	4	H	July 30
4667	Striper M	18	D	Aug 4
5022	Sutgee F	16	C	Aug 8
5305	Sorg A Art	1	M	Aug 11
5393	Swagger H Cav	4	D	Aug 12
5801	Sisson J	4	D	Aug 15
6120	Slaughterback B	15	H	Aug 23
6833	Sutgen F	16	C	Aug 25
7377	Smith F	14	E	Aug 31
7706	Starr Darius S S	2	F	Sept 2
7874	Snider J	11	B	Sept 5
8839	Scott Jas H Cav	2	B	Sept 15
9215	Stansbury E, Mar Corps			Sept 19
9514	Souls J H	15	F	Sept 22
10214	Sullivan T	11	C	Oct 2
11144	Schroder F	15	C	Oct 19
11301	Smith J	8	D	Oct 22
11333	Stanton R	14	K	Oct 23
11661	Spencer J H	2	D	Oct 30
11699	Shortman J	14	E	Oct 31
12186	Streeter J	16	B	Nov 28
12211	Stanton C	2	I	Dec 2
92	Tooley Michael	13	G	Mch 21
489	Taylor Amos	17	H	April 12
2603	Thompson Wm	18	G	June 28
2662	Truman J Cav	5	D	June 29
3466	Tyson E S	14	B	July 17
4716	Tredridge A, Musician	13	Aug	4
7366	Taylor M D	18	E	Aug 31
7801	Turk H	18	H	Sept 4
8258	Thomas J Cav	1	D	Sept 9
8259	Trainer M	6	F	Sept 9
8279	Thomas L, negro	8	D	Sept 9
9115	Taylor F	18	I	Sept 18
11393	Topper J	11	B	Oct 24
7829	Unmuch C Art	1	K	Sept 4 64
3657	Volmore J	3	K	July 18
7042	Vancotten Wm	16	D	Aug 27
7135	Vickery Wm	1	H	Aug 28
12011	Van Buren W H	16	B	Nov 16
1259	Walker Wm	6	D	May 21
1299	Worster Chas B C	5		May 23
2752	White Thos	1	D	July 1
4023	Williams D	18	D	July 26
4218	Warner S	16	E	July 20
4303	Williams Jno	4	D	July 30
5425	Walmor ——	10	D	Aug 12
6125	Wickham G H	16	B	Aug 19
6637	Wills S	15	E	Aug 23
7048	Wright C S	12	C	Aug 27
7109	Wadsworth B H	12	C	Aug 28
7254	Warner H	2	D	Aug 30
9105	Whitney J W Cav	4	K	Sept 18
9131	White Samuel	8	F	Sept 18
9677	Walker Jno, negro	8	F	Sept 24
9854	Walter I	17	B	Sept 27
10355	Wigley E	17	C	Oct 5
10374	Waters ——	8	C	Oct 5
10756	Waldo J M Art	1	K	Oct 12
11137	Williams C Art	1	K	Oct 19
11395	Wizmaker G	2	M	Oct 24
12000	Wilson C W	15	A	Nov 14
12027	Wise G B	6	F	Nov 15
6496	Yarger A	18		Aug 22
7101	Young Robt Cav	1	K	Aug 28
10754	Young F B Art	2	M	Oct 12
11373	Young J C	19	A	Oct 23
7793	Zimmerman J	17	D	Sept 4
10423	Zing P	10	C	Oct 6
11450	Zimmerman M	14	I	Oct 7

Total 399.

UNITED STATES NAVY.

No.	Name	Ship	Date
2619	Atkinson A, Nepsia		June 27 64
4698	Anker Geo, Norman		Aug 4
8071	Anderson C, Southfield		Sept 7
2919	Bradley Jno	"	July 3
3475	Broderick W		July 17
5072	Bowers W H, W Witch		Aug 8
12047	Boucher W, Shawsheen		Nov 16
1914	Carnes Wm		June 18
2149	Conant G S, Southfield		June 18
2580	Carter W J, Montg'y		June 27
6201	Collins Thos, Southfield		Aug 10
7144	Corbet E		Aug 29
7508	Connor J		Sept 1
9544	Culbert J		Sept 23
164	Dillingham J N, Housa'c		Mar 26
6437	Duffney J		Aug 22
3086	Ellis J H, Columbine		July 9
4134	Evans Jno, Shawsheen		July 28
4462	Earl J H, Paym'r Stew'd		Aug 1
5419	Foley Dan'l, Southfield		Aug 12
4605	Green G C, Southfield		Aug 3
8871	Goundy Thos		Sept 15
1087	Heald W, Canandaigua		Apr 14
1469	Hunter Jno, Seaman		May 30
2215	Hilton Jno, Johana		June 20
3448	Hodges L, Norman		July 17
3793	Hughes Benj, Wabash		July 22
5875	Heald H H, Merchantm'n		Aug 16

LIST OF THE DEAD.

No.	Name	Date
9284	Holas Thos, W'r Witch	Sept 19 64
1432	Jones Wm, Underwriter	May 28
2178	Jones Theo, "	June 19
2206	Journeay Jno, Fireman	June 19
6417	Jackson J, Shawsheen	Aug 22
8291	Johnson G P,	Sept 9
8858	James F A	Sept 15
9392	Johnson M	Sept 20
10218	Joseph F	Oct 2
602	Keefe Jno, Housatonic	Apr 18
698	Kultz A T, Ward	Apr 23
1546	Kelley Jas, Underwriter	June 1
3850	Kinney J, Water Witch	July 24
7375	Lodi Jno	Aug 31
2813	Lindersmith E, Montg'y	July 3
4201	Lawton Jas, Ladona	July 30
135	Mays A H, Mate, Norm'n	Mar 29
2452	McDonald Jno	June 25
2581	Moore A, Anna	June 27
3128	Malaby P, Montgomery	July 10
3348	Murphy M J	July 15
3529	McDonald Jno	July 17
3804	Matthews J, Underwriter	July 22
4208	McHenry D'l, Southfield	July 29
4324	McCarty T, Housatonic	July 30
4396	McVey K	July 31
4679	McTier J	Aug 4
4800	McLaughlin E	Aug 5
5485	Meldon J	Aug 13
6355	Marshall N B, Leipzig	Aug 21
6571	McDermott P, Montg'y	Aug 23
6825	Mathews W C	Aug 25
6917	McLaughlin B	Aug 26
7251	McGowan J, Powhattan	Aug 30
11863	Maston J, Ratler	Nov 6
7824	Noe M	Sept 4
2227	O'Brien Wm	June 20
3208	Ottinger M, Water Witch	July 12
3153	Page Lyman	July 11
5325	Parkham J C, Shawsheen	Aug 11
9024	Peterson J	Sept 17
2460	Quinlan N	June 25
7867	Quade M	Sept 5
2207	Ragan John, T Ward	June 20
4661	Raymond W, " "	Aug 3
5108	Roland Jno, Underwriter	Aug 9
7003	Reynolds T J	Aug 27
169	Stark John	Mar 26
2010	Sullivan J, Underwriter	June 15
2883	Smith Jno W, Southfield	July 3
3261	Sampson J R, Nav Bat	July 13
4611	Smith B N, Mendota	Aug 3
6592	Stanley Wm, Southfield	Aug 23
11290	Smith Wm, Water Witch	Oct 22
1713	Thomas Sam, Southfi'd	June 7
1851	Thomas Jno, Southfield	June 11
3757	Turner Wm,	July 1
4159	Trymer Jas, Southfield	July 28
7445	Tobin Michael,	Sept 1
8302	Ta B F, Southfield,	Sept 10
1646	Willis J P,	June 5
3004	Wilson A, Southfield,	July 7
3878	Williams M W,	July 24
4118	Willis M, Southfield,	July 28
4198	Williams C, Aries,	July 29
5820	Wordell G K,	Aug 16
5990	Warren W H,	Aug 17
6458	Wooley M,	Aug 22 64
7503	Walsh Jas,	Sept 1
8104	Welch V, Southfield,	Sept 7
10565	West Jno, Southfield,	Oct 9

TOTAL, 99.

MISCELLANEOUS.

No.	Name	Date
1460	Addley A. Citizen,	Oct 25 64
887	Amos J, Ringold Bat F	May 4
2977	Augar A,	July 7
28.	Bane S. Ringold Bat A,	Apr 1
2072	Beatty D, Ringold Bat F,	June 17
4327	Baker Jno, Teamster,	July 30
4904	Hemmar L,	Aug 6
5747	Butterfield Jas. Citizen,	Aug 15
6100	Blair H, Citizen,	Aug 18
6366	Bidwell C. Citizen Team,	Aug 21
8102	Burkhead W, Prunell's Le	Sept 7
9344	Blood G P,	Sept 20
9591	Brogdin D C,	Sept 23
10500	Burk C, Citizen,	Oct 8
10602	Bishop J, Citizen Team,	Oct 10
10963	Brown Geo, Brigge's Bat	Oct 15
12342	Boland Jas, Prunell's Cav	Dec 26
177	Cannon Wm, Teamster,	Mar 26
389	Campbell D, Ringold B E	Apr 6
431	Childers C H,	Apr 8
1195	Cobb J, Citizen Team,	May 18
1881	Clark M, Citizen Team,	June 12
3399	Cuble C, Citizen,	July 16
3972	Cregger J F, Musician,	July 25
6315	Crowley Pat,	Aug 20
9245	Carroll C, Team, 19 Art Cor	Sept 19
10485	Corbit J,	Oct 7
10872	Carey Thos,	Oct 13
11726	Collins, Cit Teamster,	Nov 1
12449	Cairoll J, Cit Teamster,	Jan 13 65
752	Deems P, Ringold Bat E	Apr 26 64
2630	Delp Geo, Cit Teamster,	June 28
4534	Davis J, Citizen,	July 30
5866	Danfirth Geo A	Aug 16
8302	Delmore W, Cit,	Sept 8
11084	Dubin M, Cit Teamster,	Oct 18
11248	Delhanta Wm, Cit,	Oct 21
182	England E,	Mar 27
3023	Evans M, Cit,	July 25
	Everett T S, Cit, Md,	Aug 30
157	Freeman Jno,	Mar 25
453	Feultly R, Cit,	Apr 9
1110	Fannon A, Cit,	May 15
2332	Faster W, Tel Operator,	June 22
2436	Farrell M Cit,	June 25
10476	Fuckson J,	Oct 7
4808	Fitzgerald ——	Aug 5
5078	Frank F M, Wilder's Bat,	Aug 8
5000	Fox Henry, Cit Teamster,	Aug 14
7643	Ford P, Teamster,	Sept 3
9064	Foucks H C, Keyes' Ind C	Sept 18
11315	Ferrall M C, Teamster,	Oct 22
2529	Gildea D, Cit,	July 1
4115	Crogran D,	July 28
4747	Gishart J,	Aug 5
6159	Graham E, Citizen,	Aug 19
7854	Gorb S,	Sept 5
9747	Goodman J O,	Sept 25
10672	Gillman John,	Oct 11

LIST OF THE DEAD.

No.	Name	Date
11862	Goodyear F, Citizen,	Nov 6 64
10717	Graves Wm E,	Oct 11
219	Heartless S,	Mar 29
264	Hammond S, Teamster,	Mar 31
605	Hoffman Chas, Cit Team,	Apr 13
1274	Harkins John, Teamster,	May 22
2370	Hammond J, Cit Team,	June 23
3222	Hudson G W, Cit Team,	July 12
4244	Hughes P,	July 20
6670	Hannay D, Cit Teamster,	Aug 18
8055	Herriage J, Teamster,	Sept 7
8756	Harkins D S, M M B,	Sept 14
9006	Hyatt J,	Sept 17
9051	Hulbert J H S,	Sept 17
9297	Hall M, A A S,	Sept 19
9425	Hart Isaac, Cit Teamster,	Sept 21
10262	Hines Daniel,	Oct 3
10331	Hopkins John,	Oct 4
11934	Heckinbridge ——,	Nov 9
12456	Harrington J,	Jan 15 65
8722	Inhagg ——,	Sept 11 64
4794	Jones Chas, Cit Teamster,	Aug 5
6854	Jacobs W C, Citizen,	Aug 25
12714	Johnson J, Cit, Canada,	Mar 1 65
2205	Kingland W H, Cit,	June 20 64
3515	Kerr E, Cit Teamster,	June 13
6273	Kins W H, Cit Teamster,	Aug 20
7804	Knight J B, Cit Teamster,	Sept 5
9467	Kellogg E L, Cit, S'g fi'ld,	Sept 21
546	Lee Jas, Cit Teamster,	Apr 14
1772	Lafferty Wm, Ring Bat,	June 5
3689	Lummo Rob't, Citizen,	July 21
10353	Linton E, Ringold Bat,	Oct 5
76	Morton J B, Ring Cav A,	Mar 20
203	Mc Mahon Pat,	Mar 23
220	Morrison F, Cit Teamster,	Mar 29
865	Mower W, Cit,	May 3
2285	Mc Atie M, Teamster,	June 21
2132	Manning B F, Cit Team,	June 24
2373	Mc Enshon Peter,	June 23
3450	Moyer J,	July 17
4017	Messenger H M, Cit,	July 26
5357	Morland J S, Cit Team,	Aug 12
5996	Mc Gee J,	Aug 17
6380	Mc Kenna F,	Aug 21
8039	Mc Guire J, Cit,	Sept 6
9135	Myers Jno,	Sept 18
9247	Mc Donald J,	Sept 19
9616	Munch Christian, Top Eng	Sept 23
12535	Mc Donald H H, Cit, Ohio,	Jan 27 65
6666	Monteith M, Cit Teamster	Aug 24 64
184	Newton Wm, Teamster,	Mar 27
7074	Nortou E, Citizen,	Aug 28
8510	Nichols J, Team, 15 Art C	Sept 12
4190	Osborne J, Citizen,	July 28
5414	Oliver W W	Aug 12
719	Pringle Wm, Cit Teamster	Apr 25
1855	Podzas L, Cit Teamster,	June 12
5920	Poole C,	Aug 17 64
8893	Powers G, Citizen,	Sept 16
9010	Potter S D,	Sept 17
9366	Phillips B B, Teamster,	Sept 20
12351	Parker Jas, Cit Teamster,	Dec 29
10100	Parkhurst W L, 1 M M B.	Sept 30
853	Quinn Jas, Citizen,	May 3
5394	Quinlan P, Cit Teamster,	Aug 12
5768	Quinn ——, Citizen,	Aug 15
3542	Reed A R, Independent,	July 18
3779	Rand J, Cit Teamster,	July 22
5936	Ronley J,	Aug 17
10111	Rendig C H, Citizen,	Oct 1
10453	Ryan John, Citizen,	Oct 7
11131	Reien R, Citizen,	Oct 18
11703	Richardson J C, 1 M M B,	Oct 30
449	Scott Blair, Citizen,	Apr 9
2431	Smith P, M M B,	June 24
2140	St Clair Benj, Cit Team,	June 25
2552	Slater Chas, Cit Team,	June 27
2959	Spicer W, Cit Teamster,	July 6
3000	Stout Chas, Citizen,	July 7
3662	Shunk J, Citizen,	July 20
4003	Smith H, Bridge's Bat,	July 25
4843	Sawyer J D,	Aug 6
9729	Stanton J, Citizen,	Sept 25
10515	Smays David,	Oct 12
136	Thompson Jno, Teamster,	Mar 24
1531	Tullis L B G, Citizen,	June 1
2693	Thompson Geo,	June 30
3400	Thomas J H, Cit Team,	July 16
3896	Taylor J W, Citizen,	July 24
12337	Tucer B, Citizen, Indiana,	Dec 26
9397	Ulmgender G, M M B, C,	Sept 21
9497	Vankirk W, Ringold Bat,	Sept 21
9688	Vandier W M, Cit,Phil,Pa	Sept 24
799	Wilkins A, Ringold Bat,	Apr 29
1032	Welsh G L, Cit Teamster,	May 14
1121	White George, Citizen,	May 15
2784	Wilson D E, Ringold Bat,	July 2
10353	Weir ——, Cit Teamster,	Oct 14
11606	Woods R C, Knapp's Bat,	Oct 23
4730	Wright Chas, Cit Team,	Aug 4
4869	Ward John, Cit Team,	Aug 6
9043	Williams F G,	Sept 17
10075	Wentgel Thos,	Sept 30
4127	Young Henry, Cit Team,	July 28
12246	Young D, Cit Teamster,	Nov 8

TOTAL, 165.

MEN THAT WERE HUNG.

1	Sarsfield Jno, 144 N Y,	July 11 64
2	Collins Wm, 88 Pa D,	July 11
3	Curtis Chas, 5 R I Art A,	July 11
4	Delaney Pat, 83 Pa E,	July 11
5	Mun A, U S Navy,	July 11
6	Rickson W R, U S Navy,	July 11

Recapitulation of Deaths by States.

ALABAMA,	15	NEW JERSEY,		170
CONNECTICUT,	315	NEW YORK,		2,572
DELAWARE,	45	NORTH CAROLINA,		17
DIST. OF COLUMBIA,	14	OHIO,		1,030
ILLINOIS,	850	PENNSYLVANIA,		1,811
INDIANA,	594	RHODE ISLAND,		74
IOWA,	174	TENNESSEE,		738
KANSAS,	5	VERMONT,		212
KENTUCKY,	436	VIRGINIA,		288
LOUISIANA,	1	WISCONSIN,		244
MAINE,	233	U. S. ARMY,		399
MARYLAND,	194	U. S. NAVY,		100
MASSACHUSETTS,	768	Citizens, Teamsters, &c.,		166
MINNESOTA,	79	Men that were hung by the Prisoners,		6
MICHIGAN,	630	Unknown U. S. Soldiers,		443
MISSOURI,	97	Died in Small Pox Hospital,		68
NEW HAMPSHIRE,	124			
TOTAL,				12,912

The following exhibit, as collated from the Hospital Register and Prison Records, will be found to be as correct as any yet published:

Total Number of Prisoners on hand at end of

APRIL, 1864,	10,427	NOVEMBER, 1864,	1,359
MAY, 1864,	18,454	DECEMBER, 1864,	4,706
JUNE, 1864,	26,367	JANUARY, 1865,	5,046
JULY, 1864,	31,678	FEBRUARY, 1865,	5,851
AUGUST, 1864,	31,693	MARCH, 1865,	3,319
SEPTEMBER, 1864,	8,218	APRIL, 1865,	51
OCTOBER, 1864,	4,208		

Deaths in Stockade and Hospital during the Existence of the Prison.

MARCH, 1864,	283	October, 1864,	4,590
APRIL, 1864,	576	NOVEMBER, 1864,	492
MAY, 1864,	708	DECEMBER, 1864,	160
JUNE, 1864,	1,201	JANUARY, 1865,	190
JULY, 1864,	1,817	FEBRUARY, 1865,	139
AUGUST, 1864,	3,076	MARCH, 1865,	192
SEPTEMBER, 1864,*	2,794	APRIL, 1865,	32
TOTAL,			12,912

* The greater number of deaths in September and October, in proportion to the number in prison, will be explained by the fact that all the well men were removed from Andersonville in these months, and none were left except the sick and wounded.

RECAPITULATION.

Day and date of greatest number of Prisoners at Andersonville — 33,114 — August 8th, 1864.

Day and date of greatest number of deaths, August 23d, 1864, 127.

Number of Prisoners received during its occupation, 45,613.

Daily average of deaths during its occupation, 29¾.

Ratio of mortality per 1,000 of mean strength, 24 per cent.

Mortality of 18,000 registered patients, 75 per cent.

The Diseases of which the Prisoners died will be found in the following classification:

Disease	Count	Disease	Count
Anasarca,	377	Hydrocele,	1
Asphyxia,	7	Hemorrhoids,	1
Ascites,	24	Jaundice,	9
Asthma,	3	Laryngitis,	4
Bronchitis,	93	Nostalgia,	7
Catarrh,	55	Nephritis,	4
Constipation,	5	Phthisis,	137
Diarrhœa, Chronic,	4,000	Pleuritis,	54
" Acute,	817	Pneumonia,	321
Debilitas,	198	Paralysis,	1
Diphtheria,	3	Rheumatism,	83
Dyspepsia,	2	Scurvy,	3,574
Diabetes,	1	Syphilis,	7
Dysenteria,	1,384	Scrofula,	3
Erysipelas,	11	Stricture,	1
Febris Typhoides,	229	Sunstroke,	52
Fistula,	2	Small Pox,	68
Fracture,	1	Vaccine Ulcers,	4
Febris Remittens,	177	Gunshot Wounds,	155
Gonorrhœa,	3	Unknown,	443
Gangrene,	678	Hung in Stockade,	6
Total,			**12,912**

A List of Officers Imprisoned at Camp Asylum, Columbia, S. C.

Aldrich C S, Cap	85th N Y Vol	Bick W C, Cap	62d Pa Vol
Austin J W, L't	5th Iowa Cav	Braiday Count S, L't	2d N J Cav
Alters J B, Cap	75th O Vol	Bulon A, L't	3d N J Cav
Albaugh Wm, Cap	51st Pa Vol	Burdick C H, Cap	1st Tenn Cav
Alger A B, L't	22d O Bat	Bartram D S, L't	17th Conn Vol
Avery W B, Cap	132d N Y Vol	Brown J A, Cap	85th N Y Vet Vol
Allender W F, L't	7th Tenn Cav	Bradley A B, R Q M	" " "
Adair W A, L't	51st Ind Vol	Butts L A, L't	" " "
Albro S A, L't	80th Ill Vol	Bowers G W, Cap	101st Pa Vol
Adams J, L't		Benner H S, Cap	" "
Allstaedt C L, Adj	54th N Y Vol	Bowers G A, L't	16th Conn Vol
Ahern M, L't	10th W Va Vol	Blakeslee B F, L't	" "
Ahlert T H, L't	45th N Y Vol	Bruns H, L't	" "
Adams C A, Cap	1st Vt Cav	Bryson R R, L't	103d Pa Vol
Alban H H, Cap	21st O Vol	Burns S D, L't	" "
Andrews H B, Cap	17th Mich Vol	Bierbower W, L't	87th Pa Vol
Apple H, L't	1st Md Cav	Beegle D F, L't	101st Pa Vol
Anderson C S, L't	3d Iowa Vol	Bryan J H, L't	18th Pa Vol
Allee A, L't	16th Ill Cav	Berry A, Cap	3d Md Cav
Abernathy H C, A Adj	" "	Bunting G, L't	5th Md Cav
Acker G D, L't	123d O Vol	Bascomb R, L't	50th N Y Vol
Adkins P, L't	2d Tenn Vol	Baldwin M R, Cap	2d Wis Vol
Aigan John, Cap	5th R I Art	Blake, L't	3d Me Vol
Adams J G B, L't	19th Mass Vol	Brown W H, L't	93d O Vol
Alexander E P, L't	26th Mich Vol	Beard J V, L't	89th O Vol
Anderson H M, L't	3d Me Vol	Byron C, Cap	3d O Vol
Anderson J F, L't	2d Pa Art	Banks B V, Cap	13th Ky Cav
Anderson R W, L't	122d O Vol	Burch J, Cap	42d Ind Vol
Andrus W R, L't	16th Conn Vol	Bailey G W, L't	3d O Vol
Abbey A L, L't	8th Mich Cav	Brownell F G, L't	51st Ind Vol
Arthur J A, Cap	8th Ky Cav	Booker A H, L't	73d Ind Vol
Arthurs S C, Cap	67th Pa Vol	Brown J L, L't	" "
Allen S, Cap	85th N Y Vet Vol	Barlow J W, L't	51st Ind Vol
Adams S B, Cap	" " "	Bath W, L't	132d N Y Vol
Andrews S T, L't	" " "	Bending H R, Cap	61st O Vol
Albright J, Cap	87th Pa Vol	Bush J G, Cap	16th Ill Cav
Abbott A O, L't	1st N Y Drag	Blinn L B, Cap	100th O Vol
Armstrong T S, L't	122d O Vol	Baldwin C W, L't	2d N J Vol
Airey W, Cap	15th Pa Cav	Bartley R, L't	U S A Sig Corps
Appleget A S, L't	2d N J Cav	Bradley G, Cap	2d N J Vol
Allen Robert, L't	2d N J Drag	Brandt C W, L't	1st N Y Vet Cav
Auer M, Cap	15th N Y Cav	Bontin C W, Cap	4th Vet Vol
Anshutz H T, L't	12th W Va Vol	Barrett D W, Cap	89th O Vol
Adams H W, L't	89th O Vol	Brandt O B, L't	17th O Vol
Austin G A, R Q M	14 & 15 Ill V Bat	Byers S H M, Adj	5th Iowa Vol
Albin H S, L't	79th Ill Vol	Barker H P, L't	1st R I Cav
Andrews E E, L't	22d Mich Vol	Boone S G, L't	88th Pa Vol
Alden G C, R Q M	112th Ill Vol	Bisbee L C, L't	16th Me Vol
Ashworth J H, Col	1st Ga U Vol	Bisbee G D, L't	" "
Adams W C, L't	2d Ky Cav	Button G W, L't	22d Mich Vol
Amory C B, Cap	A A Gen	Barker H E, L't	22d N Y Cav
Affleck E T, Adj	170th O Nat Gds	Butler T H, Col	5th Ind Cav
Alexander A H, Cap	103d Pa Vol	Bowen C D, Cap	18th Conn Vol
Abbott E A, L't	23d O Vet Vol	Bennett B, Cap	22d N Y Cav
Belger James, Cap	1st R I Art	Brush Z T, L't	100th O Vol
Baker S S, L't	6th Mo Vol	Bigley C H, L't	82d N Y Vol
Butler C P, L't	29th Ind Vol	Burns M, L't	13th N Y Cav
Baird J F, L't	1st W Va Vol	Bassett M M, L't	53d Ill Vol
Bricker W H, L't	3d Pa Vol	Bortwick N, Cap	20th O Vol

LIST OF OFFICERS.

Brown C A, L't	1st N Y Art	Ballard S H, L't	6th Mich Cav
Benson J F, Cap	120th Ill Vol	Brown J H, Cap	17th Iowa Vol
Bosford W R, L't	1st N Y Vol	Byron S, L't	2d U.S Inf
Burns J, L't	57th Pa Vol	Blaire Geo E, L't	17th O Vol
Barton J L, L't	49th Pa Vol	Bishop F P, L't	4th Tenn Cav
Beebee B C, Cap	13th Ind Vol	Bowen C T, L't	4th R I Vol
Buchanan W, L't	76th N Y Vol	Bateman Wm, L't	9th Mich Cav
Benson A N, Cap	1st D C Cav	Baird Wm, L't	23d U S C T
Barkley C, L't	149th Pa Vol	Barnum S D, Cap	" "
Blane W, L't	43d N Y Vol	Biller J N, L't	2d Pa Art
Bristol J H, L't	1st Conn Cav	Baker W F, Cap	87th Pa Vol
Burpee E A, Cap	19th Me Vol	Bowley F S, L't	30th U S C T
Bryant J W, Cap	5th N Y Cav	Boettger C, L't	2d Md Vol
Biebel H, Cap	6th Conn Vol	Bogle A, Major	35th U S C T
Bixby H L, L't	9th Me Vol	Barnard W A, L't	20th Mich Vol
Byrns J M, Cap	2d Pa R C Vol	Blasse Wm, L't	43d N Y Vol
Barrett J A, Cap	7th Pa R C Vol	Buffum M P, L't Col	4th R I Vol
Burkholder D W, L't	" " "	Brown C O, L't	31st Me Vol
Beal E, Cap	8th Tenn Vol	Beecham R K, L't	23d U S C T
Bayard G A, Cap	148th Pa Vol	Briscoe A M, L't	Cole's Md Cav
Brun S, L't	81st Ill Vol	Burbank H H, Cap	32d Me Vol
Brady W H, L't	2d Del Vol	Bearce H M, L't	" "
Breon J, L't	148th Pa Vol	Bittenger C L, L't	76th Pa Vol
Bischoff P, L't	6th U S Art	Bartlett O E, Cap	31st Me Vol
Burnett G M, L't	4th Ind Cav	Braidey A J, L't	54th Pa Vol
Blair B F, Adj	123d O Vol	Bell C A, L & A D C	
Boyce T W, L't	" "	Burton R, L & A D C	9th N Y Art
Breckenridge F A, L't		Beebe H E, L & A D C	22d N Y Cav
Boyd W J, L't	5th Mich Cav	Coleman S S, L't	12th Ky Cav
Brown W L, L't	17th Tenn Vol	Chalfant J T, Cap	11th Pa Vol
Burrows S W, L't	1st N Y Vet Cav	Call C H, Cap	29th Ill Vol
Brown S, A M Mte	U S Navy	Caswell H, L't	95th Ill Vol
Beman W M, Cap	1st Vet Cav	Carpenter E D, L't	18th Conn Vol
Boaz E P, Cap	20th Ill Vol	Caldwell C, L't	1st Wis Cav
Bryan G, Adj	18th Pa Cav	Cook A A, L't	9th O Cav
Bath H, L't	45th N Y Vol	Casdorph C H, L't	7th W Va Cav
Beadle M, L't	123d N Y Vol	Casler B G, Cap	154th N Y Vol
Bigelow A J, Cap	79th Ill Vol	Cook A L, L't	2d Pa Val
Borchess L T, Cap	67th Pa Vol	Cusac J, Cap	21st O Vol
Brown G L, L't	101st Pa Vol	Canfield S S, Cap	" "
Blanchard Geo A, Cap	85th Ill Vol	Catin M, Cap	" "
Bradford John, L't	4th N J Vol	Coffin V L, L't	31st Me Vol
Borchess T F, L't	67th Pa Vol	Chandler G A, L't	5th Me Vol
Barnes O P, L't	3d O Vol	Coren J H, L't	1st W Va Cav
Bremen S, Cap	3d Mich Vol	Culver F B, L't	123d O Vol
Brickenhoff M, L't	42d N Y Vol	Carothers J, L't	" "
Barse J R, L't	5th Mich Cav	Claghorn A C, L't	21st O Vol
Bliss A T, Cap	10th N Y Cav	Carey S E, L't	13th Mass Vol
Buckley H, L't	4th N H Vol	Campbell L A, L't	152d N Y Vol
Bader H, L't	29th Mo Vol	Carnes W C, Cap	2d Tenn Vol
Blac J G, L't	3d O Vol	Center A P, Cap	" "
Boughton S H, L't	71st Pa Vol	Carroll E, L't	11th Tenn Vol
Barnes A T, L't	14th N Y Vet Bat	Carr C W, L't	4th Vt Vol
Beasley J L, L't	81st Ill Vol	Cunningham J, L't	7th Pa R C Vol
Baker H D, Cap	120th Ill Vol	Coslett C, L't	115th Pa Vol
Burke T F, Cap	16th Conn Vol	Cooper It, L't	7th N J Vol
Barnes W J, Cap		Crawford C H, L't	183d Pa Vol
Bennett W F, Cap	39th Iowa Vol	Cromack S O, L't	77th N Y Vol
Bassett W H, L't	79th Ill Vol	Correll N O, L't	2d Vt Vol
Botts W O, L't	10th Wis Vol	Cornell C H, L't	95th N Y Vol
Biggs J, L't	123d Ill Vol	Cutter C H, L't	" "
Bennett F J, L't	18th U S Inf	Creasey G W, L't	35th Mass Vol
Brown J C, L't	15th " "	Chute R H, L't	59th " "
Bryant M C, L't	42d Ill Vol	Cross H M, L't	" "
Butler W O, L't	10th Wis Vol	Chapin H A, L't	95th N Y Vol
Brooks E P, Adj		Clyde J D, Cap	76th " "
Barringer A, L't	44th N Y Vol	Cahill W, L't	" " "

LIST OF OFFICERS.

Casler J L, L't	" " "	Cratty E G, Cap	103d Pa Vol
Chisman H, L't	7th Ind Vol	Coats H A, Cap	85th N Y Vet Vol
Cooper A, L't	12th N Y Cav	Crooks S J, Col	22d N Y Cav
Cribben H, L't	140th N Y Vol	Case S F, Cap	2d O Cav
Curtis G M, L't	" " "	Cutler J, Cap	34th O Vol
Caldwell J S, L't	16th Ill Cav	Coglin T, Cap	14th N Y H Art
Caslin C S, L't	151st N Y Vol	Cord T A, L't	19th U S Inf
Crossley S, L't	118th Pa Vol	Cloadt J, Cap	119th N Y Vol
Chauncey C R, Cap	34th Mass Vol	Calkins W W, L't	104th Ill Vol
Carlisle S B, L't	145th Pa Vol	Craig J, Cap	1st W Va Vol
Conover S D, Cap	125th Ill Vol	Colville J W, Cap	5th Mich Vol
Cole O L, L't	50th Ill Vol	Crosby T J, Cap	157th Pa Vol
Cain J H, L't	104th N Y Vol	Cohen M, Cap	4th Ky Vol
Cassell E F, L't	11th Iowa Vol	Copeland J R, Cap	7th O Vol
Chambers J H, L't	103d Pa Vol	Creps F A M, L't	77th Pa Vol
Cottingham E, L't	35th Pa Vol	Curtis R, L't	4th Ky Vol
Coddington J P, Vet Sur	8th Iowa Cav	Clements J, L't	15th Ky Vol
Cole A F, Cap	59th N Y Vol	Caldwell D B, L't	75th O Vol
Curtiss W H, Adj	19th Mass Vol	Cubbison J C, L't	101st Pa Vol
Clark J W, L't	59th N Y Vol	Crawford H P, Cap	2d Ill Cav
Clark J H, L't	1st Mass Art	Chase E E, Cap	1st R I Cav
Case D L, Jr, Adj	102d N Y Vol	Coffin G A, Adj	29th Ind Vol
Cope J D, L't	116th Pa Vol	Cockran T G, L't	77th Pa Vol
Cove J W, L't	6th W Va Cav	Conrad W F, Cap	25th Iowa Vol
Coulter W J, L't	15th Mass Vol	Carperts L M, Cap	18th Wis Vol
Cubbetson W M, L't	30th Ind Vol	Cox J L, L't	21st Ill Vol
Casey J, L't	45th N Y Vol	Cunningham M, L't	42d N Y Vol
Carter W H, L't	5th Pa R C Vol	Charters A M, L't	17th Iowa Vol
Chittenden J L, L't	5th Ind Cav	Carpenter J Q, L't	150th Pa Vol
Conney W H, L't	69th N Y Vol	Campbell B F, Cap	
Cameron P, L't	16th N Y Cav	Clark H L, L't	2d Mass Art
Campbell W F, L't	51st Pa Vol	Copeland W A, L't	10th Mich Vol
Cameron J F, L't	5th Pa Cav	Cuniffe H, L't	13th Ill Vol
Carr J P, Cap	93d Ind Vol	Carpenter E N, Cap	6th Pa Cav
Clegg M, L't	5th Ind Cav	Clemmons T, L't	13th Ill Vol
Curtice H A, L't	157th N Y Vol	Crocker Geo A, A A G	
Coffin J A, L't	" " "	Cook W C, Adj	9th Mich Cav
Collins W A, Cap	10th Wis Vol	Cowles H F, L't	18th Conn Vol
Carlisle J B, L't	2d W Va Cav	Cramer C P, L't	21st N Y Cav
Christopher W, L't	" "	Clancey C W, Lt Col	52d O Vol
Chandler G W, L't	1st W Va Cav	Coram Geo, R Q M	2d Ky Cav
Chatburn J, L't	150th Pa Vol	Case M B, L't	23d U S C T
Childs J W, L't	16th Me Vol	Cline D G, L't	75th O V M I
Chase H R, L't	1st Vt H Art	Conn C G, L't	1st M S S
Conover W H, L't	22d N Y Cav	Cook J L, L't	6th Iowa Vol
Clark J A, Cap	7th Mich Cav	Cunningham M, L't	1st Vt H Art
Cook W B, L't	140th Pa Vol	Copland C D, L't	58th Mass Vol
Califf B F, L't	2d W S S S	Chamberlain V B, Cap	7th Conn Vol
Cook E F, Major	2d N Y Cav	Catlin J E, L't	45th Pa Vol
Cooke H P, A A G		Cashell C P, L't	12th Pa Cav
Crocker H, L't	1st N J Cav	Clark M W, Cap	11th Iowa Cav
Camp T B C, Cap	52d Pa Vol	Channel J R, L't	1st Ill Art
Clark L S, Cap	62d N Y Vol	Day J W, L't	17th Mass Vol
Chapin H C, Cap	4th Vt Vol	Damrell W S, L't	13th "
Conyngham J B, Lt Col	52d Pa Vol	Dearing G A, L't	16th Me Vol
Christopher J, Cap	16th U S Inf	Duferr T J, L't	5th Mich Cav
Cochrane M A, Cap	" "	Dickerson A A, L't	16th Conn Vol
Causten M C, L't	19th U S Inf	Donaghy J, Cap	103d Pa Vol
Chubbuck D B, L't	19th Mass Vol	Davis W G, L't	27th Mass Vol
Carpenter S D, L't	3d O Vol	Day A P, L't	15th Conn Vol
Carley A A, Cap	73d Ind Vol	Dewees J H, Major	18th Pa Cav
Connelly R J, L't	73d Ill Vol	Daniels E S, Cap	35th U S C T
Cartwright A G, Cap	85th N Y Vet Vol	Dietz Henry, Cap	45th N Y Vol
Clark M L, Cap	101st Pa Vol	Dodge C C, Cap	20th Mich Vol
Compher A, Cap	" "	Dieffenbach A C, L't	73d Pa Vol
Clapp J B, Adj	16th Conn Vol	Dewees T B, L't	2d U S Cav
Case A G, L't	" "	Dooley A T, L't	51st Ind Vol

LIST OF OFFICERS.

Downing O J, Cap	2d N Y Cav	Dorr H G, A Q M	4th Mass Cav
Denny W N, Cap	57th Ind Vol	Drake J M, L't	9th N J Vol
Delano J A, L't	51st Ind Vol	Dicey E C, Cap	1st Mich S S
Davis Q R, L't	123d O Vol	Downing H A, L't	31st U S C T
Derrickson J G, Cap	66th N Y Vol	Dibeler J B, Cap	45th Pa Vol
Dean S V, L't	145th Pa Vol	Davidson J W, L't	95th O Vol
Daily W A, Cap	8th Pa Cav	Denny W N, Major	51st Ind Vol
Davis C G, L't	1st Mass Cav	Drew G H, L't	9th N H Vol
Doruschke B, Cap	26th Wis Vol	Everett Chas, L't	70th O Vol
Dennis J B, Cap	7th Conn Vol	Eastman F R, L't	2d Pa Cav
Davis L R, Cap	7th O Vol	Elkin J L F, Adj	1st N J Vol
Drake L, L't	22d Mich Vol	Eastmond O, Cap	1st N C U Vol
Dutton W G, L't	67th Pa Vol	Evans T E, L't	52d Pa Vol
Dillon C D, L't	7th Iowa Cav	Egertone J W, L't	13th Ind Vol
Drennan J S, L't	1st Vt H Art	Ellinwood W B, L't	10th Wis Vol
Deane T J, L't	5th Mich Cav	Edwards D C, L't	2d Md Vol
Dunn J, L't	64th N Y Vol	English D, Major	11th Ky Cav
Dunning A J, L't	7th N Y Art	Elder S S, Cap	1st U S Art
Davenport T F, Cap	75th O Vol	Eckings T K, L't	3d N J Vol
Davis H C, Cap	18th Conn Vol	Evans B W, Cap	4th O Cav
Davis T C, L't	38th Ill Vol	Errickson J H, L't	57th N Y Vol
Dirlan C L, Cap	72d O Vol	Eberheart H H, Cap	120th O Vol
Doughton O G, L't	111th O Vol	Eagan M, Cap	15th W Va Vol
Day J R, Cap	3d Me Vol	Evans N C, Cap	184th Pa Vol
Donovan J, L't	2d N J Vol	Eglin A R, Cap	45th O Vol
Durbrow W, Cap	40th N Y Vol	Ewen M, Cap	21st Wis Vol
Dyre E B, L't	1st Conn Cav	Eagan John, L't	1st U S Art
Dinsmore A, Cap	5th Pa Cav	Elder John, L't	8th Ind Vol
Duzenburgh A, Cap	35th N Y Vol	Edwards T D, Asst Eng	U S Navy
Dorris W C, L't	111th Ill Vol	Edminston S, L't	89th O Vol
Dodge H G, L't	2d Pa Cav	Evans H F	
Dixon A, Cap	104th N Y Vol	Eans M, Cap	15th N Y Cav
Dunn M, Major	19th Mass Vol	Elheny J L F, Adj	1st N J Vol
Doane E B, Cap	8th Iowa Cav	Flick M, L't	67th Pa Vol
Davidson J, L't	6th N Y Art	Fritz J, L't	11th Tenn Vol
Drake J W, L't	136th N Y Val	Fay S A, L't	85th N Y Vet Vol
Downs C, L't	33d N J Vol	Frost C W, L't	" " "
Davis J W, L't	115th N Y Vol	Freeman D W D, Cap	101st Pa Vol
Duven J, L't	5th N H Vol	Fiske J E, Cap	2d Mass Art
Dushane J M, Cap	142d Pa Vol	Fish O M, L't	" "
Davis W H, Cap	4th Md Vol	Fluke A L, L't	103d Pa Vol
Dircks C S F, Cap	1st Tenn Vol	Fahs J, Cap	87th Pa Vol
Devine J S, L't	71st Pa Vol	Foot M C, L't	92d N Y Vol
Diemer M, L't	10th Mo Vol	Fontaine J, L't	73d Pa Vol
Dingley F, L't	7th R I Vol	Fairbanks J, L't	72d O Vol
Durfee W H, L't	5th "	Follett W H, L't	2d Mass Art
Durboyne G, L't	66th N Y Vol	Fry Alfred, L't	73d Ind Vol
Donohey G B, Cap	7th Pa Res	Fish G W,	3d O Cav
Dieffenbach W H, L't	" " "	Frasier J, Col	140th Pa Vol
De Lay R, L't	3d Iowa Cav	Fleming C K, Major	11th Vt Vol
Demmick O W, L't	11th N H Vol	Foster J W, Cap	42d Ill Vol
Drake C H, L't	142d Pa Vol	Fales J M, L't	1st R I Cav
Dygest K S, Cap	16th Mich Vol	Finney G E, Adj	19th Ind Vol
Dick L, L't	72d O Vol	Fowler J H, L't	100th O Vol
Davis L B, Cap	93d Ind Vol	Fox G B, Major	75th O Vol
Dillon F W, Cap	1st Ky Cav	Farr W V, Cap	106th Pa Vol
Dahl O R, L't	15th Wis Vol	Forbes W H, Major	2d Mass Cav
Dickey M V, L't	94th O Vol	Ford E W, Cap	9th Minn Vol
Davis Byron, L't	71st Pa Vol	Ferris J M, L't	3d Mich Vol
Day E, Cap	89th O Vol	Fairchild H, L't	10th Wis Vol
Dalton G A, L't	22d Mich Vol	Funk W, Cap	39th N Y Vol
Dickerson E, L't	44th Wis Vol	Faye E M, L't	42d N Y Vol
Durnam T J, L't	16th U S Inf	Furgerson J, L't	1st N J Vol
Dunn H C, L't	10th Ky Vol	Flannery D, L't	4th N J Vol
Driscoll D, L't	24th Mo Vol	Fowler H M, L't	15th N J Vol
Davis E J, L't	44th Ill Vol	Fisk W M, Cap	73d N Y Vol
Dugan J, L't	35th Ind Vol	Fleeger G W, L't	11th Pa R C Vo-

LIST OF OFFICERS.

Name	Unit	Name	Unit	Name	Unit
Fagan C A, L't	11th Pa R C Vol	Getman D, Cap		10th N Y Cav
French H, L't	3d Vt Vol	Griffin H G, Lt		112th Ill Vol
Francis J L, Cap	135th O Vol	Gordon E, Lt		81st Ind Vol
Field A, L't	94th N Y Vol	Geasland S A, Lt		11th Tenn Cav
Fritchy A W, L't	26th Mo Vol	Grey F C, Lt		11th Pa Vol
Fortescue L R, L't	Signal C U S A	Green C W, Lt		44th Ind Vol
Fellows M, L't	149th Pa Vol	Goss J W, Lt		1st Mass Art
Fisher R, L't	17th Mo Vol	Grafton B, Cap		64th O Vol
Fenner W, L't	2d R I Vol	Gates J, Cap		33d O Vol
Fox J D, L't	16th Ill Cav	Grant A, Cap		19th Wis Vol
Fritze C, L't	24th Ill Vol	Green G W, Cap		19th Ind Vol
Fisher L W, L't	4th Vt Vol	Goodrich A L, Cap		8th N Y Cav
Fatzer S, L't	108th N Y Vol	Gamble N P, Lt		63d Pa Vol
Fontaine E, Lt	7th Pa R C Vol	Garbet D, Lt		77th Pa Vol
Flamsburgh D, Cap	4th Ind Bat	Good T G, Lt		1st Md Cav
Forney D, Lt	30th O Vol	Gordon H M, Lt		143d Pa Vol
Fisher S, Lt	93d Ind Vol	Gray P, Lt		77th Pa Vol
Fielder J, Cap	Eng C U S A	Gallagher J, Lt		4th O Vt Vol
Finney D S, Lt	14&15 Ill Vet Bat	Galloway J L, C'p A A G		
Fairfield O B, Lt	89th O Vol	Green E A, Lt		81st Ill Vol
Fitzpatrick L, Lt	146th N Y Vol	Green J L, A A G		U S A
Fales L D C, Lt		Gove W A, Lt		3d Mass Cav
Freeman H B, Lt	18th U S Inf	Grant S, Lt		6th Mich Art
Foster H C, Lt	23d Ind Vol	Griffin T, Adj		55th U S C T
Foley John, Lt	59th Mass Vol	Gore J B, Lt		115th Ill Vol
Faass Louis, Lt	14th N Y Art	Gross T, Lt		21st Ill Vol
Frost R J, Lt	9th Mich Cav	Gordon G C, Cap		24th Mich Vol
Fall J P, Cap	32d Me Vol	Gerhardt H, Lt		24th Ill Vol
Filler J H, Major	55th Pa Vol	Gageby J H, Lt		19th U S Inf
Fay W W, Cap	56th Mass Vol	Gutjahr C, Cap		16th Ill Vol
George G J, Lt	40th Ill Vol	Galloway ——, Lt		15th U S Inf
Gillespie J B, Cap	120th Ill Vol	Grayham P, Cap		54th Pa Vol
Gunn T M, Lt	21st Ky Vol	Godley M L, Lt		17th Iowa Vol
Gilbert E C, Cap	152d N Y Vol	Gould D, Cap		33d W Vu Vol
Gill A W H, Cap	14th N Y Vol	Grey W H, Lt		14th Ill Cav
Greble C E, Cap	8th Mich Cav	Gude A, Cap		51st Ind Vol
Green J H, Lt	100th O Vol	Glenn S A, Cap		89th O Vol
Gotshall J, Adj	55th Pa Vol	Grey Philip, Lt		72d Pa Vol
Godwin J M, Lt	12th Ind Vol	Huey Pennock, Col		8th Pa Cav
Grover J E, Lt	6th Ind Cav	Hetsler J W, Cap		9th O Cav
Gayer H, Lt	133d W Va Mil	Hicks D W, Lt		
Gatch O C, Cap	89th O Vol	Halsey T J, Major		11th N J Vol
Gross J M, Cap	18th Ky Vol	Hutchinson J, Lt		2d W Va Mt Inf
Galbraith H E, Cap	22d Mich Vol	Huffman J W, Lt		5th Iowa Vol
Goetz J, Cap	" "	Hinds H H, Lt		57th Pa Vol
Gray W L, Cap	151st Pa Vol	Hagler J S, Cap		5th Tenn Vol
Gross C M, Lt	110th O Vol	Helms M B, Lt		1st W Va Vol
Grant G W, Lt	88th Pa Vol	Hall C B, Cap		" "
Grant H D, Lt	117th N Y Vol	Hallenburg G, Lt		1st O Vol
Gray R H, Lt	15th U S Inf	Hall A M, Lt		9th Minn Vol
Gariss A J, Adj	1st Md Cav	Haveley T, Cap		79th Ill Vol
Gates A L, Lt	10th Wis Vol	Hubbard H R, Lt		119th Ill Vol
Goodwin J A, Lt	1st Mass Cav	Heffley A, Cap		142d Pa Vol
Gamble G H, Adj	8th Ill Cav	Hays A H, Cap		7th Tenn Cav
Gates R C, Lt	18th U S Inf	Hare T H, Lt		5th O Cav
Gilmore J A, Lt	79th N Y Vol	Helm J B, Lt		101st Pa Vol
Gamble H, Lt	73d Ind Vol	Heffley C P, Lt		142d Pa Vol
Grant E, Cap	1st Vt Cav	Hubbell F A, Lt		67th Pa Cav
Granger C M, Lt	88th N Y Vol	Heffner W, Lt		" "
Goodrich J O, Adj	85th N Y Vet Vol	Harrington B F, Lt		18th Pa Cav
Glazeer W W, Lt	2d N Y Cav	Hart E R, Lt		1st Vt Art
Goodin A, Lt	82d O Vol	Hanson J B, Lt		1st Mass Art
Gordon C O, Lt	1st Me Cav	Hodge W E, Lt		5th Md Vol
Green E H, Cap	107th Pa Vol	Hawkins S W, Lt		7th Tenn Cav
Gimber H W, Cap	150th Pa Vol	Henry C D, Lt		4th O Cav
Gilman ——, Lt	3d Me Vol	Hays W W, Lt		34th O Vol
Gottland C, Lt	134th N Y Vol	Hodge J F, Lt		55th Pa Vol

LIST OF OFFICERS

Hall R F, Lt	75th O Vol	Heffelfinger J, Lt	7th P R V Corps
Haight J T, Lt	8th Iowa Cav	Harvey J L, Lt	2d Pa Art
Hastings T J, Lt	15th Mass Vol	Hobart M C, Cap	7th Wis Vol
Hock A, Cap	63d N Y Vol	Hock R B, Cap	12th N Y Cav
Hill G W, Lt	7th Mich Cav	Holman W C, Lt	9th Vt Vol
Heslit J, Lt	3d Pa Cav	Hadley H V, Lt	7th Ind Vol
Hazel E J, Lt	6th Pa Cav	Hall C, Lt	13th Wis Cav
Hanon J, Lt	115th Ill Vol	Hayden J A, Cap	11th P R V Corps
Herrick L C, Lt	1st N Y Cav	Hill J B, Lt	17th Mass Vol
Hine J J, Lt	100th O Vol	Hallett M V B, Lt	2d Pa Cav
Herbert R, Lt	50th Pa Vol	Hodge W L, Cap	120th Ill Vol
Harris S, Lt	5th Mich Cav	Henry A J, Lt	" "
Heppard T H, Lt	101st Pa Vol	Hamlin S G, Cap	134th N Y Vol
Hamilton W, Lt	2d Mass Art	Holladay V G, Lt	2d Ind Cav
Hastings G L, Lt	24th N Y Bat	Havens D, Lt	85th Ill Vol
Horton S H, Lt	101st Pa Vol	Hays C A, Lt	111th Pa Vol
Huff H B, Cap	184th Pa Vol	Hastings J L, Adj	7th Pa R V Corps
Hampton C G, Lt	15th N Y Cav	Haines H A, Cap	184th Pa Vol
Hard W B, Lt	17th Mich Cav	Hunter A W, Lt	2d U S (C'd) Art
Heil J, Cap	45th N Y Cav	Harris J W, Lt	2d Ind Cav
Hauf N, Lt	" "	Heltemus J B, Cap	18th Ky Vol
Hitt W R, Cap	113th Ill Cav	Herzberg F, Lt	66th N Y Vol
Harris W, Cap	24th Mo Cav	Henry J M, Lt	154th N Y Vol
Hobbie C A, Cap	17th Conn Cav	Harris G, Lt	79th Ind Vol
Holden E, Lt	1st Vet Cav	Holt W C, Cap	6th Tenn Vol
Hedges S P, Adj	112th N Y Vol	Harrison C E, Lt	89th O Vol
Hinds H C, Lt	102d N Y Vol	Huey R, Lt	2d E Tenn Vol
Hall W P, Major	6th N Y Cav	Henderson J H, Lt	14 & 15 Ill Vet Bat
Hart R K, Cap	19th U S Inf	Higley E H, Lt	1st Vet Cav
Hodge A, Cap	80th Ill Vol	Hendryks W H, Lt	11th Mich Bat'n
Harvey W H, Lt	51st Ind Vol	Hull G W, Lt	135th O Vol
Hay D, Cap	80th Ill Vol	Hamilton W B, Lt	22d Mich Vol
Harmer R J, Lt	" "	Hendrick F, Cap	1st N Y Cav
Hart C M, Lt	45th Pa Vol	Huston J, Lt	95th O Vol
Hopper J, Lt	2d N Y Cav	Henderson R, Lt	1st Mass Art
Hand G T, Lt	51st Pa Vol	Howe C H, Lt	21st Ill Vol
Hartzog R H O, Cap	1st N Y Cav	Halderman J, Lt	129th Ill Vol
Hagler J S, Cap	5th Tenn Vol	Hymer S, Cap	115th Ill Vol
Hintz H, Cap	16th Conn Vol	Hieurod P, Cap	105th O Vol
Hunt C O, Lt	5th Me Bat	Hackett A N, Lt	110th O Vol
Halpin G, Lt	116th Pa Vol	Huntley C C, Lt	16th Ill Cav
Hagenback J C, Lt	67th Pa Vol	Hand S P, Lt	43d U S C T
Hagan P A, Lt	7th Md Vol	Hurst T B, Lt	7th Pa Res V C
Holland W R, Lt	5th Md Cav	Hale G W, Lt	101st O Vol
Hawkins H E, Cap	78th Ill Vol	Hopf Geo, Lt	2d Md Vol
Heer T A, Cap	28th O Vol	Hescock H, Cap	1st Mo Art
Hart G D, Lt	5th Pa Cav	Hill O M, Lt	23d U S C T
Hull G W, Lt	135th O Vol	Hall C T, Lt	13th Mich Vol
Hoyt H B, Cap	40th N Y Vol	Heck F W, Cap	2d Md Vol
Hamilton H E, Lt	" "	Hill V H, A Q M	
Hezelton D W, Lt	22d N Y Cav	Hogeland D B, Cap	76th Pa Vol
Hovey H, Lt	78th Ill Vol	Hood John, Lt	80th Ill Vol
Hame D J, Cap	19th Mass Vol	Hogue J B, Lt	4th Pa Cav
Holahan C P, Lt	19th Pa Cav	Holmes A J, Cap	37th Wis Vol
Hamilton H N, Lt	59th N Y Vol	Haywood L E, Lt	58th Mass Vol
Hoppin H P, Lt	2d Mass Art	Irwin C L, Lt,	78th Ill Vol
Huntington E S, Lt	11th U S Inf	Irwin S E, Lt	3d Iowa Vol
Hutchison R C, Cap	8th Mich Vol	Irwin W H, Adj	103d Pa Vol
Hoyt W H, Lt	16th Iowa Vol	Imbric J M, Cap	3d O Vol
Hart P H, Lt	19th Ind Vol	Isett J H, Major	8th Ind Cav
Hughes R M, Lt	14th Ill Cav	Irsch F, Cap	45th N Y Vol
Henckly L D, Lt	10th Wis Vol	Isham A B, Lt	7th Mich Cav
Harkness R, Major	" "	Ingleden L, Cap	
Hewitt J, Lt	105th Pa Vol	Jackson R W, Lt	21st Wis Vol
Hastings C W, Cap	12th Mass Vol	Jenkins J H, Adj	" "
Heston J, Lt	4th N J Vol	Johnson H A, Lt	3d Me Vol
Hayes E, Cap	95th N Y Vol	James H H, Lt	6th Ind Vol

LIST OF OFFICERS.

Jones S F, Cap	80th Ill Vol
Johnson G, Lt	16th Conn Vol
Judd J H, Lt	27th Mass Vol
Jacobs J W, Cap	4th Ky Vol
John E P, L't	135th O Vol
Johnson J C, Cap	149th Pa Vol
Jobe B A, Cap	11th Pa R V C
Johnson V W, L't	10th N Y Cav
Jones J A, L't	21st Ill Vol
Johnson C K, L't	1st Me Cav
Jennings J T, Cap	75th O Vol
Jones D, Cap	14th N Y Art
Judson S C, Cap	106th N Y Vol
Jenkins H, Cap	40th Mass Vol
Jackson C G, Cap	84th Pa Vol
Jones J P, L't	55th O Vol
Jenkins G W, L't	9th W Va Vol
Jones C W, L't	16th Pa Cav
Justus J C, L't	2d Pa R V C
Jackson J, L't	4th Ind Cav
Jackson J S, L't	22d Ill Vol
Jones S E, L't	7th N Y Art
Jones H, L't	5th U S Cav
Jones W, L't	38th O Vol
Jones M J, Cap	115th Ill Vol
Johnson R, Cap	6th N Y Cav
Johnson J W, L't	1st Mass Art
Johnson W N, Correspt	
Jones Alfred, R Q M	50th Pa Vet Vol
Johnson J D, Cap	10th N J Vol
Jordan E C, L't	7th Conn Vol
Jacks J, L't	15th W Va Vol
Kelley D O, L't	100th O Vol
Krohn P, L't	5th N Y Cav
Keeler A M, Cap	22d Mich Vol
Kendal T, L't	15th U S Inf
Keniston J, L't	100th Ill Vol
Keith C E, L't	19th Ill Vol
Knowles E M, L't	42d Ind Vol
Kreuger W, L't	2d Mo Vol
Kreps F A M, L't	77th Pa Vol
Kane S, L't	38th Ind Vol
Kelly D A, Cap	1st Ky Vol
Kendrick E, Adjt	10th N J Vol
Kerr S C, L't	126th O Vol
Kendall H T, Adjt	56th Pa Vol
Kelly A, L't	126th O Vol
Keen J, L't	7th Pa V R C
Kuchin A, L't	5th Md Vol
Kees G W, L't	18th Conn Vol
Kreiger A, L't	67th Pa Vol
Knowles R A, L't	116th O Vol
Knapp F H, L't	9th O Cav
Kennaly J D, L't	8th O Cav
Kempton J F, L't	75th O Vol
Kline D J, L't	75th O Vol
Kennedy J W, Lt	134th N Y V 1
Kankel R, L't	45th N Y Vol
Kidd J H, L't	1st Md Art
Kendrick R H, Lt	25th Wis Vol
Kenyon G C, Lt	17th Ill Vol
Kidder G C, Lt	118th Pa Vol
Kelly H K, Cap	118th Pa Vol
Knox G, Lt	109 Pa Vol
Kelly J M, Lt	4th Tenn Vol
Kessler J G, Cap	2d Ind Cav
Kirby W M, Lt	3d N Y Art
King T, R Q M	101st Pa Vol
Keister W H H, Lt	103d Pa Vol
Kirk J B, Lt	101st Pa Vol
Krause J, Cap	3d Pa Art
Kempton F H, Lt	58th Mass Art
Kennits H, Lt	2d Mass Vol
Kauts J D, Lt	1st Ky Cav
Kellogg H, Lt	6th Mich Cav
Kronemeyer C, Cap	52 N Y Vol
King M D, Lt	3d O Vol
Kendal J, Cap	43d Ind Vol
King G E, Cap	103d Ill Vol
Knight H B, Lt	20th Mich Vol
Kelly J B, Lt	1st Pa Cav
Kirkpatrick G W, Lt	15th Iowa Vol
Knox J C, Lt	4th Ind Cav
Kepheart J S, Lt	5th Ind Vol
Kerin J, Lt	6th U S Cav
Kenyon P D, Cap	14 & 15th Ill V B
King Abe, Lt	12th O V Inf
King John, Lt	15th Ill Cav
Kissam Edgar, Cap	9th N J Vol
Kepheart J, Lt	13th O Vol
Kelton J, Lt	2d Pa Art
Kibby G L, Lt	4th R I Vol
Kendale W M, Major	73d Ind Vol
Kost R, Lt	6th Conn Vol
Kenfield F, Cap	17th Vt Vol
King John, Lt	6th Conn Vol
Kings S B, Cap	12th Pa Cav
Lindemeyer L, Cap	45th N Y Vol
Lemson A T, Lt	104th N Y Vol
Litchfield J B, Cap.	4th Me Vol
Lombard H G, Adj	4th Mich Vol
Logan W S, Cap	17th Mich Vol
Love J E, Cap	8th Kan Vol
Lucas John, Cap	5th Ky Vol
Lovett L T, Cap	" " "
Lodge G R, Lt	53d Ill Vol
Lucas W D, Cap	5th N Y Cav
Little J S, Cap	143 Pa Vol
Lewis C E, Lt	1st N Y Drag
Laycock J B, Lt	7th Pa R V C
Lyman H H, Lt	147th N Y Vol
Larrabee W H, Lt	7th Me Vol
Lanning A, Serg	24th Mich Vol
Leigh S J, A D C	
Lee A, Lt	152d N Y Vol
Lynch C M, Major	145th Pa Vol
Lynn J, Lt	" "
Lyttle C W, Cap	" "
Loud E J C, Lt	2d Pa Art
Ludney M S, Lt	52d Pa Vol
Lewry D W, Lt	2d Pa Art
Longnecker J H, Adjt	101st Pa Vol
Landen H, Lt	16th Conn Vol
Laughlin J M, Lt	103d Pa Vol
Langworthy D A, Cap	85th N Y Vol
Lafler J A, Lt	" "
Lyman J, Lt	27th Mass Vol
Laird J O, Lt	25th U S Inf
Litchfiel A C, Lt Col	7th Mich Cav
Lym W C, Lt	22d O Vol
Lintz W J, Lt	8th Tenn Vol
Leslee J L, Lt	18th Pa Cav
Leonard A, Lt	71st N Y Vol

LIST OF OFFICERS.

Laird M. Lt	16th Iowa Vol
Luther J C, Lt	1st Pa V R C
Lemon M W, Lt	14th N Y Art
Lane L M, Lt	9th Minn Vol
Lamson T D. Lt	3d Ind Cav
Loomis A W. Lt	18th Conn Vol
Locke W H. Lt	" "
Lindsy A H, Lt	" "
Leith S. Lt	132d N Y Vol
Long C H. Lt	1st Md Vol
Lewis D B, Lt	12th Pa Cav
Livingston C H, Lt	1st W Va Cav
Law G. Cap	6th W V Cav
Loyd J K. Cap	17th Mass Vol
Leeds M A, Lt Col	153d O Vol
Lock D R. Lt	8th Ky Cav
Limbard A. Lt	M'Laughlin's Sq
Lloyd T S C. Lt	6th Ind Cav
Lawrence G H, Lt	2d N Y Md Rifles
Land J R. Cap	65th Ind Vol
Lee E N. Cap	5th Mich Cav
Larkin F A Lt	18th Ind Vol
Locklin A W. Lt	94th N Y Vol
Lang C H. Lt	59th Mass Vol
Latimer E C. Cap	27th U S C T
Lenter A P Cap	2d Tenn Inf
Myers T. L't	107th Pa Vol
Mooney J, L't	" "
Mussel O, Cap	68th N Y Vol
Millis V. L't	" "
Mosely H H, L't	25th O Vol
Makepeace A J, Cap	19th Ind Vol
McDade A. L't	154th N Y Vol
Murphy F. Cap	97th N Y Vol
Moran F. L't	73d N Y Vol
Mendenhall J A, L't	75th N Y Vol
Mell J R L't	61st N Y Vol
Morres W J. L't	5th Md Vol
Metta J S. L't	" " "
Merwin S T C. L't	18th Conn Vol
Madera W B. L't	6th W Va Vol
Meany D B. Cap	13th Pa Cav
Matherson E J. L't	18th Conn Vol
McKeag F, L't	" " "
Morningstar H. L't	87th Pa Vol
Manning J S, L't	116th O Vol
Mash P. Cap	67th Pa Vol
McNeal D L't	13th Pa Cav
Matson C C L't Col	6th Ind Cav
McCarty W W. Cap	18th O Cav
Morgan C H L't	21st Wis Cav
McGruder W H. L't	" " "
McDowal J S, Cap	77th Pa Cav
Moses H. L't	4th Ky Cav
Morrison M V B. Lt	33d O Cav
McKinison A H, Lt	10th Wis Cav
Mead L C, Lt	22d Mich Cav
McKercher D, Col	10th Wis Cav
Mathews A S. Adjt	22d Mich Vol
McGowan E Lt	29th Ind Vol
Murphy J. Lt	16th U S Inf
Mitchell J. Lt	79th Ill Vol
McCune A W. Lt	2d O Vet Vol
Muhlemon J R, Maj &c	
McNeil S. Lt	51st O Vol
Metcalf C W, Cap	42d Ind Vol
Messick J M, Lt	" " "

Mackey J T. Lt	16th U S Inf
Mahoney J S, Lt	21st O Vol
Mead W H Lt	6th Ky Cav
Moore M. Cap	29th Ind Vol
Moore G W. Cap	7th Tenn Vol
McConalee W J, Lt	14th Iowa Cav
Morton J W, Cap	4th Mass Cav
Malambre J M, Lt	75th O Vol
Morse E. Lt	78th Ill Vol
Marshall W S Major	5th Iowa Vol
McGovern J, L't	75th Pa Vol
McKinley J, L't	98th O Vol
McNiece A, L't	73d Pa Vol
Mann G, L't	80th O Vol
Moore F. L't	72d Pa Vol
Mooney A H, Cap	16th N Y Cav
McHugh J, Cap	69th Pa Vol
McFadden W M, Cap	59th N Y Vol
Monaghan J, L't	62d Pa Vol
McIntosh J C. L't	145th Pa Vol
Mather F W, L't	7th N Y Art
McCray H. Cap	115th Pa Vol
Mockrie P B, L't	7th N Y Art
May J, Cap	15th Mass Vol
Moore N H. Cap	7th N Y Art
McCutcheon E F, L't	64th N Y Vol
McWain E J, L't	1st N Y V Art
McCreary D B, L't Col	145th Pa Vol
Murry S F, Cap	2d U S S S
McKage J. Cap	184th Pa Vol
Muffley S F, Adjt	" " "
Mangus H F. L't	52d Pa Vol
McLauglin J, L't	" " "
McGinnes W A, L't	19th Mass Vol
Mathews A R. L't	1st Vt Art
Morse A. L't	" " "
Maish L. Cap	87th Pa V 1
McQuiddy ——, Cap	5th Tenn Cav
Marshall W S, Adjt	51st Ind Vol
McDill H. L't	80th Ill Vol
Maxwell C A. L't	2d O Vol
Mall D H. Cap	73d Ind Vol
Munday J W, L't	" " "
Murdock H S. L't	" " "
McHolland D A, Cap	" " "
Morey H. L't	10th N Y Cav
McColgin J, L't	7th O Cav
Morris J H. L't	4th Ky Vol
McLernan P. Major	2d N Y Cav
Mattock C P. Major,	17th Me Vol
Myers W H. L't	76th N Y Vol
McGeehan J, L't	14 th N Y Vol
Miller F C. Col	147th N Y Vol
Mitchell H W. L't	14th N Y Vol
Maltison A C Cap	12th N J Vol
Morrisy G H. A Q M,	12th Iowa
McKay D S, L't	18th Pa Cav
Mayer L L't	12th " "
Merritt H A D, L't	5th N Y Cav
Metzger J. Cap	55th Pa Vol
Moore Le Roy, Cap	72d O Vol
McCain J C, L't	9th Minn Vol
McKee T H, Cap	1st W Va Vol
McGnire T, Cap	7th Ill Vol
Miller J W, L't	14th Ill Cav
Murphy J. L't	60th N Y Vol
Mallison J, L't	94th N Y Vol

LIST OF OFFICERS.

Moulton O. L't Col	25th Mass Vol
Morgan S M, Cap	
McGraylis M. Cap	93d Ind Vol
Morgan Ben B. L't Col	75th O Vol
Mulligan J A, L't	4th M ss Cav
Mead S, Cap	111th N Y Vol
McCall O, L't	103d Pa Vol
Mullin D W, Cap	101st Pa Vol
Morrow J M, L't	" " "
McHenry C, L't	85th N Y Vet Vol
Miller W G, L't	16th Conn Vol
Mackey J F, Cap	103d Pa Vol
Morrow J J. Cap	" " "
Mathews W F. L't	1st Md Vol
Merrill H P, Cap	4th Ky Vol
Menier N J, L't	93d Ind Vol
McDonald H J, Cap	11th Conn Vol
Moodey J E L't	59th Mass Vol
Martin J C, Cap	1st Tenn Cav
Melkorn M. Cap	135th O Vol
Moon R A, L't	6th Mich Cav
Moore M M. L't	" " "
Manley J A, Cap	64th N Y Vol
Miller H, L't	17th Mich Vol
McMannus P W, Adjt	27th Mass Vol
Moses C C, Cap	58'h Pa Vol
Mudgett A G, Cap	11th Me Vol
McMahon E. L't	72d O Vol
McKinstry J, L't	16th Ill Cav
McEvoy W, Adjt	2d Ill Vol
McBeth N, L't	45th O Vol
Merry W A, L't	106th N Y Vol
Marney A, Cap	2d Tenn Vol
Moore D T, L't	" " "
Morton G C, L't	4th Pa Cav
McKay R G. L't	5th Mich Cav
Molton H. L't	1st U S Cav
Montgomery R H, L't	5th " "
Marrow H C, Ass Egr	U S N
Morgan J T, Cap	17th Mich Vol
Manning G A, Cap	2d Mass Cav
Mather E. L't	1st Vt Cav
McDonald C, L't	2d Ill Art
Moore W Q, L't	2d Md Cav
McCafferty N J, L't	4th U S Art
Millis J, L't	66th Ind Vol
McClure T W, L't	6th U S Art
McNitt R J, Cap	1st Pa Cav
Mason J, L't	13th Pa Cav
Main C A, Cap	5th Ill Cav
McDonald J, L't	2d E Tenn Vol
Morse C W, L't	16th Conn Vol
Miller C, Adjt	14th Ill Cav
McAdams J, L't	10th W Va Vol
Mayer G W, L't	37th Ind Vol
Mure C. L't	15th Mo Vol
McIntyre ——, Cap	15th Wis Vol
McCormick J. L't	21st N Y Cav
Moore L. Cap	72d O Vol
McKay R G, L't	1st Mich Cav
Marshland A J, L't	2d Pa Art
Millard R J, Cap	" " "
Mix W H, L't	19th U S Cav
Munger T J, L't	37th Wis Vol
McNure A, L't	73d Pa Vol
Mitchell H G, L't	32d Me Vol
Marshall J D, L't	57th O Vol
McLane ——, L't	9th Minn Vol
Morris W M, L't	93d Ill Vol
Norris A W, L't	107th Pa Vol
Norcross J C, L't	2d Mass Cav
Niedenhoffen C, L't	9th Minn Vol
Nyce W, L't	2d N Y Cav
Nelson W H, L't	13th U S Inf
Nutting J H, Cap	27th Mass Vol
Norris O P. L't	111th O Vol
Nelson P, Major	66th N Y Vol
Nelson A, L't	" " "
Nolan L, Cap,	2d Del Vol
Needham J B. L't	4th Vt Vol
Noggle C L, L't	2d U S Inf
Nichols C H, Cap	6th Conn Vol
Newbrant J F, L't	4th Mo Cav
Norwood J, L't	76th N Y Vol
Norton E E, Cap	24th Mich Vol
Nealy O H, L't	11th U S Inf
Netlerville W McM, L't	12th U S Inf
Nash W H. Cap	1st U S S S
Neher W, L't	7th Pa R V Cav
Newsome E, Cap	81st Ill Vol
Neal A, L't	5th Ind Cav
Nuhfer A, Cap	72d O Vol
Nolan H J, Cap	14th N Y Cav
Niswander D M, L't	2d Pa Art
Niemayer B H. L't	11th Ky Cav
Newlin C. Cap	7th Pa Cav
Nyman H J, L't	19th Mich Vol
Nulland W R, L't	5th Ind Cav
Norris J. Cap	2d Pa Art
Noyes C S, Cap	31st Me Vol
Outcolt R V, L't	135th O Vol
O'Harre J, L't	7th N Y Art
Osborne F. L't	19th Mass Vol
Ong O C, L't	2d Va Cav
Ottinger W, Cap	8th Tenn Vol
Oliphant D. L't	35th N J Vol
O'Connor W, L't	13th Pa Cav
O'Brien E Cap	29th Mo Vol
O'Shea E. L't	13th Pa Cav
Olcott D W. Cap	131th N Y Vol
O'Kain J, L't	7th Ill Cav
Oats J G, L't	3d O Vol
O'Connel P. L't	53th Pa Vol
Owens W N, Major	1st Ky Cav
Ogden J, L't	1st Wis Cav
Ogan H W, Cap	14th O Vol
O'Sullivan F J, L't	67th O Vol
Olden G C, L't	112th Ill Vol
Pickenpaugh A C, L't	6th W Va Vol
Picquet H, L't	32d Ill Vol
Parker J T, L't	13th Iowa Vol
Phinney A, L't	90th Ill Vol
Provine W M. L't	81th Ill Vol
Purcell C, L't	16th Iowa Vol
Powell W H. L't	2d Ill L Art
Parker G M. L't	45th Ill Vol
Purveance J S L't	130th Ind Vol
Pratt J E, L't	4th Vt Vol
Pemberton H V, Cap	14th N Y Art
Piffard D H, L't	" " "
Price C A, L't	5th Mich Cav
Parker E B, L't	1st Vt Art
Pumphry J B, L't	123d O Vol
Paxton W N, L't	110th Pa Vol

LIST OF OFFICERS.

Porter E. Cap	154th N Y Vol
Poole S V. Cap	" "
Potts G P, L't	151st Pa Vol
Potts J H, L't	75th O Vol
Powers J L, L't	157th N Y Vol
Pettijohn, L't	2d U S S S
Parsons W L. Major	2d Wis Vol
Parker J, Cap	1st N J Vol
Powell J P. Cap	146th N Y Vol
Paine L B, Cap	121st N Y Vol
Partridge W H L't	67th N Y Vol
Pierce H H, L't	7th Conn Vol
Pasco H S, Major	16th Conn Vol
Pitt G W. L't	85th N Y Vet
Peake I. S. L't	" " "
Pierson E C. L't	" " "
Piggott J T, Jr, Cap	8th Pa Cav
Phelps L D. L't	8th Pa Cav
Plase W B. Cap	87th U S Inf
Pentzell D, L't	4th N Y Cav
Peetrey J G. L't	95th O Vol
Powers D H. Cap	6th Mich Cav
Parmalee J A, Cap	7th Ind Vol
Penfield J A. Major	5th N Y Cav
Potter E D. L't	6th Mich Cav
Purlier H, L't	2d O Vol
Powell O, L't	42d Ill Vol
Patterson J B, L't	21st O Vol
Perley J P. L't	13th Mich Vol
Pierce G S. Cap	19th U S Inf
Perry F W, Cap	10th Wis Vol
Pulliam M D. L't	11th Ky Cav
Prather Z R. L't	116th Ill Vol
Pierson M P. L't	100th N Y Vol
Pilsbury S H, Cap	5th Me Vol
Phares W, L't	46th W Va Vol
Paul A C. A A G	
Pettit G. Cap	120th N Y Vol
Preston A L. L't	8th Mich Cav
Pendleton D B, Cap	5th Mich Cav
Porter D M. Cap	120th Ill Vol
Pennybacker E J. Cap	18th Pa Cav
Patterson F A. Cap	3d W Va Cav
Potter H C. L't	18th Pa Cav
Paul J S. L't	122d O Vol
Phillipp F, L't	5th Pa Cav
Pierce S C, Cap	3d N Y Cav
Protsman C N. L't	7th Wis Vol
Potter G A, L't	2d Ky Vol
Peters G, L't	9th N J Vol
Pitt J H, L't	118th N Y Vol
Post James. L't	149th Pa Vol
Page J E. Cap	5th Iowa Vol
Pace N C. Cap	80th Ill Vol
Piper S B. Adjt	3d O Vol
Phelps J D. Cap	73d Ind Vol
Palmer E L. L't	57th N Y Vol
Poston J L, Cap	13th Tenn Vol
Patrec L B, L't	126th O Vol
Poole J F, L't	1st W Va Cav
Peterson C J A, L't	1st R I Cav
Peck M D. L't	2d N Y Cav
Pelton E W, L't	2d Md Vol
Patterson G W, L't	135th O Vol
Price J C. L't	75th O Vol
Pain H C. L't	20th Ill Vol
Porter B B, Cap	10th N Y Art
Perrin Z L't	72d O Vol
Platt L H. L't	34th Mass Vol
Porter L G. L't	87th Ill
Paine J A. Cap	2d Ind Cav
Phelps L A. Major	5th W Va Vol
Palmer J H. L't	12th O Vol
Peckeville W F. Cap	5th Iowa Vol
Pope W A. L't	18th Wis Vol
Pyne D B. L't	3d Mo Vol
Ping T, Cap	17th Iowa Vol
Park A L't	" " "
Perrin J. Adjt	6th U S Cav
Pierce W. L't	17th Vt Vol
Phillips W B. L't	2d Pa Art
Poindexter C O, L't	31st Me Vol
Pierson A P, L't	9th Mich Cav
Phillips W E. L't	7th Conn Vol
Payne L S, Cap	100th N Y Vol
Price Chas A. L't	3d Mich Vol
Quigg D. Major	14th Ill Cav
Rees M L't	72d O Vol
Robinson J L, L't	7th Tenn Cav
Robbins H. Cap	2d Wis Vol
Rockwell W O. L't	134th N Y Vol
Robbins N A. L't	4th Me Vol
Russell J H. L't	12th Mass Vol
Rockwell J O, L't	97th N Y Vol
Richardson H, L't	19th Ind Vol
Robinson G L. L't	80th O Vol
Robertson G W, L't	22d Mich Vol
Roach S. L't	100th Ill Vol
Riggs B T, Cap	18th Ky Vol
Rice J A. Cap	73d Ill Vol
Retilley W L, L't	51st O Vol
Ray T J. L't	49th O Vol
Reynolds H. L't	42d Ill Vol
Rose W B. L't	106th Pa Cav
Rourke J, Cap	1st Ill Art
Reynolds W H. Major	14th N Y Art
Ruger J M. L't	57th Pa Vol
Richards L S, L't	1st Vt Art
Ronnels J R L't	145th Pa Vol
Rieneckar G, L't	5th Pa Cav
Rahn O, L't	184th Pa Vol
Ritter H. Cap	52d N Y Vol
Reynolds W J, Cap	75th O Vol
Reynolds E P. L't	5th Tenn Cav
Robbinson J F, L't	67th Pa Vol
Ruff J. L't	" " "
Randolph J F, Cap	123d O Vol
Robbins A, Cap	" " "
Rosenbaum O H. Cap	" " "
Rossman W C. Cap	3d O Vol
Russel M. Cap	51st Ind Vol
Randall W, L't	80th Ill Vol
Richley J A. Cap	73d Ind Vol
Roach A C, L't	51st Ind Vol
Rosencranz A C, Cap	4th Ind Cav
Rowley G A, L't	2d U S Inf
Reid J A, L't	2d N C Vol
Robinson B E, L't	95th O Vol
Ryder S B. Cap	5th N Y Cav
Robinson W A, Cap	77th Pa Vol
Roach W E, L't	49th N Y Vol
Rogers A, Cap	4th Ky Cav
Raymond H W, L't	8th N Y Art
Ross C W, L't	1st Ky Vol

LIST OF OFFICERS.

Rose J E. L't	120th Ill Vol	Sanders A H. L't Col	16th Iowa Vol
Roberts E R, L't	7th Ill Vol	Shedd W, Col	30th Ill Vol
Reed J H, L't	120th Ill Vol	Strang H W, Cap	" " "
Richard J M. L't	1st W Va Vol	Smith J H, Cap	16th Iowa Vol
Rings G. Adjt	100th O Vol	Skilton A S. Cap	57th O Vol
Rothe H L't	15th N Y Art	Shuttz W Cap	37th O Vol
Robb W J, Cap	1st W Va Vol	Smythe S S. L't	1st Ill Art
Ramsey E K L't	1st N J Vol	Smith A E, Cap	48th Ill Vol
Riley L H, L't	7th Pa R V Cps	Scott Geo. L't	10th Ind Vol
Ruby S V, L't	" " "	Swift E. L't	74th Ill Vol
Ross C H Adjt	13th Ind Vol	Sutherland G W. Adjt	126th O Vol
Risedon I, L't	11th Tenn Vol	Starkweather W L. Cap	85th N Y Vol
Robs E W. L't	1st Tenn Vol	Shaefer James Cap	101st Pa Vol
Ring A. L't	12th O Vol	Strong E E, L't	16th Conn Vol
Richardson J A. L't	2d N Y Cav	Sampson I B, Cap	2d Mass H Art
Romaine L. L't	2d N J Vol	Sinclair R B, L't	" " "
Roberts G, L't	7th N H Vol	Spence D M. L't	103d Pa Vol
Ross G. L't	7th Vt Vol	Stoke G W, L't	" " "
Rathbone T W, L't	153d O Vol	Smullen F, Cap	" " "
Rugg C L. L't	6th Ind Cav	Stewart A, Jr, Cap	
Roger J R. L't	157th Pa Vol	Sweeny J Ass Egr	U S N
Reed —— Cap	107th N Y Vol	Starr G H. Cap	104th N Y Vol
Roney J C L't	3d O Vol	Schell G L, Cap	88th Pa Vol
Robinson T B. Cap	16th Conn Vol	Seely H B, Adjt	86th N Y Vol
Richards J S, L't		Schroeders E, L't	74th Pa Vol
Russell J A Cap	98d Ill Vol	Sears D C, L't	94th N Y Vol
Rice J S. L't	13th Ind Vol	Smith J A, L't	154th N Y Vol
Reade J, L't	57th Mass Vol	Schuld G, L't	45th N Y Vol
Richards R C, Cap	45th Pa Vol	Sampson J B. L't	12th Mass Vol
Raynor A J. L't	19th U S Cav	Spring W, Cap	45th N Y Vol
Rainear L, L't	2d N J Cav	Schroeder C H. L't	12th Ill Vol
Reynolds W J. Cap	4th R I Vol	Stevens C G, L't	154th Ill Vol
Roberson J S, L't	7th Tenn Cav	Swift R R, Cap	12th Mass Vol
Riley W S. L't	21st N Y Cav	Skinner J L, L't	" " "
Randall W H. L't	1st Mich S S	Stone D, Cap	118th N Y Vol
Reir Geo W. Cap	107th N Y Vol	Spindler J. L't	73d Ill Vol
Robinson C. Cap	31st U S Cav	Spencer S A Cap	82d Ind Vol
Rorick D, A D C	31st Iowa Vol	Spufford A C, L't	41st O Vol
Reynolds B J. Cap	143d N Y Vol	Schwade J C. Cap	77th Pa Vol
Sturgeon W B. L't	107th Pa Vol	Singer G P. Cap	33d O Vol
Stover M H, L't	18th " "	Spaulding E G, L't	22d Mich Vol
Sweetland A A, L't	2d Pa Cav	Smythe W H, L't	16th U S Inf
Snyder J. Cap	14th N Y Vol	Schummerhone J, Cap	42d Ind Vol
Smith E B. L't	1st Vt Art	Schwainforth F, L't	24th Ill Vol
Stoughton H R. L't Col	2d U S S S	Sanger A W, L't	21st Ill Vol
Steele J, Major	2d Pa Cav	Spencer F, L't	17th O Vol
Smart G F C, Cap	145th Pa Vol	Simpson J D, L't	10th Ind Vol
Schurr C, L't	7th N Y Art	Stover J C, Cap	3d Tenn Vol
Shafer W H. L't	5th Pa Cav	Stevens J H. L't	5th Mc Vol
Standeford S A, L't	42d N Y Vol	Stevens F, L't	190th Pa Vol
Smith H I, Cap	53d Pa Vol	Stuart C. L't	24th N Y Vol
Sargeant M G, L't	1st Vt Art	Shanan M, L't	140th N Y Vol
Schooley D, Cap	2d Pa "	Stevens J R, Cap	40th N Y Vol
Stallman C H, L't	87th Pa Vol	Speece L B Major	7th Pa R V C
Socks J, L't	5th Md Art	Shelton W H, L't	1st N Y Art
Sweadner J. L't	" " "	Smith M S, L't	16th Mc Vol
Stewart T H. L't	" " "	Snowhite E, L't	7th Pa R V C
Stroman C P, L't	87th Pa Art	Swann E J. Cap	76th N Y Vol
Sibley H L. L't	116th O "	Sweet W H S. L't	146th N Y Vol
Smith M H, L't	123d " "	Schofield E. Cap	11th Pa R V C
Schuyler J F. L't	" " "	Steel J M, L't	1st W Va Vol
Simpson G W. L't	67th Pa "	Sitler J R L't	2d Pa Cav
Schroeder E, L't	5th Md "	Shaw J C, L't	7th O Vol
Smith J, L't	67th Pa "	Sheerd D G, L't	5th Ky Cav
Schortz D, Cap	12th Pa Cav	Shannon A L, L't	3d Ind Cav
Sheppard E A Cap	110th O Vol	Smith C B, L't	4th N Y Cav
Smith C J, Major	6th Ind Cav	Smith A M. L't	1st Tenn Cav

LIST OF OFFICERS.

Sutter C. L't	39th N Y Vol
Spaulding E J, L't	2d U S Cav
Shaffer H C. L't	2d N Y Cav
Swayzie W A, Cap	3d O Vol
Sharp E, L't	51st Ind Vol
Smith D D. Cap	1st Tenn Vol
Segar T W. L't	81st Ill Vol
Smith J C. L't	24th Ind Bat
Saber G E. L't	2d R I Cav
Sullivan J, Adjt	7th R I Vol
Smith J B. L't	5th W Va Cav
Sandon W. L't	1st Wis Cav
Sutcher C B. Cap	16th Ill Vol
Sharp G A, L't	19th Pa Cav
Stone L L. R Q M	2d Vt Vol
Smith L S, L't	14th N Y Cav
Sanford O L. Major	7th Conn Vol
Smith J P, L't	49th Pa Vol
Stevens J G. L't	52d Pa Vol
Smith T A, Major	7th Tenn Cav
Swope C T. L't	4th Ky Vol
Stewart A S. L't	4th Ky Vol
Strickland E P, L't	114th Ill Vol
Smith P. L't	4th Tenn Cav
Stanton J W. L't	5th Ind Cav
Soper M H. Major	5th Ind Cav
St John W H. L't	5th Ind Cav
Shepard E. L't	6th O Cav
Scripture F E. R Q M	7th N Y Art
Simmons A B. L't	5th Ind Cav
Starr H P, L't	22d N Y Cav
Spring B, L't	75th O Vol
Shurtz E. Cap	8th Iowa Cav
Stover A C. L't	95th O Vol
Stansbury M L, Cap	95th O Vol
Schofield R, Cap	1st Vt Cav
Stone C P. L't	1st Vt Cav
Scudder A A, R Q M	35th Pa Vol
Scoville H C. L't	92d Ill Vol
Stebbins J. L't	77th N Y Vol
Schwartz C S, L't	2d N J Cav
Sailor J, L't	13th Pa Vol
Smyser H C, L't	2d Md Vol
Scott R F. L't	11th Ky Cav
String T B. Cap	11th Ky Cav
Stewart R R. L't	2d N Y Cav
Stribling M W. L't	61st O Vol
Shoemaker F M, Cap	100th O Vol
Smith J, L't	5th Pa Cav
Stout J O. L't	McL's S O Cav
Shepstrong M N. Cap	60th O Vol
Snodgrass J G. Cap	110th O Vol
Sargent H R, Cap	32d Me "
Stanton J W, L't	5th Ind Cav
Sheehan J P. L't	31st Me Vol
Shull J F, L't	28th U S C T
Smith S B, L't	30th " "
Stauber B F, L't	20th Pa Cav
Schulter H. L't	43d N Y Vol
Sherman S U. Cap	4th R I "
Seely L D. L't	45th Pa "
Stewart R T, Cap	138th Pa Vol
Stevens Frank, L't	12th Pa V R Cps
Scott D W. Cap	23d U S Cav
Schroeder H. L't	82d Ill Vol
Septon A F. L't	8th Iowa Cav
Senter A P, Cap	2d E Tenn Cav
Scofield T D, L't	27th Mich Vol
Sanders C B, L't	30th U S Cav
Simondson P A, L't	23d U S Cav
Shaefer N W, L't	24th Ind Cav
Tuthill P A. L't	104th N Y Vol
Templeton O F. Cap	107th Pa Vol
Thonsen B E. L't	9th O Vol
Teter A J. L't	2d O Vol
Teneyck S. Cap	18th U S Inf
Tainter H S. L't	82d N Y Vol
Tanner D. L't	118th Ill Vol
Tompkins H V, L't	59th N Y Vol
Trent B W. L't	106th Pa Vol
Tyler L D C, Cap	" "
Thomas D Major	135th O Vol
Thornbury J M S't	39th Ky Vol
Thompson C H. Major	5th Ind Cav
Tillottson H H. L't	73d Ind Vol
Thomas A V. L't	" "
Thompson J S, L't	10th Vt Vol
Thorp T J, L't Col	1st N Y Drag
Terwilliger J E, L't	85th N Y Vol
Turner M C. Cap	16th Conn Vol
Tyler L E. L't	1st Conn Cav
Timpson S C. Cap	95th N Y Vol
Thayer H O, L't	67th Pa Vol
Taylor A A. L't	122d O Vol
Thompson R L't	67th Pa Vol
Tilbraud H, Cap	4th N H Vol
Thorn R F, L't	5th Ky Vol
Tinn A, L't	16th Iowa Vol
Turner J H, Cap	" "
Todd O. L't	18th Wis Vol
Tiffany A W. L't	9th Minn Vol
Taylor H. L't	55th Ind Vol
Temple H, L't	2d N Y Cav
True W M. L't	16th Ill Cav
Thompson J J T. As Sur	12th O Vol
Tibbles H G, Cap	" "
Taylor J, L't	2d Pa V R Cps
Tubbs A,	
Tower D W. L't	17th Iowa Vol
Towson F. L't	" "
Tipton A F, L't	8th Iowa Cav
Tourtillotte J, Cap	7th Conn Vol
Turner D, L't	118th Ill Vol
Tob I C. L't	15th N Y Art
Thompson J, Cap	4th O Cav
Toby J P F. L't	31st Me Vol
Tinker S H, L't	93d Ind Vol
Unthank C L. Cap	11th Ky Cav
Ullenbaugh G, L't	1st O Vol
Urwiler S C. Cap	67th Pa Vol
Ulem J. L't	3d O Vol
Uptigrove J R. L't	73d Ind Vol
Underdown J D, Cap	2d Tenn Vol
Ulffar H A. A A G	
Underwood J W, Cap	57th O Vol
Von Keiser A. Cap	30th N Y Bat
Van Netter R N. L't	1st Mich Cav
Von Valack D D. L't	12th U S Inf
Vanderheiff J W. Cap	45th N Y Vol
Velfort G. L't	54th N Y Vol
Vickers D. Major	4th N J Vol
Von Rottenburg H N. L't	103 N Y Vol
Von Helanrich G, L't Col	4th Mo Cav
Vinay F, L't	85th N Y Vol

LIST OF OFFICERS.

Van Doren D, L't	72d O Vol	Wanzer G G, Major	24th N Y Cav
Van Ness G A, L't	73d Ind Vol	Wadsworth M C, L't	16th Me Vol
Van Rensalaer C, L't	148th N Y Vol	Warchaw F, L't	51th N Y Vol
Vaughn Z, Cap	1st Me Cav	Wilson W C, Cap,	104th N Y Vol
Van Buren G M, Cap	6th N Y Cav	White H G, Cap	54th N Y Vol
Van Alin W C, L't	45th Pa Vol	Widdess C C, Cap,	150th Pa Vol
Von Bulow A, L't	3d N J Cav	Whiston D, L't	13th Mass Vol
Von Haack A, Cap	68th N Y Vol	Welsh W H H, L't	87th Pa Vol
West O W, L't	1st N Y Drag	White C W, Cap	5th W Va Cav
Warner J B, L't	8th Mich Cav	Wilson J, Cap	57th O Vol
Williams G, L't	" "	Williams W H, Cap	41st N Y Vol
Whitney M G, Cap	29th Mo Vol	Watson W L, L't	21st Wis Vol
Winters J, L't	72d O Vol	Winner C N, L't	1st O Vol
Warner J, L't	33d N J Vol	Wasson J M, L't	40th O Vol
Wheeler J F, L't	149th N Y Vol	Webb G W, Cap	2d Pa Art
West J H, Cap	11th Ky Vol	Williams R, Cap	12th O Vol
Waidmann F, L't	16th Iowa Vol	Welch J C, L't	85th N Y Vol
Walker J, L't	8th Tenn Vol	Wheeler J D, Cap,	15th Conn Vol
Western C S, L't	21st Wis Vol	Wenrick J E.	19th Pa Cav
Willets W, L't	22d Mich Vol	Williams W, L't	6th Mich Cav
Wands H P, Cap	" "	Willis W, L't	51st Ind Vol
Welker W H, L't	21st O Vol	Williams M F, L't	15th Ky Vol
Welshimer P, Cap	21st Ill Vol	Wiley M, Cap	1st Tenn Vol
Weatherby J, L't	51st O Vol	Whittaker E B, Cap	72d Pa Vol
Weesner T A, L't	14 & 15 Ill V Bat	Wallace J, L't Col	47th O Vol
Wyman E F, C S		Ward T H, L't	59th U S Cav
West D J, L't	6th Conn Vol	Wheaton J, L't	" "
Ware E W, L't	9th Me Vol	Wright R J, Cap	6th O Vol
White Dan, Col	31st Me Vol	Wilcox W H H, L't	10th N Y Cav
Washburne W, Cap	35th Mass Vol	Wallace R P, Lt	120th O Vol
Wing G H, L't	14th N Y Art	Walpole H H, Cap	122d N Y Vol
Wilder G O, Adj	15th Mass Vol	Wright J W, L't	10th Iowa Vol
Willis A R, Cap	8th Me Vol	Whittemore B W, L't	5th N Y Vol
Wilcox C W, L't	9th N H Vol	Wallace J J, L't	7th Tenn Cav
Westbrook U S, Cap	135th O Vol	Wentworth H A, L't	14th N Y H Art
Weeks E J, L't	67th Pa Vol	Wall M W, Cap	69th N Y Vol
Woodard J E, L't	18th Conn Vol	Walker W H, Lt	4th O Vol
Weakly T J, Lt	100th O Vol	Wislon E S, L't	1st Mass Cav
Wright B F, Cap	146th N Y Vol	Warren D H, Ass Surg	8th Iowa Cav
Wilson W M, Jr, Cap	122d O Vol	Wilson R P, L't	5th U S Cav
Watson J C, L't	12th O Vol	Willets W, L't	22d Mich Vol
Woodruff F M, L't	76th N Y Vol	White H, Major	
Wright D L, L't	51st Ind Vol	White G M, Cap	1st W Va Vol
Whiting J D, L't	3d O Vol	Whitney J de W	O Vet Inf
Wright W R, Cap	80th Ill Vol	Yaw E C, L't	67th N Y Vol
Wilson A, Cap	" "	York J H, L't	63d Ind Vol
Wolbach A R, L't	3d O Vol	Youtz H C, Cap	126th O Vol
Woodrow J C, L't	73d Ind Vol	Young D G, Cap	81st Ill Vol
Williamson J B, L't	14th W Va Vol	Young W J, L't	111th Ill Vol
Weaver J R, L't	18th Pa Cav	York E D, L't	2d N C U Vol
Wilson H, L't	" "	Young J W, Major,	76th N Y Vol
Worthen T A, L't	118th Ill Vol	Yates C H, L't	96th Ill Vol
Wakefield H B, Cap	55th Ind Vol	Young A, L't	4th Pa Cav
Whitman W S, Lt	66th Ind Vol	Young T P, L't	4th Ky Cav
Wiltshire J W, L't	45th O Vol	Zarracher F K, Cap	16th Pa Cav
Weddle Geo, L't	144th O Vol	Zeigler Aaron, L't	7th Pa V R C
Woodrow C W, L't	19th Iowa Vol	Zeis H, Cap	80th I U Vol
Webb G W, Cap	2d Pa Art	Zimm A, L t	15th Iowa Vol
White A B, L't	4th Pa Cav	Zobel C, L't	15th N Y Art
Warwick Jos F, L't	101st Pa Vol	Zeigler J D, L't	114th Ill Vol
Willis H H, L't	40th N Y Vol	DEATHS.	
Winship J, L't	88th Ill Vol	Eckings T R, L't	3d N J Vol
Whitney J N, L't	2d R I Cav	Henderson J H, L't	14th Ill Vet Batn
Wilson R, L't	113th Ill Vol	Jackson R W, L't	21st Wis Vol
Whitten B F, L't	9th Me Vol	Spafford A C, L't	41st O Vol
Whiteside J C, Cap	94th N Y Vol	Wenrick J E, Cap	19th Penn Cav
Warren J W, L't	1st Wis Cav	Young A, L't	4th Penn Cav

JAS. A. GARFIELD.

In the closing of this book, we deem it fitting to produce a very correct likeness of our beloved President, who lies at death's door, smitten by the hand of the assassin Guiteau. This is done more in appreciation of the peculiar sadness of the circumstances and the anxiety of the people, than because of any connection which the cut may have with the other contents of the book.

46TH CONGRESS, }
2D SESSION. } H. R. 4495.

IN THE HOUSE OF REPRESENTATIVES.
FEBRUARY 16, 1880.
Read twice, referred to the Committee on Invalid Pensions, and ordered to be printed.

Mr. Keifer, by unanimous consent, introduced the following bill:

A BILL granting pensions to certain Union soldiers and sailors of the late war of the rebellion who were confined in so called Confederate prisons.

Whereas during the late rebellion many soldiers and sailors of the Federal Army and Navy, through the fortunes of war, became prisoners and were confined in so-called Confederate prisons, to the detriment and permanent injury of their health, but whose debility is of such a general and indefinable character as to exclude them from the benefits of existing pension laws: Therefore

Be it enacted by the Senate and House of Representatives of the United States of America in Congress assembled, That the Secretary of the Interior be, and he hereby is, authorized and required to place upon the pension-rolls of the United States, upon application and proof being made to the satisfaction of the Department, all honorably discharged soldiers and sailors of the Federal Army and Navy who, during the late war, were captured and confined, during the period of six months or more, in any of the prisons or places commonly used for the confinement of prisoners by the so called Confederate authorities during the late rebellion, and who are not now beneficiaries, nor entitled to become so under existing pension laws of the United States.

Sec. 2. That such pension shall in each case begin from the date of the discharge of the soldier or sailor aforesaid from the military or naval service of the United States, and shall be at the rate of eight dollars per month in cases where the term of imprisonment shall have been more than six months and less than one year, and one dollar per month additional for each full month of such imprisonment in excess of one year. And the said pension shall be paid at the same time and in the same manner as other pensions are paid: *Provided*, That nothing in this act shall be construed to authorize the reduction or to prevent the increase of the pension of any person now receiving or entitled to receive the benefits of existing pension laws.

www.ingramcontent.com/pod-product-compliance
Lightning Source LLC
Chambersburg PA
CBHW022108230426
43672CB00008B/1315